Prentice-Hall Series in Accounting
Charles T. Horngren, Editor

AUDITING: AN INTEGRATED APPROACH, 2/E
Arens/Loebbecke

FINANCIAL STATEMENT ANALYSIS
Foster

FINANCIAL ACCOUNTING, 2/E
Granof

INTRODUCTION TO FINANCIAL ACCOUNTING
Horngren

INTRODUCTION TO MANAGEMENT ACCOUNTING, 5/E
Horngren

COST ACCOUNTING, 4/E
Horngren

CPA PROBLEMS AND APPROACHES TO SOLUTIONS, 5/E
VOLUMES I & II
Horngren/Leer

DICTIONARY FOR ACCOUNTANTS, 5/E
Kohler

A NEW INTRODUCTION TO FINANCIAL ACCOUNTING, 2/E
May/Mueller/Williams

AUDITING PRINCIPLES, 4/E
Stettler

BUDGETING, 4/E
Welsch

Charles T. Horngren

Ph.D., C.P.A.
Stanford University

FIFTH EDITION

Introduction to
MANAGEMENT ACCOUNTING

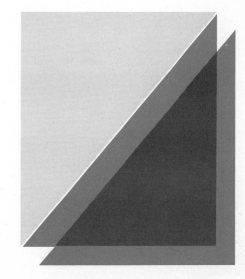

PRENTICE-HALL, INC.
ENGLEWOOD CLIFFS, NEW JERSEY 07632

Library of Congress Cataloging in Publication Data

HORNGREN, CHARLES T.
 Introduction to management accounting.

 Bibliography: p.
 Includes index.
 1. Managerial accounting.   2. Cost accounting.
I. Title.
HF5635.H814 1981   658.1'511   80-26538
ISBN-0-13-487652-0

Editorial/production supervision by *Esther S. Koehn*
Interior and cover design by *Linda Conway*
Cover photo by *Harold Sund, The Image Bank*
Manufacturing buyer: *Raymond Keating*

Printed in the United States of America

10   9   8   7   6   5   4   3   2   1

Prentice-Hall International, Inc., *London*
Prentice-Hall of Australia Pty. Limited, *Sydney*
Prentice-Hall of Canada, Ltd., *Toronto*
Prentice-Hall of India Private Limited, *New Delhi*
Prentice-Hall of Japan, Inc., *Tokyo*
Prentice-Hall of Southeast Asia Pte. Ltd., *Singapore*
Whitehall Books Limited, *Wellington, New Zealand*

to Joan, Scott, Mary, Susie, Cathy

Charles T. Horngren is the Edmund W. Littlefield Professor of Accounting at Stanford University. A graduate of Marquette University, he received his MBA from Harvard University, and his Ph.D. from the University of Chicago. He is also a recipient of an honorary DBA from Marquette University.

Professor Horngren served on the Accounting Principles Board for six years, the Financial Accounting Standards Board Advisory Council for five years, and the Council of the American Institute of Certified Public Accountants for three years.

A member of the American Accounting Association, Horngren has been its president and its director of research. He received the Outstanding Accounting Educator Award in 1973, when the association initiated an annual series of such awards.

Horngren is also a member of the National Association of Accountants, where he was on its research planning committee for three years.

Horngren is the author of three other best-selling Prentice-Hall titles—the companion to this book, *Introduction to Financial Accounting,* 1981; *Cost Accounting: A Managerial Emphasis,* fourth edition, 1977; and *CPA Problems and Approaches to Solutions,* fifth edition, 1979 (with J. A. Leer).

In recognition of his outstanding contributions to accounting education, Horngren was named the first Consulting Editor of the Prentice-Hall Series in Accounting.

CONTENTS

part two
accounting for planning and control

part three
selected topics for further study

19 FINANCIAL REPORTING AND CHANGING PRICES 577

part five
appendixes

Introduction to Management Accounting is the second member of a matched pair of books that provides full coverage of the essentials of financial and managerial accounting. The first book is *Introduction to Financial Accounting.* In combination, the pair can be used throughout two semesters or three quarters of introductory accounting.

This book is an introduction to internal accounting—most often called *management accounting.* It deals with important topics that all students of management and business should study. The book is written primarily for students who have had one or two terms of basic accounting.

It is also appropriate for continuing educational programs of varying lengths in which the students have had no formal training in accounting. My twin goals have been to choose relevant subject matter and to present it clearly.

Major revisions in the content and organization occurred in the preceding edition. This revision has concentrated on improvements in clarity, assignment materials, and consistency with the new companion volume, *Introduction to Financial Accounting.* In particular, more straightforward, easier assignment material has been introduced, covering the nuts and bolts of each chapter. At the same time, the general nature of the assignment material that has been a key to the popularity of preceding editions has been retained. In short, the assignment material as a whole has been improved. There is enormous variety and flexibility and a higher proportion of simpler, shorter problems. More than ever, this is a basic book aimed at a reader who has a minimal background in accounting, if any.

This book attempts a balanced, flexible approach. For example, it deals as much with not-for-profit, retail, wholesale, selling, and administrative situations as it does with manufacturing. The fundamental accounting concepts and techniques for planning and control are applicable to all types and functions of organizations, not just to manufacturing. This more general approach makes it easier for the student to relate the book's examples and problems to his or her particular interests. Moreover, many valuable concepts (for example, master budgets) are more easily grasped if they are not complicated by intricate manufacturing situations.

Stress is on planning and control, not on product costing for purposes of inventory valuation and income determination. This approach, which excludes the troublesome but unimportant complications introduced by changes in inventory levels, simplifies the presentation of planning and control techniques in the classroom. Instead of the simultaneous discussion of costs for control and for product costing found in most texts, this text concentrates on planning and control without dwelling on product costing at all until Chapter 13. At that point, the implications of overhead application for product costing may be considered in perspective and in relation to management policy decisions regarding the "best" inventory valuation method.

Significant changes in this edition include

1. Major changes in the assignment material, which have already been described.

2. New problems of various types are presented in nearly every chapter, often using nonmanufacturing settings such as hospitals and universities. Considerable attention is given to not-for-profit organizations.

3. Chapters 9, 10, and 11 have been condensed and combined into two chapters that show the behavioral ramifications of management accounting more concretely than before. For example, material on goal congruence and incentive is introduced in conjunction with the material on decentralization in Chapter 10.

4. Special care has been taken to permit easy use of the material on product costing. If desired, the latter may be smoothly covered almost simultaneously with related coverage of planning and control. Thus Chapter 13, "Job and Process Systems and Overhead Application," can be assigned without hesitation immediately after Chapter 3, "Introduction to Manufacturing Costs." Similarly, Chapter 14, "Overhead Application: Direct and Absorption Costing," can be assigned immediately after Chapter 7, "Flexible Budgets and Standards for Control."

5. There is a set of learning objectives at the beginning of each chapter. These enable the reader to focus on what he or she should achieve.

6. The final four chapters on financial accounting are almost completely new. They represent a self-contained explanation of basic financial accounting, which is covered in far more detail in the separate companion book, *Introduction to Financial Accounting*.

7. The student guide (by Dudley W. Curry) that is available as supplementary material features numerous changes and additions in the self-test and practice exercises for each chapter.

8. The chapter-by-chapter test bank (by Dudley W. Curry), available free to textbook adopters, has been thoroughly overhauled and considerably expanded. In addition, a computerized option is now available that facilitates the construction of tailor-made tests in volume.

ALTERNATIVE WAYS OF USING THIS BOOK

In my opinion, the first nine chapters provide the foundation of the field of management accounting. These nine chapters may be amplified by assigning the subsequent chapters in the given order, or by inserting them after the earlier chapters as desired. Such insertion may be achieved without disrupting the readers' flow of thought. The most obvious candidates for insertion are indicated below:

Chapters	1	2	3	4	5	6	7	8	9 → 10–19
		↑		↑		↑		↑	
		16		13		11		14	
		17				12			
		18							
		19							

If they are going to be covered in a course in management accounting, any or all of the financial accounting chapters (16–19) may be undertaken anytime. (For example, to provide a change of pace, I have even used such chapters in the midst of a course.)

Instructors tend to disagree markedly about the sequence of topics in a course in management accounting. Criticisms of *any* sequence in a textbook are inevitable. Consequently, this book tries to provide a modular approach that permits hopping and skipping back and forth with minimal inconvenience. In a nutshell, my rationale is to provide a loosely constrained sequence to facilitate diverse approaches to teaching. Content is of primary importance; sequence is secondary.

Teaching is highly personal and is heavily influenced by the backgrounds and interests of assorted students in miscellaneous settings. To satisfy this audience, a book must be a pliable tool, not a straitjacket.

As the author, I prefer to assign the chapters in the sequence provided in the book. But I am not enslaved by the sequence. Through the years, I have assigned an assortment of sequences, depending on the readers' backgrounds.

Part One, "Focus on Decision Making," provides a bedrock introduction, so I assign it in its entirety. Sometimes I assign Chapter 16 immediately after Chapter 1, particularly if the readers have little or no background in financial accounting. Moreover if there is time in the course for students to become more familiar with product costing, I frequently assign Chapter 13 immediately after Chapter 3. Furthermore, there is much logical appeal to studying the chapters on capital budgeting (Chapters 11 and 12) immediately after the chapters on relevant costs (Chapters 4 and 5). However, tradition has prevented my placing such chapters there, plus the fact that capital budgeting is often amply covered in other courses. In addition, the master budget is often covered in finance courses, so Chapter 6 is frequently skipped in courses in accounting.

Part Two, "Accounting for Planning and Control," emphasizes the attention-directing functions of accounting. I often assign Chapter 14 immediately after Chapter 7 because it stresses the product-costing aspects of standard costs, whereas Chapter 7 focuses on the control aspects.

Part Three, "Selected Topics for Further Study," contains chapters on capital budgeting, product costing, and quantitative techniques. These topics are important, but the decision to study them will depend on the teachers' preferences, the other courses in the curriculum, and the students' previous courses.

Part Four introduces, interprets, and appraises basic financial accounting. These chapters form a unified package that covers all elementary financial accounting in capsule form with heavy stress on interpretation and uses and, except in Chapter 16, with little attention given to the accumulation of the information. In my view, a major objective of basic financial accounting should be to equip the student with enough fundamental concepts and terminology so that he or she can reasonably comprehend any industrial corporate annual report.

Chapters 16–19 may be skipped entirely or may be used in a variety of ways:

1. In courses or executive programs where the students have *no* accounting background but where the main emphasis is on management rather than financial accounting.

2. In courses where the chapters may be used as a quick review by students who have had some financial accounting previously.

3. In courses where one or two of Chapters 16–19 may be chosen to remedy weaknesses or gaps in the background of the students.

Chapters 16–19 need not be used in total, page by page or topic by topic. The teacher is free to pick and choose those topics (particularly in Chapter 19) that seem most suitable for his or her students.

On the other hand, some teachers may want to use these chapters to teach the fundamentals of financial accounting to students with no prior background in accounting. Classroom testing has shown that such teaching can be done successfully, provided that the homework material is chosen carefully.

The front of the solutions manual contains several alternate detailed assignment schedules and ample additional recommendations to teachers regarding how best to use this book.

Acknowledgments

I have received ideas, assistance, miscellaneous critiques, and assorted assignment material in conversations and by mail from many students and professors. Each has my gratitude, but the list is too long to enumerate here.

Professor Dudley W. Curry (Southern Methodist University) has my special thanks for offering many helpful suggestions and for preparing the test bank material and the student guide that are available as supplementary material. In addition he has contributed the learning objectives for each chapter, prepared several new problems, and revised several old problems.

I am also especially grateful to Jonathan Schiff for his review of the manuscript and his preparation of Instructor Resource Outlines, available to adopters upon request.

The following professors supplied helpful reviews of the previous edition or drafts of this edition: Edward J. Blocher, Ron Burrows, J. F. Cook, David Croll, Joseph Curran, Kenneth L. Danko, Richard Gilman, and Melissa Martinson.

Alyce Adams has my special appreciation for her cheerful and skillful typing and related help. Laurie Martin also has my gratitude for ably performing assorted editorial chores. Robin Stark and Elizabeth J. Ritter deserve recognition for their flawless typing of the solutions manual.

My thanks to the American Institute of Certified Public Accountants (problem material designated as CPA), the National Association of Accountants (NAA), the Society of Management Accountants of Canada (SMA), and the Institute of Management Accounting (CMA) for their generous permission to use some of their problems and to quote from their publications.

And, finally, my thanks to Ron Ledwith, Esther Koehn, Linda Conway, and Elinor Paige at Prentice-Hall.

Comments from users are welcome.

CHARLES T. HORNGREN

part one

focus on decision making

PERSPECTIVE: SCOREKEEPING, ATTENTION DIRECTING, AND PROBLEM SOLVING

learning objectives

Learning objectives will be found at the beginning of each chapter. These objectives specify some of the important knowledge and skills you should have after completing your study of the chapter and your solving of the assignment material:

1. List the three major ends and means of an accounting system.
2. Name the basic functions of a management planning and control system and identify the main accounting activities that relate to these functions.
3. Identify the three main characteristics of service organizations that distinguish them from manufacturing organizations.
4. Distinguish between the line and staff roles in an organization.
5. Contrast the functions of controllers and treasurers.
6. Describe the two major themes of this book: cost-benefit and behavioral implications.
7. Identify the major distinctions between management accounting and financial accounting.

The main purpose of this chapter is to gain an overall view of the accountant's role in an organization. We shall see that the accountant must fulfill three jobs simultaneously: scorekeeping, attention directing, and problem solving.

Why study accounting?

Accounting is a very important subject. This opinion is widely shared, as shown by eleven hundred responses to a questionnaire sent to academicians and managers in 1979 by the American Assembly of Collegiate Schools of Business. Here are the top three courses ranked in terms of how much time and effort should be spent on each one of them:

	AMONG MANAGERS	AMONG PROFESSORS
Accounting	1	2
Finance	2	3
Economics	3	1

Because accounting is so pervasive, an understanding of its usefulness— and its limitations—is desirable for all managers in all types of organizations. Company presidents, production managers, public accountants, hospital administrators, controllers, school administrators, sales managers, and politicians are better equipped to perform their duties when they have a reasonable grasp of accounting data.

The study of management accounting can be especially fruitful because it helps us see through the eyes of those who are subject to accounting measures of performance and who often depend heavily on accounting data for guidance in decision making. There is no escaping the linkage of accounting and management, so the study of management accounting will help you regardless of whether you become a manager or an accountant, or whether you will work in retailing, manufacturing, health care, public management, or other activity.

The more that managers know about accounting, the better able they are to plan and control the operations of their organization and its subunits. Managers will be handicapped in dealing with both inside and outside parties if their comprehension of accounting is sketchy or confused. Therefore the learning of accounting is almost always a wise investment.

Many production, marketing, and government executives are stronger managers when they have a solid understanding of accounting. Moreover, their performance and their rewards are often determined by how accounting measurements are made, so they have a natural self-interest in gaining knowledge about accounting.

Applicability to nonprofit organizations

This book is aimed at a variety of readers, including students who aspire to become either managers or professional accountants. The major focus will be on profit-seeking organizations. However, the fundamental ideas also apply to not-for-profit organizations. In addition, managers of the latter typically have personal investments in profit-seeking organizations or must interact with businesses in some way.

Managers and accountants in various settings such as hospitals, universities, and government agencies have much in common with their counterparts in profit-seeking organizations. There is money to be raised and spent. There are budgets to be prepared and control systems to be designed and implemented. There is an obligation to use resources wisely. If used intelligently, accounting contributes to efficient operations. The strengthening of the accounting system was a mandatory condition imposed by the federal government in saving New York City from bankruptcy.

The overlap of government and business is everywhere. Government administrators and politicians are much better equipped to deal with problems inside and outside their organizations if they understand accounting. For example, a knowledge of accounting is crucial for decisions regarding research contracts, defense contracts, and loan guarantees. Keep in mind that decisions about loan guarantees have been made with respect to tiny businesses (for instance, through the Small Business Administration) as well as large businesses such as Lockheed and Chrysler.

Ends and means of an accounting system

An *accounting system* is a formal means of gathering data to *aid* and *coordinate* collective decisions in light of the overall goals or objectives of an organization. The accounting system is the major quantitative information system in almost every organization. An effective accounting system provides information for three broad purposes or ends: (1) internal reporting to managers, for use in planning and controlling routine operations; (2) internal reporting to managers, for use in strategic planning, that is, the making of special decisions and the formulating of overall policies and long-range plans; and (3) external reporting to stockholders, government, and other outside parties.

Both management (internal parties) and external parties share an interest in all three important purposes, but the emphases of financial accounting and of management (internal) accounting differ. Financial accounting has been mainly concerned with the third purpose and has traditionally been oriented toward the historical, stewardship aspects of external reporting.[1] The distinguishing feature of management accounting is its emphasis on the planning and control purposes. Management accounting is concerned with the accumulation, classification, and interpretation of information that assists individual executives to fulfill organizational objectives as revealed explicitly or implicitly by top management.

What means do accounting systems use to fulfill the ends? Accounting data can be classified and reclassified in countless ways. A helpful overall classification was proposed in a research study of seven large companies with geographically dispersed operations:

> By observation of the actual decision-making process, specific types of data needs were identified at particular organizational levels—the vice-presidential level, the

---

[1]For a book-length presentation of the subject, see *Introduction to Financial Accounting* (Englewood Cliffs, N.J.: Prentice-Hall), the companion to this textbook.

level of the factory manager, and the level of the factory head [foreman], for example—each involving quite distinct problems of communication for the accounting department.[2]

The research team found that three types of information, each serving as different means, often at various management levels, raise and help to answer three basic questions:

1. *Scorecard questions:* Am I doing well or badly?
2. *Attention-directing questions:* Which problems should I look into?
3. *Problem-solving questions:* Of the several ways of doing the job, which is the best?

The scorecard and attention-directing uses of data are closely related. The same data may serve a scorecard function for a foreman and an attention-directing function for the foreman's superior. For example, many accounting systems provide performance reports in which actual results are compared with previously determined budgets or standards. Such a performance report often helps to answer scorecard questions and attention-directing questions simultaneously. Furthermore, the actual results collected serve not only control purposes but also the traditional needs of financial accounting, which is chiefly concerned with the answering of scorecard questions. This collection, classification, and reporting of data is the task that dominates day-to-day accounting.

Problem-solving data may be used in long-range planning and in making special, nonrecurring decisions, such as whether to make or buy parts, replace equipment, or add or drop a product. These decisions often require expert advice from specialists such as industrial engineers, budgetary accountants, and statisticians.

In sum, the accountants task of supplying information has three facets:

1. **Scorekeeping.** The accumulation of data. This aspect of accounting enables both internal and external parties to evaluate organizational performance and position.
2. **Attention directing.** The reporting and interpreting of information that helps managers to focus on operating problems, imperfections, inefficiencies, and opportunities. This aspect of accounting helps managers to concern themselves with important aspects of operations promptly enough for effective action either through perceptive planning or through astute day-to-day supervision. Attention directing is commonly associated with current planning and control and with the analysis and investigation of recurring routine internal-accounting reports.
3. **Problem solving.** This aspect of accounting involves the concise quantification of the relative merits of possible courses of action, often with recommendations as to the best procedure. Problem solving is commonly associated with nonrecurring decisions, situations that require special accounting analyses of reports.

The above distinctions sometimes overlap or merge. Consequently, it is

[2]H. A. Simon, *Administrative Behavior,* 2nd ed. (New York: Macmillan), p. 20.

EXHIBIT 1-1. Ends and means of an accounting system

Major Ends:
Helping Decisions

Major Means:
Accounting Data

1. Managers for strategic planning and special decisions ◄ Problem solving data

2. Managers for planning and controlling routine operations ◄ Scorekeeping data / Attention directing data / Problem solving data

3. Outsiders for investors, tax collectors, regulators, and others ◄ Scorekeeping data

often difficult to pinpoint a particular accounting task as being scorekeeping, attention directing, or problem solving. Nevertheless, attempts to make these distinctions provide insight into the objectives and tasks of both accountants and managers. Exhibit 1-1 recapitulates the relationships just described. Above all, accounting systems are the means, and better decisions are the ends.

The management process and accounting

☐ NATURE OF PLANNING AND CONTROLLING

The nucleus of the management process is decision making, the purposeful choosing from among a set of alternative courses of action in light of some objective. These decisions range from the routine (making daily production schedules) to the nonroutine (launching a new product line).

Decision making underlies the commonly encountered twofold division of the management process into (1) planning and (2) control. The left-hand side of Exhibit 1-2 clearly demonstrates the planning and control cycle of current operations. **Planning** (the top box) means deciding on objectives and the means for their attainment. It provides the answers to two questions: What is desired? and When and how is it to be accomplished? **Controlling** (the two boxes labeled "Action" and "Evaluation" immediately below) means implementation of plans and the use of feedback so that objectives are optimally attained. The feedback loop is the central facet of any concept of control, and timely, systematic measurement is the chief means of providing useful feedback. Planning and controlling are so intertwined that it seems artificial to draw rigid lines of separation between them; yet at times we will find it useful to concentrate on one or the other phase of the planning-control cycle.

☐ MANAGEMENT BY EXCEPTION

The right-hand side of Exhibit 1-2 shows that accounting formalizes plans by expressing them in the language of figures as **budgets.** Accounting formalizes control as **performance reports** (the last box), which provide feedback by com-

EXHIBIT 1-2. Accounting framework for planning and control

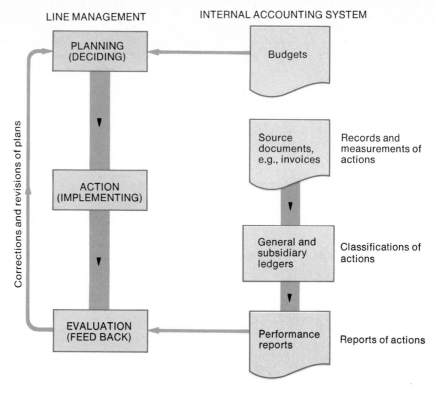

paring results with plans and by highlighting **variances** (i.e., deviations from plans).

Exhibit 1-3 shows the form of a simple performance report for a management consulting firm. Such reports spur investigation of exceptions. Operations are then brought into conformity with the plans, or the plans are revised. This is an example of management by exception.

Management by exception means that the executive's attention and effort are concentrated on the significant deviations from expected results and that the information system highlights the areas most in need of investigation. Management should not ordinarily be concerned with results that conform

EXHIBIT 1-3

Performance Report

	BUDGETED AMOUNTS	ACTUAL AMOUNTS	DEVIATIONS OR VARIANCES	EXPLANATION
Revenue from fees	xxx	xxx	xx	—
Various expenses	xxx	xxx	xx	—
Net income	xxx	xxx	xx	—

EXHIBIT
1-4

Assembly Department Budget for the Month Ended March 31, 19X1	
Material (detailed by type: metal stampings, motors, etc.)	$ 38,000
Assembly labor (detailed by job classification, number of workers, etc.)	73,000
Other labor (foremen, inspectors)	12,000
Utilities, maintenance, etc.	7,500
Supplies (small tools, lubricants, etc.)	2,500
Total	$133,000

closely to plans. However, well-conceived plans should incorporate enough discretion or flexibility so that the manager may feel free to pursue any unforeseen opportunities. In other words, the definition of control does not mean that managers should blindly cling to a preexisting plan when unfolding events indicate the desirability of actions that were not authorized specifically in the original plan.

☐ ILLUSTRATION OF THE BUDGET AND THE PERFORMANCE REPORT

An assembly department constructs electric fans. The assembly of the parts and the installation of the electric motor are basically hand operations. Each fan is inspected before being transferred to the painting department. In light of the present sales forecast, a production schedule of 4,000 window fans and 6,000 table fans is planned for the coming month. Cost classifications are shown in Exhibit 1-4, the Assembly Department Budget.

The operating plan, which is crystallized in the form of a department budget for the coming month, is prepared in conferences attended by the foreman, the foreman's supervisor, and an accountant. Each of the costs subject to the foreman's control is scrutinized. Its average amount for the past few months is often used as a guide, especially if past performance has been reasonably efficient. However, the budget is a *forecast* of costs. Each cost is projected in light of trends, price changes, alterations in product mix, specifications, labor methods, and changes in production volume from month to month. The budget is then formulated, and it becomes the foreman's target for the month.

As actual factory costs are incurred during the month, the accounting department collects them and classifies them by departments. At the end of the month (or perhaps weekly, or even daily, for such key items as materials or assembly labor), the accounting department prepares an Assembly Department Performance Report (Exhibit 1-5). In practice, this report may be very detailed and contain explanations of variances from the budget.

The foreman and his[3] superiors use this report to help appraise perform-

[3] For conciseness, "he" and "his" are usually used in this book rather than "he or she" or "his or hers" or "person." If you prefer, substitute "she" or "hers" where appropriate. Incidentally, the assignment material frequently refers to women in a variety of management roles.

EXHIBIT
1-5

Assembly Department Performance Report for the Month Ended March 31, 19X1	BUDGET	ACTUAL	VARIANCE
Material (detailed by type: metal stampings, motors, etc.)	$ 38,000	$ 39,000	$1,000 U
Assembly labor (detailed by job classification, number of workers, etc.)	73,000	74,300	1,300 U
Other labor (foremen, inspectors)	12,000	11,200	800 F
Utilities, maintenance, etc.	7,500	7,400	100 F
Supplies (small tools, lubricants, etc.)	2,500	2,600	100 U
Totals	$133,000	$134,500	$1,500 U

U = Unfavorable.
F = Favorable.

ance. The spotlight is cast on the variances—the deviations from the budget. It is through management's investigation of these variances that better ways of doing things are discovered. The budget is an aid to planning; the performance report is the tool that aids controlling. The accounting system thus helps to direct managerial attention to the exceptions. Exhibit 1-2 shows that accounting does *not* do the controlling. Controlling consists of actions performed by the managers and their subordinates and of the evaluation that follows actions. Accounting assists the managerial control function by providing prompt measurements of actions and by systematically pinpointing trouble spots. This management-by-exception approach frees managers from needless concern with those phases of operations that are adhering to plans.

Management accounting and service organizations

The basic ideas of management accounting were developed in manufacturing organizations. However, they have evolved so that they are applicable to all types of organizations, including service organizations. Service organizations or industries are defined in various ways. For our purposes, they are organizations that produce a service rather than a tangible good. Examples are public accounting firms, law firms, management consultants, real estate firms, transportation companies, banks, and hotels. Almost all nonprofit or not-for-profit[4] organizations are service industries. Examples are hospitals, schools, and a department of forestry.

The characteristics of service organizations include:

1. *Labor is intensive.* For example, the highest costs in schools and law firms are

[4] *Not-for-profit* is more accurately descriptive of these organizations, but it is more awkward than *nonprofit*, which will be used henceforth for brevity. See Chapter 10 for a fuller discussion.

wages, salaries, and payroll-related costs, not the costs relating to the use of machinery, equipment, and extensive physical facilities.

2. *Output is usually difficult to define.* For example, the output of a university might be defined as the number of degrees granted, but many critics would maintain that the real output is "what is contained in the students' brains." In such a manner the output of schools and hospitals is often idealized; attempts to measure output are often considered immoral.

3. *Major inputs and outputs cannot be stored.* For example, although raw materials and store merchandise may be stored, a hotel's available labor force and rooms are either used or unused as the day expires.

Many activities of nonprofit organizations are little different from business organizations, as these two excerpts illustrate:

> St. Mary's College aimed at luring working adults back to the campus. Backed by a yearly advertising and marketing budget of $20,000, the adult division is thriving. . . . The new adult programs are helping to carry the school financially. It's very profitable.[5]
>
> The success of the King Tut-inspired reproductions spotlights the push that many museums are making into the retail arena. Now, with Christmas approaching, once-stuffy institutions are busily advertising their wares in shops, mail-order catalogs, and tie-ins with leading department stores.[6]

In this book, references are made to service industry applications as the various management accounting techniques are discussed. A major generalization is worth mentioning at the outset. Simplicity is the watchword for installation of systems in service industries and nonprofit organizations, especially in the health industry, where highly paid professionals such as physicians barely bother with a written medical record, much less a time card. In fact, simplicity is a fine watchword for the design of any accounting system. Complexity tends to generate data-gathering and data-interpreting costs that often exceed prospective benefits. Simplicity is sometimes referred to as KISS (which means keep it simple, stupid).

Role of the accountant in the organization

☐ LINE AND STAFF AUTHORITY

The organization chart in Exhibit 1-6 portrays how many manufacturing companies are divided into subunits. In particular, consider the distinction between **line** and **staff authority.** Most organizations specify certain activities as their basic mission, such as the production and sale of goods or services. All subunits of the organization that are *directly* responsible for conducting these basic activities are called *line* departments. The others are called *staff* departments, because their principal task is to support or service the line departments. Thus staff activities are *indirectly* related to the basic activities of the organiza-

[5]"Colleges Learn to Hard Sell," *Business Week,* February 14, 1977, p. 92.

[6]"Museums Find a New Patron: The Retail Market," *Business Week,* October 24, 1979, p. 135.

EXHIBIT 1-6. Organization chart of a manufacturing company

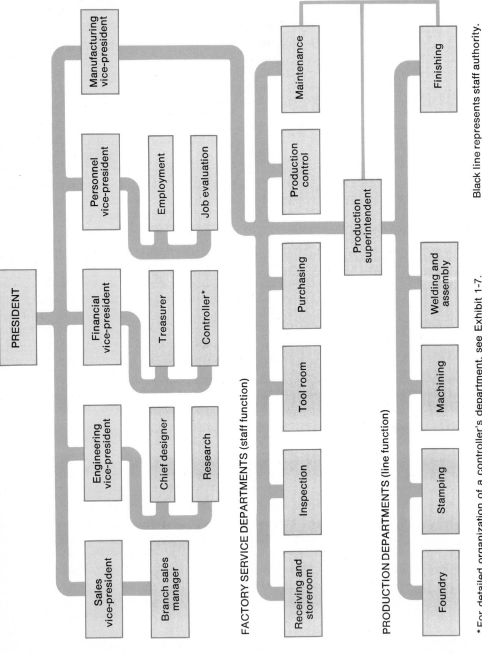

PRESIDENT

Sales vice-president

Engineering vice-president

Financial vice-president

Personnel vice-president

Manufacturing vice-president

Branch sales manager

Chief designer

Research

Treasurer

Controller*

Employment

Job evaluation

FACTORY SERVICE DEPARTMENTS (staff function)

Receiving and storeroom

Inspection

Tool room

Purchasing

Production superintendent

Production control

Maintenance

PRODUCTION DEPARTMENTS (line function)

Foundry

Stamping

Machining

Welding and assembly

Finishing

*For detailed organization of a controller's department, see Exhibit 1-7.

Black line represents staff authority.

tion. For instance, Exhibit 1-6 shows a series of factory-service departments that perform the staff functions of supporting the line functions carried on by the production departments.

The controller fills a staff role, in contrast to the line roles of sales and production executives. The accounting department has responsibility for providing other managers with specialized service, including advice and help in budgeting, analyzing variances, pricing, and the making of special decisions. The accounting department does not exercise direct authority over line departments: Its authority to prescribe uniform accounting and reporting methods is delegated to the controller by top-line management. The uniform accounting procedure is authorized by the company president and is installed for him by the controller. When the controller prescribes the line department's role in supplying accounting information, he is not speaking as the controller, a staff person; he is speaking for top-line management.

Theoretically, the controller's decisions regarding the best accounting procedures to be followed by line people are transmitted to the president. In turn, the president communicates these procedures through a manual of instructions, which comes down through the line chain of command to all people affected by the procedures. In practice, however, the daily work of the controller, and his face-to-face relationships with the production manager or foreman, may require him to direct how production records should be kept or how work tickets should be completed. The controller usually holds delegated authority from top-line management over such matters.

Exhibit 1-7 shows how a controller's department may be organized. In particular, note the distinctions between the scorekeeping, attention-directing, and problem-solving roles. Unless some internal accountants are given the latter two roles as their primary responsibilities, the scorekeeping tasks tend to be too dominating and the system less responsive to facilitating management's decision making.

☐ THE CONTROLLER

The title of controller is applied to various accounting positions, the stature and duties of which vary from company to company. In some firms the controller is little more than a glorified bookkeeper who compiles data, primarily for external reporting purposes. In General Electric the controller is a key executive who aids managerial planning and control in over 160 company subdivisions. In most firms the controller has a status somewhere between these two extremes. For example, his opinion on the tax implications of certain management decisions may be carefully weighed, yet his opinion on other aspects of these decisions may not be sought. In this book, **controller** (sometimes called **comptroller,** derived from the French *compte,* for "account") means the chief management accounting executive. We have already seen that the modern controller does not do any controlling in terms of line authority, except over his own department. Yet the modern concept of controllership maintains that, in a special sense, the controller *does* control: By reporting and interpreting relevant data, the controller exerts a force or influence or projects an attitude that impels management toward logical decisions that are consistent with objectives.

EXHIBIT 1-7. Organization chart of a controller's department

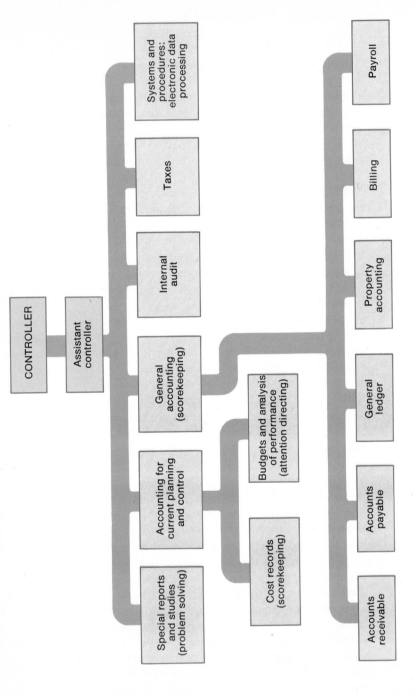

Many people confuse the offices of controller and treasurer. The Financial Executives Institute, an association of corporate treasurers and controllers, distinguishes their functions as follows:

Controllership	*Treasurership*
1. Planning for control	1. Provision of capital
2. Reporting and interpreting	2. Investor relations
3. Evaluating and consulting	3. Short-term financing
4. Tax administration	4. Banking and custody
5. Government reporting	5. Credits and collections
6. Protection of assets	6. Investments
7. Economic appraisal	7. Insurance

Note how management accounting is the controller's primary *means* of implementing the first three functions of controllership.

We shall not dwell at length on the treasurer's functions. As the seven points indicate, the treasurer is concerned mainly with financial, as distinguished from operating, problems. The exact division of various accounting and financial duties obviously varies from company to company.

The controller has been compared to the ship's navigator. The navigator, with the help of his specialized training, assists the captain. Without the navigator, the ship may flounder on reefs or miss its destination entirely, but the captain exerts his right to command. The navigator guides and informs the captain as to how well the ship is being steered. This navigator role is especially evident in points 1 through 3 of the seven functions.

Two major themes

We have already seen that management accounting is concerned with how accounting systems help collective decisions. This book emphasizes two major themes or philosophies or problems regarding the design of these systems: (a) cost-benefit and (b) behavioral implications. Both will briefly be described now; and because of their importance, both will also be mentioned often in succeeding chapters.

☐ COST-BENEFIT THEME

The **cost-benefit theme** (or call it a philosophy or state of mind if you prefer) is our fundamental approach to choosing among accounting systems and accounting methods. It will dominate this book. Systems and methods are economic goods that are available at various costs. Which system does a manager want to buy? A simple file drawer for amassing receipts and canceled checks? An elaborate budgeting system based on computerized descriptive models of the organization and its subunits? Or something in between?

Of course, the answer depends on the buyer's perceptions of the expected incremental (additional) benefits in relation to the incremental costs. For example, a hospital administrator may contemplate the installation of a TECHNI-

CON computerized system for controlling hospital operations. Such a system uses a single document of original entry for automatic accumulation of data for financial records, medical records, costs by departments, nurse staffing requirements, drug administration, billings for patients, revenue generated by physicians, and so forth. This system will lead to more efficiency, less waste, and fewer errors. But the system costs $14 million. Thus the system is not good or bad by itself. It must meet the tests of the economics of information—its value must exceed its cost.

Steak and butter may be "good buys" for many people at 50¢ per pound, but they may become "bad buys" at $5 per pound. Similarly, a particular accounting system may be a wise investment in the eyes of the buyer if it will generate a sufficiently better collective set of decisions to justify its added cost. However, an existing accounting system is only *one* source of information for decision making. In many organizations it may be more economical to gather data by one-shot special efforts than by having a ponderous system gathering data repetitively that are rarely used.

The cost-benefit theme provides innate appeal to both the hard-headed manager and the theoretician. Managers have been employing the cost-benefit test for years, even though they may not have expressed it as such. Instead, they may have referred to the theme as "having to be practical" despite what theory may say. But the cost-benefit theme has an exceedingly rich underlying theory of information economics.[7] It is good theory that can supply the missing rationale for many management practices.

☐ BEHAVIORAL THEME

Financial accounting is often looked upon as being a cold, objective discipline. But management accounting is not; it is wrapped up in behavioral ramifications. The buyer of an accounting system should be concerned with how it will affect the decisions (behavior) of the affected managers. Earlier we saw how budgets and performance reports may play a key role in helping management. Emphasis on the future is a major feature of management accounting, whereas it is not as prominent in financial accounting. Budgets are the chief devices for compelling and disciplining management planning. Without budgets, planning may not get the front-and-center focus that it usually deserves.

The performance reports that are so widely used to judge decisions, subunits, and managers have enormous influence on the behavior of the affected individuals. Performance reports not only provide feedback to improve future economic decisions but may also provide desirable or undesirable incentives. The choices of the content, format, timing, and distribution of performance reports are heavily influenced by their probable impact on incentives.

In a nutshell, management accounting can best be understood by using a cost-benefit theme coupled with an awareness of the importance of behavioral effects. Even more than financial accounting, management accounting spills

[7] J. Demski and G. Feltham, *Cost Determination: A Conceptual Approach* (Ames, Iowa: Iowa State University Press, 1976). Also see J. Demski, *Information Analysis,* 2nd ed (Reading, Mass.: Addison-Wesley Publishing Co., 1980).

over into related disciplines, such as economics, the decision sciences, and the behavioral sciences.

Management accounting and financial accounting

☐ FREEDOM OF CHOICE

Financial accounting and management accounting would be better labeled as external accounting and internal accounting, respectively. "Financial accounting" emphasizes the preparation of reports of an organization for external users such as banks and the investing public. "Management accounting" emphasizes the preparation of reports of an organization for its internal users such as presidents, deans, and head physicians.

Keep in mind that the same basic accounting system compiles the fundamental data for both financial accounting and management accounting. Furthermore, external forces (for example, income tax authorities and regulatory bodies, such as the United States Securities and Exchange Commission and the California Health Facility Commission) often limit management's choices of accounting methods. Organizations frequently limp along with a system that has been developed in response to the legal requirements imposed by external parties. In short, many existing systems are primarily oriented toward external rather than internal users.

Consider our cost-benefit theme that accounting systems are commodities like steak or butter. As just noted, generally accepted accounting standards or principles affect both internal and external accounting. However, change in internal accounting is not inhibited by generally accepted financial accounting standards. The managers who buy an internal accounting system can have anything their hearts desire—as long as they are willing to pay the price. For instance, for its own management purpose, a hospital, a manufacturer, or a university can account for its assets on the basis of *current values,* as measured by estimates of replacement costs. No outside agency can prohibit such accounting.

There are no "generally accepted management accounting principles" that forbid particular measurements. Indeed, the cost-benefit theme refrains from stating that any given accounting is bad or good. Instead, the theme says that any accounting system or method (no matter how crazy it appears at first glance) is desirable as long as it brings incremental benefits in excess of its incremental costs.

Of course, satisfying internal demands for data (as well as external demands) means that organizations may have to keep more than one set of records. At least in the United States, there is nothing immoral or unethical about having many simultaneous sets of books—but they are expensive. The cost-benefit test says that their perceived increases in benefits must exceed their perceived increases in costs. Ultimately, benefits are measured by whether better decisions are forthcoming in the form of increased net cost savings or profit (or, in the case of many nonprofit institutions, in the form of increased quality or quantity of service rendered for each dollar spent).

The major distinctions between management accounting and financial accounting are briefly enumerated below. These points will be amplified in succeeding chapters.

	MANAGEMENT ACCOUNTING	FINANCIAL ACCOUNTING
1. Primary users	Organization managers at various levels	Organization managers and outside parties such as investors and government agencies
2. Freedom of choice	No constraints other than costs in relation to benefits of improved management decisions	Constrained by generally accepted accounting principles (GAAP)
3. Behavioral implications	Concern about how measurements and reports will influence managers daily behavior	Concern about how to measure and communicate economic phenomena. Behavioral impact is secondary
4. Time focus	Future orientation: formal use of budgets as well as historical records. Example: 19X3 **budget** versus 19X3 **actual** performance	Past orientation: historical evaluation. Example: 19X3 **actual** versus 19X2 **actual** performance
5. Time span	Flexible, varying from hourly to ten or fifteen years	Less flexible. Usually one year or one quarter
6. Reports	Detailed reports: concern about details of parts of the entity, products, departments, territories, etc.	Summary reports: concern primarily with entity as a whole
7. Delineation of activities	Field is less sharply defined. Heavier use of economics, decision sciences, and behavioral sciences	Field is more sharply defined. Lighter use of related disciplines

□ EFFECTS OF REGULATION

The accounting reports to government agencies such as the Internal Revenue Service and the Securities and Exchange Commission are reports to outside parties. Hence such reports have usually been classified as subparts of financial accounting. Nevertheless, the proliferation of government regulation has definitely affected the design of internal accounting systems. Governmental agencies have broad powers, with the force of law, to subpoena any internal document deemed necessary.

One illustration of the effects of government regulation is Line of Business Reporting required by the Federal Trade Commission (FTC). These requirements call for separate income statements, balance sheet data, and statistical data for each "business," as defined by the FTC. Examples of "businesses" might be soft drinks, restaurants, beer, and tobacco activities conducted by a large company that initially produced and sold tobacco only.

Another illustration is the requirements for universities and defense contractors to allocate costs to government contracts in specified ways or risk failure to get reimbursed.

The most noteworthy illustration is probably the **Foreign Corrupt Practices Act,** which was passed by the U.S. Congress in 1977. The title is misleading because the act's provisions pertain to the internal control systems of *all* publicly held companies, *even if they conduct no business outside the United States.* The act contains not only specific prohibitions against bribery and other corrupt practices but also requirements (a) for maintaining accounting records in reasonable detail and accuracy and (b) for maintaining an appropriate system of internal accounting controls.

The largest impact of the act has been the mandatory documentation of internal control by *management* rather than only by *outside auditors.* To help management, internal auditing staffs have been markedly increased. Internal auditors help review and evaluate systems with regard to minimizing errors, fraud, and waste. More important, many internal auditing staffs have a primary responsibility for conducting **management audits,** which concentrate on reviewing and evaluating managers' actions to see whether top management's operating policies are being implemented. Incidentally, management audits are not confined to profit-seeking organizations. The General Accounting Office (GAO) of the U.S. federal government conducts these audits on a massive scale. Moreover, in 1977 a public accounting firm did a management audit of the city of New York.

The overall impact of government regulation is very controversial. Many managers insist that the extra costs of compliance far exceed any possible benefits. One benefit is that operating managers, now more than ever, must become more intimately familiar with their accounting systems. The resulting changes in the systems sometimes provide stronger controls and more informative reports. In short, outside forces may have more influence on management accounting than appears at first glance.

☐ CAREER OPPORTUNITIES

Accounting deals with all facets of a complex organization. It provides an excellent opportunity for gaining broad knowledge. Senior accountants or controllers in a corporation are sometimes picked as production or marketing executives. Why? Because they may have impressed other executives as having acquired general management skills. Accounting cuts across all management functions, including purchasing, manufacturing, wholesaling, retailing, and a variety of marketing and transportation activities. A number of recent surveys have indicated that more chief executive officers began their careers in an accounting position than in any other area such as marketing, production, or engineering.

In 1979 Korn/Ferry International, an executive recruiting firm, conducted a survey of thirty-six hundred senior-level executives (excluding presidents) working in several hundred of the largest companies in the United States. The composite executive began in accounting or finance and still believes that to be the "fast track" to the top. In particular, there is a dominance of accountants near the peak of the corporate pyramid.

The existence of high inflation has also accelerated the prominence of accounting as a major route to high-level responsibilities. A report in *Business*

SCORE-
KEEPING,
DIRECTING,
SOLVING

19

SCORE-
KEEPING,
DIRECTING,
SOLVING

19

Week (August 15, 1977, p. 84) commented: "At companies that once stressed growth and expansion beyond all else, the job of measuring the costs of doing business—and cutting them—gets the highest priority today."

Former controllers have risen to the top of such mammoth companies as General Motors, FMC, Fruehauf, and Pfizer. *Business Week* pointed out that controllers

> . . . are now getting involved with the operating side of the company, where they give advice and influence production, marketing, and investment decisions as well as corporate planning. Moreover, many controllers who have not made it to the top have won ready access to top management. . . . Probably the main reason the controller is getting the ear of top management these days is that he or she is virtually the only person familiar with all the working parts of the company.

☐ CERTIFIED MANAGEMENT ACCOUNTANT

A prominent feature of the field of financial accounting is the use of outside auditors to give assurance about the reliability of the financial information being supplied by managers. These auditors are called **Certified Public Accountants** in the United States and Chartered Accountants in many other English-speaking nations. The major U.S. professional association in the private sector that regulates the quality of outside auditors is the American Institute of Certified Public Accountants (AICPA).

The largest association of management accountants in the United States is the **National Association of Accountants** (NAA). The rise of the field of management accounting led the NAA in 1972 to establish the Institute of Management Accounting. The institute administers a program leading to the Certificate in Management Accounting (CMA).[8] The objectives of the program are three-fold:

1. To establish management accounting as a recognized profession by identifying the role of the management accountant and the underlying body of knowledge, and by outlining a course of study by which such knowledge can be acquired.
2. To foster higher educational standards in the field of management accounting.
3. To establish an objective measure of an individual's knowledge and competence in the field of management accounting.

The highlight of the program is a qualifying examination covering five parts: (1) economics and business finance, (2) organization and behavior, (3) public reporting, (4) periodic reporting for internal and external purposes, and (5) decision analysis, including modeling and information systems. The CMA designation is gaining increased stature in the management community as a credential parallel to the CPA.

[8]Information may be obtained from the Institute, 570 City Center Building, Ann Arbor, Michigan 48104.

summary

An understanding of the overall purposes of the accounting system provides perspective for the study of the usefulness of accounting to management. The accounting system of the future is likely to be a multiple-purpose system with a highly selective reporting scheme. It will be highly integrated and will serve three main purposes: (1) routine reporting to management, primarily for planning and controlling current operations (scorekeeping and attention directing); (2) special reporting to management, primarily for long-range planning and nonrecurring decisions (problem solving); and (3) routine reporting on financial results, oriented primarily for external parties (scorekeeping). The first two purposes are the distinguishing characteristics of internal accounting for planning and control.

Internal accounting is interwoven with management itself. Accounting is a service function. Internal accounting is not management as ordinarily conceived, but it helps management do a better job.

The chief of internal accounting is usually called the **controller.** The controller's responsibilities usually encompass all phases of accounting, including income taxes and routine reporting to outside parties. But accounting techniques for planning and control are the controller's main tools for helping managers to get things done. Besides being a combination scorekeeper, attention director, and problem solver, the controller must constantly provide an objective view of operations and avoid seizing or accepting line authority. The human or organizational facets of the controller's work often provide his most challenging and delicate tasks.

This book will stress two major themes: cost-benefit and behavioral implications. The choice of a system or method should be based on weighing the value of the system against its cost. This weighing often entails making predictions of how individuals will collectively behave under one system versus another. Therefore the behavioral impact of alternatives is given ample attention throughout this book.

summary problems for your review

(*Try to solve these problems before examining the solutions that follow.*)

▦ PROBLEM ONE

The scorekeeping, attention-directing, and problem-solving duties of the accountant have been described in this chapter and elsewhere in literature. The accountant's usefulness to management is said to be directly influenced by how good an attention director and problem solver he or she is.

Evaluate this contention by specifically relating the accountant's duties to the duties of operating management.

PROBLEM TWO

Using the organization charts in this chapter (Exhibits 1-6 and 1-7), answer the following questions.

1. Do the following have line or staff authority over the machine foreman: maintenance foreman, manufacturing vice-president, production superintendent, purchasing agent, storekeeper, personnel vice-president, president, chief budgetary accountant, chief internal auditor?

2. What is the general role of service departments in an organization? How are they distinguished from operating or producing departments?

3. Does the controller have line or staff authority over the cost accountants? The accounts receivable clerks?

4. What is probably the *major duty* (scorekeeping, attention directing, or problem solving) of the following:

Payroll clerk	Cost analyst
Accounts receivable clerk	Head of special reports and
Cost record clerk	studies
Head of general accounting	Head of accounting
Head of taxes	for planning and control
Head of internal auditing	Controller
Budgetary accountant	

SOLUTION TO PROBLEM ONE

Operating managers may have to be good scorekeepers, but their major duties are to concentrate on the day-to-day problems that most need attention, to make longer-range plans, and to arrive at special decisions. Accordingly, because managers are concerned mainly with attention directing and problem solving, they will obtain the most benefit from the alert internal accountant who is a useful attention director and problem solver.

SOLUTION TO PROBLEM TWO

1. The only executives having line authority over the machining foreman are the president, the manufacturing vice-president, and the production superintendent.

2. A typical company's major purpose is to produce and sell goods or services. Unless a department is directly concerned with producing or selling, it is called a service or staff department. Service departments exist only to help the production and sales departments with their major tasks: the efficient production and sale of goods or services.

3. The controller has line authority over all members of his own department, all those shown in the controller's organization chart (Exhibit 1-7).

4. The major duty of the first five—through the head of taxes—is typically scorekeeping. Attention directing is probably the major duty of the next three. Problem solving is probably the primary duty of the head of special reports and studies. The head of accounting for planning and control and the controller should be concerned with all three duties: scorekeeping, attention directing, and problem solving. However, there is a perpetual danger that day-to-day pressures will emphasize scorekeeping. Therefore accountants and managers should constantly see that attention directing and problem solving are also stressed. Otherwise the major management benefits of an accounting system may be lost.

assignment material

The assignment material for each chapter is divided into two groups: *fundamental* and *additional*. The first group consists of carefully designed, relatively straightforward material aimed at conveying the essential concepts and techniques of the particular chapter. These assignments provide a solid introduction to the major concepts of accounting for management control.

The first question in each chapter usually concerns terminology, an extremely important and often troublesome phase of the learning process. A fuzzy understanding of terms hampers the learning of concepts. Many instructors will not require written answers to the question on terminology; in this case, the reader should check his or her comprehension of new terms by consulting the glossary at the end of the book.

The second group of assignment material in each chapter should not be regarded as being inferior to the fundamental group. Many of these problems can be substituted for ones in the fundamental group.

■ FUNDAMENTAL ASSIGNMENT MATERIAL

1-1. Terminology. Define *attention directing; budget; Certified Management Accountant; Certified Public Accountant; comptroller; controller; controlling; Foreign Corrupt Practices Act; line authority; management audit; management by exception; National Association of Accountants; performance report; planning; problem solving; scorekeeping; source document; staff authority; variance.*

1-2. Role of the accountant in the organization: line and staff functions.

1. Of the following, who have line authority over a cost record clerk: budgetary accountant; head of accounting for current planning and control; head of general accounting; controller; storekeeper; production superintendent; manufacturing vice-president; president; production control chief?

2. Of the following, who have line authority over an assembler: stamping foreman; assembly foreman; production superintendent; production control chief; storekeeper; manufacturing vice-president; engineering vice-president; president; controller; budgetary accountant; cost record clerk?

1-3 Scorekeeping, attention directing, and problem solving. For each of the following, identify the function the accountant is performing—i.e., scorekeeping, attention directing, or problem solving. *Also state* whether the departments mentioned here are production or factory service departments. If a department is neither of these, name the particular department and indicate whether it is a staff or a line type.

1. Recording overtime hours of the product finishing department.

2. Compiling data for a report showing the ratio of advertising expenses to sales for each branch store.

3. Investigating reasons for increased returns and allowances for materials purchased.

4. Computing and recording end-of-year adjustments for expired fire insurance on the factory warehouse for materials.

5. Preparing a schedule of fuel costs by months and factory departments.

6. Estimating the operating costs and outputs that could be expected for each of two large metal-stamping machines offered for sale by different manufacturers. Only one of these machines is to be acquired by your company.

7. Preparing a report of overtime labor costs by production departments.

8. Posting daily cash collections to customers' accounts.

9. Estimating the costs of moving corporate headquarters to another city.

10. Daily recording of material purchase vouchers.

11. Analyzing the costs of acquiring and using each of two alternate types of welding equipment.

12. Interpreting increases in assembly labor costs per product unit.

13. Analyzing deviations from the budget of the factory maintenance department.

14. Assisting in a study by the manufacturing vice-president to determine whether to buy certain parts needed in large quantities for manufacturing our products or to acquire the manufacturing facilities needed to make these parts.

15. Allocating factory service department costs to production departments.

■ ADDITIONAL ASSIGNMENT MATERIAL

1-4. "Additional government regulation assists the development of management accounting systems." Do you agree? Explain.

1-5. Distinguish between the American Institute of CPAs and the National Association of Accountants.

1-6. What two major themes will be emphasized in succeeding chapters?

1-7. "The Foreign Corrupt Practices Act applies to bribes paid outside the United States." Do you agree? Explain.

1-8. "The accounting system is intertwined with operating management. Business operations would be a hopeless tangle without the paperwork that is so often regarded with disdain." Do you agree? Explain, giving examples.

1-9. What are the three broad purposes of an accounting system?

1-10. "The emphases of financial accounting and management accounting differ." Explain.

1-11. Distinguish between scorekeeping, attention directing, and problem solving.

1-12. Give examples of special nonrecurring decisions and of long-range planning.

1-13. Briefly describe the probable business information system of the future.

1-14. "Planning is much more vital than control." Do you agree? Explain.

1-15. Distinguish between a source document, a subsidiary ledger, and a general ledger.

1-16. Distinguish between a budget, a performance report, and a variance.

1-17. "Management by exception means abdicating management responsibility for planning and control." Do you agree? Explain.

1-18. "Good accounting provides automatic control of operations." Do you agree? Explain.

1-19. Distinguish between line and staff authority.

1-20. "The controller does control in a special sense." Explain.

1-21. "The importance of accurate source documents cannot be overemphasized." Explain.

1-22. Organization chart. Draw an organization chart for a single-factory company with the following personnel. Which represent factory service departments? Producing departments?

Punch press foreman
Vice-president and controller
Storekeeper
Drill press foreman
Production superintendent
Chairman of the board
Engineering vice-president
Manufacturing vice-president
President

Personnel vice-president
Maintenance foreman
Sales vice-president
Production control chief
Production planning chief
Assembly foreman
Purchasing agent
Secretary and treasurer

1-23. Costs and benefits. Marks & Spencer, a giant retailer in the United Kingdom, has used a cost-benefit approach to the paper bureaucracy. Looked at in isolation, each form seemed reasonable:

> . . . but in terms of the total procedure, the substantial effort required in each department to confirm the accuracy of the information or verify completion of the task seemed to be out of proportion to any value achieved. By challenging the need for detail and highlighting the fact that sensible approximation costs less, the committee succeeded in simplifying many documents and eliminating others.[9]

Describe the rationale that should underlie systems design.

1-24. Focus on financial data. *Business Week* (January 10, 1977, p. 58) reported:

> Rockwell's Anderson, a veteran of the company's automotive operations, recalls that when he sat in on meetings at Rockwell's North American Aircraft Operations in the late 1960s, "there'd be 60 or 70 guys talking technical problems, with never a word on profits." Such inattention to financial management helped Rockwell lose the F-15 fighter to McDonnell Douglas, Pentagon sources say. Anderson brought in profit-oriented executives, and he has now transformed North American's staff meetings to the point that "you seldom hear talk of technical problems any more," he says. "It's all financial."

What is your reaction to Anderson's comments? Are his comments related to management accounting?

1-25. Nonprofit systems. The following comments were made by a certified public accountant who has had extensive experience in consulting in service industries and nonprofit organizations: "Valid accounting principles are so basic that, once accepted, it seems incredible that there was ever any question. Accounting doesn't advance on theory, only when somebody's money is at stake."

REQUIRED

During the 1970s and early 1980s hospitals hired consultants in droves to install cost-accounting systems. Why hadn't hospitals used much cost accounting before?

1-26. Measuring costs and benefits. The *Wall Street Journal* (January 31, 1980, p. 1) reported:

> A score of U.S. cities—from Decatur, Ill., and Birmingham, Ala., to San Francisco and New York City—have either just completed or plan to build soon downtown

[9]Derek G. Rayner, "A Battle Won in the War on the Paper Bureaucracy," *Harvard Business Review,* January-February 1975, 14.

convention centers to help them compete for the tourist and business dollar. "There has been a sharp growth in trade shows and the work-shop and educational type of convention," says a spokesman for Grand Rapids, Mich., which just opened a $26.3 million center.

A spokesman for the Trade Show Bureau, an industry group, says more companies are using shows and conventions to build sales leads. Sources estimate it costs a firm $140 for a salesman in the field to contact a new potential customer, while the same contact at a show costs $50 or less.

(1) Explain briefly how management accountants may have arrived at the two estimated costs mentioned in the second paragraph of this extract. (2) How would you classify these accounting activities: scorekeeping, attention directing, or problem solving?

INTRODUCTION TO COST-VOLUME RELATIONSHIPS

learning objectives

When you have finished studying this chapter, you should be able to:

1. Define **variable costs** and **fixed costs** and compute the effects of changes in volume on each of these costs.
2. Construct a cost-volume-profit graph from appropriate data.
3. From given data, calculate activity volume in both total dollars and total units to (a) break even and (b) achieve a specified target profit.
4. Describe the roles of cost-volume analysis and contribution margins in management planning and control.
5. Specify the limiting assumptions that underlie cost-volume analysis.
6. Distinguish between contribution margin and gross margin.
7. Construct and interpret a P/V chart (Appendix 2A).
8. Compute cost-volume-profit relationships on an after-tax basis (Appendix 2B).

Importance of cost-volume-profit analysis

How do the costs and revenues of a hospital change as one more patient is admitted for a four-day stay? How are the costs and revenue of an airline affected when one more passenger is boarded at the last moment, or when one more flight is added to the schedule? How should the budget request by the California Department of Motor Vehicles be affected by the predicted increase in the state's population? These questions have a common theme: What will happen to financial results if a specified level of activity or volume fluctuates? Their answers are not easy to obtain, and managers usually resort to some simplifying assumptions, especially concerning cost behavior (that is, how total costs are affected as volume changes). Nevertheless, implicitly or explicitly, managers must frequently answer these questions in order to reach intelligent decisions.

The managers of profit-seeking organizations usually study the relationships of revenue (sales), expenses (costs), and net income (net profit). This study is commonly called cost-volume-profit analysis. The managers of nonprofit organizations also will benefit from the study of cost-volume-profit relationships, primarily because knowledge of how costs fluctuate in response to changes in volume is valuable regardless of whether profit is an objective. After all, no organization has unlimited resources.

The subject matter of this chapter is straightforward. No knowledge of the accountant's assumptions underlying financial reporting is required. After all, in its most fundamental sense, an income statement is merely a presentation of the financial results from matching sales and related costs.

Cost-volume relationships are important to both management and outsiders. For example, the U.S. Securities and Exchange Commission requires the management of all publicly held companies to include a "management's discussion and analysis of the statement of income" in corporate quarterly and annual reports. Some of these analyses are quite detailed, and all focus on the effects of changes in prices and physical quantities sold. The analysis of the Holiday Inns Hotel Group provides an example:

> . . . Revenues for the Hotel Group increased $60 million or 10.2 percent over 1977. The revenue improvement was primarily the result of a 3.1 percentage point occupancy gain, a 13.2 percent increase in average room rates and a 2.7 percent expansion of the Holiday Inn system.
>
> Operating income for the Hotel Group increased $26 million or 29.4 percent in 1978. Operating income margins reached 18.0 percent in 1978, up 2.7 percentage points from 1977. The improvement resulted from improved occupancy levels, higher average room rates and effective cost control programs.

Variable costs and fixed costs

Variable costs and **fixed costs** are usually defined in terms of how a total cost changes in relation to fluctuations in the quantity of some selected activity. Activity bases are diverse: They may be the number of orders processed, the number of lines billed in a billing department, the number of admissions to a theater, the number of pounds handled in a warehouse, the hours of labor worked in an assembly department, the number of rides in an amusement park, the seat-miles on an airline, the dollar sales in a grocery store, or some other index of volume.

If Watkins Products pays its door-to-door sales personnel a 40 percent straight commission, then the total cost of sales commissions should be 40 percent of the total sales dollars. If a garden shop buys bags of weed killer at $2 each, then the total cost of weed killer should be $2 times the total number of bags. These are variable costs. They are uniform *per unit*, but their *total* fluctuates in direct proportion to the total of the related activity or volume. These relationships are depicted graphically in Exhibit 2-1. The costs of most merchandise, materials, parts, supplies, commissions, and many types of labor are variable.

EXHIBIT 2-1. Variable-cost behavior

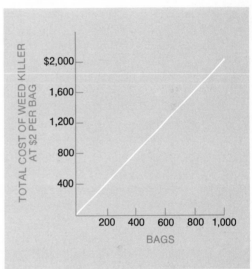

If a manufacturer of picture tubes for color television rents a factory for $100,000 per year, then the unit cost of rent applicable to each tube will depend on the total number of tubes produced. If 100,000 tubes are produced, the unit cost will be $1; if 50,000 tubes are produced, $2. This is an example of a fixed cost, a cost that does not change in *total* but becomes progressively smaller on a *per-unit* basis as volume increases. Real estate taxes, real estate insurance, many executive salaries, and straight-line depreciation charges are fixed costs.

Comparison of variable and fixed costs

Note carefully from the foregoing examples that the "variable" or "fixed" characteristic of a cost relates to its *total dollar amount* and not to its per-unit amount. A variable cost (the 40 percent sales commission) is constant per unit, and its *total* dollar amount *changes* proportionally with changes in activity or volume. A fixed cost (the factory rent) varies inversely with activity or volume changes on a per-unit basis but is *constant* in *total* dollar amount. The following diagram summarizes these relationships:

TYPE OF COST	IF ACTIVITY VOLUME INCREASES (OR DECREASES):	
	total cost	cost per unit*
Fixed costs	No change†	Decrease (or increase)
Variable costs	Increase (or decrease)	No change†

*Per unit of activity volume, for example, product units, passenger miles, sales dollars.
†When using data for making predictions, it is usually less confusing to think of fixed costs as a total and variable costs as an amount per unit of activity.

☐ RELEVANT RANGE

A fixed cost is fixed only in relationship to a given period of time—the budget period—and a given, though wide, range of activity called the **relevant range.** Fixed costs may change from budget year to budget year solely because of changes in insurance and property tax rates, executive salary levels, or rent levels. But these items are highly unlikely to change within a given year. In addition, the total budgeted fixed costs may be formulated on the basis of an expected activity level (i.e., volume), say, within a relevant planning range of 40,000 to 85,000 units of production per month. However, operations on either side of the range will result in major salary adjustments or in the layoff or hiring of personnel. For example, assume the total monthly fixed cost within the relevant range is $100,000. If operations fall below 40,000 units, changes in personnel and salaries will slash fixed costs to $60,000. If operations rise above 85,000 units, increases in personnel and salaries will raise fixed costs to $115,000.

These assumptions—a given time period and a given range—are shown graphically at the top of Exhibit 2-2. The possibility that operations will be outside the relevant range is usually remote. Therefore the three-level refinement at the top of Exhibit 2-2 is usually not graphed. A single horizontal line is usually extended through the plotted activity levels, as at the bottom of the exhibit.

☐ SOME SIMPLIFYING ASSUMPTIONS

Nearly every organization has some variable costs and some fixed costs. As you may suspect, it is often difficult to classify a cost as exactly variable or exactly fixed. Many complications arise, including the possibility of costs behaving in some nonlinear way (not behaving as a straight line). For example, as workers learn to process incoming tax forms, productivity rises. This means that total costs may behave like this:

but not like this:

EXHIBIT 2-2. Fixed costs and the relevant range

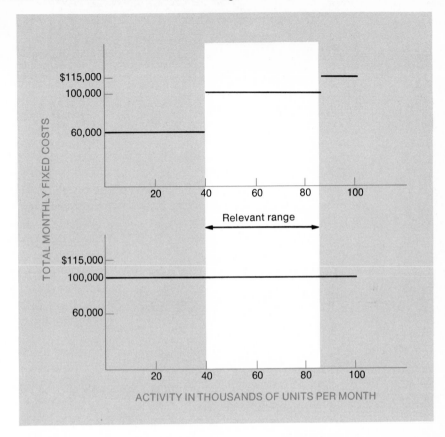

Moreover, costs may simultaneously be affected by more than one activity base. For example, the costs of shipping labor may be affected by *both* the weight and the number of units handled. We shall investigate various facets of this problem in succeeding chapters; for now, we shall assume that any cost may be classified as either variable or fixed. A given variable cost is associated with *one* measure of volume, and that relationship is linear.

Illustration of cost-volume-profit analysis

The following situation will be used to demonstrate the techniques and the analytical power of cost-volume-profit analysis. Amy Winston, the manager of food services for the state of California, is trying to decide whether to rent a line of food vending machines for the state's Sacramento buildings. Although the unit prices and acquisition costs differ among individual food items, Winston feels that an average unit selling price of 50¢ and an average unit acquisition cost of 40¢ will suffice for purposes of this analysis. The following revenue and expense relationships are predicted:

	PER UNIT	PERCENT OF SALES
Selling price	$.50	100%
Cost of each item	.40	80
Contribution margin	$.10	20%
Monthly fixed expenses:		
Rent	$1,000	
Wages for replenishing and servicing	4,500	
Other fixed expenses	500	
Total fixed expenses per month	$6,000	

The following six sections will explore various aspects of the above data. A new question or requirement will be stated at the start of each section.

☐ 1. BREAK-EVEN POINT—TWO ANALYTICAL TECHNIQUES

Express the monthly break-even point in number of units and in dollar sales.

The study of cost-volume-profit relationships is often called *break-even analysis.* The latter is a misnomer because the break-even point—the point of zero net income—is often only incidental to the planning decision at hand. Still knowledge of the break-even point provides insights into the possible riskiness of certain courses of action.

There are three basic techniques for computing a break-even point: equation, contribution margin, and graphing. The graphical technique is shown in the solution to Requirement 2.

a. **Equation technique.** This is the most general form of analysis, the one that may be adapted to any conceivable cost-volume-profit situation. You are familiar with a typical income statement. Any income statement can be expressed in equation form, as follows:

$$\text{sales} - \text{variable expenses} - \text{fixed expenses} = \text{net income} \quad (1)$$

or

$$\text{sales} = \text{variable expenses} + \text{fixed expenses} + \text{net income} \quad (1)$$

Let   X = number of units to be sold to break even. Then

$$\$.50X = \$.40X + \$6,000 + 0$$

$$\$.10X = \$6,000 + 0$$

$$X = \frac{\$6,000 + 0}{\$.10}$$

$$X = 60,000 \text{ units}$$

Total sales in the equation is a price-times-quantity relationship. In the above equation, this was expressed as $.50X. Of course, the *dollar* sales answer in this case could be obtained in shortcut fashion by multiplying

60,000 *units* by 50¢, which would yield the break-even dollar sales of $30,000. Another approach is to solve the equation method for total sales *dollars* directly. This method becomes important in those situations where *unit* price and *unit* variable costs are not given. Rather, you must work with variable cost as a *percentage* of each sales *dollar*. Moreover, most companies sell more than one product, and the overall break-even point is often expressed in sales dollars because of the variety of product lines. For example, although radios and television sets cannot be meaningfully added, their sales prices provide an automatic common denominator.

The same equation, this time using the relationship of variable costs and profits as a *percentage* of sales, may be used to obtain the sales in dollars:

Let $\qquad$ X = sales in dollars needed to break even. Then

$$X = .80X + \$6,000 + 0$$

$$.20X = \$6,000 + 0$$

$$X = \frac{\$6,000 + 0}{.20}$$

$$X = \$30,000$$

b. **Contribution-margin technique.** If algebra is not one of your strong points, you may prefer to approach cost-volume-profit relationships in the following common-sense arithmetic manner. Every unit sold generates a **contribution margin** or **marginal income,** which is the excess of the sales price over the variable expenses pertaining to the units in question:

Unit sales price	$.50
Unit variable expenses	.40
Unit contribution margin to fixed	
expenses and net income	$.10

The $.10 unit contribution is divided into total fixed expenses plus a target net income to obtain the number of *units* that must be sold to break even: ($6,000 + 0) ÷ $.10 = 60,000 units.

The computation in terms of *dollar* sales is

Sales price	100%
Variable expenses as a percentage	
of dollar sales	80
Contribution-margin ratio	20%

Therefore 20 percent of each sales dollar is the amount available for the recovery of fixed expenses and the making of net income: ($6,000 + 0) ÷ .20 = $30,000 sales needed to break even.

The terms *net income* and *net profit* are used interchangeably. Similarly, variable and fixed *expenses* and variable and fixed *costs* are used interchangeably. In this context, costs refer to the costs expiring during the period in question.

c. **Relationship of the two techniques.** Reflect on the relationship between the equation technique. Look at the second-last lines in the solutions to can see, the contribution-margin technique is merely a shortcut version of the equation technique. Look at the second-last lines in the solutions to Equation (1). They read:

TARGET VOLUME

in units	in dollars

$$\$.10X = \$6,000 + 0 \qquad .20X = \$6,000 + 0$$

$$X = \frac{\$6,000 + 0}{\$.10} \qquad X = \frac{\$6,000 + 0}{.20}$$

This gives us the shortcut general formulas:

$$\frac{\text{target volume}}{\text{in units}} = \frac{\text{fixed expenses} + \text{net income}}{\text{contribution margin per unit}} \qquad (2)$$

$$\frac{\text{target volume}}{\text{in dollars}} = \frac{\text{fixed expenses} + \text{net income}}{\text{contribution-margin ratio}} \qquad (3)$$

Which should you use, the equation or the contribution-margin technique?

Use either; the choice is a matter of personal preference or convenience within a particular case.

□ 2. GRAPHICAL TECHNIQUE

Graph the cost-volume-profit relationships in Requirement 1.

The break-even point is represented by the intersection of the sales line and the total expenses line in Exhibit 2-3. Exhibit 2-3 was constructed by using a sales line and a total expenses line that combined variable and fixed expenses. The procedure (see Exhibit 2-3) is as follows:

Step 1. Select a convenient sales volume, say 100,000 units, and plot the point for total sales dollars at that volume: $100,000 \times 50¢ = \$50,000$. Draw the revenue (i.e., sales) line from the origin to the $50,000 point.
Step 2. Draw the line showing the $6,000 fixed portion of expenses. It should be a horizontal line intersecting the vertical axis at $6,000.
Step 3. Determine the variable portion of expenses at a convenient level of activity: $100,000 \text{ units} \times \$.40 = \$40,000$. Add this to the fixed expenses: $\$40,000 + \$6,000 = \$46,000$. Plot the point for 100,000 units and $46,000. Then draw a line between this point and the $6,000 fixed cost intercept of the vertical axis. This is the total expenses line. The break-even

EXHIBIT 2-3. Cost-volume-profit graph

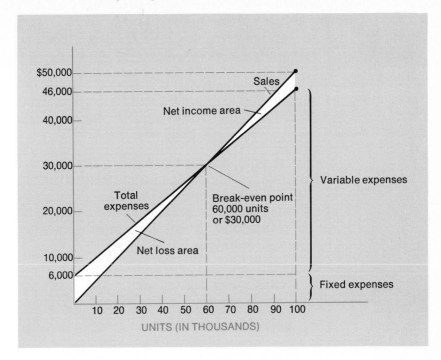

point is where this line crosses the sales line, 60,000 units or $30,000, namely where total sales revenues exactly equal total costs.

Exhibit 2-3 is the completed break-even graph. The break-even point is only one facet of this cost-volume-profit graph. More generally, the graph shows the profit or loss at *any* rate of activity. Namely, at any given volume, the vertical distance between the sales line and the total expenses line measures the net income or net loss.

The graph portrays only one of a number of methods for picturing cost-volume-profit relationships. The graph often has educational advantages because it shows potential profits over a wide range of volume more easily than numerical exhibits. Whether graphs or other types of exhibits are used depends largely on management's preference.

☐ 3. CHANGES IN FIXED EXPENSES

If the rent were doubled, find the monthly break-even point: (a) in number of units, (b) in dollar sales.

The fixed expenses would increase from $6,000 to $7,000. Then:

$$\frac{\text{target volume}}{\text{in units}} = \frac{\text{fixed expenses + net income}}{\text{contribution margin per unit}} = \frac{\$7,000}{\$.10} = \frac{70,000}{\text{units}} \quad (2)$$

$$\frac{\text{target volume}}{\text{in dollars}} = \frac{\text{fixed expenses + net income}}{\text{contribution-margin ratio}} = \frac{\$7,000}{.20} = \$35,000 \quad (3)$$

Note that a one-sixth increase in fixed expenses altered the break-even point by one-sixth: from 60,000 to 70,000 units and from $30,000 to $35,000. This relationship always exists, everything else held constant.

☐ 4. CHANGES IN CONTRIBUTION MARGIN PER UNIT

Assume that the fixed rent is unchanged. (a) If the owner is paid 1¢ per unit as additional rent, find the monthly break-even point in number of units; in dollar sales. (b) If the selling price falls from 50¢ to 45¢ per unit, and the original variable expenses are unchanged, find the monthly break-even point, in number of units; in dollar sales.

a. The variable expenses would be increased from 40¢ to 41¢, the unit contribution margin would be reduced from 10¢ to 9¢, and the contribution-margin ratio would become only 18 percent (9¢ ÷ 50¢).

The original fixed expenses of $6,000 would be unaffected, but the denominators are changed as compared with the denominators used in the solutions to Requirements 1 and 3. Thus:

$$\text{break-even point in units} = \frac{\$6,000}{\$.09} = 66,667 \text{ units} \qquad (2)$$

$$\text{break-even point in dollars} = \frac{\$6,000}{.18} = \$33,333 \qquad (3)$$

b. A change in unit contribution margin can also be caused by a change in selling price. If the selling price fell from 50¢ to 45¢, and the original variable expenses were unchanged, the unit contribution would be reduced from 10¢ to 5¢ (i.e., 45¢ − 40¢) and the break-even point would soar to 120,000 units (6,000 ÷ 5¢). The break-even point in dollars would also change, because the selling price and contribution-margin ratio change: the contribution-margin ratio would be 11.11 percent (5¢ ÷ 45¢). The break-even point, in dollars, would be $54,000 (120,000 units × 45¢), or, using the formula:

$$\text{break-even point in dollars} = \frac{\$6,000}{.1111} = \$54,000 \qquad (3)$$

☐ 5. TARGET NET PROFIT AND AN INCREMENTAL APPROACH

Refer to the original data. If Winston considers $480 per month the minimum acceptable net income, how many units will have to be sold to warrant the renting of the machines? Convert your answer into dollar sales.

$$\text{target sales volume in units} = \frac{\text{fixed expenses} + \text{net income}}{\text{contribution margin per unit}}$$

$$= \frac{\$6,000 + \$480}{\$.10} = 64,800 \text{ units} \qquad (2)$$

CHAPTER 2

36

Another way of getting the same answer is to use your knowledge of the break-even point and adopt an incremental approach. The term **incremental** is widely used in accounting. It refers to the *change* in total results (such as revenue, expenses, or income) under a new condition in comparison with some given or known condition.

In this instance, the given condition is assumed to be the 60,000-unit break-even point. All expenses would be recovered at that volume. Therefore the *change* or *increment* in net income for every unit *beyond* 60,000 would be equal to the contribution margin of $.50 − $.40 = $.10. If $480 were the target net profit, $480 ÷ 10¢ would show that the target volume must exceed the break-even volume by 4,800 units; it would therefore be 60,000 + 4,800 = 64,800 units.

The answer, in terms of *dollar* sales, can then be computed by multiplying 64,800 units by 50¢, or by using the formula:

$$\text{target sales volume in dollars} = \frac{\text{fixed expenses} + \text{net income}}{\text{contribution-margin ratio}} \tag{3}$$

$$= \frac{\$6,000 + \$480}{.20} = \$32,400$$

To solve directly for sales dollars with the alternative incremental approach, the break-even point, in dollar sales of $30,000, becomes the frame of reference. Every sales dollar beyond that point contributes 20¢ to net profit. Divide $480 by .20. The dollar sales must therefore exceed the break-even volume by $2,400 to produce a net profit of $480; thus the total dollar sales would be $30,000 + $2,400 = $32,400.

These relationships are recapitulated below:

	BREAK-EVEN POINT	INCREMENT	NEW CONDITION
Volume in units	60,000	4,800	64,800
Sales	$30,000	$2,400	$32,400
Variable expenses	24,000	1,920	25,920
Contribution margin	6,000	480	6,480
Fixed expenses	6,000	—	6,000
Net income	$ 0	$ 480	$ 480

□ 6. MULTIPLE CHANGES IN THE KEY FACTORS

Suppose, after the machines have been in place awhile, Winston is considering locking them from 6:00 P.M. to 6:00 A.M., which she estimates will save $820 in wages monthly. The cutback from 24-hour service would hurt volume substantially, because many nighttime employees use the machines. However, employees could find food elsewhere, so not too many complaints are expected. Should the machines remain available 24 hours per day? Assume that monthly sales would decline by 10,000 units from current sales of (a) 62,000 units and (b) 90,000 units.

First, whether 62,000 or 90,000 units are being sold is irrelevant to the decision at hand. The analysis of this situation consists of constructing and solving equations for conditions that prevail under either alternative and selecting the volume level that yields the highest net profit. However, the incremental approach is much quicker. What is the essence of this decision? We are asking whether the prospective savings in cost exceed the prospective loss in *total* contribution margin in dollars:

Lost total contribution margin, 10,000 units @ $.10	$1,000
Savings in fixed expenses	820
Prospective decline in net income	$ 180

Regardless of the current volume level, whether it be 62,000 or 90,000 units, if we accept the prediction that sales will decline by 10,000 units as accurate, the closing from 6:00 P.M. to 6:00 A.M. will decrease the profit by $180:

	DECLINE FROM 62,000 TO 52,000 UNITS		DECLINE FROM 90,000 TO 80,000 UNITS	
Units	62,000	52,000	90,000	80,000
Sales	$31,000	$26,000	$45,000	$40,000
Variable expenses	24,800	20,800	36,000	32,000
Contribution margin	$ 6,200	$ 5,200	$ 9,000	$ 8,000
Fixed expenses	6,000	5,180	6,000	5,180
Net Profit	$ 200	$ 20	$ 3,000	$ 2,820
Change in net profit	($180)		($180)	

Uses and limitations of cost-volume analysis

☐ OPTIMUM COMBINATION OF FACTORS

The analysis of cost-volume-profit relationships is one of management's paramount responsibilities. The knowledge of patterns of cost behavior offers insights valuable in planning and controlling short- and long-run operations. This is a major lesson of this book, so we should regard the current material as introductory. Our purpose in this chapter is to provide perspective, rather than to impart an intimate knowledge of the niceties of cost behavior.

The example of the vending machines demonstrated some valuable applications of cost-volume-profit analysis. One of management's principal duties is to discover the most profitable combination of the variable and fixed-cost factors. For example, automated machinery may be purchased, causing more fixed costs but reducing labor cost per unit. On the other hand, it may be wise to reduce fixed costs in order to obtain a more favorable combination. Thus, direct selling by a salaried sales force may be supplanted by the use of manufacturer's agents who are compensated via sales commissions (variable costs).

Generally, companies that spend heavily for advertising are willing to do so because they have high contribution margins (airlines, cigarette, and cosmetic companies). Conversely, companies with low contribution margins usually spend less for advertising and promotion (manufacturers of industrial equipment). The size of the contribution margin influences such outlays. Obviously a company with a volume of 100,000 units and a contribution margin of 10¢ per unit is not going to risk the same promotional outlay to obtain, say, a 10 percent increase in volume as a company with a contribution margin of 90¢ per unit.

Therefore, when the contribution-margin ratio is low, great increases in volume are necessary before significant increases in net profits can occur. As sales exceed the break-even point, a high contribution-margin ratio increases profits faster than a small contribution-margin ratio.

□ LIMITING ASSUMPTIONS

The notion of relevant range, which was introduced when fixed expenses were discussed, is applicable to the entire break-even graph. Almost all break-even graphs show revenue and cost lines extending back to the vertical axis. This is misleading, because the relationships depicted in such graphs are valid only within the relevant range that underlies the construction of the graph. Exhibit 2-4(B), a modification of the conventional break-even graph, partially demonstrates the multitude of assumptions that must be made in constructing the typical break-even graph. Some of these assumptions are:

1. The behavior of revenues and expenses is accurately portrayed and is linear over the relevant range. The principal differences between the accountant's break-even chart and the economist's are: (a) the accountant's sales line is drawn on the assumption that selling prices do not change with production or sales, and the economist assumes that reduced selling prices are normally associated with increased sales volume; (b) the accountant usually assumes a constant variable expense per unit, and the economist assumes that variable expense per unit does change with production.

2. Expenses may be classified into variable and fixed categories. Total varia-

EXHIBIT 2-4. Conventional and modified break-even graphs

A. CONVENTIONAL GRAPH

B. MODIFIED GRAPH

ble expenses vary directly with volume. Total fixed expenses do not change with volume.

3. Efficiency and productivity will be unchanged.

4. Sales mix will be constant. The **sales mix** is the relative combination of quantities of a variety of company products that compose total sales.

5. The difference in inventory level at the beginning and at the end of a period is insignificant. (The impact of inventory changes on cost-volume-profit analysis is discussed in Chapter 14.)

☐ CONTRIBUTION MARGIN AND GROSS MARGIN

Recall that *contribution margin* was defined as the excess of sales over *all* variable expenses. It may be expressed as a *total* absolute amount, a *unit* absolute amount, and a *percentage*. Sometimes a **variable expense ratio** or **variable cost ratio** may be encountered; it is defined as the variable expenses divided by sales. Thus a contribution margin ratio of 20 percent means that the variable cost ratio is 80 percent.

The most confusion about terms seems to be the mix-up between *contribution margin* and **gross margin** (which is also called **gross profit**). *Gross margin* is a widely used concept, particularly in the retailing industry. It is defined as the excess of sales over the **cost of goods sold** (that is, the cost of the merchandise that is acquired and resold). The following comparisons from our chapter illustration show the similarities and differences between the contribution margin and the gross margin:

Sales	$.50
Variable costs: Acquisition cost of unit sold	.40
Contribution margin and gross margin are equal	$.10

Thus the basic data for Requirement 1 resulted in no difference between the measure of contribution margin and gross margin. However, recall that Requirement 4a introduced a variable portion of rent. There would now be a difference:

	4a	1
Sales	$.50	$.50
Acquisition cost of unit sold	$.40	.40
Variable rent	.01	
Total variable expense	.41	
Contribution margin	$.09	
Gross margin		$.10

As the preceding tabulation indicates, and as the next chapter will explain more fully, contribution margin and gross margin are not the same concepts.

Contribution margin focuses on sales in relation to *all* variable cost behavior, whereas gross margin focuses on sales in relation to a lone item, the acquisition cost of the *merchandise* that has been sold.

summary

An understanding of cost behavior patterns and cost-volume-profit relationships can help guide a manager's decisions.

Variable costs (and expenses) and fixed costs (and expenses) have contrasting behavior patterns. Their relationship to sales, volume, and net profit is probably best seen on a cost-volume-profit graph. However, the graph should be used with great care. The portrayal of all profit-influencing factors on such a graph entails many assumptions that may hold over only a relatively narrow range of volume. As a tool, the graph may be compared to a meat-ax rather than to a surgeon's scalpel. Cost-volume-profit analysis, as depicted on a graph, is a framework for analysis, a vehicle for appraising overall performance, and a planning device.

The assumptions that underlie typical cost-volume-profit analysis are static. A change in one assumption (e.g., total fixed cost or the unit price of merchandise) will affect all the cost-volume-profit relationships on a given graph. The static nature of these assumptions should always be remembered by the managers who use this valuable analytical technique.

summary problem
for your review

PROBLEM

The income statement of Wiley Company is summarized as follows:

Net revenue	$800,000
Less: Expenses, including $400,000 of fixed expenses	880,000
Net loss	$ (80,000)

The manager believes that an increase of $200,000 in advertising outlays will increase sales substantially. His plan was approved by the chairman of the board.

REQUIRED

1. At what sales volume will the company break even?
2. What sales volume will result in a net profit of $40,000?

SOLUTION

1. Note that all data are expressed in dollars. No unit data are given. Most companies have many products, so the overall break-even analysis deals with dollar sales, not units. The variable expenses are $880,000 − $400,000, or $480,000. The variable expense ratio is $480,000 ÷ $800,000, or .60. Therefore the contribution-margin ratio is .40.

Let

S = break-even sales, in dollars. Then

$$S = \text{variable expenses} + \text{fixed expenses} + \text{net profit} \qquad (1)$$

$$S = .60S + (\$400,000 + \$200,000) + 0$$

$$.40S = \$600,000 + 0$$

$$S = \frac{\$600,000 + 0}{.40} = \frac{\text{fixed expenses} + \text{target net profit}}{\text{contribution-margin ratio}} \qquad (3)$$

$$S = \$1,500,000$$

2. $$\text{required sales} = \frac{\text{fixed expenses} + \text{target net profit}}{\text{contribution-margin ratio}} \qquad (3)$$

$$\text{required sales} = \frac{\$600,000 + \$40,000}{.40} = \frac{\$640,000}{.40}$$

$$\text{required sales} = \$1,600,000$$

Alternatively, we can use an incremental approach and reason that all dollar sales beyond the $1.5 million break-even point will result in a 40 percent contribution to net profit. Divide $40,000 by .40. Sales must therefore be $100,000 beyond the $1.5 million break-even point in order to produce a net profit of $40,000.

Appendix 2A: the P/V chart and sales-mix analysis

☐ THE P/V CHART

Exhibit 2-3 can be recast in another form as a so-called P/V chart (a profit-volume graph). This form is preferred by many managers who are interested mainly in the impact of changes in volume on net income. The first graph in Exhibit 2-5 illustrates the chart, using the data in our example. The chart is constructed as follows:

1. The vertical axis is net income in dollars. The horizontal axis is volume in units (or in sales dollars, in many cases).

2. At zero volume, the net loss would be approximated by the total fixed costs: $6,000 in this example.

3. A net income line will slope upward from the −$6,000 intercept at the rate of the unit contribution margin of 10¢. The line will intersect the volume axis at the break-even point of 60,000 units. Each unit sold beyond the break-even point will add 10¢ to net income. For example, at a volume

EXHIBIT 2-5. P/V chart

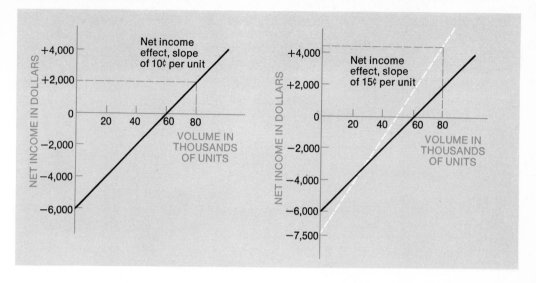

of 80,000 units, the net income would be $(80,000 - 60,000) \times 10¢ = \$2,000$.

The P/V chart provides a quick, condensed comparison of how alternatives on pricing, variable costs, or fixed costs may affect net income as volume changes. For example, the second graph in Exhibit 2-5 shows how net income and the break-even point would be affected by an increase in selling price from 50¢ to 55¢ and a $1,500 increase in rent. The unit contribution would become 15¢, and the break-even point would fall from 60,000 to 50,000 units:

new break-even point = $7,500 ÷ $.15

= 50,000 units

Note also that the net income will increase at a much faster rate as volume increases. At a volume of 80,000 units, the net income would be $(80,000 - 50,000) \times 15¢ = \$4,500$.

☐ EFFECTS OF SALES MIX

The cost-volume-profit analysis in this chapter has focused on a single line of products. In multiproduct firms, sales mix is an important factor in calculating an overall company break-even point. If the proportions of the mix change, the cost-volume-profit relationships also change. When managers choose a sales mix, it can be depicted on a break-even chart or P/V chart by assuming average revenues and costs for a given mix.

For example, suppose that a two-product company has a unit contribution margin of $1 for Product A and $2 for Product B, and that fixed costs are $100,000. The break-even point would be 100,000 units if only A were sold and 50,000 units if only B were sold. Suppose that the planned mix is three units of A for each unit of B. The contribution margin for each "package" of products

EXHIBIT 2-6. P/V chart and sales mix

would be 3 × $1 plus 1 × $2, or $5. The average contribution margin per unit of product would be $5 ÷ 4 units in each package = $1.25.[1] The break-even point, assuming that the mix is maintained, would be:

$100,000 ÷ $1.25 = 80,000 units (consisting of 60,000 units of A

and 20,000 of B)

These relationships are shown in Exhibit 2-6. The slopes of the solid lines depict the unit contribution margins of each product. The slope of the broken line depicts the average contribution per unit. Suppose that the total planned sales are 160,000 units, consisting of 120,000 units of A and 40,000 of B. Exhibit 2-6 shows that if overall unit sales and mix targets are achieved, net income would be $100,000. However, if the mix changes, net income may be much greater because the proportion of sales of B might be higher than anticipated. The opposite effect would occur if A sold in a higher proportion than expected. When the sales mix changes, the break-even point and the expected net income at various sales levels are altered.

Management's discussion and analysis of income statements often refers to the effects of changes in sales mix. For example, consider the 1979 annual report of Deere and Company, a manufacturer of farm equipment: "The increase in the ratio of cost of goods sold to net sales resulted from the higher production costs, a less favorable mix of products sold, and sales incentive programs."

---

[1]An alternate computation would use a weighted-average approach:

	PLANNED SALES	WEIGHTS	UNIT CONTRIBUTION MARGIN	WEIGHTED AVERAGE
A	3	3/4	$1.00	$ .75
B	1	1/4	2.00	.50
	4			$1.25

Appendix 2B: impact of income taxes

Private enterprises are subject to income taxes. Reconsider Requirement 5 of the basic illustration in the chapter, where the target income before income taxes was $480. If an income tax were levied at 40 percent, relationships would be:

Income before income tax	$480	100%
Income tax	192	40
Net income	$288	60%

Note that:

$$\text{income before income taxes} = \frac{\text{target after-tax net income}}{1 - \text{tax rate}}$$

$$\text{income before income taxes} = \frac{\$288}{1 - .40} = \frac{\$288}{.60} = \$480$$

Suppose the target net income after taxes were $288. The only change in the general equation approach would be:

$$\text{target sales} = \text{variable expenses} + \text{fixed expenses} + \frac{\text{target after-tax net income}}{1 - \text{tax rate}}$$

Thus, letting X be the number of units to be sold at 50¢ each with a variable cost of 40¢ each and total fixed costs of $6,000:

$$\$.50X = \$.40X + \$6,000 + \frac{\$288}{1 - .4}$$

$$\$.10X = \$6,000 + \frac{\$288}{.6}$$

$$\$.06X = \$3,600 + \$288 = \$3,888$$

$$X = \$3,888 \div \$.06 = 64,800 \text{ units}$$

Suppose the target net income after taxes were $480. The needed volume would rise to 68,000 units, as follows:

$$\$.50X = \$.40X + \$6,000 + \frac{\$480}{1 - .4}$$

$$\$.10X = \$6,000 + \frac{\$480}{.6}$$

$$\$.06X = \$3,600 + \$480 = \$4,080$$

$$X = \$4,080 \div \$.06 = 68,000 \text{ units}$$

assignment material

2-1. **Terminology.** Define *contribution margin; cost of goods sold; fixed cost; gross margin; gross profit; incremental; marginal income; relevant range; sales mix; variable cost; variable cost ratio; variable expense ratio.*

2-2. **Photocopying machines.** The Martinez Company operates and services photocopying machines located in college dormitories, libraries, hotels, and various public places. The machines are rented from the manufacturer. In addition, Martinez must rent the space occupied by the machines. Martinez has an opportunity to place some machines in ten branch libraries of a large city. The following expense and revenue relationships pertain to a contemplated expansion program of ten machines, which are rented by Martinez from a manufacturer at a flat rate per month plus one cent per copy:

Fixed monthly expenses:

Machine rental: 10 machines	$1,300
Space rental: 10 locations	400
Wages, including fringe costs, to service the additional 10 machines	500
Other fixed costs	200
Total	$2,400

Other data:

	PER COPY	PER $100 OF SALES
Selling price	$.10	100%
Cost of paper, toner, repair parts, and rental charge per copy	.06	60
Contribution margin	$.04	40%

REQUIRED

These questions relate to the above data unless otherwise noted. Ignore income taxes. *Consider each question independently.*

1. Compute the monthly break-even point in number of copies; in dollar sales.
2. Compute the company's net income if 70,000 copies were sold.
3. Suppose the space rental were doubled. Compute the monthly break-even point in number of copies; in dollar sales.
4. Refer to the original data. Suppose the manufacturer increased the rent from one to two cents per copy. Compute the monthly break-even point in number of copies.
5. Refer to the original data. Suppose the libraries were paid one cent per copy for each unit sold in excess of the break-even point. Compute the company's net income if 70,000 copies were sold.

2-3. **Exercises in cost-volume-profit relationships.** (An alternate is 2-12.) The Avanti Transportation Company specializes in hauling heavy goods over long distances. Avanti's revenue depends on both weights and mileage. Summarized budget data for next year are based on total intercity–vehicle revenue miles of 800,000:

	PER MILE
Average selling price (revenue)	$1.20
Average variable expenses	1.00
Fixed expenses, $120,000	

1. Compute the budgeted net income. Ignore income taxes.
2. Management is trying to decide how various possible conditions or decisions might affect net income. Compute the new net income for each of the following changes. Consider each case independently.
   a. A 10 percent increase in revenue miles.
   b. A 10 percent increase in sales price.
   c. A 10 percent increase in variable expenses.
   d. A 10 percent increase in fixed expenses.
   e. A 10 percent increase in fixed expenses in the form of more advertising and a 5 percent increase in revenue miles.
   f. An average decrease in selling price of 3¢ per mile and a 5 percent increase in revenue miles. Refer to the original data.
   g. An average increase in selling price of 5 percent and a 10 percent decrease in revenue miles.

◼ ADDITIONAL ASSIGNMENT MATERIAL

2-4. Why is "break-even analysis" a misnomer?

2-5. Distinguish between the equation technique and the unit contribution technique.

2-6. What are the principal differences between the accountant's and the economist's break-even graphs?

2-7. What is the sales mix?

2-8. Explain the *incremental approach* as used in cost-volume-profit analysis.

2-9. **Nature of variable and fixed costs.** "As I understand it, costs such as the salary of the vice-president of transportation operations are variable because the more traffic you handle, the less your unit cost. In contrast, costs such as fuel are fixed because each ton-mile should entail consumption of the same amount of fuel and hence bear the same unit cost." Do you agree? Explain.

2-10. **Extensions of chapter illustration.** Refer to the basic facts in the chapter illustration. Suppose the selling price was changed to 60¢ in response to a rise in unit variable cost from 40¢ to 45¢. The original data are on page 32.

1. Compute the monthly break-even point in number of units and in dollar sales.
2. Refer to the original data. If the rent were halved, what would be the monthly break-even point in number of units and in dollar sales?

2-11. **Hospital costs and pricing.** A hospital has overall variable costs of 30 percent of total revenue and fixed costs of $6.3 million per year.

1. Compute the break-even point expressed in total revenue.
2. A patient-day is often used to measure the volume of a hospital. Suppose there are going to be 20,000 patient-days next year. Compute the average daily revenue per patient necessary to break even.

2-12. **Basic review exercises.** (An alternate is 2-3.) Each problem is unrelated to the others.

1. Given: Selling price per unit, $20; total fixed expenses, $8,000; variable expenses per unit, $15. Find break-even sales in units.

2. Given: Sales, $40,000; variable expenses, $30,000; fixed expenses, $7,500; net income, $2,500. Find break-even sales.

3. Given: Selling price per unit, $30; total fixed expenses, $32,000; variable expenses per unit, $14. Find total sales in units to achieve a profit of $8,000, assuming no change in selling price.

4. Given: Sales, $50,000; variable expenses, $20,000; fixed expenses, $25,000; net income, $5,000. Assume no change in selling price; find net income if activity volume increases 10 percent.

5. Given: Selling price per unit, $40; total fixed expenses, $80,000; variable expenses per unit, $30. Assume that if variable expenses are reduced by 20 percent per unit, the total fixed expenses will be increased by 10 percent. Find the sales in units to achieve a profit of $16,000, assuming no change in selling price.

2-13. **Fixed costs and relevant range.** Horizon Computer Consultants has a substantial year-to-year fluctuation in billings to clients. Top management has the following policy regarding the employment of key professional personnel:

IF GROSS ANNUAL BILLINGS ARE	NUMBER OF PERSONS TO BE EMPLOYED	KEY PROFESSIONAL ANNUAL SALARIES AND RELATED EXPENSES
$2,000,000 or less	8	$ 800,000
$2,000,001–$2,400,000	9	900,000
$2,400,001–$2,800,000	10	1,000,000

Top management believes that a minimum of eight individuals should be retained for a year or more even if billings drop drastically below $2 million.

For the past five years, gross annual billings have fluctuated between $2,020,000 and $2,380,000. Expectations for next year are that gross billings will be between $2,100,000 and $2,300,000. What amount should be budgeted for key professional personnel? Graph the relationships on an annual basis, using the two approaches illustrated in Exhibit 2-2. Indicate the relevant range on each graph. You need not use graph paper; simply approximate the graphical relationships.

2-14. **Estimating cost behavior patterns.** The Mideastern Railroad showed the following results (in millions of dollars):

	19X3	19X2
Operating revenues	$218	$196
Operating expenses:		
Transportation	$ 87	$ 84
Maintenance of way and structures	34	32
Maintenance of equipment	37	34
Traffic	7	6
General	12	11
Payroll taxes	9	9
Property taxes	7	7
Equipment and other rentals	13	12
Total operating expenses	$206	$195
Net railway operating income	$ 12	$ 1

REQUIRED

Examine the figures in their entirety, not item by item. How do total expenses change in relation to total revenues? That is, if total revenues increase by $1,000, by how much will total expenses increase? What is the apparent contribution-margin percentage? Explain any assumptions that underlie your answer.

2-15. **Movie manager.** Joan Baker is the manager of Stanford's traditional Sunday Flicks. Each Sunday a film has two showings. The admission price is deliberately set at a very low 50¢. A maximum of 1,650 tickets are sold for each showing. The rental of the auditorium is $100 and labor is $280, including $30 for Baker. Baker must pay the film distributor a guarantee, ranging from $200 to $600 or 50 percent of gross admission receipts, whichever is higher.

Before and during the show, refreshments are sold; these sales average 12 percent of gross admission receipts and yield a contribution margin of 40 percent.

1. On June 3, Baker played *The Graduate.* The film grossed $1,400. The guarantee to the distributor was $500, or 50 percent of gross admission receipts. What operating income was produced for the Students Association, which sponsors the showings?

2. Recompute the results if the film grossed $900.

3. The "four-wall" concept is increasingly being adopted by movie producers. This means that the producer pays a fixed rental for the theater for, say, a week's showing of a movie. As a theater owner, how would you evaluate a "four-wall" offer?

2-16. Promotion of championship fight. Newspaper accounts of a Joe Frazier-Muhammad Ali boxing match stated that each fighter would receive a flat fee of $2.5 million in cash. The fight would be shown on closed-circuit television. The central promoter would collect 100 percent of the receipts and would return 30 percent to the individual local promoters. He expected to sell 1.1 million seats at a net average price of $10 each. He also was to receive $250,000 from Madison Square Garden (which had sold out its 19,500 seats, ranging from $150 for ringside down to $20, for a gross revenue of $1.25 million); he would not share the $250,000 with the local promoters.

REQUIRED

1. The central promoter is trying to decide what amount to spend for advertising. What is the most he could spend and still break even on his overall operations, assuming that he would sell 1.1 million tickets?
2. If the central promoter desired an operating income of $500,000, how many seats would have to be sold? Assume that the average price was $10 and the total fixed costs were $8 million.

2-17. Cost-volume-profit relationships and a dog track. The Multnomah Kennel Club is a dog-racing track. Its revenue is derived mainly from attendance and a fixed percentage of the parimutuel betting. Its expenses for a 90-day season are:

Wages of cashiers and ticket takers	$150,000
Commissioner's salary	20,000
Maintenance (repairs, etc.)	20,000
Utilities	30,000
Other expenses (depreciation, insurance, advertising, etc.)	100,000
Purses: Total prizes paid to winning racers	810,000

The track made a contract with the Auto Parking Association to park the cars. Auto Parking charged the track $1.80 per car. A survey revealed that on the average three persons arrived in each car and that there were no other means of transportation except by private automobiles.

The track's sources of revenue are:

Rights for concession and vending	$50,000
Admission charge (deliberately low)	$.80 per person
Percentage of bets placed	10%

REQUIRED

1. Assuming that each person bets $25 a night:
   a. How many persons have to be admitted for the track to break even for the season?

b. What is the total contribution margin at the break-even point?

c. If the desired profit for the year is $540,000, how many people would have to attend?

2. If a policy of free admission brought a 10 percent increase in attendance, what would be the new level of profit? Assume that the previous level of attendance was 600,000 people.

3. If the purses were doubled in an attempt to attract better dogs and thus increase attendance, what would be the new break-even point? Refer to the original data and assume that each person bets $25 a night.

2-18. **Hospital cost-volume-profit relationships.** Dr. Green and Dr. Jones, the two radiologists of the San Marcos Hospital, have submitted the following costs for operating the Department of Radiology:

Radiologists' salaries	30% of gross receipts
Technicians' and clerical salaries	$70,000
Supplies (fixed)	80,000
Depreciation	60,000

This year the department processed 65,000 films with three 200-milliampere X-ray machines. (Their original cost was $200,000 each, their original life expectancy, ten years.) For these processed films the average charge was $6. The 65,000 films represent maximum volume possible with the present equipment.

The physicians have submitted a request for two new 300-milliampere X-ray machines. (Their cost will be $250,000 each, their life expectancy ten years.) They will increase the capacity of the department by 35,000 films per year. Because of their special attachments (i.e., fluoroscopes) it will be possible to take more intricate films, for which a higher charge will be made. The average charge to the patient for each of these additional 35,000 films is estimated at $10. In order to operate the new machines, one highly trained technician must be hired at an annual salary of $15,000. The added capacity will increase the cost of supplies by $20,000.

REQUIRED

1. Determine the break-even point in films for the three 200-milliampere X-ray machines. How much do they contribute to the hospital's overall profits?

2. Determine the break-even point if the two new 300-milliampere X-ray machines are added to the department, assuming a sales mix based on maximum capacity. How much will be contributed to the hospital's overall profit, assuming they are operated at maximum volume?

2-19. **Church enterprise.** A California law permits a game of chance called BINGO when it is offered by specified not-for-profit institutions, including churches. Reverend John O'Toole, the pastor of a new parish in suburban Los Angeles, is investigating the desirability of conducting weekly BINGO nights. The parish has no hall, but a local hotel would be willing to commit its hall for a lump-sum rental of $300 per night. The rent would include cleaning, setting up and taking down tables and chairs, and so on.

REQUIRED

1. BINGO cards would be provided by a local printer in return for free advertising thereon. Door prizes would be donated by local merchants. The services of clerks, callers, security force, and others would be donated by volunteers. Admission would be $2.50 per person, entitling the player to one card; extra cards would be $1.50 each. Father O'Toole also learns that many persons buy extra cards, so there would be an average of four cards played per person. What is the maximum in total cash prizes that the church may award and still break even if 100 persons attend each weekly session?

2. Suppose the total cash prizes are $400. What will be the church's operating income if 50 persons attend? If 100 persons attend? If 150 persons attend? Briefly explain effects of the cost behavior on income.

3. After operating for ten months, Father O'Toole is thinking of negotiating a different rental arrangement but keeping the prize money unchanged. Suppose the rent is $200 weekly plus $1 per person. Compute the operating income for attendance of 50, 100, and 150 persons, respectively. Explain why the results differ from those in Requirement 2.

2-20. Effects of changes in costs. (CMA.) All-Day Candy Company is a wholesale distributor of candy. The company services grocery, convenience, and drugstores in a large metropolitan area.

Small but steady growth in sales has been achieved by the All-Day Candy Company over the past few years while candy prices have been increasing. The company is formulating its plans for the coming fiscal year. Presented below are the data used to project the current year's after-tax net income of $110,400.

Average selling price per box	$4.00
Average variable costs per box:	
Cost of candy	$2.00
Selling expenses	.40
Total	$2.40
Annual fixed costs	
Selling	$160,000
Administrative	280,000
Total	$440,000
Expected annual sales volume (390,000 boxes)	$1,560,000
Tax rate	40%

Manufacturers of candy have announced that they will increase prices of their products an average of 15 percent in the coming year, owing to increases in raw material (sugar, cocoa, peanuts, etc.) and labor costs. All-Day Candy Company expects that all other costs will remain at the same rates or levels as the current year.

REQUIRED

1. What is All-Day Candy Company's break-even point in boxes of candy for the current year?
2. What selling price per box must All-Day Candy Company charge to cover the 15 percent increase in the cost of candy and still maintain the current contribution-margin ratio? Read Appendix 2B. (Also see Problem 2-30.)

2-21. Traveling expenses. (A. Roberts.) Harold Nuget is a traveling inspector for the Environmental Protection Agency. He uses his own car and the agency reimburses him at 18¢ per mile. Harold claims he needs 21¢ per mile just to break even.

George Barr, the district manager, decides to look into the matter. He is able to compile the following information about Harold's expenses:

Oil change every 3,000 miles	$ 12
Maintenance (other than oil) every 6,000 miles	180
Yearly insurance	400
Auto cost $10,800 with an average cash trade-in value of $6,000; has a useful life of three years.	
Gasoline is approximately $2 per gallon and Harold averages 20 miles per gallon.	

When Harold is on the road, he averages 120 miles a day. The manager knows that Harold does not work Saturdays or Sundays, has ten working days vacation and six holidays, and spends approximately fifteen working days in the office.

1. How many miles a year would the inspector have to travel to break even at the current rate of reimbursement?
2. What would be an equitable mileage rate?

2-22. Adding a product. Jiminy's Greenlawn Tap, a pub located in a college community, serves as a gathering place for the university's more social scholars. Jiminy sells beer on draft and all brands of bottled beer at a contribution margin of 40¢ a beer.

Jiminy is considering also selling hamburgers. His reasons are twofold. First, sandwiches would attract daytime customers. A hamburger and a beer are a quick lunch. Second, he has to meet competition from other local bars, some of which provide more extensive menus.

Jiminy analyzed the costs as follows:

Monthly fixed expenses:	
Wages of cook	$1,000
Other	200
Total	$1,200

	PER HAMBURGER
Variable expenses:	
Rolls	$ .05
Meat @ $1.40 per pound	
(7 hamburgers per pound)	.20
Other	.05
Total	$ .30

Jiminy planned a selling price of $.55 per hamburger to lure many customers.

For all questions, assume a 30-day month.
1. What are the monthly and daily break-even points, in number of hamburgers?
2. What are the monthly and daily break-even points, in dollar sales?
3. At the end of two months, Jiminy finds he has sold 3,600 hamburgers. What is the net profit per month on hamburgers?
4. Jiminy thinks that at least 60 extra beers are sold per day because he has these hamburgers available. This means that 60 extra people come to the bar or that 60 buy an extra beer because they are attracted by the hamburgers. How does this affect Jiminy's monthly income?
5. Refer to Requirement 3. How many extra beers would have to be sold per day so that the overall effects of the hamburger sales on monthly operating income would be zero?

2-23. Hospital costs. (Heavily adapted from CPA.) The Lincoln Hospital operates several special departments. Each department pays space and bed charges on a fixed yearly basis, and services such as meals and laundry are charged as used. During 19X5 the pediatrics department billed each patient an average of $65 per day, had a capacity of 60 beds, and collected a gross revenue of $1,138,800. Expenses charged by the hospital to the pediatrics department for 19X5 are detailed below.

	BASIS OF ALLOCATION	
	patient-days	bed capacity
Meals	$ 42,952	
Janitorial		$ 12,800
Laundry	28,000	
Laboratory	94,800	
Maintenance	5,200	7,140
General administrative services		131,760
Rent		275,320
Pharmacy	73,800	
Other	18,048	25,980
	$262,800	$453,000

A separate contract is negotiated each year regarding nursing staff. Each nurse receives an annual salary of $15,000 from the hospital, and at the end of the year each department is charged according to the following schedule.

ANNUAL PATIENT-DAYS	NURSES SUPPLIED (assumed)
10,000–14,000	20
Over 14,000	25

You have been asked to assist the head of the Pediatrics Clinic in determining the 19X6 operating budget and renegotiating the nursing contract for 19X6. The cost system for space and services will be unchanged in 19X6.

REQUIRED

1. Considering only the space and service fees charged by the hospital (before nursing fees), how many patient-days will be required in 19X6 for the pediatrics department to break even?
2. Now *including* the nursing charges, how many patient-days will be required for the pediatrics department to break even in 19X6?
3. The head of the pediatrics department is considering offering the nursing center a flat nursing rate of $22.50 per patient-day, rather than the two-level system employed in 19X5. What will be the break-even point (in patient-days) under this plan (including the proposed nursing fee)?

2-24. **Pricing and service industries.** Most law firms have two broad ranks of attorneys: associates, who work for salaries, and partners, who share any income generated before taxes. You are an experienced associate of James Milne and Company, a small but prestigious law firm. James Milne, the senior partner, has asked you to analyze the following budget data with the aim of setting a fee structure for 19X4:

	DEPARTMENT		
	probate	tax	TOTAL
Number of partners	2	3	5
Budgeted partner-hours billable to clients	3,200	4,500	7,700
Number of associates	2	6	8
Budgeted associate-hours billable to clients	3,000	8,400	11,400
Total hours	6,200	12,900	19,100
Budgeted expenses for the firm:			
Secretarial staff and receptionist			$110,000
Library services			40,000
Rent			52,000
Janitorial services			14,000
Supplies and photocopying			30,000
Telephone			11,000
General expenses			15,000
			$272,000

Associates receive salaries and benefits of $40,000 per person per year.

James Milne kept abreast of the general pricing practices of other law firms. The billing rate for associates was $40 per hour, and he said it would be unthinkable for his firm to do otherwise. However, because of the general high quality of the work performed by his firm, the senior partner was confident that a partner could be billed out at $80 to $125 per hour. Milne also told you that, on an average, the partners expected an income after all expenses, but before income taxes, of $100,000 each.

1. Compute the average billing rate per partner-hour for 19X4.
2. All expenses for 19X4 were exactly the same as budgeted. You have been asked to repeat for 19X5 what you did in Requirement 1. All expenses are expected to be the same as the actual expenses for 19X4. However, because of their superior work in 19X4, the associates will be provided greater responsibility and greater breadth of experience. What that entailed, you learned, was that the associates would work more hours and the partners would work fewer. The budgeted billable hours for 19X5 were:

	DEPARTMENT		
	probate	tax	TOTAL
Partners	2,400	3,300	5,700
Associates	3,800	9,600	13,400
Total hours	6,200	12,900	19,100

You also learned that the partners still expected to receive $100,000 each on the average. The market remained such that an associate could still only be billed out at $40 per hour.

assignment materials for appendixes

2-25. **P/V chart.** Consider the example on page 32. Suppose the rent were cut from $1,000 to $504, the cost per item raised from 40¢ to 47¢, and the selling price raised to 55¢.

1. Compute the new break-even point in units.
2. Draw a new P/V chart similar to the second one in Exhibit 2-5, page 43.
3. Compute and plot the new net income at a volume of 80,000 units.

2-26. **P/V chart and sales mix.** The Grimm Company has three products—X, Y, and Z—having contribution margins of $2, $3, and $6, respectively. The president is planning to sell 200,000 units in the forthcoming period, consisting of 80,000 X, 100,000 Y, and 20,000 Z. The company's fixed costs for the period are $406,000.

1. What is the company's break-even point in units, assuming that the given sales mix is maintained?
2. Prepare a P/V chart for a volume of 200,000 units. Have a broken line represent the average contribution margin per unit and have solid lines represent the net income effects of each product by showing their unit contributions as the slopes of each line. What is the total contribution margin at a volume of 200,000 units? Net income?
3. What would net income become if 80,000 units of X, 80,000 units of Y, and 40,000 units of Z were sold? What would be the new break-even point if these relationships persisted in the next period?

2-27. **Product mix and break-even analysis.** The Frozen Entree Company specializes in preparing two delicious food items that are frozen and shipped to many of the finer restaurants in the New York area. As a diner orders the item, the restaurant heats and serves it. The budget data for 19X4 are:

	PRODUCT	
	veal oscar	chicken kiev
Selling price	$5	$4
Variable expenses	2	2
Contribution margin	$3	$2
Number of units expected to be sold	20,000	30,000

Fixed expenses have been assigned, $33,000 to veal and $16,000 to chicken.

REQUIRED

1. Compute the break-even point in units for each product.
2. Suppose that the entrees were made in the same facilities, delivered on the same trucks, and so on. Suppose that a local chicken processor began a competitive operation on the chicken item, cutting the price so severely that Frozen Entree instantly dropped the chicken item for all of 19X4. Suppose also that the company's fixed costs were unaffected.
   a. What would be the break-even point for the company as a whole, assuming no chicken were produced?
   b. Suppose instead that only chicken and no veal were produced. What would be the break-even point for the company as a whole?
3. Draw a break-even graph for the company as a whole, using an average selling price and an average variable expense per unit. What is the break-even point under this aggregate approach? What is the break-even point if you add together the individual break-even points that you computed in Requirement 1? Why is the aggregate break-even point different from the sum of the individual break-even points?

2-28. **Patient mix.** [Adapted from J. Suver and B. Neumann, "Patient Mix and Break-even Analysis," *Management Accounting*, LVIII, No. 7 (January 1977), 38–40.] A hospital has the following cost structure and patient mix: fixed costs, $1 million; daily revenue rate, $120; variable costs, $40 per patient-day.

Type of Patient		Reimbursement Basis per Patient-Day	
Self-pay	20%	Revenue rate	$120
Private insurance	25	Revenue rate	120
Medicare	30	Specified costs or revenue rate, whichever is lower	110
Medicaid	25	Specified costs only	100

REQUIRED

1. What level of total revenue must be achieved to break even?
2. How many patient-days must be achieved to break even? If the mix is unchanged, how many patient-days for each type of patient are necessary to break even?
3. The application of cost-volume-profit analysis in a hospital will depend on many objectives of top management. For instance, the hospital may be committed to take all types of patients as a matter of its community responsibilities. Suppose that the hospital is able to eliminate the Medicare and Medicaid patients; how many patient-days are required to break even?

COST-VOLUME
RELATIONSHIPS

2-29. **Income taxes.** Review the illustration in Appendix 2B. Suppose the income tax rate were 30 percent instead of 40 percent.

How many units would have to be sold to achieve a target net income of (1) $288 and (2) $480? Show your computations.

2-30. Income taxes. (CMA.) Refer to Problem 2-20. What volume of sales in dollars must the All-Day Candy Company achieve in the coming year to maintain the same net income after taxes as projected for the current year if the selling price of candy remains at $4 per box and the cost of candy increases 15 percent?

2-31. Multiple choice. (CMA.) Read Appendix 2B. Select the best answer for each of the following items.

1. Cost-volume-profit analysis is a technique available to management to understand better the interrelationships of several factors that affect a firm's profit. As with many such techniques, the accountant oversimplifies the real world by making assumptions. Which of the following is *not* a major assumption underlying cost-volume-profit analysis:

    a. All costs incurred by a firm can be separated into their fixed and variable components.

    b. The product selling price per unit is constant at all volume levels.

    c. Operating efficiency and employee productivity are constant at all volume levels.

    d. For multiproduct situations, the sales mix can vary at all volume levels.

    e. Costs vary only with changes in volume.

The Following Data Apply to Items 2-6.

Laraby Company produces a single product. It sold 25,000 units last year with the following results:

Sales		$625,000
Variable costs	$375,000	
Fixed costs	150,000	525,000
Net income before taxes		$100,000
Income taxes (45%)		45,000
Net income		$ 55,000

In an attempt to improve its product, Laraby is considering replacing a component part in its product that has a cost of $2.50 with a new and better part costing $4.50 per unit in the coming year. A new machine would also be needed to increase plant capacity. The machine would cost $18,000 with a useful life of six years and no salvage value. The company uses straight-line depreciation on all plant assets.

2. What was Laraby Company's break-even point in number of units last year?

    a. 6,000.   *d.* 18,000.

    b. 15,000.   *e.* none of the preceding responses

    c. 21,000.   is correct.

3. How many units of product would Laraby Company have had to sell in the last year to earn $77,000 in net income after taxes?

    a. 29,000.   *d.* 29,300.

    b. 23,000.   *e.* none of the preceding responses

    c. 22,700.   is correct.

4. If Laraby Company holds the sales price constant and makes the suggested changes, how many units of product must be sold in the coming year to break even?

    a. 15,300.   *d.* 21,000.

    b. 18,750.   *e.* none of the preceding responses

    c. 19,125.   is correct.

5. If Laraby Company holds the sales price constant and makes the suggested changes, how many units of product will the company have to sell to make the same net income after taxes as last year?

a. 31,625.

b. 31,250.

c. 33,500.

d. 25,300.

e. none of the preceding responses is correct.

6. If Laraby Company wishes to maintain the same contribution-margin ratio, what selling price per unit of product must it charge next year to cover the increased material costs?

a. $27.00.

b. $25.00.

c. $32.50.

d. $28.33.

e. none of the preceding responses is correct.

2-32. **Income taxes on hotels.** The Galvez Hotel has annual fixed costs applicable to rooms of $1.5 million for its 300-room hotel, average daily room rates of $40, and average variable costs of $6 for each room rented. It operates 365 days per year. The hotel is subject to an income tax rate of 30 percent.

REQUIRED

1. How many rooms must the hotel rent to earn a net income after taxes of $1 million? Of $500,000?
2. Compute the break-even point in number of rooms rented. What percentage occupancy for the year is needed to break even?

2-33. **Income taxes.** The Tastee Morsel Company has a chain of restaurants that operate in various local hospitals and universities. The following analysis was conducted:

Average sales check for each customer		$4.00
Costs of food	$1.50	
Other variable costs	.30	1.80
Contribution margin		$2.20

Fixed costs are $300,000 per year. The income tax rate is 40 percent.

REQUIRED

What total revenue must be achieved to obtain net income of $80,000?

chapter **3**

INTRODUCTION TO MANUFACTURING COSTS

learning objectives

When you have finished studying this chapter, you should be able to:

1. Define the following terms and concepts and explain how they are related: **cost, cost objective, cost accumulation,** and **cost allocation.**
2. Define and identify examples of each of the three major elements in the cost of a manufactured product.
3. Differentiate between product costs and period costs, identifying examples of each.
4. Explain how the financial statements of merchandisers and manufacturers differ because of the types of goods they sell.
5. Show the effects that the basic transactions of a manufacturing company can have on the balance sheet equation.
6. Construct model income statements of a manufacturing company in both the functional form and the contribution form.
7. Distinguish between job-order and process-costing systems.

Some form of cost accounting is applicable to manufacturing companies, retail stores, insurance companies, medical centers, and nearly all types of organizations. Throughout this book we shall consider both nonmanufacturing and manufacturing organizations, but we shall start with the manufacturing company because it is the most general case—embracing production, marketing, and general administration functions. You can then apply this overall framework to any organization.

Classifications of costs

☐ COST ACCUMULATION AND COST OBJECTIVES

A **cost** may be defined as a sacrifice or giving up of resources for a particular purpose. Costs are frequently measured by the monetary units (for example, dollars or francs) that must be paid for goods and services. Costs are initially recorded in elementary form and then grouped in different ways to facilitate various decisions such as evaluating managers and subunits of the organization, expanding or deleting products or territories, and replacing equipment.

To help make decisions, managers want the *cost of something*. This something is called a **cost objective,** which may be defined as *any activity for which a separate measurement of costs is desired.* Examples of cost objectives include departments, products, territories, miles driven, bricks laid, patients seen, tax bills sent, checks processed, student hours taught, and library books shelved.

The cost-accounting system typically (1) accumulates costs by some "natural" classification such as materials or labor and (2) then allocates (traces) these costs to cost objectives. Exhibit 3-1 illustrates how a company might use materials in two main departments for manufacturing several different products. Note that the cost of, say, the metal used may be accumulated initially by keeping a tabulation of the amounts withdrawn from the raw-material storage center by each department. In turn, the metal used by each department is allocated to the products worked on in that department.

Cost-accounting systems vary in complexity. They tend to become more detailed as management seeks more accurate data for decision making. In a news story about Mark Controls Company, an Evanston, Illinois, manufacturer in the valve industry, *Business Week* (August 1, 1977) said: "The key to Mark's success so far has been tough financial controls and methodical emphasis on profit margins." The company had previously relied on broad averages. The story continued: "The company set up a computerized costing system that calculated the precise cost and profit margin for each of the 15,000 products the company sold. Since then, about 15% of those products have been dropped from the company's line because they were insufficiently profitable."

How "precise" can cost allocations be? Probably never as precise as might be desired. Nevertheless, managers have increasingly discovered that reliance on broad averages is not enough in today's world.

☐ ELEMENTS OF MANUFACTURING COSTS

The same general approach of cost accumulation and cost allocation that was just illustrated for raw materials is also applicable to other manufacturing costs.

EXHIBIT 3-1. Cost accumulation and allocation

1. Cost accumulation

2. Cost allocation to cost objectives:

a) To departments*

b) To products**

*Purpose: to evaluate performance of manufacturing departments.
**Purpose: to obtain costs of various products for valuing inventory, determining income, and judging product profitability.

Manufacturing is the transformation of materials into other goods through the use of labor and factory facilities. There are three major elements in the cost of a manufactured product: (1) **direct materials,** (2) **direct labor,** and (3) **factory overhead.**

1. **Direct materials.** All materials that are physically identified as a part of the finished goods and that may be traced to the finished goods in an economically feasible way. Examples are gray iron castings, lumber, aluminum sheets, and subassemblies. Direct materials often do *not* include minor items such as nails or glue. Why? Because the costs of tracing insignificant items do not seem worth the possible benefits of having more precise product costs. Such items are usually called *supplies* or *indirect materials* and are classified as a part of the factory overhead described below.

2. **Direct labor.** All labor that is physically traceable to the finished goods in an economically feasible way. Examples are the labor of machine operators and of assemblers. Much labor, such as that of janitors, forklift-truck operators, plant guards, and storeroom clerks, is considered to be *indirect labor* because of the impossibility or economic infeasibility of tracing such activity to specific products via physical observation. Indirect labor is classified as a part of factory overhead.

3. **Factory overhead.** All costs other than direct material or direct labor that are associated with the manufacturing process. Other terms used to describe this category are **factory burden, manufacturing overhead, manufacturing expenses,** and **indirect manufacturing costs.** The last term is a clearer descriptor than factory overhead, but factory overhead

will be used most frequently in this book because it is briefer. Two major subclassifications of factory overhead are

a. **Variable factory overhead.** Examples are power, supplies, and most indirect labor. Whether the cost of a specific category of indirect labor is variable or fixed depends on its behavior in a given company. In this book, unless we specify otherwise, indirect labor will be considered a variable rather than a fixed cost.

b. **Fixed factory overhead.** Examples are supervisory salaries, property taxes, rent, insurance, and depreciation.

Two of the three major elements are sometimes combined in cost terminology as follows. *Prime cost* consists of (1) + (2), direct materials plus direct labor. *Conversion cost* consists of (2) + (3), direct labor plus factory overhead.

Relationships of income statements and balance sheets

This section assumes a basic familiarity with income statements and balance sheets, as covered by any beginning course in financial accounting or by Chapter 16. However, the reader can easily understand most of the terms explained here without having such familiarity.

☐ PRODUCT COSTS AND PERIOD COSTS

Accountants frequently refer to *product costs* and *period costs*. **Product costs** generally are identified with goods produced or purchased for resale. Product costs are initially identified as part of the inventory on hand; in turn, these product costs (inventoriable costs) become expenses (in the form of *cost of goods sold*) only when the inventory is sold. In contrast, **period costs** are costs that are being deducted as expenses during the current period without having been previously classified as product costs.

The distinctions between product costs and period costs are best understood by example. Examine the top half of Exhibit 3-2. A merchandising company (retailer or wholesaler) acquires goods for resale without changing their basic form. The *only* product cost is the purchase cost of the merchandise. Unsold goods are held as merchandise inventory cost and shown as an asset on a balance sheet. As the goods are sold, their costs become expense in the form of "cost of goods sold."

A merchandising company also has a variety of selling and administrative expenses, which are the major examples of period costs (noninventoriable costs). They are referred to as period costs because they are deducted from revenue as expenses without ever having been regarded as a part of inventory.

In manufacturing accounting, as the bottom half of Exhibit 3-2 illustrates, direct materials are transformed into salable form with the help of direct labor and factory overhead. All these costs are product costs because they are allocated to inventory until the goods are sold. As in merchandising accounting, the selling and administrative expenses are not regarded as product costs but are treated as period costs.

EXHIBIT 3-2. Relationships of product costs and period costs

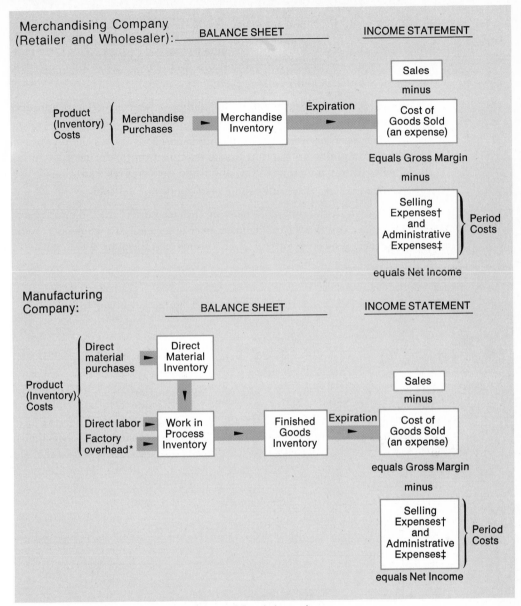

*Examples: indirect labor, factory supplies, insurance and depreciation on plant.

†Examples: insurance on salespersons' cars, depreciation on salespersons' cars, salespersons' salaries.

‡Examples: insurance on corporate headquarters building, depreciation on office equipment, clerical salaries.

Note particularly that where insurance and depreciation relate to the manufacturing function, they are inventoriable; but where they relate to selling and administration, they are not inventoriable.

☐ BALANCE SHEET PRESENTATION

As Exhibit 3-2 shows, balance sheets of manufacturers and merchandisers differ with respect to inventories. The merchandise inventory account is supplanted in a manufacturing concern by three inventory classes. The purpose of these various classifications is to trace all product costs through the production process to the time of sale. The classes are:

Direct-material inventory: materials on hand but not yet issued to the production line

Work-in-process inventory: cost of uncompleted goods still on the production line containing appropriate amounts of the three major manufacturing costs (direct material, direct labor, and factory overhead)

Finished-goods inventory: fully completed goods not yet sold

The only essential difference between the structure of the balance sheet of a manufacturer and that of the balance sheet of a retailer or wholesaler would appear in their respective current-asset sections (numbers are assumed):

Current-Asset Sections of Balance Sheets

MANUFACTURER			RETAILER OR WHOLESALER	
Cash		$ 4,000	Cash	$ 4,000
Receivables		25,000	Receivables	25,000
Finished goods	$32,000			
Work in process	22,000		Merchandise	
Direct material	23,000		inventories	77,000
Total inventories		77,000	Other current assets	1,000
Other current assets		1,000	Total current assets	$107,000
Total current assets		$107,000		

☐ UNIT COSTS FOR PRODUCT COSTING

Most often, product costing is accomplished by heavy use of unit costs. Assume the following:

Total cost of goods manufactured (10,000,000 units)	$40,000,000
Total units manufactured	10,000,000
Unit cost of product for inventory purposes ($40,000,000 ÷ 10,000,000)	$4

The unit cost facilitates the accounting for inventory valuation and income measurement. If some of the 10 million units manufactured are still unsold at the end of the period, a part of the $40 million cost of goods manufactured will be "held back" as a cost of the ending inventory of finished goods (and shown as an asset on a balance sheet). The remainder becomes "cost of goods sold" for the current period (that is, shown as an expense on the income statement).

☐ COSTS AND INCOME STATEMENTS

In the income statements, the detailed reporting of selling and administrative expenses is typically the same for manufacturing and merchandising organizations, but the cost of goods sold is different:

Manufacturer	*Retailer or Wholesaler*
Manufacturing cost of goods produced and then sold, usually composed of the three major elements of cost: direct materials, direct labor, and factory overhead	Merchandise cost of goods sold, usually composed of the purchase cost of items, including freight in, that are acquired and then resold

Consider the additional assumed details as they are presented in the model income statement of Exhibit 3-3. The $40 million cost of goods manufactured is subdivided into the major components of direct materials, direct labor, and factory overhead.

The terms "costs" and "expenses" are often used loosely by accountants and managers. "Expenses" denote all costs being deducted from (matched against) revenue in a given period. On the other hand, "costs" is a much broader

EXHIBIT 3-3

Model Income Statement, Manufacturing Company

Sales (8,000,000 units @ $10)			$80,000,000
Cost of goods manufactured and sold:			
Beginning finished-goods inventory		$ -0-	
Cost of goods manufactured:			
Direct materials used	$20,000,000		
Direct labor	12,000,000		
Factory overhead:			
Variable factory overhead	2,000,000		
Fixed factory overhead	6,000,000	40,000,000	
Cost of goods available for sale		$40,000,000	
Ending finished-goods inventory, 2,000,000 units @ $4		8,000,000	
Cost of goods sold (an expense)			32,000,000
Gross margin or gross profit			$48,000,000
Less other expenses:			
Selling costs (an expense)		$30,000,000	
General and administrative costs (an expense)		8,000,000	38,000,000
Operating income (also net income in this example)			$10,000,000

term; for example, "cost" is used to describe an asset (the cost of inventory) and an expense (the cost of goods sold). Thus manufacturing costs are funneled into an income statement as an expense (in the form of cost of goods sold) via the multistep inventory procedure, as indicated earlier in Exhibit 3-2. In contrast, selling and general administrative costs are commonly deemed expenses immediately as they are incurred.

☐ COMMON MISTAKES

Before proceeding, please take a moment to review some key distinctions made in Exhibits 3-2 and 3-3. Otherwise these new terms and classifications become blurred.

Distinguish sharply between the merchandising accounting and the manufacturing accounting for such costs as insurance, depreciation, and wages. In merchandising accounting, all such items are period costs (expenses of the current period). In manufacturing accounting, many of such items are related to production activities and thus, as factory overhead, are product costs (become expenses as the inventory is sold).

In both merchandising and manufacturing accounting, selling and general administrative costs are period costs. Thus the inventory cost of a manufactured product *excludes* sales salaries, sales commissions, advertising, legal, public relations, and the president's salary. *Manufacturing* overhead is traditionally regarded as a part of finished-goods inventory cost, whereas *selling* expenses and *general administrative* expenses are not.[1]

☐ RELATION TO BALANCE SHEET EQUATION

Exhibit 3-4 relates the theory of product costing to the analysis of the balance sheet equation. For simplicity, all acquisitions and dispositions of resources are assumed to be for cash. The same dollar amounts are used in Exhibits 3-3 and 3-4 except that Exhibit 3-4 introduces the idea of an inventory of materials. That is, $30 million of direct materials were acquired, $20 million were used, and $10 million were left in inventory at the end of the period.

Trace the effects of each summary transaction, step by step, in Exhibit 3-4. As the bottom of Exhibit 3-4 indicates, the ending balance sheet accounts would be:

Cash	$ 92,000,000	Paid-in capital	$100,000,000
Direct-materials inventory	10,000,000	Retained income	10,000,000*
Work-in-process inventory	—		
Finished-goods inventory	8,000,000		
Total assets	$110,000,000	Total equities	$110,000,000

Retained income arose because of profitable operations, which produced income of $10 million. For the detailed income statement, see Exhibit 3-3.

---

[1]Some accountants maintain that product costs become period costs as the goods are sold. In their minds, there is no difference between the terms "period costs" and "expenses," because both represent all costs that are being deducted from revenue during the current period. However, the distinction in this book consists of two steps: (1) Is the cost a product cost or a period cost? and (2) When do the product costs and the period costs become expenses? The product costs become expenses as the goods are sold, whereas the period costs become expenses as incurred.

EXHIBIT 3-4

Analysis of Balance Sheet Equation for Manufacturing Costs
(In millions of dollars)

transactions	ASSETS				= liabilities +	EQUITIES	
	cash +	direct-materials inventory +	work-in-process inventory +	finished-goods inventory		stockholders' equity paid-in capital +	retained income
Beginning balances	100				=	100	
1. Purchase of direct materials	−30	+30			=		
2. Direct materials used		−20	+20		=		
3. Acquire direct labor	−12		+12		=		
4. Acquire factory overhead	−8		+8		=		
5. Complete the goods			−40	+40	=		
6a. Revenue	+80				=		+80 (Revenue)
6b. Cost of goods sold				−32	=		−32 (Expense)
7. Selling costs	−30				=		−30 (Expense)
8. General and administrative costs	−8				=		−8 (Expense)
Ending balances	92 +	10 +	0 +	8	=	100 +	10

Admittedly, the area of manufacturing costs contains a thicket of new terms. One of your main tasks in studying this chapter is to understand these terms. For example, a distinction was made earlier in this chapter between costs that are "direct" and "indirect" with respect to a *particular* cost objective—the manufactured product. In other settings, the direct-indirect distinction may pertain to a different cost objective, for example, a department. Thus the wages of a janitor who works solely in the assembly department may be regarded as a direct cost of the department but as an indirect cost of the products worked on within that department. However, unless otherwise stated, throughout this book the direct-indirect distinction will pertain only to the *product* as the cost objective.

Two types of income statements

☐ DETAILED COSTS OF MANUFACTURING COMPANY

A fresh example may clarify many of the cost terms and distinctions explored thus far. Assume that the Samson Company for 19X2 has direct-material costs of $7 million and direct-labor costs of $4 million. Assume also that the company incurred the indirect manufacturing costs (factory overhead) illustrated in Exhibit 3-5 and the selling and administrative expenses illustrated in Exhibit 3-6. Total sales were $20 million.

Finally, assume that the units produced are equal to the units sold. That is,

---

EXHIBIT 3-5

SAMSON COMPANY
Schedules of Indirect Manufacturing Costs (which are product costs)
For the Year Ended December 31, 19X2
(In thousands of dollars)

Schedule 1: Variable Costs

Supplies (lubricants, expendable tools, coolants, sandpaper)	$ 150	
Indirect labor (janitors, forklift operators)	700	
Repairs	100	
Power	50	$1,000
Schedule 2: Fixed Costs		
Foremen's salaries	$ 200	
Employee training	90	
Factory picnic and holiday party	10	
Supervisory salaries, except foremen's salaries	700	
Depreciation, plant and equipment	1,800	
Property taxes	150	
Insurance	50	3,000
Total indirect manufacturing costs		$4,000

EXHIBIT
3-6

SAMSON COMPANY
Schedules of Selling and Administrative Expenses (which are period costs)
For the Year Ended December 31, 19X2
(In thousands of dollars)

Schedule 3: Selling Expenses

Variable:		
Sales commissions	$ 700	
Shipping expenses for products sold	300	$1,000
Fixed:		
Advertising	$ 700	
Sales salaries	1,000	
Other	300	2,000
Total selling expenses		$3,000

Schedule 4: Administrative Expenses

Variable:		
Some clerical wages	$ 80	
Computer time rented	20	$ 100
Fixed:		
Office salaries	$ 100	
Other salaries	200	
Depreciation on office facilities	100	
Public-accounting fees	40	
Legal fees	100	
Other	360	900
Total administrative expenses		$1,000

there is no change in inventory levels. In this way we avoid some complications that are unnecessary and unimportant at this stage.[2]

Note that Exhibits 3-5 and 3-6 contain subdivisions of costs between variable and fixed classifications. Many companies do not make such subdivisions. Furthermore, when such subdivisions are made, sometimes arbitrary decisions are necessary as to whether a given cost is variable or fixed, or partially variable and partially fixed (for example, repairs). Nevertheless, to aid decision making, an increasing number of companies are attempting to report the extent to which their costs are approximately variable or fixed.

☐ FUNCTIONAL APPROACH

Exhibit 3-7 presents the income statement in the form used by most companies. The theory followed is called the **functional approach** or **absorption costing** or **traditional costing** or **full costing.** It is the theory also illustrated in Exhibit 3-3, whereby all indirect manufacturing costs (both variable plus fixed factory overhead) are considered as inventoriable or product costs that become an expense in the form of manufacturing cost of goods sold as sales occur.

MANU-
FACTURING
COSTS

69

[2]These complexities are discussed in Chapters 13 and 14. (If preferred, Chapters 13 and 14 may be studied immediately after Chapters 3 and 7, respectively, without loss of continuity.)

EXHIBIT 3-7   EXHIBIT 3-8

SAMSON COMPANY Functional Income Statement for the Year Ended December 31, 19X2 (In thousands of dollars)			**SAMSON COMPANY** Contribution Income Statement for the Year Ended December 31, 19X2 (In thousands of dollars)		
Sales		$20,000	Sales		$20,000
Less **manufacturing** costs of goods sold:			Less **variable** expenses:		
Direct material	$7,000		Direct material	$ 7,000	
Direct labor	4,000		Direct labor	4,000	
Indirect **manufacturing costs** (Schedules 1 plus 2)	4,000	15,000	**Variable** indirect manufacturing (Schedule 1)	1,000	
Gross profit or gross margin		$ 5,000	Total **variable** manufacturing cost of goods sold		$12,000
Selling expenses (Schedule 3)	$3,000		**Variable** selling expenses (Schedule 3)	1,000	
Administrative expenses (Schedule 4)	1,000		**Variable** administrative expenses (Schedule 4)	100	
Total **selling** and **administrative** expenses		4,000	Total **variable** expenses		13,100
Operating income		$ 1,000	Contribution margin		$ 6,900
			Less **fixed** expenses:		
			Manufacturing (Schedule 2)	$ 3,000	
			Selling (Schedule 3)	2,000	
			Administrative (Schedule 4)	900	5,900
			Operating income		$ 1,000

Note: Schedules 1 and 2 are in Exhibit 3-5. Schedules 3 and 4 are in Exhibit 3-6.

Take a moment to compare Exhibits 3-3 and 3-7. Note that gross profit or gross margin is the difference between sales and the *manufacturing* cost of goods sold. Note too that the *primary classifications* of costs on the income statement are by three major management *functions:* manufacturing, selling, and administrative.

☐ CONTRIBUTION APPROACH

Exhibit 3-8 presents the income statement in the "contribution" form used by an increasing number of companies for internal (management accounting) purposes. Even though a standard format is used for external purposes, a company can and often does adopt a different format for internal purposes if the expected benefits of making decisions exceed the extra costs of using different reporting systems simultaneously.

The theory followed by Exhibit 3-8 has been called the **contribution approach, variable costing, direct costing,** or **marginal costing.** For decision purposes, the most important difference between the contribution approach and the functional approach is the emphasis of the former on the distinction between variable and fixed costs. The *primary classifications* of costs are by variable and fixed *cost behavior patterns,* not by *business functions.*

The contribution income statement provides a contribution margin, which is computed after deducting *all* variable costs, *including* variable selling and administrative costs. This approach facilitates the computation of the impact on net income of changes in sales, and it dovetails neatly with the cost-volume-profit analysis illustrated in the preceding chapter.

The contribution approach stresses the lump-sum amount of fixed costs to be recouped before net income emerges. This highlighting of total fixed costs helps to attract management attention to fixed-cost behavior and control when both short-run and long-run plans are being made. Keep in mind that advocates of this contribution approach do not maintain that fixed costs are unimportant or irrelevant; but they do stress that the distinctions between behaviors of variable and fixed costs are crucial for certain decisions.

The implications of the *functional approach* and the *contribution approach* for decision making are discussed in the next chapter, using Exhibits 3-7 and 3-8.

Job-order and process costing

The first section of this chapter contains a general diagram of how raw-material costs are accumulated and allocated to departments and products. Direct labor and factory overhead are allocated to products in a similar fashion. The detailed procedures for allocating costs to products vary considerably from industry to industry and company to company. Two contrasting forms of product costing are **job-order costing** and **process costing.** Their principal difference centers on the type of products that are the cost objectives. Job-order costing is found in industries such as printing, construction, and furniture manufacturing, where each unit or batch (job) of product tends to be unique and easily identifiable. Process costing is found where there is mass production of identical units through a sequence of several processes, such as mixing and cooking. Examples include flour, glass, and paint. To see the major difference between job-order costing and process costing, visualize the detail that might support the work-in-process inventory, as diagramed in Exhibit 3-9.

Job-order accounting is used in many service industries, too, such as in repairing, consulting, legal, and accounting services. Each customer order is a different job with a special account or order number. Sometimes only costs are traced directly to the job, sometimes only revenue is traced, and sometimes both. For example, automobile repair shops typically have a repair order for each car worked on, with space for allocating materials and labor. The customer is permitted to see only a copy showing the retail prices of the materials, parts, and labor billed to his or her order. If the repair manager wants cost data, he may also have a system designed so that the "actual" parts and labor costs of each order are traced to a duplicate copy of the job order. That is why you often see auto mechanics "punching in" and "punching out" on "work tickets" as each new order is worked on.

The job-order approach occurs in not-for-profit industries too. Costs or revenues may be traced to individual patients, individual social welfare cases, individual doctoral seminars, and individual research projects.

EXHIBIT 3-9. Comparison of job-order and process costing

For job-order costing:

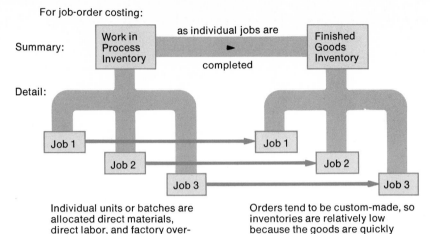

Individual units or batches are allocated direct materials, direct labor, and factory overhead

Orders tend to be custom-made, so inventories are relatively low because the goods are quickly delivered to customers

For process costing:

No distinction between individual units or batches. Materials, labor and overhead are allocated to Process 1, Process 2 and so on. As units are completed, they are transferred to Finished Goods Inventory at average unit costs.

Masses of like units carried in stock at average unit costs of production

The process-costing approach is less concerned with distinguishing among individual units of product. Instead, accumulated costs for a period, say a month, are divided by quantities produced during that period in order to get broad, average unit costs. Process costing may be adopted in nonmanufacturing activities as well as in manufacturing activities. Examples include dividing the costs of giving state automobile driver's license tests by the number of tests given and dividing the costs of an X-ray department by the number of X-rays processed.

summary

Direct material, direct labor, and factory overhead are traditionally regarded as product costs (inventoriable costs). In contrast, selling and administrative costs are accounted for as period costs and are deducted from revenue in the period incurred.

The most important aspect of intelligent cost planning and control is an understanding of cost behavior patterns and influences. The most basic behavior pattern of costs may be described as either variable or fixed. The contribution approach to preparing an income statement emphasizes this distinction and is a natural extension of the cost-volume-profit analysis used in decisions. In contrast, the functional approach emphasizes the distinction among three major management functions: manufacturing, selling, and administration.

Many new terms were introduced in this chapter. You should review them to make sure you know their exact meanings.

READERS WHO NOW DESIRE A MORE DETAILED TREATMENT OF PRODUCT COSTING (PARTICULARLY JOB-ORDER COSTING) MAY JUMP TO THE STUDY OF CHAPTER 13 WITHOUT LOSING CONTINUITY. IN TURN, CHAPTER 14 MAY BE STUDIED IMMEDIATELY AFTER CHAPTER 7 IF DESIRED.

summary problem for your review

◼ PROBLEM

1. Review the illustrations in Exhibits 3-5 through 3-8. Suppose that all variable costs fluctuate in direct proportion to units produced and sold, and that all fixed costs are unaffected over a wide range of production and sales. What would operating income have been if sales (at normal selling prices) had been $20.9 million instead of $20.0 million? Which statement, the functional income statement or the contribution income statement, did you use as a framework for your answer? Why?

2. Suppose that employee training (Exhibit 3-5) was regarded as a variable rather than a fixed cost at a rate of $90,000 ÷ 1,000,000 units, or 9¢ per unit. How would your answer in part 1 change?

◼ SOLUTION

1. Operating income would increase from $1,000,000 to $1,310,500, computed as shown at the top of the next page.

That analysis is readily calculated by using data from the contribution income statement. In contrast, the traditional functional costing income statement must be ana-

Increase in revenue	$ 900,000

Increase in total contribution margin:
Contribution-margin ratio in contribution income
  statement (Exhibit 3-8) is $6,900,000 ÷ $20,000,000 = .345

Ratio times revenue increase is .345 × $900,000	$ 310,500
Increase in fixed expenses	-0-
Operating income before increase	1,000,000
New operating income	$1,310,500

lyzed and divided into variable and fixed categories before the effect on operating income can be estimated.

    2. The contribution-margin ratio would become lower because the variable costs would be higher by 9¢ per unit: $6,810,000 ÷ $20,000,000 = $.3405.

Ratio times revenue increase is .3405 × $900,000	$ 306,450
Increase in fixed expenses	-0-
Operating income before increase	1,000,000
New operating income	$1,306,450

Appendix 3: classification of labor costs

The terminology for labor costs is usually the most confusing. Each organization seems to develop its own interpretation of various labor-cost classifications. We begin by considering some commonly encountered labor-cost terminology.

    For our purposes, we categorize the terminology as follows:

Direct labor (already defined)
Indirect labor:
    Forklift-truck operators (internal handling of materials)
    Janitors
    Plant guards
    Rework labor (time spent by direct laborers redoing defective work)
    Overtime premium paid to *all* factory workers
    Idle time
Payroll fringe costs

    All factory labor costs, other than those for direct labor, are usually classified as **indirect labor costs,** a major component of indirect manufacturing costs. The term *indirect labor* is usually divided into many subsidiary classifications. The wages of forklift-truck operators are generally not commingled with janitors' salaries, for example, although both are regarded as indirect labor.

    Costs are classified in a detailed fashion primarily in an attempt to associate a specific cost with its specific cause, or reason for incurrence. Two classes of indirect labor need special mention: overtime premium and idle time.

    Overtime premium paid to all factory workers is usually considered a part of overhead. If a lathe operator earns $8 per hour for straight time, and time and one-half for overtime, his premium is $4 per overtime hour. If he works

44 hours, including four overtime hours, in one week, his gross earnings are classified as follows:

Direct labor: 44 hours × $8	$352
Overtime premium (factory overhead): 4 hours × $4	16
Total earnings	$368

Why is overtime premium considered an indirect cost rather than direct? After all, it can usually be traced to specific batches of work. It is usually not considered a direct charge because the scheduling of production jobs is generally random. For example, assume that Jobs No. 1 through 5 are scheduled for a specific workday of ten hours, including two overtime hours. Each job requires two hours. Should the job scheduled during hours 9 and 10 be assigned the overtime premium? For example, suppose that you brought your automobile to a shop for repair by 8:00 A.M. Through random scheduling, your auto was repaired during hours 9 and 10 as Job No. 5. When you came to get your car, you learned that all the overtime premium had been added to your bill. You probably would not be overjoyed.

Thus, in most companies, the overtime premium is not allocated to any specific job. Instead, it is prorated to all jobs. The latter approach does not penalize a particular batch of work solely because it happened to be worked on during the overtime hours. Instead, the overtime premium is considered to be attributable to the heavy overall volume of work, and its cost is thus regarded as indirect manufacturing costs (factory overhead).

Another subsidiary classification of indirect-labor costs is **idle time.** This cost typically represents wages paid for unproductive time caused by machine breakdowns, material shortages, sloppy production scheduling, and the like. For example if the same lathe operator's machine broke down for three hours during the week, his earnings would be classified as follows:

Direct labor: 41 hours × $8	$328
Overtime premium (factory overhead): 4 hours × $4	16
Idle time (factory overhead): 3 hours × $8	24
Total earnings	$368

The classification of factory *payroll fringe costs* (e.g., employer contributions to social security, life insurance, health insurance, pensions, and miscellaneous other employee benefits) differs from company to company. In most companies these are classified as indirect manufacturing costs. In some companies, however, the fringe benefits related to direct labor are charged as an additional direct-labor cost. For instance, a direct laborer, such as a lathe operator whose gross wages are computed on the basis of $8 an hour, may enjoy fringe benefits totaling, say, 75¢ per hour. Most companies tend to classify the $8 as direct-labor cost and the 75¢ as factory overhead. Other companies classify the entire $8.75 as direct-labor cost. The latter approach is preferable, because most of these costs are also a fundamental part of acquiring labor services.

assignment material

■ FUNDAMENTAL ASSIGNMENT MATERIAL

3-1. **Terminology.** Define *absorption costing; contribution approach; cost; cost objective; direct costing; direct labor; direct material; factory burden; factory overhead; full costing; functional approach; idle time; indirect labor; indirect manufacturing costs; job-order costing; manufacturing expenses; manufacturing overhead; marginal costing; overtime premium; period costs; process costing; product costs; traditional costing; variable costing.*

3-2. **Straightforward income statements.** (An alternate problem is 3-28.) The Gardena Company had the following manufacturing data for the year 19X1 (in thousands of dollars):

Beginning inventories	None	Utilities—fixed portion	$ 6
Direct material purchased	$240	Indirect labor—variable portion	50
Direct material used	180	Indirect labor—fixed portion	20
Direct labor	200	Depreciation	60
Supplies	10	Property taxes	12
Utilities—variable portion	20	Supervisory salaries	50

Selling expenses were $172,000 (including $40,000 that were variable), and general administrative expenses were $100,000 (including $20,000 that were variable). Sales were $1 million.

Supplies are regarded as variable costs.

REQUIRED

1. Prepare two income statements, one using the contribution approach and one the functional approach.
2. Suppose that all variable costs fluctuate directly in proportion to sales, and that fixed costs are unaffected over a very wide range of sales. Compute the operating income if sales had been $1,150,000 instead of $1,000,000. Which income statement did you use to help obtain your answer? Why?

3-3. **Meaning of typical language.** Refer to the functional income statement of your solution to the preceding problem. Give the amounts of the following: (1) factory burden, (2) ending inventory of direct materials, (3) conversion costs, (4) manufacturing expenses, and (5) prime costs.

■ ADDITIONAL ASSIGNMENT MATERIAL

3-4. "Advertising is non-inventoriable." Explain.

3-5. "Departments are not cost objects or objects of costing." Do you agree? Explain.

3-6. "Manufacturing cost of goods sold is a special category of expense." Do you agree? Explain.

3-7. "Unexpired costs are always inventory costs." Do you agree? Explain.

3-8. "Miscellaneous supplies are always indirect costs." Do you agree? Explain.

3-9. Distinguish between the two prime costs.

3-10. "Glue or nails become an integral part of the finished product, so they would be direct material." Do you agree? Explain.

3-11. What is the advantage of the contribution approach as compared with the traditional approach?

3-12. Distinguish between manufacturing and merchandising.

3-13. Cost accumulation and allocation. The Y Company incurred raw-material costs of $200,000. The machining department used $150,000, and the finishing department, $50,000. Product A flowed through both departments, incurring 10 percent of the machining department's raw-material costs and 5 percent of the finishing department's raw material costs. What was the raw-material cost of Product A?

3-14. Cost accumulation and allocation. Examine Exhibit 3-1. Suppose a company incurred the following costs:

Direct material	$60,000
Direct labor	30,000
Manufacturing overhead	39,000

Eighty percent of the material was introduced in the machining department, but only 30 percent of the direct labor was incurred there. Manufacturing overhead incurred by each department was allocated to products in proportion to the direct-labor costs of products within the departments.

In the machining department, one-half of the direct material was used on Product X-1 and one-fourth on each of Y-1 and Z-1. Direct labor was split equally among the three products. The manufacturing overhead incurred by the machining department and allocated to all products therein amounted to $18,000.

In the finishing department, the direct-material cost was split equally among the three products. Direct labor was used as follows: 40 percent for X-1, 40 percent for Y-1, and 20 percent for Z-1. The remainder of the total manufacturing overhead cost was incurred by the finishing department.

REQUIRED

1. Compute the total costs incurred by the machining department and added by the finishing department.
2. Compute the total costs of each product that would be shown as finished-goods inventory if all the products were transferred to finished stock upon completion.

3-15. Relating costs to cost objectives. A company uses a job-order cost system. Prepare headings for two columns: (1) assembly department costs and (2) products assembled. Fill in the two columns for each of the costs below. If a specific cost is direct to the department but indirect to the product, place a D in column 1 and an I in column 2. The costs are: materials used, supplies used, assembly labor, material-handling labor (transporting materials between and within departments), depreciation—building, assembly foreman's salary, and the building and grounds supervisor's salary.

3-16. Classification of manufacturing costs. Classify each of the following as direct or indirect (D or I) with respect to product, and as variable or fixed (V or F) with respect to whether the cost fluctuates in total as activity or volume changes over wide ranges of activity. You will have two answers, D or I and V or F, for *each* of the ten items:

1. Food for a factory cafeteria
2. Factory rent
3. Salary of a factory storeroom clerk
4. Foreman training program
5. Abrasives (sandpaper, etc.)
6. Cutting bits in a machinery department
7. Workmen's compensation insurance in a factory

8. Cement for a roadbuilder
9. Steel scrap for a blast furnace
10. Paper towels for a factory washroom

3-17. **Variable costs and fixed costs; manufacturing and other costs.** For each of the numbered items, choose the appropriate classifications for a job-order manufacturing company (e.g., custom furniture, job printing). If in doubt about whether the cost behavior is basically variable or fixed, decide on the basis of whether the total cost will fluctuate substantially over a wide range of volume. Most items have two answers from among the following possibilities with respect to the cost of a particular job:

a. Variable cost
b. Fixed cost
c. General and administrative cost

d. Selling cost
e. Manufacturing costs, direct
f. Manufacturing costs, indirect
g. Other (specify)

Sample answers:

Direct material	a, e
President's salary	b, c
Bond interest expense	b, g (financial expense)

Items for your consideration:

1. Sandpaper
2. Supervisory salaries, production control
3. Supervisory salaries, assembly department
4. Supervisory salaries, factory storeroom
5. Company picnic costs
6. Overtime premium, punch press
7. Idle time, assembly
8. Freight out

9. Property taxes
10. Factory power for machines
11. Salespersons' commissions
12. Salespersons' salaries
13. Welding supplies
14. Fire loss
15. Paint for finished products
16. Heat and air-conditioning, factory
17. Material-handling labor, punch press
18. Straight-line depreciation, salespersons' automobiles

3-18. **Meaning of technical terms.** Refer to Exhibit 3-3. Give the amounts of the following with respect to the cost of goods available for sale: (1) prime costs, (2) conversion costs, (3) factory burden, and (4) manufacturing expenses.

3-19. **Product and period costs.** Refer to Exhibit 3-3. Suppose that $30 million of direct material had been purchased.

REQUIRED   Using Exhibit 3-2 as a guide, sketch how the costs in Exhibit 3-3 are related to balance sheets and income statements. In other words, prepare an exhibit like 3-2, inserting the numbers from Exhibit 3-3 to the extent you can.

3-20. **Presence of ending work in process.** Refer to Exhibits 3-3 and 3-4. Suppose that manufacturing costs were the same, but that there was an ending work-in-process inventory of $5 million. The cost of the completed goods would therefore be $35 million instead of $40 million. Assume also that sales and the cost of goods sold are unchanged.

REQUIRED   1. Recast the income statement of Exhibit 3-3.
2. What lines and ending balances would change in Exhibit 3-4 and by how much?

3-21. Balance sheet equation. Review Exhibit 3-4. Assume that the G Company had a beginning balance of $800,000 cash and paid-in capital. The following transactions occurred in 19X2 (in thousands):

1. Purchase of direct materials for cash	$350
2. Direct materials used	300
3. Acquire direct labor for cash	160
4. Acquire factory overhead for cash	200
5. Complete all goods that were started	?
6a. Revenue (all sales are for cash)	600
6b. Cost of goods sold (half of the goods completed were sold)	?
7. Selling costs for cash	100
8. General and administrative costs for cash	40

REQUIRED Prepare an analysis similar to Exhibit 3-4. What are the ending balances of cash, direct materials, finished goods, paid-in capital, and retained income?

3-22. Balance sheet equation. Refer to the preceding problem. Suppose that some goods were still in process that cost $100,000. Half the goods completed were sold. However, the same revenue was generated even though fewer goods were sold. What are the balances of all the accounts in the ending balance sheet?

3-23. Overtime premium. Please read the chapter appendix. An automobile dealer has a service department. You have brought your car for repair at 8:00 A.M. When you come to get your car after 6:00 P.M., you notice that your bill contains a charge under "labor" for "overtime premium." When you inquire about the reason for the charge, you are told, "We worked on your car from 5:00 P.M. to 6:00 P.M. Our union contract calls for wages to be paid at time-and-a-half after eight hours. Therefore our ordinary labor charge of $25 per hour was billed to you at $37.50."

REQUIRED
1. Should the overtime premium be allocated only to cars worked on during overtime hours? Explain.
2. Would your preceding answer differ if the dealer arranged to service your car at 8:00 P.M. as a special convenience to you? Explain.

3-24. Payroll fringe costs. Please read the chapter appendix. Direct labor is often accounted for at the gross wage rate, and the related "fringe costs" such as employer payroll taxes and employer contributions to health-care plans are accounted for as part of overhead. Therefore, the $9 gross pay per hour being paid to Mary Locke, a direct laborer, might cause related fringe costs of $3 per hour.

REQUIRED
1. Suppose Locke works 40 hours during a particular week as an auditor for a public accounting firm, 30 hours for Client A and 10 for Client B. What would be the cost of direct labor? Of general overhead?
2. The firm allocates costs to each client. What would be the cost of "direct labor" on the Client A job? The Client B job?
3. How would you allocate general overhead to the Client A job? The Client B job?
4. Suppose Locke works a total of 50 hours (30 for A and 20 for B), 10 of which are paid on the basis of time-and-one-half. What would be the cost of direct labor? Of general overhead?
5. Given the facts in Requirement 4, what would be the cost of "direct labor" on the Client A job? The Client B job?

3-25. Review of Chapters 2 and 3. Consider the following miscellaneous data regarding operations in 19X3 of the Gombiner Manufacturing Company (in millions):

Gross profit	$ 25	Net loss	$12
Fixed selling and		Fixed manufacturing	
administrative expenses	21	overhead	30
Direct material used	60	Direct labor	25
Sales	150		

There were no beginning or ending inventories.

REQUIRED

Compute the following (listed in no particular sequence):

1. Contribution margin in dollars.
2. Breakeven point in sales dollars.
3. Manufacturing cost of goods sold.
4. Variable selling and administrative expenses.
5. Variable manufacturing overhead.

Hint: Prepare an income statement. Fill in the known items; then solve for the unknowns.

3-26. **Review of Chapters 2 and 3.** Consider the following data of the Belmont Corporation regarding operations for 19X4:

Variable manufacturing overhead	$ 50,000
Direct labor	140,000
Break-even point (in sales dollars)	600,000
Gross profit	240,000
Direct material used	200,000
Sales	800,000
Contribution margin	360,000

There were no beginning or ending inventories. Ignore income taxes.

REQUIRED

Compute: (1) variable selling and administrative expenses, (2) fixed manufacturing overhead, and (3) fixed selling and administrative expenses. Computations need not be made in any specific order. Probably the easiest way to obtain the answers is to prepare an income statement, filling in the known items, and then solving for the unknowns.

3-27. **Prepare profit plan.** (CMA.) The Barr Food Manufacturing Company is a medium-sized publicly held corporation, producing a variety of consumer food and specialty products. Current-year data were prepared as shown below for the salad-dressing product line using five months of actual expenses and a seven-month projection. These data were prepared for a preliminary 19X9 budget meeting between the Specialty Products Division president, marketing vice-president, production vice-president, and the controller. The current-year projection was accepted as being accurate, but it was agreed that the projected income was not at a satisfactory level.

The division president stated that he wanted, at a minimum, a 15 percent increase in gross sales dollars and not less than 10 percent before-tax profit for 19X9. He also stated that he would be responsible for a $200,000 reduction in the general and administrative expenses to help achieve the profit goal.

Both the vice-president of marketing and the vice-president of production felt that the president's objectives would be difficult to achieve. However they offered the following suggestions to reach the objectives:

a. Sales volume—The current share of the salad-dressing market is 15 percent and the total salad-dressing market is expected to grow 5 percent for 19X9. Barr's

Projected Income Statement
For the Year Ended December 31, 19X8
(5 months actual; 7 months projected)
(000 omitted)

Volume in gallons	5,000
Gross sales	$30,000
Freights, allowances, discounts	3,000
Net sales	$27,000
Less manufacturing costs	
Variable	$13,500
Fixed	2,100
Depreciation	700
Total manufacturing costs	$16,300
Gross profit	$10,700
Less expenses	
Marketing	$ 4,000
Brokerage	1,650
General and administrative	2,100
Research and development	500
Total expenses	$ 8,250
Income before taxes	$ 2,450

current market share can be maintained by a marketing expenditure of $4.2 million. The two vice-presidents estimated that the market share could be increased by additional expenditures for advertising and sales promotion. For an additional expenditure of $525,000, the market share can be raised by one percentage point until the market share reaches 17 percent. To get further market penetration, an additional $875,000 must be spent for each percentage point until the market share reaches 20 percent. Any advertising and promotion expenditures beyond this level are not likely to increase the market share to more than 20 percent.

b. Selling price—The selling price will remain at $6 per gallon. The selling price is very closely related to the costs of the ingredients, which are not expected to change in 19X9 from the costs experienced in 19X8.

c. Variable manufacturing costs—Variable manufacturing costs are projected at 50 percent of the net sales dollar (gross sales less freight, allowances, and discounts).

d. Fixed manufacturing costs—An increase of $100,000 is projected for 19X9.

e. Depreciation—A projected increase in equipment will increase depreciation by $25,000 over the 19X8 projection.

f. Freight, allowances, and discounts—The current rate of 10 percent of gross sales dollars is expected to continue in 19X9.

g. Brokerage expense—A rate of 5 percent of gross sales dollars is projected for 19X9.

h. General and administrative expense—A $200,000 decrease in general and administrative expense from the 19X8 forecast is projected; this is consistent with the president's commitment.

i. Research and development expense—A 5 percent increase from the absolute dollars in the 19X8 forecast will be necessary to meet divisional research targets.

REQUIRED

1. The controller must put together a preliminary profit plan from the facts given. Can the president's objectives be achieved? If so, present the profit plan that best achieves them. If not, present the profit plan that most nearly meets the president's objectives.

2. The president's objectives, as described in the case, were stated in terms of a percentage increase in gross sales and the percentage return on sales.

a. What other measures of performance (other than sales dollars and return on sales percentage) could be used in setting objectives?

b. Discuss the advantages or disadvantages of the measures you present in relation to those in the case.

3-28. Contribution and functional income statements. (An alternate problem is 3-2.) The records of the Turlock Company for the year ended December 31, 19X2, revealed the following:

Long-term rent, factory	$ 200,000	Indirect labor (variable)	1,400,000
Factory super-intendent's salary	90,000	Fire insurance on factory equipment	10,000
Direct labor	4,000,000	Abrasives for machining	200,000
Sales	26,000,000		
Foremen's salaries	200,000	Factory methods studies	90,000
Advertising	5,690,000		
Cutting bits used	110,000	Property taxes on factory equipment	20,000
Administrative expenses (variable)	400,000	Administrative executive salaries	300,000
Direct material used	7,000,000		
Shipping expenses	590,000	Sales commissions	1,900,000
Depreciation on equipment	800,000		
Inventories	None		

1. Prepare a contribution income statement and a functional income statement. If you are in doubt about any cost behavior pattern, decide on the basis of whether the total cost in question will fluctuate substantially over a wide range of volume. Prepare a separate supporting schedule of indirect manufacturing costs subdivided between variable and fixed costs.
2. Suppose that all variable costs fluctuate directly in proportion to sales, and that fixed costs are unaffected over a very wide range of sales. What would operating income have been if production and sales had been $27 million instead of $26 million? Which income statement did you use to help get your answer? Why?

3-29. Frequently encountered terms. Refer to the functional income statement of your solution to the preceding problem. Give the amounts of the following: (1) manufacturing expenses, (2) factory burden, (3) prime costs, and (4) conversion costs.

3-30. Analysis with contribution income statement. The following data have been condensed from Draco Corporation's report of 19X3 operations (in millions of dollars):

	VARIABLE	FIXED	TOTAL
Manufacturing cost of goods sold	$400	$180	$580
Selling and administrative expenses	140	60	200
Sales			900

1. Prepare the 19X3 income statement in contribution form, ignoring income taxes.
2. Draco operations have been fairly stable from year to year. In planning for the future, top management is considering several options for changing the annual pattern of operations. You are asked to perform an analysis of their estimated effects. Use your contribution income statement as a framework to compute the estimated operating income (in millions) under each of the following separate and unrelated assumptions:
   a. Assume that a 10 percent reduction in selling prices would cause a 30 percent increase in the physical volume of goods manufactured and sold.

b. Assume that an annual expenditure of $30 million for a special sales-promotion campaign would enable the company to increase its physical volume by 10 percent with no change in selling prices.

c. Assume that a basic redesign of manufacturing operations would increase annual fixed manufacturing costs by $80 million and decrease variable manufacturing costs by 15 percent *per product unit*, but with no effect on physical volume or selling prices.

d. Assume that a basic redesign of selling and administrative operations would double the annual fixed expenses for selling and administration and increase the variable expenses for selling and administration by 25 percent *per product unit*, but would also increase physical volume by 20 percent. Selling prices would be increased by 5 percent.

RELEVANT COSTS AND SPECIAL DECISIONS – PART ONE

learning objectives

When you have finished studying this chapter, you should be able to:

1. Describe the management accountant's role in special decision situations.
2. Identify the general characteristics of information needed for making special decisions.
3. Identify the relationships among the main elements of the decision process: information, predictions, decisions, implementation, and feedback.
4. Discriminate between relevant and irrelevant information for making decisions.
5. Analyze data by the contribution approach to support a decision for accepting or rejecting a special sales order.
6. Compute a target sales price by both the contribution and absorption-costing approaches and identify their advantages and disadvantages in determining sales prices.
7. Analyze data by the relevant-cost approach to support a decision for adding or deleting a product line.
8. Analyze data to determine how to maximize profits within the constraints of a given productive capacity.

Managers' special decisions (often called *problem solving,* as described in Chapter 1) pervade a variety of areas and spans of time. By definition, special decisions occur with less regularity than the typical daily or weekly operating decisions of a hotel, hospital, or manufacturer. The pricing of an unusual sales order is an example of a special decision. Other examples are adding programs, services, or products; selecting equipment; selling products at a certain stage of manufacturing or processing them further; and repairing municipal automobiles internally or buying the repair service from outside suppliers. Unique factors bear on all these special decisions. However, there is a general approach that will help the executive make wise decisions in *any* problem-solving situation. The term "relevant" has been overworked in recent years; nevertheless the general approach herein will be labeled as the *relevant-cost approach.* Coupled with the contribution approach, the ability to distinguish relevant from irrelevant items is the key to making special decisions.

Throughout this and the next chapter, in order to concentrate on a few major points, we shall ignore the time value of money (which is discussed in Chapter 11) and income taxes (which are discussed in Chapter 12).

The accountant's role in special decisions

□ ACCURACY AND RELEVANCE

Accountants have an important role in the problem-solving process, not as the decision makers but as collectors and reporters of **relevant data.** Their reports must provide valid data—numbers that measure the quantities pertinent to the decision at hand. Many managers want the accountant to offer recommendations about the proper decision, even though the final choice always rests with the operating executive.

The distinction between precision and relevance should be kept in mind. Ideally, the data should be *precise* (accurate) and *relevant* (pertinent). However, as we shall see, figures can be precise but irrelevant, or imprecise but relevant. For example, the university president's salary may be $100,000 per year, to the penny, but may have no bearing on the question of whether to buy or rent data-processing equipment. As has often been said, it is better to be roughly right than precisely wrong.

□ QUALITATIVE AND QUANTITATIVE FACTORS

The aspects of each alternative may be divided into two broad categories, *qualitative* and *quantitative.* Qualitative factors are those for which measurement in dollars and cents is difficult and imprecise; yet a qualitative factor may easily be given more weight than a measurable saving in cost. For example, the opposition of a militant union to new labor-saving machinery may cause an executive to defer or even reject completely the contemplated installation. Or, the chance to manufacture a component oneself for less than the supplier's selling price may be rejected because acceptance might lead to the company's long-run dependency on the supplier for other subassemblies. Quantitative factors are those that may more easily be reduced to dollars and cents—for example, projected costs of alternative materials, of direct labor, and of overhead. The accountant, statistician, and mathematician try to express as many decision factors as feasible in quantitative terms. This approach reduces the number of qualitative factors to be judged.

Meaning of relevance: the major conceptual lesson

Problem solving is essentially decision making—choosing among several courses of action. The available courses of action are the result of an often time-consuming formal or informal search and screening process, perhaps carried on by a company team that includes engineers, accountants, and operating executives.

The accountant's role in problem solving is primarily that of a technical expert on cost analysis. The accountant's responsibility is to be certain that the manager is guided by relevant data, information that will lead the manager to the best decision.

☐ DEFINITION OF RELEVANCE

Consider the final stages of the decision-making process. Two (or more) courses of action are aligned, and a comparison is made. The decision is based on the difference in the effect of the two on future performance. The key question is, What difference does it make? The relevant information is the *expected future data* that will *differ* among alternatives.

The ideas in the preceding paragraph deserve elaboration because they have such wide application. Historical, or past, data have no direct bearing on the decision. Historical data may be helpful in the formulation of *predictions,* but past figures, in themselves, are irrelevant simply because they are not the expected future data that managers must use in intelligent decison making. Decisions affect the future. Nothing can alter what has already happened; all past costs are down the drain as far as current or future decisions are concerned.

Of the expected future data, only those that will differ among alternatives are relevant. Any item is irrelevant if it will remain the same regardless of the alternative selected. For instance, if the department manager's salary will be the same regardless of the products stocked, his or her salary is irrelevant to the selection of products.[1]

☐ EXAMPLES OF RELEVANCE

The following examples will help us summarize the sharp distinctions needed for proper cost analysis for special decisions.

You habitually buy gasoline from either of two nearby gasoline stations. Yesterday you noticed that one station is selling gasoline at $2.00 per gallon; the other, at $1.90. Your automobile needs gasoline, and, in making your choice of stations, you *assume* that these prices are unchanged. The relevant costs are $2.00 and $1.90, the expected future costs that will differ between the alternatives. You

---

[1] The time value of money is ignored here; it is discussed in Chapter 11. Strictly interpreted, differences in future data are affected by both magnitude and timing. Therefore, expected future data with the same magnitude but different timing can be relevant.

use your past experience (i.e., what you observed yesterday) for predicting to-day's price. Note that the relevant cost is not what you paid in the past, or what you observed yesterday, but what you *expect to pay* when you drive in to get gasoline. This cost meets our two criteria: (a) it is the expected future cost, and (b) it differs between the alternatives.

You may also plan to have your car lubricated. The recent price at each station was $8.50, and this is what you anticipate paying. This expected future cost is irrelevant, because it will be the same under either alternative. It does not meet our second criterion.

Exhibit 4-1 sketches the decision process and uses the following decision as an illustration. A manufacturer is thinking of using aluminum instead of copper in a line of desk lamps. The cost of direct material will decrease from 30¢ to 20¢. The elaborate mechanism in Exhibit 4-1 seems unnecessary for this decision. After all, the analysis in a nutshell is:

	ALUMINUM	COPPER	DIFFERENCE
Direct material	$.20	$.30	$.10

The cost of copper used for this comparison undoubtedly came from his-torical-cost records, but note that the relevant costs in the above analysis are both expected future costs.

The direct-labor cost will continue to be 70¢ per unit regardless of the material used. It is irrelevant because our second criterion—an element of differ-ence between the alternatives—is not met. Therefore we can safely exclude di-rect labor. In such a case, the following comparison would be made:

	ALUMINUM	COPPER	DIFFERENCE
Direct material	$.20	$.30	$.10
Direct labor	.70	.70	—

There is no harm in including irrelevant items in a formal analysis, pro-vided that they are included properly. However, clarity is usually enhanced by confining the reports to the relevant items only.

☐ ROLE OF PREDICTIONS

Reflect on Exhibit 4-1. It provides a helpful overview. Box 1(a) represents histor-ical accounting data that are usually supplied by the accounting system, whereas box 1(b) represents other data, such as price indices or industry statis-tics, that are usually gathered from outside the accounting system. Regardless of their source, the historical data in step 2 help the formulation of *predictions.* Although historical data are often used as a guide to predicting, they are irrele-vant per se to the decision itself.

In turn, in step 3 these predictions become inputs to the *decision model,* the method for making the choice. In this case our decision model has a simple

EXHIBIT 4-1. Decision process and role of information *(Place a clip on this page for easy reference.)*

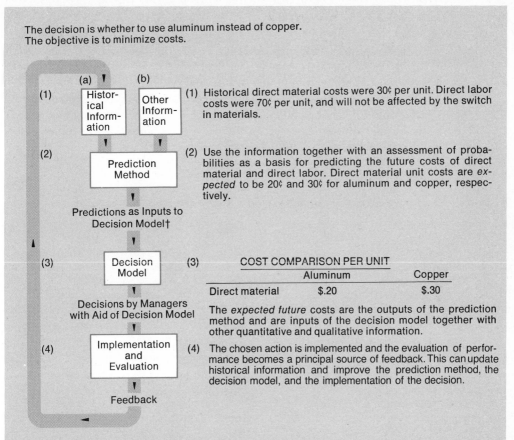

The decision is whether to use aluminum instead of copper.
The objective is to minimize costs.

(1) — (a) Historical Information / (b) Other Information

(1) Historical direct material costs were 30¢ per unit. Direct labor costs were 70¢ per unit, and will not be affected by the switch in materials.

(2) Prediction Method

Predictions as Inputs to Decision Model†

(2) Use the information together with an assessment of probabilities as a basis for predicting the future costs of direct material and direct labor. Direct material unit costs are *expected* to be 20¢ and 30¢ for aluminum and copper, respectively.

(3) Decision Model

Decisions by Managers with Aid of Decision Model

(3)

COST COMPARISON PER UNIT

	Aluminum	Copper
Direct material	$.20	$.30

The *expected future* costs are the outputs of the prediction method and are inputs of the decision model together with other quantitative and qualitative information.

(4) Implementation and Evaluation

Feedback

(4) The chosen action is implemented and the evaluation of performance becomes a principal source of feedback. This can update historical information and improve the prediction method, the decision model, and the implementation of the decision.

Note that historical data may be relevant for prediction methods.
†*Historical data are never relevant per se for decision models. Only those expected future data that are different are really relevant. For instance, in this example, direct material makes a difference and direct labor does not. Therefore,* under our definition here, *direct labor is irrelevant.*

form: compare the predicted unit costs and select the alternative bearing the lesser cost.

Exhibit 4-1 will be referred to frequently. It displays the major conceptual lesson in this chapter. This and the next chapter will show how the notion of relevant costs combined with the contribution approach may be applied to various particular decisions. Note that the analytical approach is consistent, regardless of the particular decision encountered. The contribution approach to cost analysis, which was introduced in the preceding chapter, facilitates analysis for a variety of decisions. In this chapter we shall examine the following decisions: (1) special sales orders, (2) pricing policies, (3) deleting or adding product lines or departments, and (4) using available capacity.

The special sales order

☐ ILLUSTRATIVE EXAMPLE

Consider the special sales order decision by selecting data from Exhibits 3-7 and 3-8. We are deliberately returning to these exhibits to underscore their general importance. The main data are summarized again in Exhibit 4-2.

The differences in the emphasis and format of the two income statements in Exhibit 4-2 may be unimportant as long as the accompanying cost analysis leads to the same set of decisions. But these two approaches sometimes lead to different unit costs that must be interpreted warily.

EXHIBIT 4-2. Functional and contribution forms of the income statement

SAMSON COMPANY
Income Statement
For the Year Ended December 31, 19X2
(In thousands of dollars)

FUNCTIONAL FORM		CONTRIBUTION FORM		
Sales	$20,000	Sales		$20,000
Less manufacturing cost of goods sold	15,000	Less variable expenses:		
Gross profit or gross margin	$ 5,000	Manufacturing	$12,000	
Less selling and administrative expenses	4,000	Selling and administrative	1,100	13,100
Operating income	$ 1,000	Contribution margin		$ 6,900
		Less fixed expenses:		
		Manufacturing	$3,000	
		Selling and administrative	2,900	5,900
		Operating income		$ 1,000

In our illustration, suppose that 1 million units of product, such as some automobile replacement part, were made and sold. Under the functional costing approach, the unit manufacturing cost of the product would be $15,000,000 ÷ 1,000,000, or $15 per unit. Suppose a mail-order house near year-end offered Samson $13 per unit for a 100,000-unit special order that would not affect regular business in any way, would not raise any antitrust issues concerning price discrimination, would not affect total fixed costs, would not entail any additional variable selling and administrative expenses, and would use some otherwise idle manufacturing capacity. Should Samson accept the order? Perhaps the question should be stated more sharply: What is the difference in the short-run financial results between not accepting and accepting? Again, the key question is, What difference does it make?

EXHIBIT 4-3. Comparative predicted income statements, contribution approach

For the Year Ended December 31, 19X2
(In thousands of dollars)

	WITHOUT SPECIAL ORDER, 1,000,000 UNITS	WITH SPECIAL ORDER, 1,100,000 UNITS	SPECIAL-ORDER DIFFERENCE, 100,000 UNITS total	per unit
Sales	$20,000	$21,300	$1,300	$13
Less variable expenses:				
Manufacturing	$12,000	$13,200	$1,200	$12
Selling and administrative	1,100	1,100	—	—
Total variable expenses	$13,100	$14,300	$1,200	$12
Contribution margin	$ 6,900	$ 7,000	$ 100	$ 1
Less fixed expenses:				
Manufacturing	$ 3,000	$ 3,000	—	—
Selling and administrative	2,900	2,900	—	—
Total fixed expenses	$ 5,900	$ 5,900	—	—
Operating income	$ 1,000	$ 1,100	$ 100	$ 1

(Put a clip on this page for easy reference.)

☐ CORRECT ANALYSIS

The correct analysis employs the contribution approach and concentrates on the final overall results. As Exhibit 4-3 shows, only the variable manufacturing costs are affected by the particular order, at a rate of $12 per unit. All other variable costs and all fixed costs are unaffected and may therefore be safely ignored in making this special-order pricing decision. Note how the necessary cost analysis is facilitated by the contribution approach's distinction between variable- and fixed-cost behavior patterns. The total short-run income will increase by $100,000 if the order is accepted—despite the fact that the unit selling price of $13 is less than the functional manufacturing cost of $15 computed below:

Total manufacturing costs from Exhibit 4-2	$15,000,000
Divided by units produced	1,000,000
Unit cost	$15

☐ VARIABLE AND ABSORPTION COSTING

When accountants compare the contribution and functional approaches for product costing (inventory valuation) purposes, they frequently call them the **variable-costing** and **absorption-costing** approaches, respectively. Thus, if 1 million units were produced, the unit manufacturing product cost for inventory purposes would be $12 under variable costing and $15 under absorption costing.

Variable costing differs from absorption costing in one major respect: *fixed* indirect manufacturing costs are regarded as expenses immediately and *not* as costs of the manufactured product. The implications of this theory for product costing and income measurement are explored more fully in Chapter 14, but for our immediate purposes they are unimportant.

The variable-costing and absorption-costing terms are introduced here because in practice all kinds of terms are sometimes used to denote particular costs. Be sure to get their exact meaning in a specific decision situation. For example, the terms "full cost" or "fully distributed cost" or "fully allocated cost" sometimes are used as synonyms for absorption cost. However, in other situations **"full cost"** per unit means "absorption cost *plus* an allocation of selling and administrative costs." For example, using Exhibit 4-2:

	PER UNIT
Absorption cost, $15,000,000 ÷ 1,000,000 units	$15
Selling and administrative expenses, $4,000,000 ÷ 1,000,000 units	4
Full cost	$19

For external reporting purposes, American companies must use only the $15 amount for inventory valuation. The $4 period cost must, of course, be excluded from inventory. However, you can readily see that for internal decision purposes, managers are free to allocate costs to products in any way that seems helpful. For instance, for setting long-run target prices for products, managers may desire "full-cost" computations.

☐ INCORRECT ANALYSIS

Faulty cost analysis sometimes occurs because of misinterpretation of unit fixed costs. Some managers may erroneously use the $15 unit absorption cost to make the following prediction for the year (in thousands of dollars):

	WITHOUT SPECIAL ORDER	WITH SPECIAL ORDER	SPECIAL-ORDER DIFFERENCE
Sales	20,000	21,300	1,300
Less manufacturing cost of goods sold @ $15	15,000	16,500	1,500
Gross profit	5,000	4,800	(200)
Other costs	4,000	4,000	—
Operating income	1,000	800	(200)

The $1.5 million increase in costs is computed by multiplying $15 times 100,000 units. Of course, the fallacy in this approach is the regarding of a fixed cost (fixed manufacturing cost) as though it behaved in a variable manner. Avoid the assumption that unit costs may be used indiscriminately as a basis for predicting how total costs will behave. Instead, follow what was called Robert McNamara's First Law of Analysis when he was U.S. secretary of defense: "Always start by looking at the grand total. Whatever problem you are studying, back off and look at it in the large." In this context, that law means, "Beware of unit costs. When in doubt, convert all costs into totals to get the big picture."

☐ SPREADING FIXED COSTS

As we just saw, the unit cost–total cost distinction can become particularly troublesome when analyzing fixed-cost behavior. Assume the same facts concerning the special order as before, except that the order was for 250,000 units at a selling price of $11.50. Some managers have been known to argue for acceptance of such an order as follows: Of course, we will lose 50¢ each on the variable manufacturing costs, but we will gain 60¢ per unit by spreading our fixed manufacturing costs over 1.25 million units instead of 1 million units. Consequently, we should take the offer because it represents an advantage of 10¢ per unit:

Old fixed manufacturing cost per unit, $3,000,000 ÷ 1,000,000	$3.00
New fixed manufacturing cost per unit, $3,000,000 ÷ 1,250,000	2.40
"Saving" in fixed manufacturing costs per unit	$ .60
Loss on variable manufacturing costs per unit, $11.50 − $12.00	.50
Net saving per unit in manufacturing costs	$ .10

Again, the analytical pitfalls of unit-cost analysis can be avoided by using the contribution approach and concentrating on totals (in thousands of dollars):

	WITHOUT SPECIAL ORDER	WITH SPECIAL ORDER	SPECIAL-ORDER DIFFERENCE
Sales	20,000	22,875	2,875*
Variable manufacturing costs	12,000	15,000	3,000†
Other variable costs	1,100	1,100	—
Total variable costs	13,100	16,100	3,000
Contribution margin	6,900	6,775	(125)§

*250,000 × $11.50 selling price of special order.
†250,000 × $12.00 variable manufacturing cost per unit of special order.
§250,000 × $.50 negative contribution margin per unit of special order.

Short-run income will fall by $125,000 (that is, 250,000 units × $.50) if the special order is accepted. No matter how the fixed manufacturing costs are "unitized" and "spread" over the units produced, their total of $3 million will be *unchanged* by the special order (in thousands of dollars):

	WITHOUT SPECIAL ORDER	WITH SPECIAL ORDER	SPECIAL-ORDER DIFFERENCE
Contribution margin (as above)	6,900	6,775	(125)
Fixed costs:			
As originally allocated at a per-unit rate of $3.00	3,000	} 3,000	—
As newly allocated at a per-unit rate of $2.40			
Contribution to other fixed costs and operating income	3,900	3,775	(125)

☐ TOTAL COSTS AND UNIT COSTS

The term "absorption costing" arises from the procedure of taking a cost that behaves as a fixed cost in total (the fixed manufacturing cost of $3 million) and then allocating the cost *as though it were variable*. The fixed costs are thus said to be "absorbed" by "attaching" themselves to units of product as those units are manufactured. By the end of the year, if predictions were flawless, the total fixed costs absorbed by the product would indeed exactly equal the total actual fixed costs.

Of course, predictions are rarely flawless, so the cost analysis can become more complicated. Such complexities of the role of fixed overhead in product costing are explored in detail in Chapter 14, so do not be concerned here with anything beyond the major lesson: No matter how fixed costs are spread for *unit* product-costing purposes, the *total* fixed costs will be unchanged. This is true even though fixed costs *per unit* have fallen from $3 to $2.40. The moral is: Beware of unit costs when analyzing fixed costs. Think in terms of totals instead.

To recapitulate, a common error is to regard all unit costs indiscriminately, as if all costs were variable costs. Changes in volume will affect *total* variable costs but not *total* fixed costs. The danger then is to predict total costs assuming that all unit costs are variable. The correct relationships are:

	BEHAVIOR AS VOLUME FLUCTUATES	
	variable cost	fixed cost
Cost per unit	No change	Change
Total cost	Change	No change

Role of costs in pricing

☐ FACTORS THAT INFLUENCE PRICES

Many managers say that they use cost-plus pricing—that is, they compute an average unit cost and add a "reasonable" markup that will generate an adequate return on investment. This entails circular reasoning because price, which influences sales volume, is based upon full cost, which in turn is partly determined by the underlying volume of sales. Also, the plus in cost-plus is rarely an unalterable markup. Its magnitude depends on the behavior of competitors and customers. Three major factors influence pricing decisions: customers, competitors, and costs.

Customers always have an alternative source of supply, can substitute one material for another, and may make a part rather than buy it if the vendor's prices are too high.

Competitors will usually react to price changes made by their rivals. Tinkering with prices is usually most heavily influenced by the price setter's expectations of competitors' reactions.

The maximum price that may be charged is the one that does not drive the customer away. The minimum price is zero; companies may give out free samples to gain entry into a market. A more practical guide is that, in the short run, the *minimum* price to be quoted, *subject to consideration of long-run effects,* should be the costs that may be avoided by not landing the order—often all variable costs.

□ TARGET PRICING

When a company has little influence over price, it usually sells at the market price and tries, by controlling costs, to achieve profitable operations. When a company can set its own prices, its procedures are often a combination of shrewd guessing and mysterious folklore. Often the first step is to accumulate costs and add a markup. This is the target price. Subsequent adjustments may be made "in light of market conditions."

Earlier in this chapter the relationship between "absorption cost" and "full cost" was discussed. Sometimes these terms are used interchangeably, but more often absorption cost refers to all manufacturing costs while full cost refers to all manufacturing costs plus an allocation of selling and administrative costs too. Target prices might be based on a host of different markups based on a host of different definitions of cost. Thus there are many ways to arrive at the same target price. They simply reflect different arrangements of the components of the same income statement.

However, when it is used intelligently, the contribution approach has distinct advantages over the traditional full-costing (absorption-costing) approach, which fails to highlight different cost behavior patterns.

First, the contribution approach offers more detailed information than the traditional full-costing approach because variable- and fixed-cost behavior patterns are explicitly delineated. Because the contribution approach is sensitive to cost-volume-profit relationships, it is a better, easier basis for developing pricing formulas.

Second, a normal or target-pricing formula can be as easily developed by the contribution approach as by traditional full-costing approaches. Consider the facts in Exhibit 4-2. Note that under traditional approaches the target markup percentage may be expressed as a percentage of absorption cost—that is, the total manufacturing cost—or as a percentage of some total cost in the fullest sense, whereby all selling and administrative costs are also unitized.

For a volume of 1 million units, assume that the target selling price is $20 per unit. Therefore the target percentage (sometimes called a *markup* or *markon* percentage) of the base amount to be added to the base amount to obtain a selling price of $20 would be (in thousands):

As a percentage of manufacturing cost,

$$\frac{\$20,000 - \$15,000}{\$15,000} = 33.33\%$$

Thus, $15,000 + 33.33% ($15,000) = $20,000; $20,000 ÷ 1,000 = $20.

As a percentage of manufacturing, selling, and adminstrative cost,

$$\frac{\$20,000 - (\$15,000 + \$4,000)}{(\$15,000 + \$4,000)} = 5.26\%$$

Thus, $19,000 + 5.26% ($19,000) = $20,000.

As a percentage of variable manufacturing cost,

$$\frac{\$20,000 - \$12,000}{\$12,000} = 66.67\%$$

Thus, $12,000 + 66.67% (12,000) = $20,000.

As a percentage of variable manufacturing, selling, and administrative cost,

$$\frac{\$20,000 - \$13,100}{\$13,100} = 52.67\%$$

Thus, $13,100 + 52.67% ($13,100) = $20,000.

The percentages above are only a few of the possible variations in formula approaches to pricing. Under *either* the absorption (full) costing or the contribution approach, the pricing decision maker will have a formula that will lead him or her toward the *same* target price. If the decision maker is unable to obtain such a price consistently, the company will not achieve its $1 million operating-income objective or its desired operating-income percentage of sales.

Third, the contribution approach offers insight into the short-run versus long-run effects of cutting prices on special orders. For example, assume the same cost behavior patterns as in Exhibit 4-3. The 100,000-unit order added $100,000 to operating income at a selling price of $13, which was $7 below the target selling price of $20 and $2 below the absorption cost of $15. The implication there, given all the stated assumptions, was in favor of accepting the order. No general answer can be given, but the relevant information was more easily generated by the contribution approach. Recall the possible analyses:

	CONTRIBUTION APPROACH	TRADITIONAL ABSORPTION (FULL) COSTING APPROACH
Sales, 100,000 units @ $13	$1,300,000	$ 1,300,000
Variable manufacturing costs @ $12	1,200,000	
Absorption manufacturing costs @ $15		1,500,000
Apparent change in income	$ 100,000	$ −200,000

Should the offer be accepted? Compare the two approaches. Under the traditional approach, the decision maker has no direct knowledge of cost-volume-profit relationships. The decision maker makes the decision by hunch. On the surface the offer is definitely unattractive, because the price of $13 is $2 below factory absorption costs.

Under the contribution approach, the decision maker sees a short-run advantage of $100,000 from accepting the offer. Fixed costs will be unaffected by whatever decision is made and net income will increase by $100,000. Still, there often are long-run effects to consider. Will acceptance of the offer undermine the long-run price structure? In other words, is the short-run advantage of $100,000 more than offset by high probable long-run financial disadvantages? The decision maker may think so and may reject the offer. But—and this is important—by doing so the decision maker is, in effect, saying that he or she is willing to forgo $100,000 now in order to protect his or her long-run market advantages. Generally, the decision maker can assess problems of this sort by asking whether the probability of long-run benefits is worth an "investment" equal to the foregone contribution margin ($100,000 in this case). Under traditional approaches, the decision maker must ordinarily conduct a special study to find the immediate effects. Under the contribution approach, the manager has a system that will routinely and more surely provide such information.

Our general theme of focusing on relevant costs also extends into the area of pricing. To say that the contribution approach or absorption (full-cost) approach provides the best guide to pricing decisions is a dangerous oversimplification of one of the most perplexing problems in business. Lack of understanding and judgment can lead to unprofitable pricing regardless of the kind of cost data available or cost-accounting system used.

Frequently, managers are reluctant to employ a contribution approach because of fears that variable costs will be substituted indiscriminately for full costs and will therefore lead to suicidal price cutting. This should *not* occur if the data are used wisely. However, if the top managers perceive a pronounced danger of underpricing when variable-cost data are revealed, they may justifiably prefer a full-cost approach for guiding pricing decisions.

A complete discussion of pricing is beyond the scope of this book.[2] However, a contribution approach should clarify the major classes of information that bear on the pricing decision.

Deletion or addition of products or departments

Consider a discount department store that has three major departments: groceries, general merchandise, and drugs. Management is considering dropping groceries, which have consistently shown a net loss. The present annual net income is reported at the top of the next page (in thousands of dollars).

Sometimes the terms *avoidable* and *unavoidable* costs are used in conjunction with special decison making. **Avoidable costs** are those costs that will not continue if an ongoing operation is changed or deleted; in contrast, **unavoidable costs** are those costs that will continue. Avoidable costs include department

---

[2] For example, many laws prohibit price discrimination—that is, quoting different selling prices for identical goods or services. Obviously there are also many other complications, which are explored in books on economics and marketing.

DEPARTMENTS

	total	groceries	general merchandise	drugs
Sales	$1,900	$1,000	$800	$100
Variable cost of goods sold and expenses	1,420	800	560	60
Contribution margin	$ 480 (25%)	$ 200 (20%)	$240 (30%)	$ 40 (40%)
Fixed expenses (salaries, depreciation, insurance, property taxes, etc.):				
Avoidable	$ 265	$ 150	$100	$ 15
Unavoidable	180	60	100	20
Total fixed expenses	$ 445	$ 210	$200	$ 35
Net income	$ 35	$ (10)	$ 40	$ 5

salaries and other costs that could be avoided by not operating the specific department. Unavoidable costs include many **common costs,** which are defined as those costs of facilities and services that are shared by user departments. Examples are store depreciation, heating, air conditioning, and general management expenses.

Assume first that the only alternatives to be considered are to drop or continue the grocery department. Assume further that the total assets invested would not be affected by the decision. The vacated space would be idle, and the unavoidable costs would not be changed. Which alternative would you recommend? An analysis follows (in thousands of dollars):

STORE AS A WHOLE

income statements	a keep groceries	b drop groceries	a – b difference
Sales	$1,900	$900	$1,000
Variable expenses	1,420	620	800
Contribution margin	$ 480	$280	$ 200
Avoidable fixed expenses	265	115	150
Profit contribution to common space and other unavoidable costs	$ 215	$165	$ 50
Common space and other unavoidable costs	180	180	—
Net income	$ 35	$ (15)	$ 50

The preceding analysis shows that matters would be worse, rather than better, if groceries were dropped and the vacated facilities left idle. In short, as the income statement shows, groceries bring in a contribution margin of $200,000, which is $50,000 more than the $150,000 fixed expenses that would be saved by closing the grocery department.

Assume now that the space made available by the dropping of groceries would be used by an expanded general merchandise department. The space would be occupied by merchandise that would increase sales by $500,000, generate a 30 percent contribution-margin percentage, and have avoidable fixed costs of $70,000. The operating picture would then be improved by an increase in net income of $65,000 − $35,000 = $30,000:

	TOTAL	GENERAL MERCHANDISE	DRUGS
	(in thousands of dollars)		
Sales	$1,400	$800 + $500	$100
Variable expenses	970	560 + 350	60
Contribution margin	$ 430	$240 + $150	$ 40
Avoidable fixed expenses	185	100 + 70	15
Contribution to common space and other unavoidable costs	$ 245	$140 + $ 80	$ 25
Common space and other unavoidable costs*	180		
Net income	$ 65		

*Includes former grocery fixed costs, which were allocations of common costs that will continue regardless of how the space is occupied.

As the following summary analysis demonstrates, the objective is to obtain, from a given amount of space or capacity, the maximum contribution to the payment of those costs that remain unaffected by the nature of the product sold (in thousands of dollars):

	PROFIT CONTRIBUTION OF GIVEN SPACE		
	groceries	expansion of general merchandise	difference
Sales	$1,000	$500	$500 U
Variable expenses	800	350	450 F
Contribution margin	$ 200	$150	$ 50 U
Avoidable fixed expense	150	70	80 F
Contribution to common space and other unavoidable costs	$ 50	$ 80	$ 30 F

F = Favorable difference resulting from replacing groceries with general merchandise.
U = Unfavorable difference.

In this case, the general merchandise will not achieve the dollar sales volume that groceries will, but the higher markups and the lower wage costs (mostly because of the diminished need for stocking and checkout clerks) will bring more favorable net results.

An extremely large U.S. grocery chain, A&P, ran into profit difficulties during the 1970s. It began retrenching by closing many stores. Management's lack of adequate information about individual store operations made the closing program a hit-or-miss affair. *Fortune* (November 6, 1978) reported:

> . . . Because of the absence of detailed profit-and-loss statements, and a cost-allocation system that did not reflect true costs, A&P's strategists could not be sure whether an individual store was really unprofitable. For example, distribution costs were shared equally among all the stores in a marketing area without regard to such factors as a store's distance from the warehouse. Says one close observer of the company: "When they wanted to close a store, they had to wing it. They could not make rational decisions, because they did not have a fact basis."

Contribution to profit per unit of limiting factor

When a multiple-product plant is being operated at capacity, decisions as to which orders to accept must often be made. The contribution approach is also applicable here, because the product to be pushed or the order to be accepted is the one that makes the biggest *total* profit contribution per unit of the **limiting factor.**

The contribution approach must be used wisely, however. Sometimes a major pitfall is the erroneous tendency to favor those products with the biggest contribution-margin ratios per sales dollar.

Assume that a company has two products:

	PRODUCT	
PER UNIT	A	B
Selling price	$20	$30
Variable costs	16	21
Contribution margin	$ 4	$ 9
Contribution-margin ratio	20%	30%

Which product is more profitable? Product B apparently is more profitable than A: However, one important fact has been purposely withheld—the time that it takes to produce each product. If 10,000 hours of capacity are available, and three units of A can be produced per hour in contrast to one unit of B, your choice would be A, because it contributes the most profit per hour, the *limiting, critical,* or *scarce factor* in this example:

	A	B
1. Units per hour	3	1
2. Contribution margin per unit	$4	$9
Contribution margin per hour (1) × (2)	$12	$9
Total contribution for 10,000 hours	$120,000	$90,000

The limiting, critical, or scarce factor is the item that restricts or constrains the production or sale of a given product. Thus the criterion for maximizing profits, for a given capacity, is to obtain the greatest possible contribution to profit per unit of the limiting or critical factor. The limiting factor in the above example may be machine-hours or labor-hours. In the discount store example it was square feet of floor space. It may be cubic feet of display space. In such cases, a ratio such as the conventional gross-profit percentage (gross profit ÷ selling price) is an insufficient clue to profitability because profits also depend on the stock turnover (number of times the average inventory is sold per year).

The success of the suburban discount department stores illustrates the concept of the contribution to profit per unit of limiting factor. These stores have been satisfied with subnormal markups because they have been able to increase turnover and thus increase the contribution to profit per unit of space, as Exhibit 4-4 illustrates, using hypothetical numbers.

EXHIBIT 4-4.

	REGULAR DEPARTMENT STORE	DISCOUNT DEPARTMENT STORE
Retail price	$4.00	$3.50
Cost of merchandise	3.00	3.00
Contribution to profit per unit	$1.00 (25%)	$ .50 (14+%)
Units sold per year	10,000	22,000
Total contribution to profit, assuming the same space allotment in both stores	$10,000	$11,000

summary

The accountant's role in problem solving is primarily that of a technical expert on cost analysis. The accountant's responsibility is to be certain that the manager uses **relevant data** in guiding his or her decisions. Accountants and managers must have a penetrating understanding of relevant costs.

To be relevant to a particular decision, a cost must meet two criteria: (1) it must be an expected **future** cost; and (2) it must be an element of **difference** as among the alternatives. All **past** (**historical** or **sunk**) costs are in themselves irrelevant to any **decision** about the future, although they often provide the best available basis for the **prediction** of expected future data.

The combination of the relevant costing and contribution approaches is a fundamental framework, based on economic analysis, that may be applied to a vast range of problems. The following are among the more important generalizations regarding various decisions:

1. Wherever feasible, think in terms of total costs rather than unit costs. Too often, unit costs are regarded as an adequate basis for predicting changes in total costs. This assumption is satisfactory when analyzing variable costs, but it is frequently misleading when analyzing fixed costs.

2. The contribution approach to pricing special sales orders offers helpful information because the foregone contribution can be quantified as the investment currently being made to protect long-run benefits.

3. The key to obtaining the maximum profit from a given capacity is to obtain the greatest possible contribution to profit per unit of the limiting or scarce factor.

summary problems for your review

■ PROBLEM ONE

Return to the basic illustration in Exhibit 4-3. Suppose a special order like that described in conjunction with Exhibit 4-3 had the following terms: selling price would be $13.50 instead of $13, but a manufacturer's agent who had acquired the potential order would have to be paid a flat fee of $40,000 if the order was accepted. What would be the new operating income if the order was accepted? (Exhibit 4-3 is on page 91.)

■ PROBLEM TWO

Consider the following news story:

SALT LAKE CITY (UPI)—Mayor Ted Wilson says Sen. William Proxmire, D-Wis., had better stop taking his daily $12 federally funded showers before he criticizes Salt Lake City's $145,000 wave-making machine.

Wilson awarded Proxmire a "Golden Hypocrisy" award Tuesday in exchange for the "Golden Fleece" award the senator gave the U.S. Interior Department for spending taxpayers' money to make waves in a Salt Lake swimming pool so that desert dwellers could have an aquatic experience known only to coastal swimmers.

Proxmire gives out a Golden Fleece award monthly to people, projects and organizations he believes are ripping off the taxpayers through wasteful spending.

But Wilson predicted that 180,000 people—the city's entire population—would use the pool annually. He also criticized Proxmire for taking advantage of luxuries provided for senators.

The mayor said it cost taxpayers $12.35 a day for Proxmire to shower in the Senate gymnasium after he jogs to work.

"If he showers every day the Senate is in session, it costs the taxpayer $2,470 a year for a publicly paid shower," said Wilson.

"I am giving him my Golden Hypocrisy Award in recognition of the senator's ability to find fault in others and myopically overlook his own waste."

Wilson, who was a congressional aide before his election as mayor, said he calculated the cost of a Senate shower through his own observations. He said only about 15 of the 100 senators use the gym, which costs about $200,000 a year to operate.

"This means Sen. Proxmire costs the taxpayers $12.35 every time he takes a shower."

Proxmire attacked the wave-making machine as the "biggest, most ridiculous" example of wasteful government spending during November.

He said if the government follows the rationale used to justify the wave-making machine, "hard-pressed taxpayers will next be asked to fund ski slopes in Florida, mountain scenery in Indiana, igloos in Death Valley and tropical rain forests in Wisconsin."

REQUIRED

1. Compute the total cost and the unit cost per swim per year for making waves. Assume that the equivalent of (a) 180,000 and (b) 90,000 swimmers use the pool once during the year. Also assume that the machine will last five years and will have annual fixed operating costs of $11,000 for power and maintenance.
2. Analyze Mayor Wilson's response to Senator Proxmire. Compute the number of days the Senate is usually in session per year.
3. Compute the total cost and the unit cost per visit to the gymnasium if (a) 15, (b) 30, and (c) 90 of the senators use the gym and shower each day the Senate is in session.
4. (a) How does your computation of unit cost in Requirement 3a compare with the $12.35 calculated by Wilson? (b) Give a possible explanation for the difference between Wilson's and your computations.

■ SOLUTION TO PROBLEM ONE

The easiest way to solve this part is to work from the $100,000 increase in income already shown in the final column of Exhibit 4-3:

Operating income based on $13 price	$100,000
Increase in selling price per unit is $13.50 minus $13, or $.50. Increase in revenue, $.50 × 100,000 units	50,000
Increase in fixed expenses, special fee	(40,000)
New operating income	$110,000

■ SOLUTION TO PROBLEM TWO

This problem is worthwhile because it (a) underscores the roles of total costs and unit costs in evaluating frequently encountered discussions and (b) is amusing.

1. Annual costs in total:

Depreciation, $145,000 ÷ 5	$29,000
Fixed operating costs	11,000
Total	$40,000

a. Unit costs, $40,000 ÷ 180,000 = $.2222
b. Unit costs, $40,000 ÷ 90,000 = $.4444

2. Number of days in session = $2,470 ÷ $12.35 = 200. The total cost is probably entirely fixed, except for soap, water, towels, and slight fluctuations in energy bills because of variations in hot-water usage. Wilson's analysis seems unjustified. He implies that each visit by Proxmire increases the *total* expenses of operating the gym by $12.35. In fact, each visit has virtually no effect on *total* expenses.

Students should also ponder how Wilson might have accused Proxmire of incurring a higher unit cost per shower if the senator took only one or ten showers per year instead of two hundred. When a fixed cost is divided by some unit measure of activity, the lower the activity, the higher the unit cost. See the next part for examples.

3. a.

Total operating costs per year	$200,000
Visits per year, 15 senators × 200 days ÷	3,000
Unit cost per visit and shower =	$66.67

b. If 30 senators visit, the unit cost would drop to $200,000 ÷ (30 × 200) = $200,000 ÷ 6,000 = $33.33.

c. If 90 senators visit: $200,000 ÷ (90 × 200) = $11.11.

4. a. The $66.67 is obviously much higher than the $12.35 quoted by Wilson.

b. Two possible explanations are:

Wilson erred in his computations. Wilson's criticisms of Proxmire would have been even more dramatic if they had been based on the analysis in 3a.

Another possible explanation is that Wilson conducted a sophisticated analysis and somehow decided that $12.35 represented the true variable portion of the operating costs.

assignment material

■ FUNDAMENTAL ASSIGNMENT MATERIAL

4-1 Terminology. Define *absorption costing; avoidable cost; common cost; decision model; full cost; limiting factor; relevant information; unavoidable cost; variable costing.*

4-2 Terminology and interpretations of unit costs. The following is the income statement of a manufacturer of slacks:

BULOW COMPANY
Income Statement
For the Year Ended December 31, 19X4

	TOTAL	PER UNIT
Sales	$36,000,000	$36
Less manufacturing cost of goods sold	20,000,000	20
Gross margin	$16,000,000	$16
Less selling and administrative expenses	15,000,000	15
Operating income	$ 1,000,000	$ 1

Bulow had manufactured 1 million units, which had been sold to various clothing wholesalers and department stores. At the start of 19X5, the president, Rosalie Bulow, dropped dead of a stroke. Her son, Samuel, became the new president. Sam had worked for fifteen years in the marketing phases of the business. He knew very little about accounting and manufacturing, which were his mother's strengths. Sam had several questions for you, including inquiries regarding the pricing of special orders.

REQUIRED

1. To prepare better answers, you decide to recast the income statement in contribution form. Variable manufacturing cost was $15 million. Variable selling and administrative expenses, which were mostly sales commissions, shipping

expenses, and advertising allowances paid to customers based on units sold, were $9 million.

2. Sam asks, "I can't understand financial statements until I know the meaning of various terms. In scanning my mother's assorted notes, I found the following pertaining to both total and unit costs: *functional manufacturing cost, absorption cost, variable cost, full cost, fully allocated cost, fully distributed cost, gross margin, contribution margin.* Using our data for 19X4, please give me a list of these costs, their total amounts, and their per unit amounts."

3. "Near the end of 19X4 I brought in a special order from Macy's for 50,000 slacks at $30 each. I said I'd accept a flat $8,000 sales commission instead of the usual 6 percent of selling price, but my mother refused the order. She usually upheld a relatively rigid pricing policy, saying that it was bad business to accept orders that did not at least generate full manufacturing cost plus 80 percent of full manufacturing cost.

"That policy bothered me. We had idle capacity. The way I figured, our manufacturing costs would go up by 50,000 × $20 = $1,000,000, but our selling and administrative expenses would only go up by $8,000. That would mean additional operating income of 50,000 × ($30 − $20) minus $8,000, or $500,000 minus $8,000, or $492,000. That's too much money to give up just to maintain a general pricing policy. Was my analysis of the impact on operating income correct? If not, please show me the correct additional operating income."

4. After receiving the explanations offered in Requirements 2 and 3, Sam said: "Forget that I had the Macy's order. I had an even bigger order from J. C. Penney. It was for 250,000 units and would have filled the plant completely. I told my mother I'd settle for no commission. There would have been no selling and administrative costs whatsoever because J. C. Penney would pay for the shipping and would not get any advertising allowances.

"J. C. Penney offered $14.40 per unit. Our fixed manufacturing costs would have been spread over 1.25 million instead of 1 million units. Wouldn't it have been advantageous to accept the offer? Our old fixed manufacturing costs were $5 per unit. The added volume would reduce that cost more than our loss on our variable costs per unit.

"Am I correct? What would have been the impact on total operating income if we had accepted the order?"

4-3 **Special order.** Consider the following details of the income statement of the Monarch Pen Company for the year ended December 31, 19X3:

Sales	$10,000,000
Less manufacturing cost of goods sold	6,000,000
Gross profit or gross margin	$ 4,000,000
Less selling and administrative expenses	3,100,000
Operating income	$ 900,000

Monarch's fixed manufacturing costs were $2.4 million and its fixed selling and administrative costs were $2.3 million. Sales commissions of 3 percent of sales are included in selling and administrative expenses.

The company had sold 2 million pens. Near the end of the year, McDonald's Corporation, the well-known purveyor of hamburgers, had offered to buy 150,000 pens on a special order. To fill the order, a special clip bearing the McDonald's emblem would have had to be made for each pen. McDonald's intended to use the pens in special promotions during early 19X4.

Even though Monarch had some idle plant capacity, the president rejected the McDonald's offer of $660,000 for the 150,000 pens. He said:

The McDonald's offer is too low. We'd avoid paying sales commissions, but we'd have to incur an extra cost of 20¢ per clip for the emblem and its assembly with the pens. If Monarch sells below its regular selling prices, it will begin a chain reaction of competitors' price cutting and of customers wanting special deals. I believe in pricing at no lower than 8 percent above our full costs of $9,100,000 ÷ 2,000,000 units = $4.55 per unit plus the extra 20¢ per clip less the savings in commissions.

REQUIRED

1. Using the contribution approach, prepare an analysis similar to that in Exhibit 4-3. Use four columns: without the special order, with the special order, and the special-order difference shown in total and per unit. Exhibit 4-3 is on p. 91.
2. By what percentage would operating income increase or decrease if the order had been accepted? Do you agree with the president's decision? Why?

4-4 **Analysis of unit costs.** The Porterfield Company manufactures small appliances, such as electric can openers, toasters, food mixers, and irons. The peak season is at hand, and the president is trying to decide whether to produce more of the company's standard line of can openers or its premium line that includes a built-in knife sharpener, a better finish, and a higher quality motor. The unit data follow:

	PRODUCT	
	standard	premium
Selling price	$25	$31
Direct material	$ 7	$ 9
Direct labor	2	1
Variable factory overhead	2	3
Fixed factory overhead	6	9
Total cost of goods sold	$17	$22
Gross profit per unit	$ 8	$ 9

The sales outlook is very encouraging. The plant could operate at full capacity by producing either product or both products. Both the standard and the premium products are processed through the same departments. Selling and administrative costs will not be affected by this decision, so they may be ignored.

Many of the parts are produced on automatic machinery. The factory overhead is allocated to products by developing separate rates per machine-hour for variable and fixed overhead. For example, the total fixed overhead is divided by the total machine-hours to get a rate per hour. Thus the amount of overhead allocated to products is dependent on the number of machine-hours allocated to the product. It takes one hour of machine time to produce one unit of the standard product.

Direct labor may not be proportionate with overhead because many workers operate two or more machines simultaneously.

REQUIRED

Which product should be produced? If more than one should be produced, indicate the proportions of each. Show computations. Explain your answer briefly.

■ ADDITIONAL ASSIGNMENT MATERIAL

4-5. "A ratio such as the conventional gross-profit percentage is an insufficient clue to profitability." Do you agree? Explain.

4-6. What three major factors influence pricing decisions?

4-7. Why are customers one of the three factors influencing prices?

4-8. "I don't believe in assigning only variable costs to a job for guiding pricing. This results in suicidal underpricing." Do you agree? Why?

4-9. "The distinction between precision and relevancy should be kept in mind." Explain.

4-10. Distinguish between the quantitative and qualitative aspects of decisions.

4-11. "Any future cost is relevant." Do you agree? Explain.

4-12. Why are historical or past data irrelevant to special decisions?

4-13. Give four examples of limiting or scarce factors.

4-14. **Unit costs and total costs.** You are a college professor who belongs to a faculty club. Annual dues are $120. You use the club solely for lunches, which cost $3 each. You have not used the club much in recent years and are wondering whether to continue your membership.

REQUIRED

1. You are confronted with a variable-cost plus a fixed-cost behavior pattern. Plot each on a graph, where the vertical axis is total cost and the horizontal axis is volume in number of lunches. Also plot a third graph that combines the previous two graphs.
2. What is the cost per lunch if you pay for your own lunch once a year? Twelve times a year? Two hundred times a year?
3. Suppose the average price of lunches elsewhere is $4. (a) How many lunches must you have at the faculty club so that the total costs of the lunches would be the same regardless of where you ate for that number of lunches? (b) Suppose you ate 250 lunches a year at the faculty club. How much would you save in relation to the total costs of eating elsewhere?

4-15. **Information and decisions.** Suppose a company's historical costs for the manufacture of a calculator were as follows: direct materials, $2.20 per unit; direct labor, $3.00 per unit. Management is trying to decide whether to replace some materials with different materials. The replacement should cut material costs by 10 percent per unit. However, direct-labor time will increase by 5 percent per unit. Moreover, direct-labor rates will be affected by a recent 10 percent wage increase.

Prepare an exhibit like Exhibit 4-1, showing where and how the data about direct material and direct labor fit in the decision process.

4-16. **A&P's closing of stores.** This chapter refers to the A&P's closing of stores.

_1._ The company's labor costs as a percentage of sales increased in some markets, such as the Long Island and Pittsburgh divisions, even after allowing for normal increases in wage rates. How could this effect occur?

_2._ The company manufactured many of its own products. In the mid-1970s the company operated forty-six plants. Twenty-one were bakeries. The others manufactured a variety of goods, from frozen potatoes to mouthwash. What impact would the store closings probably have on the manufacturing plants and on the total operating income?

4-17. **Profit per unit of space.**

_1._ Several successful chains of discount department stores have merchandising policies that differ considerably from those of the traditional downtown department stores. Name some characteristics of these discount stores that have contributed to their success.

_2._ Food chains have typically regarded, perhaps, 20 percent of selling price as an average target gross profit on canned goods and similar grocery items. What are the limitations of such an approach? Be specific.

4-18. Pricing a special order. The Metroproducts Corporation has an annual plant capacity of 2,400 product units. Its predicted operations for the year are:

Production and sales of 2,000 units, total sales	$90,000
Manufacturing costs:	
Fixed (total)	$30,000
Variable (per unit)	$13
Selling and administrative expenses:	
Fixed (total)	$15,000
Variable (per unit)	$4

Compute, ignoring income taxes:

1. If the company accepts a special order for 200 units at a selling price of $19 each, how would the *total* predicted net income for the year be affected, assuming no effect on regular sales at regular prices?
2. Without decreasing its total net income, what is the lowest *unit price* for which the Metroproducts Corporation could sell an additional 100 units not subject to any variable selling and administrative expenses, assuming no effect on regular sales at regular prices?
3. In solving Requirement 2 above, list the numbers given in the problem that are irrelevant (not relevant).
4. Compute the expected annual net income (with no special orders) if plant capacity can be doubled by adding additional facilities at a cost of $250,000. Assume that these facilities have an estimated life of five years with no residual scrap value, and that the current unit selling price can be maintained for all sales. Total sales are expected to equal the new plant capacity each year. No changes are expected in variable costs per unit or in total fixed costs except for depreciation.

4-19. Dropping a product line. A local Woolworth's store sells many products. It has a restaurant with a counter that extends almost the length of the store. Management is considering dropping the restaurant, which has consistently shown an operating loss. The predicted income statements, in thousands of dollars, follow (for ease of analysis, only three product lines are shown):

	TOTAL	GENERAL MERCHANDISE	GARDEN PRODUCTS	RESTAURANT
Sales	5,000	4,000	400	600
Variable expenses	3,390	2,800	200	390
Contribution margin	1,610 (32%)	1,200 (30%)	200 (50%)	210 (35%)
Fixed expenses (compensation, depreciation, property taxes, insurance, etc.)	1,110	750	50	310
Operating income	500	450	150	(100)

The $310,000 of fixed expenses include the compensation of restaurant employees of $100,000. These employees will be released if the restaurant is abandoned. All counters and equipment are fully depreciated, so none of the $310,000 pertains to such items. Furthermore, their disposal values will be exactly offset by the costs of removal and remodeling.

If the restaurant is dropped, the manager will use the vacated space for either (a) more general merchandise or (b) more garden products. The expansion of general merchandise would not entail hiring any additional salaried help, but more garden products would require an additional person at an annual cost of $25,000. The manager thinks that sales of general merchandise would increase by $300,000; garden products, by $200,000. The manager's modest predictions are partially based on the fact that she thinks the restaurant has helped lure customers to the store and thus improved overall sales. If the restaurant is closed, that lure would be gone.

REQUIRED | Should the restaurant be closed? Explain, showing computations.

4-20. **Demand analysis.** (SMA, adapted.) The Aurora Manufacturing Limited produces and sells one product. During 19X4 the company manufactured and sold 50,000 units at $25 each. Existing production capacity is 60,000 units a year.

In formulating the 19X5 budget, management is faced with a number of decisions concerning product pricing and output. The following information is available:

1. A market survey shows that the sales volume is very much dependent on the selling price. For each $1 drop in selling price, sales volume would increase by 10,000 units.

2. The company's expected cost structure for 19X5 is as follows:
   a. Fixed cost (regardless of production or sales activities), $360,000
   b. Variable costs per unit (including production, selling and administrative expenses), $16

3. To increase annual capacity from the present 60,000 to 90,000 units, additional investment for plant, building, equipment, etc., of $200,000 would be necessary. The estimated average life of the additional investment would be ten years, so the fixed costs would increase by an average of $20,000 per year. (Expansion of less than 30,000 additional units of capacity would cost only slightly less than $200,000.)

REQUIRED | Indicate, with reasons, what the level of production and the selling price should be for the coming year. Also indicate whether the company should approve the plant expansion. Show your calculations. Ignore income tax considerations and the time value of money.

4-21. **Pricing strategy.** The Germane Company has the following cost behavior pattern for the unique ashtrays that it manufactures and sells:

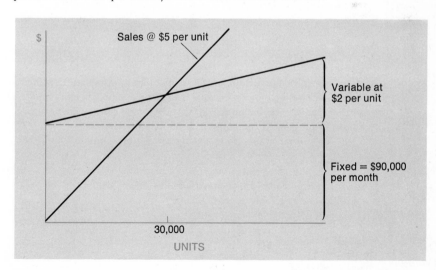

REQUIRED |
1. What is the break-even point in units?
2. If sales were at 40,000 units, would you then be inclined to cut the selling price? Why?
3. If sales were at 20,000 units, would you then be inclined to cut the selling price? Why?

4-22. Accepting a low bid. The Vittetaw Company, a maker of a variety of metal and plastic products, is in the midst of a business downturn and is saddled with many idle facilities. The National Hospital Supply Company has approached Vittetaw to produce 300,000 nonslide serving trays. National will pay $1.20 each.

Vittetaw predicts that its variable costs will be $1.30 each. However, its fixed costs, which had been averaging $1 per unit on a variety of other products, will now be spread over twice as much volume. The president commented, "Sure, we'll lose 10¢ each on the variable costs, but we'll gain 50¢ per unit by spreading our fixed costs. Therefore, we should take the offer, because it represents an advantage of 40¢ per unit."

REQUIRED

Do you agree with the president? Why? Suppose the regular business had a current volume of 300,000 units, sales of $600,000, variable costs of $390,000, and fixed costs of $300,000.

4-23. Variable costs and prices. A supplier to an automobile manufacturer has the following conversation with the manufacturer's purchasing manager:

SUPPLIER: You did not predict the heavy demands. To keep up with your unforeseen demands over the coming quarter, we will have to work six days per week instead of five. Therefore, I want a price increase in the amount of the overtime premium that I must pay.

MANUFACTURER: You have already recouped your fixed costs, so you are enjoying a hefty contribution margin on the sixth day. So quit complaining!

REQUIRED

Should the supplier get an increase in price? Explain.

4-24. Formulas for pricing. Adrian Corporation, a building contractor, constructs houses in tracts, often building as many as twenty homes simultaneously. The president of the corporation, Ms. Adrian, has budgeted costs for an expected number of houses in 19X7 as follows:

Direct materials	$2,000,000
Direct labor	1,000,000
Job construction overhead	1,000,000
Cost of jobs	$4,000,000
Selling and administrative costs	1,000,000
Total costs	$5,000,000

The job construction overhead includes approximately $400,000 of fixed costs, such as the salaries of supervisors and depreciation on equipment. The selling and administrative costs include $200,000 of variable costs, such as sales commissions and bonuses that depend fundamentally on overall profitability.

Ms. Adrian wants an operating income of $1 million for 19X7.

REQUIRED

Compute the average target profit percentage for setting prices as a percentage of
1. Prime costs (direct materials plus direct labor).
2. The full "cost of jobs."
3. The variable "cost of jobs."
4. The full "cost of jobs" plus selling and administrative costs.
5. The variable "cost of jobs" plus variable selling and administrative costs.

4-25. Pricing and contribution approach. The Big Western Transportation Company has the following operating results to date for 19X3:

Operating revenues	$50,000,000
Operating costs	40,000,000
Operating income	$10,000,000

A large Los Angeles manufacturer has inquired about whether Western would be interested in trucking a large order of its parts to San Francisco. Steve Minkler, operations manager, investigated the situation and estimated that the "fully distributed" costs of servicing the order would be $40,000. Using his general pricing formula, he quoted a price of $50,000. The manufacturer replied: "We'll give you $35,000, take it or leave it. If you do not want our business, we'll truck it ourselves or go elsewhere."

A cost analyst had recently been conducting studies of how Big Western's operating costs tended to behave. She found that $32 million of the $40 million could be characterized as variable costs. Minkler discussed the matter with her and decided that this order would probably generate cost behavior little different from Big Western's general operations.

REQUIRED

1. Using a contribution format, prepare an analysis for Minkler.
2. Should Big Western accept the order? Explain.

4-26. Pricing by auto dealers. Many automobile dealers have an operating pattern similar to that of Lance Motors, a dealer in Ohio. Each month, Lance initially aims at a unit volume quota that approximates a break-even point. Until the break-even point is reached, Lance has a policy of relatively lofty pricing, whereby the "minimum deal" must contain a sufficiently high markup to ensure a contribution to profit of no less than $250. After the break-even point is attained, Lance tends to quote lower prices for the remainder of the month.

REQUIRED

What is your opinion of this policy? As a prospective customer, how would you react to this policy?

4-27. Pricing of education. You are the director of continuing education programs for a well-known university. Courses for executives are especially popular, and you have developed an extensive menu of one-day and two-day courses that are presented in various locations throughout the nation. The performance of these courses for the current fiscal year, which is almost ended, is:

Tuition revenue	$2,000,000
Costs of courses	800,000
Contribution margin	1,200,000
General administrative expenses	300,000
Operating income	$ 900,000

The costs of the courses include fees for instructors, rentals of classrooms, advertising, and any other items, such as travel, that can be easily and exclusively identified as being caused by a particular course.

The general administrative expenses include your salary, your secretary's compensation, and related expenses, such as a lump-sum payment to the university's central offices as a share of university overhead.

The enrollment for your final course of the year is forty students, who have paid $150 each. Two days before the course is to begin, a city manager phones your office. "Do you offer discounts to nonprofit institutions?" he asks. "If so, we'll send ten managers. But our budget will not justify our spending more than $75 per person." The extra cost of including these ten managers would entail lunches at $10 each and course materials at $20 each.

REQUIRED

1. Prepare a tabulation of the performance for the full year, including the final course. Assume that the costs of the final course for the forty enrollees' instruction, travel, advertising, rental of hotel classroom, lunches, and course materials would be $2,500. Show a tabulation in four columns: before final course,

final course with forty registrants, effect of ten more registrants, and grand totals.

2. What major considerations would probably influence the pricing policies for these courses? For setting regular university tuition in private universities?

4-28. **Utilization of passenger jets.** In 19X2 Continental Air Lines, Inc., filled 50 percent of the available seats on its Boeing 707 jet flights, a record about 15 percent below the national average.

Continental could have eliminated about 4 percent of its runs and raised its average load considerably. But the improved load factor would have reduced profits. Give reasons for or against this elimination. What factors should influence an airline's scheduling policies?

When you answer this question, suppose that Continental had a basic package of 3,000 flights per month that had an average of 100 seats available per flight. Also suppose that 52 percent of the seats were filled at an average ticket price of $50 per flight. Variable costs are about 70 percent of revenue.

Continental also had a marginal package of 120 flights per month that had an average of 100 seats available per flight. Suppose that only 20 percent of the seats were filled at an average ticket price of $40 per flight. Variable costs are about 50 percent of this revenue. Prepare a tabulation of the basic package, marginal package, and total package, showing percentage of seats filled, revenue, variable expenses, and contribution margin.

4.29. **Airline costs.** An executive of Trans World Airlines (TWA) stated:

Under the Civil Aeronautics Board load factor standard, any shortfall below 55 percent is treated as presumptive managerial guilt of overscheduling. Thus, if the industry expects 116 billion *passenger miles* of traffic [a *passenger mile* is one person moved one mile], all we have to do is limit *seat miles* to 211 billion [a *seat mile* is one seat moved one mile]. . . . For us the smallest meaningful unit in capacity planning is not the seat mile, but the schedule. And each schedule generates a large, inflexible, indivisible batch of seat miles. . . . We cannot slice 5 percent off the airplane.

TWA analyzed its New York–Phoenix schedule for the year ended October 1977. This round trip produced revenues of $4.9 million. Fully allocated costs were $5.2 million, consisting of (a) $3.5 million "out-of-pocket costs" specifically created by this schedule (examples are fuel, crew pay, landing fees, and passenger-handling costs), and (b) $1.7 million of allocated fixed costs (examples are the rental of the terminal at Kennedy Airport, the depreciation on the central overhaul base in Kansas City).

REQUIRED | Should TWA give up its New York–Phoenix round-trip schedule? Explain.

4-30. **Utilization of capacity.** (CMA, adapted.) Anchor Company manufactures several different styles of jewelry cases. Management estimates that during the third quarter of 19X6 the company will be operating at 80 percent of normal capacity. Because the company desires a higher utilization of plant capacity, it will consider a special order.

Anchor has received special-order inquiries from two companies. The first is from JCP Inc., which would like to market a jewelry case similar to one of Anchor's cases. The JCP jewelry case would be marketed under JCP's own label. JCP Inc. has offered Anchor $5.75 per jewelry case for 20,000 cases to be shipped by October 1, 19X6. The cost data for the Anchor jewelry case, which would be similar to the specifications of the JCP special order, are as follows:

Regular selling price per unit	$9.00
Costs per unit:	
Raw materials	$2.50
Direct labor .5 hr @ $6	3.00
Overhead .25 machine-hr @ $4	1.00
Total costs	$6.50

According to the specifications provided by JCP Inc., the special-order case requires less-expensive raw materials, which will cost only $2.25 per case. Management has estimated that the remaining costs, labor time, and machine time will be the same as those for the Anchor jewelry case.

The second special order was submitted by the Krage Co. for 7,500 jewelry cases at $7.50 per case. These cases would be marketed under the Krage label and would have to be shipped by October 1, 19X6. The Krage jewelry case is different from any jewelry case in the Anchor line; its estimated per-unit costs are as follows:

Raw materials	$3.25
Direct labor .5 hr @ $6	3.00
Overhead .5 machine-hr @ $4	2.00
Total costs	$8.25

In addition, Anchor will incur $1,500 in additional setup costs and will have to purchase a $2,500 special device to manufacture these cases; this device will be discarded once the special order is completed.

The Anchor manufacturing capabilities are limited to the total machine-hours available. The plant capacity under normal operations is 90,000 machine-hours per year, or 7,500 machine-hours per month. The budgeted *fixed* overhead for 19X6 amounts to $216,000. All manufacturing overhead costs are applied to production on the basis of machine-hours at $4 per hour.

Anchor will have the entire third quarter to work on the special orders. Management does not expect any repeat sales to be generated from either special order. Company practice precludes Anchor from subcontracting any portion of an order when special orders are not expected to generate repeat sales.

REQUIRED

Should Anchor Company accept either special order? Justify your answer and show your calculations. *Hint:* Distinguish between variable and fixed overhead.

4-31. **Using available facilities.** The Lowe Company manufactures electronic subcomponents that can be sold at the end of Process A or can be processed further in Process B and sold as special parts for a variety of intricate electronic equipment. The entire output of Process A can be sold at a market price of $2 per unit. The output of Process B has been generating a sales price of $5.50 for three years, but the price has recently fallen to $5.10 on assorted orders.

Helen Tobin, the vice-president of marketing, has analyzed the markets and the costs. She thinks that the B output should be dropped whenever its price falls below $4.50 per unit. The total available capacity of A and B is interchangeable, so all facilities should currently be devoted to producing B. She has cited the following data:

OUTPUT OF A		
Selling price, after deducting relevant selling costs		$2.00
Direct materials	$1.00	
Direct labor	.20	
Manufacturing overhead	.60	
Cost per unit		1.80
Operating profit		$ .20

OUTPUT OF B

Selling price, after deducting relevant selling costs		$5.10
Transferred-in variable cost from A	$1.20	
Additional direct materials	1.50	
Direct labor	.40	
Manufacturing overhead	1.20	
Cost per unit		4.30
Operating profit		$ .80

Direct-materials and direct-labor costs are variable. The total overhead is fixed; it is allocated to units produced by predicting the total overhead for the coming year and dividing this total by the total hours of capacity available.

The total hours of capacity available are 600,000. It takes one hour to make 60 units of A and two hours of additional processing to make 60 units of B.

1. If the price of B for the coming year is going to be $5.10, should A be dropped and all facilities devoted to the production of B? Show computations.
2. Prepare a report for the vice-president of marketing to show the lowest possible price for B that would be acceptable.
3. Suppose that 50 percent of the manufacturing overhead were variable. Repeat Requirements 1 and 2. Do your answers change? If so, how?

4-32. Review of Chapters 2, 3, 4. The Dolphin Corporation has the following cost behavior patterns:

Production range in units	0–10,000	10,001–20,000	20,001–30,000	30,001–40,000
Fixed costs	$400,000	$560,000	$670,000	$760,000

Maximum production capacity is 40,000 units per year. Variable costs per unit are $50 at all production levels.

REQUIRED

Each situation described below is to be considered independently.
1. Production and sales are expected to be 21,000 units for the year. The sales price is $80 per unit. How many additional units need to be sold, in an unrelated market, at $70 per unit to show a total overall net income of $60,000 for the year?
2. The company has orders for 45,000 units at $80. If it desired to make a minimum overall net income of $500,000 on these 45,000 units, what unit purchase price would it be willing to pay a subcontractor for 5,000 units? Assume that the subcontractor would act as Dolphin's agent, deliver the units to customers directly, and bear all related costs of manufacture, delivery, and so forth. The customers, however, would pay Dolphin directly as the goods were delivered.
3. Production is currently expected to be 12,000 units for the year at a selling price of $80. By how much may advertising or special promotion costs be increased to bring production up to 25,000 units and still earn a total net income of 3 percent of dollar sales?
4. Net income is currently $330,000. Fixed costs are $670,000. However, competitive pressures are mounting. A 4 percent decrease in price will not affect sales volume but will decrease net income by $90,000. Compute the present volume in units and the selling price per unit (which is *not* $80). Refer to the original data.

114

RELEVANT COSTS AND SPECIAL DECISIONS – PART TWO

learning objectives

When you have finished studying this chapter, you should be able to:

1. Analyze given data to support a decision to make or buy certain parts or products.
2. Identify the opportunity-cost concept and apply it to an analysis for choosing the best use of available facilities.
3. Identify the uses and limitations of allocating joint costs.
4. Use either an incremental analysis or an opportunity-cost analysis to determine whether individual joint products should be processed beyond the split-off point.
5. Distinguish between relevant and irrelevant items in arriving at decisions concerning disposal of obsolete inventory and replacement of equipment.
6. Identify the nature, causes, and remedies of a serious motivational problem that might block a desirable decision to dispose of old equipment and replace it with new equipment.

The key question in relevant-cost analysis was introduced and explained in the preceding chapter: What difference does it make? This chapter extends the application of such analysis. The contribution approach is illustrated for make-or-buy decisions and sell-or-process-further decisions. Particular attention is given to the relationships between past and future data, using the decision to replace equipment as an illustration.

Make or buy

☐ MAKE OR BUY AND IDLE FACILITIES

Manufacturers are often confronted with the question of whether to make or buy a product. For example, should we manufacture our own parts and sub-assemblies or buy them from vendors? The qualitative factors may be of paramount importance. Sometimes the manufacture of parts requires special know-how, unusually skilled labor, rare materials, and the like. The desire to control the quality of parts is often the determining factor in the decision to make them. Then, too, companies hesitate to destroy mutually advantageous long-run relationships by erratic order giving, which results from making parts during slack times and buying them during prosperous times. They may have difficulty in obtaining any parts during boom times, when there are shortages of material and workers and no shortage of sales orders.

What are the quantitative factors relevant to the decision of whether to make or buy? The answer, again, depends on the context. A key factor is whether there are idle facilities. Many companies make parts only when their facilities cannot be used to better advantage.

Assume that the following costs are reported:

B COMPANY Cost of Making Part No. 900	TOTAL COST FOR 20,000 UNITS	COST PER UNIT
Direct material	$ 20,000	$ 1
Direct labor	80,000	4
Variable factory overhead	40,000	2
Fixed factory overhead	80,000	4
Total costs	$220,000	$11

Another manufacturer offers to sell B Company the same part for $10. Should B Company make or buy the part?

Although the $11 unit cost shown above seemingly indicates that the company should buy, the answer is rarely obvious. The key question is the difference in expected future costs as between the alternatives. If the $4 fixed overhead assigned to each unit represents those costs (e.g., depreciation, property taxes, insurance, allocated executive salaries) that will continue regardless of the decision, the entire $4 becomes irrelevant.

Again, it is risky to say categorically that only the variable costs are relevant. Perhaps $1 of the fixed costs will be saved if the parts are bought instead of made. For instance, suppose $20,000 is the salary of a supervisor who will be released or transferred to another productive assignment. In other words, fixed costs that may be avoided in the future are relevant.

For the moment, let us assume that the capacity now used to make parts will become idle if the parts are purchased. The relevant computations follow:

	PER UNIT		TOTALS	
	make	buy	make	buy
Direct material	$1		$ 20,000	
Direct labor	4		80,000	
Variable factory overhead	2		40,000	
Fixed factory overhead that can be avoided by not making (supervisor's salary)	1		20,000	
Total relevant costs	$8	$10	$160,000	$200,000
Difference in favor of making		$2	$40,000	

☐ ESSENCE OF MAKE OR BUY: UTILIZATION OF FACILITIES

The choice in our example is not really whether to make or buy; it is how best to utilize available facilities. Although the data above indicate that making the part is the better choice, the figures are not conclusive—primarily because we have no idea of what can be done with the manufacturing facilities if the component is bought. Only if the released facilities are to remain idle are the figures above valid.

If the released facilities can be used advantageously in some other manufacturing activity (to produce a contribution to profits of, say, $55,000) or can be rented out (say, for $35,000), these alternatives also may merit consideration. The two courses of action have become four (figures are in thousands):

	MAKE	BUY AND LEAVE FACILITIES IDLE	BUY AND RENT	BUY AND USE FACILITIES FOR OTHER PRODUCTS
Rent revenue	$ —	$ —	$ 35	$ —
Contribution from other products	—	—	—	55
Obtaining of parts	(160)	(200)	(200)	(200)
Net relevant costs	$(160)	$(200)	$(165)	$(145)

The analysis indicates that buying the parts and using the vacated facilities for the production of other products is the alternative that should yield best results in this case.

In sum, the make-or-buy decision should focus on relevant costs in a particular decision context. In all cases, companies should relate make-or-buy decisions to the long-run policies for the use of capacity:

> One company stated that it solicits subcontract work for *other* manufacturers during periods when sales of its own products do not fully utilize the plant, but that such work cannot be carried on regularly without expansion of its plant. The profit margin on subcontracts is not sufficiently large to cover these addtional costs and hence work is accepted only when other business is lacking. The same company sometimes meets a period of high volume by *purchasing* parts or having them made by subcontractors. While the cost of such parts is usually higher than the cost to make them in the company's own plant, the additional cost is less than it would be if they were made on equipment which could be used only part of the time.[1]

Opportunity costs

An **opportunity cost** is the *maximum* available contribution forgone by using limited resources for a particular purpose. It represents a forsaken alternative, so the "cost" differs from the usual kind in the sense that it is not the *outlay cost* that accountants and managers typically encounter and discuss. An **outlay cost** entails a cash disbursement sooner or later; that is, the outlay-cost idea provides the basis for the typical historical-cost valuations of assets.

Consider a hospital administrator who is trying to decide how to use some space vacated by the pediatrics clinic. The administrator has tabulated three choices in a straightforward way. The numbers favor laboratory testing, which will generate a contribution to income that is $30,000 greater than that of the eye clinic:

	(1) EXPAND LABORATORY TESTING	(2) EXPAND EYE CLINIC	(3) RENT TO GIFT SHOP MANAGER*
Expected future revenue	$70,000	$50,000	$4,000
Expected future costs	30,000	40,000	—
Contribution to income	$40,000	$10,000	$4,000

The gift shop is run by an independent retailer who pays the hospital a yearly rental. She wants to expand her present space.

In fact the manager may have a dozen possible uses for that space. Instead of listing all of them, he may pick the *best* (the rental) from among the ten alternatives that he does not want to consider in any detail and incorporate the forgone contribution as a cost of his final two alternatives. Therefore, the above data could be tabulated as on page 119, using the notion of opportunity cost.

The numbers have been analyzed correctly under both tabulations. They show a $30,000 difference in favor of the laboratory and thus answer the key query: What difference does it make? A comparison of the two tabulations

[1] *The Analysis of Cost-Volume-Profit Relationships,* National Association of Accountants, Research Series No. 17, p. 552.

	(1) EXPAND LABORATORY TESTING		(2) EXPAND EYE CLINIC	
Expected future revenue		$70,000		$50,000
Expected future costs:				
Outlay costs	$30,000		$40,000	
Opportunity cost— rent forgone	4,000	34,000	4,000	44,000
Contribution to income		$36,000		$ 6,000

shows how the concept of opportunity cost is a practical means of narrowing the number of alternatives under consideration.

Sometimes an individual may want to focus on only two alternatives from the start. For instance, Joan Bickerton, a certified public accountant, may be employed by a large accounting firm at a salary of $35,000 per year. She may want to begin her own independent practice. Her analysis of alternatives follows:

	INDEPENDENT PRACTICE	EMPLOYEE
Revenue	$90,000	$35,000
Costs	43,000	—
Net income	$47,000	$35,000

Like many individuals, Bickerton may prefer to tabulate the numerical effects as follows:

	INDEPENDENT PRACTICE	
Revenue		$90,000
Costs:		
Outlay costs	$43,000	
Opportunity cost— forgone salary	35,000	78,000
Net income		$12,000

The correct key difference, $12,000, will be generated by either tabulation. Some accountants and managers regard the opportunity-cost format of the second tabulation as being more confusing than the straightforward presentation of the first tabulation. Choose either approach. The choice is a matter of taste. Obviously, if the choice is framed as in the second tabulation (entering practice versus not entering), the failure to recognize an opportunity cost will misstate the difference between alternatives.

Note that opportunity costs are seldom incorporated into formal accounting systems, particularly for external reporting. Such costs represent incomes forgone by rejecting alternatives; therefore opportunity costs do not involve cash receipts or outlays. Accountants usually confine their recording to those events that ultimately involve exchanges of assets. Accountants confine their history to alternatives selected rather than those rejected, primarily because of the impracticality or impossibility of accumulating meaningful data on what might have been.

Joint product costs and incremental costs

☐ NATURE OF JOINT PRODUCTS

The preceding chapter referred to **common costs** as the cost of facilities and services shared by user departments. Sometimes accountants use the term *common cost* as a synonym for *joint cost*. In this book, however, *joint* will be restricted to the narrower meaning of **joint product costs.** The latter term is defined as the costs of manufactured goods of relatively significant sales values that are produced by a process or a series of processes and that are not identifiable as different individual products until after a certain stage of production known as the **split-off point.** Examples include petroleum products, chemicals, lumber, flour milling, leather tanning, copper mining, soap making, and meat packing. A meat-packing company cannot kill a sirloin steak; it has to slaughter a steer, which supplies various cuts of dressed meat, hides, and trimmings.

The split-off point is that juncture of production where the joint products become individually identifiable. Any costs beyond that stage are called *separable costs* because they are not part of the joint process and can be exclusively identified with individual products.

An illustration should clarify the meaning of these new terms. Suppose that a company produces two chemical products, X and Y, as a result of a particular joint process. The joint-processing cost is $100,000. Both products are sold to the petroleum industry to be used as ingredients of gasoline. The relationships follow:

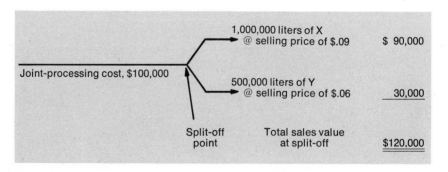

	1,000,000 liters of X @ selling price of $.09	$ 90,000
Joint-processing cost, $100,000	500,000 liters of Y @ selling price of $.06	30,000
Split-off point	Total sales value at split-off	$120,000

☐ SELL OR PROCESS FURTHER

Management frequently faces decisions of whether to sell joint products at split-off or to process some or all products further. Suppose the 500,000 liters of Y can be processed further and sold to the plastics industry as Product YA, an ingredient for plastic sheeting, at an additional cost of 8¢ per liter for manufacturing and distribution. The net sales price of YA would be 16¢ per liter.

Product X will be sold at the split-off point, but management is undecided about Product Y. Should Y be sold or should it be processed into YA? The joint costs must be incurred to reach the split-off point, so they do not differ among alternatives and are completely irrelevant to the question of whether to sell or process further. The only approach that will yield valid results is to concentrate on the separable costs and revenue *beyond* split-off, as shown in Exhibit 5-1.

EXHIBIT 5-1

	SELL AT SPLIT-OFF AS Y	PROCESS FURTHER AS YA	DIFFERENCE
Revenue	$30,000	$80,000	$50,000
Separable costs beyond split-off, @ $.08	—	40,000	40,000
Income effects	$30,000	$40,000	$10,000

This analysis shows that it would be $10,000 more profitable to process Y beyond split-off than to sell Y at split-off. Briefly, it is profitable to extend processing or to incur additional distribution costs on a joint product if the difference in revenue exceeds the difference in expenses.

For decisions regarding whether to sell or process further, the most straightforward analysis is as shown above. Alternatively, an opportunity-cost format would be:

	PROCESS FURTHER	
Revenue		$80,000
Outlay cost: separable cost beyond split-off, @ $.08	$40,000	
Opportunity cost: sales value of Y at split-off	30,000	70,000
Income effects		$10,000

This format merely is a different way of recognizing another alternative (sell Y at split-off) when considering the decision to process further individually. When they are properly analyzed, decision alternatives may be compared either by excluding the idea of opportunity costs altogether, as Exhibit 5-1 shows, or by encompassing opportunity costs, as is shown here. The key difference, $10,000, is generated either way.

☐ INCREMENTAL OR DIFFERENTIAL COSTS

SPECIAL DECISIONS— PART TWO

Two important points deserve mentioning here. First, the allocation of joint costs would not affect the decision, as Exhibit 5-2 demonstrates. The joint costs are not allocated in the exhibit, but no matter how they might be allocated, the total income effects would be unchanged.

Second, the title of the last column in Exhibit 5-2 contains terms that are frequently encountered in cost analysis for special decisions. **Incremental costs**

EXHIBIT 5-2

Firm as a Whole							
	ALTERNATIVE ONE			**ALTERNATIVE TWO**			incremental or differential
	x	y	total	x	ya	total	
Revenue	$90,000	$30,000	$120,000	$90,000	$80,000	$170,000	$50,000
Joint costs			$100,000		—	$100,000	—
Separable costs			—		40,000	40,000	40,000
Total costs			$100,000			$140,000	$40,000
Income effects			$ 20,000			$ 30,000	$10,000

(sometimes called **differential costs**) are, in any given situation, the difference between the total costs of each alternative. In this situation, the *incremental revenue* is $50,000, the *incremental cost* is $40,000, and the *incremental income* is $10,000. Each is the difference between the corresponding items under the alternatives being considered. In an analysis that showed only the differences, called an *incremental analysis,* only column 3 would be shown. In a *total analysis* all three sets of columns are shown. The choice of an incremental or a total analysis is a matter of individual preference.

☐ DANGER OF ALLOCATION

Earlier discussions in this and the preceding chapter have emphasized the desirability of concentrating on totals and of carefully examining unit costs and allocations of fixed costs. For example, the total common costs may only be partially affected by changes in departments or products. Similarly, the allocations of joint product costs to units of product is fraught with analytical perils.

Joint product costs are routinely allocated to products for purposes of inventory valuation and income determination. For example, some of the costs attributable to product X will ordinarily be allocated to any ending inventory of X. Such allocations are useful for inventory purposes *only.* For decisions of selling a joint product or processing it further, joint cost allocations should be ignored. Not only are they irrelevant, they may be downright misleading.

Two conventional ways of allocating joint costs to products are widely used: *physical units* and *relative sales values.* If physical units were used, the joint costs would be allocated as follows:

	LITERS	WEIGHTING	ALLOCATION OF JOINT COSTS	VALUE AT SPLIT-OFF
X	1,000,000	10/15 × $100,000	$ 66,667	$ 90,000
Y	500,000	5/15 × $100,000	33,333	30,000
	1,500,000		$100,000	$120,000

This approach shows that the $33,333 joint cost of producing Y exceeds its $30,000 value at split-off, seemingly indicating that Y should not be produced. However, such an allocation is not helpful in making production decisions.

Neither of the two products could be produced separately. In such a case, as we have already seen, the allocation of joint costs would not be relevant in deciding what to do with each product individually after split-off.

Costing in proportion to *relative sales values* at split-off is another popular way of allocating joint costs:

	RELATIVE SALES VALUE	WEIGHTING	ALLOCATION OF JOINT COSTS
X	$ 90,000	90/120 × $100,000	$ 75,000
Y	30,000	30/120 × $100,000	25,000
	$120,000		$100,000

Now each product would be assigned a joint cost portion that is less than its value at split-off. Note how the allocation of a cost to a particular product such as Y is dependent not only on the sales value of Y but also on the sales value of X. However, here again the joint cost allocation has no bearing on whether Y should be sold as Y or processed further to become YA.

Irrelevance of past costs

As defined early in Chapter 4, a relevant cost is (a) an expected future cost (b) that will differ among alternatives. The contribution aspect of relevant-cost analysis has shown that those expected future costs that will not differ are irrelevant to choosing among alternatives. Now we return to the idea that all past costs are also irrelevant to such decisions.

☐ OBSOLETE INVENTORY

A company has 100 obsolete missile parts that are carried in inventory at a manufacturing cost of $100,000. The parts can be (1) remachined for $30,000, and then sold for $50,000; or (2) scrapped for $5,000. Which should be done?

This is an unfortunate situation; yet the $100,000 cost is irrelevant to the decision to remachine or scrap. The only relevant factors are the expected future revenue and costs:

	REMACHINE	SCRAP	DIFFERENCE
Expected future revenue	$ 50,000	$ 5,000	$45,000
Expected future costs	30,000	—	30,000
Relevant excess of revenue over costs	$ 20,000	$ 5,000	$15,000
Accumulated historical inventory costs*	100,000	100,000	—
Net overall loss on project	$(80,000)	$(95,000)	$15,000

Irrelevant because it is not an element of difference as between the alternatives.

We could completely ignore the **historical cost** and still arrive at the $15,000 difference, the key figure in the analysis.

For now, we shall not consider all aspects of equipment-replacement decisions, but we shall turn to one that is widely misunderstood—the role of the book value of the old equipment. **Book value** is defined here as the original (historical) acquisition cost of a fixed asset less its accumulated depreciation. Suppose that an old machine has four years of useful life remaining, originally costing $10,000, has accumulated depreciation of $6,000, and thus has a book value of $4,000. It can be sold for $2,500 cash now, but it will have no disposal value at the end of the four years. A new machine, which (to simplify the analysis) will also have a useful life of four years, is available for $6,000. The new machine will reduce cash operating costs (maintenance, power, repairs, coolants, and the like) from $5,000 to $3,000 annually, but it will have no disposal value at the end of four years. Prepare a comparative analysis of the two alternatives.

Before making such an analysis, we consider some important concepts. The most widely misunderstood facet of replacement analysis is the role of the book value of the old equipment in the decision. The book value, in this context, is sometimes called a **sunk cost,** which is really just another term for historical or past cost. All historical costs are always irrelevant to choosing among alternative courses of action. Therefore the book value of the old equipment is always irrelevant to replacement decisions. At one time or another, we all like to think that we can soothe our wounded pride arising from having made a bad purchase decision by using the item instead of replacing it. The fallacy here is in erroneously thinking that a current or future action can influence the long-run impact of a past outlay. All past costs are down the drain. *Nothing* can change what has already happened.

We can apply our definition of decision relevance to four commonly encountered items:

1. *Book value of old equipment.* Irrelevant, because it is a past (historical) cost. Therefore depreciation on old equipment is irrelevant.

2. *Disposal value of old equipment.* Relevant (ordinarily), because it is an expected future inflow that usually differs among alternatives.

3. *Gain or loss on disposal.* This is the algebraic difference between 1 and 2. It is therefore a meaningless combination of book value, which is always irrelevant, and disposal value, which is usually relevant. The combination form, *loss* (or *gain*) *on disposal,* blurs the distinction between the irrelevant book value and the relevant disposal value. Consequently, it is best to think of each separately.[2]

4. *Cost of new equipment.* Relevant, because it is an expected future outflow that will differ among alternatives. Therefore depreciation on new equipment is relevant.

---

[2]For simplicity, we ignore income tax considerations and the effects of the interest value of money in this chapter. But book value is irrelevant even if income taxes are considered, because the relevant item is then the tax cash flow, not the book value. Using the approach in Exhibit 4-1, the book value is essential information for the *prediction method* (step 2), but the expected future income tax cash outflows are the relevant information for the *decision model* (step 3). The prediction method would be: Disposal value, $2,500 − Book value, $4,000 = Loss on disposal, $1,500. If the income tax rate is 50 percent, the income tax cash saving would be $750. This $750 would be the expected future cash flow that is relevant input to the decision model. For elaboration, see Chapter 12.

EXHIBIT 5-3

Cost Comparison—Replacement of Equipment
Including Relevant and Irrelevant Items

	FOUR YEARS TOGETHER			ANNUALIZED (DIVIDED BY 4)		
	keep	replace	difference	keep	replace	difference
Cash operating costs	$20,000	$12,000	$8,000	$5,000	$3,000	$2,000
Old equipment (book value):						
Periodic write-off as depreciation	4,000	—	—	1,000	—	—
or						
Lump-sum write-off		4,000*	—	—	1,000	—
Disposal value	—	−2,500*	2,500	—	−625	625
New machine, written off periodically as depreciation	—	6,000	−6,000	—	1,500	−1,500
Total costs	$24,000	$19,500	$4,500	$6,000	$4,875	$1,125

*In a formal income statement, these two items would be combined as "loss on disposal" of $1,500.

Exhibit 5-3 should clarify the above assertions. It deserves close study. Book value of old equipment is irrelevant regardless of the decision-making technique used. The "difference" columns in Exhibit 5-3 show that the $4,000 book value of the old equipment is not an element of difference between alternatives and could be completely ignored without changing the $1,125 difference in average annual net income. No matter what the *timing* of the charge against revenue, the *amount* charged is still $4,000, regardless of any available alternative. In either event, the undepreciated cost will be written off with the same ultimate effect on profit.[3] The $4,000 creeps into the income statement either as a $4,000 offset against the $2,500 proceeds to obtain the $1,500 *loss on disposal* in one year, or as $1,000 depreciation in each of four years. But how it appears is irrelevant to the replacement decision. In contrast, the $1,500 annual depreciation on the new equipment *is* relevant because the total $6,000 depreciation is a future cost that may be avoided by not replacing.

The advantage of replacement is $4,500 for the four years together; the average annual advantage is $1,125.

☐ EXAMINING ALTERNATIVES OVER THE LONG RUN

The foregoing is the first example that has looked beyond one year. A useful technique is to view the alternatives over their entire lives and then to compute annual average results. In this way, peculiar nonrecurring items (such as loss on

[3]We are deliberately ignoring income tax factors for the time being. If income taxes are considered, the *timing* of the writing off of fixed-asset costs may influence income tax payments. In this example, there will be a small real difference: the present value of $40,000 as a tax deduction now versus the present value of a $10,000 tax deduction each year for four years. But this difference in *future* income tax flows is the *relevant* item—not the book value of the old fixed asset per se. See Chapter 12.

EXHIBIT 5-4

Cost Comparison—Replacement of Equipment, Relevant Items Only

	FOUR YEARS TOGETHER			ANNUALIZED (DIVIDED BY 4)		
	keep	replace	difference	keep	replace	difference
Cash operating costs	$20,000	$12,000	$8,000	$5,000	$3,000	$2,000
Disposal value of old equipment	—	−2,500	2,500	—	−625	625
Depreciation—new equipment	—	6,000	−6,000	—	1,500	−1,500
Total relevant costs	$20,000	$15,500	$4,500	$5,000	$3,875	$1,125

disposal) will not obstruct the long-run view that must necessarily be taken in almost all special managerial decisions.

Exhibit 5-4 concentrates on relevant items only. Note that the same answer (the $4,500 net difference) will be produced even though the book value is completely omitted from the calculations. The only relevant items are the cash operating costs, the disposal value of the old equipment, and the depreciation on the new equipment. To demonstrate that the amount of the book value will not affect the answer, suppose the book value of the old equipment is $500,000 rather than $4,000. Your final answer will not be changed. The cumulative advantage of replacement will still be $4,500. (If you are in doubt, rework this example, using $500,000 as the book value.)

Motivation and conflict of models

☐ INFLUENCE OF LOSS

Recall that Exhibit 4-1 contained a series of boxes that stressed the relationship among historical costs, prediction methods, decision models, implementation and evaluation of performance, and feedback. Reconsider these relationships in conjunction with our illustration of equipment replacement. If the decision model says that the comparison should be on the total change in costs over the four years, as was assumed in our analysis, the choice would be to replace. Would the manager use that decision model? The answer might depend on how his or her performance was being evaluated. Conflict arises when managers are told to use one model for decision making, and their performance is then evaluated via a performance evaluation model that is inconsistent with the decision model. In this instance, if the manager's performance were to be evaluated by the typical accrual accounting model, a loss of $1,500 on the disposal of the old equipment would appear for the first year under the "replace" choice, but not under the "keep" choice.

Note the motivational factors here. A manager may be reluctant to replace simply because the large loss on disposal would severely harm his or her reported profit performance in the first year. Many managers and accountants would not replace the old machine because it would entail recognizing the $1,500 "loss on disposal," whereas retention would allow spreading the $4,000 book value over four years in the form of "depreciation expense" (a more appealing term than "loss on disposal"). This demonstrates how overemphasis on short-run income may conflict with the objective of maximizing income over the long run, especially if managers are transferred periodically to different responsibilities.

☐ DISTINGUISHING BETWEEN DECISIONS

Review Exhibit 4-1. Step 4, the evaluation of performance, is the means of gathering feedback on one decision (Decision A) that often sharpens the predictions of a second decision (Decision B). Feedback on Decision A helps Decision B, feedback on B helps Decision C, and so forth. Thus the feedback provided by the evaluation of performance is a major way of improving decisions. However, the financial impact of Decision B should not be mingled with the financial impact of Decision A. The analysis of relevant data should not mix the evaluation of Decision A with the steps of Decision B. For example, Decision B should not be forced to bear any "loss" already suffered by Decision A.

The equipment illustration demonstrates that the blunders of a Decision A should not become inputs to the decision model for a Decision B. In this example, having the loss from Decision A (the old decision to buy the existing equipment) affect the measurement of Year 1's performance for Decision B (replacing) would be faulty thinking. That is, Decisions A and B should be analyzed separately. The analytical difficulties are imposing, because the performance evaluation model (which is based on the typical accrual accounting model) does not ordinarily distinguish various special decisions. Instead, these decisions become mixed together, sometimes in ways that may lead to the wrong choice when Decision B is made.

How are Decisions A and B related? In equipment-replacement decisions, the feedback regarding Decision A may easily affect the predictions concerning Decision B. For instance, if existing equipment was supposed to last ten years, and it only lasted six, how credible is the new prediction that the proposed equipment will last, say, four years? Thus the evaluation of the performance of past decisions provides vital feedback that should improve later decisions.

☐ RECONCILING THE MODELS

The conflict between decision models and performance evaluation models just described is a pervasive problem in practice. Unfortunately, there are no easy solutions. In theory, the synchronization of these models seems obvious. Merely design a performance evaluation model that harmonizes exactly with the decision model. In our equipment example, this would mean predicting year-by-year income effects over the planning horizon for four years, noting that the first year would be poor, and following up accordingly.

The trouble is that systems rarely accommodate each decision in this fashion, one at a time. Consequently, the results of a single decision are encompassed along with many other decisions in an overall performance report. In such cases, the manager may predict the first-year effects and be inhibited from taking the longer view that may be preferable in the eyes of top management.

This one-year-at-a-time approach is especially prevalent in many not-for-profit organizations, where budgets are approved on a year-to-year basis and the use of feedback is not well developed. Occasionally, managers will be tempted to underestimate costs in order to obtain initial approval and then come back year after year for supplementary amounts that were not provided for in the original budget request. Moreover, through the years many colleges and universities have accepted donations for new facilities such as buildings and research equipment without providing sufficiently for lifelong maintenance and repairs. There is a danger that the value of such resources will be exceeded by the costs of operating them.

Irrelevance of future costs that will not differ

The past costs in the preceding two examples were not an element of difference among the alternatives. As noted, the $100,000 inventory and the $4,000 book value were included under both alternatives and were irrelevant because they were the same for each alternative under consideration.

There are also expected *future* costs that may be irrelevant because they will be the same under all feasible alternatives. These, too, may be safely ignored for a particular decision. The salaries of many members of top management are illustrations of expected future costs that will not be affected by the decision at hand.

Other examples include many fixed costs that will be unaffected by such considerations as whether Machine A or Machine B is selected, or whether a special order is accepted. However, it is not merely a case of saying that fixed costs are irrelevant and variable costs are relevant. Variable costs can be irrelevant. For instance, sales commissions might be paid on an order regardless of whether the order is filled from Plant A or Plant B. Variable costs are irrelevant whenever they do not differ among the alternatives at hand. Our preceding example showed that fixed costs (cost of new equipment) can be relevant. Fixed costs are relevant whenever they differ under the alternatives at hand.

Beware of unit costs

The pricing illustration in the preceding chapter showed that unit costs should be analyzed with care in decision making. There are two major ways to go wrong; (a) the inclusion of irrelevant costs, such as the $3 allocation of unavoidable fixed costs in the make-or-buy example that would result in a unit cost of $11 instead of the relevant unit cost of $8; and (b) comparisons of unit costs not computed on the same volume basis, as the following example demonstrates. Generally, it is advisable to use total costs rather than unit costs. Then, if desired, the totals may be unitized. Machinery sales personnel, for example, often brag about the low unit costs of using the new machines. Sometimes they neglect to point out that the unit costs are based on outputs far in excess of the volume of activity of their prospective customer.

Assume that a new $100,000 machine with a five-year life can produce 100,000 units a year at a variable cost of $1 per unit, as opposed to a variable cost per unit of $1.50 with an old machine. Is the new machine a worthwhile acquisition?

It is attractive at first glance. If the customer produces 100,000 units, unit-cost comparisons are valid, provided that new depreciation is also considered. Assume that the disposal value of the old equipment is zero. Because depreciation is an allocation of historical cost, the depreciation on the old machine is irrelevant. In contrast, the depreciation on the new machine is relevant, because the new machine entails a future cost that can be avoided by not acquiring it:

	OLD MACHINE	NEW MACHINE
Units	100,000	100,000
Variable costs	$150,000	$100,000
Straight-line depreciation	–	20,000
Total relevant costs	$150,000	$120,000
Unit relevant costs	$ 1.50	$ 1.20

However, if the customer's expected volume is only 30,000 units a year, the unit costs change:

	OLD MACHINE	NEW MACHINE
Units	30,000	30,000
Variable costs	$45,000	$30,000
Straight-line depreciation	–	20,000
Total relevant costs	$ 45,000	$50,000
Unit relevant costs	$ 1.50	$1.6667

Decision models and uncertainty

The decision models illustrated in this and the preceding chapter employed accrual accounting models, whereby the effects on net income under various alternatives were compared and the alternative with the best income effect was chosen. Other decision models are discussed in later chapters. (For example, Chapters 11 and 12 cover discounted-cash-flow models for equipment-replacement decisions. Many readers may prefer to jump directly to Chapters 11 and 12 immediately after completing their study of this chapter. This can be done without breaking continuity.)

It is vitally important to recognize that throughout this and other chapters, dollar amounts of future sales and operating costs are assumed to be known with certainty in order to highlight and to simplify various important points. In practice, the forecasting of these key figures is generally the most difficult aspect of decision analysis. For elaboration, see Chapter 15, which explores the implications of uncertainty in decision contexts.

summary

Relevant-cost analysis, which makes heavy use of the contribution approach, concentrates on expected future data that will differ among alternatives. As Exhibit 4-1 shows, clear distinctions should be made between past data, which may be helpful in formulating predictions, and the predicted data that are the inputs to decision models.

Highlights of this approach are (1) each cost used must be an expected **future** cost, and (2) it must be an element of **difference** among the alternatives. All **past** (**historical** or **sunk**) costs are in themselves irrelevant to any decision about the future, although they often provide the best available basis for the prediction of expected future data.

The combination of the relevant-costing and contribution approaches is a fundamental framework, based on economic analysis, that may be applied to a vast range of problems. The following are among the more important generalizations regarding various decisions:

1. Make-or-buy decisions are, fundamentally, examples of obtaining the most profitable utilization of given facilities.

2. Sometimes the notion of an opportunity cost is helpful in cost analysis. An opportunity cost is the maximum sacrifice in rejecting an alternative; it is the maximum earning that might have been obtained if the productive good, service, or capacity had been applied to some alternative use. The opportunity-cost approach does not affect the important final differences between the courses of action, but the format of the analysis differs.

3. Joint product costs are irrelevant in decisions about whether to sell at split-off or process further.

4. Incremental costs or differential costs are the differences in the total costs under each alternative.

5. The book value of old equipment is always irrelevant in replacement decisions. This cost is often called a **sunk cost.** Disposal value, however, is generally relevant.

6. Generally, it is advisable to use total costs, rather than unit costs, in cost analysis.

7. Managers are often motivated to reject desirable economic decisions because of a conflict between the measures used in the decision model and the performance evaluation model.

summary problem for your review

■ PROBLEM

Exhibit 5-5 contains data for the Block Company for the year just ended. The company makes parts that are used in the final assembly of its finished product.

EXHIBIT 5-5

	A + B COMPANY AS A WHOLE	A FINISHED PRODUCT*	B PARTS
Sales: 100,000 units, @ $100	$10,000,000		
Variable costs:			
Direct material	$ 4,900,000	$4,400,000	$ 500,000
Direct labor	700,000	400,000	300,000
Variable factory overhead	300,000	100,000	200,000
Other variable costs	100,000	100,000	—
Sales commissions, @ 10% of sales	1,000,000	1,000,000	—
Total variable costs	$ 7,000,000	$6,000,000	$1,000,000
Contribution margin	$ 3,000,000		
Separable fixed costs	$ 2,300,000	$1,900,000	$ 400,000
Common fixed costs	400,000	320,000	80,000
Total fixed costs	$ 2,700,000	$2,220,000	$ 480,000
Operating income	$ 300,000		

*Not including the cost of parts (column B).

REQUIRED

1. During the year, a prospective customer in an unrelated market offered $82,000 for 1,000 finished units. The latter would be in addition to the 100,000 units sold. The regular sales commission rate would have been paid. The president rejected the order because "it was below our costs of $97 per unit." What would operating income have been if the order had been accepted?

2. A supplier offered to manufacture the year's supply of 100,000 parts for $13.50 each. What would be the effect on operating income if the Block Company purchased rather than made the parts? Assume that $350,000 of the separable fixed costs assigned to parts would have been avoided if the parts were purchased.

3. The company could have purchased the parts for $13.50 each and used the vacated space for the manufacture of a deluxe version of their major product. Assume that 20,000 deluxe units could have been made (and sold in addition to the 100,000 regular units) at a unit variable cost of $70, exclusive of parts and exclusive of the 10 percent sales commission. The sales price would have been $110. All of the fixed costs pertaining to the parts would have continued, because these costs related primarily to the manufacturing facilities utilized. What would operating income have been if Block had bought the necessary parts and made and sold the deluxe units?

1. Costs of filling special order:

Direct material	$49,000
Direct labor	7,000
Variable factory overhead	3,000
Other variable costs	1,000
Sales commission, @ 10% of $82,000	8,200
Total variable costs	$68,200
Selling price	82,000
Contribution margin	$13,800

Net income would have been $300,000 + $13,800, or $313,800, if the order had been accepted. In a sense, the decision to reject the offer implies that the Block Company is willing to invest $13,800 in immediate gains forgone (an opportunity cost) in order to preserve the long-run selling-price structure.

2. Assuming that $350,000 of the fixed costs could have been avoided by not making the parts and that the other fixed costs would have been continued, the alternatives can be summarized as follows:

	MAKE	BUY
Purchase cost		$1,350,000
Variable costs	$1,000,000	
Avoidable fixed costs	350,000	
Total relevant costs	$1,350,000	$1,350,000

If the facilities used for parts were to become idle, the Block Company would be indifferent as to whether to make or buy. Operating income would be unaffected.

3.

Sales would increase by 20,000 units, @ $110		$2,200,000
Variable costs exclusive of parts would increase by 20,000 units, @ $70	$1,400,000	
Plus the sales commission, 10% of $2,200,000	220,000	1,620,000
Contribution margin on 20,000 units		$ 580,000
Parts: 120,000 rather than 100,000 would be needed		
Buy 120,000, @ $13.50	$1,620,000	
Make 100,000, @ $10 (only the variable costs are relevant)	1,000,000	
Excess cost of outside purchase		620,000
Fixed costs, unchanged		—
Disadvantage of making deluxe units		$ (40,000)

Operating income would decline to $260,000 ($300,000 − $40,000, the disadvantage of selling the deluxe units). The deluxe units bring in a contribution margin of $580,000, but the additional costs of buying rather than making parts is $620,000, leading to a new disadvantage of $40,000.

assignment material

5-1. Terminology. Define *book value; common cost; differential cost; historical cost; incremental cost; joint product costs; opportunity cost; outlay cost; split-off point; sunk cost.*

5-2. Replacing old equipment. (An alternate is 5-30.) Suppose that a university's old photocopying machine has three years of useful life remaining. It originally cost $15,000, has accumulated depreciation of $6,000, and thus has a book value of $9,000. It can be sold for $5,700 cash now, but it will have no disposal value at the end of three years.

A new machine will have a useful life of three years. It is available for $12,000. It will have no disposal value at the end of three years. The new machine will reduce cash operating costs for power, maintenance, toner, and supplies from $8,000 to $5,000 annually. Income taxes and the time value of money are to be ignored.

REQUIRED

1. Prepare a cost comparison similar to Exhibit 5-4. Which alternative seems preferable?
2. Prepare a cost comparison similar to Exhibit 5-5. Which tabulation is clearer, this one or the one in Requirement 1?
3. Prepare a simple "shortcut" or direct analysis to support your choice of alternatives.

5-3. Decision and performance models. (An alternate is 5-31.) Refer to the preceding problem.

1. Suppose the "decision model" favored by top management consisted of a comparison of a three-year accumulation of cash under each alternative. As the manager of office operations, which alternative would you choose? Why?

2. Suppose the "performance evaluation" model emphasized the minimization of overall costs of photocopying operations for the first year. Which alternative would you choose?

5-4. "I had a chance to rent my summer cottage for two weeks for $150. But I chose to have it idle. I didn't want strangers living in my summer house." What term in this chapter describes the $150? Why?

5-5. There are two major reasons why unit costs should be analyzed with care in decision making. What are they?

5-6. "Accountants do not formally record opportunity costs in the accounting records." Why?

5-7. Distinguish between an opportunity cost and an outlay cost.

5-8. Distinguish between an incremental cost and a differential cost.

5-9. "Past costs are indeed relevant in most instances, because they provide the point of departure for the entire decision process." Do you agree? Why?

5-10. Which of the following items are relevant in replacement decisions. Explain.
a. Book value of old equipment.
b. Disposal value of old equipment.
c. Cost of new equipment.

5-11. "No technique applicable to the problem of joint product costing should be used for management decisions regarding whether a product should be sold at the split-off point or processed further." Do you agree? Explain.

5-12. "Incremental cost is the addition to costs from the manufacture of one unit." Do you agree? Explain.

5-13. **Relevant investment.** Tom Thorp had obtained a new truck with a list price, including options, of $10,000. The dealer had given him a "generous trade-in allowance" of $3,000 on his old truck that had a wholesale price of $2,000. Sales tax was $600.

The annual cash operating costs of the old truck were $3,000. The new truck was expected to reduce these costs by one-third.

REQUIRED

Compute the original investment in the new truck. Explain your reasoning.

5-14. **Opportunity cost.** Juanita Morales is a sole practitioner as a certified public accountant. She enjoys her work, is very skilled, and is in heavy demand. Morales has raised her fees considerably during the past two years, but she is unable to accept all the clients who want her accounting services.

Morales has worked an average of nine hours daily, six days a week, for forty-eight weeks a year. Her fees average $125 per hour. Her variable costs are negligible and may be ignored for decision purposes. Ignore income taxes.

REQUIRED

1. Morales wants to reduce her hours. She is considering not working on Saturdays, but instead working ten hours daily on Mondays through Fridays. What would be her annual income (a) if she continues to work the same schedule as before and (b) if she adopts the new schedule?
2. What would be her opportunity cost for the year of not working the extra hours?
3. Suppose that Morales has definitely decided to adopt the new schedule. She loves to play golf. If she plays golf during half a Saturday when she otherwise would not be doing work for clients, what is her opportunity cost of playing golf?

5-15. **Opportunity costs.** A private university has been suffering from declining enrollments. Its student union building is underutilized. A small delicatessen had been operating in some of the space, but it has been losing money for many months.

Alice Adams, the head administrator of the building, is trying to decide whether to:

a. Close the delicatessen. Occupy the space by expanding the adjacent variety store, which has been reasonably profitable for several years. The expected future revenue from the new space would be $100,000. Expected future costs would be $90,000.

b. Replace the delicatessen with a gift and paperback book shop. The expected future revenue per year from the new shop would be $80,000; expected future costs, $50,000.

c. Replace the delicatessen with a Baskin-Robbins ice-cream store run by a local businesswoman. She would pay annual rent of $8,000.

REQUIRED

1. Tabulate the total relevant costs of the decision alternatives. Omit the concept of opportunity cost in your first tabulation, but use it in your second tabulation.
2. As the administrator, which tabulation would you prefer to receive? Which decision alternative seems most attractive? Why?

5-16. **Hotel rooms and opportunity costs.** The Sheraton Corporation operates many hotels throughout the world. One of its New York hotels is facing difficult times because of the opening of several new competing hotels.

To accommodate its flight personnel, American Airlines has offered Sheraton a contract for the coming year that provides a rate of $50 per night per room for a minimum of fifty rooms for 365 nights. This contract would assure Sheraton of selling fifty rooms of space nightly, even if some of the rooms are vacant on some nights.

The Sheraton manager has mixed feelings about the contract. On several peak nights during the year, the hotel could sell the same space for $95 per room.

REQUIRED

1. Suppose the contract is signed. What is the opportunity cost of the fifty rooms on October 20, the night of a big convention of retailers when every midtown hotel room is occupied? What is the opportunity cost on December 28, when only ten of these rooms would be expected to be rented at an average rate of $75?
2. If the year-round rate per room averaged $90, what percentage of occupancy of the fifty rooms in question would have to be rented to make Sheraton indifferent about accepting the offer?

5-17. **Make or buy.** McCain Company manufactures automobile parts. It frequently subcontracts work to other manufacturers, depending on whether McCain's facilities are fully occupied. McCain is about to make some final decisions regarding the use of its manufacturing facilities for the coming year.

The following are the costs of making Part K426, a key component of an emission control system:

	TOTAL COST FOR 60,000 UNITS	COST PER UNIT
Direct material	$ 300,000	$ 5
Direct labor	480,000	8
Variable factory overhead	360,000	6
Fixed factory overhead	300,000	5
Total manufacturing costs	$1,440,000	$24

Another manufacturer has offered to sell the same part to McCain for $22 each. The fixed overhead consists of depreciation, property taxes, insurance, and supervisory salaries. All of the fixed overhead would continue if McCain bought the component, except that the costs of $120,000 pertaining to some supervisory and custodial personnel could be avoided.

REQUIRED

1. Assume that the capacity now used to make parts will become idle if the parts are purchased. Should the parts be made or bought? Show computations.
2. Assume that the capacity now used to make parts will either (a) be rented to a nearby manufacturer for $50,000 for the year or (b) be used to make carburetors that will yield a profit contribution of $80,000. Should Part K426 be made or bought? Show computations.

5-18. **Conceptual approach.** A large automobile-parts plant was constructed four years ago in an Ohio city served by two railroads. The PC Railroad purchased forty specialized 60-foot freight cars as a direct result of the additional traffic generated by the new plant. The investment was based on an estimated useful life of twenty years.

Now the competing railroad has offered to service the plant with new 86-foot freight cars, which would enable more efficient shipping operations at the plant. The automobile company has threatened to switch carriers unless PC Railroad buys ten new 86-foot freight cars.

The PC marketing management wants to buy the new cars, but PC operating management says: "The new investment is undesirable. It really consists of the new outlay plus the loss on the old freight cars. The old cars must be written down to a low salvage value if they cannot be used as originally intended."

Evaluate the comments. What is the correct conceptual approach to the quantitative analysis in this decision?

5-19. Meaning of allocation of joint costs.

1. Examine the illustration on joint costs that appears in this chapter. Suppose the joint costs were allocated on the basis of liters. Prepare an income statement by product line on the assumption that Product Y was (a) sold at split-off, or (b) processed further.

2. Repeat Requirement 1, assuming that the joint costs were allocated on the basis of net realizable values (relative sales values) at split-off.

3. Which set of income statements is more meaningful, those in Requirement 1 or in 2? Why?

5-20. Sell or process joint products.
The Raymond Company manufactured three joint products at a joint cost of $600,000. These products were processed further and sold as follows:

PRODUCT	SALES	ADDITIONAL PROCESSING COSTS
X	$ 400,000	$100,000
Y	700,000	320,000
Z	300,000	130,000
	$1,400,000	$550,000

If the company had pursued its opportunities to sell at split-off directly to other processors, sales would have been: X, $250,000; Y, $400,000; and Z, $100,000.

The company expects to operate at the same level of production and sales in the forthcoming year.

Consider all the available information, and assume that all costs incurred after split-off are variable.
1. Could the company increase operating income by altering its processing decisions? If so, what would be the expected overall operating income?
2. Which products would be processed further and which should be sold at split-off?

5-21. Joint costs and decisions.
The Coast Chemical Company has a batch process whereby 1,400 gallons of raw material are transformed into 200 pounds of X-1 and 600 pounds of X-2. Although the joint costs of their production are $1,200, both products are worthless at their split-off point. Additional separable costs of $350 are necessary to give X-1 a sales value of $1,000 as Product A. Similarly, additional separable costs of $150 are necessary to give X-2 a sales value of $1,000 as Product B.

You are in charge of the batch process and the marketing of both products. (Show your computations for each answer.)
1. a. Assuming that you believe in assigning joint costs on a physical basis, allocate the operating profit of $300 per batch to Products A and B.
   b. Would you stop processing one of the products? Why?
2. a. Assuming that you believe in assigning joint costs on a net-realizable-value (relative-sales-value) basis, allocate the operating profit of $300 per batch to Products A and B. If there is no market for X-1 and X-2 at their split-off point, a net realizable value is usually imputed by taking the ultimate sales values at the point of sale and working backward to obtain approximated

"synthetic" relative sales values at the split-off point. These synthetic values are then used as weights for allocating the joint costs to the products.

b. You have internal product-profitability reports in which joint costs are assigned on a net-realizable-value basis. Your chief engineer says that, after seeing these reports, he has developed a method of obtaining more of Product B and correspondingly less of Product A from each batch, without changing the per-pound cost factors. Would you approve of this new method? Why? What would the overall operating profit be if 100 more pounds of B were produced and 100 less pounds of A?

5-22. **Joint products.** (CPA.) From a particular joint process, Watkins Company produces three products, X, Y, and Z. Each product may be sold at the point of split-off or processed further. Additional processing requires no special facilities, and production costs of further processing are entirely variable and traceable to the products involved. In 19X3 all three products were processed beyond split-off. Joint production costs for the year were $60,000. Sales values and costs needed to evaluate Watkins's 19X3 production policy follow:

PRODUCT	UNITS PRODUCED	NET REALIZABLE VALUES (SALES VALUES) AT SPLIT-OFF	ADDITIONAL COSTS AND SALES VALUES IF PROCESSED FURTHER sales values	added costs
X	6,000	$25,000	$42,000	$9,000
Y	4,000	41,000	45,000	7,000
Z	2,000	24,000	32,000	8,000

Joint costs are allocated to the products in proportion to the relative physical volume of output.

1. For units of Z, the unit production cost most relevant to a sell-or-process-further decision is

a. $5.
b. $12.
c. $4.
d. $9.

2. To maximize profits, Watkins should subject the following products to additional processing:

a. X only.
b. X, Y, and Z.
c. Y and Z only.
d. Z only.

5-23. **Joint costs.** Two products, A and B, had been allocated $30,000 of joint costs each, using the net-realizable-value method. Net realizable value is the ultimate selling price less separable costs of completion and marketing. The products' ultimate sales values were $70,000 and $90,000, respectively. The separable costs for A were $20,000. What were the separable costs for B?

5-24. **Sell equipment.** (H. Schaefer.) Dearborn Company is phasing out a production process during the next twelve months. The process uses a piece of special-purpose equipment that has a remaining book value of $10,000 (straight time) per year and the equipment consumes $1,000 of power annually. The production supervisor earns $18,000 annually and spends about 10 percent of his time supervising this process. Building depreciation allocated to the process amounts to $1,500 per year.

During the phase-out period the equipment operator will work about 20 percent more time at overtime rates (time-and-one-half) performing some manual tasks. This causes the supervisor to consider the possibility of performing the process manually— 100 percent, without the equipment. The equipment can be sold today for $7,000. If the process is done manually, the existing operator will not have to work overtime, but a second operator will have to be hired at $9,000 per year. The equipment can be sold at the end of the phase-out period for $4,000.

Should the process be performed with the equipment or 100 percent manually (without the equipment)? Support your answer with quantitative analysis. Do *not* consider the effect of taxes or the time value of money.

5-25. New machine. A new $200,000 machine is expected to have a four-year life and a terminal value of zero. It can produce 80,000 units a year at a variable cost of $2 per unit. The variable cost is $3 per unit with an old machine, which has a book value of $80,000. It is being depreciated on a straight-line basis at $20,000 per year. It too is expected to have a terminal value of zero. Its current disposal value is also zero because it is highly specialized equipment.

The salesman of the new machine prepared the following comparison:

	NEW MACHINE	OLD MACHINE
Units	80,000	80,000
Variable costs	$160,000	$240,000
Straight-line depreciation	50,000	20,000
Total cost	$210,000	$260,000
Unit cost	$ 2.625	$ 3.25

He said, "The new machine is obviously a worthwhile acquisition. You will save 62 1/2¢ for every unit you produce."

1. Do you agree wth the salesman's analysis? If not, how would you change it? Be specific.
2. Prepare an analysis of total and unit costs if the annual volume is 40,000 units.
3. At what annual volume would both the old and new machines have the same total relevant costs?

5-26. Discontinuation of product. (CMA, adapted.) The Scio Division of Georgetown Inc. manufactures and sells four related product lines. Each product is produced at one or more of the three manufacturing plants of the division. The accompanying table presents a product line profitability statement for the year ended December 31, 19X7, which shows a loss for the baseball equipment line. A similar loss is projected for 19X8.

The baseball equipment is manufactured in the Evanston Plant. Some football equipment and all miscellaneous sports items are also processed through this plant. A few of the miscellaneous items are manufactured, and the remainder are purchased for resale. The item purchased for resale is recorded as materials in the records. A separate production line is used to produce the products of each product line.

The accompanying schedule presents the costs incurred at the Evanston Plant in 19X7. Inventories at the end of the year were substantially identical to those at the beginning of the year.

The management of Georgetown Inc. has requested a profitability study of the baseball equipment line to determine if the line should be discontinued. The marketing department of the Scio Division and the accounting department at the plant have developed the following additional data to be used in the study:

a. If the baseball equipment line is discontinued, the company will lose approximately 10 percent of its sales in each of the other lines.

b. The equipment now used in the manufacture of baseball equipment is quite specialized. It has a current salvage value of $105,000 and a remaining useful life of five years. This equipment cannot be used elsewhere in the company.

c. The plant space now occupied by the baseball equipment line could be closed off from the rest of the plant and rented for $175,000 per year.

Product Line Profitability—19X7
(000 omitted)

	FOOTBALL EQUIPMENT	BASEBALL EQUIPMENT	HOCKEY EQUIPMENT	MISCELLANEOUS SPORTS ITEMS	TOTAL
Sales	$2,200	$1,000	$1,500	$500	$5,200
Costs of goods sold:					
Material	$ 400	$ 175	$ 300	$ 90	$ 965
Labor and variable overhead	800	400	600	60	1,860
Fixed overhead	350	275	100	50	775
Total	$1,550	$ 850	$1,000	$200	$3,600
Gross profit	$ 650	$ 150	$ 500	$300	$1,600
Selling expense:					
Variable	$ 440	$ 200	$ 300	$100	$1,040
Fixed	100	50	100	50	300
Corporate administration expenses	48	24	36	12	120
Total	$ 588	$ 274	$ 436	$162	$1,460
Contribution to corporation	$ 62	$ (124)	$ 64	$138	$ 140

Evanston Plant Costs—19X7
(000 omitted)

	FOOTBALL EQUIPMENT	BASEBALL EQUIPMENT	MISCELLANEOUS SPORTS ITEMS	TOTAL
Material	$100	$175	$ 90	$ 365
Labor	$100	$200	$ 30	$ 330
Variable overhead:				
Supplies	$ 85	$ 60	$ 12	$ 157
Power	50	110	7	167
Other	15	30	11	56
Subtotal	$150	$200	$ 30	$ 380
Fixed overhead:				
Supervision*	$ 25	$ 30	$ 21	$ 76
Depreciation†	40	115	14	169
Plant rentals‡	35	105	10	150
Other§	20	25	5	50
Subtotal	$120	$275	$ 50	$ 445
Total costs	$470	$850	$200	$1,520

* The supervision costs represent salary and benefit costs of the supervisors in charge of each product line.
† Depression cost for machinery and equipment is charged to the product line on which the machinery is used.
‡ The plant is leased. The lease rentals are charged to the product lines on the basis of square feet occupied.
§ Other fixed-overhead costs are the cost of plant administration and are allocated arbitrarily by management decision.

d. If the line is discontinued, the supervisor of the baseball equipment line will be released. In keeping with company policy, he would receive severance pay of $5,000.

e. The company has been able to invest excess funds at 10 percent per annum.

REQUIRED

1. Should Georgetown Inc. discontinue the baseball equipment line? Support your answer with appropriate calculations and qualitative arguments.
2. A member of the board of directors of Georgetown Inc. has inquired whether the information regarding the discontinuance of product lines should be included in the financial statements on a regular monthly basis for all product lines. Draft a memorandum in response to the board member's inquiry. Your memorandum should (a) state why or why not this information should be included in the regular monthly financial statements distributed to the board and (b) detail the reasons for your response.

SPECIAL DECISIONS— PART TWO

5-27. **Make or buy.** The Rohr Company's old equipment for making subassemblies is worn out. The company is considering two courses of action: (a) completely replacing the old equipment with new equipment, or (b) buying subassemblies from a reliable outside supplier, who has quoted a unit price of $1 on a seven-year contract for a minimum of 50,000 units per year.

Production was 60,000 units in each of the past two years. Future needs for the next seven years are not expected to fluctuate beyond 50,000 to 70,000 units per year. Cost records for the past two years reveal the following unit costs of manufacturing the subassembly:

Direct material	$ .25
Direct labor	.40
Variable overhead	.10
Fixed overhead (including $.10 depreciation and $.10 for supervision and other direct departmental fixed overhead)	.25
	$1.00

The new equipment will cost $188,000 cash, will last seven years, and will have a disposal value of $20,000. The current disposal value of the old equipment is $10,000.

The salesman for the new equipment has summarized his position as follows: The increase in machine speeds will reduce direct labor and variable overhead by 35¢ per unit. Consider last year's experience of one of your major competitors with identical equipment. They produced 100,000 units under operating conditions very comparable to yours and showed the following unit costs:

Direct material	$.25
Direct labor	.10
Variable overhead	.05
Fixed overhead, including $.24 depreciation	.40
	$.80

REQUIRED

For purposes of this case, assume that any idle facilities cannot be put to alternative use. Also assume that 5¢ of the old Rohr unit cost is allocated fixed overhead that will be unaffected by the decision.

1. The president asks you to compare the alternatives on a total-annual-cost basis and on a per-unit basis for annual needs of 60,000 units. Which alternative seems more attractive?

2. Would your answer to Requirement 1 change if the needs were 50,000 units? 70,000 units? At what volume level would Rohr be indifferent between make and buy? Show your computations.

3. What factors, other than the above, should the accountant bring to the attention of management to assist them in making their decision? Include the considerations that might be applied to the outside supplier.

For additional analyses, see Problems 11-35 and 12-30.

5-28. **Review of Chapters 2–5.** (CMA, adapted.) The Keylo Co. manufactures a line of plastic products that are sold through hardware stores. The company sales have declined slightly for the past two years, leaving it with idle plants and equipment.

A Keylo engineer met a former college classmate while attending a recent convention of machinery builders. The classmate is employed by the Paddington Co., which is also in the plastic products business. During the course of their conversation, it became evident that Keylo might be able to make a particular product for Paddington with the currently unused equipment and space.

The following requirements were specified by Paddington for the new product:

1. Paddington needs 80,000 units per year for the next three years.

2. The product is to be built to Paddington specifications.

3. Keylo is not to enter into the independent production of the product during the three-year contract.

4. Paddington would provide Keylo, without charge, a special machine to finish the product. The machine becomes the property of Keylo at the end of the three-year period.

Although Keylo is not operating at capacity, the company generated a profit last year, as is shown in its income statement.

Keylo Co.
Income Statement
For the fiscal Year Ended October 31, 19X7
(000 omitted)

	DOLLAR AMOUNT	PERCENT
Sales	$1,500	100%
Cost of goods sold:		
Material	$ 200	13%
Direct labor	400	27
Overhead*	390	26
Cost of goods sold	$ 990	66%
Gross margin before depreciation on idle capacity	$ 510	34%
Depreciation on idle capacity	10	1
Gross margin	$ 500	33%
Operating expenses:		
Sales commissions	$ 60	4%
Sales administration	30	2
General administration	110	7
Total operating expenses	$ 200	13%
Income before income taxes	$ 300	20%
Income taxes (40%)	120	8
Net income	$ 180	12%

*Schedule of manufacturing overhead:

Variable	
Indirect labor	$100
Supplies	40
Power	120
Fixed costs applied	
Administration	60
Depreciation	70
	$390

The Keylo engineering, production, and accounting departments agreed upon the following facts if the contracts were accepted:

1. Manufacturing:

a. The present idle capacity would be fully used.

b. One additional supervisor would be required; the annual salary would be $15,000 at the present rates.

c. The annual requirements for material and labor would increase by 10 percent at current prices.

d. The power and supply requirements would increase by 10 percent at current prices due to the reactivation of idle machines.

e. The machine provided by Paddington would increase the annual power and supply costs by $10,000 and $4,000, respectively, at current prices.

f. The Paddington machine would have no value to Keylo at the end of the contract.

2. Sales:

    a. A sales commission of $10,000 would be paid to the salespersons arranging the contract.

    b. No additional sales administrative costs would be incurred.

3. General administration: No additional general administrative costs would be incurred.

4. Other information:

    a. Estimated cost increases due to inflation for the entire three-year period are shown below.

Material	5%
Labor	10%
Power	20%
Depreciation	0
Sales commissions	0
Income taxes	0
All other items	10%

    b. Inventory balances, which have remained stable for the past three years, will not be increased or decreased by the production of the new product.

1. Calculate the total price needed for the three-year order (240,000 units) if the company wants to add to its net income in an amount equal to 10 percent after taxes on the sales price of this order.
2. Calculate the total price for the three-year order (240,000 units) if this order were to contribute nothing to net income.
3. Would the answer you calculated in Requirement 2 above contribute to existing fixed costs? Explain.

5-29. **Relevant costs of auto ownership.** Joan Robbins, a dairy inspector for the state of Wisconsin, used her private automobile for work purposes and was reimbursed by the state at a rate of 22¢ per mile. Robbins was unhappy about the rate, so she was particularly interested in a publication of the Federal Highway Administration, "The Cost of Owning and Operating an Automobile."

The publication contained a "work sheet for first-year auto costs":

```
 1. Amount paid for your car . . . . . . . . . . . . . . . . . . . .    $ . . . . . . . . .
 2. First-year mileage . . . . . . . . . . . . . . . . . . . . . . . .      . . . . . . . . .
 3. First-year depreciation . . . . . . . . . . . . . . . . . . . .    $ . . . . . . . . .
 4. Insurance . . . . . . . . . . . . . . . . . . . . . . . . . . . .    $ . . . . . . . . .
 5. License, other fees or taxes . . . . . . . . . . . . . . . .    $ . . . . . . . . .
 6. Interest on auto loan . . . . . . . . . . . . . . . . . . . . .    $ . . . . . . . . .
 7. Maintenance, repairs, tires . . . . . . . . . . . . . . . . .    $ . . . . . . . . .
 8. Fuel and oil . . . . . . . . . . . . . . . . . . . . . . . . . . .    $ . . . . . . . . .
 9. Parking, garaging, tolls . . . . . . . . . . . . . . . . . . .    $ . . . . . . . . .
10. Total of Lines 3 through 9 . . . . . . . . . . . . . . . . . .    $ . . . . . . . . .
11. Line 10 divided by Line 2 . . . . . . . . . . . . . . . . . .    $ . . . . . . . . .
       Line 11 is your first-year per-mile cost.
```

Robbins paid $9,000 for her new car. She expected to drive it 20,000 miles per year. The highway administration work sheet calls for depreciation at 33 percent of original cost for the first year, 25 percent the second year, and 20 percent the third year.

Insurance is $400. License and other fees amount to $200. Interest on her $6,000 auto loan is $720 for the first year, $480 for the second year, and $240 for the third year. The highway booklet said that the following charges might be expected for maintenance for every 10,000 miles: $120 for the first year, $240 for the second year, and $480 for the third year. Parking and tolls would cost an average of 1¢ per mile, and fuel and oil 6¢ per mile.

1. Compute the total first-year cost of automobile ownership. Compute the cost per mile if the following miles were driven: 10,000, 20,000, and 30,000.
2. Is the reimbursement rate of 22¢ a "fair" rate?
3. Joan and a friend use her car for a 400-mile journey. They agree in advance "to split the costs of using the car, fifty-fifty." How much should Joan's friend pay?
4. What if Joan had paid cash for her car rather than borrowed $6,000? Would the costs change? By how much? Explain.
5. Suppose Joan were thinking of buying a second car exactly like the first and on the same financial terms, but she would confine the second car to personal use of 5,000 miles per year. The total mileage of the two cars taken together would still be 20,000 miles. What would be the first-year cost of operating a second car? The average unit cost? What costs are relevant? Why?
6. Robbins has owned the car one year. She has switched to a local job that does not require a car. What costs are relevant to the question of selling the car and using other means of transportation?

5-30. **Role of old equipment in replacement.** (An alternate is 5-2.) On January 2, 19X1, the Buxton Company installed a brand-new $81,000 special molding machine for producing a new product. The product and the machine have an expected life of three years. The machine's expected disposal value at the end of three years is zero.

On January 3, 19X1, Jim Swain, a star salesman for a machine tool manufacturer, tells Mr. Buxton: "I wish I had known earlier of your purchase plans. I can supply you with a technically superior machine for $100,000. The old machine can be sold for $16,000. I guarantee that our machine will save $35,000 per year in cash operating costs, although it too will have no disposal value at the end of three years."

Mr. Buxton examines some technical data. Although he had confidence in Swain's claims, Buxton contends: "I'm locked in now. My alternatives are clear: (a) disposal will result in a loss; (b) keeping and using the 'old' equipment avoids such a loss. I have brains enough to avoid a loss when my other alternative is recognizing a loss. We've got to use that equipment till we get our money out of it."

The annual operating costs of the old machine are expected to be $60,000, exclusive of depreciation. Sales, all in cash, will be $900,000 per year. Other annual cash expenses will be $800,000 regardless of this decision. Assume that the equipment in question is the company's only fixed asset. Note that the facts in this problem are probed more deeply in Problems 11-25 and 12-28.

Ignore income taxes and the time value of money.
1. Prepare statements of cash receipts and disbursements as they would appear in each of the next three years under both alternatives. What is the total net difference in cash flow for the three years?
2. Prepare income statements as they would appear in each of the next three years under both alternatives. Assume straight-line depreciation. What is the total difference in net income for the three years?
3. Assume that the cost of the "old" equipment was $1 million rather than $81,000. Would the net difference computed in Requirements 1 and 2 change? Explain.
4. As Jim Swain, reply to Buxton's contentions.
5. What are the irrelevant items in each of your presentations for Requirements 1 and 2? Why are they irrelevant?

5-31. **Decision and performance models.** (An alternate is 5-3.) Refer to the preceding problem.

1. Suppose the "decision model" favored by top management consisted of a comparison of a three-year accumulation of wealth under each alternative. Which alterna-

tive would you choose? Why? (Accumulation of wealth means cumulative increase in cash.)

2. Suppose the "performance evaluation model" emphasized the net income of a subunit (such as a division) each year rather than considering each project, one by one. Which alternative would you choose? Why?

3. Suppose the same quantitative data existed, but the "enterprise" was a post office of the U.S. Postal Service. Would your answers to the first two parts change? Why?

part two

accounting for planning and control

chapter **6**

THE MASTER BUDGET: THE OVERALL PLAN

learning objectives

When you have finished studying this chapter, you should be able to:

1. Define **budget** and identify its major advantages to an organization.
2. Distinguish between master budgets and capital budgets.
3. Distinguish between operating budgets and financial budgets.
4. List the principal steps in preparing a master budget.
5. Construct the supporting schedules and main statements for a master budget.
6. Identify the two primary uses of a financial-planning model.

Management—and many investors and bank loan officers—have become increasingly aware of the merits of formal business plans. This chapter provides a condensed view of the overall business plan for the forthcoming year (or less)—the master budget. The major technical work of the budgetary accountant involves expected future data rather than historical data. There is also a major philosophical difference: The advocates of budgeting maintain that the process of preparing the budget forces executives to become better administrators. Budgeting puts planning where it belongs—in the forefront of the manager's mind.

This chapter provides a bird's-eye view of planning for the organization as a whole. We will see that planning requires all the functions of a business to blend together. We will see the importance of an accurate sales forecast. Most of all, we should begin to appreciate why budgeting is helpful. Budgeting is primarily attention directing, because it helps managers to focus on operating or financial problems early enough for effective planning or action.

This book stresses how accounting helps the *operating* performance of management (how effectively assets are acquired and utilized). But the *financing* function (how funds for investment in assets are obtained) is also important. That is why this chapter examines cash budgets as well as operating budgets. Successful organizations are usually characterized by both superior operating management *and* superior financial management. Business failures are frequently traceable to management's shirking of the financial aspects of its responsibilities.

Characteristics of budgets

□ DEFINITION OF BUDGET

A budget is a formal quantitative expression of management plans. The master budget summarizes the goals of all subunits of an organization—sales, production, distribution, and finance. It quantifies targets for sales, production, net income, and cash position, and for any other objective that management specifies. The master budget usually consists of a statement of expected future income, a balance sheet, a statement of cash receipts and disbursements, and supporting schedules.[1] These statements are the culmination of a series of planning decisions arising from a detailed, rigorous look at the organization's future.

Of course, budgets can also be used on an individual level. For instance, a student may budget in a detailed or general way regarding food for the coming week or month, hours of study before examinations, and so forth.

□ ADVANTAGES OF BUDGETS

Many skeptics who have never used budgets are quick to state, "I suppose budgeting is okay for the other fellow's business, but *my* business is different. There are too many uncertainties and complications to make budgeting worthwhile for me." But the same managers, when prodded for details, usually reveal that

---

[1] A master budget also contains a statement of changes in financial position, which is described in Chapter 17.

they are planning incessantly, but in an informal way. Perhaps the best way to combat such a short-sighted attitude is to name others in the same industry who are zealous about budgeting and who, inevitably, are among the industry's leaders. An organization that adopts formal budgeting usually becomes rapidly convinced of its helpfulness and would not consider regressing to its old-fashioned, nonbudgeting days. The benefits of budgeting almost always clearly outweigh the cost and the effort.

Some kind of budget program is bound to be useful to any organization, regardless of its size or its uncertainties. The major benefits are:

1. Budgeting, by formalizing their responsibilities for planning, compels managers to think ahead.
2. Budgeting provides definite expectations that are the best framework for judging subsequent performance.
3. Budgeting aids managers in coordinating their efforts, so that the objectives of the organization as a whole harmonize with the objectives of its parts.

☐ FORMALIZATION OF PLANNING

The principal advantage of budgeting is probably that it forces managers to think ahead—to anticipate and prepare for changing conditions. The budgeting process makes planning an explicit management responsibility. Too often, managers operate from day to day, extinguishing one business brush fire after another. They simply have no time for any tough-minded thinking beyond the next day's problems. Planning takes a back seat or is actually obliterated by workaday pressures.

The trouble with the day-to-day approach to managing an organization is that objectives are never crystallized. Without goals, company operations lack direction, problems are not foreseen, and results are hard to interpret. Advocates of budgeting correctly maintain that most business emergencies can be avoided by careful planning.

☐ EXPECTATIONS AS A FRAMEWORK FOR JUDGING PERFORMANCE

As a basis for judging actual results, budgeted goals and performance are generally regarded as being more appropriate than past performance. The news that a company had sales of $10 million this year, as compared with $8 million the previous year, may or may not indicate that the company has been effective and has achieved maximum success. Perhaps sales should have been $11 million this year. The major drawback of using historical data for judging performance is that inefficiencies may be concealed in the past performance. Moreover, the usefulness of comparisons with the past is also limited by intervening changes in economic conditions, technology, competitive maneuvers, personnel, and so forth.

Another benefit of budgeting is that key personnel are informed of what is expected of them. Nobody likes to drift along, not knowing what his or her boss expects or hopes to achieve.

Coordination is the meshing and balancing of an organization's resources so that its overall objectives are attained—so that the goals of the individual manager harmonize with goals of the organization as a whole. The budget is the means for communicating overall objectives and for blending the objectives of all departments.

Coordination requires, for example, that purchasing officers integrate their plans with production requirements, and that production officers use the sales budget to help them anticipate and plan for the manpower and plant facilities they will require. The budgetary process obliges executives to visualize the relationship of their department to other departments, and to the company as a whole.

A budget is not a cure-all for existing organizational ills. It will not solve the problems created by a bumbling management or a faulty information system. The budget is a device whose value depends on its being administered astutely in conjunction with an information system that is attuned to a coordinated organization.

Human relations

Middle management's attitude toward budgets will be heavily influenced by the attitude of top management. The chief executives must offer wholehearted support if a budgetary program is to achieve maximum benefits.

The ability to adhere to a budget is often an important factor in judging a manager's performance, and naturally, budgets are usually not the most popular aspect of a manager's professional life. Budgets pinpoint a manager's performance and direct his or her superior's attention to trouble spots. Few individuals are ecstatic about any techniques used by the boss to check their performance. Budgets are therefore sometimes regarded by middle management as embodiments of nickel-nursing, restrictive, negative top-management attitudes.

These misconceptions can be overcome by persuasive education and salesmanship. The budget should not be an unpleasant instrument for harassing the employee. Properly used, it will be a positive aid in setting standards of performance, in motivating toward goals, in metering results, and in directing attention to the areas that need investigation. *The budget is inanimate;* however, its administration is a delicate task, because everyone it affects must understand and accept the notion that the budget is primarily designed to help, not hinder.

The supreme importance of the human relations aspects of budgeting cannot be overemphasized. Too often, top management and its accountants are overly concerned with the mechanics of budgets, whereas the effectiveness of any budgeting system depends directly on whether the managers it affects understand it and accept it. Ideally, managers should be cooperative and cost-conscious. This subject is explored more fully in Chapters 9 and 10.

Types of budgets

The planning horizon for budgeting may vary from a year or less to many years, depending on budget objectives and on the uncertainties involved. Long-range budgets, called *capital budgets,* are often prepared for particular projects such as equipment purchases, locations of plant, and additions of product lines. **Master budgets,** which consolidate an organization's overall plans for a shorter span of time, are usually prepared on an annual basis. The annual budget may be subdivided on a month-to-month basis, or perhaps on a monthly basis for the first quarter and on a quarterly basis for the three remaining quarters.

Continuous budgets are increasingly being used. These are master budgets that perpetually add a month in the future as the month just ended is dropped. Continuous budgets are desirable because they compel managers to think specifically about the forthcoming twelve months and thus maintain a stable planning horizon.

□ CLASSIFICATION OF BUDGETS

The terms used to describe assorted budget schedules vary from company to company. Sometimes budgets are called **pro-forma** statements because they are forecasted financial statements, in contrast to statements of actual results.

Budgets, accompanied by subsidiary schedules, may be classified as follows:

1. Master budget
   a. Operating budget
      (1) Sales budget
      (2) Production budget (for manufacturing companies)
         (a) Materials used and material purchases
         (b) Direct labor
         (c) Indirect manufacturing overhead
         (d) Changes in inventory levels
      (3) Cost-of-goods-sold budget (for merchandising and manufacturing companies)
      (4) Selling-expense budget
      (5) Administrative-expense budget
   b. Financial budget
      (1) Cash budget: cash receipts and disbursements
      (2) Budgeted balance sheet
      (3) Budgeted statement of changes in financial position or budgeted statement of sources and applications of funds
2. Special budget reports
   a. Performance reports (comparisons of results with plans)
   b. Capital budgets (long-range expectations for specific projects)

Illustration of preparation of a master budget

Try to prepare the budget schedules required for the solution of this illustrative problem. Use the basic steps described after the problem. Do not rush. This is a comprehensive illustration that will require some step-by-step thinking and some reflection before a full understanding can be achieved. Although this illustration may seem largely mechanical, remember that the master-budgeting process generates key decisions regarding pricing, product lines, capital expenditures, research and development, personnel assignments, and so forth. Therefore the first draft of a budget leads to decisions that prompt subsequent drafts before a final budget is chosen. Suppose that R Company is a retailer of a wide variety of household items. The company rents a number of retail stores and also has a local door-to-door sales force.

The R Company's newly hired accountant has persuaded management to prepare a budget to aid financial and operating decisions. Because this is the company's first attempt at formal budgeting, the planning horizon is only four months, April through July. In the past, sales have increased during the spring season. Collections lag behind and cash is needed for purchases, wages, and other operating outlays. In the past, the company has met this cash squeeze with the help of six-month loans from banks.

Exhibit 6-1 is the closing balance sheet for the fiscal year just ended. Sales in March were $40,000. Monthly sales are forecasted as follows:

April	$50,000	July	$50,000
May	$80,000	August	$40,000
June	$60,000		

Sales consist of 60 percent cash and 40 percent credit. All credit accounts are collected in the month following the sales. The accounts receivable on March 31 represent credit sales made in March (40 percent of $40,000). Uncollectible accounts are negligible and are to be ignored.

At the end of any month, the R Company wishes to maintain a basic inventory of $20,000 plus 80 percent of the cost of goods to be sold in the following month. The cost of merchandise sold averages 70 percent of sales. Therefore the inventory, on March 31, is $20,000 + .8 (.7 × April sales of $50,000) = $20,000 + $28,000 = $48,000. The purchase terms available to the R Company are net, 30 days. Fifty percent of a given month's purchases is paid during that month and 50 percent during the following month.

Wages and commissions are paid semimonthly, half a month after they are earned. They are divided into two portions: monthly fixed wages of $2,500 and commissions, equal to 15 percent of sales, which are uniform throughout each month. Therefore the March 31 balance of Accrued Wages and Commissions Payable consists of (.5 × $2,500) + .5 (.15 × $40,000) = $1,250 + $3,000 = $4,250. This $4,250 will be paid on April 15. A used delivery truck will be purchased for $3,000 cash in April.

EXHIBIT
6-1

R COMPANY
Balance Sheet
March 31, 19X1

ASSETS

Current assets:		
Cash	$10,000	
Accounts receivable, net (.4 × March sales of $40,000)	16,000	
Merchandise inventory, $20,000 + .8 (.7 × April sales of $50,000)	48,000	
Unexpired insurance	1,800	$ 75,800
Plant assets:		
Equipment, fixtures, and other	$37,000	
Accumulated depreciation	12,800	24,200
Total assets		$100,000

EQUITIES

Current liabilities:		
Accounts payable (.5 × March purchase of $33,600)	$16,800	
Accrued wages and commissions payable ($1,250 + $3,000)	4,250	$ 21,050
Owners' equity		78,950
Total equities		$100,000

Other monthly expenses are:

Miscellaneous expenses	5% of sales, paid as incurred
Rent	$2,000, paid as incurred
Insurance	$200 expiration per month
Depreciation, including truck	$500

The company desires to maintain a minimum cash balance of $10,000 at the end of each month. Money can be borrowed or repaid in multiples of $1,000, at an interest rate of 18 percent per annum. Management does not want to borrow any more cash than necessary and wants to repay as promptly as possible. At the time the principal is repaid, interest is computed and paid only on the portion of principal that is repaid. Assume that borrowing takes place at the beginning, and repayment at the end, of the months in question.

Special note: By now it must be obvious that a basic knowledge of financial accounting (see Chapter 16) is necessary to cope with this illustrative problem.
1. Using the data given, prepare the following detailed schedules:
   a. Sales forecast
   b. Cash collection from customers

c. Purchases

d. Disbursements for purchases

e. Wages and commissions

f. Disbursements for wages and commissions

2. Using the data given and the schedules you have compiled, prepare the following major statements:

a. Budgeted income statement for four months ending July 31, 19X1

b. Budgeted statement of cash receipts and disbursements by months, including details of borrowings, repayments, and interest

c. Budgeted balance sheet as of July 31, 19X1

☐ SOLUTION SCHEDULES a–f

	MARCH	APRIL	MAY	JUNE	JULY	APRIL–JULY TOTAL
Schedule a: Sales Forecast						
Credit sales, 40%	$16,000	$20,000	$ 32,000	$24,000	$20,000	
Cash sales, 60%	24,000	30,000	48,000	36,000	30,000	
Total sales, 100%	$40,000	$50,000	$ 80,000	$60,000	$50,000	$240,000
Schedule b: Cash Collections						
Cash sales this month		$30,000	$ 48,000	$36,000	$30,000	
100% of last month's credit sales		16,000	20,000	32,000	24,000	
Total collections		$46,000	$ 68,000	$68,000	$54,000	
Schedule c: Purchases						
Ending inventory	$48,000	$64,800	$ 53,600	$48,000	$42,400	
Cost of goods sold	28,000*	35,000	56,000	42,000	35,000	$168,000
Total needed	$76,000	$99,800	$109,600	$90,000	$77,400	
Beginning inventory	42,400†	48,000	64,800	53,600	48,000	
Purchases	$33,600	$51,800	$ 44,800	$36,400	$29,400	
Schedule d: Disbursements for Purchases						
50% of last month's purchases		$16,800	$ 25,900	$22,400	$18,200	
50% of this month's purchases		25,900	22,400	18,200	14,700	
Disbursements for merchandise		$42,700	$ 48,300	$40,600	$32,900	
Schedule e: Wages and Commissions						
Wages, all fixed	$ 2,500	$ 2,500	$ 2,500	$ 2,500	$ 2,500	
Commissions (15% of current month's sales)	6,000	7,500	12,000	9,000	7,500	
Total	$ 8,500	$10,000	$ 14,500	$11,500	$10,000	$ 46,000
Schedule f: Disbursements for Wages and Commissions						
50% of last month's expenses		$ 4,250	$ 5,000	$ 7,250	$ 5,750	
50% of this month's expenses		5,000	7,250	5,750	5,000	
Total		$ 9,250	$ 12,250	$13,000	$10,750	

*.7 × March sales of $40,000 = $28,000.

†$20,000 + .8(.7 × March sales of $40,000) = $20,000 + $22,400 = $42,400.

For consistency with the numbering scheme used in this book, label your responses to Requirement 2 as Exhibits 6-2, 6-3, and 6-4, respectively. Note that Schedules a, c, and e will be needed to prepare Exhibit 6-2, and Schedules b, d, and f will be needed to prepare Exhibit 6-3.

☐ BASIC STEPS IN PREPARING MASTER BUDGET

The basic steps in preparing budgeted financial statements follow. Use the steps to prepare your own schedules. Then examine the schedules in the Solution.

Step 1. The sales forecast (Schedule *a*) is the starting point for budgeting, because inventory levels, purchases, and operating expenses are generally geared to the rate of sales activity. Trace the final column in Schedule *a* to Exhibit 6-2. In nonprofit organizations, forecasts of revenue or some level of services are also the focal point for budgeting. Examples are patient revenues expected by hospitals and donations to be received by churches. If no revenues are generated, as in the instances of municipal fire protection, a desired level of service is predetermined.

Step 2. After sales are budgeted, the purchases budget (Schedule *c*) may be prepared. The total merchandise needed will be the sum of the desired ending inventory plus the amount needed to fulfill budgeted sales demand. The total need will be partially met by the beginning inventory; the remainder must come from planned purchases. Therefore these purchases are computed as follows: Purchases = Desired ending inventory + Cost of goods sold − Beginning inventory. Trace the final column of Schedule *c* to Exhibit 6-2.

Step 3. The budgeting of operating expenses is dependent on various factors. Many operating expenses are directly influenced by month-to-month fluctuations in sales volume. Examples are sales commissions and delivery expenses. Other expenses are not directly influenced (e.g., rent, insurance, depreciation, certain types of payroll). In this solution, Schedule *e* should be prepared for wages and commissions. Trace the final column of Schedule *e* to Exibit 6-2. The other operating expenses are entered in the budgeted income statement, as shown in Exhibit 6-2.

Step 4. Steps 1 through 3 will provide enough information for a budgeted statement of income from operations (Exhibit 6-2).

EXHIBIT 6-2

R COMPANY
Budgeted Income Statement
For the Four Months Ended July 31, 19X1

	DATA		SOURCE OF DATA
Sales		$240,000	Schedule a
Cost of goods sold		168,000	Schedule c
Gross margin		$ 72,000	
Operating expenses:			
Wages and commissions	$46,000		Schedule e
Rent	8,000		*
Miscellaneous expenses	12,000		5% of sales
Insurance	800		*
Depreciation	2,000	68,800	*
Income from operations		$ 3,200	
Interest expense		675	Exhibit 6-3
Net income		$ 2,525	

Monthly amounts are given in the statement of the problem.

Step 5. Predict the month-to-month effects on the cash position of the level of operations summarized in Exhibit 6-2. The preparation of the cash budget (Exhibit 6-3) is explained below.

☐ EXPLANATION OF CASH BUDGET

The **cash budget** (budgeted statement of cash receipts and disbursements, Exhibit 6-3) has the following major sections:

w. The beginning cash balance plus cash receipts yield the total cash available for needs, before financing. Cash receipts depend on collections from customers' accounts receivable and cash sales (Schedule *b*) and on other operating sources such as miscellaneous rental income. Trace Schedule *b* to Exhibit 6-3. Studies of the collectibility of accounts receivable are a prerequisite to accurate forecasting. Key factors include collection experience and average time lag between sales and collections.

EXHIBIT 6-3

R COMPANY
Budgeted Statement of Cash Receipts and Disbursements
For the Four Months Ended July 31, 19X1

		APRIL	MAY	JUNE	JULY
	Cash balance, beginning	$10,000	$10,550	$10,970	$10,965
	Cash receipts:				
	Collections from customers (Schedule b)	46,000	68,000	68,000	54,000
w.	*Total cash available for needs, before financing	56,000	78,550	78,970	64,965
	Cash disbursements:				
	Merchandise (Schedule d)	42,700	48,300	40,600	32,900
	Wages and commissions (Schedule f)	9,250	12,250	13,000	10,750
	Miscellaneous expenses, 5% of sales	2,500	4,000	3,000	2,500
	Rent	2,000	2,000	2,000	2,000
	Truck purchase	3,000	—	—	—
x.	Total disbursements	59,450	66,550	58,600	48,150
	Minimum cash balance desired	10,000	10,000	10,000	10,000
	Total cash needed	69,450	76,550	68,600	58,150
	Excess (deficiency) of total cash available over total cash needed before current financing	(13,450)	2,000	10,370	6,815
	Financing:				
	Borrowings (at beginning)	14,000†			
	Repayments (at end)	—	(1,000)	(9,000)	(4,000)
	Interest (at 18% per annum)‡	—	(30)	(405)	(240)
y.	Total effects of financing	14,000	(1,030)	(9,405)	(4,240)
z.	Cash balance, ending (w + y − x)	$10,550	$10,970	$10,965	$12,575

Note: *Expired insurance and depreciation do not entail cash outlays.*
Letters are keyed to the explanation in the text.
†*Borrowings and repayments of principal are made in multiples of $1,000, at an interest rate of 18 percent per annum.*
‡*Interest computations: .18 × $1,000 × 2/12 = $30; .18 × $9,000 × 3/12 = $405; .18 × $4,000 × 4/12 = $240.*

x. Cash disbursements:

(1) Purchases depend on the credit terms extended by suppliers and the bill-paying habits of the buyer (Schedule *d*, which should be traced to Exhibit 6-3).

(2) Payroll depends on wage, salary, or commission terms and on payroll dates (Schedule *f*, which should be traced to Exhibit 6-3).

(3) Other costs and expenses depend on timing and credit terms. Note that depreciation does not entail a cash outlay.

(4) Other disbursements include outlays for fixed assets, long-term investments, installment payments on purchases, and the like. In this problem, the only "other disbursement" is $3,000 for the truck.

y. Financing requirements depend on how the total cash available *w* (in Exhibit 6-3) compares with the total cash needed. Needs include the disbursements *x* plus the ending cash balance *z* desired. The financing plans will depend on the relationship of cash available to cash sought. If there is an excess, loans may be repaid or temporary investments made. The pertinent outlays for interest expenses are usually contained in this section of the cash budget. Trace the calculated interest expense to Exhibit 6-2, which will then be complete (ignoring income taxes).

z. The ending cash balance is $w + y - x$. Financing *y* may have a positive (borrowing) or a negative (repayment) effect on the cash balance. The illustrative cash budget shows the pattern of short-term, self-liquidating financing. Seasonal peaks often result in heavy drains on cash, for merchandise purchases and operating expenses, before the sales are made and cash collected from customers. The resulting loan is self-liquidating—that is, the borrowed money is used to acquire merchandise for sale, and the proceeds from the sale are used to repay the loan. This "working-capital cycle" moves from cash to inventory to receivables and back to cash.

Cash budgets help management to avoid having unnecessary idle cash, on the one hand, and unnecessary nerve-racking cash deficiencies, on the other. An astutely mapped financing program keeps cash balances in reasonable relation to needs.

□ BUDGETED BALANCE SHEET

The final step is the preparation of the budgeted balance sheet (Exhibit 6-4). Each item is projected in accordance with the business plan as expressed in the previous schedules. Specifically, the beginning balances at March 31 would be increased or decreased in light of the expected cash receipts and disbursements in Exhibit 6-3 and in light of the effects of noncash items appearing on the income statement in Exhibit 6-2. For example, unexpired insurance of $1,800 (the balance on March 31) minus the $800 expiring over four months would affect the balance sheet, even though it is a noncash item.

When the complete master budget is formulated, management can consider all the major financial statements as a basis for changing the course of events. For example, the initial formulation may prompt management to try new sales strategies to generate more demand. Or management may explore the effects of various ways of adjusting the timing of receipts and disbursements. In

EXHIBIT 6-4

R COMPANY
Budgeted Balance Sheet
July 31, 19X1

ASSETS

Current assets:
Cash (Exhibit 6-3)	$12,575	
Accounts receivable (.40 × July sales of $50,000) (Schedule a)	20,000	
Merchandise inventory (Schedule c)	42,400	
Unexpired insurance ($1,800 old balance − $800 expired)	1,000	$ 75,975

Plant:
Equipment, fixtures, and other ($37,000 + truck, $3,000)	$40,000	
Accumulated depreciation ($12,800 + $2,000 depreciation)	14,800	25,200
Total assets		$101,175

EQUITIES

Current liabilities:
Accounts payable (.5 × July purchases of $29,400) (Schedule d)	$14,700	
Accrued wages and commissions payable (.5 × $10,000) (Scheaule e)	5,000	$ 19,700
Owners' equity ($78,950 + $2,525 net income)		81,475
Total equities		$101,175

Note: *Beginning balances were used as a start for the computations of unexpired insurance, plant, and owners' equity.*

any event, the first draft of the master budget is rarely the final draft. In this way, the budgeting process becomes an integral part of the management process itself in the sense that *planning* and *budgetng* are indistinguishable.

The difficulties of sales forecasting

As you have seen in the foregoing illustration, the sales forecast is the foundation of the entire master budget. The accuracy of estimated production schedules and of cost to be incurred depends on the detail and accuracy, in dollars and in units, of the forecasted sales.

The sales forecast is usually prepared under the direction of the top sales executive. All of the following factors are important: (1) past patterns of sales; (2) the estimates made by the sales force; (3) general economic and competitive conditions; (4) specific interrelationships of sales and economic indicators, such as gross national product or industrial production indexes; (5) changes in prices; (6) market research studies; and (7) advertising and sales promotion plans.

Sales forecasting usually combines various techniques. Opinions of the sales staff are sought. Statistical methods are often used. Correlations between sales and economic indicators help make sales forecasts more reliable. In most cases, the quantitative analysis provided by economists and members of the market research staff provide valuable help but not outright answers. The opinions of line management heavily influence the final setting of sales forecasts.

Pricing policies can have pronounced effects on sales. Management's assessment of price elasticities (the effect of price changes on the physical volume sold) will influence the sales forecast. A company may not offer the same unit price to all customers (because of differences in costs of serving different markets). In such cases, a detailed analysis of both units to be sold as well as dollar sales is needed for each price category before a final sales forecast can be aggregated.

Sales forecasting is still somewhat mystical, but its procedures are becoming more formal and are being viewed more seriously because of the intensity of competitive pressures. Although this book does not encompass a detailed discussion of the preparation of the sales budget, the importance of an accurate sales forecast cannot be overstressed.

In recent years, the formal use of statistical probabilities has been applied to the problem of sales forecasting. (See Chapter 15 for an elaboration.) Moreover, financial-planning models and simulation have enabled managers to get a quantitative grasp on the ramifications of various sales strategies.[2]

Governments and other nonprofit organizations also face a problem similar to sales forecasting. For example, the budget for city revenues may depend on a variety of items such as predicted property taxes, traffic fines, parking fees, and city income taxes. In turn, property taxes depend on the extent of new construction and general increases in real estate values. Thus the budget is based on a variety of assumptions and past results.

Financial-planning models and simulation

In most cases, the master budget is the best practical approximation to a formal model of the total organization: its objectives, its inputs, and its outputs. If the master budget serves as a "total decision model" for top management, then decisions about strategies for the forthcoming period may be formulated and altered during the budgetary process. Traditionally, this has been a step-by-step process whereby tentative plans are gradually revised as executives exchange views on various aspects of expected activities.

In the future, much of the interaction and interdependence of the decisions will probably be formalized in mathematical simulation models—"total models" that are sometimes called financial-planning models.[3] These models are mathematical statements of the relationships in the organization among all the operating and financial activities, and of other major internal and external factors that may affect decisions.

Financial models include all the ingredients for preparing a master budget. However, they can also be used for long-range planning decisions. For

[2]For a survey of forecasting techniques, see S. Makridakis and S. Wheelwright, "Forecasting: Issues & Challenges for Marketing Management," *Journal of Marketing,* October 1977, pp. 24–38. Also see Wheelwright and Makridakis, *Forecasting Methods for Management,* 3rd. ed. (New York, John Wiley, 1980).

[3] Vincent R. LoCascio, "Financial Planning Models," *Financial Executive,* Vol. 40, No. 3.

example, if managers want to predict the impact of adding a new product line, they can obtain budgeted financial statements for many future years. For instance, at Dow Chemical Company, 140 separate cost inputs, constantly revised, are fed into the model. Such factors as major raw-material costs and prices by country and region are monitored weekly. Multiple contingency plans rather than a single master plan are used more widely than before.[4]

Many models are constructed and working. They are used for budgeting, for revising budgets with little incremental effort, and for comparing a variety of decision alternatives as they affect the entire firm. The models speed the budgetary process because the sensitivity of income and cash flows to various decisions can be tested promptly via a simulation. Management can react quickly to events and to revisions in predictions of various aspects of operations. Moreover, mathematical probabilities can be incorporated into these models, so that uncertainty can be dealt with explicitly rather than informally.

The computer has enabled managers to shorten their reaction time. For example, at a New Jersey utility, Public Service Electric and Gas Company, the total corporate plan is run once a day, on average. Measures are generated of the financial impact on costs and equipment utilization of such business decisions as a cutback in fuel purchases during an unexpectedly warm winter week. Equally important is the speed of the computer. The executive vice-president said, "If an oil embargo were announced tomorrow, within 24 hours we would know the major impact of it and could begin reacting."[5]

summary

The master budget expresses management's overall operating and financing plan. It outlines company objectives and steps for achieving them. The budgetary process compels managers to think ahead and to prepare for changing conditions. Budgets are aids in setting standards of performance, motivating personnel toward goals, measuring results, and directing attention to the areas that most need investigation.

The human factors in budgeting are more important than the mechanics. Top management must support a budgetary program wholeheartedly. The job of educating personnel and selling them on the budget is everlasting, but essential, if those who are affected by the budget are to understand it and accept it. The master budget should be a powerful aid to the most crucial decisions of top management. Often it falls far short of that role because its potential is misunderstood. Instead of being regarded as a management tool, in many cases the budget is unfortunately looked upon as a necessary evil.

The cornerstone of the budget is the sales forecast. All current operating and financial planning is generally tied to the expected volume of sales.

[4] "What-if Help for Management," *Business Week,* January 21, 1980, p. 73.
[5] "Computer Games That Planners Play," *Business Week,* December 18, 1978, p. 66.

■ PROBLEM

Before attempting to solve the homework problems, review the R Company illustration in this chapter.

assignment material

■ FUNDAMENTAL ASSIGNMENT MATERIAL

6-1. **Terminology.** Define *cash budget; continuous budget; master budget; pro-forma statements.*

6-2. **Master budget.** (Alternate to 6-26 and 6-27.) One of your duties as the manager of the North Park Store of a large retail chain is to prepare the quarterly budget. It is the policy of your company to have each store of this size begin each month with a bank balance of $8,000. Any excess over this amount at the *end* of the month is to be sent promptly to the corporate headquarters. Any deficiency below $8,000 is to be sent to the North Park Store. (Assume that such deficiency payments are made at the *beginning* of the month.) These amounts are accounted for simply by adjusting North Park's owners' equity account, and no interest charges are involved. The central office handles all requirements for reporting and paying income taxes. Therefore your budget will be prepared entirely on a pretax basis. The following data are available to you at June 30, 19X4:

a. Actual and Budgeted Sales, 19X4

April	$200,000
May	150,000
June	100,000
July	100,000
August	150,000
September	200,000
October	200,000
November	250,000

b. Balance Sheet, June 30, 19X4

Cash	$ 8,000
Receivables (merchandise)	110,000
Inventory	55,000
Fixtures	100,000
Total assets	$273,000
Payables (merchandise)	$ 55,000
Owners' equity	218,000
Total equities	$273,000

c. Average gross profit rate: 45 percent.

d. Merchandise purchases each month are geared exactly to the sales requirements of the following month, and they are paid in cash in the month following purchase.

e. Cash payments are expected as follows:

Variable expenses (paid in month of sale):	
Employee compensation and fringe benefits	25% of sales
Other operating expenses	5% of sales
Fixed expenses (paid in month of sale):	
Rent, property taxes, insurance, etc.	$5,000 per month

f. Depreciation of fixtures is $1,000 per month.

g. Cash sales average 20 percent of total sales, the remainder being credit sales. The accounts receivable from credit sales are 75 percent collected in the month after sale, the other 25 percent being collected in the next following month. Ignore uncollectible accounts. The $110,000 of receivables in the June 30 balance sheet consist solely of the accounts from credit sales for May and June: $(.25 \times .80 \times \$150,000) + (.80 \times \$100,000) = \$30,000 + \$80,000 = \$110,000$.

Prepare the following budgeted schedules and statements for the third quarter (the three months ending September 30, 19X4):
1. Sales and cash collections of accounts receivable: each month and total for the quarter.
2. Purchases and cash disbursements for purchases: each month and total for the quarter.
3. Cash disbursements for expenses: each month and total for the quarter.
4. Summary of all cash receipts, disbursements, and balances: each month only.
5. Income statement: quarter totals only.
6. Balance sheet, September 30, 19X4.

Show support for all amounts used in schedules and statements.

ADDITIONAL ASSIGNMENT MATERIAL

6-3. What factors influence the sales forecast?

6-4. "There are too many uncertainties and complications to make budgeting worthwhile in my business." Do you agree? Explain.

6-5. What is the major technical difference between historical and budgeted financial statements?

6-6. What are the major benefits of budgeting?

6-7. Why is budgeted performance better than past performance, as a basis for judging actual results?

6-8. What is *coordination?*

6-9. "Education and salesmanship are key features of budgeting." Explain.

6-10. "Capital budgets are plans for managing long-term debt and common stock." Do you agree? Explain.

6-11. "*Pro-forma* statements are those statements prepared in conjunction with continuous budgets." Do you agree? Explain.

6-12. What is the difference between an operating budget and a financial budget?

6-13. Why is the sales forecast the starting point for budgeting?

6-14. What is a self-liquidating loan?

6-15. What is the principal objective of a cash budget?

6-16. Miscellaneous computations. (H. Schaefer.) These questions relate to the preparation of budgets for *the year 19X6.* Each question is independent of the others.

a. Sales are predicted to be 30,000 units per month for the first six months and 40,000 units per month for the last six months. The January 1 balance in Accounts Receivable is $50,000. The accounts receivable are predicted to experience a one-month turnover cycle. The predicted sales price is $2. All sales are on a credit basis. Compute (1) predicted sales revenue, (2) predicted December 31 balance in Accounts Receivable, (3) predicted cash collections from accounts receivable.

b. The January 1 balance in Prepaid Rent is $400. Rent is paid on the last day of the month prior to the month for which it applies; e.g., the April rent is paid on March 31. The present rent contract is for $400 per month, and the last payment is scheduled for May 31. A new contract is expected to be signed for $500 per month, the first payment being on June 30. The new contract is expected to be in effect for twelve months. Compute (1) predicted rent expense, (2) predicted December 31 balance in Prepaid Rent, (3) predicted cash payments for rent.

6-17. **Cash collection budget.** Volyum Company's experience indicates that cash collections from customers tend to occur in the following pattern:

Collected within cash discount period in month of sale	50%
Collected within cash discount period in first month after month of sale	10
Collected after cash discount period in first month after month of sale	25
Collected after cash discount period in second month after month of sale	13
Never collected	2
Total	100%
Cash discount allowable as a percentage of invoice price	1%

Compute the total cash budgeted to be collected in March if sales are predicted as $200,000 for January, $300,000 for February, and $400,000 for March.

6-18. **Budget computations for purchases and borrowing.** Nuts & Bolts, Inc., needs your help in computing two of the estimates for its budget for a certain period.

a. The company plans to produce during the period 15,000 units of Product X and 20,000 units of Product Y. It uses 5 units of material K for each X and 3 units of K for each Y. The beginning inventory of K is 12,000 units, and the desired ending inventory is 18,000 units. How many K units must your company purchase during the period?

b. The company forecasts cash receipts of $330,000 and cash disbursements of $365,000. If the beginning cash balance is $26,000 and the desired ending cash balance is $20,000, how much cash must be borrowed during the period?

6-19. **Multiple choice.** (CPA.) The Zel Co., a wholesaler, budgeted the following sales for the indicated months:

	June 19X1	July 19X1	August 19X1
Sales on account	$1,500,000	$1,600,000	$1,700,000
Cash sales	200,000	210,000	220,000
Total sales	$1,700,000	$1,810,000	$1,920,000

All merchandise is marked up to sell at its invoice cost plus 25 percent. Merchandise inventories at the beginning of each month are at 30 percent of that month's projected cost of goods sold.

1. The cost of goods sold for the month of June 19X1 is anticipated to be (a) $1,530,000, (b) $1,402,500, (c) $1,275,000, (d) $1,190,000, (e) none of these.

2. Merchandise purchases for July 19X1 are anticipated to be (a) $1,605,500, (b) $1,474,400, (c) $1,448,000, (d) $1,382,250, (e) none of these.

6-20. **Cash budget.** Dorothy Lucks is the proprietor of the D. Lucks Catering Service, which specializes in wedding receptions. She is concerned about her ability to meet certain payment deadlines in November 19X1, particularly a $10,000 bank loan due November 13 with $1,000 interest. She has asked you to prepare her cash budget for November. The following additional information is available to you:

November food and beverage purchases, 60% to be paid in November, total	$21,000
Payrolls and subcontractors' charges due in November	7,800
November installment due for equipment bought last year	300
October 31 trade payables for food and beverage, 80% of which must be paid in November, total	12,000
Accrued payroll taxes and other expenses of October to be paid in full in November	800
Expected beginning cash balance for November	1,400
Utilities and other expenses to be paid in November	600
October 31 customer receivables, 90% collection expected in November, total	15,000
Estimated November sales, 75% collection expected in month of sale, total	40,000
Depreciation expense on equipment for November	200

REQUIRED

1. Prepare a cash budget showing the expected cash receipts and disbursements for November and the forecasted cash balance at the end of the month.
2. Compute the following amounts:
   a. The minimum estimated percentage of collection of November sales that would still leave an ending cash balance of at least $1,000
   b. The minimum total November sales that would still leave an ending cash balance of at least $1,300, given the same 75% estimated collection percentage of November sales.

6-21. **Multiple choice.** (CPA, adapted.) Select the best answer for each item. Give supporting computations.

The Dilly Company marks up all merchandise at 25 percent of gross purchase price. All purchases are made on account with terms of 1/10, net/60. Purchase discounts, which are recorded as miscellaneous income, are always taken. Normally, 60 percent of each month's purchases are paid for in the month of purchase, while the other 40 percent are paid during the first ten days of the first month after purchase. Inventories of merchandise at the end of each month are kept at 30 percent of the next month's projected cost of goods sold.

Terms for sales on account are 2/10, net/30. Cash sales are not subject to discount. Fifty percent of each month's sales on account are collected during the month of sale, 45 percent are collected in the succeeding month, and the remainder are usually uncollectible. Seventy percent of the collections in the month of sale are subject to discount, while 10 percent of the collections in the succeeding month are subject to discount.

Projected sales data for selected months follow:

	SALES ON ACCOUNT—GROSS	CASH SALES
December	$1,900,000	$400,000
January	1,500,000	250,000
February	1,700,000	350,000
March	1,600,000	300,000

1. Projected gross purchases for January are
   a. $1,400,000.   d. $1,248,000.
   b. $1,470,000.   e. None of these.
   c. $1,472,000.
2. Projected inventory at the end of December is
   a. $420,000.   d. $393,750.
   b. $441,600.   e. None of these.
   c. $552,000.

3. Projected payments to suppliers during February are
   a. $1,551,200.
   b. $1,535,688.
   c. $1,528,560.
   d. $1,509,552.
   e. None of these.

4. Projected sales discounts to be taken by customers making remittances during February are
   a. $5,250.
   b. $15,925.
   c. $30,500.
   d. $11,900.
   e. None of these.

5. Projected total collections from customers during February are
   a. $1,875,000.
   b. $1,861,750.
   c. $1,511,750.
   d. $1,188,100.
   e. None of these.

Hints: 1/10, net/60 means that 1 percent of the gross purchase price may be deducted as a purchase discount if payment is made within ten days. In any event, the invoice is payable within sixty days. Similar reasoning applies to sales terms. This problem requires painstaking attention to detail.

6-22. **Importance of sales forecast.** The seven local supermarkets of Little Giant, a regional grocery chain, sell a small (one-half pound) jar of mixed nuts and a large (one pound) jar of the same kind of nuts. Both sizes sell at the same $2 price per pound (net weight). The nuts are purchased from a local fruit and nut broker for 90¢ per pound. The jars are purchased from a nearby container manufacturer for 20¢ for the small size and 25¢ for the large size. No changes are expected in any of the purchasing and selling prices. Little Giant uses its central warehouse for mixing the nuts and packing them in the jars.

Compared with last year, the company's top management expects a 2 percent increase this year in total dollar sales of staple groceries and a 20 percent increase in total dollar sales of "luxury"-type foods. However, Federal Reserve statistics show food store sales to be 3 percent over last year, from the period from January 1 to September 30.

Last year the company sold 30,000 small jars of nuts and 14,000 large jars during November and December. This year the October 31 inventories are:

Nuts (pounds)	800
Small jars	300
Large jars	400

The December 31 target inventories are:

Nuts (pounds)	400
Small jars	200
Large jars	100

It is near the end of October. Orders must be placed today for delivery by November 1. These orders are to provide sufficient stock to last through the Christmas season.

REQUIRED

Compute the following:

1. Budgeted sales of small jars of nuts, in pounds, total dollars, and number of jars, for November and December.
2. Budgeted sales of large jars of nuts, in pounds, total dollars, and number of jars, for November and December.
3. Pounds and total cost of needed nut purchases.
4. Numbers and total cost of needed jar purchases:
   a. Small size
   b. Large size

6-23. **Sales forecasting.** In each of the accompanying diagrams A through E, the dollar value of a sales order is contrasted with the quantity of product or service sold. Assume a single product in each case.

REQUIRED

1. What pricing policy is reflected by these order patterns (assuming that all customers are rational)?
2. Why are these patterns relevant to a sales forecast?

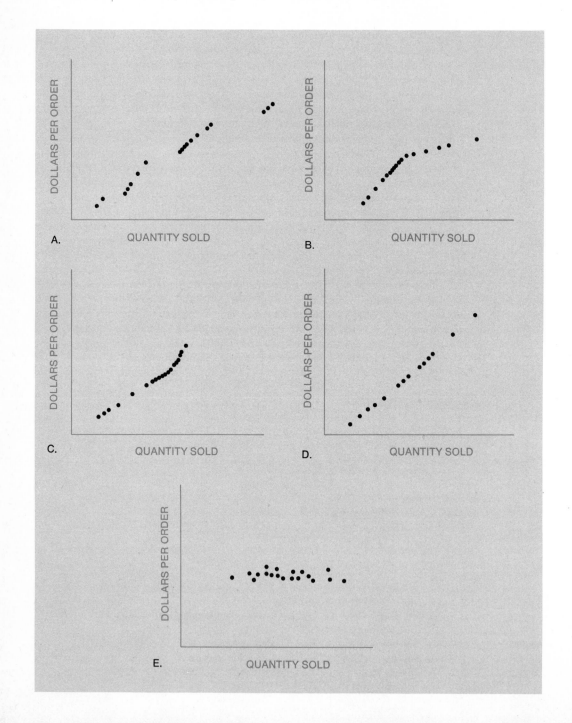

6-24. Budgeting for educational institution. (CMA.) United Business Education, Inc. (UBE), is a nonprofit organization that sponsors a wide variety of management seminars throughout the United States. In addition, it is heavily involved in research into improved methods of educating and motivating business executives. The seminar activity is largely supported by fees and the research program from member dues.

UBE operates on a calendar-year basis and is in the process of finalizing the budget for 19X9. The following information has been taken from approved plans, which are still tentative at this time.

Seminar Program

Revenue—The scheduled number of programs should produce $12 million of revenue for the year. Each program is budgeted to produce the same amount of revenue. The revenue is collected during the month the program is offered. The programs are scheduled so that 12 percent of the revenue is collected in each of the first five months of the year. The remaining programs, accounting for the remaining 40 percent of the revenue, are distributed evenly through the months of September, October, and November. No programs are offered in the other four months of the year.

Direct Expenses—The seminar expenses are made up of three segments:

● Instructors' fees are paid at the rate of 70 percent of the seminar revenue in the month following the seminar. The instructors are considered independent contractors and are not eligible for UBE employee benefits.

● Facilities fees total $5.6 million for the year. They are the same for each program and are paid in the month the program is given.

● Annual promotional costs of $1 million are spent equally in all months except June and July when there is no promotional effort.

Research Program

Research Grants—The research program has a large number of projects nearing completion. The other main research activity this year includes the feasibility studies for new projects to be started after 19X9. As a result, the total grant expense of $3 million for 19X9 is expected to be paid out at the rate of $500,000 per month during the first six months of the year.

Salaries and Other UBE Expenses

Office Lease—Annual amount of $240,000 paid monthly at the beginning of each month.

General Administrative Expenses (telephone, supplies, postage, etc.)—$1.5 million annually, or $125,000 a month.

Depreciation Expense—$240,000 a year.

General UBE Promotion—Annual cost of $600,000, paid monthly.

Salaries and Benefits—

NUMBER OF EMPLOYEES	ANNUAL SALARY PAID MONTHLY	TOTAL ANNUAL SALARIES
1	$50,000	$ 50,000
3	40,000	120,000
4	30,000	120,000
15	25,000	375,000
5	15,000	75,000
22	10,000	220,000
50		$960,000

Employee benefits amount to $240,000, or 25 percent of annual salaries. Except for the pension contribution, the benefits are paid as salaries are paid. The annual pension payment of $24,000, based on 2.5 percent of salaries (included in the total benefits and the 25 percent rate), is due April 15, 19X9.

Other Information

Membership Income—UBE has 100,000 members, each of whom pays an annual fee of $100. The fee for the calendar year is invoiced in late June. The collection schedule is as follows.

July	60%
August	30
September	5
October	5
	100%

Capital Expenditures—The capital expenditures program calls for a total of $510,000 in cash payments to be spread evenly over the first five months of 19X9.

Cash and Temporary Investments at January 1, 19X9, are estimated at $750,000.

1. Prepare a budget of the annual cash receipts and disbursements for UBE, Inc., for 19X9.
2. Prepare a cash budget for UBE, Inc., for January 19X9.
3. Using the information you developed in Requirements 1 and 2, identify two important operating problems of UBE, Inc.

6-25. **Cash budget.** The Laser Element Company deals in a single standard element used by many electronics firms. Each unit is purchased for $20 and sold for $30. Actual and budgeted sales in total dollars for selected months of 19X2 and for the fiscal year are:

May	$ 25,000
June	90,000
July	72,000
August	54,000
Year	720,000

Account balances at July 1, 19X2, included:

Cash	$ 1,300	Accounts receivable,	
Merchandise inventory	24,000	merchandise	$39,000
		Accounts payable,	
		merchandise	18,000

Two-thirds of the company's merchandise purchases are paid for in the month of purchase, the remainder in the following month. Standard planning requires that the end-of-month merchandise inventory be 50 percent of the budgeted sales in units for the following month.

Sales terms include a 2 percent cash discount if payment is made by the end of the calendar month. Past experience indicates that 50 percent of the billings will be collected during the month of sale, 40 percent in the following calendar month, 8 percent in the next following calendar month. Two percent will be uncollectible. The company's fiscal year begins May 1.

Exclusive of bad debts, total budgeted selling and general administrative expenses for the fiscal year are estimated at $137,000, of which $42,000 is fixed expense (inclusive of an $18,000 annual depreciation charge). These fixed expenses are incurred uniformly throughout the year. The balance of the selling and general administrative expenses varies with sales. Expenses are paid as incurred.

Prepare the following for the month of July 19X2:
1. Schedule of estimated cash collections of accounts receivable.
2. Schedule of estimated cash payments for merchandise.
3. Schedule of selling and general administrative expenses, including estimated cash payments.
4. Summary of estimated cash receipts and disbursements.

6-26. Prepare master budget. (Alternate to 6-2 and 6-27.) The Medal Company's recent and forecasted sales for certain months in 19X2 and 19X3 are:

July 19X2	$ 75,000	November	$150,000
August	50,000	December	75,000
September	50,000	January 19X3	90,000
October	125,000	February	80,000

The September 30, 19X2, balance sheet shows:

ASSETS		EQUITIES	
Cash	$ 3,000	Accounts payable	
Accounts receivable		(merchandise)	$ 70,000
(merchandise)	30,000	Dividends payable	1,500
Inventory	75,000	Rent payable	17,500
Prepaid insurance	1,800	Total liabilities	$ 89,000
Fixtures, net	20,000	Stockholders' equity	40,800
Total assets	$129,800	Total equities	$129,800

You are to prepare a master budget for the three months ending December 31, 19X2. Sales are forecasted at an average price that is twice the average cost per unit. Monthly operating expenses are as follows:

Wages and salaries	$38,000
Insurance expired	200
Depreciation	300
Miscellaneous	3,000
Rent	500 + 10% of sales

Cash dividends of $1,500 are to be paid quarterly, beginning October 15, and are declared on the fifteenth of the previous month. All operating expenses are paid as incurred, except insurance, depreciation, and rent. Rent of $500 is paid at the beginning of each month, and the additional 10 percent of sales is paid quarterly on the tenth of the month following the quarter. The next settlement is due October 10.

The company desires an ending minimum cash balance of $3,000 each month. Inventories are supposed to equal 120 percent of the next month's sales in units. Purchases during any given month are paid in full during the following month. All sales are on credit, payable within thirty days, but experience has shown that 50 percent of current sales are collected in the current month, 40 percent in the next month, and 10 percent in the month thereafter. Bad debts are negligible.

Money can be borrowed and repaid in multiples of $1,000 at an interest rate of 18 percent per annum. Management wants to minimize borrowing and repay rapidly. At the time the principal is repaid, interest is computed and paid on the portion of principal that is repaid. Assume that borrowing takes place at the beginning, and repayments at the end, of the months in question. Money is never borrowed at the beginning and repaid at the end of the *same* month. Compute interest to the nearest dollar. Ignore income taxes.

REQUIRED

1. Prepare a master budget, including a budgeted income statement, a balance sheet, a statement of cash receipts and disbursements, and supporting schedules.
2. Explain why there is a need for a bank loan and what operating sources provide the cash for the repayment of the bank loan.

6-27. Deviations from master budget. (Alternate to 6-2 and 6-26.) Review the major illustration in the chapter. It is the end of July. Operations have been exactly in accordance with the budget, expect that July sales were $40,000 instead of $50,000. Purchases for July were not affected by the drop in sales, but commissions, cash, accounts receivable, and notes payable were among the accounts affected.

Prepare a summary analysis of the effects. That is, how would Schedules *a*, *b*, *e*, and *f* be affected, as well as Exhibits 6-2, 6-3, and 6-4? Include a list of all new balances in Exhibit 6-4.

suggested readings

ARMSTRONG, J., *Long-Range Forecasting.* New York: John Wiley, 1978.

BUTLER, W., R. KAVESH, and R. PLATT, eds., *Methods and Techniques of Business Forecasting.* Englewood Cliffs, N.J.: Prentice-Hall, 1974.

CONFERENCE BOARD, *Sales Forecasting.* New York: The Conference Board, 1978.

WELSCH, G., *Budgeting: Profit Planning and Control,* 4th ed. Englewood Cliffs, N.J.: Prentice-Hall, 1976.

WHEELWRIGHT, S., and S. MAKRIDAKIS, *Forecasting Methods for Management,* 3rd ed. New York: John Wiley, 1980.

FLEXIBLE BUDGETS AND STANDARDS FOR CONTROL

learning objectives

When you have finished studying this chapter, you should be able to:

1. Distinguish between static budgets and flexible budgets.
2. Compute and use a budget formula in the construction of a flexible budget.
3. Use the flexible-budget approach to compute (a) marketing variance and (b) total variance due to price changes and inefficiency.
4. List the five usual stages in the evolution of a control system for an organization.
5. Distinguish between budget amounts and standard amounts.
6. Distinguish between perfection standards and currently attainable standards.
7. Compute the price and efficiency variances for direct material and direct labor.
8. Identify the typical responsibilities for controlling variances in material and labor costs.

The essence of control is feedback—the comparison of actual performance with planned performance. Flexible budgets and standard costs are major attention-directing techniques for planning and for providing feedback regarding individual costs. Throughout this chapter, to stress some basic ideas, we shall continue to assume that each cost is either variable or fixed; in the next chapter we shall consider various cost behavior patterns in more detail.

Flexible budgets

☐ STATIC-BUDGET COMPARISONS

As Chapter 6 shows, budgets may be developed on a companywide basis to cover all activities, from sales to direct materials to sweeping compounds, and from spending on a new plant to expected drains on petty cash. A budget may be expressed on an accrual basis or on a cash-flow basis; it may be highly condensed or exceedingly detailed. All the budgets discussed in Chapter 6 are *static* (inflexible). A **static budget** is defined as a budget prepared for only one level of activity (e.g., volume of sales). To illustrate: A typical master-planning budget is a plan tailored to a single target volume level of, say, 100,000 units. All results would be compared with the original plan, regardless of changes in ensuing conditions—even though, for example, volume turned out to be only 90,000 units instead of the original 100,000.

Consider a simplified illustration. Suppose that the Dominion Company, a one-department firm, manufactured and sold a special kind of carry-on flight luggage that required several hand operations. The product had some variations, but it was viewed essentially as a single product bearing one selling price.

The master budget for the forthcoming month included the condensed income statement shown in Exhibit 7-1, column 2. The actual results are in column 1. The master budget called for the production and sales of 9,000 units, but only 7,000 units were actually produced and sold. There were no beginning or ending inventories.

The master budget was based on detailed expectations for the given month, including a careful forecast of sales. The performance report in Exhibit 7-1 compares the actual results with the master budget. **Performance report** is a general term that usually means a comparison of actual results with some budget. In particular, note that the volume of activity, as measured by sales, was substantially below the budget. The budget in Exhibit 7-1 is an example of a static budget.

Exhibit 7-1 is difficult to analyze. Recall that Chapter 1 defined *variance* as a deviation of an actual result from the expected or budgeted result. Clearly, sales are below expectations, but the favorable variances regarding the variable costs are deceptive. Considering the lower-than-projected level of activity, was cost control really satisfactory? The comparison of actual results with a static budget does not give much help in answering that question.

☐ FLEXIBLE-BUDGET COMPARISONS

As president of the Dominion Company, you would probably want a performance report that better pinpoints some major variances between the master

EXHIBIT
7-1

DOMINION COMPANY
Performance Report Using Static Budget
For the Month Ended June 30, 19X1

	ACTUAL	MASTER (STATIC) BUDGET	VARIANCE
Units	7,000	9,000	2,000
Sales	$168,000	$216,000	$48,000 U
Variable costs:			
Direct material	$ 21,350	$ 27,000	$ 5,650 F
Direct labor	61,500	72,000	10,500 F
Labor to transport materials internally and provide general support	11,100	14,400	3,300 F
Idle time	3,550	3,600	50 F
Cleanup time	2,500	2,700	200 F
Other indirect labor	800	900	100 F
Miscellaneous supplies	4,700	5,400	700 F
Variable manufacturing costs	$105,500	$126,000	$20,500 F
Shipping expenses (selling)	5,000	5,400	400 F
Duplication, telephone, etc. (administrative)	2,000	1,800	200 U
Total variable costs	$112,500	$133,200	$20,700 F
Contribution margin	$ 55,500	$ 82,800	$27,300 U
Fixed costs:			
Factory supervision	$ 14,700	$ 14,400	$ 300 U
Rent of factory	5,000	5,000	—
Depreciation of factory equipment	15,000	15,000	—
Other fixed factory costs	2,600	2,600	—
Fixed manufacturing costs	$ 37,300	$ 37,000	$ 300 U
Fixed selling and administrative costs	33,000	33,000	—
Total fixed costs	$ 70,300	$ 70,000	$ 300 U
Operating income (loss)	$ (14,800)	$ 12,800	$27,600 U

F = Favorable cost variances occur when actual costs are less than budgeted costs.
U = Unfavorable cost variances occur when actual costs are greater than budgeted costs.

budget and the actual results. To get a better basis for analysis, a flexible budget is introduced. The **flexible budget** (also called **variable budget**) is based on knowledge of cost behavior patterns. It is prepared for a range, rather than a single level, of activity; it is essentially a set of budgets that may be tailored to any level of activity. Ideally, the flexible budget is compiled after obtaining a detailed analysis of how each cost is affected by changes in activity. Exhibit 7-2 shows how a flexible budget might appear.

The costs in Exhibit 7-2 may be graphed as in Exhibit 7-3. As these exhibits show, a mathematical function or formula can summarize the cost behavior

**FLEXIBLE
BUDGET
CONTROLS**

EXHIBIT 7-2

DOMINION COMPANY
Flexible Budget
For the Month Ended June 30, 19X1

	BUDGET FORMULA PER UNIT	VARIOUS LEVELS OF ACTIVITY		
Units	—	7,000	8,000	9,000
Sales	$24.00	$168,000	$192,000	$216,000
Variable costs:				
Direct material	$ 3.00	$ 21,000	$ 24,000	$ 27,000
Direct labor	8.00	56,000	64,000	72,000
Labor to transport materials internally and provide general support	1.60	11,200	12,800	14,400
Idle time	.40	2,800	3,200	3,600
Cleanup time	.30	2,100	2,400	2,700
Other indirect labor	.10	700	800	900
Miscellaneous supplies	.60	4,200	4,800	5,400
Variable manufacturing costs	$14.00	$ 98,000	$112,000	$126,000
Shipping expenses (selling)	.60	4,200	4,800	5,400
Duplication, telephone, etc.	.20	1,400	1,600	1,800
Total variable costs	$14.80	$103,600	$118,400	$133,200
Contribution margin	$ 9.20	$ 64,400	$ 73,600	$ 82,800
Fixed costs:				
Factory supervision		$ 14,400	$ 14,400	$ 14,400
Rent of factory		5,000	5,000	5,000
Depreciation of factory equipment		15,000	15,000	15,000
Other fixed factory costs		2,600	2,600	2,600
Fixed manufacturing costs		$ 37,000	$ 37,000	$ 37,000
Fixed selling and administrative costs		33,000	33,000	33,000
Total fixed costs*		$ 70,000	$ 70,000	$ 70,000
Operating income (loss)		$ (5,600)	$ 3,600	$ 12,800

Note that the budget formula for fixed costs is $70,000 per month. Therefore the budget formula for total costs is $14.80 per unit plus $70,000 per month. The graph in Exhibit 7-3 portrays these relationships.

as $70,000 per month plus $14.80 per unit. Although we have assumed that the graph is valid for the range of 7,000 to 9,000 units, costs are unlikely to behave in accordance with such a pat formula beyond either side of this range. Inasmuch as the activity was 7,000 units, the pertinent flexible budget is in the 7,000-unit column of Exhibit 7-2.

Flexible budgets have the following distinguishing features: (a) they are prepared for a range of activity instead of a single level; (b) they supply a

EXHIBIT 7-3. Dominion Company graph of flexible budget of costs

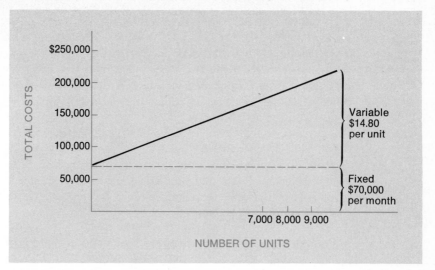

dynamic basis for comparison because they are automatically geared to changes in volume.

The flexible-budget approach says, "Give me any activity level you choose, and I'll provide a budget tailored to that particular volume." Flexible budgets may be useful both before and after the period in question. They may be helpful when managers are trying to choose among various ranges of activity for planning purposes. They may also be helpful at the end of the period when managers are trying to analyze actual results.

☐ ISOLATING THE VARIANCES

Pause a moment to reflect on the analytical problem. The company had an original plan, and the president may seek an explanation of why the plan was not achieved; in other words, a manager may desire a more penetrating analysis of the variances in Exhibit 7-1. The analysis may become quite detailed. However, as a start, consider how the variances may be divided into two major categories:

1. Variances from a revenue target (sometimes called a volume target or, in the case of a production manager, a scheduled production target).[1] In this book, this variance will be called a **marketing variance**, although its label will vary from company to company. It emphasizes the idea that the marketing function usually has the primary responsibility for reaching the sales level called for in the master budget.

---

[1] Sometimes this is generically called an *effectiveness* variance, as distinguished from all other measures, which are loosely called *efficiency* variances. Effectiveness is the accomplishment of a predetermined objective. Efficiency is an optimum relationship between input and output. Given any level of output, did the manager control his inputs as he should have? Performance may be both effective and efficient, but either condition can occur without the other. For example, a company may set 200,000 units as a production objective. Subsequently, because of material shortages, only 150,000 units may be produced with 100 percent efficiency—performance would be ineffective but efficient. In contrast, 200,000 units may be produced on schedule but with a considerable waste of labor and materials—performance would be effective but inefficient.

2. Variances arising from changes in unit prices (or unit costs) and from inefficient utilization of inputs, here called **price** and **efficiency variances.**

The trouble with the static budget, as Exhibit 7-1 shows, is its failure to distinguish between these two facets of a manager's performance. However, Exhibit 7-4 gives a condensed view of how these variances can be isolated by using a flexible budget as an explanatory bridge between the master (static) budget and the actual results.

Column 4 in Exhibit 7-4 focuses on the marketing variance. It shows that the underachievement of sales by 2,000 units and $48,000 resulted in an $18,400 decrease in attained contribution margin and hence an $18,400 decrease in operating income. Note that unit prices are held constant in this part of the analysis—that is, the net marketing variance is computed by using the budgeted contribution margin per unit:

net marketing variance = budgeted unit contribution margin × difference between the master budgeted sales in units and the actual sales in units

$$= \$9.20 \times (9,000 - 7,000) = \$18,400, \text{ unfavorable}$$

Without the flexible budget in column 3, this marketing variance cannot be isolated.

Column 2 focuses on the variances arising from price changes and inefficient uses of inputs. The focus is on the difference between actual costs and flexible budgeted costs when *both* are at the 7,000-unit level of activity. Again,

EXHIBIT 7-4

DOMINION COMPANY
Summary of Performance
For the Month Ended June 30, 19X1

	(1)	(2) (1) − (3)	(3)	(4) (3) − (5)	(5)
	ACTUAL RESULTS AT ACTUAL PRICES*	VARIANCES BECAUSE OF PRICE CHANGES AND INEFFICIENCY†	FLEXIBLE BUDGET FOR ACTUAL OUTPUT ACHIEVED‡	MARKETING VARIANCES	MASTER (STATIC) BUDGET*
Physical units	7,000	—	7,000	2,000	9,000
Sales	$168,000	$ —	$168,000	$48,000	$216,000
Variable costs	112,500	8,900 U	103,600	29,600	133,200
Contribution margin	$ 55,500	$8,900 U	$ 64,400	$18,400	$ 82,800
Fixed costs	70,300	300 U	70,000	—	70,000
Operating income	$(14,800)	$9,200 U	$ (5,600)	$18,400 U	$ 12,800

U = *Unfavorable.*
Figures are from Exhibit 7-1.
†*Figures are shown in more detail in Exhibit 7-5.*
‡*Figures are from the 7,000-unit column in Exhibit 7-2.*

without the flexible budget in column 3, these variances cannot be separated from the effects of changes in sales volume.

If the president wants to pursue this analysis of cost control beyond the summary in Exhibit 7-4, the cost performance report in Exhibit 7-5 may be of help. Even if the president were not interested in probing further, some lower-level managers might be so inclined. Exhibit 7-5 gives a line-by-line sizeup, showing how most of the costs that had favorable variances when a static budget

EXHIBIT 7-5

DOMINION COMPANY
Cost Control Performance Report
For the Month Ended June 30, 19X1

	ACTUAL COSTS INCURRED	FLEXIBLE BUDGET*	VARIANCES BECAUSE OF PRICE CHANGES AND INEFFICIENCY†	EXPLANATION
Units	7,000	7,000	—	
Variable costs:				
Direct material	$ 21,350	$ 21,000	$ 350 U	Lower prices, but higher usage
Direct labor	61,500	56,000	5,500 U	Higher wage rates and higher usage
Labor to transport materials internally and provide general support	11,100	11,200	100 F	
Idle time	3,550	2,800	750 U	Excessive machine breakdowns
Cleanup time	2,500	2,100	400 U	Needs more investigation
Other indirect labor	800	700	100 U	
Miscellaneous supplies	4,700	4,200	500 U	Higher prices and higher usage
Variable manufacturing costs	$105,500	$ 98,000	$7,500 U	
Shipping expenses (selling)	5,000	4,200	800 U	Use of air freight
Duplication, telephone, etc.	2,000	1,400	600 U	Needs more investigation
Total variable costs	$112,500	$103,600	$8,900 U	
Fixed costs:				
Factory supervision	$ 14,700	$ 14,400	$ 300 U	Unanticipated raise
Rent of factory	5,000	5,000	—	
Depreciation of factory equipment	15,000	15,000	—	
Other fixed factory costs	2,600	2,600	—	
Fixed manufacturing costs	$ 37,300	$ 37,000	$ 300 U	
Fixed selling and administrative costs	33,000	33,000	—	
Total fixed costs	$ 70,300	$ 70,000	$ 300 U	
Total variable and fixed costs	$182,800	$173,600	$9,200 U	

F = *Favorable.* U = *Unfavorable.*
*From 7,000-unit column in Exhibit 7-2.
† This represents a line-by-line breakdown of the variances in column 2 of Exhibit 7-4.

was used as a basis for comparison have, in reality, unfavorable variances. These "price and efficiency variances" may be analyzed in even more depth by being subdivided further, at least for the more important material and labor costs, as shown later in the section "Standards for Material and Labor."

□ DEVELOPMENT OF CONTROL SYSTEMS

In most organizations, systems for accumulating and analyzing data evolve gradually. For example, when small businesses are founded, planning and control decisions are based at first almost wholly on the manager's *physical observations* of operations. It does not take long for the manager to realize that keeping some *historical records* would be a net benefit. That is, the additional bookkeeping costs are clearly outweighed by the greater likelihood of a series of better decisions regarding extensions of trade credit to customers, negotiating with suppliers and bankers, and so on. Furthermore, comparing the current period's sales, costs, or income with the preceding period's helps in the evaluation of performance and the preparation of new plans.

Physical observation and historical records, however, are often not enough. Managers desire to reduce emergency decision making by doing more careful planning, and the *master (static) budget* is helpful in this regard. Furthermore, the master budget provides a better benchmark for evaluating performance. That is, managers want to know more than how they have done currently in relation to last period's performance; they also want to know how they have done *currently* in relation to their *current* targeted performance.

This chapter has shown that some managers are willing to pay for more help in the form of *flexible budgets,* which are key aids in mapping an explanatory trail from the master budget to the actual results.

Thus the evolution of control systems is often from physical observation, to historical records, to master (static) budgets, to flexible budgets (and standard costs, which are described in the next section). Note that one control tool does not *replace* another; instead, each control tool is *added* to the others. The systems become more costly, but they are perceived by the managers who buy them as leading to net benefits in the form of a better set of collective operating decisions.

This concludes the presentation of an overall view of flexible budgets and standards. Subsequent sections probe the subject more deeply.

Standards for material and labor

Standard costs are the building blocks of a budgeting and feedback system. A **standard cost** is a carefully predetermined cost that should be attained, usually expressed per unit.

□ DIFFERENCE BETWEEN STANDARDS AND BUDGETS

How does a standard amount differ from a budget amount? If standards are currently attainable, as they are assumed to be in this book, there is no conceptual difference. However, as it is most widely used, the term *standard cost* refers to a *single* unit. In contrast, the term *budgeted cost* refers to a *total*. For example, the standard cost of direct material in Exhibit 7-2 shows:

	BUDGET FORMULA PER UNIT	FLEXIBLE BUDGET FOR VARIOUS LEVELS OF ACTIVITY		
Units	1	7,000	8,000	9,000
Direct material	$3.00	$21,000	$24,000	$27,000

The standard cost is $3 per unit. The budgeted cost is $21,000 if 7,000 units are to be produced. It may help to think of a standard as a budget for the production of a single unit. In many companies, the terms *budgeted performance* and *standard performance* are used interchangeably.

In practice, direct material and direct labor are often said to be controlled with the help of *standard costs,* whereas all other costs are usually said to be controlled with the help of *departmental overhead budgets.* This distinction probably arose because of different timing and control techniques for various costs. Direct material and direct labor are generally relatively costly and are easily identifiable for control purposes. Therefore techniques for planning and controlling these costs are relatively refined. Overhead costs are combinations of many individual items, none of which justifies an elaborate control system. In consequence, use of direct material may be closely watched on an hourly basis; direct labor, on a daily basis; and factory overhead, on a weekly or monthly basis.

All this leads to the following straightforward approach (using assumed figures), which we will pursue throughout the remainder of this book. The *standard* is a *unit* idea; the *budget* is a *total* idea. Using the data in Exhibit 7-2:

	STANDARDS		
	(1) standard inputs allowed for each unit of output achieved	(2) standard price per unit of input	BUDGET FOR 7,000 UNITS OF OUTPUT*
Direct material	5 pounds	$ .60	$21,000
Direct labor	2 hours	4.00	56,000
Other costs (detailed)	Various	Various	96,600

*Col. (1) × (2) × 7,000.

☐ ROLE OF PAST EXPERIENCE

The study of past behavior patterns is typically a fundamental step in formulating a standard or a budgeted cost. Although the study of past cost behavior is a useful starting point, a budgeted cost should not merely be an extension of past experience. Inefficiencies may be reflected in prior costs. Changes in technology, equipment, and methods also limit the usefulness of comparisons with the past. Also, performance should be judged in relation to some currently attainable goal, one that may be reached by skilled, diligent, superior effort. Concern with the past is justified only insofar as it helps prediction. Management wishes to plan what costs *should be,* not what costs *have been.*

What standard of expected performance should be used? Should it be so severe that it is rarely, if ever, attained? Should it be attainable 50 percent of the time? Eighty percent? Twenty percent? Individuals who have worked a lifetime in setting standards for performance cannot agree, so there are no universal answers to these questions.

Two types of standards deserve mention here, perfection standards and currently attainable standards. *Perfection standards* (often also called *ideal standards*) are expressions of the absolute minimum costs possible under the best conceivable conditions, using existing specifications and equipment. No provision is made for shrinkage, spoilage, machine breakdowns, and the like. Those who favor this approach maintain that the resulting unfavorable variances will constantly remind managers of the perpetual need for improvement in all phases of operations. These standards are not widely used, however, because they have an adverse effect on employee motivation. Employees tend to ignore unreasonable goals.

Currently attainable standards are those that can be achieved by *very efficient* operations. Expectations are set high enough so that employees regard their fulfillment as possible, though perhaps not probable. Allowances are made for normal shrinkage, waste, and machine breakdowns. Variances tend to be unfavorable, but managers accept the standards as being reasonable goals.

The major reasons for using currently attainable standards are:

1. The resulting standard costs serve multiple purposes. For example, the same cost may be used for cash budgeting, inventory valuation, and budgeting departmental performance. In contrast, perfection standards cannot be used per se for cash budgeting, because financial planning will be thrown off.[2]

2. They have a desirable motivational impact on employees. The standard represents reasonable future performance, not fanciful ideal goals or antiquated goals geared to past performance.

☐ PRICE AND EFFICIENCY VARIANCES

The assessment of performance is facilitated by separating the items that are subject to the manager's direct influence from those that are not. The general approach is to separate *price* factors from *efficiency* factors. Price factors are less subject to immediate control than are efficiency factors, principally because of external forces, such as general economic conditions and unforeseeable price

---

[2] If standards are not currently attainable because they are perfection or outdated, the amount budgeted for financial (cash) planning purposes has to differ from the standard. Otherwise, projected income and cash disbursements will be forecasted incorrectly. In such cases, ideal or outdated standards may be used for compiling performance reports, but "expected variances" are stipulated in the master budget for financial planning. For example, if unusually strict labor standards are used, the standard cost per finished unit may be $8 despite the fact that top management anticipates an unfavorable performance variance of 40¢ per unit. In the master budget, the total labor costs would be $8.40 per unit: $8 plus an expected variance of 40¢.

changes. Even when price factors are regarded as outside of company control, it is still desirable to isolate them to obtain a sharper focus on the efficient usage of the goods or services in question.

To see how the analysis of variances can be pursued more fully, reconsider the direct material and direct labor in Exhibit 7-5. The variances there can be subdivided into two major types: *price* and *efficiency*.[3]

To demonstrate this general approach for direct material and direct labor, we continue our illustration and assume that the following actually occurred:

Direct material: 36,810 pounds of inputs used at an actual unit price of 58¢ for a total actual cost of $21,350.

Direct labor: 15,000 hours of inputs were used at an actual hourly price (rate) of $4.10, for a total actual cost of $61,500.

The **budget variance** for materials may be analyzed as follows:

Price variance
= Actual inputs used × Difference between the actual unit price and the standard unit price
= 36,810 pounds × ($.58 − $.60)
= $736 F

Efficiency variance
= Standard unit price × Difference between the actual inputs used and the standard inputs allowed for the outputs achieved
= $.60 × [36,810 − (7,000 units of finished product × 5 pounds of materials per unit)]
= $.60 × (36,810 − 35,000)
= $.60 × 1,810 = $1,086 U

Flexible-budget variance explained
= Price variance + Efficiency variance
= $736 F + $1,086 U
= $736 + (−$1,086) = $−350 Unfavorable

"Efficiency" is a relative measure that is often expressed as the ratio of inputs to outputs. That is, the concept of efficiency requires our knowing both *inputs* and *outputs* and their interrelationship. "Perfect" efficiency would be some approximation of an optimal relationship between inputs and outputs.

Variance analysis does *not* provide any answers. But it raises questions, provides clues, and directs attention. For instance, one possible explanation, among many, for this set of variances is that a manager might have made a trade-off and lost—that is, the manager might have purchased, at a favorable price, some materials that were slightly substandard, resulting in excessive waste as indicated by the unfavorable efficiency variance.

---

[3] *Price* and *efficiency* will be used throughout this book to describe these two classes of variances. In practice, the price variance is often called a **rate** variance when it is used in conjunction with labor. Similarly, the efficiency variance is often called a **usage** or **quantity** variance when it is used in conjunction with materials.

The analysis for direct labor is similar:

Price variance	$= 15,000 \text{ hours} \times (\$4.10 - \$4.00)$
	$= 15,000 \times \$.10 = \$1,500 \text{ U}$
Efficiency variance	$= \$4.00 \times [15,000 - (7,000 \text{ product}$
	units $\times$ 2 allowed hours of labor
	per unit)]
	$= \$4.00 \times 1,000 = \$4,000 \text{ U}$
Flexible-budget variance explained	$= \$1,500 \text{ U} + \$4,000 \text{ U} = \$5,500 \text{ U}$

EXHIBIT 7-6. General approach to analysis of variable-cost variances

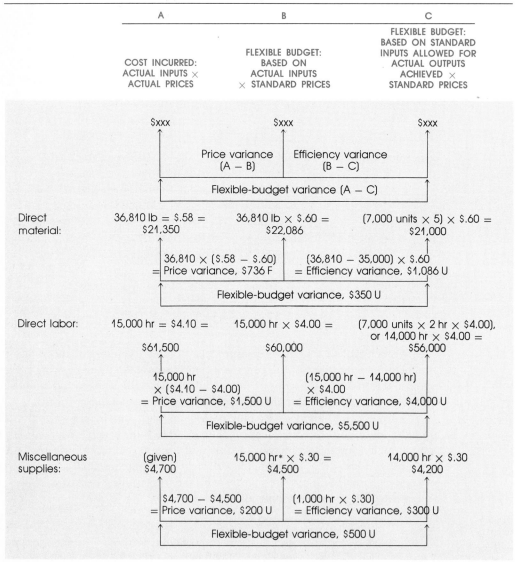

U = *Unfavorable.* F = *Favorable.*
For comments, see the section "Limitations of Price and Efficiency Variances" in text.

Evidently, direct labor warrants further investigation, because it is easily the largest variance of all.

☐ A GENERAL APPROACH

Exhibit 7-6 presents the foregoing analysis in a format that deserves close study. The general approach is at the top of the exhibit; the specific applications then follow. Even though the exhibit may seem unnecessarily complex at first, its repeated use will solidify your understanding of variance analysis. Of course, the other budget variances in Exhibit 7-5 could be further analyzed in the same manner in which direct material and direct labor are analyzed in Exhibit 7-6. The pursuit of such a detailed investigation depends on the manager's perception as to whether the extra benefits will exceed the extra cost of such detective work.

☐ GRAPHICAL APPROACH

A graphical approach sometimes clarifies the relationships. For example, the direct-labor analysis in the middle of Exhibit 7-6 is also portrayed in Exhibit 7-7. The cost function is linear, sloping upward at a standard rate (price) of $4 per hour.

EXHIBIT 7-7. Graphical analysis of direct labor

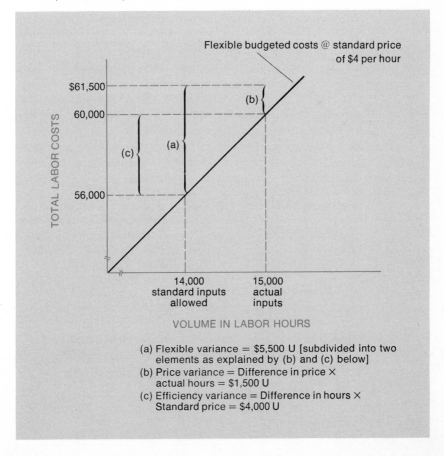

Flexible budgeted costs @ standard price of $4 per hour

TOTAL LABOR COSTS

$61,500
60,000
(b)
(c)
(a)
56,000

14,000
standard inputs
allowed

15,000
actual
inputs

VOLUME IN LABOR HOURS

(a) Flexible variance = $5,500 U [subdivided into two elements as explained by (b) and (c) below]
(b) Price variance = Difference in price × actual hours = $1,500 U
(c) Efficiency variance = Difference in hours × Standard price = $4,000 U

Note that volume is expressed in hours instead of in physical units of product. This is a common practice. Most departments have a variety of products; when the variety of units is added together, the result is frequently a nonsensical sum. Therefore all units of output are expressed in terms of the standard inputs of hours allowed for their production. Hours thus become the common denominator for measuring total volume. Production, instead of being expressed as, say, 12,000 chairs and 3,000 tables, is frequently expressed as 14,000 *standard hours allowed* (or *standard hours worked,* or *standard hours earned,* or most accurately as *standard hours of input allowed for outputs achieved*).

Another key idea illustrated in Exhibits 7-6 and 7-7 is the versatility of the flexible budget. A flexible budget is geared to volume, and Exhibit 7-7 shows that volume can be measured in terms of *actual inputs* alone, *actual outputs achieved* alone, or both. Both measures are shown in the graph; they are necessary to obtain separate identification of price and efficiency variances.

When used in this book, unless stated otherwise, the term *flexible-budget variance* will mean the difference between columns A and C in Exhibit 7-6, the difference between actual costs and the flexible budget based on the standard inputs allowed for actual outputs achieved.

Please reread the preceding four paragraphs before going on. They contain key ideas and terms that warrant scrutiny.

☐ LIMITATIONS OF PRICE AND EFFICIENCY VARIANCES

The division of variances into two neat categories of "price" and "efficiency" is a good first step. However, it is a crude split, and its limitations should be kept in mind. In particular, the individual overhead items may be hard to subdivide in this way. For instance, the flexible budget for supplies is budgeted in Exhibit 7-5 at $4,200, based on a formula of 60¢ per unit.

In practice, a simple but fragile assumption underlies the usual efficiency-variance computation for variable-overhead items: Variable-overhead costs fluctuate in direct proportion to direct-labor hours. Therefore the efficiency variance for a variable-overhead item such as supplies is a measure of the extra overhead (or savings) incurred *solely* because the actual *direct-labor hours* used differed from the standard hours allowed:

overhead efficiency variance = standard overhead rate per hour ×
(actual direct-labor hours of inputs
− standard direct-labor hours allowed)
= $.30 × (15,000 − 14,000)
= $300 unfavorable

Because direct labor was inefficiently used by 1,000 hours under this approach, we would expect the related usage of supplies to be proportionately excessive wholly because of labor inefficiency. However, whether in fact this direct relationship exists depends on specific circumstances.

To recapitulate, ponder why there was a $500 supplies variance in Exhibit 7-5. The implications of the analysis in Exhibit 7-6 are on the top of the next page.

Above all, the limitations of these analyses of variances should be underscored. The *only* way to discover why overhead performance did not agree with a budget is to investigate possible causes, line item by line item. However, the

Actual costs	$4,700
Efficiency variance—The amount that would be expected to be incurred **because of the inefficient use of direct labor,** 1,000 hr × $.30 =	$300
Price variance—The amount unexplained by the efficiency variance. It could arise from unit price changes for various supplies—but it could also arise simply from the general waste and sloppy use of these supplies. In short, this, too, could be partially or completely traceable to **more inefficiency,** even though it is labeled as a price variance. (Incidentally, for this reason, many practitioners call this type of overhead variance a **spending** variance rather than a price variance).	200
Budget variance	500
Budgeted amount in flexible budget	$4,200

price-efficiency distinctions provide a handy springboard for a more rigorous analysis.

Controllability and variances

☐ RESPONSIBILITY FOR MATERIAL VARIANCES

In most companies, the *acquisition* of materials or merchandise entails different control decisions than their *use*. The purchasing executive of a manufacturing company worries about getting raw materials at favorable prices, whereas the production executive concentrates on using them efficiently. The merchandise manager of a large grocery company will be responsible for skillful buying of foodstuffs, but the store manager will be responsible for their sale and for minimizing losses from shrinkage, shoplifting, and the like. Thus the responsibility for price variances usually rests with the purchasing officer, and the responsibility for efficiency variances usually rests with the production manager or sales manager.

Price variances are often regarded as measures of forecasting ability rather than of failure to buy at specified prices. Some control over the price variance is obtainable by getting many quotations, buying in economical lots, taking advantage of cash discounts, and selecting the most economical means of delivery. Price variances may lead to decisions to change suppliers or freight carriers.

However, failure to meet price standards may result from a sudden rush of sales orders or from unanticipated changes in production schedules, which in turn may require the purchasing officer to buy at uneconomical prices or to request delivery by air freight. In such cases, the responsibility may rest with the sales manager or the head of production scheduling, rather than with the purchasing officer.

☐ RESPONSIBILITY FOR LABOR VARIANCES

In most companies, because of union contracts or other predictable factors, labor prices can be foreseen with much greater accuracy than can prices of materials. Therefore labor price variances tend to be relatively insignificant.

185

Labor, unlike material and supplies, cannot ordinarily be stored for later use. The acquisition and use of labor occur simultaneously. For these reasons, labor rate variances are usually charged to the same manager who is responsible for labor usage.

Labor price variances may be traceable to faulty predictions of the labor rates. However, the more likely causes include (1) the use of a single average standard labor price for a given operation that is, in fact, performed by individuals earning slightly different rates because of seniority; (2) the assignment of a worker earning, perhaps, $6 per hour to a given operation that should be appointed to a less-skilled worker earning, say, $4 per hour; and (3) the payment of hourly rates, instead of prescribed piece rates, because of low productivity.

☐ CAUSES OF EFFICIENCY VARIANCES

The general approach to analyzing efficiency variances is probably best exemplified by the control of direct materials in standard cost systems. The budget of the production department manager is usually based on a *standard formula* or a Standard Bill of Materials. This is a specification of the physical quantities allowed for producing a specified number of acceptable finished units. These quantities are then compared with the quantities actually used.

What does the manager do with the variances? The manager seeks explanations for their existence. Common causes of efficiency variances include improper handling, inferior quality of material, poor workmanship, changes in methods, new workers, slow machines, broken cutting tools, and faulty blueprints.

☐ TRADE-OFFS AMONG VARIANCES

Variance analysis can be useful for focusing on how various aspects of operations are meeting expectations. However, a standard cost system should not be a straitjacket that prevents the manager from aiming at the overall organization objectives. Too often, each unfavorable variance is regarded as, ipso facto, bad; and each favorable variance is regarded as, ipso facto, good.

Managers sometimes deliberately acquire off-standard material at unusually low prices. They hope that the favorable price variances will exceed any resulting unfavorable efficiency variances caused by heavy spoilage or unusual labor-hours. Thus, if the manager guesses correctly, the decision was favorable despite the unfavorable label pinned on the efficiency variances. Because there are so many interdependencies among activities, an "unfavorable" or a "favorable" label should not lead the manager to jump to conclusions. By themselves, such labels merely raise questions and provide clues. They are attention directors, not answer givers. The chapter appendix discusses these interdependencies in more depth.

☐ WHEN TO INVESTIGATE VARIANCES

When should variances be investigated? Frequently the answer is based on subjective judgments, hunches, guesses, and rules of thumb. The most troublesome aspect of feedback is in deciding when a variance is significant enough to warrant management's attention. For some items, a small deviation may prompt follow-up. For other items, a minimum dollar amount or 5, 10, or 25 percent deviations from budget may be necessary before investigations commence. Of course, a 4 percent variance in a $1 million material cost may deserve more attention than a 20 percent variance in a $10,000 repair cost. Therefore rules such as "Investigate all variances exceeding $5,000, or 25 percent of standard cost, whichever is lower" are common.

Variance analysis is subject to the same cost-benefit test as other phases of an information system. The trouble with the foregoing rules of thumb is that they are too frequently based on subjective assessments, guesses, or hunches. The field of statistics offers tools to help reduce these subjective features. These tools help answer the cost-benefit question, and they help separate variances caused by random events from variances that are controllable.

Accounting systems have traditionally implied that a standard is a single acceptable measure. Practically, the accountant (and everybody else) realizes that the standard is a *band* or *range* of possible acceptable outcomes. Consequently, the accountant expects variances to fluctuate randomly within some normal limits. A random variance, by definition, calls for no corrective action to an existing process. In short, random variances are attributable to chance rather than to management's implementation decisions.

summary

Management is best aided by carefully prepared standards and budgets representing what should be accomplished. These standards should be based on material specifications and on work measurement rather than on past performance, because the latter too often conceals past inefficiencies.

Currently attainable standards are the most widely used because they usually have the most desirable motivational impact and because they may be used for a variety of accounting purposes, including financial planning, as well as for monitoring departmental performance.

When standards are currently attainable, there is no logical difference between standards and budgets. A standard is a unit concept, whereas a budget is a total concept. In a sense, the standard is the budget for one unit.

Flexible budgets are geared to changing levels of activity rather than to a single static level. They may be tailored to a particular level of sales or production volume—before or after the fact. They tell how much cost should be or should have been incurred for any level of output, which is usually expressed either in product units of output or in standard direct-labor hours allowed for that output.

The evaluation of performance is aided by a feedback comparison of actual results with budgeted expectations, as summarized in Exhibit 7-4. The flexible-budget idea helps managers to get an explanation of why the master budget was not achieved. Variances are often divided into marketing, price, and efficiency variances. In practice, the efficiency factors are more important because they are subject to more direct management influence than are prices of materials or labor.

There is a similarity in approach to the control of all costs that are regarded as variable. The price variance is the difference in price multiplied by actual quantity. The efficiency variance is the difference in quantity multiplied by standard price.

Variances raise questions; they do not provide answers. The analysis and follow-up of variances are the keys to successful management control. Variances provide clues, jog memories, and open pertinent avenues for management investigation. If managers do not do anything with the variances, then either the reporting system needs overhauling or the managers need to be educated and convinced of the benefits that can be derived from a careful analysis of the variances.

Variance analysis is subject to the same cost-benefit test as other phases of an information system. The decision on whether to investigate a variance depends on expected net benefits.

CHAPTER 14, WHICH MAY BE STUDIED NOW IF DESIRED, PROBES THE ANALYSIS OF VARIANCES IN MORE DEPTH, PARTICULARLY WITH RESPECT TO FIXED OVERHEAD AND INVENTORIES.

summary problem for your review

PROBLEM

The following questions are based on the data contained in the illustration used in the chapter:

1. Suppose that actual production and sales were 8,500 units instead of 7,000 units. (a) Compute the marketing variance. Is the performance of the marketing function the sole explanation for this variance? Why? (b) Using a flexible budget, compute the budgeted contribution margin, budgeted operating income, budgeted direct material, and budgeted direct labor.

2. Suppose the following were the actual results for the production of 8,500 units:

Direct material: 46,000 pounds of inputs were used at an actual unit price of 55¢, for a total actual cost of $25,300.

Direct labor: 16,500 hours of inputs were used at an actual hourly price (rate) of $4.20, for a total actual cost of $69,300.

Compute the flexible budget variance and the price and efficiency variances for direct material and direct labor. Present your answers in the form shown in Exhibit 7-6.

3. Suppose that the company is organized so that the purchasing manager bears the primary responsibility for the acquisition prices of materials, and the production manager bears the primary responsibility for efficiency but no responsibility for unit prices. Assume the same facts as in Requirement 2, except that the purchasing manager acquired 60,000 pounds of materials. This means that there is an ending inventory of 14,000 pounds. Would your variance analysis of materials in Requirement 2 change? Why? Show computations to support your answer.

▪ SOLUTION

1. (a) **Marketing variance = Budgeted unit contribution margin × Difference between the master-budgeted sales in units and the actual sales in units**
= $9.20 × (9,000 − 8,500) = $4,600 U

This variance is labeled as a marketing variance because it quantifies the impact on net income of the deviation from an original sales target—while holding price and efficiency factors constant. Of course, the failure to reach target sales may be traceable to a number of causes beyond the control of the marketing force, including strikes, material shortages, and storms.

(b) The budget formulas in Exhibit 7-2 are the basis for the following answers:

Budgeted contribution margin = $9.20 × 8,500 = $78,200
Budgeted operating income = $78,200 − $70,000 fixed costs = $8,200
Budgeted direct material = $3.00 × 8,500 = $25,500
Budgeted direct labor = $8.00 × 8,500 = $68,000

2.

	COST INCURRED: ACTUAL INPUTS × ACTUAL PRICE	FLEXIBLE BUDGET: BASED ON ACTUAL QUANTITY × STANDARD PRICE	FLEXIBLE BUDGET: BASED ON STANDARD INPUTS ALLOWED FOR ACTUAL OUTPUTS ACHIEVED × STANDARD PRICES
Direct material:	46,000 lb × $.55 =	46,000 lb × $.60 =	(8,500 units × 5) × $.60 =
	$25,300	$27,600	$25,500

46,000 × ($.55 − $.60)
= Price variance, $2,300 F

(46,000 − 42,500) × $.60
= Efficiency variance, $2,100 U

Flexible-budget variance, $200 F

Direct labor:	16,500 hr × $4.20 =	16,500 hr × $4 =	(8,500 units × 2 hr × $4), or 17,000 hr × $4 = $68,000
	$69,300	$66,000	

16,500 × ($4.20 − $4)
= Price variance, $3,300 U

(16,500 − 17,000) × $4
= Efficiency variance, $2,000 F

Flexible-budget variance, $1,300 U

3. Whether the variance analysis in Requirement 2 would change depends on how the information system is designed. In many organizations, price variances for materials are isolated at the most logical control point—time of purchase rather than time of use. In turn, the production or operating departments that later use the materials are always charged at some predetermined so-called budget or standard unit price, never at actual unit prices. Under this procedure the price-variance analysis would be conducted in the purchasing department and the efficiency-variance analysis in the production department. This represents a slight modification of the approach in Requirement 2 as follows:

CONTROL POINT	COST INCURRED: ACTUAL QUANTITY × ACTUAL PRICE	ACTUAL QUANTITY × STANDARD PRICE	FLEXIBLE BUDGET: STANDARD QUANTITY ALLOWED × STANDARD PRICE
Purchasing department	60,000 lb × $.55 = $33,000	60,000 lb × $.60 = $36,000	
		60,000 × ($.55 − $.60) = Price variance, $3,000 F	
Production department		46,000 lb × $.60 = $27,600	42,500 lb × $.60 = $25,500
		(46,000 lb − 42,500) × $.60 = Efficiency variance, $2,100 U	

Note that the efficiency variance is the same in Requirements 2 and 3.

Appendix 7: mutual price and efficiency effects

The usual breakdown of variances into price and efficiency is not theoretically perfect because there may be a small mutual price-efficiency effect. A production foreman and a purchasing agent might argue over the following situation. The direct material is 1,000 pounds @ $1 and is intended to produce 1,000 good finished units. The performance report shows the use of 1,150 pounds @ $1.20 to produce 1,000 good finished units.

The ordinary analysis of variances would appear as follows:

Actual quantity × Actual price, or 1,150 × $1.20 =		$1,380
Price variance = Difference in price × Actual pounds = ($1.20 − $1) × 1,150 =	$230 U	
Efficiency variance = Difference in quantity × Standard price = (1,150 − 1,000) × $1 =	150 U	
Total variance explained		380 U
Standard quantity of inputs allowed for units produced × Standard price = 1,000 × $1 =		$1,000

The small area in the upper right-hand corner of the graphic analysis (Exhibit 7-8) may be the area of controversy. The purchasing officer might readily accept responsibility for the price variance on the 1,000 pounds in the standard allowance but might also claim that the extra $30 buried in the $230 total variance is more properly attributable to the production foreman. After all, if the foreman had produced in accordance with the standard, the extra 150 pounds would not have been needed. But this distinction is not often made, simply because it usually involves a small sum. However, we should be aware that the conventional variance analysis, which includes the joint price-efficiency variance ($30, in this case) as a part of an overall price variance, has logical deficiencies.

In practice, the efficiency variance is considered much more important than the price variance because the manager can exert more direct influence over the efficiency variance. Consequently, the performance report on efficiency should minimize the possibility of the production manager's criticisms of any

EXHIBIT 7-8. Graphic analysis of variances

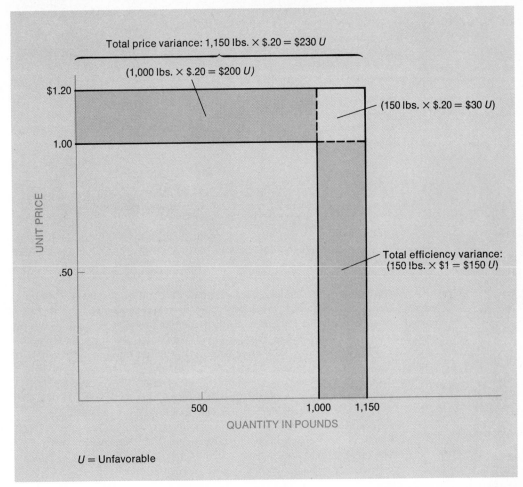

accounting or measurement methods. Joint price-efficiency variance is less likely to cause arguments if it is buried in the total price variance than if it is buried in the efficiency variance.

assignment material

■ FUNDAMENTAL ASSIGNMENT MATERIAL

7-1. Terminology. Define *budget variance; currently attainable standards; efficiency variance; flexible budget; marketing variance; performance report; price variance; quantity variance; rate variance; spending variance; standard cost; static budget; usage variance; variable budget.*

7-2. Flexible and static budgets. (An alternate is Problem 7-24.) The Middle Transportation Company used a budget based on expectations for the month of March. The condensed performance report for a Missouri branch was (in dollars):

	ACTUAL	BUDGET	VARIANCE
Revenues	3,600,000	4,000,000	400,000 U
Variable payroll	1,656,000	1,800,000	144,000 F
Fuel	940,000	1,000,000	60,000 F
Repairs and maintenance	115,000	120,000	5,000 F
Supplies and miscellaneous	79,000	80,000	1,000 F
Total variable costs*	2,790,000	3,000,000	210,000 F
Supervision	100,000	100,000	—
Rent	200,000	200,000	—
Depreciation	400,000	400,000	—
Other fixed costs	100,000	100,000	—
Total fixed costs	800,000	800,000	—
Total costs charged against revenue	3,590,000	3,800,000	210,000 F
Operating income	10,000	200,000	190,000 U

U = *Unfavorable.* F = *Favorable.*

For purposes of this analysis, assume that all these costs are totally variable. In practice, many are mixed and must be split into variable and fixed components before a meaningful analysis can be made. Also assume that the mix of services remains unchanged.

The branch manager was displeased about the inability to obtain the budgeted revenues. However, he consoled himself with the thought that his performance in cost control was favorable. Otherwise the branch's operating income would have been even lower.

A new vice-president of operations, Lawrence Beech, assumed his new duties on March 1. Beech had previously worked for a competitor. He commented on the performance report as follows: "This report might be a starting place for evaluating performance, but the report does little to help me appraise how well the branch manager has controlled costs. There must be a more helpful way to get an analytical handle on performance."

REQUIRED

1. Prepare a columnar flexible budget for expected costs at $3, $4, and $5 million levels of revenue. Include both variable and fixed costs in your budget.
2. Express Requirement 1 in formula form. That is, what are the fixed costs per month and by what percentage of revenue do variable costs fluctuate?
3. Prepare a performance report similar to Exhibit 7-4 that explains why the originally budgeted operating income was not attained.

7-3. Direct-material and direct-labor variances. The Kenneth Company manufactures metal giftware that is hand-shaped and hand-painted. The following standards were developed for a luxury line of vases:

	STANDARD INPUTS ALLOWED FOR EACH UNIT OF OUTPUT ACHIEVED	STANDARD PRICE PER UNIT OF INPUT
Direct materials	12 ounces	$ 4.00 per pound
Direct labor	.5 hour	20.00 per hour

During April, 50,000 vases were scheduled for production. However, only 48,000 were actually produced.

Direct materials used amounted to 40,000 pounds at a unit price of $3.50 per pound. Direct labor actually was paid $21.00 per hour, and 26,000 hours were used.

REQUIRED

1. Compute the standard cost per vase for direct materials and direct labor. (There are sixteen ounces in one pound.)
2. Compute the price variances and efficiency variances for direct materials and direct labor.
3. Based on these sketchy data, what clues for investigation are provided by the variances?

7-4. "Price variances should be computed even if prices are regarded as outside of company control." Do you agree? Explain.

7-5. "Failure to meet price standards is the responsibility of the purchasing officer." Do you agree? Explain.

7-6. Why do labor price variances tend to be insignificant?

7-7. What are the key questions in the analysis and follow-up of variances?

7-8. What are some common causes of quantity variances?

7-9. Why is the joint price-quantity variance buried in the price variance rather than in the quantity variance?

7-10. What two basic questions must be asked in approaching the control of all costs?

7-11. Why do the techniques for controlling overhead differ from those for controlling direct material and direct labor?

7-12. "The flex in the flexible budget relates solely to variable costs." Do you agree? Explain.

7-13. How does the overhead price variance differ from the labor price variance?

7-14. Why are standard hours superior to actual hours as an index of activity?

7-15. "A standard is a band or range of acceptable outcomes." Criticize.

7-16. What are standard costs? Why is their use preferable to comparisons of actual data with past data?

7-17. "Direct material and direct labor may be included in a flexible budget." Do you agree? Explain.

7-18. Why should a budgeted cost not be merely an extension of past experience?

7-19. Distinguish between perfection and currently attainable standards.

7-20. What is the difference between a standard amount and a budget amount?

7-21. What are expected variances?

7-22. **National Park Service.** The National Park Service prepared the following budget for one of its national parks for 19X4:

Revenue from fees	$4,000,000
Variable costs (miscellaneous)	400,000
Contribution margin	$3,600,000
Fixed costs (miscellaneous)	3,600,000
Operating income	$ 0

The fees were based on an average of 50,000 vehicle-admission days (vehicles multiplied by number of days in parks) per week for the twenty-week season, multiplied by average entry and other fees of $4 per vehicle-admission day.

The season was booming for the first four weeks. However, there was a wave of thievery and violence during the fifth week. Grizzly bears killed four campers during the sixth week and two during the seventh week. As a result, the number of visitors to the park dropped sharply during the remainder of the season.

Total revenue fell by $1 million. Moreover, extra rangers and police had to be hired at a cost of $200,000. The latter was regarded as a fixed cost.

REQUIRED

Prepare a columnar summary of performance, showing the original budget, marketing variance, and actual results.

7-23. Explanation of variance in income. The H & R Income Tax Service processes income tax returns that result in standard contribution margins averaging 60 percent of dollar sales and average selling prices of $30 per return. Average productivity is four returns per hour. Some preparers work for sales commissions and others for an hourly rate. The master budget for 19X2 had predicted sales of 900,000 returns, but only 800,000 returns were processed.

Fixed costs of rent, supervision, advertising, and other items were budgeted at $11 million, but they were exceeded by $1 million because of extra advertising in an attempt to boost revenue.

There were no variances from the average selling prices, but the actual commissions paid to preparers and the actual productivity per hour resulted in flexible-budget variances (that is, total price and efficiency variances) for variable costs of $1.1 million unfavorable.

The president was unhappy because the budgeted operating income of $5.2 million was not achieved. He said, "Sure, we had unfavorable variable-cost variances, but our operating income was down far more than that. Please explain why."

REQUIRED

Explain why the budgeted operating income was not attained. Use a presentation similar to Exhibit 7-4. Enough data have been given to permit you to construct the complete exhibit by filling in the known items and then computing the unknown. Complete your explanation by summarizing what happened, using no more than three sentences.

7-24. University flexible budgeting. (CMA, adapted.) The University of Boyne offers an extensive continuing education program in many cities throughout the state. For the convenience of its faculty and administrative staff and also to save costs, the university operates a motor pool. The motor pool operated with twenty vehicles until February of this year, when an additional automobile was acquired. The motor pool furnishes gasoline, oil, and other supplies for the cars and hires one mechanic who does routine maintenance and minor repairs. Major repairs are done at a nearby commercial garage. A supervisor manages the operations.

Each year the supervisor prepares an operating budget, informing university management of the funds needed to operate the pool. Depreciation on the automobiles is recorded in the budget in order to determine the costs per mile.

The schedule below presents the annual budget approved by the university. The actual costs for March are compared with one-twelfth of the annual budget.

The annual budget was constructed upon the following assumptions:
a. 20 automobiles in the pool
b. 30,000 miles per year per automobile

UNIVERSITY MOTOR POOL
Budget Report
For March 19X6

	ANNUAL BUDGET	ONE-MONTH BUDGET	MARCH ACTUAL	OVER* UNDER
Gasoline	$ 72,000	$ 6,000	$ 9,100	$3,100*
Oil, minor repairs, parts, and supplies	3,600	300	380	80*
Outside repairs	2,700	225	50	175
Insurance	6,000	500	525	25*
Salaries and benefits	30,000	2,500	2,500	—
Depreciation	26,400	2,200	2,310	110*
	$130,700	$11,725	$14,865	$3,140*
Total miles	600,000	50,000	63,000	
Cost per mile	$ .2178	$ .2345	$ .2360	
Number of automobiles	20	20	21	

c. 15 miles per gallon per automobile

d. $1.80 per gallon of gas

e. $.006 per mile for oil, minor repairs, parts, and supplies

f. $135 per automobile in outside repairs

The supervisor is unhappy with the monthly report comparing budget and actual costs for March; he claims it presents his performance unfairly. His previous employer used flexible budgeting to compare actual costs with budgeted amounts.

REQUIRED

1. Employing flexible-budgeting techniques, prepare a report that shows budgeted amounts, actual costs, and monthly variation for March.
2. Explain briefly the basis of your budget figure for outside repairs.

7-25. Standard material allowances. (CMA) Danson Company is a chemical manufacturer that supplies industrial users. The company plans to introduce a new chemical solution and needs to develop a standard product cost for this new solution.

The new chemical solution is made by combining a chemical compound (nyclyn) and a solution (salex), boiling the mixture, adding a second compound (protet), and bottling the resulting solution in 10-liter containers. The initial mix, which is 10 liters in volume, consists of 12 kilograms of nyclyn and 9.6 liters of salex. A 20 percent reduction in volume occurs during the boiling process. The solution is then cooled slightly before 5 kilograms of protet are added; the addition of protet does not affect the total liquid volume.

The purchase prices of the raw materials used in the manufacture of this new chemical solution are as follows:

Nyclyn	$1.30 per kilogram
Salex	1.80 per liter
Protet	2.40 per kilogram

REQUIRED

Determine the standard quantity for each of the raw materials needed to produce a 10-liter container of Danson Company's new chemical solution and the standard materials cost of a 10-liter container of the new product.

7-26. Explanation of variance in income. The Sarah Company based its master budget for 19X2 on an expected sales volume of 110,000 units, at an average unit selling price of $25. Costs were expected to be:

STANDARD VARIABLE COSTS PER UNIT		TOTAL FIXED COSTS	
Direct material	$ 9.00	Manufacturing	$600,000
Direct labor	5.00	Nonmanufacturing	250,000
Factory overhead	1.00	Total fixed costs	$850,000
Order filling	.75		
Administrative	.25		
Total variable costs per unit	$16.00		

Standard costs and flexible budgets were used. There were no beginning or ending inventories. During 19X2, 97,000 units were produced and sold. The only variances were an unfavorable efficiency variance for direct labor ($15,000) and variable factory overhead ($3,000).

REQUIRED

Prepare two sets of reports: (a) a summary of performance similar to Exhibit 7-4, and (b) a cost control performance report similar to Exhibit 7-5.

7-27. Explanation of variance in income. The Ilima Company had been unable to change its formal records in accordance with more liberal direct-labor efficiency specifications for 19X2. Instead, the company provided for an "expected direct-labor efficiency variance" of $10,000, unfavorable, in its master budget. Expected net income was $60,000, based on expected production and sales of 100,000 units at an average unit contribution margin of $2. Total fixed expenses for the year, budgeted and actual, were $130,000.

Actual results proceeded exactly according to plan until the last quarter of the year, which was marked by a general lull in business conditions plus some weakness in prices. Ilima had to cut selling prices on the final 20,000 units sold by an average of 20¢ per unit without being able to cut unit variable costs. The company scheduled, produced, and sold a total of 92,000 units for the year. There were no beginning or ending inventories.

REQUIRED

Complete the following schedule:

1. Master-budgeted net income	$XXX
2. Actual net income	XXX
Variance to be explained	$XXX
Explained as follows:	
3. Marketing variance (describe fully)	$XXX
4. Other variances, if any (describe fully)	XXX
Total variance explained	$XXX

7-28. Material and labor variances. The standard direct-material allowance for a lighting fixture is one pound per unit. The standard cost per pound is $5. In the month of April, 12,000 pounds of materials (input) were acquired and were used to produce 11,400 fixtures. The actual cost per pound was $5.40.

The standard direct labor allowed to produce one fixture was twenty minutes at an hourly rate of $19. It actually took 4,100 hours to produce the 11,400 fixtures. Because some new workers were used at lower rates, the actual average hourly wage rate was $18.

REQUIRED

1. Compute the price and efficiency variances for direct materials and direct labor.
2. What clues for possible investigation are provided by the variances?

7-29. Straightforward variance analysis. The Kirby Company uses a standard cost system. The month's data regarding its single product follow:

Material purchased and used, 6,700 lb
Direct-labor costs incurred, 11,000 hours, $41,800
Variable overhead costs incurred, $9,500
Finished units produced, 2,000
Actual material cost, $.90 per pound
Variable overhead rate, $.90 per hour
Standard direct-labor cost, $4 per hour
Standard material cost, $1 per pound
Standard pounds of material in a finished unit, 3
Standard direct-labor hours per finished unit, 5

REQUIRED

Prepare schedules of all variances, using the format of Exhibit 7-6.

7-30. Hospital costs. A hospital cafeteria used a flexible budget. The expectation for January volume was 20,000 meals. Hourly paid extra dishwashers were budgeted at $4,000, computed on the basis of an average wage rate of $4 per hour. The following data were compiled for January, when 20,000 meals were actually served and the dishwashers actually worked 1,200 hours:

	ACTUAL	BUDGET	VARIANCE
Dietary department:			
Wages—dishwashers	$4,560	$4,000	$560 U

U = *Unfavorable.*

REQUIRED

1. Compute the price and efficiency variances. What might be some possible reasons for the variances?
2. Suppose 24,000 meals had been served. Compute the price and efficiency variances.

7-31. Direct labor and variable overhead. The Klein Company has a standard cost and flexible-budget system. The condensed results for a recent month were:

	FLEXIBLE-BUDGET VARIANCE	BUDGETED BEHAVIOR PER DIRECT-LABOR HOUR
Indirect labor	$15,000 U	$ 5
Power	4,000 U	2
Lubricants and factory supplies	5,000 F	3
Miscellaneous	3,000 U	2
Total variable overhead	$17,000 U	$12

The scheduled production had been 30,000 units in 25,000 direct-labor hours allowed. However, storm damage resulted in the production of only 26,400 units. The standard wage rate was $18 per hour, which was $2 more than the actual hourly rate. Actual direct-labor hours of input were 24,000.

REQUIRED

1. Prepare a detailed performance report. Show two major sections: direct labor and variable overhead.
2. Using the format of Exhibit 7-6, prepare a summary analysis of price and efficiency variances for direct labor and for the total variable overhead.
3. Explain the differences and similarities between the direct-labor and variable-overhead variances. Describe some likely causes of the overhead variances.

7-32. Variance analysis. The Sheehan Company uses a flexible budget and standard costs. The production manager is responsible for all variances except material price variances, which are the responsibility of the head of the purchasing department. Summarized operating data for the past month are:

Direct material: Purchases 100,000 lbs. @ $8.70. Standard price, $9.00 per lb. Actually used, 90,000 lbs. Standard allowance per unit produced, 1.5 lbs.

Direct labor: Standard allowed per unit of output, 15 minutes. Standard price (rate) for its highly skilled labor per hour, $24. Actual costs, 14,500 hours @ $23.50, or $340,750.

Variable manufacturing overhead: Budget formula is $9.60 per hour. Actual costs, $150,000.

Finished units produced, 54,000.

REQUIRED

1. See the format for Requirement 3 of the solution to the "Summary Problem for Your Review." Using that format, present the price and efficiency variances for material, direct labor, and variable manufacturing overhead.
2. What is the budget allowance for direct labor? Would it be any different if production were 60,000 units?

7-33. **Graphical analysis of direct labor.** An air-conditioning service company uses "mechanics" to rebuild and maintain equipment. It has developed flexible budgets and standards for much of its work. The following partially completed graph displays a recent month's performance of direct labor regarding the jobs subject to these standards:

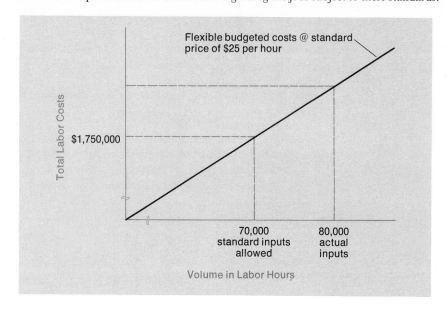

The standard inputs allowed for the actual output achieved were 70,000 hours. The mechanics have a strong union. They earn $30 per hour. Apprentices earn less, and they do some of the same work as the mechanics; thus the average standard price per hour is $25. Because a higher than usual proportion of apprentices worked last month, the actual amounts paid were $23 per hour for a total of 80,000 hours of input, or $1,840,000.

REQUIRED

1. Compute the price and efficiency variances for direct labor.
2. Complete and fully label the graph. Enter and identify the flexible-budget variance, the price variance, and the efficiency variance.

7-34. **Analyzing direct labor.** (CMA.) The Felton Company manufactures a complete line of radios. Because a large number of models have plastic cases, the company has its own molding department for producing the cases. The month of April was devoted to the production of the plastic case for one of the portable radios—Model SX76.

The molding department has two operations—molding and trimming. There is no interaction of labor in these two operations. The standard labor cost for producing ten plastic cases for Model SX76 is as follows:

Molders	.50 hr @ $6 =	$3
Trimmers	.25 hr @ $4 =	1
		$4

During April, 70,000 plastic cases were produced in the molding department. However, 10 percent (7,000) had to be discarded as defective at final inspection. The purchasing department had changed to a new plastic supplier to take advantage of a lower price for comparable plastic. The new plastic turned out to be of a lower quality and resulted in the rejection of completed cases.

Direct-labor hours of input and direct-labor costs charged to the molding department are shown below.

Actual Direct-Labor Costs in the Molding Department

Molders	3,800 hr @ $6.25 =	$23,750
Trimmers	1,600 hr @ $4.15 =	6,640
		$30,390

As a result of poor scheduling by the production scheduling department, the foreman of the molding department had to shift molders to the trimming operation for 200 hours during April. The company paid the molding workers their regular hourly rate even though they were performing a lower-rated task. No significant loss of efficiency was caused by the shift. In addition, the foreman of the department indicated that 75 hours and 35 hours of idle time occurred in the molding and trimming operations, respectively, as a result of unexpected machinery repairs required during the month.

1. The monthly report, which compares actual costs with standard cost of output for the month of April, shows the following labor variance for the molding department:

Actual labor costs for April	$30,390
Standard labor cost of output (63,000 × $4/10)	25,200
Unfavorable labor variance	$ 5,190

This variance is significantly higher than normal, and management would like an explanation. Prepare a detailed analysis of the unfavorable labor variance for the molding department that shows the variance resulting from (1) labor rates, (2) labor substitution, (3) material substitution, (4) operating efficiency, and (5) idle time.

2. The foreman of the molding department is concerned with the large variances charged to his department. He feels that the variances due to labor substitution and change in raw materials should not be charged to his department. Does the foreman have a valid argument? Briefly justify your position.

7-35. Labor variances. The city of Houston has a sign shop where street signs of all kinds are manufactured and repaired. The manager of the shop uses standards to judge performance. However, because a clerk mistakenly discarded some labor records, the manager has only partial data for October. He knows that the total direct-labor variance was $880, favorable, and that the standard labor price was $6 per hour. Moreover, a recent pay raise produced an unfavorable labor price variance for October of $320. The actual hours of input were 1,600.

REQUIRED

1. Find the actual labor price per hour.
2. Determine the standard hours allowed for the output achieved.

7-36. Variable-overhead variances. You have been asked to prepare an analysis of the overhead costs in the billing department of a hospital. As an initial step, you prepare a summary of some events that bear on overhead for the most recent period. The variable-overhead budget variance was $4,000, unfavorable. The standard variable-overhead price per billing was 5¢. Ten bills per hour is regarded as standard productivity per clerk. The total overhead incurred was $168,500, of which $110,000 was fixed. There were no variances for fixed overhead. The variable-overhead price variance was $2,000, favorable.

REQUIRED

Find the following:
1. Variable-overhead efficiency variance.
2. Actual hours of input.
3. Standard hours allowed for output achieved.

7-37. Combined or joint price-quantity variance and incentives. Read the chapter appendix. The Howell Company had an incentive system that rewarded managers each Christmas for cost savings on materials. The manager of purchasing received 10 percent of any favorable price variance accumulated for the fiscal year ending November 30. Similarly, the production manager received 10 percent of the favorable efficiency (quantity) variances. In addition, each manager received 10 percent of the favorable net material variances. Note, however, that all variances were included in the computations—that is, an unfavorable variance in one month would offset a favorable variance in another month.

In the opinion of the company president, this system had worked reasonably well in past years. Of course, because of the sensitivity of the incentive system, the standards were carefully specified and adjusted each quarter. Only minimal inventories were kept at any time. Bonuses had varied from zero to 20 percent of the managers' base salaries. The purchasing manager's base salary for a recent fiscal year ending November 30 was $24,000; the production manager's was $30,000.

The operating results on Material A for a recent month were:

Purchase-price variance	$ 72,000 U
Efficiency variance	36,000 U
Net material variance	$108,000 U

Two pounds of Material A was the standard quantity allowed for every unit of a particular finished product, a chemical used in petroleum refining. One hundred thousand units of the chemical had been manufactured. The average price actually paid for Material A was 30¢ per pound in excess of the standard price.

REQUIRED

1. What number of pounds of Material A was purchased?
2. Find the standard price per pound of Material A.
3. What is the total standard cost allowed for material components of the finished product?
4. As the purchasing manager, what is your opinion of the bonus system? Would your answer be the same if the actual raw-material price paid had been 70¢ per pound? Explain fully.
5. As the production manager, what is your opinion of the bonus system? Why?
6. Why is part of the bonus dependent on the net material variance?
7. Assume that some bonus system tied to variance analysis is maintained. What changes would you recommend?

7-38. Review of major points in chapter. The following questions are based on the data contained in the illustration used in the chapter:

1. Suppose that actual production and sales were 8,000 units instead of 7,000 units. (a) Compute the marketing variance. Is the performance of the marketing function the sole explanation for this variance? Why? (b) Using a flexible budget, compute the budgeted contribution margin, the budgeted operating income, budgeted direct material, and budgeted direct labor.

2. Suppose the following were the actual results for the production of 8,000 units:

Direct material: 42,000 pounds were used at an actual unit price of 56¢, for a total actual cost of $23,520.

Direct labor: 16,500 hours were used at an actual hourly rate of $4.10, for a total actual cost of $67,650.

Compute the flexible-budget variance and the price and efficiency variances for direct materials and direct labor. Present your answers in the form shown in Exhibit 7-6.

3. Suppose the company is organized so that the purchasing manager bears primary responsibility for the acquisition prices of materials, and the production manager bears the primary responsibility for efficiency but no responsibility for unit prices. Assume the same facts as in Requirement 2, except that the purchasing manager acquired 60,000 pounds of materials. This means that there is an ending inventory of 18,000 pounds. Would your variance analysis of materials in Requirement 2 change? Why? Show your computations.

7-39. Review problem on standards and flexible budgets; answers provided. The Kowloon Company makes a variety of leather goods. It uses standard costs and a flexible budget to aid planning and control. Budgeted variable overhead at a 60,000-direct-labor-hour level is $36,000.

During April the company had an unfavorable variable-overhead efficiency variance of $1,200. Material purchases were $322,500. Actual direct-labor costs incurred were $187,600. The direct-labor efficiency variance was $6,000, unfavorable. The actual average wage price was 20¢ lower than the average standard wage price.

The company uses a variable-overhead rate of 20 percent of standard direct-labor *cost* for flexible budgeting purposes. Actual variable overhead for the month was $41,000.

REQUIRED

Compute the following amounts; then use *U* or *F* to indicate whether requested variances are favorable or unfavorable.

1. Standard direct-labor cost per hour.
2. Actual direct-labor hours worked.
3. Total direct-labor price variance.
4. Total flexible budget for direct-labor costs.
5. Total direct-labor variance.
6. Variable-overhead price variance in total.

Answers to Problem 7-39

1. $3. The variable-overhead price is $.60, obtained by dividing $36,000 by 60,000 hours. Therefore the direct-labor price must be $.60 ÷ .20 = $3.

2. 67,000 hours. Actual costs, $187,600 ÷ ($3 − $.20) = 67,000 hours.

3. $13,400 F. 67,000 actual hours × $.20 = $13,400.

4. $195,000. Efficiency variance was $6,000, unfavorable. Therefore, excess hours must have been $6,000 ÷ $3 = 2,000. Consequently, standard hours allowed must be 67,000 − 2,000 = 65,000. Flexible budget = 65,000 × $3 = $195,000.

5. $7,400 F. $195,000 − $187,600 = $7,400 F;   or $13,400 F − $6,000 U = $7,400 F.

6. $800 U.   Flexible budget = 65,000 × $.60 = $39,000.   Total variance = $41,000 − $39,000 = $2,000 U.   Price variance = $2,000 − $1,200 efficiency variance = $800 U.

7-40. Review problem on standards and flexible budgets. The Faber Company uses a flexible budget and standard costs to aid planning and control. At a 60,000-direct-labor-hour level, budgeted variable overhead is $30,000 and budgeted direct labor is $240,000.

The following are some results for August:

Variable-overhead budget variance	$ 12,500 U
Variable-overhead efficiency variance	9,500 U
Actual direct-labor costs incurred	294,000
Material purchase price variance (based on goods purchased)	16,000 F
Material efficiency variance	9,000 U

The standard price per pound of direct material is $1.50. The standard allowance is one pound of direct material for each unit of finished product. Ninety thousand finished units of product were produced during August. There was no beginning or ending work in process. In July the material efficiency variance was $1,000, favorable, and the purchase price variance was 20¢ per pound unfavorable. In August the purchase price variance was 10¢ per pound.

In July labor troubles caused an immense slowdown in the pace of production. There had been an unfavorable direct-labor efficiency variance of $60,000; there was no labor price variance. These troubles had persisted in August—some workers quit. Their replacements had to be hired at higher rates (prices) which had to be extended to all workers. The actual average wage rate in August exceeded the standard average wage rate by 20¢ per hour.

REQUIRED

Establish the following for the month of August:
1. Total pounds of direct material purchased.
2. Total number of pounds of excess material usage.
3. Variable-overhead price variance.
4. Total number of actual hours worked.
5. Total number of standard hours allowed for the finished units produced.

suggested readings

BEYER, R., and D. TRAWICKI, *Profitability Accounting for Planning and Control,* 2nd ed. New York: Ronald Press, 1972. Especially strong in the area of flexible budgeting.

HORNGREN, C., *Cost Accounting: A Managerial Emphasis,* 4th ed. Englewood Cliffs, N.J.: Prentice-Hall, Inc., 1977.

VARIATIONS OF COST BEHAVIOR PATTERNS

learning objectives

When you have finished studying this chapter, you should be able to:

1. Distinguish between committed and discretionary fixed costs and between engineered and discretionary variable costs.
2. Define **work measurement** and identify its objective.
3. Use the engineered-cost approach to compute the flexible-budget cost and the budget variance for a given expense.
4. Describe the basic ideas of zero-based budgeting.
5. Identify the two major assumptions on which the determination of cost behavior patterns is usually based.
6. Identify each of the elements in the mathematical formula for a linear-cost function.
7. Identify the two principal criteria for accepting and using a particular cost function.
8. Use the high-low method for measuring the fixed and variable elements of a mixed cost.

When we refer to **cost behavior patterns,** we generally mean the relationship of total costs to changes in the volume of activity. Until this chapter, we have concentrated on two basic linear-cost behavior patterns: variable and fixed. Now we shall examine some variations of these patterns that have proven helpful for planning and control. Then we shall explore the problem of how to determine cost behavior patterns so that useful predictions and evaluations may be made.

Engineered, discretionary, and committed costs

During the 1960s, a classification of costs evolved as follows:

FIXED COSTS:	VARIABLE COSTS:
Committed Discretionary	Engineered Discretionary*

Only a few variable costs belong in the discretionary classification, as explained below.

We shall describe these types of costs, beginning with **committed fixed costs.**

☐ FIXED COSTS AND CAPACITY

Fixed costs, also called *capacity costs,* measure the cost of providing the capability to operate at a particular capacity for such activities as manufacturing, sales, administration, and research. They reflect the capability for sustaining a planned volume of activity.

The size of fixed costs is influenced by long-run marketing conditions, technology, and the methods and strategies of management. Examples of the methods and strategies of management include sales salaries versus sales commissions and one-shift versus two-shift operations. Fixed costs are often the result of a trade-off decision whereby lower variable costs are attained in exchange for higher fixed costs. For example, automatic equipment may be acquired by banks, post offices, or hospitals to reduce labor costs.

Generally, a heavier proportion of fixed to variable costs lessens management's ability to respond to short-run changes in economic conditions and opportunities. Still, unwillingness to incur fixed costs reveals an aversion to risk that may exclude a company from profitable ventures. For instance, the launching of new products often requires very large fixed costs for research, advertising, equipment, and working capital.

☐ COMMITTED FIXED COSTS

For planning and control, fixed costs may be usefully subdivided into committed and discretionary categories. Committed fixed costs consist largely of those fixed costs that arise from the possession of plant, of equipment, and of a basic organization. Examples are depreciation, property taxes, rent, insurance, and the salaries of key personnel. These costs are affected primarily by long-run sales forecasts that, in turn, indicate the long-run capacity needs.

The behavior of committed fixed costs may best be viewed by assuming a zero volume of activity in an enterprise that fully expects to resume normal activity (for example, during a strike or a shortage of materials that forces a complete shutdown of activity). The committed fixed costs are all those organization and plant costs that continue to be incurred and that cannot be reduced without injuring the organization's competence to meet long-range goals. Committed fixed costs are the least responsive of the fixed costs, because they tend to be less affected by month-to-month and year-to-year decisions.

In planning, the focus is on the impact of these costs over a number of years. Such planning usually requires tailoring the capacity to future demand for the organization's products in the most economical manner. For example, should the store size be 50,000 square feet, or 80,000, or 100,000? Should the gasoline station have one, or two, or more stalls for servicing automobiles? Such decisions usually involve selecting the point of optimal trade-off between present and future operating costs. That is, constructing excess capacity now may save costs in the long run, because construction costs per square foot may be much higher later. On the other hand, if the forecast demand never develops, the organization may have to bear the costs of owning facilities that are idle.

These decisions regarding capital expenditures are generally shown in an annual budget called the *capital budget* or *capital-spending budget*. As you recall, the *master budget* is based primarily on the annual sales forecast, the cornerstone of budgeting. Similarly, all capital-spending decisions are ultimately based on long-range sales forecasts. Capital budgeting is discussed in Chapter 11.

Once buildings are constructed and equipment is installed, little can be done in day-to-day operations to affect the *total level* of committed costs. From a control standpoint, the objective is usually to increase current utilization of facilities, because this will ordinarily increase net income.

There is another aspect to the control problem, however. A follow-up, or audit, is needed to find out how well the ensuing utilization harmonizes with the decision that authorized the facilities in the first place. The latter approach helps management to evaluate the wisdom of its past long-range decisions and, in turn, should improve the quality of future decisions.

☐ DISCRETIONARY FIXED COSTS

Discretionary fixed costs (sometimes called **managed** or **programmed costs**) are fixed costs (a) that arise from periodic (usually yearly) **budget appropriation** decisions that directly reflect top-management policies regarding the maximum permissible amounts to be incurred, and (b) that do not have a demonstrable optimum relationship between inputs (as measured by the costs) and outputs (as measured by sales, services, or production). Discretionary costs may have no particular relation to volume of activity. Examples vary among organizations and include child day-care services, staging an opera, research and development, advertising, sales promotion, charitable donations, management consulting services, and many employee-training programs. Conceivably, such costs could be reduced almost entirely for a given year in dire times, whereas the committed costs would be much more difficult to reduce.

Discretionary fixed costs are decided upon by management at the start of the budget period. Goals are selected, the means for their attainment are chosen, the maximum expense to be incurred is specified, and the total amount to be spent is appropriated. For example, a state government may appropriate $5 million for an advertising campaign to encourage tourism. In the give-and-take process of preparing the master budget, the discretionary costs are the most likely to be revised.

Discretionary fixed costs represent an assortment of manufacturing, selling, administrative, and research items. For example, a large portion of discretionary fixed costs may consist of salaries for sales personnel, accountants, clerks, and engineers, and often appear in the income statement lumped under the heading "General Selling and Administrative Expense." As in the case of committed costs, the resources acquired should be carefully planned and fully utilized if net income is to be maximized. Unlike committed costs, discretionary costs can be influenced more easily from period to period. It is also harder to measure the utilization of resources acquired via discretionary costs, principally because the results of services such as creative personnel, advertising, research, and training programs are much more difficult to isolate and quantify than the results of utilizing plants and equipment to make products.

The behavior of some discretionary fixed costs is easy to delineate. Advertising, research, donations, and training programs, for example, are usually formulated with certain objectives in mind. The execution of such projects is measured by comparing total expenditures with the appropriation. Because the tendency is to spend the entire budget appropriation, the resulting dollar variances are generally trivial. But planning is far more important than this kind of day-to-day control. The perfect execution of an advertising program—in the sense that the full amount authorized was spent in specified media at predetermined times—will be fruitless if the advertisements are unimaginative and lifeless and if they reach the wrong audience.

The most noteworthy aspect of discretionary fixed costs is that, unlike most other costs, they are not subject to ordinary engineering input-output analysis. For example, an optimum relationship between inputs and outputs can be specified for direct materials because it takes three pounds or five gallons or two square feet to make a finished product. In contrast, we are usually unsure of the "correct" amount of advertising, research, management training, donations, management consulting costs, police protection, and programs for health care, education, or consumer protection.

The U.S. Department of Education can quantify the inputs (for example, the amount spent on planning, research, and evaluation and on writing regulations), but the outputs and the relation between inputs and outputs are harder to quantify. Systems can be designed to ensure that the research and the regulations are concerned with the subjects deemed most important by the decision makers, but there is no convincing way of knowing how much is enough in any absolute sense.

☐ ENGINEERED AND DISCRETIONARY VARIABLE COSTS

An engineered cost is any cost that has an explicit, specified physical relationship with a selected measure of activity. Most variable costs fit this classification. An "engineered" variable cost exists when an optimum relationship between inputs and outputs has been carefully determined by work-measurement techniques, which are described below. In fact, **efficiency** has been defined as just such an optimum relationship. For example, an automobile may have exact specifications: one battery, one radiator, two fan belts, and so forth. Direct material and direct labor are prime examples of engineered costs.

Many managers and accountants tend to use "variable cost" and "engineered cost" interchangeably, as if they were syonymous. Usually, this error is harmless. However, as noted at the start of the chapter, although most variable costs are engineered, some fit a discretionary classification; depending on management policy, other costs may go up and down with sales (or production) merely because management has predetermined that the organization can afford to spend a certain percentage of the sales dollar for items such as research, donations, and advertising. Such discretionary costs would have a graphical pattern of variability, but not for the same reasons as direct materials or direct labor. An increase in these costs may be due to management's authorization to spend "because we can afford it" rather than to an engineered cause-and-effect relationship between such costs and sales.

Engineered versus discretionary costs

□ WORK MEASUREMENT FOR CONTROL

Work measurement is the careful analysis of a task, its size, the methods used in its performance, and its efficiency. Its objective is to determine the workload in an operation and the number of employees necesary to perform that work efficiently.

The work-measurement approach is based on a fundamental premise: Permanent improvement in any performance is impossible unless the work is measured. The premise is a natural accompaniment for the definition of *efficiency*, which is an optimal relationship between inputs and outputs. Therefore, to know whether efficiency exists, we must have some quantification of both inputs and outputs.

□ ORIGINS OF WORK MEASUREMENT

Work-measurement techniques were initially developed for planning and control of manufacturing rather than of nonmanufacturing activities. This occurred because inputs and ouputs in the manufacturing areas are easier to identify and measure. The measurement of direct material consumed and finished units produced is straightforward. It is much more difficult to obtain a measurement for relating the inputs of advertising and sales promotion activity to the outputs of sales or contribution margins.

As the input-output relationships become less defined, management tends to abandon any formal work-measurement techniques and, instead, relies almost wholly on the individual and his or her supervisor for sucessful control. Consequently, the role of physical observation is paramount and formal cost control is approached from a discretionary-cost rather than from an engineered-cost (work-measurement) viewpoint, especially in many areas of nonmanufacturing. However, despite the difficulties of implementation, work measurement is getting more attention from nonmanufacturing organizations as they seek to improve their efficiency.

In recent years, work measurement has been extended into nonprofit organizations as well as into the selling and administrative clerical areas of profit-seeking organizations. In fact, federal government agencies are heavy users of work measurement in such diverse areas as the auditing of income tax returns, the processing of social security checks, and the sorting of mail.

☐ CONTROL-FACTOR UNITS

The specific techniques used to measure the work include time and motion study, observation of a random sample of the work (work sampling), and the estimation, by a work-measurement analyst and a line supervisor, of the amount of time required for the work (time analysis).

The workload is often expressed in **control-factor units,** which are used in formulating the budget. For example, the control-factor units in a payroll department might include operations performed on time cards, on notices of change in the labor rate, on notices of employee promotion, on new employment and termination reports, and on routine weekly and monthly reports. All of these would be timed. The estimated workload would then be used for determining the required labor force and budgetary allowance.

Examples of other operations and appropriate control-factor units include:

Operation	Unit of measure (control-factor unit)
Billing	Lines per hour
Warehouse labor	Pounds or cases handled per day
Packing	Pieces packed per hour
Posting accounts receivable	Postings per hour
Mailing	Pieces mailed per hour

☐ THE ENGINEERED-COST APPROACH

There is much disagreement about how clerical costs should be controlled. Advocates of work measurement favor a more rigorous approach, which essentially regards these costs as engineered. In practice, a discretionary-fixed-cost approach is more often found.

Assume that ten payroll clerks are employed by a government agency, and that each clerk's operating efficiency *should be* the processing of the payroll records of 500 employees per month. This might be called the *perfection standard* for the work. In the month of June, the payroll records of 4,700 individuals were processed by these ten clerks. Each clerk earns $1,800 per month.

The engineered-cost approach to this situation is to base the budget formula on the unit cost of the individual pay record processed: $1,800 ÷ 500 records, or $3.60. Therefore the budget allowance for payroll-clerk labor would be $3.60 × 4,700, or $16,920. Assume that the ten employees worked throughout the month. The performance report on the top of the next page would be prepared (*U* means unfavorable).

Essentially, two decisions must be made in this operation. The first is a policy decision: How many clerks do we need? How flexible should we be? How divisible is the task? Should we use part-time help? Should we hire and fire as the volume of work fluctuates? The implication of these questions is that once

	ACTUAL COST	FLEXIBLE BUDGET: TOTAL STANDARD INPUTS ALLOWED FOR ACTUAL OUTPUT PRODUCED	BUDGET VARIANCE
	(10 × $1,800)	(4,700 × $3.60)	
Payroll-clerk labor	$18,000	$16,920	$1,080 U

the hiring decision is made, the total costs incurred can be predicted easily—$18,000 in our example.

The second decision concentrates on day-to-day control, on how efficiently the given resources are being utilized. The work-measurement approach is an explicit and formal attempt to measure the utilization of resources by

1. Assuming a proportionately variable budget and the complete divisibility of the workload into small units.

2. Generating a budget variance that assumes a comparison of actual costs with the perfection standard—the cost that would be incurred if payroll-clerk labor could be turned on and off like a faucet. In this case, the variance of $1,080 informs management that there was overstaffing. The workload capability was 5,000 pay records, not the 4,700 actually processed. The extra cost of $1,080 resulted from operating in a way that does not attain the lowest possible cost. The $1,080 might also be considered as the amount that management is currently investing to provide stability in the work force.

Critics of work measurement will often assert that such a formal approach is not worth its cost because strong labor unions and other forces prevent managers from fine-tuning the size of the work force. Defenders of work measurement will respond that managers must know the costs of various labor policies. For instance, if the cost of overstaffing becomes exorbitant, the pertinent provisions in a labor contract may become key bargaining issues when the contract is about to be renewed.

☐ THE DISCRETIONARY-FIXED-COST APPROACH

Work-measurement techniques are not used in the vast majority of organizations. Consequently, the tendency is to rely on the experience of the department head and his or her superior for judging the size of the work force needed to carry out the department's functions. There is a genuine reluctance to overhire because there is a corresponding slowness in discharging or laying off people when volume slackens. As a result, temporary peak loads are often met by hiring temporary workers or by having the regular employees work overtime.

In most cases, the relevant range of activity during the budget period can be predicted with assurance, and the work force needed for the marketing and administrative functions can readily be determined. If management refuses, consciously or unconsciously, to control costs in rigid accordance with short-run fluctuations in activity, these costs become discretionary—that is, their total amount is relatively fixed and unresponsive to short-run variations in volume.

The practical effects of the discretionary-fixed-cost approach are that the budgeted costs and the actual costs tend to be very close, so that resulting budget variances are small. Follow-ups to see that the available resources are being fully and efficiently utilized are regarded as the managers' responsibility, a duty that can be carried through by face-to-face control and by records of physical quantities (for example, pounds handled per day in a warehouse, pieces mailed per hour in a mailing room) that do not have to be formally integrated into the accounting records in dollar terms.

Hence there is a conflict between common practice and the objective of work measurement, which is to treat most costs as engineered and to therefore subject them to short-range management control. The moral is that management's attitudes and its planning and controlling decisions often determine whether a cost is discretionary fixed or engineered variable. A change in policy can transform a budgeted fixed cost into a budgeted variable cost, and vice versa.

In sum, the two approaches may be compared as in Exhibit 8-1. The graphs there provide an overview of how differing philosophies of budgeting and control may be adopted for a cost that has *the same underlying behavior pattern*.

☐ CHOOSING AMONG CONTROL SYSTEMS

As we have just seen, costs may be divided for planning and control purposes as follows:

TYPE OF COST	MAJOR CONTROL TECHNIQUES	TIME SPAN AND FEEDBACK
Engineered	Flexible budgets and standards	Short
Discretionary	Physical observation and budget negotiation	Longer
Committed	Capital budgeting[1]	Longest

From time to time, you will undoubtedly find these distinctions among engineered, discretionary, and committed costs to be useful. However, these are subjective decisions, so expect some ambiguity as to whether a given cost is, say, committed or discretionary. For example, the salaries of supervisory or other highly prized personnel that would be kept on the payroll at zero activity levels are often regarded as committed costs; but some organizations may classify them as discretionary costs. Arguments about whether such types of costs should be classified as committed or discretionary are a waste of time—these matters must be settled on a case-by-case basis. In a given organization, quick agreement regarding an appropriate classification is usually possible.

The section on work measurement illustrates the overall theme of this book regarding control systems. Two alternative systems have been *described*, but note that one is not *advocated* here as being superior to the other. Such judgments can safely be made only in the specific circumstances facing a given organization.

Although a particular *system* has not been advocated here, a *method for*

[1]Discussed in Chapters 11 and 12.

EXHIBIT
8-1

	BUDGET AS AN ENGINEERED VARIABLE COST	BUDGET AS A DISCRETIONARY FIXED COST
Actual cost incurred	$18,000	$18,000
Budget allowance	16,920*	18,000
Variance	1,080 U	0

*Rate = $18,000 ÷ 5,000 records, or $3.60 per record; total = 4,700 records @ $3.60 = $16,920.

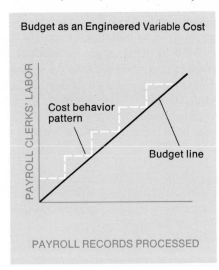

Budget as an Engineered Variable Cost

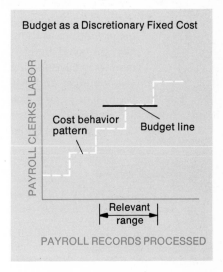

Budget as a Discretionary Fixed Cost

choosing among the systems is favored. Essentially, it is the cost-benefit method. That is, the manager or systems designer should assess (1) the expected benefits from, say, a proposed clerical work-measurement system in the form of a better collective set of operating behavior or decisions against (2) the expected costs of a more formal system, including behavioral costs and the costs of educating employees.

Budgeting of discretionary fixed costs

☐ BUDGETING AS ONGOING PROCEDURE

Because managers of all organizations are unsure about what amount for a discretionary cost is "correct" or "right" or "optimum," they frequently rely on industry or company tradition or custom for deciding on a budgeted amount. For example, a lump sum of 2 percent of last year's sales may be appropriated for the forthcoming year's research budget.

By definition, discretionary costs are not subject to scientific input-output analysis. Nevertheless, managers have attempted to pinpoint relative priorities. For instance, some organizations ask their managers to specify the activities that would be added or cut back if the budgetary allowance were increased or decreased, respectively. This ploy requires the manager to conduct more than the superficial analysis that often accompanies the budgetary ritual.

A hallmark of the evolution of management accounting systems has been the tendency to subject an increasing number of cost categories to work measurement or some type of more formal scrutiny. For example, some discretionary costs such as clerical costs are transformed into engineered costs.

Consider another example of trying to improve budgeting. From time to time, catchy words and phrases arise to describe new budgeting techniques or variations of old ones. An example is **zero-based budgeting,** which arose as a response to the problems of controlling discretionary costs and which refers to the practice of having a manager justify his or her department's activities from the ground up as though they were being initiated for the first time. Traditionally, proposed budgets have been justified on an incremental basis. That is, managers have tended to prepare new budgets in terms of changes from last year's budget and results. In contrast, zero-based budgeting gets back to the bedrock questions such as why does this activity or department exist and what are or should be its goals or objectives.

Zero-based budgeting has been receiving increased attention in non-profit organizations:

> Zero-based budgeting is especially adaptable to discretionary cost areas in which service and support are the primary outputs. It is this characteristic that has attracted the interest of governmental officials, as most expenditures of government can be classified as discretionary in nature.[2]

☐ EXPERIENCE TO DATE

Zero-based budgeting has been adopted by at least twelve state governments. The general idea is for low-level managers to construct alternative budgets for each activity. These alternatives are combined into so-called decision packages.

One alternative says what would occur if the activity were simply eliminated. Another alternative explains how the agency would adapt to a budget cut. Other alternatives indicate what will be achieved with the existing budget and with extra money if supplied.

Charles Travis, the Texas governor's budget chief, has commented on the advantages of zero-based budgeting: "The system itself doesn't save money. What it does is provide better information for the decision makers."[3] The Georgia study[4] cited the same advantage plus two others: (1) more careful planning before the budget itself is prepared and (2) increased involvement of lower-level personnel in the state's budgetary process.

The biggest disadvantage is the cost of zero-based budget preparation in terms of time and effort. For example, a proposed study of one portion of the Federal Elementary and Secondary Education Act will last seven years and cost $7 million during the first year alone. Thus, in some organizations the costs may exceed any expected benefits.

---

[2]See G. Minmier and R. Hermanson, "A Look at Zero Base Budgeting—The Georgia Experience," *Atlanta Economic Review,* 26, No. 4 (July-August 1976), 6. The practice originally arose in Texas Instruments Company. For elaboration of procedures and descriptions, see Peter A. Phyrr, "Zero-Base Budgeting," *Harvard Business Review,* November-December 1970, pp. 111–21.

[3]"Zero-Based Budgeting," *U.S. News & World Report,* September 20, 1976, p. 80.

[4]Minmier and Hermanson, "The Georgia Experience," p. 11.

Is complete zero-based budgeting on an annual basis a feasible way to plan? Many critics think that such a traumatic, costly analysis is desirable every five or six years, but not every year. Accordingly, some states (including Colorado and Florida) have passed "sunset laws" that provide a termination date for each state regulatory agency. As the date approaches, a performance review is conducted to determine whether the agency's life should be extended.

Determining how costs behave

☐ MAJOR ASSUMPTIONS

Before costs can be classified and appropriately controlled, managers must be familiar with how the costs in question behave. As we know, costs often do not fit snugly into strictly variable and strictly fixed categories. Instead, there are a variety of *cost behavior patterns,* more technically described as *cost functions.* A **cost function** is a relationship between two or more variables. The dependent variable is frequently denoted as *y* (for example, some measure of total cost of repairs); the independent variable, as *x* (for example, some measure of activity or volume of inputs or outputs). The problem facing the accountant or manager is frequently called **cost estimation** or **cost approximation,** which is the attempt to specify some underlying relation between *x* and *y* over a stipulated *relevant range* of *x* that may be of interest. That is, given any quantification of the independent variable *x* (e.g., total miles driven), how much will the dependent variable *y* be (e.g., total repair costs)?

In practice, such cost approximations are typically based on two major simplifying and often heroic assumptions:

1. The cost function is linear over the relevant range. This straight-line approximation is often regarded as sufficiently precise for most decision uses.
2. The "true" cost behavior can be sufficiently explained by one independent variable (miles driven) instead of more than one (miles driven, weather, weight carried, model year of the vehicle, and so forth).

☐ FOCUS ON COSTS AND BENEFITS

As this book has stressed, whether these simplifying assumptions are justified is a cost-benefit question to be answered on a situation-by-situation basis. The manager tends to rely on exceedingly rough approximations until he or she realizes that buying finer cost estimation models may lead to net collective benefits from more desirable operating decisions.

To summarize, given assumptions of linearity and of one independent variable, each item of cost has some underlying "true" behavior pattern, whose expected value, $E(y)$, has the form:

$$E(y) = A + Bx$$

where A and B are the true (but unknown) parameters. (A **parameter** is a constant, such as A, or a coefficient, such as B, in a model or system of equations.)

Working with historical data, the cost analyst usually develops a formula approximation of the underlying relationship:

$$y' = a + bx$$

where y' is the calculated value as distinguished from the observed value y, and a and b are the approximations of the true A and B.

☐ CRITERIA FOR CHOOSING FUNCTIONS

The critical tasks in choosing among possible cost functions are to approximate the appropriate slope coefficient (defined as the amount of increase in y for each unit increase in x) and the constant or intercept (defined as the value of y when x is zero). The cost function is determined on the basis of some plausible theory that supports the relationships between the dependent and the independent variable—not on the basis of sample observations alone. There are many variables that move together and are therefore referred to as being highly *correlated*. But no conclusions about causes and effects are warranted. For instance, studies have shown a high positive correlation between teachers' salaries and liquor consumption. There are also many teacher members of Alcoholics Anonymous, but no cause-and-effect relationships have been demonstrated.

The following criteria should help in obtaining accurate approximations of cost functions:

1. *Economic plausibility.* The relationship must be credible. Physical observation, when it is possible, probably provides the best evidence of a relationship. The engineered-cost approach described earlier is an example of heavy reliance on observed technical relationships between inputs and outputs.

2. *Goodness of fit.* The cost analyst uses tests of closeness of fit for personal reassurance about the choice of a plausible cost function. Such tests, which are briefly described later, may be limited to scatter diagrams or may entail full-fledged formal statistical **regression analysis.**[5]

Note especially that both of these criteria are used together in choosing a cost function; each is a check on the other. Knowledge of both cost accounting and operations is helpful. For example, repairs are often made when output is low because the machines can be taken out of service at these times. Therefore, if repair costs were recorded as each repair was made, scatter diagrams and regression analysis would show repair costs declining as output increased, whereas engineers know that the *timing* of the repair is often discretionary—the true cause-and-effect relationship is a tendency for many repair costs to increase (perhaps in steplike fashion) as activity increases. Consequently, these costs

[5]In the latter case, so-called specification analysis is also conducted to be sure that certain assumptions are satisfied. Then the sample values a and b are the best available estimates of the population values A and B. For an expanded discussion, see C. Horngren, *Cost Accounting: A Managerial Emphasis,* 4th ed. (Englewood Cliffs, N.J.: Prentice-Hall, 1977), Chap. 25.

should be analyzed separately; otherwise the true extent of variability of costs with output will be masked.[6]

Note too how criteria 1 and 2 interrelate. For example, a clerical overhead cost may show a high correlation with the number of records processed and an even higher correlation with the number of factory machine-hours worked. Our knowledge of operations confirms the first relationship; in contrast, there is a less convincing theoretical basis for the second.

□ VARIETY OF COST FUNCTIONS

To illustrate the major types of cost functions, we now examine the corresponding graphic solutions to the basic formula: $y' = a + bx$.

A *proportionately variable cost* is the classical variable cost that we introduced in Chapter 2. Its total fluctuates in direct proportion to changes in x:

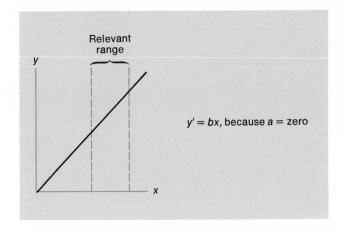

Relevant range

y

$y' = bx$, because a = zero

x

A *fixed cost* does not fluctuate in total as x changes within the relevant range:

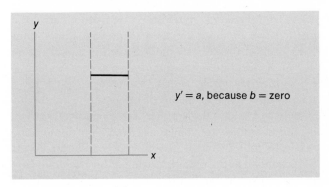

y

$y' = a$, because b = zero

x

A *mixed* or *semivariable cost* is a combination of variable and fixed elements. That is, its total fluctuates as x changes within the relevant range, but not in direct proportion. Instead, its behavior accords with the basic formula:

[6]George J. Benston, "Multiple Regression Analysis of Cost Behavior," *Accounting Review*, 41, No. 4, 663.

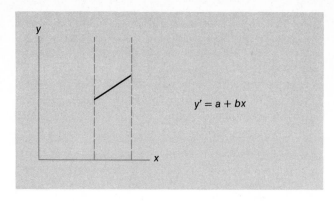

A *step-function* cost is nonlinear because of the breaks in its behavior pattern:

There would be three cost approximations, depending on the place within the relevant range:
$y' = a, y'_2 = a_2, y'_3 = a_3$

☐ METHODS OF LINEAR APPROXIMATION

There are many methods of approximating cost functions, including (a) *the industrial engineering method,* (b) *account analysis,* (c) *high-low points,* (d) *visual fit,* (e) *simple regression,* and (f) *multiple regression.* These methods are not mutually exclusive; frequently, two or more are used to prevent major blunders. In many organizations, each of these six methods is used in succession over the years as the need for more accurate approximations becomes evident.

The *industrial engineering method,* sometimes called the *analytic method,* searches for the most efficient means of obtaining wanted output. It entails a systematic review of materials, supplies, labor, support services, and facilities. Time and motion studies are sometimes used. Any input-output relationship that is physically observable is an obvious candidate for the engineering method. For example, in the manufacturing of bicycles, one handlebar and two wheels are needed per bicycle. But the engineering method is of little help when relationships are infeasible or impossible to observe on an individual cost basis. Examples are relationships between various overhead costs and output. Then other methods come to the fore.

In *account analysis,* the analyst proceeds through the detailed ledger accounts, one by one, and classifies each into one of two categories, variable or fixed. In so doing, analysts may use their past experience intuitively and nothing else. More likely, they will at least study how total costs behave over a few periods before making judgments.

An examination of the accounts is obviously a necessary first step, no matter whether cost functions are approximated by means of simple inspection of the accounts or by multiple regression. Familiarity with the data is needed to avoid the analytical pitfalls that abound in regression analysis.

A major disadvantage of the account classification method is its inherent subjectivity. The *high-low* method is slightly less subjective because at least it employs a series of samples and relies on two of their results, the highest cost and the lowest cost. It will be illustrated in a subsequent section.

The *visual-fit, simple-regression,* and *multiple-regression* methods have a distinct advantage because all sample points are used in determining the cost function. A visual fit is applied by drawing a straight line through the cost points on a scatter diagram, which consists of a plotting on a graph of individual dots that represent various experienced costs at various activity levels. The line in Exhibit 8-2 could have been fitted visually.

There are no objective tests to ensure that the line fitted visually is the most accurate representation of the underlying data. Consequently, regression analysis is a more systematic approach.[7] Under certain assumptions, it has measures of probable error. Regression analysis refers to the measurement of the average amount of change in one variable (e.g., shipping cost) that is associated with unit increases in the amounts of one or more other variables. When only two variables are studied (e.g., shipping costs in relation to units shipped), the analysis is called *simple regression;* when more than two variables are studied (e.g., shipping costs in relation to units shipped and to the weight of those units shipped), it is called *multiple regression.*[8]

Approximating a cost function

□ MIXED COSTS

We have previously discussed the nature of the proportionately variable cost, the fixed cost, and the step-function cost, so this section will concentrate on the *mixed cost* (often called *semivariable cost*). Exhibit 8-2 gives a closer look at a mixed cost. The fixed portion is usually the result of *providing* the capability to operate at a particular capacity, whereas the variable portion is the result of *using* the available capacity. For example, a copy-making machine often has a fixed monthly rental plus a variable cost based on the copies produced. Other examples include costs of rented trucks, power, telephone, repairs and maintenance, clerks, accountants, and janitors.

Ideally, there should be no accounts for mixed costs. All such costs should be subdivided into two accounts, one for the variable portion and one for the fixed portion. In practice, these distinctions are rarely made in the recording process, because of the difficulty of analyzing day-to-day cost data into variable and fixed sections. Costs such as power, indirect labor, repairs, and maintenance

[7]For elaboration, see Horngren, *Cost Accounting,* Chap. 25.
[8]For elaboration, see Benston, "Multiple Regression Analysis of Cost Behavior," pp. 657–72.

EXHIBIT 8-2. Mixed cost

are generally accounted for in total. It is typically very difficult to decide, as such costs are incurred, whether a particular invoice or work ticket represents a variable or fixed item. Moreover, even if it were possible to make such distinctions, the advantages might not be worth the additional clerical effort and costs. Whenever cost classifications are too refined, the perpetual problem of getting accurate source documents is intensified.

In sum, mixed costs are merely a blend of two unlike cost behavior patterns; they do not entail new conceptual approaches. Anybody who obtains a working knowledge of the planning and controlling of variable and fixed costs, separately, can adapt to a mixed-cost situation when necessary.

In practice, where a report is divided into two main cost classifications, variable and fixed, mixed costs tend to be included in the variable category even though they may not have purely variable behavior. At first glance, such arbitrary classification may seem undesirable and misleading. However, within a particular organization, the users of the reports usually have an intimate knowledge of the fundamental characteristics of the cost in question. Therefore they can temper their interpretation accordingly.

☐ BUDGETING MIXED COSTS

How should mixed costs be budgeted? Sometimes it is relatively easy to separate the cost into its fixed and variable elements. For example, the rental for a leased computer or photographic reproduction machine may be subdivided:

Photocopying costs—variable @ 3¢ per copy	xxxx
Photocopying costs—fixed @ $200 per month	xxxx

Alternatively, a flexible budget may be prepared that contains a single-line item:

Photocopying costs ($200 per month
  plus 3¢ per copy)

XXXX	XXXX	XXXX

Other mixed costs are harder to analyze: For example, how do repairs and maintenance, indirect factory labor, clerical labor, and miscellaneous overhead relate to decisions concerning changes in general volume of work in the form of more sales, more inquiries, more telephone calls, more letters, and so forth? The relationships are often hazy and difficult to pinpoint in any systematic way. Still, the decision makers want to know how these costs are affected by volume so that they can weigh their operating alternatives more intelligently.

☐ DATA FOR ILLUSTRATION

The city of Northvale operates several municipal golf courses that require varying maintenance attention, depending on the season of the year. The assistant city manager has begun to collect data on the cost of repairing the various types of power equipment used (for example, golf carts and power lawn mowers). She is concerned because repairs have been billed individually by an outside firm as each piece of equipment fails to perform. She is considering various alternatives, including buying a service contract for a flat fee or creating her own equipment repair department.

    To date she has compiled the following data:

	GROUNDSKEEPER LABOR-HOURS (x)	REPAIR EXPENSE (y)
August	2,200	$2,300
September	2,300	2,500
October	1,900	2,000
November	1,200	2,000
December	1,200	2,000
January	900	1,500
February	700	1,400
March	1,100	1,400
April	1,400	1,600

She realizes that much more data should be gathered before jumping to conclusions about how costs behave. She also wishes that more detailed classifications were available (for example, by acreage in specific golf courses, by types and age of equipment, and perhaps by number of rounds played at each course). But she has decided to use the above data as a start.

☐ ANALYSIS OF GRAPHS

The first graph in Exhibit 8-3 is a scatter diagram of the preceding data. The analyst should scrutinize the data to see whether a strong relationship exists between the costs of repair and groundskeeper labor-hours. Also, the analyst uses the scatter diagram as a key to deciding whether the relationship can be

EXHIBIT 8-3

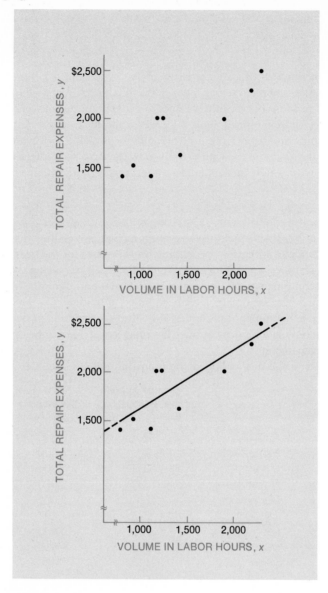

followed sufficiently closely by a *linear* approximation—that is, a straight line fitted through the dots.

The second graph in Exhibit 8-3 shows the straight line that has been fitted by the *statistical method of least squares,* which is described in more detail in the appendix to this chapter. The formula for the straight line is:

$$y' = a + bx$$

$$y' = \$983 + \$.609x$$

That is, repair costs fluctuate over the relevant range of 700 to 2,300 hours at a rate of $983 per month plus $.609 per labor-hour.

☐ FOCUS ON RELEVANT RANGE

The line in Exhibit 8-3 is extended backward from the relevant range to inter-sect the y-axis at $983. The extension is deliberately shown as a dashed line to emphasize the focus on the relevant range. The manager is concerned with how costs behave within the relevant range, not with how they behave at zero vol-ume. Therefore the $983 intercept must be kept in perspective. It is often called a fixed cost, but it is really a fixed or constant component of the formula that provides the best available linear approximation of how a mixed cost behaves within the relevant range. The manager is ordinarily not concerned about cost behavior at extremely low or high volumes.

☐ USE OF HIGH-LOW METHOD

The high-low method uses two observations rather than all the observations for constructing the line. A high representative point (rather than an "outlier" that seems nonrepresentative) and a low representative point are chosen. The result-ant line is extended back to intersect the vertical axis. The intercept becomes the "fixed" portion and the slope becomes the "variable" portion of the formula for the mixed cost.

The same results can be achieved via algebra:

	LABOR-HOURS (x)	REPAIR EXPENSE (y)
High (h)	2,300	$2,500
Low (l)	700	1,400
Difference	1,600	$1,100

$$\text{variable rate} = \frac{y_h - y_l}{x_h - x_l} = \frac{\$1,100}{1,600} = \$.6875 \text{ per labor-hour}$$

fixed overhead component = total mixed cost less variable component

$$\text{at } x_h = \$2,500 - \$.6875(2,300)$$
$$= \$2,500 - \$1,581 = \$919$$

or

$$\text{at } x_l = \$1,400 - \$.6875(700)$$
$$= \$1,400 - \$481 = \$919$$

Therefore,

mixed-cost formula = $919 per month plus $.6875 per labor-hour

Compare this high-low formula with the least-squares formula, which was $983 per month plus $.609 per labor-hour. At a 1,000-hour level of volume, cost predictions would be:

high-low formula: . $919 + $.6875(1,000) = $1,606.50

least-squares formula: $983 + $.609(1,000) = $1,592.00

In this illustration, the differences seem too small to have any influence on decisions. However, the high-low method is statistically inefficient. For example, if 40 data points were available, the high-low would use only 2 and disregard the other 38. Because of the danger of relying on extreme points, which may not be representative of normal situations, the high-low method is not recommended.

EXHIBIT 8-4

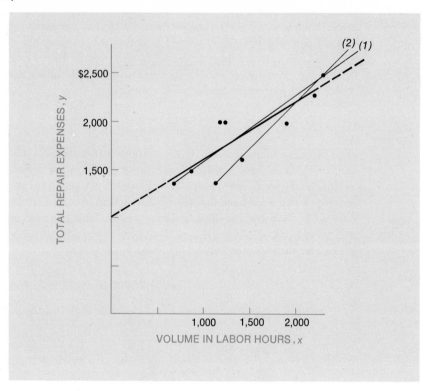

☐ UNRELIABILITY OF HIGH-LOW METHOD

The graph in Exhibit 8-4 shows the unreliability of the high-low method. The graph is merely the second one of Exhibit 8-3, which showed a least-squares line fitted to the data, plus two high-low lines, marked as (1) and (2). High-low line (1) is the one we just computed algebraically. High-low line (2) is based on the choice of the alternative low point in the data:

	LABOR-HOURS (x)	REPAIR EXPENSES (y)
High (h)	2,300	$2,500
Low (l)	1,100	1,400
Difference	1,200	$1,100

$$\text{variable rate} = \frac{y_h - y_l}{x_h - x_l} = \frac{\$1,100}{1,200} = \$.9167 \text{ per labor-hour}$$

fixed-overhead component = total mixed cost less variable component

$$\text{at } x_h = \$2,500 - \$.9167(2,300)$$
$$= \$2,500 - \$2,108 = \$392$$

or

$$\text{at } x_l = \$1,400 - \$.9167(1,100)$$
$$= \$1,400 - \$1,008 = \$392$$

Therefore,

mixed-cost formula = $392 per month plus $.9167 per labor-hour

Thus we have two strikingly different mixed-cost formulas provided by the same high-low method. The watchword is beware. Use all, or nearly all, the data points, not just two, as a basis for cost estimation.

summary

Managers who know cost behavior patterns are better equipped to make intelligent planning and control decisions. The division of costs into engineered, discretionary, and committed categories highlights the major factors that influence cost incurrence. Management policies often determine whether a cost will be planned and controlled as an engineered cost or as a discretionary cost.

Predictions of how costs will behave in response to various actions usually have an important bearing on a wide number of decisions. The cost function used to make these predictions is usually a simplification of underlying relationships. Whether this simplification is justified depends on how sensitive the manager's decisions are to the errors that the simplifications may generate. In some cases, additional accuracy may not make any difference; in other cases, it may be significant. The choice of a cost function is a decision concerning the cost and benefits of information.

summary problems
for your review

PROBLEM ONE

Reconsider the first illustration in the chapter. Suppose that eleven employees worked throughout the month, but that only 5,000 pay records were processed.

REQUIRED

1. Prepare a performance report that presents actual, budgeted, and budget variance columns for the month. Use (a) a discretionary-cost approach and (b) an engineered-cost approach.

2. Suppose the workers have been reasonably efficient. What do the budget variances in 1a and 1b tell the manager?

3. Assume that an engineered-cost approach to control is used, even though management has deliberately overstaffed. This means that management must provide for an "expected variance" or "budgeted variance" for cash-planning purposes. For preparing a budgeted statement of cash receipts and disbursements, what amount would be budgeted for payroll-clerk labor?

▧ PROBLEM TWO

The Delite Company has its own power plant. All costs related to the production of power have been charged to a single account, Power. We know that the total cost for power was $24,000 in one month and $28,000 in another month. Total machine-hours in those months were 120,000 and 160,000, respectively. Express the cost behavior pattern of the Power account in formula form.

▧ SOLUTION TO PROBLEM ONE

1. a. Discretionary-fixed-cost approach:

	ACTUAL COST	BUDGET	BUDGET VARIANCE
Payroll-clerk labor (11 × $1,800)	$19,800	$19,800	—

b. Engineered-variable-cost approach:

	ACTUAL COST	FLEXIBLE BUDGET: TOTAL STANDARD INPUTS ALLOWED FOR ACTUAL OUTPUTS ACHIEVED (5,000 × 3.60)	BUDGET VARIANCE in dollars	BUDGET VARIANCE in equivalent persons
Payroll-clerk labor	$19,800	$18,000	$1,800 U	1.0 U

Note the addition of an equivalent-persons column that was not required here, nor was it illustrated earlier. Many managers want this information because it provides a gauge of the physical extent of overstaffing.

2. Managers control operations in many ways. A basic way is physical observation, which is always used regardless of what accounting approach is favored. The budget variance in 1a tells the manager nothing. A discretionary-cost approach essentially determines a flat amount to be spent for a given planning period and relies on physical observation or other informal ways to judge if the "right" amount of cost is being incurred.

The budget variance in 1b measures the extra amount the manager is paying to keep a stable work force. Proponents of this approach maintain that the variance of $1,800 or one equivalent person keeps management abreast of the extra costs of maintaining the current number of personnel. This work-measurement approach maintains that clerical workloads must be formally measured before control can really succeed.

The chapter emphasizes that management attitudes and policies are often of determining importance in characterizing a cost as fixed or variable. If managers think that the incremental benefits from a formal engineered-variable-cost approach do not justify its incremental costs, they will continue to rely on a discretionary-cost approach. Thus there is no single "best" way to control costs. The preferable way depends on the type of organization and type of operations subject to control.

3. This question was included here to call attention to the fact that management may use one budget figure for motivation and control and a different budget figure for cash planning. The master budget would include $19,800 as a part of the budgeted statement of cash receipts and disbursements. A detailed presentation would show:

Payroll-clerk labor:

Flexible control-budget allowance	$18,000
Expected flexible control-budget variance	1,800
Total budget allowance for cash disbursements	$19,800

■ SOLUTION TO PROBLEM TWO

$$\text{variable rate} = \frac{\text{change in mixed cost}}{\text{change in volume}} = \frac{\$28,000 - \$24,000}{160,000 - 120,000}$$

$$= \frac{\$4,000}{40,000} = \$.10 \text{ per machine-hour}$$

fixed component = total mixed cost less variable component
at 160,000-hour level = $28,000 − $.10(160,000) = $12,000
or, at 120,000-hour level = $24,000 − $.10(120,000) − $12,000
cost formula = $12,000 per month + $.10 per machine-hour

Appendix 8: method of least squares

The method of least squares is the most accurate device for formulating the *past behavior* of a mixed cost.

The line itself is not plotted visually, however; it is located by means of two simultaneous linear equations:

$$\Sigma xy = a\Sigma x + b\Sigma x^2 \qquad \text{(1)}$$

$$\Sigma y = na + b\Sigma x \qquad \text{(2)}$$

where a is the fixed component, b is the variable cost rate, x is the activity measure, y is the mixed cost, n is the number of observations, and the Greek letter Σ (sigma) means summation.

For example, assume that nine monthly observations of repair costs are to be used as a basis for developing a budget formula. A scatter diagram indicates a mixed-cost behavior in the form $y = a + bx$. Computation of the budget formula by the method of least squares is shown in Exhibit 8-5. Substitute the values from Exhibit 8-5 into Equations (1) and (2):

$$\$25,520,000 = 12,900a + 12,090,000b \qquad \text{(1)}$$

$$\$16,700 = 9a + 12,900b \qquad \text{(2)}$$

repeat equation (1): $\$25,520,000 = 12,900a + 21,090,000b$

multiply equation (2) by 1,433.3333
(which is 12,900 ÷ 9): $\$23,936,667 = 12,900a + 18,490,000b$
subtract: $\$1,583,333 = 2,600,000b$

$$b = \$.6089742$$

substitute $.6089742 for b in
equation (2):

$$\$16,700 = 9a + 12,900(\$.6089742)$$
$$\$16,700 = 9a + \$7,855.7671$$
$$9a = \$8,844.233$$
$$a = \$982.69255$$

Therefore the formula for the total repair expenses is $983 per month plus $.609 per labor-hour.

A scatter diagram should also be prepared to see whether the derived line seems to fit the existing cost data to a satisfactory degree. If not, then factors other than volume or activity have also significantly affected total cost behavior. In such instances, multiple regression techniques may have to be used.

EXHIBIT 8-5

Least-Squares Computation of Budget Formula for Mixed Cost

MONTH	LABOR-HOURS x	TOTAL MIXED COST y	xy	x^2
August	2,200	$ 2,300	$ 5,060,000	4,840,000
September	2,300	2,500	5,750,000	5,290,000
October	1,900	2,000	3,800,000	3,610,000
November	1,200	2,000	2,400,000	1,440,000
December	1,200	2,000	2,400,000	1,440,000
January	900	1,500	1,350,000	810,000
February	700	1,400	980,000	490,000
March	1,100	1,400	1,540,000	1,210,000
April	1,400	1,600	2,240,000	1,960,000
	12,900	$16,700	$25,520,000	21,090,000

SOURCE: *Adapted from "Separating and Using Costs as Fixed and Variable," N.A.A. Bulletin,* Accounting Practice Report No. 10 (*New York, June 1960*), *p. 13. For a more thorough explanation, see any basic text in statistics or Horngren,* Cost Accounting, *Chap. 25.*

assignment material

■ FUNDAMENTAL ASSIGNMENT MATERIAL

8-1. **Terminology:** Define *budget appropriation; committed fixed costs; control-factor unit; cost approximation; cost behavior pattern; cost estimation; cost function; discretionary costs; efficiency; managed (or programmed) costs; parameter; regression analyses; work measurement; zero-based budgeting.*

8-2. **Clerical work measurement.** The Mohr Company has many small accounts receivable. Work measurement of billing labor has shown that a billing clerk can process

2,000 customers' accounts per month. The company employs thirty billing clerks at an annual salary of $9,600 each. The outlook for next year is for a decline in the number of customers, from 59,900 to 56,300 per month.

REQUIRED

1. Assume that management has decided to continue to employ the thirty clerks despite the expected drop in billings. Show two approaches, the engineered-cost approach and the discretionary-fixed-cost approach, to the budgeting of billing labor. Show how the *performance report* for the year would appear under each approach.
2. Assume that the workers are reasonably efficient. (a) Interpret the budget variances under the engineered-cost approach and the discretionary-fixed-cost approach. (b) What should management do to exert better control over clerical costs?
3. Some managers favor using tight budgets as motivating devices for controlling operations. In these cases, the managers really expect an unfavorable variance and must allow, in financial planning, for such a variance so that adequate cash will be available as needed. What would be the budgeted variance, also sometimes called expected variance, in this instance?

8-3. **Types of cost behavior.** Identify the following as (a) proportionately variable costs, (b) discretionary fixed costs, (c) committed fixed costs, (d) mixed or semivariable costs, (e) step-function costs, (f) discretionary variable costs, and (g) engineered variable costs.

1. Advertising allowances granted to wholesalers by Schlitz Brewing Company on a per-case basis.

2. Total repairs and maintenance of a school building.

3. Straight-line depreciation on desks in the office of a certified public accountant.

4. Rental payment by the Federal Bureau of Investigation on a five-year lease for office space in a private office building.

5. Sales commissions based on revenue dollars. Payments made to advertising salespersons employed by radio station KCBS, San Francisco.

6. Advertising costs, a lump sum budgeted and paid by Coca-Cola.

7. Crew supervisor in a Sears mail-order house. A new supervisor is added for every seven workers employed.

8. Public relations employee compensation paid by Mobil Oil Company.

9. Jet fuel costs of United Airlines.

10. Compensation of lawyers employed internally for Ford Motor Company.

11. Total costs of renting trucks by the city of Palo Alto. Charge is a lump sum of $300 per month plus 20¢ per mile.

8-4. **High-low method.** The controller of an electronics manufacturer has asked you to develop a formula for the mixed cost behavior pattern of repair and maintenance costs of some automatic machinery. She requested that you do the best you can with the following sketchy data for the past two years:

YEAR	ACTIVITY IN MACHINE-HOURS	TOTAL REPAIR AND MAINTENANCE COSTS
19X1	20,000	$11,000
19X2	30,000	16,000

■ ADDITIONAL ASSIGNMENT MATERIAL

8-5. What is *work measurement?*

8-6. Why are committed costs the stickiest of the fixed costs?

8-7. "An unfavorable variance for discretionary costs would measure the failure to spend the entire appropriation." Do you agree? Explain.

8-8. Why are fixed costs also called capacity costs?

8-9. How do committed costs differ from discretionary costs?

8-10. How do the methods and philosophies of management affect cost behavior?

8-11. "Ideally, there should be no accounts for mixed costs." Explain.

8-12. Describe how mixed costs are budgeted.

8-13. "Variable costs are those that should fluctuate directly in proportion to sales." Do you agree? Explain.

8-14. How does the basic behavior of the cost of raw materials differ from that of clerical services?

8-15. "For practical budgeting purposes, costs do not have to be proportionately variable in order to be regarded as variable." Explain.

8-16. "The objective in controlling step costs is to attain activity at the highest volume for any given step." Explain.

8-17. What is the primary determinant of the level of committed costs?

8-18. What is the primary determinant of the level of discretionary costs?

8-19. "Planning is far more important than day-to-day control of discretionary costs." Do you agree? Explain.

8-20. **Attitudes toward work measurement.** At a management conference, a proponent of work measurement stated, "Before you can control, you must measure." Another executive complained, "Why bother to measure when work rules and guaranteed employment provisions in labor union contracts prevent discharging workers, using part-time employment, and using overtime!"

REQUIRED

Evaluate these comments. Summarize your personal attitudes toward the use of work measurement.

8-21. **Government work measurement.** The auditor general of the state of California conducted a study of the Department of Motor Vehicles. The auditor's report said that the department's work standards, which were set in 1939, allow ten minutes for typing and processing a driver's license application. But a 1977 study of 40 of its 147 field offices showed that it takes only six minutes. The report said: "The continued use of the ten-minute standard results in the overstaffing of 158 positions at an unnecessary annual cost of $1.9 million."

REQUIRED

Name four governmental activities that are likely candidates for using work measurement as a means for control.

8-22. **Government work measurement.** The Internal Revenue Service has an auditing system where an auditor scrutinizes income tax returns after they have been prescreened with the help of computer tests for normal ranges of deductions claimed by taxpayers. A standard cost of $4 per tax return has been used, based on work-measurement studies that allow twenty minutes per return. Each agent has a workweek of five days at eight hours per day.

The audit supervisor has the following data regarding performance for the most recent four-week period, when 8,000 returns were processed.

	ACTUAL COSTS	FLEXIBLE BUDGET	VARIANCE
Salaries	$38,400*	?	?

*20 auditors × $480 salary per week × 4 weeks.

1. Compute the flexible-budget allowance and the variance.
2. The supervisor believes that audit work should be conducted more productively and that superfluous personnel should be transferred to field audits. If the above data are representative, how many auditors should be transferred?
3. Enumerate some possible reasons for the variance.

8-23. **Work measurement in a hospital.** Susan Buretta, the chief administrator of a large hospital, had a clerical work-measurement study performed regarding billing procedures. A standard rate of processing five bills per hour was established. The study revealed that the average bill contained 30 lines. Each billing clerk cost the hospital $15 per hour, including fringe benefits. Each worked eight hours per day, five days per week.

1. During a recent four-week period, eight clerks worked full time and 4,800 bills were processed. Prepare a performance report, showing actual cost, flexible budget, and budget variance.
2. Buretta asks you to express the variance in terms of "equivalent persons."
3. After seeing the performance report, Buretta informed the supervisor of billing that the staff would have to be reduced by the number of equivalent persons indicated by the budget variance. Upset, the supervisor took a careful random sample of 400 bills. Her count showed a total of 16,000 lines in the sample. As the supervisor, prepare a response to Buretta.

8-24. **Zero-based budgeting.** (CMA.) There has been much recent publicity about a budgeting system called "zero-based" budgeting. The system can be applied in governmental, not-for-profit, and profit-making organizations. Its proponents believe it represents a significant change in the budgeting process for most types of organizations and that it therefore leads to more effective use of limited resources.

1. Describe the zero-based budgeting system.
2. Explain how the proponents of zero-based budgeting say it differs from the traditional budgeting process.
3. Identify the advantages and disadvantages of the zero-based budgeting system.

8-25. **Cost behavior patterns.** A hospital administrator has asked you to classify the following costs as either (a) variable, (b) step-function, (c) mixed, (d) discretionary fixed, or (e) committed fixed:
1. Salary of a medical intern
2. Head of nursing
3. Salaries of security personnel
4. Leasing costs of X-ray equipment, $4,000 per year plus $.29 per film
5. Support costs for arthritis research
6. Medical insurance for all full-time employees
7. Drugs for patients
8. Costs of services of hospital consulting firm
9. Straight-line depreciation on typewriters
10. Nursing supervisors (one added for every six nurses added)

8-26. **Various cost behavior patterns.** In practice, there is often a tendency to simplify approximations of cost behavior patterns, even though the "true" underlying behavior is not simple. Choose from among the accompanying graphs A through H the one that matches the numbered items. Indicate by letter which graph best fits each of the situations described.

The vertical axes of the graphs represent total dollars of factory costs incurred, and the horizontal axes represent total production. The graphs may be used more than once.

1. Natural gas bill consisting of a fixed component, plus a constant variable cost per thousand cubic feet after a specified number of cubic feet are used

2. Availability of quantity discounts, where the cost per unit falls as each price break is reached

3. Price rise of an increasingly scarce raw material as the volume used increases

4. Cost of sheet steel for a manufacturer of refrigerators

5. Guaranteed annual wage plan, whereby workers get paid for 40 hours of work per week at zero or low levels of production that require working only a few hours weekly

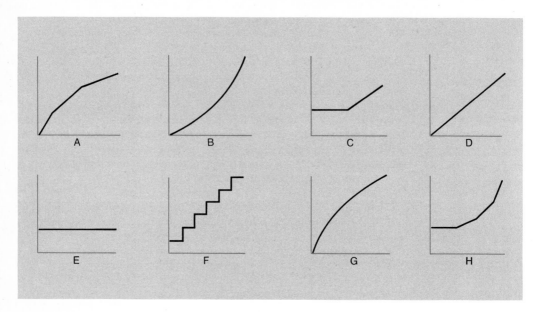

6. Cost of machining labor that tends to decrease per unit as workers gain experience

7. Depreciation on a straight-line basis

8. Water bill under drought conditions, which entails a flat fee for the first 100,000 gallons and then an increasing unit cost for every additional batch of 10,000 gallons used

9. Salaries of assistant foremen, where one assistant foreman is added for every ten assembly workers added

8-27. **Hospital X-ray costs.** The chief radiologist of City Hospital favors buying some new X-ray equipment. She maintains that quicker and better-quality service can be provided. The chief administrator of the hospital thinks that the present equipment will suffice. However, monthly repairs and maintenance costs will probably continue their recent upward direction.

Data for the relevant range in recent months reveal:

	HIGH VOLUME	LOW VOLUME
X-ray films	8,000	5,000
Repair cost	$4,000	$2,800

REQUIRED

You have been asked to approximate the fundamental variable- and fixed-cost behavior. Also prepare a freehand graph to show the administrator.

8-28. **College income.** Many private universities try to recover about one-third of their total costs from tuition revenue. The remainder is recovered via endowment income and charitable donations. Stanford University is preparing a budgeted income statement for the coming fiscal year, which will end on August 31, 19X6. Tuition revenue for the past two fiscal years was:19X5, $54 million; and 19X4, $48 million. Total expenses were: 19X5, $165.6 million; and 19X4, $153.6 million. No tuition rate changes occurred in 19X4 or 19X5. If the tuition rate is not changed in 19X6, tuition revenue is expected to be $60 million.

REQUIRED

1. What is the implied cost behavior pattern faced by the university? That is, what is the university's fixed- and variable-cost equation in relation to tuition revenue?
2. If historical patterns persist, what total expenses are expected by the university in 19X6?
3. What are the analytical defects in using the volume of tuition revenue as a basis for predicting costs? As financial vice-president of the university, what basis would you prefer?

8-29. **Rudiments of least-squares analysis.** (Adapted from an analysis prepared by Robert Keyes.) Assume that train-miles traveled (and total costs y) are a function of the gross ton-miles x (tons times miles) of work to be performed. The records show (additional zeros omitted to simplify the computations):

DATE	(x) GROSS TON-MILES	(y) TOTAL COSTS
10-1	800	$350
10-2	1,200	350
10-3	400	150
10-4	1,600	550

This example is used only to illustrate the methods that can be used for determining similar information. If, as in this instance, the number of observations is small, additional analysis should be performed to determine whether the results are reliable.

REQUIRED

1. Draw a scatter diagram.
2. Use simple regression to fit a line to the data. What is the equation of the line? Plot the line.

8-30. **Method of least squares and sales forecasts.** (SMA, adapted.) The Progressive Company Ltd. has recorded the following sales since its inception in 19M2:

19M2	$ 10,000	19M8	$125,000
19M3	20,000	19M9	150,000
19M4	30,000	19N0	180,000
19M5	45,000	19N1	220,000
19M6	70,000	19N2	270,000
19M7	90,000		

REQUIRED

1. Calculate 19N3 sales, using the least-squares method.
2. If the directors have determined from an outside consultant that the cyclical factor in 19N4 will cause sales to be 10 percent above the forecast trend, what will they amount to?

COST
BEHAVIOR
VARIATIONS

8-31. **Least-squares analysis.** Suppose that a manufacturer is troubled by fluctuations in labor productivity and wants to compute how direct-labor costs are related to the various sizes of batches of output. The workers in question set up their own jobs on complex machinery. The following data show the results of a random sample of ten batches of a given kind:

BATCH SIZE x	DIRECT-LABOR COSTS y	BATCH SIZE x	DIRECT-LABOR COSTS y
15	$180	25	300
12	140	22	270
20	230	9	110
17	190	18	240
12	160	30	320

REQUIRED

1. Prepare a scatter diagram.
2. Using least-squares analysis, compute the equation of the line relating labor costs and size of batch.
3. Predict the labor costs for a lot size of 20.
4. Using a high-low method, repeat Requirements 2 and 3. Should the manager use the high-low method or the least-squares method? Explain.

8-32. **Nonlinear costs.** The printing office of the state of New York has used a flexible budget for the overhead of one of it press departments. In April the actual overhead costs incurred in the department were $149,800. The actual outputs achieved should have taken 16,900 standard allowed hours. However, 19,600 hours of input were actually used.

The total overhead is budgeted at $127,200 for a level of 16,000 hours and $144,000 for a level of 20,000 hours.

REQUIRED

1. Calculate the flexible-budget variance for April. Divide the variance into a price (spending) variance and an efficiency variance.
2. The political climate placed much emphasis on shutting down government departments and buying many products and services from private enterprises. As a result, the manager of the press department became very concerned about cost controls. A study conducted from May through November developed the following refined approximation for predicting overhead in relation to direct-labor hours (DLH):

$$\text{total overhead} = \$64{,}000 + \$3 \text{ DLH} + \$90 \sqrt{\text{DLH}}$$

Suppose this cost function had been used in April as the flexible-budget formula, instead of the linear-budget formula used previously. Calculate the same types of variances as described in Requirement 1. Compare the magnitudes of the variances in Requirement 1 with those in Requirement 2.

8-33. **Nonlinear behavior.** The following graph contains a linear function, which is the linear approximation of the nonlinear "true" cost function also shown.

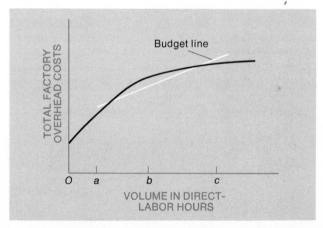

1. Will the flexible budget be higher or lower than what the budgeted "true" costs would be at *Oa, Ob,* and *Oc?*
2. Would you prefer to use the "true" cost curve for budgeting and for decision purposes? Why?

8-34. **Nonlinear behavior and banking.** Managers are often troubled by not really knowing how overhead is affected by their operating decisions. As a result, they are uncomfortable when they use the simple "linear approximations" that are commonly encountered. Suppose a bank is contemplating the introduction of a new "one-price" banking service, whereby a flat monthly fee will provide a combination of "free" checking, safety deposit, and other services.

Suppose the underlying (but unidentified) overhead-cost behavior would be:

VOLUME LEVEL IN NUMBER OF ACCOUNTS	TOTAL OVERHEAD COSTS PER YEAR
1,000	$34,000
2,000	40,000
3,000	45,000
4,000	49,000
5,000	64,000
6,000	85,000

1. A committee is trying to predict what costs are relevant. After much heated discussion, predictions were made for two "representative" volumes: 2,000 accounts and 5,000 accounts. A flexible budget was to be constructed based on a "high-low" analysis of these two volumes. Compute the formula for the flexible-budget line.
2. What predictions would be produced by the flexible budget developed in Requirement 1 for each of the tabulated levels of activity? Use a table to compare these predictions with the "true" cost behavior, showing the difference between the "true" cost behavior and the linear approximation.
3. Plot the two sets of predictions on a graph.
4. Assume that the new service has been introduced. The manager in charge is convinced that a special television campaign can increase volume from the current level of 2,000 accounts to a level of 4,000 accounts. These additional accounts would bring an additional contribution to income of $64,000 before considering the predicted increase in total overhead cost and before considering the cost of $50,000 for the television campaign. If the manager were guided by the linear flexible-budget formula, would he launch the campaign? Show computations. If he did launch the campaign, by how much would income change if 2,000 more accounts were achieved?
5. As an operating manager responsible for budgetary control of overhead, would you regard the linear budget allowances for 4,000 and 6,000 accounts as too tight or too loose? Why?
6. A top executive of the bank commented, "I think we should have a more accurate budgetary system." Do you agree? Explain.

8-35. **Two independent variables in hospital.** The underlying cost behavior pattern of overhead in South Chicago Hospital is linear but affected by two independent variables: number of patients and the number of days each patient stays. The latter, called *patient-days,* is computed by multiplying the number of patients times the days each stayed. The number of patients influences costs because the first day of the stay tends to require more overhead costs than subsequent days. In sum, the actual cost behavior pattern is:

$$\text{total overhead} = a + bx_1 + cx_2$$

where a = intercept, b = rate per patient-day, and c = rate per patient.

For simplicity, the flexible budget for overall overhead behavior is based on patient-days:

$$\text{total overhead} = a + bx_1$$

At the end of a period, the hospital administrator was disturbed that the overhead variance was highly unfavorable. He commented. "A large part of that variance is attributable to Medicare and similar reimbursement plans. Some people place aged parents in the hospital for a couple of days go away for a short holiday."

REQUIRED

Given these facts and the underlying cost behavior, was the flexible-budget variance overstated or understated? Suppose the more costly and more accurate flexible-budget formula had been developed. Would the variance be higher or lower than the variance produced by the simple formula? Why?

8-36. **Temporary versus permanent help.** The Central States Division of Lawrence's Famous Candies, Inc., is responsible for filling all orders, in an area comprising fifteen midwestern states, for the product, a high-grade candy which is retailed in many fine stores from coast to coast. The clerical work incidental to filling an order has traditionally been done by a staff of seven persons who work a five-day week of eight hours per day. Their salary and fringe benefits total $1,800 each per month. To uphold quality, the company has a longstanding policy of not using overtime. Assume, for simplicity, that each month consists of exactly twenty working days.

Sheila Matson, the division manager, has noticed that the workers are idle during part of the day during some parts of the year. A strong union prevents the division from sending permanent employees home early in order to reduce their compensation. However, the union will provide temporary help (one-day minimum) for $120 per worker per day. In turn, the workers pay some of their compensation to the union. Matson is considering reducing the permanent staff and hiring temporary help during peak periods.

Matson learned that the New York division routinely hires temporary help for the same duty, but with some loss of efficiency. Temporary help can process only 35 orders per day, whereas permanent help can process 40 orders per day.

The month-to-month sales record, expressed in terms of orders filled, has been as follows for the past five years:

January	4,800	May	4,400	September	4,400
February	4,800	June	4,000	October	4,800
March	4,800	July	4,000	November	5,600
April	5,600	August	4,000	December	5,600

REQUIRED

Should the division manager retain all seven clerks? If not, how many should she retain? Sales fluctuate significantly from month to month, but not from year to year. Any fluctuation within a given month is so minor that it can be absorbed by a slight delay. For computational simplicity, the manager assumes that sales are constant throughout the month.

chapter **9**

RESPONSIBILITY ACCOUNTING AND COST ALLOCATION

learning objectives

When you have finished studying this chapter, you should be able to:

1. Define and contrast cost centers, profit centers, and investment centers, and explain how a responsibility accounting structure can promote desirable management behavior.
2. Recognize the major purposes for allocating costs.
3. Prepare a segmented income statement, using the contribution approach to cost allocation.
4. Distinguish between the economic performance of an organization segment and the performance of the segment manager.
5. Use recommended guidelines to allocate the variable and fixed costs of service departments to other organization segments.
6. Identify the principal approaches to solving the allocation problem for the central costs of an organization.
7. Use the direct and step-down methods to allocate service department costs to user departments.

This chapter is the first of a two-chapter overview of how management accounting systems are designed. It describes some typical approaches and focuses on the factors that should influence management's choice of systems. We learn that no single system is inherently superior to another. The "best" system is the one that consistently leads to a collective set of subordinate managers' decisions that are desired by higher-level managers.

General ideas of responsibility accounting

☐ RESPONSIBILITY ACCOUNTING AND MOTIVATION

Ideally, organizations are structured by top managers who subdivide activities and stipulate a hierarchy of managers who oversee some predetermined sphere of activities and who have some latitude to make decisions in that sphere. Some type of responsibility accounting usually accompanies this delegation of decision making. **Responsibility accounting** is a system of accounting that recognizes various responsibility centers throughout the organization and reflects the plans and actions of each of these centers by assigning particular revenues and costs to the one having the pertinent responsibility. It is also called **profitability accounting** and **activity accounting.**

Responsibility accounting emphasizes a major lesson for both managers and accountants—that is, the behavior of managers is often heavily influenced by how their performance is measured. Thus accounting is usually far from being a sterile, secondary part of a manager's professional life. Instead, the accounting system often plays a key role in motivating managers toward or away from the desires of top management. The motivational impact of the responsibility approach is described in the following:

> The sales department requests a rush production. The plant scheduler argues that it will disrupt his production and cost a substantial though not clearly determined amount of money. The answer coming from sales is: "Do you want to take the responsibility of losing the X Company as a customer?" Of course the production scheduler does not want to take such a responsibility, and he gives up, but not before a heavy exchange of arguments and the accumulation of a substantial backlog of ill feeling. Analysis of the payroll in the assembly department, determining the costs involved in getting out rush orders, eliminated the cause for argument. Henceforth, any rush order was accepted with a smile by the production scheduler, who made sure that the extra cost would be duly recorded and charged to the sales department—"no questions asked." As a result, the tension created by rush orders disappeared completely; and, somehow, the number of rush orders requested by the sales department was progressively reduced to an insignificant level.[1]

☐ COST CENTERS AND PROFIT CENTERS

Areas of responsibility take many forms, including

1. **Cost centers**—formal reporting of costs only
2. **Profit centers**—formal reporting of revenues and expenses

---

[1]Raymond Villers, "Control and Freedom in a Decentralized Company," *Harvard Business Review*, XXXII, No. 2, 95.

EXHIBIT 9-1. Siesta Motels, Inc. Simplified Organization Chart

3. **Investment centers**—formal reporting of revenues, expenses, and related investment

A **cost center** is the smallest segment of activity or area of responsibility for which costs are accumulated. Typically, cost centers are departments, but in some instances a department may contain several cost centers. For example, although an assembly department may be supervised by one foreman, it may contain several assembly lines. Sometimes each assembly line is regarded as a separate cost center with its own assistant foreman.

A **profit center** is a segment of a business, often called a division, that is responsible for both revenue and expenses.[2] An **investment center** goes a step further; its success is measured not only by its income but also by relating that income to its invested capital. In practice, the term *investment center* is not widely used. Instead, *profit center* is used indiscriminately to describe segments that are always assigned responsibility for revenue and expenses but may or may not be assigned responsibility for the related invested capital.

☐ ILLUSTRATION OF RESPONSIBILITY ACCOUNTING

The simplified organization chart in Exhibit 9-1 will be the basis for our illustration of how responsibility accounting is used in the motel industry. The manager at the motel level has freedom to make many operating decisions, including some repairs and building improvements.

Exhibit 9-2 provides an overall view of responsibility reporting. Start with the lowest level and work toward the top. See how the reports are integrated through three levels of responsibility. All the variances may be subdivided for further analysis, either in these reports or in more detailed reports.

[2]In some settings, particularly in nonprofit organizations, the term *revenue center* is used instead of *profit center* because profit (as ordinarily conceived) is not the primary mission of the subunit. For example, an army motor pool might be called a revenue center if it charged users for its vehicles instead of not charging.

EXHIBIT 9-2

SIESTA MOTELS, INC.
Responsibility Accounting at Various Levels
(In thousands of dollars)

PRESIDENT'S MONTHLY RESPONSIBILITY REPORT

	budget		variance: favorable (unfavorable)	
	this month	year to date	this month	year to date
President's office	(90)	(300)	(9)	(30)
Western vice-president	297	850	8	50
Midwestern vice-president	400	1,300	20	(100)
Eastern vice-president	350	1,050	30	130
Others	300	1,000	50	100
Operating income	1,257	3,900	99	150

WESTERN VICE-PRESIDENT'S MONTHLY RESPONSIBILITY REPORT

	budget		variance: favorable (unfavorable)	
	this month	year to date	this month	year to date
Vice-president's office	(20)	(40)	(2)	4
Salinas	29	(20)	(1)	(5)
Los Banos	38	133	3	16
Merced	30	90	2	10
Others	220	687	(10)	25
Operating income	297	850	(8)	50

LOS BANOS MANAGER'S MONTHLY RESPONSIBILITY REPORT

	budget		variance: favorable (unfavorable)	
	this month	year to date	this month	year to date
Revenue	80	250	5	15
Housekeeping and supplies	12	30	1	4
Heat, light, power	3	10	(1)	(2)
Advertising and promotion	2	7	—	(2)
Repairs and maintenance	4	10	(2)	(1)
General	11	30	—	2
Depreciation	10	30	—	—
Total expenses	42	117	(2)	1
Operating income	38	133	3	16

Trace the $38,000 total from the Los Banos manager's report to the Western vice-president's report. The vice-president's report merely summarizes the final results of the motels under his jurisdiction. He may also want copies of the detailed statements for each motel manager responsible to him.

Also trace the $297,000 total from the Western vice-president's report to the president's report. The president's report includes data for her own corporate office plus a summarization of the entire company's operating income performance.

☐ FORMAT OF FEEDBACK REPORTS

This set of illustrative reports shows only the budgeted amount and the variance, which is defined as the difference between the budgeted and the actual amounts. This places the focus on the variances and illustrates *management by exception*, which means that the executive's attention is concentrated on the important deviations from budgeted items. In this way, managers do not waste time on those parts of the reports that reflect smoothly running phases of operations.

Of course, this illustration represents only one possible means of presenting a report of performance. Another common reporting method shows three sets of dollar figures instead of two sets. Moreover, the variances could also be expressed in terms of percentages of budgeted amounts. For example, revenue in Los Banos could appear as follows:

	budget		actual results		variance: favorable (unfavorable)		variance: percent of budgeted amount	
	this month	year to date	this month	year to date	this month	year to date	this month	year to date
Revenue	$80	$250	$85	$265	$5	$15	6.3%	6.0%

The full performance report would contain a similar line-by-line analysis of all items.

Other data are often included in performance evaluation reports. For example, the motel industry characteristically includes the percentage of occupancy of rooms and the average rate per room. Restaurants will show the number of meals served and the average selling price per meal.

The exact format adopted in a particular organization depends heavily on user preferences. For instance, some companies focus on the budgeted income statement for the year. As each month unfolds, the managers receive the original plan *for the year* compared against the revised plan *for the year*. The revised plan provides management with the best available prediction of how the year's results will eventually turn out.

Even though formats and intent of responsibility reports may be geared to satisfy the preferences of the managers in a particular organization, the following fundamentals are typically followed:

1. Show total costs, unit costs, and physical amounts of inputs and outputs. Most managers prefer simple reports. Consequently, some of these data may be omitted or condensed; when in doubt, more data rather than less data are furnished.

2. Keep the terminology, time spans, and various internal reports consistent. In this way, budgeted figures can easily be compared with actual results and with budgets and actual results of previous and future periods.

☐ RESPONSIBILITY AND INCENTIVE

Responsibility accounting has innate attraction for most top managers because it facilitates the delegation of decision making. That is, each middle manager is given command of a subunit together with some authority. In return, responsibility accounting supplies the basic means of evaluating each manager's performance. Consequently, in addition to keeping top management informed, a responsibility accounting system helps give individual managers incentive via performance reports.

A **controllable cost** has been defined as any cost that is subject to the influence of a given *manager* of a given *responsibility center* for a given *time span*. The degree of controllability is often hard to establish. To try to focus on the manager's performance as an individual administrator, responsibility reporting often excludes or segregates items that are judged as not subject to the manager's control. For example, a foreman's performance report may be confined to usage of direct material, direct labor, and supplies, and exclude depreciation, rent, and property taxes. In a prison or hospital, or in many hotels, the costs on a laundry department performance report might be confined to soap and labor; depreciation on the building and equipment would be excluded.

☐ WHO GETS BLAMED?

Responsibility accounting, budgets, variances, and the entire library of accounting techniques are basically neutral devices. However, they are frequently misused as negative weapons, as being a means of placing blame or finding fault. Viewed positively, they are a means of assisting managers so that future improvements in decisions are more easily attained. Moreover, they facilitate the delegation of decision making to lower levels, and autonomy is almost always treasured by managers.

The "blame-placing" attitude reveals a misunderstanding of the rationale of responsibility accounting, which basically asks, "Which individual in the organization is in the best position to explain why a specific outcome occurred? Let's trace costs down to that level so that the feedback coming from performance evaluation is as well informed as feasible."

In many circumstances, the degree of the manager's control or influence over the outcome may be minimal—but responsibility accounting still is favored. For example, the price of gold to a jewelry manufacturer may be beyond the influence of anybody within the organization. Still, somebody usually is in the best position to explain the *price* of gold, and another is in the best position to explain the *quantity* of gold consumed. The latter individual typically has a budget based on a standard (budgeted) unit price of gold rather than on its actual unit price.

In sum, responsibility accounting presses accountability down to the person who has the greatest potential day-to-day influence over the revenue or cost in question. This person must bear the responsibility, and so must his or her superiors. And this person's fundamental reporting responsibility is to explain the outcome regardless of the degree of his or her personal influence over the result.

Cost allocation in general

To be credible, responsibility accounting depends on appropriate cost allocations. The term **cost allocation** is used here as general label for all tracing of various costs to cost objectives such as departments or products. Like air and water, problems of cost allocation are everywhere. University presidents, city managers, hospital administrators, and corporate executives inevitably face these difficult problems. This section describes some general approaches to the solutions, but there are no easy answers.

☐ COST ALLOCATION AS A TERM

As Chapter 3 pointed out, cost allocation is fundamentally a problem of linking (1) some cost or groups of costs with (2) one or more cost objectives (examples are products, departments, and divisions). In short, cost allocation tries to identify (1) with (2) via some cost function. Cost-allocation bases are the means of establishing these links or cost functions, preferably using some cause-and-effect logic.

For example, major costs, such as newsprint for a newspaper and direct professional labor for a law firm, may be allocated to departments, jobs, and projects on an item-by-item basis, using cost-allocation bases such as tonnage consumed or direct-labor hours used. Other costs, taken one at a time, are not important enough to justify being allocated individually. These costs are *pooled* (that is, grouped together in some plausible way) and then allocated as pools. An example would be a university's allocating the operating costs of a registrar's office to its colleges on the basis of the number of students in each college.

The literature is not consistent in the use of terms in this area, so be sure to pinpoint the meaning of terms in specific situations. You may encounter terms such as *allocate, reallocate, trace, assign, distribute, redistribute, load, apportion,* and *reapportion* being used interchangeably to describe the same cost-accounting practice. The terms *apply* or *absorb* tend to have the narrower meaning of costs traced to *products* rather than to *departments*.

☐ FOUR PURPOSES OF ALLOCATION

What logic should be used for allocating costs from one segment to other segments of an organization? This question bothers many internal users and suppliers of services in all organizations, including nonprofit organizations. The answer should begin with a determination of the principal purpose or purposes of the cost allocation.

Costs are allocated for four major purposes:

1. *To predict the economic effects of planning and control decisions.* Examples are the addition of a new course in a university, the addition of a new flight or an additional passenger on an airline, and the addition of a new specialty in a medical clinic. Some costs are obviously associated with particular decisions. Other costs are admittedly associated, but the nature of the association is hard to establish in any convincing way.

2. *To obtain desired motivation.* Cost allocations are sometimes made to promote goal coordination and incentives. Examples are decisions to allocate or not to allocate a given cost, depending on top management's predictions regarding collective management behavior. Consequently, in some organizations there is no cost allocation for legal or internal auditing services or internal management consulting services because top management wants to encourage their use. In other organizations, there is a cost allocation for such items to spur managers to take an interest in a particular activity or to compare the costs and benefits of the use of specified services. Examples are allocations of research costs and of "carrying" costs, such as an "opportunity" or "imputed" interest cost on receivables or inventories.

3. *To compute income and asset valuations.* Costs are allocated to products and projects to measure their inventory costs and their profit contributions.

4. *To obtain a mutually agreeable price.* The best examples are in regulated industries and in government contracts based on a negotiated price that provides for costs plus some profit based on costs.[3] These contracts are used when ordinary market prices do not seem applicable. In these instances, cost allocations become substitutes for the usual working of the marketplace. That is, cost allocations are a way of arriving at a "fair" price—even if cause-and-effect logic may be hard to find.

Ideally, all four purposes would be served simultaneously by a single cost allocation. The allocation of raw-material usage to departments, products, managers, and contracts might reach this ideal occasionally. But thousands of managers and accountants will testify that for most costs the ideal is rarely achieved. Instead, cost allocations are often a major source of discontent and confusion to the affected parties. When all four purposes are unattainable simultaneously, the manager and the accountant should start attacking a cost-allocation problem by trying to identify which of the purposes should dominate in the particular situation at hand.

---

[3] "A Whole New Way to Figure AT&T's Rates," *Business Week,* February 14, 1977, pp. 86–89, reports that American Telephone and Telegraph Co. will have a future rate structure tied more closely to the "fully distributed cost" of providing various services: "In the past, it has figured rates on new services according to a complex formula that relied heavily on the incremental costs that such a service was deemed to impose on overall operations. The FCC and Bell's competitors argued that this basis was unfair, since Bell's monopoly business—ordinary telephone service—bore most of the company's costs and thus subsidized the newer services (p. 88)." Regarding government contracts, see the statements on cost allocation being issued by the Cost Accounting Standards Board, 441 G Street N.W., Washington, D.C. 20548.

The contribution approach to allocation

Many organizations combine the contribution approach and responsibility accounting; they report by cost behavior pattern as well as by degrees of controllability. To do so, they must contend with problems of cost allocation. Consider an illustration of a retail grocery company. It might have the basic organizational design shown in Exhibit 9-3.

Exhibit 9-4 displays the contribution approach to reporting and cost allocation. Study this important exhibit carefully. It provides perspective on how a reporting system can be designed to stress cost behavior patterns, controllability, manager performance, and subunit performance simultaneously.

□ CONTRIBUTION MARGIN

As demonstrated in previous chapters, the contribution margin, which is revenues minus all variable expenses [line (a) in Exhibit 9-4], is especially helpful for predicting the impact on income of short-run changes in volume. Incidentally, in this case, if management prefers, a gross margin or gross profit (revenue minus the cost of the merchandise sold) could be inserted just after cost of merchandise sold. This is a good example of how gross margin and contribution margin

EXHIBIT 9-3. Organization chart of retail grocery company

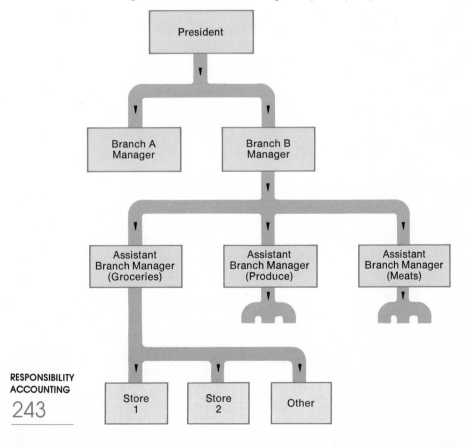

EXHIBIT 9-4

The Contribution Approach:
Model Income Statement, by Segments*
(in thousands of dollars)

	retail food company as a whole	company breakdown into two divisions		possible breakdown of branch B only				possible breakdown of branch B, meats only		
		branch A	branch B	not allocated†	groceries	produce	meats	not allocated†	store 1	store 2
Net sales	$4,000	$1,500	$2,500	—	$1,300	$300	$900	—	$600	$300
Variable costs:										
Cost of merchandise sold	$3,000	$1,100	$1,900	—	$1,000	$230	$670	—	$450	$220
Variable operating expenses	260	100	160	—	100	10	50	—	35	15
Total variable costs	$3,260	$1,200	$2,060	—	$1,100	$240	$720	—	$485	$235
(a) Contribution margin	$ 740	$ 300	$ 440	—	$ 200	$ 60	$180	—	$115	$ 65
Less: Fixed costs controllable by segment managers‡	260	100	160	$ 20	40	10	90	$ 30	35	25
(b) Contribution controllable by segment managers	$ 480	$ 200	$ 280	$(20)	$ 160	$ 50	$ 90	$(30)	$ 80	$ 40
Less: Fixed costs controllable by others§	200	90	110	20	40	10	40	10	22	8
(c) Contribution by segments	$ 280	$ 110	$ 170	$(40)	$ 120	$ 40	$ 50	$(40)	$ 58	$ 32
Less: Unallocated costs‖	100									
(d) Income before income taxes	$ 180									

*Three different types of segments are illustrated here: branches, product lines, and stores. As you read across, note that the focus becomes narrower: from Branch A and B, to Branch B only, to Meats in Branch B only.

† Only those costs clearly identifiable to a product line should be allocated.

‡ Examples are certain advertising, sales promotion, salespersons' salaries, management consulting, training and supervision costs.

§ Examples are depreciation, property taxes, insurance, and perhaps the segment manager's salary.

‖ These costs are not clearly or practically allocable to any segment except by some highly questionable allocation base.

differ. The principal example of variable operating expenses are the wages and payroll-related costs for most store personnel.

Any expected changes in income may be quickly calculated by multiplying increases in dollar sales by the contribution-margin ratio. Suppose the contribution-margin ratio for meats is 20 percent. Then a $1,000 increase in sales of meats should produce a $200 increase in income (.20 × $1,000 = $200). (This assumes, of course, no changes in selling prices or operating conditions.)

☐ SEGMENT AND MANAGER PERFORMANCE

A **segment** is defined as any part of an organization or line of activity for which separate determination of revenue and costs is obtained. When they analyze performance, many proponents of responsibility accounting distinguish sharply between the *segment* (department, division, store, motel) as an economic investment and the *manager* as a professional decision maker. Managers frequently have little influence over many factors that affect economic performance. For instance, the manager of a motel may be relatively helpless if an energy crisis reduces automobile traffic or if unseasonable weather ruins the ski season.

Similarly, the manager of a retail store may have influence over some local advertising but not other advertising, some fixed salaries but not other salaries, and so forth. Moreover, the meat manager at both the branch and store levels for the retail grocery company may have zero influence over store depreciation and the president's salary.

☐ CONTRIBUTION CONTROLLABLE BY SEGMENT MANAGERS

The controllable contribution [item (b) in Exhibit 9-4] and the segment contribution [item (c) in Exhibit 9-4] are attempts to underscore the distinction between subunit (segment) performance and manager performance.

The term "segment managers" is used in the exhibit to represent a general description of the manager of any subunit of any organization. Examples are nursing supervisors, shipping room foremen, police captains, and fire station chiefs.

Note that fixed costs controllable by the segment manager are deducted from the contribution margin to obtain the contribution controllable by segment managers. These are usually discretionary fixed costs. Examples of these discretionary costs are some local advertising but not all advertising and some fixed salaries but not the manager's own salary.

In many organizations, managers have some latitude to trade off some variable costs for fixed costs. To save variable material and labor costs, managers might make heavier outlays for machinery, labor-saving devices, quality control inspectors, maintenance, management consulting fees, employee training programs, and so on. Moreover, decisions on advertising, research, and sales promotion have effects on sales volumes and hence on contribution margins. That is why the contribution margin is not a satisfactory measure of manager performance. However, the controllable contribution attempts to capture the results of these trade-offs.

The distinctions in Exhibit 9-4 among which items belong in what cost classification are inevitably not clear-cut. For example, determining controllability is always a problem when service department costs are allocated to other departments. Should the store manager bear a part of the branch headquarters costs? If so, how much and on what basis? How much, if any, store depreciation or lease rentals should be deducted in computing the controllable contribution? There are no pat answers to these questions. They are worked out somehow from organization to organization. Again, for management control purposes there are no constraints of external accounting principles[4] on designing acceptable management accounting systems. The answers depend fundamentally on what reporting system will bring the most net benefits in terms of motivation and collective decisions.

Consider the fixed costs that are deducted between items (a) and (b) in Exhibit 9-4. The "not allocated" columns show amounts of $20,000 and $30,000, respectively. This approach recognizes that perhaps some clusters of costs should not be allocated below specified levels in the organization's hierarchy. For instance, the $20,000 may include secretarial salaries of the Branch B general manager that may not be allocated; similarly, the $30,000 in that same line may include costs of general meat advertisements that may not be allocated to individual stores.

□ CONTRIBUTION BY SEGMENTS

The contribution by segments, line (c) in Exhibit 9-4, is an attempt to approximate the economic *performance of the segment*, as distinguished from the *performance of its manager*. The "fixed costs controllable by others" typically include committed costs (such as depreciation and property taxes) and discretionary costs (such as the subunit manager's salary). These costs are examples of items that are minimally influenced by the segment manager within a reporting period of a year or less.

Exhibit 9-4 shows an "unallocated costs" line immediately before line (d). They might include central corporate costs such as the costs of the president's office and many costs of the legal and accounting activities. When a persuasive "cause-and-effect" or "benefits-received" justification for allocating such costs cannot be found, many organizations favor not allocating them to segments.

The contribution approach highlights the relative objectivity of various measures of performance evaluation. The contribution margin tends to be the most objective. As you read downward, the allocations become more difficult, and the resulting measures of contributions or income become more subject to dispute. In contrast, the traditional functional approach to income statements rarely hesitates to use full-cost allocations. Therefore it tends to offer less-sharp distinctions between variable and fixed costs and between controllable and uncontrollable costs.

---

[4]FASB *Statement No. 14,* "Financial Reporting for Segments of a Business Enterprise," requires that companies' external financial statements include information about operations in different industries, foreign operations and export sales, and major customers. Disclosure of profit contribution (revenue less only those operating expenses that are directly traceable to a segment) is encouraged but not required.

How to allocate for planning and control

□ GENERAL GUIDES

What causes costs to occur? The *causes* of costs are the very same activities that are usually chosen to be cost objectives. Examples are products produced, letters typed, and patients seen. The *effects* of these activities are various costs. Therefore the manager and the accountant should search for some cost-allocation base that establishes a convincing relationship between the cause and the effect and that permits reliable predictions of how costs will be affected by decisions regarding the activities.

The preferred guides for allocating service department costs are:

1. Use responsibility accounting and flexible budgets for each service (staff) department, just as they are used for each production or operating (line) department. When feasible, maintain distinctions between variable-cost pools and fixed-cost pools.

2. Allocate variable- and fixed-cost pools separately. This is sometimes called the dual method of allocation. Note that one service department (such as a computer department) can contain a variable-cost pool and a fixed-cost pool. That is, costs may be pooled within and among departments if desired.

3. Establish part or all of the details regarding cost allocation in advance of rendering the service rather than after the fact.

□ USING THE GUIDES

To illustrate these guides, consider a simplified example of a computer department of a university that serves two major users, the School of Earth Sciences and the School of Engineering. The computer mainframe was acquired on a five-year lease that is not cancelable unless prohibitive cost penalties are paid.

How should costs be allocated to the user departments? Suppose there are two major purposes for the allocation: (1) predicting economic effects of the use of the computer and (2) motivating toward optimal usage. Apply the guides enumerated earlier:

1. Analyze the costs of the computer department in detail. Divide the costs into two pools, one for variable costs and one for fixed costs. Suppose the flexible-budget formula for the forthcoming fiscal year is $100,000 monthly fixed costs plus $200 variable cost per hour of computer time used.

2. Allocate the variable-cost pool and the fixed-cost pool separately.

3. Establish the details regarding the cost allocation in advance.

Guides (2) and (3) will be considered together in the following sections on variable-cost pools and fixed-cost pools.

☐ VARIABLE-COST POOL

Ideally, the variable-cost pool should be allocated as follows:

(budgeted unit rate) × (actual quantities of service units used)

The cause-and-effect relationship is clear: the heavier the usage, the higher the total costs. In this example, the rate used would be the budgeted rate of $200 per hour.

The use of *budgeted* cost rates rather than *actual* cost rates for allocating variable costs of service departments protects the using departments from intervening price fluctuations and also often protects them from inefficiencies.

The most desirable procedure for allocating variable-cost pools is to know the complete cost of various services in advance. For example, the cost of a repair job would be predetermined based on budgeted cost rates multiplied by the budgeted or standard hours of input allowed for accomplishing specified repairs. User department managers sometimes complain more vigorously about the poor management of a service department than about the choice of a cost-allocation base (such as direct-labor dollars or number of employees). Such complaints are less likely if the service department managers have budget responsibility and the user departments are protected from short-run price fluctuations and inefficiencies.

☐ FIXED-COST POOL

Ideally, the fixed-cost pool should be allocated as follows:

(Budgeted fraction of capacity available for use)
× (Total budgeted fixed costs)

Before exploring the implications of this approach, consider our example. Suppose that the deans had originally predicted the following long-run average monthly usage: earth sciences, 210 hours, and engineering, 490 hours, a total of 700 hours. The fixed-cost pool would be allocated as follows:

	EARTH SCIENCES	ENGINEERING
Fixed costs per month:		
210/700, or 30% of $100,000	$30,000	
490/700, or 70% of $100,000		$70,000

This predetermined lump-sum approach is based on the long-run capacity *available* to the user, regardless of actual usage from month to month. The reasoning is that the level of fixed costs is affected by long-range planning regarding the overall level of service and the *relative* expected usage, not by *short-run* fluctuations in service levels and relative usage.

A major strength of the use of capacity *available* rather than capacity *used* for allocating *budgeted* fixed costs is that short-run allocations to user departments are not affected by the *actual* usage of *other* user departments. Such a budgeted lump-sum approach is more likely to have the desired motivational effects with respect to the ordering of service in both the short run and the long run.

☐ FIXED POOL AND ACTUAL USAGE

In practice, the use of capacity available as a base for allocating fixed-cost pools is often not followed. Instead, actual usage is the base employed. Suppose the computer department allocated the total actual costs after the fact, a weakness followed by many service departments. At the end of the month, total *actual* costs would be allocated in proportion to the *actual* hours used by the consuming departments. Compare the costs borne by the two schools:

If 600 hours are used:

Total costs incurred, $100,000 + 600 ($200) = $220,000	
Earth Sciences: 200/600 × $220,000 =	$ 73,333
Engineering: 400/600 × $220,000 =	146,667
Total cost allocated	$220,000

What happens if Earth Sciences uses only 100 hours during the following month, while Engineering still uses 400 hours?

If 500 hours are used:

Total costs incurred, $100,000 + 500 ($200) = $200,000	
Earth Sciences: 100/500 × $200,000 =	$ 40,000
Engineering: 400/500 × $200,000 =	160,000
Total cost allocated	$200,000

Engineering has done nothing differently, but it must bear higher costs of $13,333, an increase of 9 percent. Its short-run costs are dependent on what *other* consumers have used, not on its own actions. This phenomenon is caused by a faulty allocation method for the *fixed* portion of total costs, a method whereby the allocations are highly sensitive to fluctuations in the actual volumes used by the various consuming departments. This weakness is avoided by the dual approach that provides for a predetermined lump-sum allocation of fixed costs.

To consider further the use of *budgeted* rates for allocating *variable* costs, return to our data for 600 hours. Suppose that inefficiencies in the computer department caused the variable costs to be $140,000 instead of the 600 hours × $200, or $120,000 budgeted. A common weakness of cost allocation is to allocate the costs of inefficiencies to the consumer departments. To remedy this weakness, many cost allocation schemes would allocate only the $120,000 to the consuming departments and would let the $20,000 remain as an unallocated unfavorable budget variance of the computer department. This is responsibility accounting in action, and it reduces the resentment of user managers. The allocation of costs of inefficiency seems unjustified because the "consuming departments" have to bear another department's cost of waste.

Most consumers prefer to know the total price in advance. They become nervous when an automobile mechanic or a contractor undertakes a job without specifying prices. As a minimum, they like to know the hourly rates that they must bear.

Cost-allocation systems should motivate the service department manager to control operating costs. Therefore predetermined unit prices (at least) should be used. Where feasible, predetermined total prices should be used for various kinds of work based on flexible budgets and standards.

To illustrate, when we have our automobiles repaired, we are routinely given firm total prices for various types of services. Furthermore, in the short run these prices are not affected by the volume of work handled on a particular day. Imagine your feelings if you came to an automobile service department to get your car and were told: "Our daily fixed overhead is $1,000. Yours was the only car in our shop today,[5] so we are charging you the full $1,000. If we had processed 100 cars today, your charge would have been only $10."

☐ TROUBLES WITH USING LUMP SUMS

If fixed costs are allocated on the basis of long-range plans, there is a natural tendency on the part of consumers to underestimate their planned usage and thus obtain a smaller fraction of the cost allocation. Top management can counteract these tendencies by monitoring predictions and by following up and utilizing feedback to keep future predictions more honest.

In some organizations there are even definite rewards in the form of salary increases for managers who are skillful as accurate predictors. Moreover, some cost-allocation methods provide for penalties for underpredictions. For example, if a manager predicts usage of 210 hours and then demands 300 hours, either he doesn't get the hours or he pays a dear price for every hour beyond 210.

☐ ALLOCATING CENTRAL COSTS

Many central costs, such as the president's salary and related expenses, public relations, legal, income tax planning, companywide advertising, and basic research, are difficult to allocate in any feasible, convincing way. Therefore many companies do not allocate them at all. Other companies use allocation bases such as the revenue of each division, the cost of goods sold of each division, or the total costs of each division (before allocation of the central costs).

The desperate search for such allocation bases is a manifestation of a widespread, deep-seated belief that all costs must somehow be fully allocated to all parts of the organization. The flimsy assumptions that might underlie such allocations are widely recognized, but most managers accept them as a fact of a manager's life—as long as all managers seem to be treated alike and thus "fairly."

The use of the above bases may provide a rough indication of cause-and-effect relationships. Basically, however, they represent a "soak-the-rich" or "ability-to-bear" philosophy of cost allocation. For example, the costs of compa-

[5]Similarly, consider a news reporter's comment on medical costs: "When they thought I had a heart attack, I was glad to know they were giving me the Rolls Royce treatment. For 30 hours of observation in a coronary ward the bill topped $700. The cost was higher than needed because I was the only one in it."

nywide advertising, such as the goodwill sponsorship of a program on a non-commercial television station, might be allocated to all products and divisions on the basis of the dollar sales in each. But such costs precede sales. They are discretionary costs as determined by management policies, not by sales results.

Again, if these costs are to be allocated, the use of *budgeted* sales or some other *budgeted* allocation base is preferred to the use of *actual* sales. At least this method means that the short-run costs of a given consuming department will not be affected by the fortunes of other consuming departments.

For example, suppose central advertising were allocated on the basis of potential sales in two territories:

	TERRITORY A	B	TOTAL	PERCENT
Budgeted sales	$500	$500	$1,000	100%
Central advertising allocated	$ 50	$ 50	$ 100	10%

Consider the possible differences in allocations when actual sales become known:

	TERRITORIES A	B
Actual sales	$300	$600
Central advertising:		
1. Allocated on basis of budgeted sales	$50	$50
or		
2. Allocated on basis of actual sales	$33	$67

Compare allocation 1 with 2. Allocation 1 is preferable. It indicates a low ratio of sales to advertising in Territory A. It directs attention to where it is deserved. In contrast, allocation 2 soaks Territory B with more advertising cost because of the *achieved* results and relieves Territory A because it had lesser success. This is another example of the analytical confusion that can arise when cost allocations to one consuming department are dependent on the activity of other consuming departments.

The product-costing purpose

☐ RELATING COSTS TO OUTPUTS

Until this point, we have concentrated on cost allocation to divisions, depart-ments, and similar segments of an entity. Cost allocation is often carried one step further—to the outputs of these departments, however defined. Examples are *products* such as automobiles, furniture, and newspapers. Other examples are personal *services,* such as hospitalization and education.

Costs are allocated to products for inventory valuation purposes and for decision purposes such as pricing, adding products, and promoting products. Cost allocation is also performed for cost reimbursement purposes. For example, many public and private health programs reimburse hospitals for the "costs" of rendering services to patients.

The general approach to allocating costs to final products or services is:

1. Prepare budgets for all departments, including the *operating* (*line*) or *production* or *revenue-producing* departments that work directly on the final product or service and the *service* (*staff* or *support*) departments that help the operating departments.
2. Choose the most logical cost allocation bases that seem economically feasible.
3. Allocate the costs of the service departments to the operating departments. The operating departments now have been allocated all the costs: their direct department costs and the service department costs.
4. Allocate (apply) the total costs accumulated in item 3 to the products or services that are the outputs of the operating departments.

□ ALLOCATION OF SERVICE DEPARTMENT COSTS

The foregoing steps can be illustrated in a hospital setting. The output of a hospital is not as easy to define as the output of a factory. The objective is the improved health of patients, but that is hard to quantify. Consequently, the output of revenue-producing departments might be the following:

DEPARTMENT	MEASURES OF OUTPUT*
Radiology	X-ray films processed
Laboratory	Tests administered
Daily patient services†	Patient-days of care (that is, the number of patients multiplied by the number of days of each patient's stay)

*These become the product cost objectives, the various revenue-producing activities of a hospital.
† There would be many of these departments, such as obstetrics, pediatrics, and orthopedics. Moreover, there may be both in-patient and out-patient care.

As you undoubtedly suspect, the allocation of hospital costs to cost objectives is marked by trade-offs between costs and the possible benefits to be derived from more elaborate cost allocations. Because hospitals are often reimbursed by government agencies based on allocated costs, hospital administrators have become increasingly interested in how the costs of various departments might be allocated to the measures of revenue-producing output.

To keep the data manageable, suppose there are only three service departments in addition to the revenue-producing departments just mentioned: Administrative and Fiscal Services, Plant Operations and Maintenance, and Laundry.

1. *Prepare departmental budgets.* All six departments would prepare responsibility-center budgets for operating their own areas as efficiently and effectively as possible. These budgets would be confined to their "direct departmental costs" that are the primary responsibility of the particular department manager. Examples of such costs are salaries and supplies.

2. *Choose allocation bases.* Common allocation bases for various hospital service departments are shown in Exhibit 9-5. Exhibit 9-6 shows the allocation bases and relationships of our sample hospital.

3. *Allocate service department costs.* There are two popular ways to allocate:

   Method One, **Direct Method.** As the name implies, this method ignores other service departments when any given service department's costs are allocated to the revenue-producing (operating) departments. For example, as Exhibit 9-7 shows, the service rendered by Plant operations and Maintenance to Laundry is not considered. The direct method is popular. Its outstanding virtue is simplicity.

   Method Two, **Step-down Method.** Hospitals are increasingly being required to use this method, which has been used by many manufacturing companies for years. As Exhibit 9-7 shows, the step-down method recog-

---

EXHIBIT 9-5

Hospital Cost-Allocation Bases*

Purchasing—Costs of supplies used by each center; "other" direct expenses.

Nursing service, administrative office—Hours of nursing service supervised; estimated supervision time.

Pharmacy—Amount of requisitions priced at retail; number of requisitions; special studies.

Medical records—Estimated time spent on records; number of patient-days; number of admissions.

Admitting—Number of admissions.

Plant operations and maintenance—Square feet of area occupied; work orders

Laundry and linens—Pounds of soiled laundry processed; pounds weighted by degree of care (nurses' uniforms would be double- or triple-weighted to allow for starching or pressing).

Administrative and Fiscal Services—Accumulated costs in each department before these costs are allocated; number of personnel. This is a general cost center that should be subdivided into several cost centers and be allocated on different bases.

RESPONSIBILITY ACCOUNTING

*For a thorough discussion, see Cost Finding and Rate Setting for Hospitals (*Chicago: American Hospital Association*).

EXHIBIT 9-6

Cost-Allocation Bases by Department

	service departments			revenue departments		
	adminis-trative fiscal services	plant operations and maintenance	laundry	radiology	laboratory	daily patient services
Direct departmental costs	$ —	$800,000	$200,000	$1,000,000	$400,000	$1,600,000
Square feet occupied	—	—	5,000	12,000	3,000	80,000
Pounds	—	—	—	80,000	20,000	300,000

nizes that service departments render their benefits to other service departments as well as to revenue-producing departments. A sequence of allocations is chosen, usually by starting with the service department that renders the greatest service (as measured by costs) to the greatest number of other departments. The last service department in the sequence is the one that renders the least service to the least number of other departments. Therefore, once a department's costs are allocated to other departments, no subsequent service department costs are allocated back to it.

Administrative and Fiscal Services will be allocated on the basis of the relative costs of other departments and will be allocated first. Because it would be nonsense to allocate its own costs to itself, its costs are not included in the allocation base.

Plant Operations and Maintenance will be allocated second on the basis of square feet occupied, and none will be allocated back to Administrative and Fiscal Services. Therefore no square footage is presented for these two departments in this exhibit.

Laundry will be allocated third; none will be allocated back to the first two departments, *even though the first two departments may have used laundry services.* Sometimes special studies of relative usage of services are made to establish what percentage should go to various consuming departments. For example, the hospital administrator's salary might be allocated separately in proportion to the time she spends on each department. This allocation might be unchanged for a year or two. Similarly, laundry might be weighed periodically on a sampling basis and the results used as a predetermined means of allocation for a year regardless of interim usage.

4. *Allocate (apply) the total costs to products.* The final step is sometimes called *cost application,* whereby total departmental costs are applied to a revenue-producing product. Our illustration in Exhibit 9-7 is a hospital, but the same fundamental approach is used for manufactured products, for research projects in universities, and for client cases in social welfare departments.

Compare Methods One and Two in Exhibit 9-7. In many instances, the final product costs may not differ enough to warrant investing in a

EXHIBIT 9-7

Allocation of Service Department Costs: Two Methods

ALLOCATION BASE—FROM EXHIBIT 9-6	ADMINISTRATIVE AND FISCAL SERVICES (ACCUMULATED COSTS)	PLANT OPERATIONS AND MAINTENANCE (SQ. FOOTAGE)	LAUNDRY (LB)	RADIOLOGY	LABORATORY	DAILY PATIENT SERVICES
Method One, Direct Method						
Direct departmental costs before allocation	$1,000,000	$800,000	$200,000	$1,000,000	$400,000	$1,600,000
Administrative and fiscal services	(1,000,000)	—	—	333,333*	133,333	533,334
Plant operations and maintenance		(800,000)	—	101,052†	25,263	673,685
Laundry			(200,000)	40,000‡	10,000	150,000
Total budgeted costs				$1,474,385	$568,596	$2,957,019
Product output in films, tests, and patient-days, respectively				60,000	50,000	30,000
Cost per unit of output				$ 24.573	$ 11.372	$ 98.567
Method Two, Step-down Method						
Direct department costs before allocation	$1,000,000	$800,000	$200,000	$1,000,000	$400,000	$1,600,000
Administrative and fiscal services	(1,000,000)	200,000§	50,000	250,000	100,000	400,000
Plant operations and maintenance		(1,000,000)	50,000‖	120,000	30,000	800,000
Laundry			(300,000)	60,000#	15,000	225,000
Total budgeted costs				$1,430,000	$545,000	$3,025,000
Product output in films, tests, and patient-days, respectively				60,000	50,000	30,000
Cost per unit of output				$ 23.833	$ 10.900	$ 100.833

Notes: *The cost-allocation bases are from Exhibit 9-6:*

$1,000,000 ÷ ($1,000,000 + $400,000 + $1,600,000) = 33 1/3%; 33 1/3% × $1,000,000 = $333,333; etc.

†$800,000 ÷ (12,000 + 3,000 + 80,000) = $8.4210526; $8.4210526 × 12,000 sq.ft. = $101,052; etc.

‡$200,000 ÷ (80,000 + 20,000 + 300,000) = $.50; $.50 × 80,000 = $40,000; etc.

§$1,000,000 ÷ ($800,000 + $200,000 + $1,000,000 + $400,000 + $1,600,000) = 25%; 25% × $800,000 = $200,000; etc.

‖$1,000,000 ÷ (5,000 + 12,000 + 3,000 + 80,000) = $10.00; $10.00 × 5,000 sq. ft. = $50,000; etc.

#$300,000 ÷ (80,000 + 20,000 + 300,000) = $.75; $.75 × 80,000 = $60,000; etc.

cost-allocation method that is any fancier than the direct method.[6] But sometimes even small differences may be significant to a government agency or anybody paying for a large volume of services based on costs. For example, in Exhibit 9-7 the "cost" of an "average" laboratory test is either $11.37 or $10.90. This may be significant for the fiscal committee of the hospital's board of trustees, who must decide on hospital prices. Thus, cost allocation often is a technique that helps answer the vital question, "Who should pay for what, and how much?"

Summary

Responsibility accounting assigns particular revenues and costs to the individual in the organization who has the greatest potential day-to-day influence over them. The aim is **not** to place blame. Rather, it is to evaluate performance and provide feedback so that future operations can be improved. Costs are allocated for four major purposes: (1) prediction of economic effects of decisions, (2) motivation, (3) income and asset measurement, and (4) pricing.

The contribution approach to the income statement and to the problems of cost allocation is accounting's most effective method of helping management to evaluate performance and make decisions. Allocations are made with thoughtful regard for the purpose of the information being compiled. Various subdivisions of net income are drawn for different purposes. The contribution approach distinguishes sharply between various degrees of objectivity in cost allocations.

Where feasible, fixed costs of service departments should be reallocated by using predetermined monthly lump sums for providing a basic capacity to serve. Variable costs should be reallocated by using a predetermined standard unit rate for the services actually utilized.

The complexity of a cost-allocation method should be influenced by how the results of the alternative allocation methods affect decisions. Full-cost allocations are widespread, apparently because accountants and managers feel that these methods generally induce better decisions than partial-cost allocations.

[6]The most defensible theoretical accuracy is generated by the *reciprocal method,* which is rarely used in practice because of its complexity. Simultaneous equations and linear algebra are used to solve for the impact of mutually interacting services, such as between Administrative and Fiscal Services and Plant Operations. See C. Horngren, *Cost Accounting: A Managerial Emphasis,* 4th ed. (Englewood Cliffs, N.J.: Prentice-Hall, 1977), Chap. 16.

summary problem
for your review

PROBLEM

Review the section "How to Allocate for Planning and Control" and the example of the use of the computer by the university. Recall that the flexible-budget formula was $100,000 monthly plus $200 per hour of computer time used. Based on long-run predicted usage, the fixed costs were allocated on a lump-sum basis, 30 percent to Earth Sciences and 70 percent to Engineering.

  1. Show the total allocation if Earth Sciences used 210 hours and Engineering used 420 hours in a given month. Assume that the actual costs coincided exactly with the flexible-budgeted amount.

  2. Assume the same facts as in part 1, except that the fixed costs were allocated on the basis of actual hours of usage. Show the total allocation of costs to each school. As the dean of Earth Sciences, would you prefer this method or the method in part 1? Explain.

■ SOLUTION

1.

	EARTH SCIENCES	ENGINEERING
Fixed costs per month:		
210/700, or 30% of $100,000	$30,000	
490/700, or 70% of $100,000		$ 70,000
Variable costs @ $200 per hour:		
210 hours	42,000	
420 hours		84,000
Total costs	$72,000	$154,000

2.

	EARTH SCIENCES	ENGINEERING
Fixed costs per month:		
210/630 × $100,000	$33,333	
420/630 × $100,000		$ 66,667
Variable costs, as before	42,000	84,000
Total costs	$75,333	$150,667

The dean of Earth Sciences would probably be unhappy. His school has operated exactly in accordance with the long-range plan. Nevertheless, Earth Sciences is bearing an extra $3,333 of fixed costs because of what *another* consumer is using. He would prefer the method in part 1 because it insulates Earth Sciences from short-run fluctuations in costs caused by the actions of other users.

assignment material

9-1. Terminology. Define *allocation; controllable cost; cost application; cost centers; investment centers; profit centers; responsibility accounting; segment; step-down method.*

9-2. Responsibility of purchasing agent. Stribling Electronics Company, a privately held enterprise, has a subcontract from a large aerospace company on the West Coast. Although Stribling was low bidder, the aerospace company was reluctant to award the business to Stribling, a newcomer to this kind of activity. Consequently, Stribling assured the aerospace company of its financial strength by submitting its audited financial statements. Moreover, Stribling agreed to a penalty clause of $2,000 per day to be paid by Stribling for each day of late delivery for whatever cause.

Linda Yu, the Stribling purchasing agent, is responsible for acquiring materials and parts in time to meet production schedules. She placed an order with a Stribling supplier for a critical manufactured component. The supplier, who had a reliable record for meeting schedules, gave Yu an acceptable delivery date. Yu checked up several times and was assured that the component would arrive at Stribling on schedule.

On the date specified by the supplier for shipment to Stribling, Yu was informed that the component had been damaged during final inspection. It was delivered ten days late. Yu had allowed four extra days for possible delays, but Stribling was six days late in delivering to the aerospace company. Hence a penalty of $12,000 was paid.

REQUIRED | What department should bear the penalty? Why?

9-3. Fundamentals of cost allocation. The costs of energy have soared, and the power department of a heavily mechanized plant has installed meters in each of its two consuming departments. The power department's basic costs behave in a pattern of $6,000 monthly plus $.40 per machine-hour used in the consuming departments, although the managers have never studied the costs very carefully and are not conscious of such a pattern.

REQUIRED

1. Assume that the company fully allocates all service department costs to its two consuming departments by using a single combined overhead rate on the basis of actual hours used. Assume that the power costs behaved exactly as described. If Department 1 used 5,000 hours and Department 2 used 5,000 hours, how much costs would be allocated to each department? Repeat your computations, assuming that the second operating department used only 3,000 hours. (Note that total costs will be lower.) What is the lesson to be learned from comparing your two sets of computations?
2. Suppose that the service department's fundamental readiness to serve was based on long-run expected activity of 4,000 machine-hours per month in Department 1 and 6,000 hours in Department 2. The company became aware of its cost behavior pattern and decided to reallocate fixed cost on a predetermined lump-sum basis and variable costs on a predetermined standard cost-per-hour basis.
   a. Show the allocations to both departments at a 10,000-hour level and an 8,000-hour level. Compare the results with those in Requirement 1. Explain the differences.
   b. Suppose that the service department had inefficiencies and price and rate changes at a 10,000-hour level. The service department incurred costs of

$11,000 instead of the $10,000 originally budgeted. How would this change the cost reallocations under the method in Requirement 1 and under the alternative method just computed? Be specific.

9-4. **Allocating central costs.** The Centrex Railroad showed the following for 19X3 (in millions):

	TOTAL	DIVISIONS northern	middle	southern
Revenues	$500	$200	$200	$100
Allocated central general and administrative costs	15	6	6	3

The indicated costs were those general corporate headquarters costs that were allocated in proportion to actual revenue achieved. Examples of such costs are the salaries of the president and other top officers and central rent, utilities, depreciation, public relations, and advertising. The costs shown here did not include any headquarters costs specifically identified with divisions. Examples of the latter are data processing and internal auditing, which were allocated based on time spent.

In 19X4 the total costs and revenues in question were unchanged. Northern's revenue went from $200 to $250 million because of higher grain traffic. Middle's revenue fell to $150 million because coal traffic decreased. Southern's revenue was unchanged.

REQUIRED

1. Calculate each division's share of central general and administrative costs for 19X4.
2. As compared with 19X3, how would each division manager feel about the cost allocations in 19X4? What are the weaknesses of using revenue as a basis for cost allocation?
3. Suppose that budgeted revenues for 19X4 were $150, $250, and $100 million for each division, respectively. Using budgeted revenues as an allocation base, compute the allocations to each division for 19X4. Is this method preferable to that used in Requirement 1? Explain.
4. Why do many managers and accountants oppose allocating any central costs that are not specifically identifiable with divisions?

9-5. "Variable costs are controllable and fixed costs are uncontrollable." Do you agree? Explain.

9-6. "Managers may trade off variable costs for fixed costs." Give three examples.

9-7. What two major factors influence controllability?

9-8. "Material costs are controllable by a production department foreman." Do you agree? Explain.

9-9. "The contribution margin is the best measure of short-run performance." Do you agree? Why?

9-10. What is the most controversial aspect of the contribution approach to cost allocation?

9-11. Give three guides for the allocation of service department costs.

9-12. "A commonly misused basis for allocation is dollar sales." Explain.

9-13. How should national advertising costs be allocated to territories?

9-14. Give five terms that are sometimes used as substitutes for the term *allocate*.

9-15. How do the terms *apply* or *absorb* differ from *allocate?*

9-16. What is *dual allocation?*

9-17. "Always try to distinguish between the performance of a segment and its manager." Why?

9-18. "Symmetry in reporting is not a basic principle of management accounting." Explain.

9-19. Give four examples of segments.

9-20. **Hospital depreciation allocation.** Many hospital accounting systems are designed so that depreciation on buildings and fixed equipment is collected in a separate cost pool and then allocated to departments, usually on the basis of square feet of space occupied. In contrast, depreciation of major movable equipment is allocated directly to the departments that use such equipment.

Is square feet a logical allocation base? Explain.

9-21. **Responsibility accounting.** (CMA, adapted.) The Fillep Company operates a standard cost system. The variances for each department are calculated and reported to the department manager. It is expected that the manager will use the information to improve his operations and recognize that it is used by his superiors when they are evaluating his performance.

John Smith was recently appointed manager of the assembly department of the company. He has complained that the system as designed is disadvantageous to his department. Included among the variances charged to the departments is one for rejected units. The inspection occurs at the end of the assembly department. The inspectors attempt to identify the cause of the rejection so that the departments where the error occurred can be charged with it. But not all errors can easily be identified with a department. The nonidentified units are totaled and apportioned to the departments according to the number of identified errors. The variance for rejected units in each department is a combination of the errors caused by the department plus a portion of the unidentified causes of rejects.

REQUIRED

1. Is John Smith's complaint valid? Explain the reason(s) for your answer.
2. What would you recommend that the company do to solve its problem with John Smith and his complaint?

9-22. **Responsibility for a stable employment policy.** The Fast-Weld Metal Fabricating Company has been manufacturing machine tools for a number of years and has an industrywide reputation for doing high-quality work. The company has been faced with irregularity of output over the years. It has been company policy to lay off welders as soon as there was insufficient work to keep them busy, and to rehire them when demand warranted. The company, however, now has poor labor relations and finds it very difficult to hire good welders because of its layoff policy. Consequently, the quality of the work has continually been declining.

The plant manager has proposed that the welders, who earn $6 per hour, be retained during slow periods to do menial plant maintenance work that is normally performed by workers earning $3.85 per hour in the plant maintenance department.

You, as controller, must decide the most meaningful accounting procedure to handle the wages of the welders doing plant maintenance work. What department or departments should be charged with this work, and at what rate? Discuss the implications of your plan.

9-23. **Cost of passenger traffic.** Southern Pacific Railroad (SP) has a commuter operation that services passengers along a route between San Jose and San Francisco. Problems of cost allocation were highlighted in a 1978 news story about SP's application to the Public Utilities Commission (PUC) for a rate increase. The PUC staff claimed that the "avoidable annual cost" of running the operation was $700,000, in contrast to SP officials' claim of a loss of $9 million. PUC's estimate was based on what SP would be able to save if it shut down the commuter operation.

The SP loss estimate was based on a "full-allocation-of-costs" method, which allocates a share of common maintenance and overhead costs to the passenger service.

If the PUC accepted its own estimate, a 25 percent fare increase would have been justified, whereas SP sought a 96 percent fare increase.

The PUC stressed that commuter costs represent less than one percent of the systemwide costs of SP, and that 57 percent of the commuter costs are derived from some type of allocation method—sharing the costs of other operations.

SP's representative stated that "avoidable cost" is not an appropriate way to allocate costs. He said that "it is not fair to include just so-called above-the-rail costs" because there are other real costs associated with commuter service. Examples are maintaining smoother connections and making more frequent track inspections.

REQUIRED

1. As Public Utilities commissioner, what approach toward cost allocation would you favor for making decisions regarding fares? Explain.
2. How would fluctuations in freight traffic affect commuter costs under the SP method?

9-24. **Responsibility accounting, profit centers, and the contribution approach.** Consider the following data for the year's operations of an automobile dealer:

General dealership overhead	$ 100,000
Advertising of vehicles	100,000
Sales commissions, vehicles	40,000
Sales salaries, vehicles	50,000
Sales of vehicles	2,000,000
Sales of parts and service	500,000
Cost of vehicle sales	1,600,000
Parts and service materials	150,000
Parts and service labor	200,000
Parts and service overhead	50,000

The president of the dealership has long regarded the markup on material and labor for the parts and service activity as the amount that is supposed to cover all parts and service overhead plus all general overhead of the dealership. In other words, the parts and service department is viewed as a cost-recovery operation, and the sales of vehicles as the income-producing activity.

REQUIRED

1. Prepare a departmentalized operating statement that harmonizes with the views of the president.
2. Prepare an alternative operating statement that would reflect a different view of the dealership operations. Assume that $10,000 and $50,000 of the $100,000 general overhead can be allocated with confidence to the parts and service department and to sales of vehicles, respectively. The remaining $40,000 cannot be allocated except in some highly arbitrary manner.
3. Comment on the relative merits of Requirements 1 and 2.

9-25. **Divisional contribution, performance, and segment margins.** The president of the Midwestern Railroad wants to obtain an overview of his operations, particularly with respect to comparing freight and passenger business. He has heard about some new "contribution" approaches to cost allocations that emphasize cost behavior patterns and so-called *contribution margins, contributions controllable by segment managers,* and *contributions by segments.* Pertinent data for the year ended December 31, 19X2, follow:

Total revenue was $100 million, of which $90 million was freight traffic and $10 million was passenger traffic. Fifty percent of the latter was generated by Division 1; 40 percent by Division 2; and 10 percent by Division 3.

Total variable costs were $56 million, of which $44 million was freight traffic. Of the $12 million allocable to passenger traffic, $4.4, $3.7, and $3.9 million could be allocated to Divisions 1, 2, and 3, respectively.

Total separable discretionary fixed costs were $10 million, of which $9.5 million applied to freight traffic. Of the remainder, $100,000 could not be allocated to specific divisions, although it was clearly traceable to passenger traffic in general. Divisions 1, 2, and 3 should be allocated $300,000, $70,000, and $30,000, respectively.

Total separable committed costs, which were not regarded as being controllable by segment managers, were $30 million, of which 90 percent was allocable to freight traffic. Of the 10 percent traceable to passenger traffic, Divisions 1, 2, and 3 should be allocated $1.8 million, $420,000, and $180,000, respectively; the balance was unallocable to a specific division.

The common fixed costs not clearly allocable to any part of the company amounted to $1 million.

REQUIRED

1. The president asks you to prepare statements, dividing the data for the company as a whole between the freight and passenger traffic and then subdividing the passenger traffic into three divisions.
2. Some competing railroads actively promote a series of one-day sightseeing tours on summer weekends. Most often, these tours are timed so that the cars with the tourists are hitched on with regularly scheduled passenger trains. What costs are relevant for making decisions to run such tours? Other railroads, facing the same general cost picture, refuse to conduct such sightseeing tours. Why?
3. For purposes of this analysis, even though the numbers may be unrealistic, suppose that Division 2's figures represented a specific run for a train instead of a division. Suppose further that the railroad has petitioned government authorities for permission to drop Division 2. What would be the effect on overall company net income for 19X3, assuming that the figures are accurate and that 19X3 operations are in all other respects a duplication of 19X2 operations?

9-26. **Contribution approach to allocation.** (CMA, adapted.) Pralina Products Company is a regional firm that has three major product lines—cereals, breakfast bars, and dog food. The income statement for the year ended April 30, 1978, is shown on facing page; the statement was prepared by product line using absorption (full) costing.

Other Data

1. Cost of sales. The company's inventories of raw materials and finished products do not vary significantly from year to year. The inventories at April 30, 1978, were essentially identical to those at April 30,1977.

Factory overhead was applied to products at 120 percent of direct-labor dollars. The factory overhead costs for the 1977–78 fiscal year were as follows:

Variable indirect labor and supplies	$ 15,000
Variable employee benefits on factory labor	30,000
Supervisory salaries and related benefits	35,000
Plant occupancy costs	100,000
	$180,000

There was no overapplied or underapplied overhead at year-end.

2. Advertising. The company has been unable to determine any direct causal relationship between the level of sales volume and the level of advertising expenditures. However, because management believes advertising is necessary, an annual advertising

PRALINA PRODUCTS COMPANY
Income Statement
For the Year Ended April 30, 1978
(000 omitted)

	CEREALS	BREAKFAST BARS	DOG FOOD	TOTAL
Sales in pounds	2,000	500	500	3,000
Revenue from sales	$1,000	$400	$200	$1,600
Cost of sales:				
Raw materials	$ 330	$160	$100	$ 590
Direct labor	90	40	20	150
Factory overhead	108	48	24	180
Total cost of sales	$ 528	$248	$144	$ 920
Gross margin	$ 472	$152	$ 56	$ 680
Operating expenses:				
Selling expenses:				
Advertising	$ 50	$ 30	$ 20	$ 100
Commissions	50	40	20	110
Salaries and related benefits	30	20	10	60
Total selling expenses	$ 130	$ 90	$ 50	$ 270
General and administrative expenses:				
Licenses	$ 50	$ 20	$ 15	$ 85
Salaries and related benefits	60	25	15	100
Total general and administrative expenses	$ 110	$ 45	$ 30	$ 185
Total operating expenses	$ 240	$135	$ 80	$ 455
Operating income	$ 232	$ 17	$ (24)	$ 225

program is implemented for each product line. Each product line is advertised independently of the others.

3. *Commissions.* Sales commissions are paid to the sales force at the rates of 5 percent on the cereals and 10 percent on the breakfast bars and dog food.

4. *Licenses.* Various licenses are required for each product line. These are renewed annually for each product line.

5. *Salaries and related benefits.* Sales and general and administrative personnel devote time and effort to all product lines. Their salaries and wages are allocated on the basis of management's estimates of time spent on each product line.

REQUIRED

The controller of Pralina Products Company has recommended that the company do a cost-volume-profit (CVP) analysis of its operations. As a first step, the controller has requested that you prepare a revised income statement for Pralina Products Company that employs a product contribution margin format which will be useful in CVP analysis. The statement should show the profit contribution for each product line and the operating income for the company as a whole.

9-27. **Hospital cost allocation.** The amount of time necessary to perform various laboratory tests varies with their complexity. The health-care industry has developed standards for repetitive tests. These standards are not necessarily expressed in absolute amounts of time, but in terms of comparative times to perform one test versus another. For instance, the obtaining of a white-cell count takes 60 percent of the time it takes to get a measure of sugar in the blood:

RESPONSIBILITY
ACCOUNTING

263

	NUMBER OF TESTS PERFORMED	WEIGHTING
Sugar quantitative	2,375	1.0
White-cell count	4,675	0.6
Sedimentation rate	3,280	0.7
Tissues, surgical	603	10.0
Bleeding time	2,340	0.8
Chlorides	584	1.9

The total costs of these tests were $164,880. What cost rate should be used for each test as a basis for reimbursements from health-care agencies?

9-28. **Hospital allocation base.** Catherine Glazer, the administrator of Mayo Hospital, has been having disputes with auditors from government agencies and health insurance companies concerning cost allocations. Consequently, she wants to revise the hospital's accounting system to obtain cost allocations more related to causes and effects. Glazer asks you, "Please develop a better cost-allocation base for laundry costs—but don't get too fancy."

You find that the laundry does an enormous daily volume. Items processed include the usual linens for beds plus uniforms for a variety of hospital personnel. Sixty percent of the 30,000 pounds of items for the department of surgery were ten times as expensive to process as regular laundry, mainly because of extra materials and hand-work.

Last month was a typical month. The $131,400 of laundry costs had been allocated on the basis of 438,000 pounds processed for all departments, or 30¢ per pound.

REQUIRED

1. Revise the cost-allocation base and calculate the new cost-allocation rate. Ignore the special requirements other than those of the department of surgery.
2. Calculate the total cost charged to surgery using the old base and the new base.

9-29. **Allocation of costs.** The Torrance Transportation Company has one service department and two operating departments. A flexible budget is used. The budgeted cost behavior pattern of the service department is $500,000 monthly plus 80¢ per 1,000 ton-miles operated in Departments P and Q. (Ton-miles are the number of tons carried times the number of miles traveled.) The actual monthly costs of the service department are allocated on the basis of the ton-miles operated.

REQUIRED

1. Torrance processed 400 million ton-miles of traffic in April, half in each operating department. The actual costs of the service department were exactly equal to those predicted by the flexible budget. Compute the costs that would be allocated to each operating department.
2. Suppose Department P's region was plagued by strikes, so that the freight handled was much lower than originally anticipated. P moved only 100 million ton-miles of traffic. Department Q handled 200 million ton-miles. The actual costs were exactly as budgeted for this lower level of activity. Compute the costs that would be allocated to P and Q. Note that the total costs will be lower.
3. Refer to the facts in Requirement 1. Various inefficiencies caused the service department to incur costs of $900,000. Compute the costs to be allocated to P and Q. Are the allocations justified? If not, what improvement do you suggest?
4. Refer to the facts in Requirement 2. Assume that assorted investment outlays for equipment and space in the service department were made to provide a basic maximum capacity to serve Department P at a level of 390,000 ton-miles and Department Q at a level of 210,000 ton-miles. Suppose fixed costs are allocated on the basis of this capacity to serve. Variable costs are allocated by

using a predetermined standard rate per 1,000 ton-miles. Compute the costs to be allocated to each department. What are the advantages of this method over other methods?

9-30. **Step-down and direct allocations.** A factory has six departments with budgeted overhead costs as shown below. These are direct departmental overhead costs before allocation:

PRODUCTION DEPARTMENTS:		SERVICE DEPARTMENTS:	
Machining	$310,000	Administration	$240,000
Assembly	220,000	Cafeteria (net loss)	50,000
Finishing	155,000	Engineering	600,000

Other budgeted data are:

	NUMBER OF EMPLOYEES	TOTAL LABOR-HOURS	ENGINEERING HOURS*
Machining	55	100,000	18,000
Assembly	110	230,000	9,000
Finishing	35	70,000	3,000
Administration	20	30,000	—
Cafeteria	10	20,000	—
Engineering	40	60,000	—
Total	270	510,000	30,000

Engineering hours of work identifiable with production departments.

Bases for allocating service department costs are:

Administration: total labor-hours
Cafeteria: number of employees
Engineering: engineering hours

REQUIRED

1. Prepare schedules to allocate service department costs, showing all computations:
   a. By the direct method
   b. By the step-down method, allocating costs in this order: administration, cafeteria, engineering
2. Compare the results of the two methods. Which method do you favor? Why?

9-31. **Overhead allocation and application rates.** (Knowledge of Chapter 13 is helpful.) The Speed Retarder Equipment Company has only two production departments, Machining and Assembly, and it wishes to apply the overhead costs of these to the various jobs worked on. However, there are five service departments, and their overhead costs must also be absorbed in some way by the individual jobs. Various budgeted data are available:

DEPARTMENT	DIRECT-LABOR HOURS	NUMBER OF EMPLOYEES	SQUARE FEET OF FLOOR SPACE OCCUPIED	TOTAL LABOR-HOURS	NUMBER OF REQUISITIONS
Building and grounds	—	20	—	—	200
Personnel	—	10	4,000	—	100
General factory administration	—	70	14,000	—	100
Cafeteria	—	20	8,000	2,000	300
Storeroom	—	10	14,000	2,000	—
Machining	10,000	100	60,000	16,000	4,000
Assembly	30,000	200	100,000	34,000	2,000
Total	40,000	430	200,000	54,000	6,700

Budgeted overhead costs before allocation are:

Building and grounds	$ 24,000
Personnel	2,400
General factory administration	62,616
Cafeteria—operating loss	3,936
Storeroom	6,408
Machining	83,280
Assembly	117,360
Total	$300,000

1. Prepare a schedule showing allocation of service overhead costs by the direct method, using the following allocation bases:
   Building and grounds: square feet
   Personnel: employees
   Factory administration: total labor-hours
   Cafeteria: employees
   Storeroom: requisitions
   Also compute the overhead rate per direct-labor hour that would be used by Machining and Assembly.
2. Prepare a schedule showing allocation of service overhead costs by the step-down method. Use the same allocation bases, but with appropriate rates. Use the following order of departmental allocation: Building and Grounds, Personnel, Factory Administration, Cafeteria, Storeroom. Also compute the overhead rate per direct-labor hour that would be used by Machining and Assembly.
3. Compute the blanket plantwide factory-overhead application rate, assuming that direct-labor hours are used as a cost-allocation base.
4. Using the following information about two jobs, compute three different total-overhead costs for each job, using rates developed in Requirements 1, 2, and 3 above.

	direct-labor hours		
	machining	assembly	total
Job 6071	10	70	80
Job 6072	50	30	80

9-32. **Interdependence of drugstore departments.** Jane Hobbs, the owner of a small drugstore, is considering dropping a short-order restaurant department and confining the store to two departments: drugs and sundries (candy, magazines, cosmetics, and so on).

Other small drugstores have reported that the dropping of a restaurant department causes drug sales to decline 10 percent and sundry sales to decline 5 percent.

The store employs two pharmacists at yearly salaries of $25,000 each. Compensation to the restaurant counter employees totals $20,000 per year. Past experience indicates that one pharmacist is required for every $100,000 of drug sales.

In 19X3 the following data were recorded:

	DRUGS	RESTAURANT COUNTER	SUNDRIES
Sales	$200,000	$40,000	$80,000
Cost of goods sold	100,000	28,000	64,000

The restaurant counter employees spend about 30 percent of their time handling sundry items. Without them, the pharmacists would have to help with sundry sales. Because of the resulting inconvenience to customers, drug sales would fall an additional 5 percent of current sales.

(Round all computations to the nearest $1,000):

1. Compute the "contribution" of each department, where *contribution* is defined as sales less cost of goods sold less employee compensation.

2. Compute the new "contribution" if the restaurant counter were dropped. Based on the computations in Requirements 1 and 2, should the counter be dropped?

3. Assume that the owner considered the lunch counter a complete nuisance and has closed it. However, in an effort to regain lost drug sales, she is now considering cutting prices on certain manufactured drugs. She estimates that these discounts would amount to $2,000 a year, but that they would increase gross current drug sales (that is, expressed in terms of current prices before discounts) by $20,000. This course of action would have an insignificant effect on sundry sales other than the effects already considered in Requirement 2. Should she cut the prices?

4. Return to your computations in Requirement 2. Prepare a statement that measures the current performance of each of the two departments. Defend your method of allocating costs.

9-33. **Review of Chapters 1–9.** (H. Schaefer.) As you are about to depart on a business trip, your accountant hands you the following information about your Singapore division:

a. Master budget for the fiscal year just ended on October 31, 19X1:

Sales	$700,000
Manufacturing cost of goods sold	560,000
Manufacturing margin	$140,000
Selling and administrative expenses	100,000
Operating income	$ 40,000

b. Budgeted sales and production mix:

Product A	40,000 units
Product B	60,000 units

c. Standard variable manufacturing cost per unit:

Product A

Direct material	10 pieces	@ $0.25	$2.50
Direct labor	1 hour	@ $3.00	3.00
Variable overhead	1 hour	@ $2.00	2.00
			$7.50

Product B

Direct material	5 pounds	@ $0.10	$0.50
Direct labor	.3 hours	@ $2.50	0.75
Variable overhead	.3 hours	@ $2.50	0.75
			$2.00

d. All budgeted selling and administrative expenses are common, fixed expenses; 60 percent are discretionary expenses.

e. Actual income statement for the fiscal year ended October 31, 19X1:

Sales	$700,000
Manufacturing cost of goods sold	571,400
Manufacturing margin	$128,600
Selling and administrative expenses	97,000
Operating income	$ 31,600

f. Actual sales and production mix:

Product A	42,000 units
Product B	56,000 units

g. Budgeted and actual sales prices:

Product A	$10
Product B	5

h. Schedule of the actual *variable* manufacturing cost of goods sold by product; actual quantities in parentheses:

Product A:	Material	$106,800	(427,200 pieces)
	Labor	123,900	(42,000 hours)
	Overhead	86,100	(42,000 hours)
Product B:	Material	33,600	(280,000 pounds)
	Labor	42,500	(17,000 hours)
	Overhead	42,500	(17,000 hours)
		$435,400	

i. Products A and B are manufactured in separate facilities. Of the *budgeted* fixed manufacturing cost, $120,000 is separable as follows: $40,000 to product A and $80,000 to product B. Ten percent of these separable costs are discretionary. All other budgeted fixed manufacturing expenses, separable and common, are committed.

The purpose of your business trip is a board of directors meeting. During the meeting it is quite likely that some of the information from your accountant will be discussed. In anticipation you set out to prepare answers to possible questions. (There are no beginning or ending inventories.)

1. Determine the firm's *budgeted* break-even point, overall contribution-margin ratio, and contribution margins per unit by product.

2. Considering products A and B as *segments* of the firm, find the *budgeted* "contribution by segments" for each.

3. It is decided to allocate the *budgeted* selling and administrative expenses to the segments (in part 2 above) as follows: committed costs on the basis of budgeted unit sales mix and discretionary costs on the basis of actual unit sales mix. What are the final expense allocations? Briefly appraise the allocation method.

4. How would you respond to a proposal to base commissions to salespersons on the sales (revenue) value of orders received? Assume all salespersons have the opportunity to sell both products.

5. Determine the firm's *actual* "contribution margin" and "contribution controllable by segment managers" for the fiscal year ended October 31, 19X1. Assume *no* variances in committed fixed costs.

6. Determine the "marketing variance" for each product for the fiscal year ended October 31, 19X1.

7. Determine and identify all variances in *variable* manufacturing costs by product for the fiscal year ended October 31, 19X1.

suggested readings

ANTHONY, R., and R. HERZLINGER, *Management Control in Nonprofit Organizations.* rev. ed. Homewood, Ill.: Richard D. Irwin, 1980.

CAPLAN, EDWIN H., *Management Accounting and Behavioral Science.* Reading, Mass.: Addison-Wesley, 1971.

CAPLAN, EDWIN H., and J. CHAMPOUX, *Cases in Management Accounting: Context and Behavior.* New York: National Association of Accountants, 1978.

HOPWOOD, A., *Accounting and Human Behavior.* Englewood Cliffs, N.J.: Prentice-Hall, 1976.

LAWLER, E., and J. RHODE, *Information and Control in Organizations.* Pacific Palisades, Calif.: Goodyear, 1976.

LIKERT, RENSIS, *The Human Organization, Its Management and Value.* New York: McGraw-Hill, 1967.

LIVINGSTONE, J. L., ed., *Managerial Accounting: The Behavioral Foundations.* Columbus, Ohio: Grid, 1975.

SCHIFF, JONATHAN B., *Readings in Managerial Accounting.* Princeton, N.J.: Dow Jones/Arno Press Books, 1980.

SCHIFF, M., and Y. LEWIN, eds., *Behavioral Aspects of Accounting.* Englewood Cliffs, N.J.: Prentice-Hall, 1974.

PROFIT CENTERS AND TRANSFER PRICING

learning objectives

When you have finished studying this chapter, you should be able to:

1. Describe the role of management accounting systems in relation to top-management goals and subgoals and in relation to organization structure.
2. Explain the implications of goal congruence and incentives in the design of systems.
3. Define **decentralization** and identify its expected benefits and costs.
4. Define **transfer prices** and identify their purpose.
5. Identify the relative advantages and disadvantages of basing transfer prices on total costs, variable costs, and market prices.
6. Compute ROI and residual income and contrast them as criteria for judging the performance of organization segments.
7. Identify the relative advantages and disadvantages of using various bases for measuring the invested capital used by organization segments.

This chapter continues the overview of management control systems that was introduced in the preceding chapter. Special attention is given to how to judge one system versus another and to two widely used aids in measuring performance: (1) transfer prices and (2) rate of return on investment (hereafter often called ROI).

Judging a management control system

How should managers and accountants judge a management accounting system, often called a management control system? Too often, judgments focus on physical or data-processing aspects, emphasizing the detection of fraud and compliance with various legal requirements. However, a broader focus is preferable. Systems exist primarily to improve the collective decisions within an organization.

☐ TOP-MANAGEMENT GOALS AND SUBGOALS

The starting point for judging a system is the specification of a top-management goal (or set of goals). Some managements will delineate a single goal, such as the maximization of profit over the long run. Such a lofty overall goal is too vague for most subordinates. Consequently, many organizations specify multiple goals and accompany them with some form of measurement for evaluating performance.[1]

Top management's subgoals are frequently called by other names, such as *key-result areas, critical success factors, key variables,* or *critical variables.* Some critics maintain that they should not be called goals at all; instead they should be labeled as key *means* of obtaining a single, dominant overall goal such as long-run profitability.

To illustrate the use of multiple goals, consider the General Electric Company, which has stated that organizational performance will be measured in the following eight areas:

1. Profitability
2. Market position
3. Productivity
4. Product leadership
5. Personnel development
6. Employee attitudes
7. Public responsibility
8. Balance between short-range and long-range goals

Note that the first goal, profitability, usually is measured in terms of a single year's results. The thrust of the other goals is to offset the inclination of managers to maximize short-run profits to the detriment of long-run profits.

Overstress on any single goal, whether it be short-run profits or some other goal, usually does not promote long-run profitability. Instead, coordination of goals is blocked; one goal may be achieved while others are neglected:

---

[1] Some organizations express goals in unique ways. For example, consider the Gavilan Bank of Gilroy, California, Report to Shareholders, 1976: "Greed is our vital force. It is the major influence in our program of expansion . . . . As Samuel Butler said, 'Money is always on the brain so long as there is a brain in reasonable order.'"

> *Example.* The Moscow Cable Company decided to reduce copper wastage and actually slashed it by 60 percent in a given year. The value of the scrap recovered was only $40,000 instead of the $100,000 originally budgeted. However, when top management in the central government perceived this to be an undesirable short-fall of value, the plant was fined $45,000 for not meeting its scrap budget.

As the Moscow Cable example illustrates, the design of a system includes choosing accounting reports that evaluate performance and affect rewards or penalties. Managers often face trade-off decisions. That is, which goals should be emphasized or de-emphasized? For example, one way to increase market position, at least in the short run, is to cut selling prices. In turn, however, profitability may be hurt. These trade-offs, this juggling of goals, are major keys to the successes or failures of the managers and the segments they oversee.

☐ WORKING WITHIN CONSTRAINTS

Systems should be distinguished from *goals* and from **organization structures.** The latter are defined here as the way top management has arranged the lines of responsibility within an entity. For example, one company may be organized primarily by *functions,* such as manufacturing and sales; another company by *divisions* bearing profit responsibility, such as the eastern and western divisions; and other companies by some hybrid arrangement.

Occasionally the systems designer may be in a position to persuade top management that goals or organization structures deserve revamping before the system is redesigned. But most of the time, changes in control systems are piecemeal improvements rather than grandiose replacements. Thus, typically the designer must work within the constraints of given goals and organization structures.

To recapitulate, the judge or designer of systems should ordinarily consider the following:

1. Top-management goals
2. Subgoals or key-result areas
3. Trade-offs among the goals in items 1 and 2
4. Organization structure
5. Systems design in light of the above

An illustration may clarify these distinctions. Suppose top managers specify their goal: Earnings for the coming year should be $50 million. They may use the accounting system to communicate and enforce this goal. Near the end of the year, if the earnings prospects are gloomy, top managers may exert immense pressure to reach the budgeted target. To reach the earnings goal, subordinates may be inclined to reduce current expenses by postponing outlays for maintenance, sales promotion, or research, even though such decisions could cripple future earning power.

We may deplore these decisions, but our criticism should be aimed at top management's choice of goals rather than at the system. Given the goal, the accounting system performed admirably as the helpmate of top management.

The system should be judged in light of the goals, whatever they may be. In this example, the top-management goal was actually achieved; the trouble was that the goals may not have been appropriate.

Similarly, top management may be heavily committed to a favored organization structure, such as a university's heavy or light use of formal departments organized by subject area (for example, a department of marketing, a department of statistics). Most often, the design of the system must be made within the given structure.

☐ COSTS, CONGRUENCE, INCENTIVE

Three major problems dominate the final selection of a management accounting system: costs, congruence, and incentive:

1. The selection of a system should be governed by weighing the collective costs and benefits, given the particular circumstances of the specific organization. The benefits are often difficult to measure. The overall cost-benefit theme basically says that all systems are imperfect and that System A is superior to System B if A is likely to generate a more desirable set of collective operating decisions after due consideration is given to the costs of A and B.

2. Goal congruence exists when individuals and groups aim at the goals desired by top management. Goal congruence is achieved as managers, when working in their own perceived best interests, make decisions that harmonize with the overall objectives of top management. The challenge is to specify goals (or behaviors) to induce (or at least not discourage) decisions that will blend with top-management goals.

3. Incentive is a matter of degree; it is maximized when individuals and groups *strive* (run rather than walk) toward their goals. Goal congruence can exist with little incentive, and vice versa. For example, students can enroll for a university course because their goal is to learn about, say, managing a government agency. The dean of the school, the professors, and the students may share the same goal. But goal congruence is not enough. Educators also introduce incentives in the form of a grading system.

Grading is a formal tool of *performance evaluation*, as are accounting performance reports in various organizations. Performance evaluation is a widely used means of improving incentives because most individuals tend to perform better when they expect such feedback.[2]

During the course some students may be irresistibly tempted to skip class sessions and play tennis instead. This would be an example of having plenty of incentive aimed at a different and less-important goal. Similarly, managers may eagerly pursue sales in the aggregate without paying sufficient attention to the specified and most important goal of profits, which may be affected differently by different products.

---

[2]Incentives are also provided by compensation. Sometimes a large fraction of executive compensation is based on accounting measurements. For example, a prospectus issued by Golden Nugget, Inc., a Nevada casino operator, said: ". . . the Company entered into a five-year employment contract with an executive and director providing for a salary of $25 per day for each day worked during the term thereof and additional compensation equivalent to $16\frac{2}{3}$ percent of the operating income from the game of poker."

Motivation has been defined as the need to achieve some *selected goal* (the goal-congruence problem) together with the *resulting drive* (the incentive problem) that influences action toward that goal. So the systems designer's problems of goal congruence and incentive may be wrapped together as the problem of motivation—a problem that often is fruitfully divided into its congruence and incentive aspects. Hereafter in this book, the terms "motivational" or "motivation" will refer to both the goal-congruence effects and the incentive effects.

Obtaining goal congruence and incentive is essentially a behavioral problem. The incessant focus is on the motivational impact of a particular accounting system or method versus another system or method. It may seem strange to view accounting systems in terms of their behavioral effects, but the task of the accountant is more complex, more ill-structured, and more affected by the human aspects than many people believe at first glance. A simple awareness of the importance of goal congruence and the incentive impact of systems is at least a first step toward getting a perspective on the design of accounting systems and the selection of accounting techniques.

Evolution of accounting techniques

Reconsider the ideas introduced in Chapter 7 in the section "Development of Control Systems." As organizations grow, managers cope with their responsibilities by delegating their decision-making powers to subordinates and by coordinating activities through informal and formal control systems, most notably the accounting system. The initial stages of organizations are usually marked by heavy reliance on personal observation and light reliance on formal accounting techniques. But the founders soon learn that accounting techniques can improve decisions. The evolution occurs as follows:

1. *Physical observation.* Managers rely on their eyes and ears to obtain their objectives.
2. *Historical records.* The manager quickly finds that records help operations. Moreover, assorted records must be kept to satisfy legal requirements such as income tax laws. The cost-benefit tests of system design are easily met; without such records, the manager faces lawsuits, fines, or worse.
3. *Static budgets.* The manager finds that historical records are often insufficient because they do not draw attention to the right questions. For example, the manager may be depressed if he discovers that his hospital's actual revenue in 1981 was only $50 million instead of the $55 million of the previous year. But he may be even more depressed if the budgeted 1981 revenue was $62 million. The key question, then, is not How did we do in comparison with last year? but How did we do in comparison with our targets for the current year?
4. *Flexible budgets and standards.* Many organizations introduce these techniques to obtain a sharper focus on explaining the separate impact on operations of price, efficiency, and volume factors.
5. *Profit centers.* Organizations use these devices to evaluate the performance of subunits that are assigned responsibility for revenue as well as costs and to provide better motivation.

Reflect on this evolution. Steps 1 and 3 through 5 are usually taken voluntarily rather than being imposed by outside forces. Thus the cost-benefit tests induce managers to invest in more sophisticated accounting systems as their organizations become harder to control. Furthermore, these new features are *additions* to the old features instead of *replacements* for them.

The conceptual overview here is that systems are typically changed on an incremental basis when top management predicts that the benefits from better collective decisions (improved goal congruence and incentive) will exceed the additional costs.

Decentralization

☐ COSTS AND BENEFITS

Decentralization is the delegation of the freedom to make decisions. The lower in the organization that this freedom exists, the greater the decentralization. Decentralization is a matter of degree along a continuum:

The benefits of decentralization include: (1) the lower-level managers have the best knowledge concerning local conditions and therefore are able to make better decisions than their superiors; (2) managers acquire the ability to make decisions and other management skills that assist their movement upward in the organization; and (3) managers enjoy higher status from being independent and thus are better motivated.

The costs of decentralization include: (1) managers may make dysfunctional decisions (a) by focusing on and acting to improve their own subunit's performance at the expense of the organization, or (b) by not being aware of all relevant facts; (2) managers tend to duplicate central services that might be less expensive when centralized (accounting, advertising, and personnel are examples); and (3) costs of accumulating and processing information frequently rise. The last is exemplified by responsibility accounting reports that represent a necessary counterbalance to the extension of freedom to make decisions. It is also exemplified by the time that subunit managers often spend with one another in negotiating prices for goods or services that are transferred internally.

Decentralization is more popular in profit-seeking organizations (where outputs and inputs can be measured) than in nonprofit organizations:

. . . considerable latitude can safely be given to the operating manager . . . . If poor decisions are made, these are soon revealed through the signal of inadequate profits. Without such a signal, such latitude is dangerous . . . . The budgeting process is extremely important in a nonprofit organization. When resource allocation decisions cannot safely be decentralized, the budget is an essential device for communicating how operating managers are expected to act.[3]

□ MIDDLE GROUND

Philosophies of decentralization differ considerably. Cost-benefit considerations usually result in some management decisions being highly decentralized and vice versa. To illustrate, much of the controller's problem-solving and attention-directing functions may be found at the lower levels, whereas income tax planning and mass scorekeeping such as payroll may be highly centralized.

Decentralization tends to be most successful when the segments or subunits are relatively independent of one another—that is, the decisions of one manager will not affect the fortunes of another manager. If subunits do much internal buying or selling, much buying from the same outside suppliers, or much selling to the same outside markets, they are candidates for heavier centralization.

An earlier part of this chapter stressed cost-benefit tests, goal congruence, and incentive as three major problems that must be considered when designing a control system. A fourth problem, autonomy, must be added if management has pondered the pros and cons and has decided in favor of heavy decentralization. The control system should be designed to respect autonomy to the extent specified by top management. In other words, when top managers openly commit themselves to decentralization, they must refrain from interfering in local decisions (except in rare instances).

□ MEANING OF PROFIT CENTERS

Do not confuse **profit centers** (accountability for revenue and expenses) with **decentralization** (freedom to make decisions). They are entirely separate concepts, although profit centers clearly are accounting devices that aim to facilitate decentralization. However, one can exist without the other. Some profit-center managers possess vast freedom to make decisions concerning labor contracts, supplier choices, equipment purchases, personnel decisions, and so on. In contrast, other profit-center managers may have to obtain top-management permission for almost all the decisions just mentioned. Indeed, some cost centers may be more heavily decentralized than profit centers if the cost-center managers have more freedom to make decisions.

Transfer pricing

□ NATURE OF TRANSFER PRICING

Transfer prices are associated with goods or services that are exchanged among the subunits of an organization. Most often, the term is associated with materials, parts, or finished goods. In a most fundamental sense, all cost allocation is a form of transfer pricing, although how to charge the costs of a personnel depart-

---

[3]R. Anthony and R. Herzlinger, *Management Control in Nonprofit Organizations*, rev. ed. (Homewood, Ill.: Richard D. Irwin, 1980), p. 77.

ment to the subunits of a hospital, for example, is referred to as a cost-allocation problem, not a transfer-pricing problem.

Why do transfer-pricing systems exist? The principal reason is to communicate data that help solve the problems of cost-benefit trade-offs, goal congruence, incentive, and autonomy. Transfer-pricing systems are judged as all facets of control systems should be judged—by determining whether top-management objectives are being obtained as efficiently and effectively as feasible.

Organizations solve their problems by using market prices for some transfers, standard costs for other transfers, negotiated prices for other transfers, and so forth. Therefore, do not expect to obtain a lone, universally applicable answer in the area of transfer pricing. It is a subject of continuous concern to top management. Whenever there is a lull in a conversation with a manager, try asking, "Do you have any transfer-pricing problems?" The response is usually, "Let me tell you about the peculiar transfer-pricing difficulties in my organization."

☐ TRANSFERS AT COST

When the "transfer price" is some version of cost, such transfer pricing is indistinguishable from the "cost allocation" of interdepartmental services that was discussed in the preceding chapter. Therefore, if you want to study the options and pitfalls of "transfer pricing at cost," merely substitute those words for "cost allocation" as you review the section "How to Allocate for Planning and Control" in the preceding chapter.

As an example of a pitfall, transferring at *actual* cost is generally not recommended because it fails to provide the buying subunit with a reliable basis for planning. More important, it fails to provide the supplying division with the incentive to control its costs. Inefficiencies are merely passed along to the buying division. Thus the general recommendation of using budgeted or standard costs instead of actual costs applies to all forms of cost allocation, whether the allocation is called transfer pricing, cost reallocation, or by some other name.

☐ MARKET PRICE

When an organization has profit centers, market price should be the prime candidate for setting transfer prices. In this way, the buyers and sellers systematically keep abreast of their internal and external opportunities, and problems of goal congruence, incentive, and autonomy are minimized.

Frequently, internal transfers are made at market-price-minus. That is, the supplier division may avoid some shipping or marketing costs by transferring goods to another division instead of marketing them to outside customers. These savings are often deducted when the transfer price is agreed upon.

Sometimes market prices fail to be used because they are nonexistent, inapplicable, or impossible to determine. For example, no intermediate markets may exist for specialized parts, or markets may be too thin or scattered to permit the determination of a credible price. In these instances, versions of "cost-plus-a-profit" are used that are supposed to provide a "fair" or "equitable" substitute for regular market prices.

Although market prices have innate appeal in a profit-center context, they are not cure-all answers to transfer-pricing problems. To illustrate, consider the analysis in Exhibit 10-1. Division A produces a part that may be sold either to outside customers or to Division B, which incorporates the part into a finished product that is then sold to outside customers. The selling prices and "variable" costs per unit are shown in the exhibit. Whether the part should be manufactured by Division A and transferred to Division B depends on the existence of idle capacity in Division A (insufficient demand from outside customers).

EXHIBIT 10-1

Analysis of Market Prices

DIVISION A		DIVISION B			
Market price of finished part to outsiders	$15	Sales price of finished product			$17
Variable costs per unit	6	Variable costs:			
Contribution margin	$ 9	Division A		$6	
		Division B			
Total contribution for 10,000 units	$90,000	Processing	$4		
		Selling	4	8	14
		Contribution margin			$ 3
		Total contribution for 10,000 units		$30,000	

As Exhibit 10-1 shows, if there were no idle capacity in Division A, the optimum action would be for A to sell outside at $15, because Division B would incur $8 of variable costs but add only $2 to the selling price of the product ($17 − $15). Using market price would provide the correct congruence and incentive for such a decision, because, if the part were transferred, Division B's cost would rise to $15 + $8 = $23, which would be $6 higher than B's prospective revenue of $17 per unit. So B would choose not to buy from A at the $15 market price.

As Exhibit 10-1 also shows, if there were idle capacity in Division A, the optimum action would be to produce the part and transfer it to Division B. If there were no production and transfer, Division B and the company as a whole would forgo a total contribution of $30,000. In this situation, variable cost[4] would be the better basis for transfer pricing and would lead to the optimum decision for the firm as a whole.

☐ DYSFUNCTIONAL BEHAVIOR

Reconsider the situation depicted in Exhibit 10-1. If there were idle capacity in Division A, the optimum transfer price would be the $6 variable cost. Neverthe-

---

[4]"Variable" is used here (but with misgivings) because the term is so widely used in the literature and in practice. "Variable" should be interpreted broadly here as including all pertinent "outlay" costs (those additional costs that will be incurred by the production of the units in question.) For example, if a special lump-sum outlay such as a setup cost were engendered by the order for 10,000 units, it would be added to the "variable" costs in Exhibit 10-1 for purposes of this analysis.

less, in a decentralized company the Division A manager, working in his own best interests, may argue that the transfer price should be based on the $15 market price rather than $6. If his subunit is a profit center, his incentive is to obtain as high a price as possible above the $6 variable cost, because such a price maximizes the contribution to the subunit profit. (Of course, the latter statement assumes that the number of units transferred will be unaffected by the transfer price—an assumption that is often shaky.)

So the solutions to the problems of goal congruence and incentive may conflict. From the companywide viewpoint, the desired transfers may not occur because each subunit manager, pursuing his own best interest, could decide against a transfer. This is an example of **dysfunctional behavior**, which is defined as actions taken in conflict with top-management goals. These conflicts are sometimes overcome by having a superior manager impose a "fair" transfer price and insist that a transfer be made. But the managers of subunits within an organization that has an announced policy of decentralization often regard such orders as undermining their autonomy. So the imposition of a price may solve the congruence and incentive problem but intensify the autonomy problem. Transfer pricing thus becomes a delicate balancing act in systems design.

The general difficulties are exemplified by the following:

> Levels of the subunits tried to make their results look good at each other's expense. One widespread result: Inflated transfer payments among the Gulf subunits as each one vied to boost its own bottom line. A top manager commented, "Gulf doesn't ring the cash register until we've made an outside sale."[5]

☐ USE OF INCENTIVES

What should top management of a decentralized organization do if it sees dysfunctional decisions being made at the subunit level? As usual, the answer is "It depends." If top management steps in and forces transfers, it undermines autonomy. This may have to be done occasionally, but if top management imposes its will too often, the organization is in substance being recentralized. Of course, if the decision were indeed not to give autonomy, the organization could be redesigned by combining the two subunits.

Top managers who are proponents of decentralization will be more reluctant to impose their desires. Instead, they will make sure that both A and B managers understand all the facts, are good company citizens, and will make sacrifices for the company as a whole. If they think a dysfunctional decision is going to be made anyway, some top managers swallow hard and accept the subunit manager's judgments.

Keep in mind that a decentralized setup is usually initiated primarily because top managers think that the subunit managers have more information at the local level that permits these subordinates to make better collective decisions about all sorts of options. Therefore, second-guessing the local managers really means that the top manager is saying, "I know more than you do about the condition of the local markets."

Being a good corporate citizen may be one way to appeal to subunit

[5]"Gulf Oil Goes Back to What It Knows Best," *Business Week,* January 31, 1977, p. 80. Richard Vancil, *Decentralization: Managerial Ambiguity by Design* (New York: Financial Executives Research Foundation, 1979), covers problems of decentralization and transfer pricing in more depth.

managers to make goal-congruent decisions, but building in some formal incentives typically is far more persuasive. As a result, some companies would try various incentives in reaction to our illustration in Exhibit 10-1. For example, the contribution to the company as a whole, $30,000 in the idle-capacity case, would be split between A and B, perhaps equally, perhaps in proportion to the variable costs of each, or perhaps via negotiation.[6]

The need for many transfer prices

Previous sections have pointed out that there is seldom a single transfer price that will ensure the desired decisions. The "correct" transfer price depends on the economic and legal circumstances and the decision at hand. We may want one transfer price for congruence and a second for incentive. Furthermore, the optimal price for either may differ from that employed for tax reporting or for other external needs.

Income taxes, property taxes, and tariffs often influence the setting of transfer prices so that the firm as a whole will benefit, even though the performance of a subunit may suffer. To minimize tariffs and domestic income taxes, a company may want to set an unusually low selling price for a domestic division that ships goods to foreign subsidiaries in countries where the prevailing tax rates are lower. To maximize tax deductions for percentage depletion allowances, which are based on revenue, a petroleum company may want to transfer crude oil to other subunits at as high a price as legally possible.

Transfer pricing is also influenced in some situations because of state fair-trade laws and national antitrust acts. Because of the differences in national tax structures around the world or because of the differences in the incomes of various divisions and subsidiaries, the firm may wish to shift profits and "dump" goods, if legally possible. These considerations are additional illustrations of the limits of decentralization where heavy interdependencies exist and of why the same company may use different transfer prices for different purposes.

Measures of profitability

☐ RETURN ON INVESTMENT

A favorite objective of top management is to maximize profitability. The trouble is that profitability does not mean the same thing to all people. Is it net income? Income before taxes? Net income percentage based on revenue? Is it an absolute amount? A percentage?

Too often, managers stress net income or income percentages without tying the measure into the investment associated with the generating of the income. A better test of profitability is the rate of return on investment (ROI). That is, given the same risks, for any given amount of resources required, the investor wants the maximum income. To say that Project A has an income of

[6]Other examples include using the dual allocation described in the preceding chapter—that is, transfer at standard variable cost. In addition, a predetermined lump-sum charge is made for fixed costs, based on a long-run commitment of the buyer to support the supplier. In this way the buyer's month-to-month decisions are not influenced by the supplier's fixed costs.

$200,000 and Project B has an income of $150,000 is an insufficient statement about profitability. The required investment in A may be $500,000, and the required investment in B may be only $150,000. Based on rate of return, all other things being equal, A's return would be much less than B's.

The ROI measure is a useful common denominator. It can be compared with rates inside and outside the organization and with opportunities in other projects and industries. It is affected by two major ingredients:

$$\frac{\text{rate of return on}}{\text{invested capital}} = \frac{\text{income}}{\text{invested capital}}$$

$$= \frac{\text{income}}{\text{revenue}} \times \frac{\text{revenue}}{\text{invested capital}}$$

$$= \text{income percentage of revenue} \times \text{capital turnover}$$

The terms of this equation are deliberately vague at this point because various versions of income, revenue, and invested capital are possible. Ponder the components of the equation. The rate of return is the result of the combination of two items, **income percentage of revenue** and **capital turnover**. An improvement in either without changing the other will improve the rate of return on invested capital.

Consider an example of these relationships:

	RATE OF RETURN ON INVESTED CAPITAL		$\dfrac{\text{INCOME}}{\text{REVENUE}}$	$\times$	$\dfrac{\text{REVENUE}}{\text{INVESTED CAPITAL}}$
Present outlook	20%	=	$\dfrac{16}{100}$	$\times$	$\dfrac{100}{80}$
Alternatives:					
1. Increase income percentage by reducing expenses	25%	=	$\dfrac{20}{100}$	$\times$	$\dfrac{100}{80}$
2. Increase turnover by decreasing investment in inventories	25%	=	$\dfrac{16}{100}$	$\times$	$\dfrac{100}{64}$

Alternative 1 is a popular way to improve performance. An alert management tries to decrease expenses without reducing sales in proportion or to boost sales without increasing related expenses in proportion.

Alternative 2 is less popular, but it may be a quicker way to improve performance. Increasing this turnover of invested capital means generating higher revenue for each dollar invested in such assets as cash, receivables, or inventories. There is an optimal level of investment in these assets. Having too much is wasteful, but having too little may hurt credit standing and the ability to compete for sales.

☐ ROI OR RESIDUAL INCOME?

Most managers agree that the rate of return on investment is the ultimate test of profitability. Intelligently used, ROI can help guide decision making. However, some companies favor emphasizing an *absolute amount* of income rather than a *rate* of return. This approach is called *residual income* (RI). For example, residual income may be defined as follows:

	FIGURES ASSUMED
Divisional net income after taxes	$900,000
Minus imputed interest on average invested capital	800,000
Equals residual income	$100,000

Suppose that the average invested capital in the division for the year was $10 million. The corporate headquarters assesses an "imputed" interest charge of 8 percent (.08 × $10,000,000 = $800,000). The word "imputed" in this context means that the charge is made regardless of whether the corporation as a whole has actually incurred an interest cost in the ordinary sense of a cash disbursement. The rate represents the minimum acceptable rate for investments in that division.

Why do some companies (such as General Electric) prefer RI to ROI? The ROI approach shows:

Divisional net income after taxes	$900,000
Average invested capital	$10,000,000
Return on investment	9%

Residual income is favored for reasons of goal congruence and incentive. Under ROI, the basic message is, "Go forth and maximize your rate of return, a percentage." Thus managers of highly profitable divisions may be reluctant to invest in projects at, say 8 percent if their division is currently earning, say, 18 percent, because their average ROI would be reduced.

From the viewpoint of the company as a whole, top management may want this division manager to accept any projects that earn 8 percent or more. Under RI, the manager would be inclined to invest in projects earning more than 8 percent even if his or her division were currently earning 18 percent. The basic message is, "Go forth and maximize residual income, an absolute amount."

Distinction between managers and investments

As Chapter 9 explained (see Exhibit 9-4), a distinction should be made between the performance of the division manager and the performance of the division as an investment by the corporation. Managers should be evaluated on the basis of their controllable performance (in many cases some controllable contribution in relation to controllable investment). For other decisions, "such as new investment or a withdrawal of funds from the division, the important thing is the success or failure of the divisional venture, not of the men who run it."[7]

[7]David Solomons, *Divisional Performance: Measurement and Control* (Homewood, Ill.: Richard D. Irwin, 1968), p. 84. Solomons also discusses residual income.

This distinction helps clarify some vexing difficulties. For example, top management may want to use an investment base to gauge the economic performance of a retail store, but the *manager* may best be judged by focusing on income and forgetting about any investment allocations. If investment is assigned to the manager, the aim should be to assign controllable investment only. Controllability depends on what *decisions* managers can make regarding the size of the investment base. In a highly decentralized company, for instance, the manager can influence the size of all his or her assets and can exercise judgment regarding the appropriate amount of short-term credit and perhaps some long-term credit.

Key role of budget

☐ MANAGEMENT BY OBJECTIVES

Management by objectives (MBO) is a term that describes the joint formulation by a manager and his superior of a set of goals and of plans for achieving the goals for a forthcoming period.[8] For our purposes here, the terms *goals* and *objectives* are synonyms. The plans often take the form of a responsibility accounting budget (together with supplementary goals such as levels of management training and safety that may not be incorporated into the accounting budget). The manager's performance is then evaluated in relation to these agreed-upon budgeted objectives.

Regardless of whether it is so labeled, a management-by-objectives approach lessens the complaints about lack of controllability because of its stress on *budgeted results.* That is, a budget is negotiated between a particular manager and his or her superior for a *particular* time period and a *particular* set of expected outside and inside influences. In this way, a manager may more readily accept an assignment to a less successful subunit. This is preferable to a system that emphasizes absolute profitability for its own sake. Unless focus is placed on currently attainable results, able managers will be reluctant to accept responsibility for subunits that are in economic trouble.

Thus, skillful budgeting and intelligent performance evaluation will go a long way toward overcoming the common lament: "I'm being held responsible for costs beyond my control."

☐ TAILORING BUDGETS FOR MANAGERS

Many of the troublesome motivational effects of performance evaluation systems can be minimized by the astute use of budgets. The desirability of tailoring a budget to particular managers cannot be overemphazised. For example, either an ROI or an RI system can promote goal congruence and incentive if top management gets everybody to focus on what is currently attainable in the forthcoming budget period. Typically, divisional managers do not have complete freedom to make major investment decisions without checking with senior management.

[8]G. Odiorne, *Management Decisions by Objectives* (Englewood Cliffs, N.J.: Prentice-Hall, 1970); and R. Brady, "MBO Goes to Work in the Public Sector," *Harvard Business Review,* March-April 1973, pp. 65–74.

In sum, our cost-benefit approach provides no universal answers with respect to such controversial issues as historical values versus current values or return on investment versus residual income. Instead, each organization must judge for itself whether an alternate control system or accounting technique will improve collective decision making. The latter is the central criterion.

Too often, the literature engages in pro-and-con discussion about which alternative is more perfect or truer than another in some logical sense. The cost-benefit approach is not concerned with "truth" or "perfection" by itself. Instead, it asks, "Do you think your perceived 'truer' or 'more logical' system is worth its added cost? Or will our existing imperfect system provide about the same set of decisions if it is skillfully administered?"[9]

Definitions of invested capital and income

Consider the following balance sheet classifications:

Current assets	$ 400,000		Current liabilities	$ 200,000
Property, plant and equipment	800,000		Long-term liabilities	400,000
Construction in progress	100,000		Stockholders' equity	700,000
Total assets	$1,300,000		Total equities	$1,300,000

Possible definitions of invested capital include

1. *Total assets.* All assets are included, $1,300,000.

2. *Total assets employed.* All assets except agreed-upon exclusions of vacant land or construction in progress, $1,300,000 − $100,000 = $1,200,000.

3. *Total assets less current liabilities.* All assets except that portion supplied by short-term creditors, $1,300,000 − $200,000 = $1,100,000. This is sometimes expressed as *long-term invested capital;* note that it can also be computed by adding the long-term liabilities and the stockholders' equity, $400,000 + $700,000 = $1,100,000.

4. *Stockholders' equity.* Focuses on the investment of the owners of the business, $700,000.

All of the above are computed as averages for the period under review. These averages may be based simply on the beginning and ending balances or on more complicated averages that weigh changes in investments through the months.

For measuring the performance of division managers, any of the three asset bases is recommended rather than stockholders' equity. If the division manager's mission is to utilize all assets as best he or she can without regard to

[9]For an expanded discussion, see C. Horngren, "Budgets, Respect, and Inflation," *Journal of Accountancy,* March 1980. Also see James S. Reece and William R. Cool, "Measuring Investment Center Performance," *Harvard Business Review,* May-June 1978, p. 28.

their financing, then base 1 is best. If top management directs the manager to carry extra assets that are not currently productive, then base 2 is best. If the manager has direct control over obtaining short-term credit and bank loans, then base 3 is best.[10] In practice, base 1 is used most often, although base 3 is not far behind.

A few companies allocate long-term debt to their divisions and thus have an approximation of the stockholders' equity in each division. However, this practice has doubtful merit. Division managers typically have little responsibility for the long-term *financial* management of their divisions, as distinguished from *operating* management. You might compare how the investment base of a division manager of Company A might differ radically from the investment base of a comparable division manager of Company B, if A bore heavy long-term debt and B were debt-free.

☐ ALLOCATION TO DIVISIONS

Various definitions of income for the segments of an organization were discussed in the preceding chapter, so they will not be repeated here. Just as cost allocations affect income, asset allocations affect the invested capital of particular divisions. The aim is to allocate in a manner that will be goal-congruent, will provide incentive, and will recognize autonomy insofar as possible. Incidentally, as long as the managers feel that they are being treated uniformly, they tend to be more tolerant of the imperfections of the allocation.

A frequent criterion for asset allocation is avoidability. That is, the amount allocable to any given segment for the purpose of evaluating the division's performance is the amount that the corporation as a whole could avoid by not having that segment. Commonly used bases for allocation, when assets are not directly identifiable with a specific division, include:

ASSET CLASS	POSSIBLE ALLOCATION BASE
Corporate cash	Budgeted cash needs, as discussed below
Receivables	Sales weighted by payment terms
Inventories	Budgeted sales or usage
Plant and equipment	Usage of services in terms of long-run forecasts of demand or area occupied

The allocation of central corporate assets often parallels the allocation of central corporate costs. Where the allocation of an asset would indeed be arbitrary, many managers feel that it is better not to allocate.

Should cash be included under controllable investment if the balances are strictly controlled by corporate headquarters? Arguments can be made for both sides, but the manager is usually regarded as being responsible for the volume of business generated by the division. In turn, this volume is likely to have a direct effect on the overall cash needs of the corporation.

[10] Reece and Cool, "Measuring Investment Center Performance," surveyed the practices of 620 companies. Of these, 459 used investment centers; 51 percent deducted external current payables in calculating an investment center's asset base.

Central control of cash is usually undertaken to reduce the holdings from what would be used if each division had a separate account. Fluctuations in cash needs of each division will be somewhat offsetting, and backup borrowing power is increased. These factors make allocation of cash to the subunits difficult.

The allocation of cash on the basis of sales dollars seldom gets at the economic rationale of cash holdings. As Chapter 6 explains, cash needs are influenced by a host of factors, including payment terms of customers and creditors.

If the criterion of avoidability is used, the cash assignments should be done in recognition of offsetting "portfolio" effects. For example, Division A might have a cash deficiency of $1 million in February, but Division B might have an offsetting cash excess of $1 million. Taken together for the year, Divisions A, B, C, D, and others might require a combined investment in cash of, say, $16 million if each were independent entities but only $8 million if cash were controlled centrally. Hence, if Division C would ordinarily require a $4 million investment in cash as a separate entity, it would be allocated an investment of only $2 million as a subunit of a company where cash was controlled centrally.

Measurement alternatives

☐ VALUATION OF ASSETS

There is a widespread tendency to have one asset measure serve many masters. Should the assets contained in the investment base be valued at net book value (original cost less accumulated depreciation), some version of current value, or some other way? Practice is overwhelmingly in favor of using net book value:[11]

	NUMBER	PERCENTAGE
Gross book value	63	14%
Net book value	389	85
Replacement cost	10	2
Other	2	0
No answer	8	2
Total	472*	103%

Number of responding companies was 459. Includes multiple responses. Note that only 2 percent used replacement cost, a remarkably low percentage in light of the inflation of the 1970s.

Historical cost has been widely criticized for many years as providing a faulty basis for decision making and performance evaluation. As Chapters 4 and 5 point out, historical costs are irrelevant per se for making economic decisions. Despite these criticisms, and despite the increasing external requirements for using current values such as replacement costs for asset valuation,[12] managers have been slow to depart from historical cost.

[11]Reece and Cool, "Measuring Investment Center Performance," p. 42.

[12]See Chapter 19 for a discussion of the use of current values and general price-level indexes as a basis of asset valuation and income measurement.

Why is historical cost so widely used? Some critics would say that sheer ignorance is the explanation. But a more persuasive answer comes from cost-benefit analysis. Accounting systems are costly. Historical records must be kept for many legal purposes; therefore they are already in place. No additional money must be spent to obtain an evaluation of performance based on the historical-cost system. Furthermore, many managements believe that such a system provides the desired goal congruence and incentive. That is, a more sophisticated system will not radically improve the collective operating decisions that are desired. In short, the historical-cost system is good enough for the *routine* evaluation of performance. In nonroutine instances, such as replacing equipment or deleting a product line, managers will conduct special studies to gather any current valuations that seem relevant.

The impending required introduction in external reporting of "current costs" in the United Kingdom and Australia and the required disclosures of "current costs" in American external reporting will probably also cause their wider use internally. Thus, such current-value information will have to be gathered in a routine manner to satisfy external requirements. When current values are already available, the incremental costs (including the costs of educating users, which are high) of using such values for internal performance measurement purposes are much less imposing than when current values must be installed from scratch.

□ PLANT AND EQUIPMENT: GROSS OR NET?

Although net book value is extensively used, gross book value was used by 14 percent of the companies surveyed. The proponents of gross book value maintain that it facilitates comparisons between years and between plants or divisions.

Consider an example of a $600,000 piece of equipment with a three-year life and no residual value:

YEAR	OPERATING INCOME BEFORE DEPRECIATION	DEPRECIATION	OPERATING INCOME	AVERAGE INVESTMENT			
				net book value	rate of return	gross book value	rate of return
1	$260,000	$200,000	$60,000	$500,000	12%	$600,000	10%
2	260,000	200,000	60,000	300,000	20%	600,000	10%
3	260,000	200,000	60,000	100,000	60%	600,000	10%

The rate of return on net book value goes up as the equipment ages; note that it could increase even if operating income gradually declined through the years. In contrast, the rate of return on gross book value is unchanged if operating income does not change; moreover, the rate would decrease if operating income gradually declined through the years.

The advocates of using net book value maintain:

1. It is less confusing because it is consistent with the assets shown on the conventional balance sheet and with the net income computations.

2. The major criticism of net book value is not peculiar to its use for ROI purposes. It is really a criticism of using historical cost as a basis for evaluation.

This author is not enchanted with the gross book value method because of its inherent inconsistency. To show depreciation on an income statement and not deduct it on the balance sheet seems like an awkward means of remedying some peculiarities of historical-cost accounting. Instead, if net book value is yielding unsatisfactory measures of performance, serious consideration should be given to revising the straight-line patterns of depreciation[13] or to using current values.

Choosing desired rates of return

Whatever their merits, neither the ROI nor the residual-income method can be used without considering the cost of capital. Critical questions include (a) what minimum rates to specify; (b) when and by how much minimum rates should be altered; and (c) whether the same minimum rates should be used in each segment of the organization. If a uniform rate is used and many divisions are currently earning different rates, the use of a very low rate will surely drive ROI down toward such a rate. Moreover, frequent changes in the rate may be demoralizing as well as nonoptimal. For example, it might lead to acceptance of an 11 percent prospective return when the minimum rate is 11 percent, and rejection of a 15 percent prospective rate when the minimum rate is 16 percent.

Modern financial theory supports the use of different rates for different divisions. Portfolio theory provides the analytical framework for the investment decision under uncertainty. The firm would be viewed as a collection of different classes of assets whose income streams bear different risks. The minimum desired rates of return are functions of risk. Various divisions face different risks. Therefore a different minimum desired rate should be used for each division, based on the relative investment risk of each.[14]

The Reece and Cool survey revealed the following practices:

Survey question: If you use ROI (alone or with residual income), how do you set an investment center's target or budgeted ROI percentage?

Survey responses:

	NUMBER	PERCENTAGE
All investment centers are expected to earn the same ROI	30	7%
Each investment center is assigned its own target ROI based on its profit potential	294	64
Investment centers are not given target ROIs	105	23
No answer or not applicable	30	7
Total	459	101%*

Because of rounding.

[13] Solomons, *Divisional Performance,* p. 135. He discusses these issues at length on pp. 134–42.

[14] James Van Horne, *Financial Management and Policy,* 5th ed. (Englewood Cliffs, N.J.: Prentice-Hall, 1980), Chap. 8, gives a detailed discussion of the finance issues summarized here.

The majority practice is roughly consistent with modern financial theory. Note also how a budgeted ROI can be adjusted to allow for special circumstances facing a division. In developing target rates within a division, top management would be consistent with modern financial theory by using different rates for different divisional assets. For example, one rate may be used for investments in current assets and another rate for plant assets.

Alternatives of timing

Accounting textbooks, including this one, do not discuss at length the problem of timing. However, timing is an important factor to consider when an information system is designed. For instance, the costs of gathering and processing information and the need for frequent feedback for controlling current operations may lead to using historical-cost measures rather than replacement costs. The need for replacement costs, realizable values, and economic values tends to be less frequent, so the systems are not designed for providing such information routinely.

Admittedly, this point was made earlier in the chapter. Nevertheless, it is repeated here because it is a likely explanation of why actual practice seems to differ so markedly from what theory may prefer. The essence of the matter is that management seems unwilling to pay for more elegant information because its extra costs exceed its prospective benefits.

Another aspect of timing underscores why management accounting systems are seldom static. A system that works well in 1980 may not suffice in 1985. Why? Because top management's desires and the attitudes of various managers may change. For example, top management may not allocate the costs of the internal auditing department in 1980 in order to encourage all managers to use auditing services. In 1985 top management may begin allocating auditing services in order to discourage use.

Why profit centers?

The literature contains many criticisms of profit centers on the grounds that managers are given profit responsibility without commensurate authority. Therefore, the criticism continues, the profit center is "artificial" because the manager is not free to make a sufficient number of the decisions that affect his or her profit.

Such criticisms confuse profit centers and decentralization; early in this chapter, we stressed that one can exist without the other. The fundamental question in deciding between using a cost center or a profit center for a given subunit is not whether heavy decentralization exists. Instead, the fundamental question is, "Will a profit center better solve the problems of goal congruence and incentive than a cost center? In other words, do I predict that a profit center will induce the managers to make a better collective set of decisions from the viewpoint of the organization as a whole?"

All control systems are imperfect. Judgments about their merits should concentrate on which alternative system will bring the actions top management seeks. For example, a plant may be a "natural" cost center because the plant manager has no influence over decisions concerning the marketing of its products. Still, some companies impose profit responsibility on the plant manager by either creating some transfer price above cost or by including the marketing costs on the plant manager's income statement. Why? Because it has changed the plant manager's behavior. How? Instead of being concerned solely with running an efficient cost center, the plant manager now "naturally" considers quality control more carefully and reacts to customers' special requests more sympathetically. The profit center obtained the desired plant-manager behavior that the cost center failed to achieve.

From the viewpoint of top management, plant managers often have more influence on sales than is apparent at first glance. This is an example of how systems may evolve from cost centers to profit centers and an example of the first-line importance of predicting behavioral effects when an accounting control system is designed.

Control systems in nonprofit organizations

Most nonprofit organizations have more difficulty in identifying objectives or goals than do profit-seeking organizations. There is no profit, no "bottom line" that so often serves as a powerful incentive in private industry. Furthermore, monetary incentives are generally less effective in nonprofit organizations. For example, many managers seek positions in nonprofit organizations primarily for nonmonetary rewards.

Control systems in nonprofit organizations will never be as highly developed as in profit-seeking organizations for several reasons, including:

1. Organizational goals or objectives are less clear. Moreover, they are often multiple, requiring trade-offs.
2. Professionals (for example, teachers, attorneys, physicians, scientists, economists) tend to dominate nonprofit organizations. They are usually less receptive to the installation or improvement of formal control systems.[15]
3. Measurements are more difficult:
   a. There is no profit measure.
   b. There are heavy amounts of discretionary fixed costs.
   c. The relationships of inputs to outputs are hard to specify and measure. Attempts to relate inputs to outputs via work measurement are often resisted.

Additional difficulties arise because of the lesser role of the marketplace, the greater role of politics, and the vague sense of responsibility because "ownership" of nonprofit organizations is often ill-defined.

Budgeting was originally developed in the public sector as a way of providing accountability. However, the management uses of budgets have been unimpressive. Too often, the budget is regarded as a means of obtaining money, not as a means of planning and control. Thus the process of budgeting in the public sector is often a matter of playing bargaining games with higher authorities to get the largest possible authorization of discretionary fixed costs.

---

[15] Anthony and Herzlinger, *Nonprofit Organizations*, pp. 34–58, discuss differences between nonprofit and other organizations. Also see R. Anthony and J. Dearden, *Management Control Systems*, 4th ed. (Homewood Ill.: Richard D. Irwin, 1980), Chap. 16.

summary

The starting point for judging a management accounting or management control system is the specification of top-management goals and subgoals. Systems typically are designed within the constraints of a given set of goals and a given organization structure. The final selection of a system depends on costs, congruence, and incentive. Above all, top management should predict which alternative system is more likely to produce the best collective set of operating decisions in light of the costs of the systems.

As organizations grow, decentralization of some management functions becomes desirable. Decentralization immediately raises problems of obtaining decisions that are coordinated with the objectives of the organization as a whole. Ideally, planning and control systems should provide information that (a) aims managers toward decisions that are goal-congruent, (b) provides feedback (evaluation of performance) that improves incentive and future decisions, and (c) preserves autonomy. Note that the common thread of these problems is motivation.

Transfer-pricing systems are often used as a means of communicating data among subunits. There is rarely a single transfer price that will serve all requirements. Instead, there may be one transfer price for making a particular production decision, another for evaluating performance, and another for minimizing tariffs or income taxes. The choice of transfer-pricing systems must contend with problems of cost-benefit trade-offs, goal congruence, incentives, and autonomy.

Many techniques, such as ROI or residual income, fall far short of the ideal goals stipulated above. Nevertheless, in practice their conceptual shortcomings may be unimportant; often they are the best techniques available for obtaining the perceived top-management goals.

Despite the theoretical attractiveness of various nonhistorical accounting methods, most managements have apparently decided that a historical-cost system is good enough for the **routine** evaluation of managers. Evidently this crude approach provides the desired motivational effects and gives clues as to whether to invest or disinvest in a particular division. The investment decision is evidently not routine enough to justify gathering information regarding replacement costs or realizable values except as special decisions arise.

Profit centers are usually associated with heavily decentralized organizations, whereas cost centers are usually associated with heavily centralized organizations. However, profit centers and decentralization are separate ideas; one can exist without the other.

Although this point was not mentioned in the chapter, any control system requires enthusiastic support from senior management if it is to be taken seriously by subordinates. Indeed, top-management support is so important that it deserves nearly as much prominence as goal congruence and incentive as a major problem in designing systems.

summary problems
for your review

PROBLEM ONE

Examine Exhibit 10-1. In addition to the data there, suppose that Division A has fixed manufacturing costs of $400,000 and expected annual production of 100,000 units. The "full absorption cost" per unit was computed as follows:

Variable costs per unit	$ 6
Fixed costs, $400,000 ÷ 100,000 units	4
Full absorption cost per unit	$10

REQUIRED

Assume that Division A has idle capacity. Division B is considering whether to buy 10,000 units to be processed further and sold for $17. The additional costs shown in Exhibit 10-1 for Division B would prevail. If transfers were based on absorption cost, would the B manager buy? Why? Would the company as a whole benefit if the B manager decided to buy? Why?

PROBLEM TWO

A division has assets of $200,000 and operating income of $60,000.

1. What is the division's ROI?

2. If interest is imputed at 14 percent, what is the residual income?

3. What effects on management behavior can be expected if ROI is used to gauge performance?

4. What effects on management behavior can be expected if residual income is used to gauge performance?

SOLUTION TO PROBLEM ONE

B would not buy. Absorption costing may occasionally lead to dysfunctional decisions. The absorption-costing transfer price of $10 would make the acquisition of parts unattractive to B:

Division B:			
Sales price of final product			$ 17
Deduct costs:			
Transfer price per unit paid to A (absorption cost)		$10	
Additional costs (from Exhibit 10-1):			
Processing	$4		
Selling	4	8	
Total costs to B			18
Contribution to profit of B			$ −1
Contribution to company as a whole (from Exhibit 10-1)			$ 3

As Exhibit 10-1 shows, the company as a whole would benefit by $30,000 ($10,000 units × $3) if the units were transferred.

The major lesson here is that, when idle capacity exists in the supplier division, transfer prices based on absorption costs may induce the wrong decisions. Working in his or her own best interests, the B manager has no incentive to buy from A.

1. $60,000 \div \$200,000 = 30\%$

2. $60,000 - .14(\$200,000) = \$60,000 - \$28,000 = \$32,000$

3. If ROI is used, the manager is prone to reject projects that do not earn an ROI of at least 30 percent. From the viewpoint of the organization as a whole, this may be undesirable because its best investment opportunities may lie in that division at a rate of, say, 22 percent. If a division is enjoying a high ROI, it is less likely to expand if it is judged via ROI than if it is judged via residual income.

4. If residual income is used, the manager is inclined to accept all projects whose expected ROI exceeds the minimum desired rate. The manager's division is more likely to expand, because his or her goal is to maximize a dollar amount rather than a rate.

assignment material

■ FUNDAMENTAL ASSIGNMENT MATERIAL

10-1. Terminology. Define *capital turnover; decentralization; dysfunctional behavior; goal congruence; incentive; organization structure; profit center; transfer price.*

10-2. Rate of return and transfer pricing. A company division manager has tentatively placed a selling price of $2 on his product. His division's asset and cost structure follows:

Cash	$ 10,000
Receivables	20,000
Inventories	70,000
Fixed assets, net	100,000
	$200,000

Fixed overhead	$80,000
Variable costs	$1.50 per unit
Desired rate of return of operating income divided by average assets available	20%

1. a. How many units must be sold in order to obtain the desired rate of return?
   b. What would be the expected asset turnover?
   c. What would be the operating income percentage on dollar sales?
2. a. What rate of return would be earned on available assets if the selling price were $1.90 and the sales volume 280,000 units?
   b. If the selling price were $2.20 and sales volume 200,000 units?
3. Assume that 40,000 of a normal total volume of 240,000 units are usually sold each year to another division of the same company. The two division managers are currently trying to agree on a transfer price for the coming year. The buying division manager has offered $1.80, claiming that he can buy the units from another company at that price. The selling division manager has decided that he can eliminate $10,000 of inventories, $10,000 of fixed assets, and $8,000 of fixed overhead if he does not sell to the other division. Should he sell for $1.80? Show computations to support your answer.

10-3. Transfer-pricing dispute. A manufacturer of auto parts is heavily decentralized. For example, each division manager has complete authority to decide whether to buy or sell inside or outside the company. Division B has routinely acquired a transmission component from Division A for many years. Nevertheless, when A announced a price increase from $18 to $20, B's management decided to purchase the component from an outside supplier at $18.

Division A had recently purchased some specialized equipment that was used primarily to make the component in question. The manager said that the resulting high depreciation charges justified the price increase. He asked the president to instruct Division B to buy from A at the $20 price. He supplied the following:

B's annual purchases of component	100,000 units
A's variable costs per unit	$17
A's fixed costs per unit	$ 3

REQUIRED

1. Suppose that there are no alternative uses of the A facilities. Will the company as a whole benefit if B purchases from the outside suppliers for $18 per unit? Show computations.

2. Suppose the equipment and other facilities of A were assigned to other manufacturing operations. Without such equipment and facilities, the conduct of these other operations would require an additional annual outlay of $140,000. Should B buy the component from outsiders at $18 per unit?

3. Suppose there are no alternative uses for A's internal facilities and that the selling price of outsiders falls to $15. Should B purchase from outsiders?

4. As the president, how would you respond to the manager of A? Would your response differ, depending on the specific situations described in Requirements 1 through 3 above? Why?

ADDITIONAL ASSIGNMENT MATERIAL

10-4. "There are corporate objectives other than profit." Name four.

10-5. What is the most important question in judging the effectiveness of a measure of performance?

10-6. What eight areas has General Electric Company used to avoid overemphasis of one performance measure?

10-7. Give three examples of how managers may improve short-run performance to the detriment of long-run results.

10-8. "The essence of decentralization is the use of profit centers." Do you agree? Explain.

10-9. What is the major benefit of the ROI technique for measuring performance?

10-10. "There is an optimum level of investment in any asset." Explain.

10-11. "Just as there may be different costs for different purposes, there may be different rates of return for different purposes." Explain.

10-12. Why are cost-based transfer prices in common use?

10-13. Why are transfer-pricing systems needed?

10-14. Why are interest expense and income taxes ordinarily excluded in computing incomes that are related to asset bases?

10-15. Simple calculations. You are given the following data:

Sales	$100,000,000
Invested capital	$20,000,000
Return on investment	10%

1. Turnover of capital.
2. Net income.
3. Net income as a percentage of sales.

10-16. Comparison of asset and equity bases. Company A has assets of $1 million and a long-term, 6 percent debt of $500,000. Company B has assets of $1 million and no long-term debt. The annual operating income (before interest) of both companies is $200,000.

Compute the rate of return on:
1. Assets available.
2. Stockholders' equity.
Evaluate the relative merits of each base for appraising operating management.

10-17. Using gross or net book value of fixed assets. Assume that a particular plant acquires $400,000 of fixed assets with a useful life of four years and no residual value. Straight-line depreciation will be used. The plant manager is judged on income in relation to these fixed assets. Annual net income, after deducting depreciation, is $40,000.

Assume that sales, and all expenses except depreciation, are on a cash basis. Dividends equal net income. Thus, cash in the amount of the depreciation charge will accumulate each year. The plant manager's performance is judged in relation to fixed assets because all current assets, including cash, are considered under central-company control.

1. Prepare a comparative tabulation of the plant's rate of return and the company's overall rate of return based on:
   a. Gross (i.e., original cost) assets.
   b. Net book value of assets. Assume (unrealistically) that any cash accumulated remains idle.
2. Evaluate the relative merits of gross assets and net book value of assets as investment bases.

10-18. Margins and turnover. Return on investment is often expressed as the product of two components—capital turnover and margin on sales. You are considering investing in one of three companies, all in the same industry, and are given the following information:

	COMPANY		
	X	Y	Z
Sales	$5,000,000	$ 2,500,000	$50,000,000
Income	500,000	250,000	250,000
Capital	2,000,000	20,000,000	20,000,000

1. Why would you desire the breakdown of return on investment into margin on sales and turnover on capital?
2. Compute the margin on sales, turnover on capital, and return on investment for the three companies, and comment on the relative performance of the companies as thoroughly as the data permit.

10-19. ROI or residual income. W. R. Drace Co. is a large integrated conglomerate with shipping, metals, and mining operations throughout the world. The general manager of the ferrous metals division has been directed to submit his proposed capital budget for 19X1 for inclusion in the companywide budget.

The division manager has for consideration the following projects, all of which require an outlay of capital. All projects have equal risk.

PROJECT	INVESTMENT REQUIRED	RETURN
1	$6,000,000	$1,380,000
2	2,400,000	768,000
3	1,750,000	245,000
4	1,200,000	216,000
5	800,000	160,000
6	350,000	98,000

The division manager must decide which of the projects to take. The company has a cost of capital of 15 percent. An amount of $15 million is available to the division for investment purposes.

REQUIRED

1. What will be the total investment, total return, return on capital invested, and residual income of the rational division manager if
   a. The company has a rule that all projects promising at least 20 percent or more should be taken.
   b. The division manager is evaluated on his ability to maximize his return on capital invested (assume that this is a new division with no invested capital).
   c. The division manager is expected to maximize residual income as computed by using the 15 percent cost of capital.
2. Which of the three approaches will induce the most effective investment policy for the company as a whole?

10-20. **Evaluating divisional performance.** As the chief executive officer of Acme Company, you examined the following measures of the performance of three divisions (in thousands of dollars):

| | NET ASSETS BASED ON | | OPERATING INCOME BASED ON* | |
DIVISION	HISTORICAL COST	REPLACEMENT COST	HISTORICAL COST	REPLACEMENT COST
X	10,000	10,000	1,800	1,800
Y	30,000	37,500	4,500	4,100
Z	20,000	32,000	3,200	2,600

*The differences in operating income between historical and replacement cost are attributable to the differences in depreciation expenses.

REQUIRED

1. Calculate for each division the rate of return on net assets and the residual income based on historical cost and on replacement cost. For purposes of calculating residual income, use 10 percent as the minimum desired rate of return.
2. Rank the performance of each division under each of the four different measures computed in Requirement 1.
3. What do these measures indicate about the performance of the divisions? Of the division managers? Which measure do you prefer? Why?

10-21. **Management by objectives.** (CMA.) John Press is the chief executive officer of Manfield Company. Press has a financial management background and is known throughout the organization as a "no-nonsense" executive. When Press became chief executive officer, he emphasized cost reduction and savings and introduced a comprehensive cost control and budget system. The company goals and budget plans were established by Press and given to his subordinates for implementation. Some of the company's key executives were dismissed or demoted for failing to meet projected budget plans. Under the leadership of John Press, Manfield has once again become financially stable and profitable after several years of poor performance.

Recently Press has become concerned with the human side of the organization and has become interested in the management technique referred to as "management by objectives" (MBO). If there are enough positive benefits of MBO, he plans to implement the system throughout the company. However, he realizes that he does not fully understand MBO because he does not understand how it differs from the current system of establishing firm objectives and budget plans.

REQUIRED

1. Briefly explain what "management by objectives" entails and identify its advantages and disadvantages.
2. Does the management style of John Press incorporate the human value premises and goals of MBO? Explain your answer.

10-22. **Multiple goals and profitability.**[16] The following are multiple goals of the General Electric Company:

1. Profitability
2. Market position
3. Productivity
4. Product leadership
5. Personnel development
6. Employee attitudes
7. Public responsibility
8. Balance between short-range and long-range goals

General Electric is a Goliath corporation with sales of about $25 billion and assets of $19 billion in 1980. It had approximately 170 responsibility centers called "departments," but that is a deceiving term. In most other companies, these departments would be called divisions. For example, some GE departments have sales of over $300 million.

Each department manager's performance is evaluated annually in relation to the specified multiple goals. A special measurements group was set up in 1952 to devise ways of quantifying accomplishments in each of the areas. In this way, the evaluation of performance would become more objective as the various measures were developed and improved.

REQUIRED

1. How would you measure performance in each of these areas? Be specific.
2. Can the other goals be encompassed as ingredients of a formal measure of profitability? In other words, can profitability *per se* be defined to include the other goals?

10-23. **Salesmen's compensation plan.** You are sales manager of a manufacturing firm whose sales are subject to month-to-month variations, depending upon the individual salesman's efforts. A new salary-plus-bonus plan has been in effect for four months and you are reviewing a sales performance report. The plan provides for a base salary of $400 per month, a $500 bonus each month if the salesman's monthly quota is met, and an additional commission of 5 percent on all sales over the monthly quota.

		SALESMAN A	SALESMAN B	SALESMAN C
January	Quota	$30,000	$10,000	$50,000
	Actual	10,000	10,000	60,000
February	Quota	$10,300	$10,300	$61,800
	Actual	20,000	10,300	40,000
March	Quota	$20,600	$10,600	$41,200
	Actual	35,000	5,000	60,000
April	Quota	$36,050	$ 5,150	$61,800
	Actual	15,000	5,200	37,000

Evaluate the compensation plan. Be specific. What changes would you recommend?

[16] Adapted from a problem originally appearing in R. H. Hassler and Neil E. Harlan, *Cases in Controllership* (Englewood Cliffs, N.J.: Prentice-Hall).

10-24. Variable cost as a transfer price. A product's variable cost is $2 and its market value is $3 at a transfer point from Division S to Division P. Division P's variable cost of processing the product further is $2.25, and the selling price of the final product is $4.75.

REQUIRED

1. Prepare a tabulation of the contribution margin per unit for Division P performance and overall performance under the two alternatives of (a) processing further and (b) selling to outsiders at the transfer point.
2. As Division P manager, which alternative would you choose? Explain.

10-25. Transfer pricing. Refer to Problem 10-3, Requirement 1 only. Suppose that Division A could modify the component at an additional variable cost of $2 per unit and sell the 100,000 units to other customers for $22 each. Then would the entire company benefit if B purchased the 100,000 components from outsiders at $18 per unit?

10-26. Transfer pricing. Newmill Enterprises runs a chain of drive-in hamburger stands on Cape Cod during the ten-week summer season. The manager of each stand is told to act as if he owned the stand and is judged on his profit performance. Newmill Enterprises has rented a soft-ice-cream machine for the summer, to supply its stands with ice cream for their frappés. Rent for the machine is $1,000. Newmill is not allowed to sell ice cream to other dealers because it cannot obtain a dairy license. The manager of the ice-cream machine charges the stands $3 per gallon. Operating figures for the machine for the summer are as follows:

Sales to the stands (10,000 gallons at $3)		$30,000
Variable costs, @ $1.60 per gallon	$16,000	
Fixed costs:		
Rental of machine	1,000	
Other fixed costs	4,000	21,000
Operating margin		$ 9,000

The manager of the Clam Bar, one of the Newmill drive-ins, is seeking permission to make a contract to buy ice cream from an outside supplier at $2.40 a gallon. The Clam Bar uses 2,000 gallons of soft ice cream during the summer. Frank Redmond, controller of Newmill Enterprises, refers this request to you. You determine that the Other Fixed Costs of operating the machine will decrease by $500 if the Clam Bar purchases from an outside supplier. He wants an analysis of the request in terms of overall company objectives and an explanation of your conclusion. What is the appropriate transfer price?

10-27. Transfer-pricing concession. (CMA, adapted.) The Ajax Division of Gunnco Corporation, operating at capacity, has been asked by the Defco Division of Gunnco to supply it with Electrical Fitting No. 1726. Ajax sells this part to its regular customers for $7.50 each. Defco, which is operating at 50 percent capacity, is willing to pay $5 each for the fitting. Defco will put the fitting into a brake unit that it is manufacturing on essentially a cost-plus basis for a commercial airplane manufacturer.

Ajax has a variable cost of producing fitting No. 1726 of $4.25. The cost of the brake unit as being built by Defco is as follows:

Purchased parts—outside vendors	$22.50
Ajax fitting No. 1726	5.00
Other variable costs	14.00
Fixed overhead and administration	8.00
	$49.50

Defco believes the price concession is necessary to get the job.

The company uses return on investment and dollar profits in the measurement of division and division-manager performance.

REQUIRED

1. Consider that you are the division controller of Ajax. Would you recommend that Ajax supply fitting No. 1726 to Defco? Why or why not? (Ignore any income tax issues.)
2. Would it be to the short-run economic advantage of the Gunnco Corporation for the Ajax Division to supply the Defco Division with fitting No. 1726 at $5 each? (Ignore any income tax issues.) Explain your answer.
3. Discuss the organizational and manager-behavior difficulties, if any, inherent in this situation. As the Gunnco controller, what would you advise the Gunnco Corporation president do in this situation?

10-28. **Profit centers and transfer pricing in an automobile dealership.** A large automobile dealership is installing a responsibility accounting system and three profit centers: parts and service; new vehicles; and used vehicles. Each department manager has been told to run his shop as if he were in business for himself. However, there are interdepartmental dealings. For example:

a. The parts and service department prepares new cars for final delivery and repairs used cars prior to resale.

b. The used-car department's major source of inventory has been cars traded in in part payment for new cars.

The owner of the dealership has asked you to draft a company policy statement on transfer pricing, together with specific rules to be applied to the examples cited. He has told you that clarity is of paramount importance because your statement will be relied upon for settling transfer-pricing disputes.

10-29. **Role of economic value and replacement value.** "To me, economic value is the only justifiable basis for measuring plant assets for purposes of evaluating performance. By economic value, I mean the present value of expected future services. Still, we do not even do this upon acquisition of new assets—that is, we may compute a positive net present value, using discounted cash flow; but we record the asset at no more than its cost. In this way, the excess present value is not shown in the initial balance sheet. Moreover, the use of replacement costs in subsequent years is also unlikely to result in showing economic values; the replacement cost will probably be less than the economic value at any given instant of an asset's life.

"Market values are totally unappealing to me because they represent a second-best alternative value—that is, they ordinarily represent the maximum amount obtainable from an alternative that has been rejected. Obviously, if the market value exceeds the economic value of the assets in use, they should be sold. However, in most instances, the opposite is true; market values of individual assets are far below their economic value in use.

"The obtaining and recording of total present values of individual assets based on discounted-cash-flow techniques is an infeasible alternative. I, therefore, conclude that replacement cost (less accumulated depreciation) of similar assets producing similar services is the best practical approximation of the economic value of the assets in use. Of course, it will facilitate the evaluation of the division's performance more easily than the division manager's performance."

REQUIRED

Critically evaluate the above comments. Please do not wander; concentrate on the issues described by the quotation.

10-30. **Human-resource accounting.** The Barry Corporation is a producer of leisure footwear in Columbus, Ohio. The company has been a pioneer in so-called human-resource accounting, an outgrowth of research conducted by Rensis Likert, a social psychologist, and others.

For many years, Likert has stressed that accounting systems encourage the misuse of human resources because of undue emphasis on short-run profits. According to Likert, the attempts to maximize immediate earnings have induced managers to exert too much pressure for productivity and to have uneconomical layoffs and discharges. Why? Because increases in employee turnover and later additional spending for hiring and training more than offset the immediate savings. Likert advocates incorporating human-resource accounting as part of the formal accounting system.

Many variations of human-resource accounting are possible. The Barry Corporation has taken a minimum step by recording as assets the outlays for recruiting and training managers. These investments in human assets are then amortized over the expected useful lives of the employees.

Data from the human-resource system have not been incorporated into the company's audited financial statements. Nevertheless, as seen in Exhibit 10-2 (shown on the following page), the company's annual reports have contained a *supplementary* balance sheet and income statement. These include the human-resource effects along with the company's conventionally reported financial data.

REQUIRED

1. Were new investments in human assets during 19X7 undertaken more rapidly than they were written off? Explain, using the figures given in Exhibit 10-2.
2. Do you favor implementing human-resource accounting for internal-reporting purposes? Why do you think Likert prefers human-resource accounting to the use of less-formal measures, such as employee-attitude surveys, absenteeism, and employee-turnover rate? Be specific.

10-31. **Transfer-pricing principles.** A consulting firm, INO, is decentralized with twenty-five offices around the country. The headquarters is based in Orange County, California. Another operating division is located in Los Angeles, fifty miles away. A subsidiary printing operation, We Print, is located in the headquarters building. Top management has indicated the desirability of the Los Angeles office's utilizing We Print for printing reports. All charges are eventually billed to the client, but INO was concerned about keeping such charges competitive.

We Print charges Los Angeles the following:

Photographing page for offset printing (a setup cost)	$.30
Printing cost per page	$.015

At this rate, We Print sales have a 60 percent contribution margin to fixed overhead.

Outside bids for 50 copies of a 135-page report needed immediately have been:

EZ Print	$145.00
Quick Service	$128.25
Fast Print	$132.00

These three printers are located within a five-mile radius of INO Los Angeles and can have the reports ready in two days. A messenger would have to be sent to drop off the original and pick up the copies. The messenger usually goes to headquarters, but, in the past, special trips have been required to deliver the original or pick up the copies. It takes three to four days to get the copies from We Print (because of the extra scheduling difficulties in delivery and pickup).

Quality control of We Print is poor. Reports received in the past have had wrinkled pages and have occasionally been miscollated or had pages deleted. (In one circumstance an intracompany memorandum indicating INO's economic straits was inserted in a report. Fortunately, the Los Angeles office detected the error before the report was

EXHIBIT 10-2

R. G. BARRY CORPORATION AND SUBSIDIARIES PRO FORMA
(Conventional and Human-Resource Accounting)
Balance Sheet

ASSETS	19X7 CONVENTIONAL AND HUMAN RESOURCE	19X7 CONVENTIONAL ONLY
Total current assets	$16,408	$16,408
Net property, plant and equipment	3,371	3,371
Excess of purchase price over net assets acquired	1,288	1,288
Deferred financing costs	183	183
Net investments in human resources	**1,779**	—
Other assets	232	232
	$23,264*	$21,484*

LIABILITIES AND STOCKHOLDERS' EQUITY

Total current liabilities	3,218	3,218
Long-term debt, excluding current installments	7,285	7,285
Deferred compensation	116	116
Deferred federal income tax based upon full tax deduction for human-resource costs	**889**	—
Stockholders' equity:		
Capital stock	1,818	1,818
Additional capital in excess of par value	5,047	5,047
Retained earnings:		
Financial	3,998	3,998
Human resources	**889**	—
	$23,264	$21,484

Statement of Income

Net sales	$39,162	$39,162
Cost of sales	25,667	25,667
Gross profit	13,494	13,494
Selling, general and administrative expenses	10,190	10,190
Operating income	3,303	3,303
Interest expense	549	549
Income before federal income taxes	2,754	2,754
Net increase in human-resource investment	**218**	—
Adjusted income before federal income taxes	2,973	2,754
Federal income taxes	1,414	1,305
Net income	$ 1,558	$ 1,449

000's deleted, so totals may appear slightly inaccurate.

distributed to the clients.) The degree of quality control in the three outside print shops is unknown.

(Although the differences in costs may seem immaterial in this case, regard the numbers as significant for purposes of focusing on the key issues.)

REQUIRED

1. If you were the decision maker at INO Los Angeles, to which print shop would you give the business? Is this an optimal economic decision from the entire corporation's point of view?
2. What would be the ideal transfer price in this case, if based only on economic considerations?
3. Time is an important factor in maintaining the goodwill of the client. There is potential return business from this client. Given this perspective, what might be the optimal decision for the company?
4. Comment on the wisdom of top management in indicating that We Print should be utilized.

10-32. **Responsibility accounting and decisions.** Easthall Company, a manufacturer of a variety of small appliances, has an engineering consulting department (ECD). The department's major task has been to help the production departments improve their operating methods and processes.

For several years, the consulting services have been charged to the production departments based on a signed agreement between the managers involved. The agreement specifies the scope of the project, the predicted savings, and the number of consulting hours required. The charge to the production department is based on the costs to the engineering department of the services rendered. For example, senior engineer hours cost more per hour than junior engineer hours. An overhead cost is included. The agreement is really a "fixed-price" contract. That is, the production manager knows his total cost of the project in advance. A recent survey revealed that production managers have a high level of confidence in the engineers.

The ECD department manager oversees the work of about forty engineers and ten draftsmen. He reports to the engineering manager, who reports to the vice-president of manufacturing. The ECD manager has the freedom to increase or decrease the number of engineers under his supervision. The ECD manager's performance is based on many factors, including the annual incremental savings to the company in excess of the costs of operating the ECD department.

The production departments are profit centers. Their goods are transferred to subsequent departments, such as a sales department or sales division, at prices that approximate market prices for similar products.

Top management is seriously considering a "no-charge" plan. That is, engineering services would be rendered to the production departments at absolutely no cost. Proponents of the new plan maintain that it would motivate the production managers to take keener advantage of engineering talent. In all other respects, the new system would be unchanged from the present system.

REQUIRED

1. Compare the present and proposed plans. What are their strong and weak points? In particular, will the ECD manager tend to hire the "optimal" amount of engineering talent?
2. Which plan do you favor? Why?

suggested readings

ANTHONY, R. N., and J. DEARDEN, *Management Control Systems: Cases and Readings,* 4th ed. Homewood, Ill.: Richard D. Irwin, 1980.

DERMER, J. *Management Planning and Control Systems.* Homewood, Ill.: Richard D. Irwin, 1977.

GOLDSCHMIDT, YAAQOV, *Information for Management Decisions.* Ithaca, N.Y., and London: Cornell University Press, 1970.

HORNGREN, CHARLES T., *Cost Accounting: A Managerial Emphasis,* 4th ed. Chaps. 6, 22, 23. Englewood Cliffs, N.J.: Prentice-Hall, 1977.

SOLOMONS, DAVID, *Divisional Performance: Measurement and Control.* New York: Financial Executives Research Foundation, 1965. Reprinted in paperback form in 1968 by Richard D. Irwin.

VANCIL, RICHARD, *Decentralization: Managerial Ambiguity by Design.* New York: Financial Executives Research Foundation, 1979.

part three

selected topics for further study

chapter **11**

CAPITAL
BUDGETING

learning objectives

When you have finished studying this chapter, you should be able to:

1. Identify the assumptions of the discounted-cash-flow (DCF) models.
2. Compute a project's net present value (NPV).
3. Compute a project's internal rate of return (IRR).
4. Apply the decision rules for the two DCF models (NPV and IRR).
5. Use sensitivity analysis in evaluating projects.
6. Use the incremental approach in determining the NPV difference between two projects.
7. Use the payback model and the accounting-rate-of-return model and compare them with the DCF models.
8. Identify the methods for reconciling the conflict between using a DCF model for making a decision and the accrual accounting model for evaluating the related performance.

Should we replace the equipment? Should we add this product to our line? Managers must make these and similar decisions having long-range implications; they are called **capital-budgeting** decisions. Capital-budgeting decisions are faced by managers in all types of organizations, including religious, medical, and governmental subunits. Many different decision models are used for capital budgeting. In this chapter we deal mostly with the accountant's problem-solving function; we compare the uses and limitations of various capital-budgeting models, with particular emphasis on relevant-cost analysis.

Focus on programs or projects

The planning and controlling of operations typically have a *time-period* focus. For example, the chief administrator of a university will be concerned with all activities for a given academic year. But the administrator will also be concerned with longer-range matters that tend to have an individual *program* or *project* focus. Examples are new programs in educational administration or health-care education, joint law-management programs, new athletic facilities, new trucks, or new parking lots. In fact, the ideas of *portfolio theory* in finance have sometimes been extended so that the operating management of many organizations is perceived as the ongoing overseeing of a collection of individual investments.

This chapter concentrates on the planning and controlling of those programs or projects that affect more than one year's financial results. Such decisions inevitably entail investments of resources that are often called *capital outlays*. Hence the term *capital budgeting* has arisen to describe the long-term planning for making and financing such outlays.

Capital-budgeting problems affect almost all organizations. For example, decisions about hospital location, size, and equipment are usually crucial because of the magnitude of the financial stakes and the murkiness of future developments, particularly in technology. Because the unknowable factors are many, well-managed organizations tend to gather and quantify as many knowable factors as is feasible before a decision is made. In addition, because organizations have limited resources, they must choose *among* various investments. Thus a basis of comparison must be established. In response to these concerns, many decision models have evolved, including discounted cash flow (DCF), payback, and accrual accounting models. The DCF model is becoming increasingly popular and is conceptually more attractive than the other two models.

Discounted-cash-flow model

☐ MAJOR ASPECTS OF DCF

The old adage that a bird in the hand is worth two in the bush is applicable to the management of money. A dollar in the hand today is worth more than a dollar to be received (or spent) five years from today, because the use of money has a cost (interest), just as the use of a building or an automobile may have a cost (rent). Because the discounted-cash-flow model explicitly and systematically weighs the time value of money, it is the best method to use for long-range decisions.

Another major aspect of DCF is its focus on *cash* inflows and outflows rather than on *net income* as computed in the accrual accounting sense. As we shall see, the student without a strong accounting background has an advantage here. He or she does not have to unlearn the accrual concepts of accounting, which the accounting student often incorrectly tries to inject into discounted-cash-flow analysis.

There are two main variations of DCF: (a) net present value and (b) internal rate of return. A brief summary of the tables and formulas used is included in Appendix B at the end of this book. Do not be frightened by the mathematics of compound interest. We shall confine our study to present-value tables, which may seem imposing but which are simple enough to be taught in many grade-school arithmetic courses. Before reading on, be sure you understand Appendix B at the end of this book.

Example. The following example will be used to illustrate the concepts. A buildings and grounds manager of a campus of the University of California is contemplating the purchase of some lawn maintenance equipment that will increase efficiency and produce cash operating savings of $2,000 per year. The useful life of this project is four years, after which the equipment will have a net disposal value of zero. Assume that the equipment will cost $6,074 now and that the minimum desired rate of return is 10 percent per year.

REQUIRED

1. Compute the project's net present value.
2. Compute the expected internal rate of return on the project.

☐ NET PRESENT VALUE

One type of discounted-cash-flow approach may be called the **net-present-value method.** It assumes some minimum desired rate of return. All expected future cash flows are discounted to the present, using this minimum desired rate. If the result is positive, the project is desirable, and vice versa. When choosing among several investments, the one with the largest net present value is most desirable.

Requirement 1 of our example will be used to demonstrate the net-present-value approach. Exhibit 11-1 shows a net present value of $264, so the investment is desirable. The manager would be able to invest $264 more, or a total of $6,338 (i.e., $6,074 + $264), and still earn 10 percent on the project.

The higher the minimum desired rate of return, the less the manager would be willing to invest in this project. At a rate of 16 percent, the net present value would be $−478 (i.e., $2,000 × 2.798 = $5,596, which is $478 less than the required investment of $6,074). (Present-value factor, 2.798, is taken from Table 2 at the end of this book.) When the desired rate of return is 16 percent, rather than 10 percent, the project is undesirable at a price of $6,074.

☐ ASSUMPTIONS OF DCF MODEL

Before proceeding, consider the assumptions of the DCF model. First, the model assumes a world of certainty: You are absolutely sure that the predicted cash flows will occur at the times specified. Second, the model assumes that the origi-

EXHIBIT 11-1

Original investment, $6,074. Useful life, 4 years. Annual cash inflow from operations, $2,000. Minimum desired rate of return, 10 percent. Cash outflows are in parentheses; cash inflows are not.

	PRESENT VALUE OF $1, DISCOUNTED @ 10%	TOTAL PRESENT VALUE	SKETCH OF CASH FLOWS AT END OF YEAR				
			0	1	2	3	4
Approach 1: Discounting Each Year's Cash Inflow Separately*							
Cash flows:							
Annual savings	.909	$ 1,818		$2,000			
	.826	1,652			$2,000		
	.751	1,502				$2,000	
	.683	1,366					$2,000
Present value of future inflows		$ 6,338					
Initial outlay	1.000	(6,074)	$(6,074)				
Net present value		$ 264					
Approach 2: Using Annuity Table†							
Annual savings	3.170	$ 6,340		$2,000	$2,000	$2,000	$2,000
Initial outlay	1.000	(6,074)	$(6,074)				
Net present value		$ 264‡					

*Present values from Table 1, Appendix B, at the end of this book. (You may wish to put a paper clip on the page.)
†Present annuity values from Table 2. (Incidentally, hand-held calculators may give slightly different answers than tables.)
‡Rounded.

nal amount of the investment can be looked upon as being either borrowed or loaned at some specified rate of return.

The assumptions of certainty and the interest effects apply to the net-present-value DCF model as follows. The net present value of $264 (as computed in Exhibit 11-1) implies that if you borrowed $6,074 from a bank at 10 percent per annum, invested in the project, and repaid the loan with the project cash savings, you would accumulate the same net amount of money as if you deposited $264 in a savings institution at 10 percent interest.

Exhibit 11-2 demonstrates these relationships. Suppose that at time zero a friend offered you $264 for the project that you had invested in thirty seconds before and that he would assume the obligation to pay the bank loan. You accept and invest the $264 in a savings account at a compound interest rate of 10 percent per annum. In our assumed world of certainty, you would be serenely indifferent as between the two alternatives. Pause a moment and study Exhibit 11-2.

EXHIBIT 11-2

alternative one: invest and hold the project.

year	(1) loan balance at beginning of year	(2) interest at 10% per year	(3) (1) + (2) accumulated amount at end of year	(4) cash for repayment of loan	(5) (3) − (4) loan balance at end of year
1	$6,074	$607	$6,681	$2,000	$4,681
2	4,681	468	5,149	2,000	3,149
3	3,149	315	3,464	2,000	1,464
4	1,464	146	1,610	2,000	390*

*After repayment of the final $1,610 loan installment, the investor in the project would have $390 left over from the $2,000 cash provided by the project at the end of the fourth year. Therefore the investor would be $390 wealthier at the end of the fourth year.

alternative two: invest, sell the project for $264 an instant after inception, and deposit the $264 in a savings institution paying 10 percent interest compounded annually.

year	(1) investment balance at beginning of year	(2) interest at 10% per year	(3) (1) + (2) accumulated amount at end of year
1	$264	$26	$290
2	290	29	319
3	319	32	351
4	351	35	386†

† The investor would have the same amount of wealth at the end of four years as in Alternative One. The $4 difference between the $386 and the $390 in Alternative One is because of the accumulation of a number of small differences from rounding off amounts. Note especially that stating the net present value at $264 at time zero is equivalent to stating the future amount at $386. The investor is indifferent (given equal riskiness of the two choices) as to whether he has $264 today or $386 four years hence.

☐ INTERNAL RATE OF RETURN

Now consider Requirement 2. The **internal rate of return** has been defined as "the maximum rate of interest that could be paid for the capital employed over the life of an investment without loss on the project."[1] This rate corresponds to the effective rate of interest so widely computed for bonds purchased or sold at discounts or premiums. Alternatively, the *internal rate of return* can be defined as

[1] *Return on Capital as a Guide to Managerial Decisions,* National Association of Accountants, Research Report No. 35 (New York), p. 57.

the discount rate that makes the present value of the anticipated cash flows from a project equal to the cost of the project, i.e., the discount rate that produces a zero net present value.

The mechanics of computing the internal rate of return are not too imposing when the annual cash inflows are uniform. In Exhibit 11-3, the following equation is used:

$6,074 = present value of annuity of $2,000 at X percent for 4 years, or what factor F in Table 2 (end of the book) will satisfy the following equation:

$$\$6,074 = \$2,000\ F$$

$$F = \frac{\$6,074}{\$2,000} = 3.037$$

EXHIBIT 11-3

Two Proofs of Internal Rate of Return

original investment, $6,074
useful life, 4 years
annual cash inflow from operations, $2,000
rate of return (selected by trial-and-error methods), 12 percent

	present value of $1, discounted at 12%	total present value	sketch of cash flows at end of year				
			0	1	2	3	4
Approach 1: Discounting Each Year's Cash Inflow Separately*							
Cash flows:							
Annual savings	.893	$ 1,786		$2,000			
	.797	1,594			$2,000		
	.712	1,424				$2,000	
	.636	1,272					$2,000
Present value of future inflows		$ 6,074†					
Initial outlay	1.000	(6,074)	$(6,074)				
Net present value (the zero difference proves that the rate of return is 12 percent)		$ 0					
Approach 2: Using Annuity Table‡							
Annual savings	3.037	$ 6,074		$2,000	$2,000	$2,000	$2,000
Initial outlay	1.000	(6,074)	$(6,074)				
Net present value		$ 0					

*Present values from Table 1, Appendix B, at the end of this book.
†Sum is really $6,076, but is rounded.
‡Present values of annuity from Table 2, Appendix B, at the end of this book.
Compare Table 2 with Table 1 in Appendix B. Note that Table 1 is the fundamental table, and Table 2 can only be used as a shortcut when a series of uniform cash flows occur; that is, Table 2 accomplishes in one computation what Table 1 accomplishes in four computations. Table 2 is really compiled by using the basic present-value factors in Table 1; for example, 3.037 is equal to the sum (rounded) of .893 + .797 + .712 + .636.

On the Period 4 line of Table 2, find the column that is closest to 3.037. It happens to be exactly 12 percent.

But suppose that the cash inflow were $1,800 instead of $2,000:

$$\$6,074 = \$1,800\ F$$

$$F = \frac{\$6,074}{\$1,800} = 3.374$$

On the Period 4 line of Table 2, the column closest to 3.374 is 8 percent. This may be close enough for most purposes. To obtain a more accurate rate, interpolation is needed:

PRESENT-VALUE
FACTORS

6%	3.465	3.465
True rate		3.374
8%	3.312	
Difference	.153	.091

$$\text{true rate} = 6\% + \frac{.091}{.153}\ (2\%) = 7.2\%$$

These hand computations become more complex when the cash inflows and outflows are not uniform. Then trial-and-error methods are needed. See the appendix to this chapter for examples. Of course, in practice, canned computer programs are commonly available for such computations.

☐ MEANING OF INTERNAL RATE

Exhibit 11-3 shows that $6,074 is the present value, at a rate of return of 12 percent, of a four-year stream of inflows of $2,000 in cash. Twelve percent is the rate that equates the amount invested ($6,074) with the present value of the cash inflows ($2,000 per year for four years). In other words, if money were borrowed at an effective interest rate of 12 percent, as Exhibit 11-4 shows, the cash inflow produced by the project would exactly repay the hypothetical loan plus the interest over the four years.

Exhibit 11-4 can be interpreted from either the borrower's or the lender's vantage point. Suppose you borrowed $6,074 from a bank at an interest rate of 12 percent per annum, invested in the project, and repaid the loan with the project cash flows of $2,000 per year. Each $2,000 payment would represent interest of 12 percent plus a reduction of the loan balance. At a rate of 12 percent, the borrower would end up with an accumulated wealth of zero. Obviously, if the borrower could borrow at 12 percent, and the project could generate cash at more than the 12 percent rate (that is, in excess of $2,000 annually), the borrower would be able to keep some cash—and the internal rate of return, *by definition,* would exceed 12 percent. Again the internal rate of return is that which would provide a net present value of zero (no more, no less).

EXHIBIT 11-4

Same data as in Exhibit 11-3. Original investment, $6,074; Useful life, 4 years; Annual cash inflow from operations $2,000; Rate of return, 12 percent. Unrecovered investment at the beginning of each year earns interest for the whole year. Annual cash inflows are received at the end of each year.

year	(1) loan balance at beginning of year	(2) interest at 12% per year	(3) (1) + (2) accumulated amount at end of year	(4) cash for repayment of loan	(5) (3) − (4) loan balance at end of year
1	$6,074	$729	$6,803	$2,000	$4,803
2	4,803	576	5,379	2,000	3,379
3	3,379	405	3,784	2,000	1,784
4	1,784	216*	2,000	2,000	0

*Rounded.

☐ DEPRECIATION AND DISCOUNTED CASH FLOW

Students are often mystified by the apparent exclusion of depreciation from discounted-cash-flow computations. A common homework error is to deduct depreciation. This is a misunderstanding of one of the basic ideas involved in the concept of the discounting. Because the discounted-cash-flow approach is fundamentally based on inflows and outflows of *cash* and not on the *accrual* concepts of revenues and expenses, no adjustments should be made to the cash flows for the periodic allocation of cost called depreciation expense (which is not a cash flow). In the discounted-cash-flow approach, the initial cost of an asset is usually regarded as a *lump-sum* outflow of cash at time zero. Therefore it is wrong to deduct depreciation from operating cash inflows before consulting present-value tables. To deduct periodic depreciation would be a double counting of a cost that has already been considered as a lump-sum outflow.

☐ REVIEW OF DECISION RULES

Review the basic ideas of discounted cash flow. The decision maker cannot readily compare an outflow of $6,074 with a series of future inflows of $2,000 each because the outflows and inflows do not occur simultaneously. The net-present-value model expresses all amounts in equivalent terms (in today's dollars at time zero). An interest rate is used to measure the decision maker's time preference for money. At a rate of 12 percent, the comparison would be:

Outflow in today's dollars	$(6,074)
Inflow equivalent in today's dollars @ 12%	6,074
Net present value	$ 0

Therefore, at a time preference for money of 12 percent, the decision maker is indifferent about having $6,074 now or a stream of four annual inflows of $2,000 each. If the interest rate were 16 percent, the decision maker would find the project unattractive because the net present value would be negative:

Outflow	$(6,074)
Inflow equivalent in today's dollars @ 16% = $2,000 × 2.798 (from Table 2) =	5,596
Net present value	$(478)

We can summarize the decision rules offered by these two models as follows:

Net Present Value

1. Calculate the net present value, using the minimum desired rate of return as the discount rate.
2. If the net present value is zero or positive, accept the project; if negative, reject the project.

Internal Rate of Return

1. Using present-value tables, compute the internal rate of return by trial-and-error interpolation.
2. If this rate equals or exceeds the minimum desired rate of return, accept the project; if not, reject the project.

☐ TWO SIMPLIFYING ASSUMPTIONS

Two simplifying assumptions are being made here and throughout this book:

a. For simplicity in the use of tables, all operating cash inflows or outflows are assumed to take place at the *end* of the years in question. This is unrealistic because such cash flows ordinarily occur irregularly throughout the given year, rather than in lump sums at the end of the year. Compound-interest tables especially tailored for these more realistic conditions are available, but we shall not consider them here.[2]

b. We assume that the cost of capital is known, is given; it is the minimum desired rate of return, an opportunity investment rate on alternative uses of the funds to be invested. The cost of capital is discussed more fully in the next section.

☐ CHOOSING THE MINIMUM DESIRED RATE

Business Week (December 18, 1978, p. 86) provided an example of using a discounted-cash-flow model:

> Like many of the amounts being paid in big acquisitions of the last year, the $350 million that Eaton Corp. will have paid this January to acquire Cutler-Hammer Inc. appears to be a stiff price. . . . Eaton is justifying the price in large part by

[2]See J. Bracken and C. Christenson, *Tables for Use in Analyzing Business Decisions* (Homewood, Ill.: Richard D. Irwin).

using an old but increasingly popular financial tool: discounted cash flow analysis (DCF). To set the price, Eaton projected the future cash flows it expects from Cutler over the next 5 to 10 years and then discounted them, using a rate that reflects the risks involved in the investment and the time value of the money used. Eaton figures that, based on DCF, Cutler will return at least 12% on its $350 million outlay.

Depending on risk (that is, the degree of variability in the likely rate of return) and available alternatives, investors usually have some notion of a minimum rate of return that would make various projects desirable investments. This minimum rate is often called the *cost of capital, hurdle rate, cutoff rate, target rate,* or *discount rate*. The problem of choosing the minimum acceptable rate of return is complex and is really more a problem of finance[3] than of accounting. In this book we shall assume that the minimum acceptable rate of return is given to the accountant by management, and that it represents the rate that can be earned by the best alternative uses of investment capital.

Note too that we concentrate here on the *investing* decisions, as distinguished from the *financing* decisions. That is, the minimum desired rate is not affected by whether the *specific project* is financed by all debt, all ownership capital, or some of both. Thus the cost of capital is not "interest expense" on borrowed money as the accountant ordinarily conceives it. For example, a mortgage-free house still has a cost of capital—the maximum amount that could be earned with the proceeds if the house were sold.[4]

Capital budgeting and nonprofit organizations

Religious, educational, health-care, governmental, and other nonprofit organizations face a variety of capital-budgeting decisions. Examples include investments in buildings, equipment, weapons systems, and research programs. Thus, even when no revenue is involved, organizations try to choose projects with the least cost for any given set of objectives.

The unsettled question of the appropriate discount rate plagues all types of organizations, profit-seeking and not-for-profit. One thing is certain: As New York City has discovered, capital is not cost-free. A discussion of the appropriate hurdle rate is beyond the scope of this book. Nearly all U.S. departments use 10 percent. It represents a crude approximation of the opportunity cost to the economy of having investments made by public agencies instead of by private organizations.[5]

---

[3]For an excellent discussion, see the chapter on cost of capital in James C. Van Horne, *Financial Management and Policy,* 5th ed. (Englewood Cliffs, N.J.: Prentice-Hall, 1980).

[4]Avoid a piecemeal approach. It is near-sighted to think that the appropriate hurdle rate is the interest expense on any financing associated with a specific project. Under this faulty approach, a project will be accepted as long as its expected internal rate of return exceeds the interest rate on funds that might be borrowed to finance the project. Thus a project will be desirable if it has an expected internal rate of 11 percent and a borrowing rate of 9 percent. The trouble here is that a series of such decisions will lead to a staggering debt that will cause the borrowing rate to skyrocket or will result in an inability to borrow at all. Conceivably, during the next year, some other project might have an expected internal rate of 16 percent and will have to be rejected, even though it is the most profitable in the series, because the heavy debt permits no further borrowing.

[5]See H. Bierman and S. Smidt, *The Capital Budgeting Decision,* 5th ed. (New York: Macmillan, 1980), Chap. 24; and R. Anthony and R. Herzlinger, *Management Control in Nonprofit Organizations* rev. ed. (Homewood, Ill.: Richard D. Irwin, 1980), pp. 292–294.

Progress in management practices and in the use of sophisticated techniques has generally tended to be faster in profit-seeking organizations. Although DCF is used by federal departments, it is almost unknown at state and local levels of government. Thus there are many opportunities to introduce improved analytical techniques. In general, managers have more opportunities in nonprofit than in profit-seeking organizations to contribute to improved decision making by introducing newer management decision models such as DCF.

Uncertainty and sensitivity analysis

☐ NO SINGLE WAY

In this and other chapters, we almost always work with the expected values (single dollar amounts) of cash flows in order to emphasize and simplify various important points. These cash flows are subject to varying degrees of risk or uncertainty, defined here as the possibility that the actual cash flow will deviate from the expected cash flow. Nevertheless, as a minimum, a manager must predict the probable outcome of various alternative projects. These expected values really should be analyzed in conjunction with probability distributions, as we see in Chapter 15. However, to stress the fundamental differences among various decision models, in this chapter we deal only with the expected values.

General Electric Company requires planners to use more than just a single number, such as return on investment or assets, to justify programs. "In the last five years we have come to realize that a single-number criterion doesn't work. People can make that number come out whatever way they want."[6]

An alternative to developing probability distributions of anticipated cash flows is to use elaborate screening devices in the early stages of the decision. Consider the Monsanto Company:

> Projects are initiated with greater care than in the past. For instance, 47 planning units within Monsanto's six operating companies prepare two-page business-direction papers, which include financial data such as rates of return, information on market shares and competition, as well as an analysis of technology in the field. Top corporate management and operating executives then sift through proposed capital programs and assign priorities. A three-year list of projects is maintained. At present, about 200 are on the drawing boards . . . ; each involves a minimum investment of $2 million and must be cleared by the board of directors.[7]

Other ways to allow for uncertainty include the use of (a) high minimum desired rate of return, (b) short expected useful lives, (c) pessimistic predictions of annual cash flows, (d) simultaneous comparisons of optimistic, pessimistic, and best-guess predictions, and (e) sensitivity analysis.[8] Sensitivity analysis is a "what-if" technique that measures how the expected values in a decision model will be affected by changes in the data. In the context of capital budgeting,

---

[6]"The Opposites: GE Grows While Westinghouse Shrinks," *Business Week,* January 31, 1977, p. 64.

[7]*Wall Street Journal,* December 30, 1976, pp. 1, 7.

[8]For a survey of how firms deal with uncertainty, see J. Fremgen, "Capital Budgeting Practices: A Survey," *Management Accounting,* May 1973, pp. 19–25.

sensitivity analyis answers the question: "How will my internal rate of return or net present value be changed if my predictions of useful life or the cash flows are inaccurate?"

☐ APPLYING SENSITIVITY ANALYSIS

Although sensitivity analysis may be conducted at any time, it is usually conducted before a decision is made. Suppose that in Exhibit 11-1 the cash inflows were $1,500 annually instead of $2,000. What would be the net present value? The annuity factor of 3.170 would be multiplied by $1,500, producing a gross present value of $4,755 and a negative net present value of $4,755 − $6,074, or $−1,319. Alternatively, management may want to know how far cash inflows will have to fall to break even on the investment. In this context, "break even" means the point of indifference, the point where the net present value is zero. Let X = annual cash inflows and let net present value = 0; then

$$0 = 3.170(X) - 6,074$$

$$X = \frac{6,074}{3.170} = \$1,916$$

Thus cash inflows can drop only $84 ($2,000 − $1,916) annually to reach the point of indifference regarding the investment.

Another critical factor is useful life. If useful life were only three years, the gross present value would be $2,000 multiplied by 2.487 (from the Period 3 row in Table 2, Appendix B) or $4,974, again producing a negative net present value, $4,974 − $6,074, or $−1,100.

These calculations can also be used in testing the sensitivity of rates of return. As we saw in the section on "Internal Rate of Return," a fall in the annual cash inflow from $2,000 to $1,800 reduces the rate of return from 12 percent to 7.2 percent.

Of course, sensitivity analysis works both ways. It can measure the potential increases in net present value or rate of return as well as the decreases. The major contribution of sensitivity analysis is that it provides an immediate financial measure of the consequences of possible errors in forecasting. Therefore it can be very useful because it helps focus on decisions that may be very sensitive indeed, and it eases the manager's mind about decisions that are not so sensitive.

In addition, sensitivity analysis is applicable to the comparison of various capital-budgeting decision models. In other words, the results under the discounted-cash-flow model may be compared with the results, using the same basic data, generated under simpler models such as payback and accounting rate of return (discussed later in this chapter).

The net-present-value comparison of two projects

☐ INCREMENTAL VERSUS TOTAL PROJECT APPROACH

The mechanics of compound interest may appear formidable to those readers who are encountering them for the first time. However, a little practice with the interest tables should easily clarify the mechanical aspect. More important, we shall now combine some relevant cost analysis with the discounted-cash-flow approach. Consider the following example:

A company owns a packaging machine, which was purchased three years ago for $56,000. It has a remaining useful life of five years but will require a major overhaul at the end of two more years at a cost of $10,000. Its disposal value now is $20,000; in five years its disposal value is expected to be $8,000, assuming that the $10,000 major overhaul will be done on schedule. The cash operating costs of this machine are expected to be $40,000 annually.

A salesman has offered a substitute machine for $51,000, or for $31,000 plus the old machine. The new machine will reduce annual cash operating costs by $10,000, will not require any overhauls, will have a useful life of five years, and will have a disposal value of $3,000.

Assume that the minimum desired rate of return is 14 percent. Using the net-present-value technique, show whether the new machine should be purchased, using (1) a **total project approach;** (2) an **incremental approach.** Try to solve before examining the solution.

A difficult part of long-range decision making is the structuring of the data. We want to see the effects of each alternative on future cash flows. The focus here is on bona fide cash transactions, not on opportunity costs. Using an opportunity-cost approach may yield the same answers, but repeated classroom experimentation with various analytical methods has convinced the author that the following steps are likely to be the clearest:

Step 1. Arrange the relevant cash flows by project, so that a sharp distinction is made between total project flows and incremental flows. The incremental flows are merely algebraic differences between two alternatives. (There are always at least two alternatives. One is the status quo—i.e., doing nothing.) Exhibit 11-5 shows how the cash flows for each alternative are sketched.

Step 2. Discount the expected cash flows and choose the project with the least cost or the greatest benefit. Both the total project approach and the incremental approach are illustrated in Exhibit 11-5; which one you use is a matter of preference. However, to develop confidence in this area, you should work with both at the start. One approach can serve as proof of the accuracy of the other. In this example, the $8,425 net difference in favor of replacement is the ultimate result under either approach.

□ ANALYSIS OF TYPICAL ITEMS
UNDER DISCOUNTED CASH FLOW

1. **Future disposal values.** The disposal value at the date of termination of a project is an increase in the cash inflow in the year of disposal. Errors in forecasting terminal disposal values are usually not crucial because the present value is usually small.

2. **Current disposal values and required investment.** There are a number of correct ways to analyze this item, all having the same ultimate effect on the decision. Probably the simplest way was illustrated in Exhibit 11-5, where the $20,000 was offset against the $51,000 purchase price, and the actual cash outgo was shown. Generally, the required investment is most easily measured by offsetting the current disposal value of the old assets against the gross cost of the new assets.

3. **Investments in receivables and inventories.** Investments in receivables, inventories, and intangible assets are basically no different from investments in

EXHIBIT 11-5

Total Project versus Incremental Approach to Net Present Value

	PRESENT-VALUE DISCOUNT FACTOR, @ 14%	TOTAL PRESENT VALUE	SKETCH OF CASH FLOWS AT END OF YEAR					
			0	1	2	3	4	5
TOTAL PROJECT APPROACH								
A. Replace								
Recurring cash operating costs, using an annuity table*	3.433	$(102,990)		($30,000)	($30,000)	($30,000)	($30,000)	($30,000)
Disposal value, end of Year 5	.519	1,557						3,000
Initial required investment	1.000	(31,000)	($31,000)					
Present value of net cash outflows		$(132,433)						
B. Keep								
Recurring cash operating costs, using an annuity table*	3.433	$(137,320)		($40,000)	($40,000)	($40,000)	($40,000)	($40,000)
Overhaul, end of Year 2	.769	(7,690)			(10,000)			
Disposal value, end of Year 5	.519	4,152						8,000
Present value of net cash outflows		$(140,858)						
Difference in favor of replacement		$ 8,425						
INCREMENTAL APPROACH								
A – B Analysis Confined to Differences								
Recurring cash operating savings, using an annuity table*	3.433	$ 34,330		$10,000	$10,000	$10,000	$10,000	$10,000
Overhaul avoided, end of Year 2	.769	7,690			$10,000			
Difference in disposal values, end of Year 5	.519	(2,595)						(5,000)
Incremental initial investment	1.000	(31,000)	($31,000)					
Net present value of replacement		$ 8,425						

*Table 2 at end of book.

plant and equipment. In the discounted-cash-flow model, the initial outlays are entered in the sketch of cash flows at time zero. At the end of the useful life of the project, the original outlays for machines may not be recouped at all or may be partially recouped in the amount of the salvage values. In contrast, the entire original investments in receivables and inventories are usually recouped. Therefore, except that their expected "disposal" values are different, all investments are typically regarded as outflows at time zero, and their terminal disposal values are regarded as inflows at the end of the project's useful life.

Thus the expansion of a retail store entails an additional investment in a building and fixtures *plus* inventories. Such investments would be shown in the format of Exhibit 11-5 as follows (numbers assumed):

	SKETCH OF CASH FLOWS					
End of Year	0	1	2		19	20
Investment in building and fixtures	(10)					1
Investment in working capital (inventories)	(6)					6

As the sketch shows, the residual value of the building and fixtures might be small. However, the entire investment in inventories would ordinarily be recouped when the venture was terminated.

4. **Book value and depreciation.** Depreciation is a phenomenon of accrual accounting that entails an allocation of cost, not a specific cash outlay. Depreciation and book value are ignored in discounted-cash-flow approaches for the reasons mentioned earlier in this chapter.

5. **Income taxes.** In practice, comparison between alternatives is best made after considering tax effects, because the tax impact may alter the picture. (The effects of income taxes are considered in Chapter 12 and may be studied now if desired.)

6. **Overhead analysis.** In relevant-cost analysis, only the overhead that will differ among alternatives is pertinent. There is need for careful study of the fixed overhead under the available alternatives. In practice, this is an extremely difficult phase of cost analysis, because it is hard to relate the individual costs to any single project.

7. **Unequal lives.** Where projects have unequal lives, comparisons may be made over the useful life either of the longer-lived project or of the shorter-lived one. For our purposes, we will estimate what the residual values will be at the end of the longer-lived project. We must also assume a reinvestment at the end of the shorter-lived project. This makes sense primarily because the decision makers should extend their time horizon as far as possible. If they are considering a longer-lived project, they should give serious consideration to what would be done in the time interval between the termination dates of the shorter-lived and longer-lived projects.

8. **Mutually exclusive projects.** When the projects are mutually exclusive, so that the acceptance of one automatically entails the rejection of the other

(e.g., buying Dodge or Ford trucks), the project that maximizes wealth measured in net present value in dollars should be undertaken.

9. **A word of caution.** The foregoing material has been an *introduction* to the area of capital budgeting, which is, in practice, complicated by a variety of factors: unequal lives; major differences in the size of alternative investments; peculiarities in internal rate-of-return computations; various ways of allowing for uncertainty (see Chapter 15); changes, over time, in desired rates of return; the indivisibility of projects in relation to a fixed overall capital-budget appropriation; and more. These niceties are beyond the scope of this introduction to capital budgeting, but the "Suggested Readings" at the end of the chapter will help you pursue the subject in more depth.

Capital budgeting and inflation

As we have observed in our everyday living, inflation—the decline in the general purchasing power of the monetary unit—is pervasive and persistent. Investors typically cope with the risks of inflation by increasing their hurdle rate to incorporate their expected rate of inflation. For instance, if 8 percent inflation is expected, a hurdle rate of 10 percent without inflation becomes 18 percent with inflation.

DCF models should be adjusted for expected inflation in an internally consistent fashion. That is, if the discount rate of, say, 18 percent includes an element attributable to expected inflation, the predicted annual cash flows should also be adjusted for expected inflation. A common error is to adjust only one of the two factors. Both the *hurdle rate* and the *annual cash flows* should be adjusted.

The adjustment of the annual cash flow is made by either (a) using a general price-level index or (b) preferably using a specific index such as a wage index or a materials index. For example, suppose that a hospital is contemplating the purchase of some new dishwashing equipment that will save labor costs of $20,000 per year in terms of 19X0 dollars. If a 10 percent rise in labor rates is expected each year, the savings in 19X1 would be shown as $20,000 × 1.10 = $22,000; in 19X2 as $20,000 × (1.10)^2 = $24,200; and so forth.

The foregoing method expresses predictions in terms of the monetary units (the then-current dollars) that are supposed to appear at any given time. In this way, subsequent auditing of the capital budgeting is straightforward.[9]

Other models for analyzing long-range decisions

Although discounted-cash-flow models for business decisions are being increasingly used, they are still relatively new, having been developed and applied for the first time on any wide scale in the 1950s. There are other models with which

---

[9]Another way of allowing for inflation is to think in terms of "real" monetary units (real dollars) exclusively. To be consistent, the DCF model would use an inflation-free hurdle rate plus inflation-free annual cash flows. Using the above numbers, the 18 percent hurdle rate would be lowered to exclude the expected inflation rate, the $20,000 labor savings in 19X0 dollars would be used in 19X1, 19X2, and so forth. Properly used, both ways lead to the same net present values. See Bierman and Smidt, *Capital Budgeting Decision*, Chap. 22.

the manager should at least be somewhat familiar, because they are entrenched in many businesses.[10]

These models, which we are about to explain, are conceptually inferior to discounted-cash-flow approaches. Then why do we bother studying them? First, because changes in business practice occur slowly. Second, because where older models such as payback are in use, they should be used properly, even if better models are available. The situation is similar to using a pocket knife instead of a scalpel for removing a person's appendix. If the pocket knife is used by a knowledgeable and skilled surgeon, the chances for success are much better than if it is used by a bumbling layperson.

Of course, as always, the accountant and manager face a cost-and-value-of-information decision when they choose a decision model. Reluctance to use discounted-cash-flow models may be justified if the more familiar payback model or other models lead to the same investment decisions.

One existing technique may be called the emergency-persuasion method. No formal planning is used. Fixed assets are operated until they crumble, product lines are carried until they are obliterated by competition, and requests by a manager for authorization of capital outlays are judged on the basis of past operating performance regardless of its relevance to the decision at hand. These approaches to capital budgeting are examples of the unscientific management that often leads to bankruptcy.

☐ PAYBACK MODEL

Payback, or **payout,** or **payoff,** is the measure of the time it will take to recoup, in the form of cash inflow from operations, the initial dollars of outlay. Assume that $12,000 is spent for a machine with an estimated useful life of eight years. Annual savings of $4,000 in cash outflow are expected from operations. Depreciation is ignored. The payback calculations follow:

$$P = \frac{I}{O} = \frac{\$12,000}{\$4,000} = 3 \text{ years} \tag{1}$$

where P is the payback time, I is the initial incremental amount of outlay, and O is the uniform annual incremental cash inflow from operations.

The payback model merely measures how quickly investment dollars may be recouped; it does *not* measure profitability. This is its major weakness, because

---

[10]Thomas Klammer, "Empirical Evidence of the Adoption of Sophisticated Capital Budgeting Techniques," *Journal of Business,* Vol. VL, No. 3 (October 1972), surveyed 369 large firms and received 184 responses. Fifty-seven percent of the firms responding indicated that they used discounted-cash-flow techniques in 1970, as compared with only 19 percent in 1959:

	PERCENTAGE USING IN:		
	1970	1964	1959
Discounting	57	38	19
Accounting rate of return	26	30	34
Payback	12	24	34
Urgency	5	8	13
	100	100	100

For a description of practices in the 1970s, see S. Hayes, "Capital Commitments and the High Cost of Money," *Harvard Business Review,* May-June 1977, pp. 155-61.

a shorter payback time does not necessarily mean that one project is preferable to another.

For instance, assume that an alternative to the $12,000 machine is a $10,000 machine whose operation will also result in a reduction of $4,000 annually in cash outflow. Then

$$P_1 = \frac{\$12,000}{\$4,000} = 3.0 \text{ years}$$

$$P_2 = \frac{\$10,000}{\$4,000} = 2.5 \text{ years}$$

The payback criterion indicates that the $10,000 machine is more desirable. However, one fact about the $10,000 machine has been purposely withheld. Its useful life is only 2.5 years. Ignoring the impact of compound interest for the moment, the $10,000 machine results in zero benefit, while the $12,000 machine generates cash inflows for five years beyond its payback period.

The main objective in investing is profit, not the recapturing of the initial outlay. If a company wants to recover its outlay fast, it need not spend in the first place. Then no waiting time is necessary; the payback time is zero. When a wealthy investor was assured by the promoter of a risky oil venture that he would have his money back within two years, the investor replied, "I already have my money."

The payback approach may also be applied to the data in Exhibit 11-5. What is the payback time?

$$P = \frac{I}{O} = \frac{\$31,000}{\$10,000} = 3.1 \text{ years}$$

However, the formula may be used with assurance only when there are uniform cash inflows from operations. In this instance, $10,000 is saved by avoiding an overhaul at the end of the second year. When cash inflows are not uniform, the payback computation must take a cumulative form—that is, each year's net cash flows are accumulated until the initial investment is recouped:

YEAR	INITIAL INVESTMENT	NET CASH INFLOWS each year	NET CASH INFLOWS accumulated
0	$31,000	—	—
1	—	$10,000	$10,000
2	—	20,000	30,000
2.1	—	1,000	31,000

The payback time is slightly beyond the second year. Straight-line interpolation within the third year reveals that the final $1,000 needed to recoup the investment would be forthcoming in 2.1 years.

☐ ACCOUNTING RATE-OF-RETURN MODEL

The label for the **accounting rate-of-return** model or method is not uniform. It is also known as the *unadjusted rate-of-return model,* the *financial-statement model,* the *book-value model,* the *rate-of-return on assets model,* and the *approximate rate-of-return* *model.* Its computations supposedly dovetail most closely with conventional accounting models of calculating income and required investment. However, the dovetailing objective is not easily attained, because the purposes of the computations differ. The most troublesome aspects are depreciation and decisions concerning capitalization versus expense. For example, advertising and research are usually expensed, even though they may often be viewed as long-range investments.

The equations for the accounting rate of return are:

$$\text{accounting rate of return} = \frac{\text{increase in future average annual net income}}{\text{initial increase in required investment}} \quad (2)$$

$$R = \frac{O - D}{I} \quad (3)$$

where R is the average annual rate of return on initial additional investment, O is the average annual incremental cash inflow from operations, D is the incremental average annual depreciation, and I is the initial incremental amount invested.

Assume the same facts as in our payback illustration: cost of machine, $12,000; useful life, eight years; estimated disposal value, zero; and expected annual savings in annual cash outflow from operations, $4,000. Annual depreciation would be $12,000 ÷ 8 = $1,500. Substitute these values in Equation (3):

$$R = \frac{\$4,000 - \$1,500}{\$12,000} = 20.8\%$$

☐ WEIGHING DOLLARS DIFFERENTLY

The accounting model ignores the time value of money. Expected future dollars are unrealistically and erroneously regarded as equal to present dollars. The discounted-cash-flow model explicitly allows for the force of interest and the exact timing of cash flows. In contrast, the accounting model is based on *annual averages.* To illustrate, consider a petroleum company with three potential projects to choose from: an expansion of an existing gasoline station, an investment in an oil well, and the purchase of a new gasoline station. To simplify the calculations, assume a three-year life for each project. Exhibit 11-6 summarizes the comparisons. Note that the accounting rate of return would indicate that all three projects are equally desirable and that the internal rate of return properly discriminates in favor of earlier cash inflows.

Thus the conflict of purposes is highlighted in Exhibit 11-6. The accounting model utilizes concepts of capital and income that were originally designed for the quite different purpose of accounting for periodic income and financial position. In the accounting model, the initial capital calculation is subject to questionable asset-versus-expense decisions (e.g., allocation of costs of research or of sales promotion outlays), while the effects of interest on the timing of cash flows are ignored. The resulting accounting rate of return may be far from the real mark.[11]

[11] For illustrations of the details, subtleties, and complexities of the unadjusted (accounting) rate of return, see Charles T. Horngren, *Cost Accounting: A Managerial Emphasis,* 4th ed. (Englewood Cliffs, N.J.: Prentice-Hall, 1977), Chaps. 11 and 12.

EXHIBIT 11-6

	EXPANSION OF EXISTING GASOLINE STATION	INVESTMENT IN AN OIL WELL	PURCHASE OF NEW GASOLINE STATION
Initial investment	$ 90,000	$ 90,000	$ 90,000
Cash inflows from operations:			
Year 1	$ 40,000	$ 80,000	$ 20,000
Year 2	40,000	30,000	40,000
Year 3	40,000	10,000	60,000
Totals	$120,000	$120,000	$120,000
Average annual cash inflow	$ 40,000	$ 40,000	$ 40,000
Less: Average annual depreciation ($90,000 ÷ 3)	30,000	30,000	30,000
Increase in average annual net income	$ 10,000	$ 10,000	$ 10,000
Accounting rate of return on initial investment	11.1%	11.1%	11.1%
Internal rate of return, using discounted-cash-flow techniques	16.0%*	23.2%*	13.8%*

*Computed by trial-and-error approaches using Tables 1 and 2 at the end of the book. See the appendix to this chapter for a detailed explanation.

However, the accounting model usually facilitates follow-up, because the same approach is used in the forecast as is used in the accounts. Yet exceptions to this ideal situation often occur, commonly arising from the inclusion in the forecast of some initial investment items that are not handled in the same manner in the subsequent accounting records. For example, the accounting for trade-ins and disposal values varies considerably. In practice, spot checks are frequently used on key items.

Conflict of models

☐ NATURE OF CONFLICT

Many managers are reluctant to accept DCF models as the best way to make capital-budgeting decisions. Their reluctance stems from the wide usage of the accrual accounting model for evaluating performance. That is, managers become frustrated if they are instructed to use a DCF model for making decisions that are evaluated later by a non-DCF model, such as the typical accrual accounting rate-of-return model.

To illustrate, consider the potential conflict that might arise in the first example of this chapter. Recall that the expected rate of return was 12 percent, based on an outlay of $6,074 that would generate cash savings of $2,000 for each of four years and no terminal disposal value. Under accrual accounting, using straight-line depreciation, the first-year evaluation of performance would be:

Cash operating savings	$2,000
Straight-line depreciation, $6,074 \div 4 =$	1,519
Effect on net income	$ 481
Accounting rate of return on initial book value, $481 \div $6,074 =$	7.9%

Given the above facts, many managers of profit-seeking organizations (where performance is evaluated by accrual accounting models) would be inclined against replacing the equipment despite the internal rate of 12 percent. Such negative inclinations are especially likely where managers are transferred to new positions every year or two. As Chapter 5 indicated, the reluctance to replace is reinforced (see Problems 5-3 and 5-30) if a heavy book loss on old equipment would appear in Year 1's accrual income statement—even though such a loss would be irrelevant in a properly constructed decision model.

☐ RECONCILIATION OF CONFLICT

How can the foregoing conflict be reconciled? An obvious solution would be to use the same model for decisions and for evaluating performance. The accrual accounting model is often dominant for evaluating all sorts of performance; that is why many organizations use it for both purposes and do not use a DCF model at all. Critics claim that this nonuse of DCF may lead to many instances of poor capital-budgeting decisions.

Another obvious solution would be to use DCF for both capital-budgeting decisions and the performance evaluation audit. Several organizations use sampling procedures to perform such audits. A major reason for not auditing all capital-budgeting decisions routinely is that most accounting systems are designed to evaluate operating performances of products, departments, divisions, territories, and so on. In contrast, capital-budgeting decisions frequently deal with individual *projects*, not the collection of projects that are usually being managed simultaneously by divisional or department managers.

Some companies have solved the conflict by a dual approach. Managers use both the DCF model and the accrual accounting model at decision-making time. The decision is based on the DCF model, but the performance evaluation is tied back to the accrual accounting model.

The conflicts between the longstanding, pervasive accrual accounting model and various formal decision models represent one of the most serious unsolved problems in the design of management control systems. Top management cannot expect goal congruence if it favors the use of one collection of models for decisions and the use of other models for performance evaluaton.[12]

[12] See Horngren, *Cost Accounting,* Chap. 23, for a fuller discussion. Also see Y. Ijiri, "Recovery Rate and Cash Flow Accounting," *Financial Executive,* XLVII (March, 1980).

summary

Product costing, income determination, and the planning and controlling of operations have a current-time-period orientation. Special decisions and long-range planning have primarily a project orientation. There is a danger in using ordinary accounting data for special purposes. Discounted-cash-flow techniques have been developed for the making of special decisions and for long-range planning because the time value of money becomes extremely important when projects extend beyond one or two years.

The field of capital budgeting is important because lump-sum expenditures on long-life projects have far-reaching effects on profit and on a business's flexibility. It is imperative that management develop its plans carefully and base them on reliable forecasting procedures. Capital budgeting is long-term planning for proposed capital outlays and their financing. Projects are accepted if their rate of return exceeds a minimum desired rate of return.

Because the discounted-cash-flow model explicitly and automatically weighs the time value of money, it is the best method to use for long-range decisions. The overriding goal is maximum long-run net cash inflows.

The discounted-cash-flow model has two variations: internal rate of return and net present value. Both models take into account the timing of cash flows and are thus superior to other methods.

The payback model is a popular approach to capital-spending decisions. It is simple and easily understood, but it neglects profitability.

The accounting rate-of-return model is also widely used in capital budgeting, although it is conceptually inferior to discounted-cash-flow models. It fails to recognize explicitly the time value of money. Instead, the accounting model depends on averaging techniques that may yield inaccurate answers, particularly when cash flows are not uniform through the life of a project.

A serious practical impediment to the adoption of discounted-cash-flow models is the widespread use of conventional accrual models for evaluating performance. Frequently, the optimal decision under discounted cash flow will not produce a good showing in the early years, when performance is computed under conventional accounting methods. For example, heavy depreciation charges and the expensing rather than capitalizing of initial development costs will hurt reported income for the first year.

summary problem for your review

PROBLEM

Review the problem and solution shown in Exhibit 11-5. Conduct a sensitivity analysis as indicated below. Consider each requirement as independent of other requirements.

1. Compute the net present value if the minimum desired rate of return were 20 percent.

2. Compute the net present value if predicted cash operating costs were $35,000 instead of $30,000.

3. By how much may the cash operating savings fall before reaching the point of indifference, the point where the net present value of the project is zero, using the original discount rate of 14 percent?

SOLUTION

1. Either the total project or the incremental approach could be used. The incremental approach would show:

	TOTAL PRESENT VALUE
Recurring cash operating savings, using an annuity table (Table 2): 2.991 × $10,000 =	$29,910
Overhaul avoided: .694 × $10,000 =	6,940
Difference in disposal values: .402 × $5,000 =	(2,010)
Incremental initial investment	(31,000)
Net present value of replacement	$ 3,840

2. Net present value in Exhibit 11-5		$ 8,425
Present value of original $10,000 annual cash operating savings, given in Exhibit 11-5	$34,330	
Present value of reduced savings of $5,000, which is 50 percent of above	17,165	
Decrease in net present value		17,165
New net present value		$(8,740)

3. Let x = annual cash operating savings and let net present value = 0. Then

$$0 = 3.433(X) + \$7{,}690 - \$2{,}595 - \$31{,}000$$
$$3.433X = \$25{,}905$$
$$X = \$\ 7{,}546$$

(Note that the $7,690, $2,595, and $31,000 are at the bottom of Exhibit 11-5.)

If the annual savings fall from $10,000 to $7,546, a decrease of $2,454, the point of indifference will be reached.

An alternative way to obtain the same answer would be to divide the net present value of $8,425 (see bottom of Exhibit 11-5) by 3.433, obtaining $2,454, the amount of the annual difference in savings that will eliminate the $8,425 of net present value.

Appendix 11:
calculations of internal rates
of return

☐ EXPANSION OF EXISTING GASOLINE STATION

(Data are from Exhibit 11-6.)

$90,000 = Present value of annuity of $40,000 at x percent for three years, or what factor F in the table of the present values of an annuity will satisfy the following equation:

$90,000 = $40,000F
F = $90,000 ÷ $40,000 = 2.250

Now, on the Year 3 line of Table 2 at the end of the book, find the column that is closest to 2.250. You will find that 2.250 is extremely close to a rate of return of 16 percent—so close that straight-line interpolation is unnecessary between 14 percent and 16 percent. Therefore the internal rate of return is 16 percent.

☐ INVESTMENT IN AN OIL WELL

Trial-and-error methods must be used to calculate the rate of return that will equate the future cash flows with the $90,000 initial investment. As a start, note that the 16 percent rate was applicable to a uniform annual cash inflow. But now use Table 1 (end of the book) because the flows are not uniform, and try a higher rate, 22 percent, because you know that the cash inflows are coming in more quickly than under the uniform inflow:

		TRIAL AT 22 PERCENT		TRIAL AT 24 PERCENT	
YEAR	CASH INFLOWS	present-value factor	total present value	present-value factor	total present value
1	$80,000	.820	$65,600	.806	$64,480
2	30,000	.672	20,160	.650	19,500
3	10,000	.551	5,510	.524	5,240
			$91,270		$89,220

The true rate lies somewhere between 22 and 24 percent and can be approximated by straight-line interpolation:

INTERPOLATION		TOTAL PRESENT VALUES	
22%		$91,270	$91,270
True rate			90,000
24%		89,220	
Difference		$ 2,050	$ 1,270

Therefore

$$\text{true rate:} = 22\% + \frac{1{,}270}{2{,}050} \times 2\%$$

$$= 22\% + 1.2\% = 23.2\%$$

☐ PURCHASE OF A NEW GASOLINE STATION

In contrast to the oil-well project, this venture will have slowly increasing cash inflows. The trial rate should be much lower than the 16 percent rate applicable to the expansion project. Let us try 12 percent:

| | | TRIAL AT 12 PERCENT | | TRIAL AT 14 PERCENT | |
| | | present-value factor | total present value | present-value factor | total present value |
YEAR	CASH INFLOWS				
1	$20,000	.893	$17,860	.877	$17,540
2	40,000	.797	31,880	.769	30,760
3	60,000	.712	42,720	.675	40,500
			$92,460		$88,800

INTERPOLATION	TOTAL PRESENT VALUES	
12%	$92,460	$92,460
True rate		90,000
14%	88,800	
	$ 3,660	$ 2,460

$$\text{true rate:} = 12\% + \frac{2{,}460}{3{,}660} \times 2\%$$

$$= 12\% + 1.3\% = 13.3\%$$

assignment material

Special Note: Ignore income taxes. The effects of income taxes are considered in Chapter 12.

▓ FUNDAMENTAL ASSIGNMENT MATERIAL

11-1. Terminology. Define *accounting method; accounting rate of return; book-value method; capital budgeting; incremental approach; internal rate of return; net-present-value method; payback; payoff; payout; total project approach.*

11-2. Exercises in compound interest: answers supplied.[13] Use the appropriate interest table to compute the following:

a. It is your sixty-fifth birthday. You plan to work five more years before retiring. Then you want to take $5,000 for a round-the-world tour. What lump sum do you have to invest now in order to accumulate the $5,000? Assume that your minimum desired rate of return is

(1) 4 percent, compounded annually
(2) 10 percent, compounded annually
(3) 20 percent, compounded annually

b. You want to spend $500 on a vacation at the end of each of the next five years. What lump sum do you have to invest now in order to take the five vacations? Assume that your minimum desired rate of return is

(1) 4 percent, compounded annually
(2) 10 percent, compounded annually
(3) 20 percent, compounded annually

c. At age sixty, you find that your employer is moving to another location. You receive termination pay of $5,000. You have some savings and wonder whether to retire now.

(1) If you invest the $5,000 now at 4 percent, compounded annually, how much money can you withdraw from your account each year so that at the end of five years there will be a zero balance?

(2) If you invest it at 10 percent?

d. At 16 percent, compounded annually, which of the following plans is more desirable in terms of present values? Show computations to support your answer.

	ANNUAL CASH INFLOWS	
year	mining	farming
1	$10,000	$ 2,000
2	8,000	4,000
3	6,000	6,000
4	4,000	8,000
5	2,000	10,000
	$30,000	$30,000

11-3. Comparison of models. Midtown University is considering the purchase of a new printing machine at a cost of $28,000. This machine should save $7,000 in cash operating costs per year. Its estimated useful life is seven years, and it will have zero terminal value.

REQUIRED

1. Calculate the payback time.
2. Calculate the net present value if the minimum desired rate of return is 12 percent. Should the university buy? Why?
3. Calculate the internal rate of return.

11-4. Sensitivity analysis. The All Directions Railroad is considering the replacement of an old power jack tamper used in the maintenance of track with a new improved version that should save $5,000 per year in net cash operating costs.

The old equipment has zero disposal value, but it could be used indefinitely. The estimated useful life of the new equipment is twelve years, and it will cost $20,000.

REQUIRED

1. What is the payback time?
2. Compute the internal rate of return.

[13]The answers appear at the end of the assignment material for this chapter.

3. Management is unsure about the useful life. What would be the rate of return if the useful life were (a) six years instead of twelve and (b) twenty years instead of twelve?

4. Suppose the life will be twelve years but the savings will be $3,000 per year instead of $5,000. What would be the rate of return?

5. Suppose the annual savings will be $4,000 for eight years. What would be the rate of return?

■ ADDITIONAL ASSIGNMENT MATERIAL

11-5. According to Alexander Pope (1688–1744), "A little learning is a dangerous thing." How might this apply in capital budgeting?

11-6. State a rule that can serve as a general guide to capital-budgeting decisions.

11-7. "If discounted-cash-flow approaches are superior to the payback and the accounting methods, why should we bother to learn the others? All it does is confuse things." Answer this contention.

11-8. What is the basic flaw in the payback model?

11-9. How can the payback model be helpful in capital budgeting?

11-10. Compare the accounting rate-of-return approach and the discounted-cash-flow approach to the consideration of the time value of money.

11-11. "The higher the interest rate, the less I worry about errors in predicting terminal values." Do you agree? Explain.

11-12. "Double-counting occurs if depreciation is separately considered in discounted-cash-flow analysis." Do you agree? Explain.

11-13. "Problem solving is project-oriented rather than time-period-oriented." Explain.

11-14. Why is capital budgeting likely to receive increasing attention?

11-15. Why is discounted cash flow a superior method for capital budgeting?

11-16. Why should depreciation be excluded from discounted-cash-flow computations?

11-17. Can net present value ever be negative? Why?

11-18. "The higher the minimum rate of return desired, the higher the price that a company will be willing to pay for cost-saving equipment." Do you agree? Explain.

11-19. Why should the incremental approach to alternatives always lead to the same decision as the total project approach?

11-20. "Current disposal values of equipment are always relevant to a replacement decision." Do you agree? Explain.

11-21. "Discounted-cash-flow approaches will not work if the competing projects have unequal lives." Do you agree? Explain.

11-22. **Illustration of trial-and-error method of computing rate of return.** Study Exhibit 11-3. Suppose the annual cash inflow will be $2,500 rather than $2,000.

REQUIRED | What is the internal rate of return?

11-23. **New equipment.** The Vail Company has offered to sell some new packaging equipment to the Aspen Company. The list price is $40,000, but Vail has agreed to accept some old equipment in trade. A trade-in allowance of $6,000 was agreed upon. The old equipment was carried at a book value of $7,700 and could be sold outright for $5,000 cash. Cash operating savings are expected to be $5,000 annually for the next twelve years. The minimum desired rate of return is 12 percent. The old equipment has a remaining useful life of twelve years. Both the old and the new equipment will have zero disposal values twelve years from now.

REQUIRED

Should Aspen buy the new equipment? Show your computations, using the net-present-value method. Ignore income taxes.

11-24. Assumptions of DCF model. (R. Jaffee.) A superintendent of a school district has asked you to explain the assumptions underlying the discounted-cash-flow model. He has just learned the *mechanics* of calculating net present value, but he is unclear on its *meaning* and its implications for financial analysis.

Prepare a memorandum of explanation for the superintendent, using an example of an initial investment of $1,000, a project life of three years, and an operating cash savings of $500 at the end of each of the three years. Assume that the minimum desired rate of return is 10 percent. Use Exhibit 11-2 as a guide for preparing your presentation. The superintendent admires clarity.

11-25. Replacement of equipment. Refer to Problem 5-30. Assume that the new equipment will cost $100,000 in cash, and that the old machine cost $81,000 and can be sold now for $16,000 cash.

REQUIRED

1. Compute the net present value of the proposed investment in new equipment, assuming that the minimum desired rate of return is 10 percent.
2. What will be the internal rate of return?
3. How long is the payback period on the incremental investment?

11-26. Present values of cash flows. Pristine Products has just been established. Operating plans indicate the following expected cash flows:

	OUTFLOWS	INFLOWS
Initial investment now	$210,000	$ —
End of year: One	150,000	200,000
Two	200,000	250,000
Three	250,000	300,000
Four	300,000	400,000
Five	300,000	400,000

REQUIRED

1. Compute the net present value for all of these cash flows. This should be a single amount. Use a discount rate of 14 percent.
2. Is the internal rate of return more than 14 percent or less than 14 percent? Why?

11-27. Replacement decision for railway equipment. The St. Paul Railroad is considering replacement of a Kalamazoo Power Jack Tamper, used for maintenance of track, with a new automatic raising device that can be attached to a production tamper.

The present power jack tamper cost $18,000 five years ago and has an estimated life of twelve years. A year from now the machine will require a major overhaul estimated to cost $5,000. It can be disposed of now via an outright cash sale for $2,500. There will be no value at the end of twelve years.

The automatic raising attachment has a delivered selling price of $74,000 and an estimated life of twelve years. Because of anticipated future developments in combined maintenance machines, it is felt that the machine should be disposed of at the end of the seventh year to take advantage of newly developed machines. Estimated sale value at end of seven years is $5,000.

Tests have shown that the automatic raising machine will produce a more uniform surface on the track than the power jack tamper now in use. The new equipment will eliminate one laborer whose annual compensation, including fringe benefits, is $30,000.

Track maintenance work is seasonal, and the equipment normally works from May 1 to October 31 each year. Machine operators and laborers are transferred to other work after October 31, at the same rate of pay.

The salesman claims that the annual normal maintenance of the new machine will run about $1,000 per year. Because the automatic raising machine is more complicated than the manually operated machine, it is felt that it will require a thorough overhaul at the end of the fourth year at an estimated cost of $7,000.

Records show the annual normal maintenance of the Kalamazoo machine to be $1,200. Fuel consumption of the two machines is equal.

Should the St. Paul keep or replace the Kalamazoo Power Jack Tamper? A 10 percent rate of return is desired. Compute present values.

The railroad is not currently paying any income tax.

11-28. **Replacing office equipment.** Harvard University is considering replacing its present manual bookkeeping machines (NCR) with faster machines purchased from IBM. The administration is very concerned about the rising costs of operations during the last decade.

In order to convert to IBM, two operators would have to be sent to school. Required remodeling would cost $6,000.

Harvard's three NCR machines were purchased for $10,000 each, five years ago. Their expected life was ten years. Their resale value now is $3,000 each and will be zero in five more years. The total cost of the new IBM equipment will be $50,000; it will have zero disposal value in five years.

The three NCR operators are paid $8 an hour each. They usually work a forty-hour week. Machine breakdowns occur monthly on each machine, resulting in repair costs of $50 per month and overtime of four hours, at time-and-one-half, per machine per month, to complete the normal monthly workload. Paper, supplies, etc., cost $100 a month for each NCR.

The IBM system will require only two regular operators, on a regular workweek of forty hours each, to do the same work. Rates are $10 an hour, and no overtime is expected. Paper, supplies, etc., will cost $3,300 annually. Maintenance and repairs are fully serviced by IBM for $1,050 annually. (Assume a 52-week year.)

REQUIRED

1. Using discounted-cash-flow techniques, compute the present value of all relevant cash flows, under both alternatives, for the five-year period discounted at 12 percent.
2. Should Harvard keep the NCR machines or replace them, if the decision is based solely on the given data?
3. What other considerations might affect the decision?

11-29. **Minimizing transportation costs.** The Wriston Company produces industrial and residential lighting fixtures at its manufacturing facility located in Los Angeles. Shipment of company products to an eastern warehouse is presently handled by common carriers at a rate of 20¢ per pound of fixtures. The warehouse is located in Cleveland, 2,500 miles from Los Angeles.

The treasurer of Wriston Company is presently considering whether to purchase a truck for transporting products to the eastern warehouse. The following data on the truck are available:

Purchase price	$50,000
Useful life	5 years
Salvage value after 5 years	$5,000
Capacity of truck	10,000 lbs.
Cash costs of operating truck	$.80 per mile

The treasurer feels that an investment in this truck is particularly attractive because of his successful negotiation with X Company to back-haul X's products from Cleveland to Los Angeles on every return trip from the warehouse. X has agreed to pay Wriston $2,400 per load of X's products hauled from Cleveland to Los Angeles up to and including 100 loads per year.

Wriston's marketing manager has estimated that 500,000 pounds of fixtures will have to be shipped to the eastern warehouse each year for the next five years. The truck will be fully loaded on each round trip.

Ignore income taxes. For income tax effects, see Problem 12-29.

1. Assume that Wriston requires a minimum rate of return of 20 percent. Should the truck be purchased? Show computations to support your answer.
2. What is the minimum number of trips that must be guaranteed by the X Company to make the deal acceptable to Wriston, based on the above numbers alone?
3. What qualitative factors might influence your decision? Be specific.

11-30. **Investment in machine and working capital.** The Schultz Company has an old machine with a net disposal value of $10,000 now and $4,000 five years from now. A new Rapido machine is offered for $60,000 cash or $50,000 with a trade-in. The new machine will result in an annual operating cash outflow of $40,000 as compared with the old machine's annual outflow of $50,000. The disposal value of the new machine five years hence will be $4,000.

Because the new machine will produce output more rapidly, the average investment in inventories will be $160,000 by using the new machine instead of $200,000.

The minimum desired rate of return is 20 percent. The company uses discounted-cash-flow techniques to guide these decisions.

Should the Rapido machine be acquired? Show your calculations. Company procedures require the computing of the present value of each alternative. The most desirable alternative is the one with the least cost. Assume PV of $1 at 20 percent for five years, $.40; PV of annuity of $1 at 20 percent for five years, $3.

11-31. **Uses of warehouse: review of Chapters 5 and 11.**

a. The Hiller Company is currently leasing one of its warehouses to another company for $3,000 per year, on a month-to-month basis.

b. The estimated sales value of the warehouse is $30,000. This price is likely to remain unchanged indefinitely—even if a contemplated public expressway results in the building's condemnation. The building originally cost $20,000 and is being depreciated at $500 annually. Its net book value is $9,000.

c. The Hiller Company is seriously considering converting the warehouse into a retail outlet for selling furniture at ridiculously low discount prices. Such an endeavor would entail remodeling, at a cost of $15,000. The remodeling would be extremely modest because the major attraction would be flimsy furniture at rock-bottom prices. The remodeling can be accomplished over a single weekend.

d. The inventory, cash, and receivables needed to open and sustain the retail outlet would be $50,000. This total is fully recoverable whenever operations terminate.

e. The president, who paid an expressway engineer $1,000 to discover when and where the expressway will be built, is virtually certain that the warehouse will be available for no more than four years. He has asked you to give him an analysis of whether the company should continue to lease the warehouse or convert it to a retail outlet, assuming that the minimum annual rate of return desired is 14 percent over a four-year planning horizon. Estimated annual operating data, exclusive of depreciation, are:

f.	Sales				$200,000
g.	Operating expenses				177,000
h.	Nonrecurring sales promotion costs at *beginning* of Year 1				20,000
i.	Nonrecurring termination costs at *end* of Year 4				10,000

The president has definitely decided not to sell the warehouse until forced to by condemnation proceedings.

REQUIRED

1. Show how you would handle the *individual* items on the company's analysis form, which is set up as follows:

		NET PRESENT	CASH FLOWS IN YEAR				
ITEM	DESCRIPTION	VALUE	0	1	2	3	4
a.							
b.							
.							
.							
.							
h.							
i.							

Use the following present-value factors: PV of $1 = $.60 and the PV of an annuity of $1 = $2.90. Ignore income taxes. If you think an item is irrelevant, leave the space blank.

2. After analyzing all the relevant data, compute the net present value. Indicate which course of action, based on the data alone, should be taken.

11-32. **Cafeteria facilities.** The cafeteria of an office building is open 250 days a year. It offers typical cafeteria-line service. At the noon meal (open to the public), serving-line facilities can accommodate 200 people per hour for the two-hour serving period. The average customer has a thirty-minute lunch hour. Serving facilities are unable to handle the overflow of noon customers with the result that, daily, 200 dissatisfied customers who do not wish to stand in line choose to eat elsewhere. Projected over a year, this results in a considerable loss to the cafeteria.

To tap this excess demand, the cafeteria is considering two alternatives: (a) installing two vending machines, at a cost of $5,000 apiece; or (b) completely revamping present serving-line facilities with new equipment, at a cost of $80,000. The vending machines and serving-line equipment have a useful life of ten years and will be depreciated on a straight-line basis. The minimum desired rate of return for the cafeteria is 10 percent. The average sale is $1.50, with a contribution margin of 30 percent. This will remain the same if new serving-line facilities are installed.

Data for alternative *a* (vending machines) are as follows:

Service cost per year is $300; salvage value of each machine at the end of ten years is $500.

Contribution margin is 20 percent. It is estimated that 60 percent of the dissatisfied customers will use the vending machines and spend an average of $1.50. The estimated salvage value of the present equipment will net $2,000 at the end of the ten-year period.

Data for alternative *b* (new serving-line facilities) are as follows:

Yearly salary for an extra part-time clerk is $4,000; salvage value of old equipment is $5,000; salvage value of new equipment, at the end of ten years, is $10,000; cost of dismantling old equipment is $1,000. It is estimated that all the previously dissatisfied customers will use the new facilities.

All other costs are the same under both alternatives and need not be considered.

| Using the net-present-value model, which is the better alternative?

11-33. Accounting rate of return. Refer to Problem 11-3. Using the accounting rate-of-return model, what is the rate of return on the initial investment?

11-34. Comparison of investment models. Maria's Pizza Company makes and sells frozen pizzas to local retail outlets. Maria has just inherited $10,000 and has decided to invest it in the business. She is trying to decide between:

Alternative *a:* Buy a $10,000 contract, payable immediately, from a local reputable sales promotion agency. The agency would provide various advertising services, as specified in the contract, over the next ten years. Maria is convinced that the sales promotion would increase cash inflow from operations, through increased volume, by $2,000 a year for the first five years, and by $1,000 per year thereafter. There would be no effect after the ten years had elapsed.

Alternative *b:* Buy new mixing and packaging equipment, at a cost of $10,000, which would reduce operating cash outflows by $1,500 per year for the next ten years. The equipment would have zero salvage value at the end of the ten years.

Ignore any tax effect.

REQUIRED | 1. Compute the rates of return on initial investment by the accounting model for both alternatives.
2. Compute the rates of return by the discounted-cash-flow model for both alternatives.
3. Are the rates of return different under the discounted-cash-flow model? Explain.

11-35. Make or buy, discounted cash flow, and accounting rate of return. Refer to Problem 5-27, Requirement 1.

1. Using a net-present-value analysis, which alternative is more attractive? Assume that the minimum rate of return desired is 8 percent.

2. Using the accounting rate-of-return method, what is the rate of return on the initial investment?

11-36. Evaluation of payback model. The Knickel Oil Company has two methods of evaluating the attractiveness of oil-drilling proposals, the *payback method* and the so-called *cumulative profitability method*. The supervisor of drilling explained to some visitors that the most recent project, which was begun two days previously, will have an investment of $108,000, a nine-month payback time, and a cumulative profitability ratio of 2.3.

When asked to explain the latter, he replied, "We take the total expected production over the life of the well and figure the overall profitability by dividing its associated cash inflow by the original investment."

REQUIRED | 1. What was the expected cash inflow from operations for the first year?
2. What was the total expected cash inflow from operations for the useful life of the project?
3. Evaluate the validity of the computation in Requirement 2 in comparison with (a) the payback model and (b) the discounted-cash-flow model. Be specific. This is the most important part of the problem.

11-37. Audit of projects. (CMA.) Dickson Inc. has formal policies and procedures to screen and ultimately approve capital projects. Proposed capital projects are classified as one of the following types:

- Expansion requiring new plant and equipment

• Expansion by replacement of present equipment with more productive equipment

• Replacement of old equipment with new equipment of similar quality

All expansion projects and replacement projects that will cost more than $50,000 must be submitted to the top-management capital investment committee for approval. The investment committee evaluates proposed projects by considering the costs and benefits outlined in the supporting proposal and the long-range effects on the company. The projected revenue and/or expense effects of the projects, once operational, are included in the proposal. Once a project is accepted, the committee approves an expenditure budget for the project from its inception until it becomes operational. The expenditures required each year for the expansions or replacements are also incorporated into Dickson's annual budget procedure. The budgeted revenue and/or cost effects of the projects, for the periods in which they become operational, are incorporated into the five-year forecast.

Dickson Inc. does not have a procedure for evaluating projects once they have been implemented and become operational. The vice-president of finance has recommended that Dickson establish a postcompletion audit program to evaluate its capital expenditure projects.

REQUIRED

1. Discuss the benefits a company could derive from a postcompletion audit program for capital expenditure projects.
2. Discuss the practical difficulties in collecting and accumulating information that would be used to evaluate a capital project once it becomes operational.

11-38. **New equipment and analysis of operating costs: accounting rate of return.** The processing department of Rho Company has incurred the following costs in producing 150,000 units, which is normal volume, during the past year:

Variable	$100,000
Fixed	50,000
	$150,000

The department has been offered some new processing equipment. The salesman says that the new equipment will reduce unit costs by 20¢. The department's old equipment has a remaining useful life of five years, has zero disposal value now, and is being depreciated on a straight-line basis at $5,000 annually. The new equipment's straight-line depreciation would be $30,000 annually. It would last five years and have no disposal value. The salesman pointed out that overall unit costs now are $1, whereas the new equipment is being used by one of Rho's competitors to produce an identical product at a unit cost of 80¢, computed as follows:

Variable costs	$ 80,000
Fixed costs*	80,000
Total costs	$160,000
Divide by units produced	200,000
Cost per unit	$ .80

*Fixed costs include $30,000 depreciation on the new equipment. Rho's supervisory payroll is $10,000 less than this competitor's.

The salesman stated that a saving of 20¢ per unit would add $30,000 to Rho's annual net income.

REQUIRED

1. Show *specifically* how the salesman computed Rho's costs and prospective savings.
2. As adviser to the Rho Company, evaluate the salesman's contentions and prepare a quantitative summary to support your recommendations for Rho's best

course of action. Include the accounting rate-of-return method and the net-present-value method in your evaluation. Assume that Rho's minimum desired rate of return is 10 percent.

11-39. **Replacement decision.** Amtrak, a passenger train company subsidized wholly by the U.S. government, has included a dining car on the lone passenger train it operates from Buffalo to Albany, N.Y. Yearly operations of the dining car have shown a consistent loss, which is expected to persist, as follows:

Revenue (in cash)		$200,000
Expenses for food, supplies, etc. (in cash)	$100,000	
Salaries	110,000	210,000
Net loss (ignore depreciation on the dining car itself)		($ 10,000)

The Auto-vend Company has offered to sell automatic vending machines to Amtrak for $22,000, less a $3,000 trade-in allowance on old equipment (which is carried at $3,000 book value, and which can be sold outright for $3,000 cash) now used in the dining car operation. The useful life of the vending equipment is estimated at ten years, with zero scrap value. Experience elsewhere has led executives to predict that the equipment will serve 50 percent more food than the dining car, but prices will be 50 percent less, so the new gross receipts will probably be $150,000. The variety and mix of food sold are expected to be the same as for the dining car. A catering company will completely service and supply the machines, paying 10 percent of gross receipts to the Amtrak company and bearing all costs of food, repairs, etc. All dining car employees will be discharged immediately. Their termination pay will total $30,000. However, an attendant who has some general knowledge of vending machines will be needed for one shift per day. The annual cost to Amtrak for the attendant will be $14,000.

For political and other reasons, the railroad will definitely not abandon its food service. The old equipment will have zero scrap value at the end of ten years.

REQUIRED

Using the above data, carefully compute the following. Label computations. Ignore income taxes.

1. The incremental net present value, in dollars, of the proposed investment. Assume that Congress has specified that a minimum desired rate of return of 10 percent be used for these types of investments. For this problem, assume that the PV of $1 at 10 percent to be received at the end of ten years is $.400 and that the PV of an annuity of $1 at 10 percent for ten years is $6.000.
2. What would be the minimum amount of annual *revenue* that Amtrak would have to receive from the catering company to justify making the investment? Show computations.

11-40. **Sensitivity of capital budgeting and inflation.** The president of the Haywood Company, a London manufacturer, is considering whether to invest £100,000 in some automatic equipment that will last five years, have zero scrap value, and produce cash savings in materials and labor usage as follows, using 19X0 prices and wage rates (in pounds sterling):

YEAR	19X1	19X2	19X3	19X4	19X5
	20,000	20,000	30,000	30,000	20,000

The minimum desired rate of return, which embodies an element attributable to inflation, is 12 percent per year. For purposes of this problem, assume that the present values of £1 at the end of each year are .89, .80, .71, .64, and .57, respectively. All analysis will be conducted on a before-tax basis.

1. Compute the net present value of the project, using the above data.
2. Ms. Haywood is virtually certain that inflation will continue, although she is uncertain about its degree. She hopes that government control over prices and wages will dampen inflation, but she thinks that the existing rate of inflation, 6 percent annually, will prevail over the next five years. She wants to pinpoint price changes more precisely with respect to the materials and labor question, but she thinks 6 percent is probably as good an overall guess as any.

   One pound invested at time zero will grow as follows, if the rates of interest are (rounded to the second decimal place):

END OF PERIOD	4%	6%	8%
1	1.04	1.06	1.08
2	1.08	1.12	1.17
3	1.12	1.19	1.26
4	1.17	1.26	1.36
5	1.22	1.34	1.47

   Compute the net present value of the project, using the above data and an inflation rate of 6 percent through the five-year period. To make the decision model internally consistent, the cash savings should be adjusted upward in accordance with the 6 percent inflation rate. That is, there will be 6 percent inflation in Year 1. (The analysis in Requirements 1 and 2 should be identical, except for adjusting the savings upward.)
3. Compare your results in Requirements 1 and 2. What generalizations seem warranted?

■ SOLUTIONS TO EXERCISES
IN COMPOUND INTEREST, PROBLEM 11-2

The general approach to these exercises centers on one fundamental question: Which of the two basic tables am I dealing with? No calculations should be made until after this question is answered with assurance. If you made any errors, it is possible that you used the wrong table.

a. From Table 1, at the end of the book:
   (1) $4,110
   (2) $3,105
   (3) $2,010

The $5,000 is an *amount* or *future worth*. You want the present value of that amount:

$$PV = \frac{S}{(1 + i)^n}$$

The conversion factor, $1/(1 + i)^n$, is on line 5 of Table 1. Substituting:

PV = $5,000(.822) = $4,110   (1)
PV = $5,000(.621) = $3,105   (2)
PV = $5,000(.402) = $2,010   (3)

Note that the higher the interest rate, the lower the present value.

b. From Table 2, at the end of the book:
   (1) $2,226.00
   (2) $1,895.50
   (3) $1,495.50

The $500 withdrawal is a uniform annual amount, an annuity. You need to find the present value of an annuity for five years:

$$PV_A = \text{Annual withdrawal (F), where F is the conversion factor.}$$

Substituting:

$$PV_A = \$500(4.452) = \$2,226.00 \tag{1}$$
$$PV_A = \$500(3.791) = \$1,895.50 \tag{2}$$
$$PV_A = \$500(2.991) = \$1,495.50 \tag{3}$$

c. From Table 2:
   (1) $1,123.09
   (2) $1,318.91

You have $5,000, the present value of your contemplated annuity. You must find the annuity that will just exhaust the invested principal in five years:

$$PV_A = \text{Annual withdrawal (F)} \tag{1}$$

$$\$5,000 = \text{Annual withdrawal (4.452)}$$
$$\text{Annual withdrawal} = \$5,000 \div 4.452$$
$$= \$1,123.09$$
$$\$5,000 = \text{Annual withdrawal (3.791)} \tag{2}$$
$$\text{Annual withdrawal} = \$5,000 \div 3.791$$
$$= \$1,318.91$$

d. From Table 1: Mining is preferable; its present value exceeds farming by $3,852. Note that the nearer dollars are more valuable than the distant dollars.

YEAR	PRESENT-VALUE @ 16 PERCENT FROM TABLE 1	PRESENT VALUE OF MINING	PRESENT VALUE OF FARMING
1	.862	$8,620	$1,724
2	.743	5,944	2,972
3	.641	3,846	3,846
4	.552	2,208	4,416
5	.476	952	4,760
		$21,570	$17,718

suggested readings

BIERMAN, H., and S. SMIDT, *The Capital Budgeting Decision*, 5th ed. New York: Macmillan, 1980.

BOWER, J., *Managing the Resource Allocation Process.* Boston: Harvard Business School, 1970.

CLARK, J., T. HINDELANG, and R. PRITCHARD, *Capital Budgeting.* Englewood Cliffs, N.J.: Prentice-Hall, 1979.

VAN HORNE, JAMES C., *Financial Management and Policy*, 5th ed. Englewood Cliffs, N.J.: Prentice-Hall, 1980.

chapter **12**

IMPACT OF INCOME TAXES ON MANAGEMENT PLANNING

learning objectives

When you have finished studying this chapter, you should be able to:

1. Analyze a typical income statement to determine the net after-tax cash inflow from operations.
2. Compute the after-tax present values of projects involving straight-line depreciation and sum-of-the-years'-digits depreciation.
3. Explain the effect of an investment tax credit on net present value.
4. Distinguish between the typical income tax effects of each of the following pairs of planning alternatives:
   a. Selecting the corporate form of business organization instead of the partnership or proprietorship form
   b. Using the LIFO inventory method instead of the FIFO method
   c. Making donations to charitable or educational organizations in the form of property instead of cash
   d. Applying a net operating loss to several years instead of a single year
   e. Investing in tax-exempt bonds instead of taxable bonds
   f. Taking certain gains and losses in the same year instead of different years
   g. Allocating a larger portion of a lump-sum purchase price of assets to land or goodwill instead of other types of assets
   h. Using debt in the capital structure instead of capital stock
   i. Using the cash accounting method instead of the accrual accounting method
   j. Reporting sales on the installment basis instead of the regular basis
   k. Investing in bonds instead of common stock

Income taxes influence nearly all business decisions. In this chapter we show how income taxes may be reckoned with in decision making. Our focus is on corporations rather than on individuals or partnerships.

Managers have an obligation to avoid income taxes. Avoidance is not evasion. Avoidance is the use of legal means to minimize tax payments; evasion is the use of illegal means. Income tax problems are often exceedingly complex, so qualified counsel should be sought whenever the slightest doubt exists.

We are especially concerned with the effect of income taxes on the choice of depreciation methods and on capital-budgeting decisions. However, other topics will also be explored—the tax effects of last-in, first-out inventory valuations, of charitable contributions, and some miscellaneous matters. Obviously, in one chapter we can only scratch the surface of this vast and complicated subject.

Income taxes and capital budgeting

☐ GENERAL CHARACTERISTICS

Income taxes are cash disbursements. Income taxes can influence the *amount* and/or the *timing* of cash flows. Their basic role in capital budgeting is no different from that of any other cash disbursement. However, taxes tend to narrow the cash differences between projects. Cash savings in operations will cause an increase in net taxable income and thus an increase in tax outlays. A 60 percent income tax rate reduces the net attractiveness of $1 million in cash operating savings to $400,000.

As of 1980, U.S. federal income tax rates on ordinary corporate taxable income vary from 17 to 40 percent of the first $100,000 per year. Taxable income over $100,000 is taxed at 46 percent. These rates are sometimes subject to additional surcharges that may vary from year to year. State income tax rates vary considerably. In many instances, state plus federal income tax rates are more than 50 percent. We use a 60 percent rate in several examples to facilitate computations.

☐ EFFECTS OF DEPRECIATION DEDUCTIONS

Exhibit 12-1 shows the interrelationship of income before taxes, income taxes, and depreciation. Please examine this exhibit carefully before reading on. Assume that the company has a single fixed asset, purchased for $100,000 cash, which has a four-year life and zero disposal value. The purchase cost, less the estimated disposal value, is tax-deductible in the form of yearly depreciation. Depreciation deductions (and similar deductions that are noncash expenses when deducted) have been called **tax shields** because they protect that amount of income from taxation. The term *tax shield* seems apt at first glance, but note that all deductions from gross income are really tax shields (including cost of goods sold, donations to charities, officer salaries, and so forth).

As Exhibit 12-2 shows, the asset represents a valuable future tax deduction of $100,000. The present value of this deduction depends directly on its specific yearly effects on future income tax payments. Therefore the present value is influenced by the depreciation method selected, the tax rates, and the discount rate.

EXHIBIT 12-1

TRADITIONAL INCOME STATEMENT

(S) Sales	$130,000
(E) Less: Expenses, excluding depreciation	$ 70,000
(D)　　　Depreciation (straight line)	25,000
Total expenses	$ 95,000
Income before taxes	$ 35,000
(T) Income taxes @ 60%	21,000
(I) Net income	$ 14,000

Total after-tax effect on cash is
either S − E − T = $130,000 − $70,000 − $21,000 = $ 39,000
　　　or I + D = 　$14,000 + $25,000 = $39,000

ANALYSIS OF THE ABOVE FOR CAPITAL BUDGETING

(S − E) Cash inflow from operations:	$130,000 − $70,000 =	$ 60,000
Income tax effects, @ 60%		36,000
After-tax effects of operations (excluding depreciation)		$ 24,000
Effect of depreciation:		
(D) Straight-line depreciation: $100,000 ÷ 4 = $25,000		
Income tax savings @ 60%		15,000
Total after-tax effect on cash		$ 39,000

☐ THE BEST DEPRECIATION METHOD

The three most popular depreciation methods in the United States are
straight-line depreciation, sum-of-the-years'-digits, and **double-declining-balance.** The effects of the first two are shown in Exhibit 12-2.[1] Note that
the present value of the income tax savings is greater if straight-line depreciation
is *not* used. The general decision rule is to select accelerated methods because, as
compared with the straight-line method, they maximize the present values of
income tax savings. The cumulative *dollar* tax bills may not change when the

---

[1]Double-declining-balance depreciation (DDB) is computed as follows:

　　a. Compute rate (ignoring the terminal value) by dividing 100% by the years of useful life.
Then double the rate. In our example, 100% ÷ 4 years = 25%. The DDB rate would be 2 × 25%, or
50%.

　　b. To compute the depreciation for any year, multiply the beginning book value by the DDB
rate: 50% × $100,000 = $50,000 for the first year; 50% × ($100,000 − $50,000) = $25,000 for the
second year; etc. Unmodified, this method will never fully depreciate the existing book value.
Therefore, in the later years of an asset's life, companies are permitted to switch to a straight-line
method.

EXHIBIT 12-2

After-Tax Effects of Depreciation

Assume: Original cost of equipment $100,000; four-year life; zero disposal value; annual cash inflow from operations, $60,000; income tax rate, 60 percent; minimum desired after-tax rate of return, 12 percent.

Straight-Line Depreciation

Annual depreciation: $100,000 ÷ 4 = $25,000

Cash effects: savings in income tax disbursements,
@ 60% = .60 × $25,000 = $15,000

	12% DISCOUNT FACTOR, FROM APPROPRIATE TABLES	TOTAL PRESENT VALUE, @ 12%
	3.037	$45,555

Sum-of-the-Years'-Digits Depreciation

YEAR	MULTIPLIER*	DEDUCTION	CASH EFFECTS: INCOME TAX SAVINGS, @ 60%	12% DISCOUNT FACTOR, FROM APPROPRIATE TABLES	TOTAL PRESENT VALUE, @ 12%
1	4/10	$40,000	$24,000	.893	$21,432
2	3/10	30,000	18,000	.797	14,346
3	2/10	20,000	12,000	.712	8,544
4	1/10	10,000	6,000	.636	3,816
Total present value					$48,138

SKETCH OF CASH FLOWS AT END OF YEAR

0	1	2	3	4
$—	$15,000	$15,000	$15,000	$15,000
	$24,000	$18,000	$12,000	$ 6,000

---

*The denominator for the sum-of-the-years'-digits method is:

$$S = \frac{n(n + 1)}{2}$$

or

$$1 + 2 + 3 + 4 = 10$$

$$S = \frac{4(4 + 1)}{2} = 4 \times 2.5 = 10$$

where S = sum of the digits
n = years of estimated useful life

years are taken together, but the early write-offs defer tax outlays to future periods. The measure of the latter advantage depends on the rate of return that can be gained from funds that would otherwise have been paid as income taxes. The mottoes in income tax planning are: When there is a legal choice, take the deduction sooner rather than later; and Recognize taxable income later rather than sooner.

☐ COMPREHENSIVE ILLUSTRATION
EFFECTS OF INCOME TAXES ON CASH FLOW

The easiest way to visualize the effects of income taxes on cash flow is by a step-by-step analysis of a concrete situation. The following illustration is the same one used in the example in Chapter 11 (p. 319). However, an after-tax discount rate is now going to be used, and all income tax effects—including gains and losses on disposals—will now be considered.

A company owns a packaging machine, which was purchased three years ago for $56,000. It has a remaining useful life of five years, providing that it has a major overhaul, at the end of two more years of life, at a cost of $10,000, fully deductible in that year for income tax purposes. Its disposal value now is $20,000; in five years, its disposal value will be $8,000. The cash operating costs of this machine are expected to continue at $40,000 annually. The company has not used a residual value in allocating depreciation for tax purposes.[2] Accumulated straight-line depreciation is $21,000.

A manufacturer has offered a substitute machine for $51,000 in cash. The new machine will reduce annual cash operating costs by $10,000, will not require any overhauls, will have a useful life of five years, and will have a disposal value of $3,000. The company would use sum-of-the-years'-digits depreciation for tax purposes, with no provision for residual value.

REQUIRED

Assume that the minimum desired rate of return, after taxes, is 6 percent. Using the net-present-value technique, show whether the new machine should be purchased (a) under a total project approach; (b) under an incremental approach. Assume that income tax rates are 60 percent on ordinary income. Assume that all taxes are paid in the same year in which the taxable income is earned. Also, assume that the zero residual values used in computing depreciation for tax purposes will not be challenged by the Internal Revenue Service.

Exhibits 12-3 and 12-4 show the complete solution. The following steps are recommended. The pertinent income tax aspects will be considered as each step is discussed.

Step 1. *General Approach.* Review the example in Chapter 11 (p. 319). The general approach to these decisions is unchanged by income tax considerations.

Step 2. *Cash Operating Costs and Depreciation.* Cash operating costs and their income tax effects are separated from the depreciation effects on cash. These can be combined, if preferred. However, the approach illustrated facilitates

[2]For computing depreciation, the *Internal Revenue Code* allows a taxpayer to ignore the expected terminal residual value as long as it does not exceed 10 percent of the original cost. The assumption here is that when the machine was originally purchased, the expected terminal residual value was less than $5,600. Of course, intervening inflation can increase the residual values as stated in dollars, but such a happening will not affect the original depreciation schedule after it is set.

EXHIBIT 12-3

After-tax Analysis of Equipment Replacement:
Total Project Approach

		PRESENT-VALUE DISCOUNT FACTORS, @ 6%	TOTAL PRESENT VALUE	SKETCH OF CASH FLOWS AT END OF YEAR					
				0	1	2	3	4	5

(A) Replace

			PRESENT-VALUE DISCOUNT FACTORS, @ 6%	TOTAL PRESENT VALUE	0	1	2	3	4	5
Recurring cash operating costs		$30,000								
Income tax savings. @ 60%		18,000								
After-tax effect on cash		$12,000	4.212	$(50,544)		($12,000)	($12,000)	($12,000)	($12,000)	($12,000)

Depreciation deductions (sum of digits
1 + 2 + 3 + 4 + 5 = 15):

YEAR	MULTIPLIED BY $51,000	DEDUCTION	CASH EFFECTS: INCOME TAX SAVINGS, @ 60%	PRESENT-VALUE DISCOUNT FACTORS, @ 6%	TOTAL PRESENT VALUE	0	1	2	3	4	5
1	5/15	$17,000	$10,200	.943	9,619		10,200				
2	4/15	13,600	8,160	.890	7,262			8,160			
3	3/15	10,200	6,120	.840	5,141				6,120		
4	2/15	6,800	4,080	.792	3,231					4,080	
5	1/15	3,400	2,040	.747	1,524						2,040

		PRESENT-VALUE DISCOUNT FACTORS, @ 6%	TOTAL PRESENT VALUE	0	1	2	3	4	5
Residual value, all subject to tax because book value will be zero	$ 3,000								
Less: 60% income tax	1,800								
Total after-tax effect on cash	$ 1,200	.747	896						1,200
Initial required investment, actual cash outflow: $51,000	$51,000	1.000	(51,000)	($51,000)					

EXHIBIT 12-3—(Continued)

Disposal of old equipment:

Book value now:

$56,000 − $21,000* = $35,000

Selling price	$20,000			
Net loss	20,000			
	$15,000			
Tax savings	× .60			
	9,000			
Total after-tax effect on cash	$29,000	1.000	29,000	29,000
Total present value of all cash flows			$(44,871)	

(B) Keep

		PV factor	Present value					
Recurring cash operating costs	$40,000							
Income tax savings, @ 60%	24,000							
After-tax effect on cash	$16,000	4.212	$(67,392)	($16,000)	($16,000)	($16,000)	($16,000)	
Savings in income tax disbursements because of depreciation, @ 60% = .60 × $7,000*	4,200	4.212	17,690	4,200	4,200	4,200	4,200	4,200
Residual value, all subject to tax	$ 8,000							
Less: 60% income tax	4,800							
Total after-tax effect on cash	$ 3,200	.747	2,390					3,200
Overhaul, end of Year 2	$10,000							
Income tax savings, @ 60%	6,000							
Total after-tax effect on cash	$ 4,000	.890	(3,560)	(4,000)				
Total present value of all cash flows			$(50,872)					
Difference in favor of replacement			$ 6,001					

Depreciation of old equipment is $56,000 ÷ 8 years = $7,000 per year.

EXHIBIT 12-4

After-tax Analysis of Equipment Replacement
Incremental Approach

Analysis confined to differences between
(**A**) and (**B**) in Exhibit 12-3:

Recurring operating savings,
$40,000 − $30,000 .... $10,000

Income tax, @ 60% 6,000

After-tax effect on cash .... $ 4,000

Differences in depreciation:

YEAR	REPLACE	KEEP	DIFFERENCE	CASH INCOME TAX EFFECT, @ 60%	PRESENT-VALUE DISCOUNT FACTORS @ 6%	TOTAL PRESENT VALUES
	$17,000 − $7,000					
1	$17,000	$7,000	$10,000	$6,000	.943	5,658
2	13,600	7,000	6,600	3,960	.890	3,524
3	10,200	7,000	3,200	1,920	.840	1,614
4	6,800	7,000	(200)	(120)	.792	(95)
5	3,400	7,000	(3,600)	(2,160)	.747	(1,614)

Difference in disposal value, end of Year 5
(see Exhibit 12-3 for details):
$1,200 − $3,200 = $(2,000) .... .747 .... (1,494)

Overhaul avoided, end of Year 2,
after-tax effect on cash .... .890 3,560

Incremental initial investment
(see Exhibit 12-3 for details): $51,000 − $29,000 .... 1.000 ... (22,000)

Net present value of replacement .... $ 6,001

SKETCH OF CASH FLOWS AT END OF YEAR

	0	1	2	3	4	5
		$4,000	$4,000	$4,000	$4,000	$4,000
		6,000	3,960	1,920	(120)	(2,160)
			4,000			(2,000)
	($22,000)					

4.212 .... $ 16,848

comparisons of alternative depreciation effects and permits the use of annuity tables for the cash operating costs when they do not differ from year to year.

This illustration, in which we assume that any given cash flows and related tax flows occur in the same period, could be refined to account for any possible lags. For instance, the pretax operating cash inflows may occur in Year 1, and some related tax outflows may not occur until April in Year 2. For simplicity, we are ignoring this possibility.

Step 3. Disposals of Equipment. In general, gains and losses on disposals of equipment are taxed in the same way as ordinary gains and losses.[3]

Exhibit 12-3 is an analysis of the alternative dispositions of the asset. Disposal at the end of Year 5 entails the cash effect of the selling price, subject to a 60 percent tax. The tax is on the *gain,* the excess of the selling price over book value; the book value was zero in this case.

Immediate replacement entails the disposal of the old equipment at a loss. This loss is fully deductible from current income, so the cash-flow computations become a bit more subtle. The net loss must be computed to isolate its effects on current income tax, but the total cash-inflow effect is the selling price plus the current income tax benefit.

Step 4. Total Project or Incremental Approach? The relative merits of the total project and the incremental approaches were discussed in Chapter 11. Exhibits 12-3 and 12-4 demonstrate these approaches. Either yields the same net answer in favor of replacement. Note, however, that the incremental approach rapidly becomes unwieldy when computations become intricate. This becomes even more apparent when three or more alternatives are being considered.

□ INCOME TAX COMPLICATIONS

In the foregoing illustration, believe it or not, we deliberately avoided many possible income tax complications. As all taxpaying citizens know, income taxes are affected by many intricacies, including progressive tax rates, loss carrybacks and carryforwards, a variety of depreciation options, state income taxes, short- and long-term gains, distinctions between capital assets and other assets, offsets of losses against related gains, exchanges of property of like kind, exempt income, and so forth. Moreover, since the early 1970s most depreciable assets have qualified for an **investment tax credit,** which is generally an immediate income tax credit of 10 percent of the initial cost. This credit is a lump-sum reduction of the income tax cash outflow at time zero or in Year 1. For example, an investment of $500,000 would generate an investment tax credit that would reduce

---

[3]In this case, the old equipment was sold outright. Where there is a trade-in of old equipment for new equipment of like kind, special income tax rules result in the gain or loss being added to, or deducted from, the capitalized value of the new equipment. The gain or loss is not recognized in the year of disposal; instead, it is spread over the life of the new asset as an adjustment of the new depreciation charges.

Many gains on the sale of specified assets qualify for taxation at the *capital gains* tax rate, which is currently 30 percent for corporations. A *capital gain* is the profit on the sale of an asset that is typically not held for resale in the ordinary course of business. Examples of such assets are investments in stocks and bonds, land, and equipment.

Before 1962, gains from disposal of equipment were taxed at the existing capital gains rate. Since then, the general rule has been that gain on sale of equipment is not a capital gain except in special circumstances. This complicates the effect on taxes of gains arising on disposal, frequently resulting in part of the gains being taxed at ordinary income tax rates and part at capital gain rates. For simplicity, this chapter does not introduce the latter complication.

current income tax outflows by .10 × $500,000, or $50,000. Furthermore, the full original cost, less the estimated disposal value, is deductible in the form of yearly depreciation.[4]

Keep in mind that miscellaneous changes in the tax law occur each year. For example, the investment tax credit has been suspended, reinstated, and changed in many respects through the years.

Miscellaneous tax-planning matters

□ FORM OF ORGANIZATION

The corporation is a distinct business entity subject to separate corporate income taxes. In contrast, individual proprietorships and partnerships are not separate entities for income tax purposes. Instead, their income is attributed to the owners as individuals regardless of whether they make any cash withdrawals from the business. These distinctions are shown in Exhibit 12-5.

For a corporation, reasonable salaries paid to officers who are also stockholders are deductible for income tax purposes. For partnerships or proprietorships, no deductions are allowed for owners' salaries or for interest expense on invested ownership capital.

Corporate income is subject to double taxation. First, it is taxed to the separate entity. Second, any cash dividends are taxed to the individual at the recipient's income tax rate.

What form of business organization should be chosen? The answer depends on a myriad of legal and tax considerations, including the extent of personal liability of the owners for business debts, ease of transfer of ownership,

EXHIBIT 12-5 Diagram of tax effects of form of business organization

[4]For a book-length discussion of these and other complications, see W. L. Raby, *The Income Tax and Business Decisions,* 4th ed. (Englewood Cliffs, N.J.: Prentice-Hall, 1978).

and expected life of the business. But the personal income tax bracket of the owners is often paramount. For example, suppose an individual with a marginal income tax rate of 70 percent (because of other income) is considering how to organize his solely owned business.

Operating data may be analyzed as follows:

	CORPORATION		PROPRIETORSHIP (OR PARTNERSHIP)	
Sales (all for cash)		$200,000		$200,000
Operating expenses:				
Owner's salary	$20,000*		$ 20,000†	
Other expenses	150,000*	170,000	150,000*	170,000
Income before income taxes		$ 30,000		$ 30,000
Corporate income taxes, federal and state		6,100		—
Net income		$ 23,900		$ 30,000
Cash dividends		$ 23,900	Withdrawals	30,000†
Net income retained		$ —		$ —

*For simplicity, assume these are all cash expenses.
†Note that these amounts can be any number without affecting the personal tax liability. "Salaries" and withdrawals are irrelevant as far as income tax liability is concerned. In this case, the proprietor will be subject to personal income taxes on the entity income of $30,000 plus the $20,000 owner's salary.

   Incidentally, partnerships must file information returns disclosing the determination of net income and the share of each partner. However, under the income tax law, proprietorships and partnerships are regarded as a conduit through which taxable income flows to the owners. Thus, although salaries paid to proprietors and partners are deducted here in computing entity income, they must be reported as income by the recipients on their personal tax returns. In essence, then, the income tax laws would regard the entity income shown here ($30,000) and the owner's salary ($20,000) as arbitrary splits of a $50,000 income taxable to the owner. Therefore, if the owner wants to label the entity income as $40,000 and the salary as $10,000, it makes no difference regarding his taxable income, which will be $50,000 regardless. Furthermore, if the owner withdraws zero or $100,000, his taxable income will still be $50,000.

If the personal income tax brackets are low, the noncorporate forms may become more attractive. But high-bracket taxpayers will almost always find the corporate form more attractive if they do not need cash dividends.

☐ CHANGES IN INCOME TAX RATES

During World War II and the Korean War, the United States imposed an excess profits tax that considerably boosted effective income tax rates. At the time, the prospect of changes in income tax rates in a given year or series of years influenced management planning extensively. If income taxes were going to rise in the next year, the tendency would be to postpone certain expenses (e.g., repairs, advertising, legal services, purchases of supplies not usually inventoried) and to accelerate revenue recognition by boosting production to fill any existing orders before the higher tax rates took effect.

☐ LIFO OR FIFO

The income tax planner does not have to be directly concerned with the relative conceptual merits of LIFO (last-in, first-out) or FIFO (first-in, first-out) inventory methods. The most desirable inventory method is that which postpones income tax payments, perhaps permanently. For instance, an expansion coupled with increasing price levels favors LIFO rather than FIFO; under LIFO, the highest (most recent) costs will be released to expense sooner rather than later.

The adoption of LIFO by over half of the large American companies is directly attributable to the income tax benefits rather than to the conceptual justification of more "realistic" income measures so often cited. The only tax-planning reasons for not adopting LIFO would be (1) the negligible prospect of income tax savings because of expected long-run declines in prices; (2) stability of prices; and (3) insignificance of inventories to particular organizations, such as service businesses.

If the prices of inventory are expected to rise, a company should adopt LIFO. The annual savings in cash flow will have compound effects and will result in a substantial financial advantage. Raby illustrates these effects:

> Assume an effective income tax rate of 50 percent and after-tax rate of return of 7 percent. Inventory is $1,000,000 at time of adoption of Lifo. Prices increase in a straight line, so that inventory in Year 1 is $1,100,000 under Fifo but still $1,000,000 under Lifo; in Year 2 Fifo inventory is $1,200,000; in Year 3, $1,300,000; and so forth throughout 20 years. Meanwhile, Lifo inventory stays at $1,000,000, and income tax savings of $50,000 annually, invested at 7 percent compounded annually, will accumulate to $2,049,750 more assets under Lifo.[5]

☐ EFFECT OF LIFO ON PURCHASE DECISIONS

When prices are rising, it may be advantageous—subject to prudent restraint as to maximum and minimum inventory levels—to buy unusually heavy amounts of inventory near year-end, particularly if income tax rates are likely to fall. For example, assume that a company has made the following transactions during 19X1, its first year in business:

Sales: 10 units, @ $5   Purchases: 8 units, @ $2
                                         3 units, @ $3

Decision: Buy six more units, near year-end, @ $4? Current income tax rates, 50 percent, are expected to decline to 40 percent next year. Prices on inventory are not expected to decline next year.

		COMPARISON OF ALTERNATIVES	
		do not buy	buy 6 more units
Sales: 10 units, @ $5		$50	$50
Cost of goods sold (LIFO basis):			
3 units, @ $3 =	$ 9		
7 units, @ $2 =	14	23	
or			
6 units, @ $4 =	$24		
3 units, @ $3 =	9		
1 unit, @ $2 =	2		35
Gross margin		$27	$15

[5]Raby, *Income Tax*, p. 321.

Tax savings: 50 percent of ($27 − $15) = $6 this year. The effects on later years' taxes will depend on inventory levels, prices, and tax rates.

Tax savings can be generated because LIFO permits management to influence immediate net income by its purchasing decisions. In contrast, FIFO results would be unaffected by this decision:

		do not buy	buy 6 more units
Sales		$50	$50
Cost of goods sold (FIFO basis):			
8 units, @ $2 =	$16		
2 units, @ $3 =	6	22	22
Gross margin		$28	$28

☐ CONTRIBUTIONS OF PROPERTY RATHER THAN CASH

Donations to qualifying charitable, educational, and similar institutions are generally deductible, up to specified maximum limits, in computing income taxes. Giving property (such as marketable securities or land) rather than cash is more beneficial to both the donor and the donee. The reason is that any increase in the value of the property is not taxed, but the tax deduction is the fair market value of the contributed asset. For example:

Market price	$400,000
Cost of property	100,000
Capital gain	$300,000
Capital gain tax, @ 30%	$ 90,000*
Cash received by donor after tax, $400,000 − $90,000	$310,000

*For corporations, a capital gain on qualifying assets held more than one year is subject to a maximum tax at a rate of 30 percent, rather than at ordinary income tax rates. The tax law specifies which assets are subject to the capital gains rate (the most notable are land and marketable securities). Gains on sales of inventories and receivables are taxed at ordinary rates, while gains on sales of depreciable property are also taxed as ordinary income in many cases. However, the entire problem of computing taxes on long-term gains is too complex to be covered in this introductory chapter. Moreover, the contribution of appreciated property is subject to some complicated rules and limitations.

	sell, and donate cash	donate outright
Income tax effects of contribution:		
Deduction	$310,000	$400,000
Assumed income tax rate of 50%	×.50	×.50
Income tax savings of donor	$155,000	$200,000
Charitable institution can receive:		
Cash = $400,000 in cash − $90,000 tax, or	$310,000	
Property, and then sell it for cash		$400,000

As the tabulation shows, compared with a cash donation, the direct donation of property can enable the donor to reap larger tax savings while the donee also receives a larger benefit. Therefore, charitable institutions have tried to attract donations by stressing the tax-saving features of giving property rather than cash.

☐ OPERATING LOSSES

The net operating loss of a corporation may be used to offset net income by being carried back to each of the three preceding years and carried forward to each of the seven following years. This sequence must be followed strictly. No part of a given year's loss may be used to offset the second preceding year's income until all of the third preceding year's income has been absorbed. In short, a net operating loss enables the corporation to obtain tax refunds related to past years' operations or to reduce tax disbursements in future years.

The tax effects of a 19X4 net operating loss of $100,000 may be illustrated as follows (note that any loss carryforward unused after seven years becomes nondeductible):[6]

	NET INCOME (LOSS)	19X4 CARRYBACK OR CARRYFORWARD	TAXABLE INCOME
19X1	$ 5,000	$(5,000)	—
19X2	15,000	(15,000)	—
19X3	35,000	(35,000)	—
19X4	(100,000)	—	—
19X5	5,000	(5,000)	—
19X6	8,000	(8,000)	—
19X7	10,000	(10,000)	—
19X8	10,000	(10,000)	—
19X9	5,000	(5,000)	—
19X0	1,000	(1,000)	
19X1	2,000	(2,000)	
Used		(96,000)	
Unused and nondeductible		(4,000)	
Accounted for		(100,000)	

Strangely enough, a company may properly view a loss carryforward as an "asset," for planning purposes. It represents a valuable tax deduction as long as profitable operations are forthcoming. If the tax rate is 46 percent, a loss carryforward of $100,000 represents future tax savings of $46,000. In certain cases, this may prompt corporations to buy other profitable companies at higher-than-usual prices.

Suppose that Company A has a potential net operating cash inflow of $200,000 per year for the next five years. Suppose further that two companies, X

[6]A taxpayer may elect *not* to carry the loss back. The election is made annually and will not increase the carryover period. Such an election would generally be made only where carryback of the loss would cause tax credits utilized in the preceding years to expire unused.

and Y, are interested in buying Company A. Company X has a $1 million net operating loss carryforward that can be offset against the next five years' net taxable income. Company Y has no such loss carryforward. Both companies are willing to buy all the capital stock of Company A at a price not to exceed the present value of the five years' after-tax cash inflows, discounted at 8 percent. What are the maximum prices that Company X and Company Y are willing to pay? Calculations follow:

Company Y

After-tax net cash inflow of Company A is $200,000	
less .46(200,000)	= $108,000
Present value of an annuity of $1, @ 8%, for 5 years	× 3.993
Maximum price	$431,244

Company X

After-tax net cash inflow of Company A would be the entire $200,000, because of the $1,000,000 loss carried forward over a five-year period	$200,000
Present value of an annuity of $1, @ 8%, for 5 years	× 3.993
Maximum price	$798,600

The relevance of the loss carryforward in the Company X analysis depends on the available alternatives. Perhaps the carryforward can be used to offset Company X's future taxable income—that is, there is danger of double-counting the carryforward. It cannot be used to offset both the Company A income and the Company X income.[7]

☐ TAX-FREE INTEREST

Interest on the bonds issued by a city, state, and certain nonprofit organizations is nontaxable to the investor. Because of this feature, such bonds have a lower pretax yield than industrial bonds. However, the high-bracket taxpayer and corporations will usually find tax-exempt bonds more attractive:

	NON-TAX-EXEMPT INDUSTRIAL BOND: COUPON RATE, 8%	TAX-EXEMPT MUNICIPAL BOND: COUPON RATE, 5%
Investment in bonds	$100,000	$100,000
Interest income before taxes	$ 8,000	$ 5,000
Income taxes, @ 50%	4,000	—
Net income, after taxes	$ 4,000	$ 5,000

[7]A carryover may be disallowed if there has been a "substantial change" in ownership. These intricate rules severely limit the ability to "sell" a loss carryforward. Nevertheless, note that a holder of a loss carryforward can use it to offset future profits from other segments of the business. Therefore the holder would be more reluctant than otherwise to sell the business bearing the loss carryforward, which is an asset in the sense that it represents reductions of future income tax outflows.

Investments in stocks and bonds are usually cited as a common example of capital assets. The Internal Revenue Service defines capital assets negatively as being all assets except inventory, trade receivables, copyrights, depreciable property, and real property used in a trade or business. Unless a corporation has an operating loss, the gains from the sale of capital assets held more than one year are taxed at a maximum of 30 percent.

Depreciable property and real property used in a trade or business are not capital assets. Nevertheless, a special rule regarding these "Section 1231 assets" permits treating certain gains as long-term capital gains and certain losses as ordinary losses. If net gains exceed net losses, all the gains and losses are regarded as long-term capital gains and losses. If net losses exceed net gains, all the gains and losses are regarded as ordinary items in computing taxable income. Because the losses offset the gains dollar for dollar, the shrewd tax planner tries to time his or her transactions so that losses occur in one year and gains in another.

For example, assume that a company owns two parcels of land. One parcel can be sold at a capital gain of $500,000, the other at a capital loss of $500,000. If both were sold in the same year, the loss would offset the gain, and there would be no impact on taxes. If they were sold in separate years, the tax bill would be 30 percent of $500,000 in one year, or $150,000, and lower (assuming an ordinary tax rate of 46 percent) by $230,000 in the next year. The second strategy would thus save the company $80,000 in income tax disbursements.

☐ OTHER GENERAL CONSIDERATIONS

Purchases of assets. When a group of long-lived assets is acquired for a single overall price, care must be taken to see that as much of the total cost as permissible is allocated to those assets whose costs will be depreciated or amortized for income tax purposes. Otherwise the excess of the total cost over those parts allocated is assigned to land and/or goodwill, which are not subject to amortization for income tax purposes. For example, suppose a purchaser paid $10 million for a group of assets having a book value of $6 million; individual assets such as inventories, buildings, and equipment would tend to be revalued upward.

Use of debt in the capital structure. Interest is deductible as an expense; dividends are not. Therefore the relative after-tax cash drains on corporations favor using as much debt in the capital structure as seems prudent. Assume a 50 percent tax rate:

	PRETAX COST	AFTER-TAX COST
8% Bonds payable	8%	4%
10% Preferred stock	10%	10%

Research and development. There is conceptual merit in capitalizing many research costs for internal purposes. These costs are then amortized over future periods. From a tax-planning standpoint, however, research costs should be deducted as quickly as possible.

Cash versus accrual accounting methods. The cash method of accounting allows more taxpayer control over the timing of revenue and expense than the accrual method. For example, a legal expense attributable to services rendered in December 19X1 might be deductible in either 19X1 or 19X2, depending on whether the cash disbursement is made in December or delayed until January. However, where inventories exist, companies must use the accrual basis for income tax purposes.

Deferral of income. Among the many ways of deferring income are installment sales methods, whereby income is geared to cash receipts rather than point of sale.

For example, a furniture store's taxable income for its first year in business could be computed as follows:

	REGULAR BASIS	INSTALLMENT BASIS
Installment sales	$500,000	
Cost of goods sold	300,000	
Gross profit, @ 40%	$200,000	$160,000*
Expenses	150,000	150,000
Net taxable income	$ 50,000	$ 10,000

*Forty percent of current installment collections of $400,000. Unrealized gross profit is 40 percent of ending receivables: 40 percent of $100,000, or $40,000.

If the owner chooses to report income on the installment basis, income tax on the uncollected gross profit—which is 40 percent of $100,000 (i.e., $500,000 − $400,000), or $40,000—is deferred until the years when the installments are collected.

Also available is the discretionary timing of shipments of merchandise to customers. At year-end, the choice between making a shipment at December 31 or January 1 can have a significant impact on income taxes, because the sale can thus be included in either of the two adjacent calendar years.

Dividends received. Corporations can generally exclude 85 percent of dividends received from taxable domestic corporations; in other words, only 15 percent of the dividend is taxable to the recipient. This provision enhances the attractiveness of investing excess cash in common stock rather than in federal or corporate bonds, whose interest is fully taxable.

☐ DESIRABILITY OF LOSSES

The often-heard expression "What the heck, it's deductible" sometimes warps perspective. Even though losses bring income tax savings and gains bring additional income taxes, gains are still more desirable than losses. For example, business land (see earlier section, "Capital Gains Alternative") that cost

$300,000 a few years ago and is sold now, would have the following effect at two different selling prices:

	GAIN		LOSS	
Selling price	$1,000,000	$1,000,000	$ 100,000	$100,000
Cost	300,000		300,000	
Gain (loss)	$ 700,000		$(200,000)	
Tax, @ 30% of $700,000		−210,000		
Tax savings, @ 60% of $200,000				+120,000
Net cash effect		$ 790,000		$220,000

summary

Income tax is a significant cost of conducting business. No accountant or manager should be indifferent to its impact. Income taxes may be necessary evils, but this does not mean that management should be resigned to tax burdens. Intelligent planning, assisted by expert advice, can minimize income taxes.

Income taxes are sometimes too influential in business decisions. Their effects may be overemphasized. The ogre of the income tax may reduce the emphasis on efficiency and may unduly hamper risk taking. Income tax is only one of a number of variables that bear on business administration.

summary problem for your review

▦ PROBLEM

The Flan Company estimates that it can save $2,500 per year in annual cash operating costs for the next five years if it buys a special-purpose machine at a cost of $9,000. Residual value is expected to be $900, although no residual value is being provided for in using sum-of-the-years'-digits depreciation for tax purposes. The minimum desired rate of return, after taxes, is 10 percent. Assume the income tax rate is 40 percent. Using discounted-cash-flow techniques, show whether the investment is desirable.

▦ SOLUTION

There is a net disadvantage in purchasing because the net present value is slightly negative, indicating an internal rate of return a shade below the minimum desired rate of 10 percent. However, such a slight quantitative disadvantage could be more than offset by positive factors not quantified here. The complete analysis is on the accompanying page.

	PRESENT-VALUE DISCOUNT FACTORS, @ 10%	TOTAL PRESENT VALUES
Recurring cash operating savings $2,500		
Income taxes @ 40% 1,000		
After-tax cash operating savings $1,500	3.791	$ 5,686

SKETCH OF CASH FLOWS AT END OF YEAR

0	1	2	3	4	5
	$1,500	$1,500	$1,500	$1,500	$1,500

YEAR	MULTI-PLIED BY $9,000	DEDUC-TION	INCOME TAX SAVINGS, @ 40%	PRESENT-VALUE DISCOUNT FACTORS, @ 10%	TOTAL PRESENT VALUES	0	1	2	3	4	5
1	5/15	$3,000	$1,200	.909	1,091		1,200				
2	4/15	2,400	960	.826	793			960			
3	3/15	1,800	720	.751	541				720		
4	2/15	1,200	480	.683	328					480	
5	1/15	600	240	.621	149						240

Residual value, all subject to tax because book value will be zero $900

Less: 40% income tax on disposal gain* 360

		Net cash inflow $540	.621	335						540

Initial required investment (9,000)		(9,000)	(9,000) at year 0

Net present value of all cash flows $(77)

*Assume that ordinary income tax rates, not capital gains rates, apply.

assignment material

12-1. **Terminology.** Define *double-declining-balance depreciation; investment tax credit; straight-line depreciation; sum-of-the-years'-digits depreciation; tax shield.*

12-2. **After-tax cash from sale of assets.** (An alternate is 12-24.) Given for Fluent Dinero Corporation:

	CASE 1	CASE 2
Equipment cost	$360,000	$280,000
Estimated useful life (years)	10	10
Forecasted terminal scrap value at end of estimated useful life	$ 30,000	$ 20,000
Depreciation method: straight-line		
Actual sales price when sold at end of eighth year	$ 86,000	$ 92,000
Income tax rate (applies to all gains and losses)	55%	40%

REQUIRED

Compute for each case the total after-tax effect on cash from a single transaction, the cash sale of the equipment at end of the eighth year of use.

12-3. **Purchase of equipment.** The O'Hara Company is planning to spend $40,000 for a specialized machine for making electronic components. The machine is expected to save $13,500 in cash operating costs for each of the next four years. A major overhaul costing $4,000 will occur at the end of the second year and is fully deductible in that year for income tax purposes.

The expected terminal value is $3,000, but no terminal value is being provided for in using the sum-of-the-years'-digits depreciation method for tax purposes.

The minimum desired rate of return after taxes is 12 percent. The applicable income tax rate is 60 percent.

REQUIRED

1. Using the net-present-value model, show whether the investment is desirable.
2. Suppose an investment tax credit of 10 percent were available on all new assets acquired having useful lives in excess of three years. Would your answer in Requirement 1 change?

12-4. **Tax shield and depreciation methods.** A company has just paid $42,000 for some equipment that will have a six-year life and no residual value. The minimum rate of return desired, after taxes, is 10 percent.

The president has attended a management conference luncheon where an accounting professor adamantly stated: "Not using accelerated depreciation for tax purposes is outright financial stupidity." The president has a perpetual fear of rises in income tax rates and has favored straight-line depreciation "to have greater deductions against future income when taxes are higher."

He is having second thoughts now and has asked you to prepare a financial analysis of the dollar benefits of using sum-of-the-years'-digits depreciation instead of straight-line depreciation under the following assumptions: (a) income tax rates of 60 percent throughout the coming six years, and (b) income tax rates of 60 percent for the first three years and 80 percent for the subsequent three years.

12-5. Explain why accelerated depreciation methods are superior to straight-line methods for income tax purposes.

12-6. "Immediate disposal of equipment, rather than its continued use, results in a full tax deduction of the undepreciated cost now—rather than having such a deduction spread over future years in the form of annual depreciation." Do you agree? Explain, using the $35,000 cost of old equipment in Exhibit 12-3 as a basis for your discussion. (Exhibit 12-3 is on page 348.)

12-7. Name some income tax complications that were ignored in Exhibits 12-3 and 12-4.

12-8. What is an *investment credit?*

12-9. Why does LIFO save income taxes when prices are rising?

12-10. "If income tax rates are likely to rise, the tendency would be to increase year-end purchases of inventory under LIFO." Do you agree? Explain.

12-11. Distinguish between tax avoidance and tax evasion.

12-12. "Tax planning is unimportant because the total income tax bill will be the same in the long run, regardless of short-run maneuvering." Do you agree? Explain.

12-13. What are the major influences on the present value of a tax deduction?

12-14. Why have charitable institutions tried to attract donations in the form of property rather than cash?

12-15. How was it possible that the drug companies' net income was increased in 1962 by their contribution to the ransom of Cuban prisoners?

12-16. "A loss carryforward has an economic value." Explain.

12-17. "An investment tax credit of $100,000 saves income taxes by $100,000 multiplied by the applicable income tax rate." Do you agree? Explain.

12-18. "New equipment cost $800,000 cash. There was an investment tax credit of $80,000. Consequently, $720,000, less the estimated disposal value, is deductible in the form of yearly depreciation for income tax purposes." Do you agree? Explain.

12-19. **Switch from LIFO to FIFO.** Effective January 1, 1970, Chrysler Corporation adopted the FIFO method for inventories previously valued by the LIFO method. The 1970 annual report stated: "This . . . makes the financial statements with respect to inventory valuation comparable with those of the other United States automobile manufacturers."

The *Wall Street Journal* reported:

The change improved Chrysler's 1970 financial results several ways. Besides narrowing the 1970 loss by $20 million it improved Chrysler's working capital. The change also made the comparison with 1969 earnings look somewhat more favorable because, upon restatement, Chrysler's 1969 profit was raised only $10.2 million from the original figures.

Finally, the change helped Chrysler's balance sheet by boosting inventories, and thus current assets, by $150 million at the end of 1970 over what they would have been under LIFO. As Chrysler's profit has collapsed over the last two years and its financial position tightened, auto analysts have eyed warily Chrysler's shrinking ratio of current assets to current liabilities.

Chrysler's current liabilities shrank last year because it was able to pay off sizable amounts of short-term debt with the help of a $200 million long-term financing last winter. Chrysler's short-term debt stood at $374 million at year-end, down from $477 million a year earlier but up slightly from $370 million on Sept. 30. Chrysler's cash and marketable securities shrank during the year to $156.4 million at year-end, down from $309.3 million a year earlier and $220 million on Sept. 30.

To get the improvements in its balance sheet and results, however, Chrysler paid a price. Roger Helder, vice president and comptroller, said Chrysler owed the government $53 million in tax savings it accumulated by using the LIFO method since it switched from FIFO in 1957. The major advantage of LIFO is that it holds down profit and thus tax liabilities. The other three major auto makers stayed on the FIFO method. Mr. Helder said Chrysler now has to pay back that $53 million to the government over 20 years, which will boost Chrysler's tax bills about $3 million a year.

REQUIRED

Given the content of this text chapter, do you think the Chrysler decision to switch from LIFO to FIFO was beneficial to its stockholders? Explain, being as specific and using as many data as you can.

12-20. **Timing of gains and losses.** A company owns 10,000 shares each of the common stock of Company A and Company B. The Company A stock was acquired ten years ago for $100,000. It can now be sold for $400,000. The Company B stock was purchased five years ago for $900,000. It can now be sold for $600,000. It is now near the end of year 19X1. Capital gains tax rate is 30 percent, and ordinary income tax rate is 40 percent.

REQUIRED

1. If all the stock were sold in 19X1, what would be the effect on income taxes?
2. If the Company B stock were sold in 19X1, and the Company A stock were sold in 19X2, what would be the effect on income taxes? Assume that these are the only transactions affecting capital gains or losses. Which strategy will save the most income taxes? How much would be saved?

12-21. **Donations of property rather than cash.** The Mandrake Company has 100 shares of Florence common stock that were acquired four years ago at $70 per share. Current market price is $120 per share. Income tax rates are 60 percent on ordinary income and 25 percent on capital gains. Compare the effects on Mandrake's income taxes of (1) selling the stock and donating the net cash after taxes to a university, and (2) donating the stock outright. How much cash will the university net under each plan, assuming that all donations of property are immediately converted into cash?

12-22. **Loss carryforward and purchase of a business.** Company G's potential net operating cash inflow, before taxes, for the next five years is $500,000 annually. Two companies, P and Q, are interested in buying all of the capital stock of Company G. Company P has a $2.5 million net operating loss, which it can carry forward to offset the next five years' net taxable income. Company Q has no such loss carryforward. Both companies are willing to buy all the capital stock of Company G at a price not to exceed the present value of the five years' cash inflow after taxes, discounted at 10 percent.

REQUIRED

What are the maximum prices that Company P and Company Q are willing to pay? Show your calculations. The ordinary income tax rate is 40 percent and the capital gains rate is 30 percent.

12-23. **Form of organization.** X and Y are attempting to decide whether to organize their new business as a corporation or as a partnership. Each will invest $100,000 and will receive annual compensation for services of $20,000 each. Sales will be $900,000 and cash expenses other than owners' salaries will be $760,000. All plant assets are rented, so there is no depreciation.

Each owner is in a 60 percent marginal income tax bracket. The corporate tax rate averages out at 41.5 percent of taxable income.

REQUIRED

1. Suppose that dividends or withdrawals are equal to net income. What is the income subject to tax for the corporation? The partnership? How much cash will be available to the business and to each owner after taxes?
2. Suppose that no dividends are paid. Suppose also that the withdrawals of the partners are equal to the salary equivalent of $20,000 each plus an additional withdrawal for payment of additional income taxes on the portion of partnership income that is not withdrawn. For the corporation and the partnership forms of organization, compute the cash available to each owner after taxes and the cash available to the business for expansion.

12-24. Income taxes and disposal of assets. (An alternate is 12-2.) Assume that income tax rates are 40 percent.

1. The book value of an old machine is $12,000. It will be sold for $18,000 cash. What is the total effect of this decision on cash after taxes?

2. The book value of an old machine is $11,000. It will be sold for $7,000 cash. What is the total effect of this decision on cash after taxes?

12-25. Football coaching contract. (H. Schaefer.) Bo Hays, a successful college football coach, has just signed a "million-dollar-plus" contract to coach a new professional team. The contract is a personal services contract for five years with the team's owner, I. M. Rich (if the team is disbanded Bo can still collect from Rich). Under the terms of the contract, Bo will be paid $150,000 cash at the start of the contract plus $150,000 at the end of each of the five years. Rich also agrees to buy a $200,000 house that Bo can use rent-free for all five years.

Rich earns a substantial income from numerous business ventures. His marginal tax rate is about 60 percent. Bo's cash salary payments are tax deductible to Rich, as are the depreciation expenses on the house. Rich decides to depreciate the house over a 20-year life with zero salvage value using the straight-line method of depreciation. Rich is certain the house can be sold at the end of five years for a price equal to its remaining book value.

REQUIRED

1. Determine Rich's yearly after-tax cash flows under Bo's contract.
2. Given your answers to Requirement 1, calculate the net present value of the costs of Bo's contract to Rich, assuming Rich employs a 10 percent minimum desired rate of return. Show your calculations clearly and in an orderly fashion. You may round to the nearest thousand dollars.

12-26. Present value of after-tax cash flows. Rose Optometrics, Inc., is planning to buy new equipment to produce a new product. Estimated data are:

Cash cost of new equipment now	$400,000
Estimated life in years	10
Terminal salvage value	$ 50,000
Incremental revenues per year	$300,000
Incremental expenses per year other than depreciation	$165,000

Use the straight-line method for depreciation and assume a 60 percent flat rate for income taxes. All revenue and expenses other than depreciation will be received or paid in cash. Use a 14 percent discount rate.

Compute:

1. Depreciation expense per year.
2. Anticipated net income per year.
3. Annual net cash inflow.
4. Payback period.
5. Accounting rate of return on initial investment.
6. Net present value.

12-27. Multiple choice: double-declining-balance. (CMA, adapted.)

DISCOUNT FACTORS FOR 10% (ROUNDED)

period	present value of $1	present value of an annuity of $1 per period
1	.91	.91
2	.83	1.74
3	.75	2.49
4	.68	3.17

The following data apply to items 1–6:

Rockyford Co. must replace some machinery. This machinery has zero book value but its current market value is $1,800. One possible alternative is to invest in new machinery which has a cost of $40,000. This new machinery would produce estimated annual pretax operating cash savings of $12,500. The estimated useful life of the new machinery is four years. Rockyford uses straight-line depreciation for book purposes and the double-declining-balance method for tax purposes. The company does *not* switch from double-declining-balance depreciation to straight-line in the later years of an asset's life. The new machinery would have an estimated salvage value of $2,000 at the end of four years; however, the salvage value can be ignored for the purpose of depreciation because it does not represent at least 10 percent of the cost of the asset. The investment in this new machinery would require an additional investment in working capital of $3,000.

If Rockyford accepts this investment proposal, the disposal of the old machinery and the investment in the new equipment will take place on December 31, 1981. The cash flows from the investment will occur during the calendar years 1982–85.

Rockyford is subject to a 40 percent income tax rate for all ordinary income and capital gains and has a 10 percent after-tax cost of capital. All operating and tax cash flows are assumed to occur at year-end.

Select the best answer for each of the following items.

1. The present value of the after-tax cash flow arising from the disposal of the old machinery in 1981 is
   a. $6,638
   b. $720
   c. $1,800
   d. $1,080
   e. Some answer other than these

2. The present value of the after-tax cash flows for all four years (1982–85) attributable to the operating cash savings is
   a. $23,775
   b. $39,625
   c. $36,555
   d. $15,850
   e. Some amount other than these

3. The present value of the tax savings effect for depreciation for the first year is
   a. $7,280
   b. $10,920
   c. $6,916
   d. $3,640
   e. Some amount other than these

4. The present value of the after-tax cash flows arising from the disposal of the new machinery at its salvage value at the end of 1985 (Year 4) is
   a. $1,360
   b. $1,224
   c. $1,564
   d. $1,496
   e. Some amount other than these

5. The present value of the net effect on the income tax payments related to the project in 1983 (Year 2) is
   a. $3,320 inflow
   b. $4,150 outflow
   c. $830 outflow
   d. $830 inflow
   e. Some amount other than these

6. Rockyford's additional investment in working capital of $3,000 required in 1981 is
   a. A sunk cost that is not recovered
   b. Considered part of the initial investment when determining the net present value
   c. Spread over the four-year life of the asset as a cash outflow
   d. Depreciated as if it were part of the cost of the new machinery
   e. Ignored

7. Ander Co. can invest $4,980 in a piece of equipment with a three-year life. If the minimum desired rate of return is 10 percent after taxes and the annual expected cash savings net of taxes is $2,500, the amount (rounded to the nearest dollar) by which the annual cash flows could change before the company would be indifferent to acquiring the equipment is a
   a. Decrease of $415
   b. Decrease of $2,480
   c. Decrease of $1,245
   d. Decrease of $500
   e. Decrease of $2,000

8. The accountant of Ronier, Inc., has prepared an analysis of a proposed capital project using discounted-cash-flow techniques. One manager has questioned the accuracy of the results because the discount factors employed in the analysis have assumed the cash flows occurred at the end of the year when the cash flows actually occurred uniformly throughout each year. The net present value calculated by the accountant
   a. Will not be in error
   b. Will be slightly overstated
   c. Will be unusable for actual decision making
   d. Will be slightly understated but usable
   e. Will produce an error the direction of which is undeterminable

12-28. **Income taxes and replacement of equipment.** Refer to Problem 5-30. Assume that income tax rates are 60 percent. The minimum desired rate of return, after taxes, is 6 percent. Using the net-present-value technique, show whether the proposed equipment should be purchased. Present your solution on both a total project approach and an incremental approach. For illustrative purposes, assume that old equipment would have been depreciated on a straight-line basis and the proposed equipment on a sum-of-the-years'-digits basis.

12-29. **Minimizing transportation costs.** Refer to Assignment 11-29, but ignore the requirements there and make the following assumptions:
   a. Wriston requires a minimum 10 percent after-tax rate of return.
   b. A 40 percent tax rate.

c. Sum-of-the-years'-digits depreciation with an allowance for the $5,000 salvage value of the truck.

d. No investment tax credit.

REQUIRED 1. Should the truck be purchased? Show computations to support your answer.
2. What qualitative factors might influence your decision? Be specific.

12-30. **Income taxes and make or buy.** Refer to Problem 5-27, Requirement 1. Assume a tax rate of 40 percent. The minimum desired rate of return, after taxes, is 6 percent. Using the net-present-value technique, show whether the proposed purchase from the outside supplier is desirable. Use both a total project approach and an incremental approach. Assume straight-line depreciation.

12-31. **Correction of faulty analysis.** (CMA.) Wisconsin Products Company manufactures several different products. One of the firm's principal products sells for $20 per unit. The sales manager of Wisconsin Products has stated repeatedly that he could sell more units of this product if they were available. In an attempt to substantiate his claim, the sales manager conducted a market research study last year at a cost of $44,000 to determine potential demand for this product. The study indicated that Wisconsin Products could sell 18,000 units of this product annually for the next five years.

The equipment currently in use has the capacity to produce 11,000 units annually. The variable production costs are $9 per unit. The equipment has a book value of $60,000 and a remaining useful life of five years. The salvage value of the equipment is negligible now and will be zero in five years.

A maximum of 20,000 units could be produced annually on the new machinery which can be purchased. The new equipment costs $300,000 and has an estimated useful life of five years with no salvage value at the end of the five years. Wisconsin Product's production manager has estimated that the new equipment would provide increased production efficiencies that would reduce the variable production costs to $7 per unit.

Wisconsin Products Company uses straight-line depreciation on all of its equipment for tax purposes. The firm is subject to a 40 percent tax rate, and its after-tax cost of capital is 15 percent.

The sales manager felt so strongly about the need for additional capacity that he attempted to prepare an economic justification for the equipment, although this was not one of his responsibilities. His analysis, as shown in the accompanying tables, disappointed him because it did not justify acquiring the equipment.

Required Investment

Purchase price of new equipment		$300,000
Disposal of existing equipment:		
Loss on disposal	$60,000	
Less tax benefit (40%)	24,000	36,000
Cost of market research study		44,000
Total investment		$380,000

Annual Returns

Contribution margin from product:	
Using the new equipment [18,000 × ($20 − 7)]	$234,000
Using the existing equipment [11,000 × ($20 − 9)]	121,000
Increase in contribution margin	$113,000
Less depreciation	60,000
Increase in before-tax income	$ 53,000
Income tax (40%)	21,200
Increase in income	$ 31,800
Less 15% cost of capital on the additional investment required (.15 × $380,000)	57,000
Net annual return of proposed investment in new equipment	$ (25,200)

1. The controller of Wisconsin Products Company plans to prepare a discounted-cash-flow analysis for this investment proposal. The controller has asked you to prepare corrected calculations of
   a. The required investment in the new equipment, and
   b. The recurring annual cash flows.
   Explain the treatment of each item of your corrected calculations that is treated differently from the original analysis prepared by the sales manager.
2. Calculate the net present value of the proposed investment in the new equipment. Round your discount factors to two places.

12-32. **Oil exploration.** (J. Patell.) During 19X6 Green and Trunk Oil Drilling expended $800,000 on oil exploration in Texarkana and succeeded in locating a small deposit. However, the nature of the oil-bearing formation (a salt dome) necessitates some long-range planning decisions now, before full-scale production begins.

Standard drilling and production equipment will require an immediate investment of $1 million. In addition, a sum of $100,000 must be deposited in advance with the Environmental Protection Agency as assurance that complete land reclamation will be provided by G&T when the well is finally closed down; the sum is returned in full plus 5 percent nontaxable annual interest if the required reclamation is performed. G&T estimates that the well will be productive for five years, and thus the investment will be depreciated on a straight-line basis over the five-year life. Owing to the size and shape of the formation, however, the oil production rate will not be constant over the five years. G&T's geologists predict that the well will yield approximately $500,000 worth of crude oil for each of the first three years, but the yield will drop to $400,000 in the fourth and fifth years *under normal production procedures*. Operating costs are estimated at $100,000 yearly for the entire life, and the land reclamation should require $50,000 at the end of the fifth year (fully tax deductible).

A secondary planning problem also must be solved now. Advanced forced-water pumping techniques have recently been perfected that would enable G&T to maintain the pressure in the well during Years 4 and 5 such that there would actually be *no decrease* in the flow rate. This technology would require an outlay of $50,000 at the end of Year 3 (to be depreciated over the last two years on a straight-line basis), but there would be no increase in annual operating expenses. Unfortunately, the initial production equipment would also have to be modified to accept the additional equipment later, raising the initial outlay from $1 million to $1.1 million.

Green and Trunk pays a 40 percent corporate income tax and uses a 12 percent after-tax opportunity rate in evaluating investment proposals. For computational simplicity, assume all operating cash flows and tax payments occur at the *end* of the year.

Assume that Green and Trunk will have enough taxable income from other sources to utilize all tax benefits from this project. The future amount of $1.00 at 5 percent is $1.00 $(1.05)^5 = \$1.2763$.

1. Assuming that G&T is going to develop the well, should the original equipment be constructed to accept the later addition of forced-water extraction gear? Support your answer with a net-present-value calculation.
2. Given your decision in Requirement 1, what is the net present value now to G&T of investing in production equipment and developing the well?

chapter **13**

JOB AND PROCESS SYSTEMS AND OVERHEAD APPLICATION

learning objectives

When you have finished studying this chapter, you should be able to:

1. Identify the dual purposes of cost accounting systems and their respective cost objectives.
2. Distinguish between the two fundamental types of product-costing systems: job-order and process.
3. Compute predetermined factory overhead rates, factory overhead applied to production, and the amounts of overapplied and underapplied factory overhead.
4. Indicate how the following are related within the job-cost system for a manufacturing company: the three basic elements of manufacturing cost, the principal inventories, and the cost of goods sold.
5. Identify the meaning and purpose of normalized overhead rates.
6. Describe the two methods and their rationale for disposing of underapplied and overapplied overhead at the end of a year.
7. Explain the distinction between actual costing and normal costing, and describe the usual blend of these followed in practice.
8. Identify the main differences in extending the job-costing approach to nonprofit organizations.
9. Prepare journal entries and ledger postings for a job-costing system (Appendix 13A).
10. Compute equivalent units as used in process costing (Appendix 13B).

Thus far, we have paid little attention to the product costing–income determination purpose of an accounting system. The purpose of this and the next chapter is to show how data may be accumulated within an accounting system and how various alternative methods of applying costs to products affect inventories and income determination. These are essentially scorekeeping tasks. Management makes policy decisions, at one time or another, regarding methods of product costing. Because such decisions affect the way net income will be determined, managers should know the various approaches to product costing. Moreover, as we have seen previously, a knowledge of product-costing techniques will enhance a manager's understanding of product costs, particularly when the latter are used for pricing and evaluating product lines.

Keep in mind that product costing is separable from control. That is, a good planning and control system may be coupled with any of a number of product-costing practices. In short, how costs are held back in inventory and released to expense should have little bearing (except for income tax planning described in Chapter 12) on the planning and controlling decisions of intelligent managers.

This chapter is designed so that it may be studied immediately after Chapter 3 without loss of continuity. Therefore, to begin, please review the first two sections of Chapter 3 ("Classifications of Costs" and "Relationships of Income Statements and Balance Sheets") and the Chapter 3 Appendix ("Classification of Labor Costs"). It is not necessary to review the other parts of Chapter 3.

Our focus in this and the next chapter is on manufacturing costs, because accountants view selling, administrative, and other nonmanufacturing costs as being expenses immediately and therefore totally excludable from costs of *product*.

Control and product-costing purposes

☐ TWO PURPOSES AND TWO COST OBJECTIVES

Recall that Chapter 3 defined *cost objective* as any activity for which a separate measurement of costs is desired. Two principal cost objectives were illustrated: departments and products. Cost accounting systems have a twofold purpose fulfilled by their day-to-day operations: (1) allocate costs to departments for planning and control, hereafter for brevity's sake often called *control*, and (2) allocate costs to units of product for *product costing*.

Suppose a firm had direct-material usage of $10,000, direct-labor usage of $8,000, and manufacturing overhead incurred, $4,000, half of each of these in Department A and half in Department B. Three jobs (three special orders for batches of living room furniture) were started and completed, passing through both departments. Each received varying attention and effort, and therefore different costs were allocated to each job, as assumed in Exhibit 13-1.

If the jobs in Exhibit 13-1 are not completed at the end of the accounting period, their costs are the measure of the inventory of Work in Process. As the jobs are completed, their costs are transferred to another inventory, Finished Goods.

Direct material may be acquired and stored as Direct-Materials Inventory before it is requisitioned for use by departments. In schematic form, the flow of

EXHIBIT 13-1

Cost Allocation for Two Purposes

	total	department A			department B		
		direct materials	direct labor	factory overhead	direct materials	direct labor	factory overhead
1. Control purpose	$22,000	$5,000	$4,000	$2,000	$5,000	$4,000	$2,000
2. Product-costing purpose:							
Job 1	$ 7,500	$1,000	$2,000	$1,000	$2,000	$1,000	$ 500
Job 2	7,550	2,000	1,500	750	1,800	1,000	500
Job 3	6,950	2,000	500	250	1,200	2,000	1,000
Costs accounted for	$22,000	$5,000	$4,000	$2,000	$5,000	$4,000	$2,000
In schematic form:							

1. Control purpose

2. Product costing purpose:

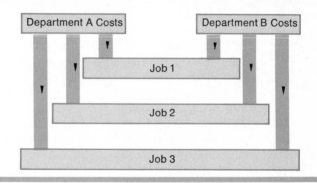

direct materials is shown in Exhibit 13-2. Pause and examine the exhibit before reading on.

☐ DISTINCTION BETWEEN JOB COSTING AND PROCESS COSTING

Two extremes of product costing are usually termed **job-order costing** and **process costing.** *Job-order* (or *job-cost* or *production-order*) accounting methods were just illustrated. They are used by companies whose products are readily identified by individual units or batches, each of which receives varying degrees of attention and skill. Industries that commonly use job-order methods include construction, printing, aircraft, furniture, and machinery.

Process costing is most often found in such industries as chemicals, oil, textiles, plastics, paints, flour, canneries, rubber, lumber, food processors, glass, mining, cement, and meat packing. In these there is mass production of like units, which usually pass in continuous fashion through a series of uniform production steps called *operations* or *processes.* This is in contrast to the production of tailor-made or unique goods, such as special-purpose machinery or printing.

Where manufacturing is conducted by continuous operations, costs are accumulated by departments (sometimes called *operations* or *processes*). The center of attention is the total department costs for a given time period in relation to the units processed. Accumulated department costs are divided by quantities

EXHIBIT 13-2. Flow of direct materials

Acquisition and storage

1. Control purpose, requisition by department

2. Product costing purpose, to Work in Process

Transfer to Finished Goods as Job 1 is completed

Direct Material Inventory

Department A

Job 1   Job 2   Job 3

Fin-ished Goods (from Job 1)

produced during a given period in order to get broad, average unit costs. Then unit costs are multiplied by units transferred to obtain total costs applied to those units.

The distinction between the job-cost and the process-cost methods centers largely on how product costing is accomplished. Unlike process costing, which deals with broad averages and great masses of like units, the essential feature of the job-cost method is the attempt to apply costs to specific jobs, which may consist of either a single physical unit (such as a custom sofa) or a few like units (such as a dozen tables) in a distinct batch or job lot.

In job costing, the costs in Exhibit 13-1 might be applicable to, say, three different batches of furniture, each bearing a differing assortment of direct materials, direct labor, and manufacturing overhead. However, to indicate the essence of the process-costing system, assume the total costs of $22,000 in Exhibit 13-1 are applicable to several manufacturing processes for the production of a *single product:* 22,000 gallons of chemicals at a unit cost of $1 per gallon of finished product:

1. Control purpose

2. Product costing purpose

Department A Costs   Department B Costs

22,000 gallons of product @ $1.00

The most important point is that product costing is an *averaging* process. The unit cost used for inventory purposes is the result of taking some accumulated cost that has been allocated to production departments and dividing it by some measure of production. The basic distinction between job-order costing and process costing is the breadth of the denominator: In job-order costing, it is small (for example, one painting, one hundred advertising circulars, or one special packaging machine); but in process costing, it is large (for example, thousands of pounds, gallons, or board feet).

Illustration of job-order costing

This section illustrates the principal aspects of the job-costing system. The first appendix to this chapter presents some technical details of job costing: source documents, journal entries, and ledgers. The second appendix explains some process-costing procedures.

☐ COST APPLICATION

Consider a new term, *cost application*, often called *cost absorption*. Until now the term cost allocation has been used indiscriminately to refer to the identifying or tracing of accumulated costs to *any* cost objective (whether a department or a product). Indeed, *cost allocation* is a general or generic term. However, when costs are allocated *to products*, the process of allocation is frequently called *application* or *absorption*. These latter terms will be used in this chapter. In any event, be alert to obtain the exact meanings of such terms when you encounter them in practice.

☐ PREDETERMINED OVERHEAD APPLICATION RATES

To show how factory overhead is applied to jobs, consider the Singapore Electronics Company, which has a job-order cost system with the following inventories on December 31, 19X1:

Direct materials (12 types)	$110,000
Work in process	—
Finished goods (leftover units from two jobs)	12,000

The following manufacturing overhead budget has been prepared for the coming year, 19X2:

	MACHINING	ASSEMBLY
Indirect labor	$69,600	$ 28,800
Supplies	14,400	5,400
Utilities	20,000	9,000
Repairs	10,000	6,000
Factory rent	24,000	16,800
Supervision	18,600	20,400
Depreciation on equipment	114,000	14,400
Insurance, property taxes, etc.	7,200	2,400
	$277,800	$103,200

In order to cost units as they are worked on, a job-cost sheet is prepared for each job as it begins. Three classes of costs are applied to the units as they pass through the departments: Material requisitions are used to apply costs of direct material; work tickets are used to apply costs of direct labor; and predetermined overhead rates are used to apply manufacturing overhead. The overhead rates are as follows:

	YEAR 19X2	
	MACHINING	ASSEMBLY
Budgeted manufacturing overhead	$277,800	$103,200
Budgeted machine-hours	69,450	
Budgeted direct-labor cost		$206,400
Predetermined overhead rate, per machine-hour: $277,800 ÷ 69,450 =	$4	
Predetermined overhead rate, per direct-labor dollar: $103,200 ÷ $206,400 =		50%

Overhead is a conglomeration of items which, unlike direct material or direct labor, cannot conveniently be applied on an individual basis. But the commonly accepted theory is that overhead is an integral part of a product's cost. Therefore it is applied in an indirect manner, using a cost-allocation base that is common to all jobs worked on and that is the best available index of the product's relative utilization of, or benefits from, the overhead items. In other words, there should be a strong correlation between the factory overhead incurred and the base chosen for its application, such as machine-hours or direct-labor cost.

Two or more machines in the machining department can often be operated simultaneously by a single direct laborer. Because utilization of machines is the major overhead cost in the machining department, machine-hours are the base for application of overhead costs. This necessitates keeping track of the machine-hours used for each job and thus creates an added clerical cost. Both direct-labor costs and machine-hours must be accumulated for each job.

In contrast, the workers in the assembly department are paid uniform hourly rates, so the cost of direct labor is an accurate reflection of the relative attention and effort devoted to various jobs. No separate job records have to be kept of the labor *hours.* All that is needed is to apply the 50 percent overhead rate to the cost of direct labor already applied to the job. Of course, if the hourly labor rates differed greatly for individuals performing identical tasks, hours of labor, rather than dollars spent for labor, would have to be used as a base. Otherwise a $9-per-hour worker would cause more overhead to be applied than a $8-per-hour worker, despite the probability that the same time would be taken and the same facilities utilized by each employee to do the same work.

These overhead rates will be used throughout the year to cost the various jobs as they are worked on by each department. All overhead will be applied to all jobs worked on during the year, in proportion to either the machine-hours or direct-labor costs of each job. If management predictions are accurate, the total overhead applied to the year's jobs on the basis of these predetermined rates should be equal to the total overhead costs actually incurred.

☐ THE YEAR'S EVENTS

In January 19X2 several jobs were begun. For example, Job 404 was begun and completed. Exhibit 13-3 is the completed job-cost sheet.

EXHIBIT 13-3. Completed job-cost sheet

Job Order No. ____404____

MACHINING DEPARTMENT						
REFERENCE	DATE	QUANTITY		UNIT COST	AMOUNT	SUMMARY
Direct material:						
Type M—Various requisitions	Various	900		$2.00	$1,800	
Type N—Various requisitions	Various	900		5.00	4,500	$ 6,300
Direct labor:						
Various work tickets	Various	320 hrs		9.00	2,880	2,880
Factory overhead applied		425 mach. hrs		4.00	1,700	1,700
Total machining						$10,880
ASSEMBLY DEPARTMENT						
(Entries would be similar to above)						XXX
Total assembly (assumed)						$ 2,000
Total product cost						$12,880

The bulk of the scorekeeping is a detailed recording and summarization of source documents such as requisitions, work tickets, and invoices.

The following is a summary of events for the year 19X2:

		MACHINING	ASSEMBLY	TOTAL
1.	Direct materials purchased	—	—	$1,900,000
2.	Direct materials requisitioned	$1,000,000	$890,000	1,890,000
3.	Direct-labor costs incurred	200,000	190,000	390,000
4a.	Factory overhead **incurred**	290,000	102,000	392,000
4b.	Factory overhead **applied:**			
	50% of direct-labor costs		95,000	95,000
	70,000 machine-hours @ $4	280,000		280,000
5.	Cost of goods completed	—	—	2,500,000
6a.	Sales	—	—	4,000,000
6b.	Cost of goods sold	—	—	2,480,000

The accounting for these events is displayed in Exhibit 13-4. The accumulated data would be allocated to departments and then to products. (If you wish a more detailed discussion, see the first appendix to this chapter.) These costs would appear in the financial statements for the year as shown in Exhibit 13-5, which warrants your close scrutiny. (Note how Exhibit 13-5 parallels the ideas in Chapter 3, Exhibit 3-2, page 63.)

Problems of overhead application

Most managements desire a close approximation of the costs of different products before the end of a fiscal period. Essentially, this need is for pricing, income determination, and inventory valuation. Moreover, there is a growing objection

EXHIBIT 13-4. Control and product-costing illustration (in dollars)

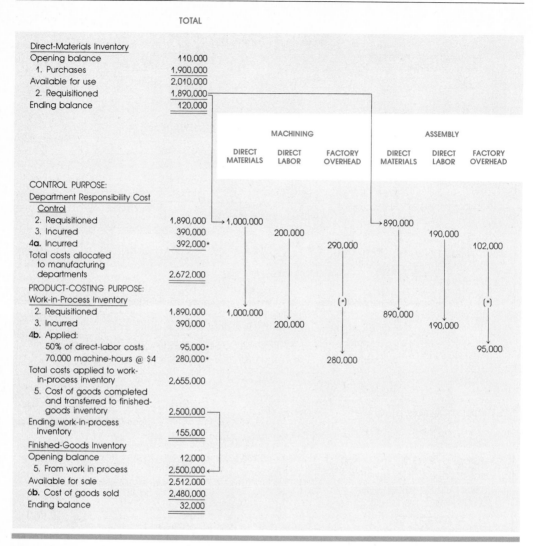

TOTAL

	TOTAL		MACHINING			ASSEMBLY		
			DIRECT MATERIALS	DIRECT LABOR	FACTORY OVERHEAD	DIRECT MATERIALS	DIRECT LABOR	FACTORY OVERHEAD
Direct-Materials Inventory								
Opening balance	110,000							
1. Purchases	1,900,000							
Available for use	2,010,000							
2. Requisitioned	1,890,000							
Ending balance	120,000							
CONTROL PURPOSE:								
Department Responsibility Cost Control								
2. Requisitioned	1,890,000		1,000,000			890,000		
3. Incurred	390,000			200,000			190,000	
4a. Incurred	392,000*				290,000			102,000
Total costs allocated to manufacturing departments	2,672,000							
PRODUCT-COSTING PURPOSE:								
Work-in-Process Inventory					(*)			(*)
2. Requisitioned	1,890,000		1,000,000			890,000		
3. Incurred	390,000			200,000			190,000	
4b. Applied:								
50% of direct-labor costs	95,000*							95,000
70,000 machine-hours @ $4	280,000*				280,000			
Total costs applied to work-in-process inventory	2,655,000							
5. Cost of goods completed and transferred to finished-goods inventory	2,500,000							
Ending work-in-process inventory	155,000							
Finished-Goods Inventory								
Opening balance	12,000							
5. From work in process	2,500,000							
Available for sale	2,512,000							
6b. Cost of goods sold	2,480,000							
Ending balance	32,000							

*The $17,000 difference is underapplied overhead, $392,000 − ($95,000 + $280,000), which is explained later in the text.

to the view that all costs incurred must be fully applied to the products. Some costs result from inefficiency, and these can hardly be viewed as being inventoriable as assets. Customers are rarely willing to pay for inefficiency.

☐ NORMALIZED OVERHEAD RATES

Basically, Exhibit 13-4 demonstrates the **normal costing** approach. Overhead application rates are predetermined by dividing total *budgeted* overhead by an appropriate base such as machine-hours, direct-labor hours, or direct-labor dollars. The idea is to use an annual average overhead rate consistently throughout the year, for product costing, without altering it from day to day and from

EXHIBIT 13-5. Relation of costs to financial statements

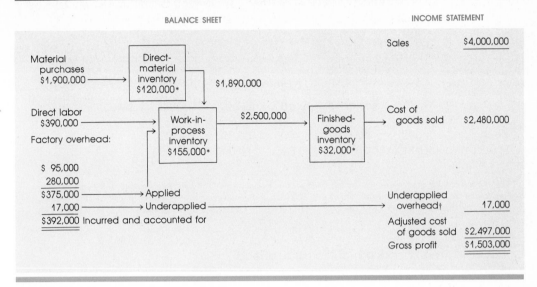

*Ending balance.
†Explained in the next section.

month to month. The resultant normal product costs include an average or normalized chunk of overhead.

As actual overhead costs are incurred by departments from month to month, they are charged, in detail, to the departments. These actual costs are accumulated weekly or monthly and are then compared with budgeted costs to obtain budget variances for performance evaluation. This *control* process is completely divorced from the *product-costing* process of applying overhead to specific jobs.

During the year and at year-end, it is unlikely that the amount incurred and applied will be equal. This variance between incurred and applied cost may be analyzed. The following are usually contributory causes: poor forecasting; inefficient use of overhead items; price changes in individual overhead items; erratic behavior of individual overhead items (e.g., repairs made only during slack time); calendar variations (i.e., 20 workdays in one month, 22 in the next); and, probably most important, operating at a different level of volume than the level used as a denominator in calculating the predetermined overhead rate (e.g., using 100,000 direct-labor hours as the denominator and then working only 80,000 hours).

All these peculiarities of overhead are commingled in an annual overhead pool. Thus an annual rate is predetermined and used regardless of the month-to-month peculiarities of specific overhead costs. Such an approach is more defensible than, say, applying the actual overhead for each month, because a *normal* product cost is more meaningful, and more representative for inventory-costing purposes, than a so-called actual product cost that is distorted by month-to-month fluctuations in production volume and by the erratic behavior of many overhead costs. For example, the employees of a gypsum plant had the privilege of buying company-made items "at cost." It was a joke common among employees to buy "at cost" during high-volume months. Unit costs were then lower under the actual overhead application system in use, whereby overhead rates would fall as volume soared, and vice versa:

| | ACTUAL OVERHEAD | | | DIRECT-LABOR HOURS | ACTUAL OVERHEAD APPLICATION RATE*PER DIRECT-LABOR HOUR |
	variable	fixed	total		
Peak-volume month	$60,000	$40,000	$100,000	100,000	$1.00
Low-volume month	30,000	40,000	70,000	50,000	1.40

*This overall rate can be separated into two rates, one for variable and one for fixed overhead. Note that the presence of fixed overhead causes the fluctuation in unit costs from $1.00 to $1.40. The variable rate is $.60 an hour in both months, but the fixed rate is $.40 in the peak-volume month ($40,000 ÷ 100,000) and $.80 in the low-volume month ($40,000 ÷ 50,000).

EXHIBIT 13-6. Disposition of factory overhead

Method One: Proration Among Inventories

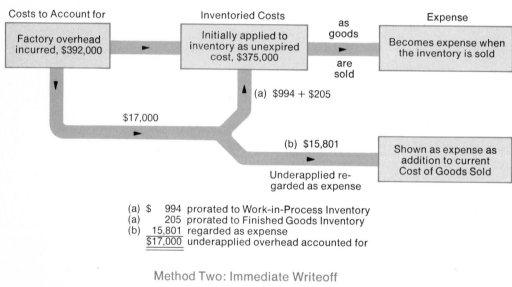

(a) $ 994 prorated to Work-in-Process Inventory
(a) 205 prorated to Finished Goods Inventory
(b) 15,801 regarded as expense
$17,000 underapplied overhead accounted for

Method Two: Immediate Writeoff

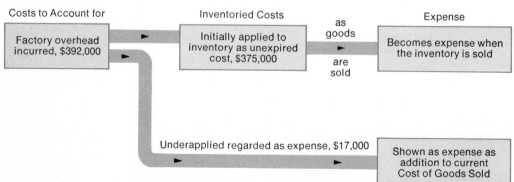

Another example of the difficulties of product costing was cited by James Lorie, who, after completing a consulting task for Chrysler Corporation in the middle 1950s, asked some top Chrysler executives if he could buy an Imperial automobile directly from the company "at cost." The response was, "We'll be happy to sell an Imperial to you at cost, which this year happens to be 120 percent of list price."

☐ DISPOSITION OF UNDERAPPLIED OR OVERAPPLIED OVERHEAD

When predetermined rates are used, the difference between incurred and applied overhead is typically allowed to accumulate during the year. When the amount applied to product exceeds the amount incurred by the departments, the difference is called **overapplied** or *overabsorbed* **overhead**; when the amount is applied is less than incurred, the difference is called **underapplied**, or *underabsorbed* **overhead**. At year-end, the difference (which was $17,000 in Exhibit 13-4) is disposed of in one of two major ways, as shown in Exhibit 13-6:

1. *Proration.* This method prorates underapplied overhead among the accounts where the costs of the 19X2 jobs worked on are now lodged. Theoretically, if the objective is to obtain as accurate a cost allocation as possible, all of the overhead costs of the individual jobs worked on should be recomputed, using the actual rather than the original predetermined rates. This approach is rarely feasible, so the best practical attack is probably to prorate on the basis of the total manufacturing costs of the 19X2 jobs in each of three accounts (Work in Process, $155,000; Finished Goods, $32,000; and Cost of Goods Sold, $2,480,000), assuming that the beginning Finished-Goods Inventory was sold during 19X2:

	(1) UNADJUSTED BALANCE, END OF 19X2*	(2) DEDUCT 19X1 JOBS	(3) (1) – (2) BASIS FOR PRORATION
Work in Process	$ 155,000	$ —	$ 155,000
Finished Goods	32,000	—	32,000
Cost of Goods Sold	2,480,000	12,000	2,468,000
			$2,655,000

	(4) PRORATION OF UNDERAPPLIED OVERHEAD	(1) + (4) ADJUSTED BALANCE END OF 19X2
	155/2,655 × 17,000 = $ 994	$ 155,994
	32/2,655 × 17,000 = 205	32,205
	2,468/2,655 × 17,000 = 15,801	2,495,801
	$17,000	

*See Exhibits 13-4 and 13-5 for details.

The amounts prorated to inventories here are not significant. In practical situations, prorating is done only when inventory valuations would be significantly affected.

2. *Immediate write-off.* This is the most widely used approach; it was used in Exhibit 13-5. The $17,000 is regarded as a reduction in current income via adding the underapplied overhead to the cost of goods sold. (The same logic is followed for overapplied overhead, except that the result would be an addition to current income because cost of goods sold would be lessened.)

The theory underlying the direct write-off is that most of the goods worked on have been sold, and a more elaborate method of disposition is not worth the extra trouble. Another justification is that the extra overhead costs represented by underapplied overhead do not qualify as part of ending inventory costs because they do not represent assets. They should be written off because they largely represent inefficiency or the underutilization of available facilities.

In sum, overhead applications will rarely coincide with overhead incurrence (e.g., entry 4*b* in Exhibit 13-4 will not exactly offset entry 4*a*). A difference will arise (i.e., entry 4*b*, compared with entry 4*a*, shows a $17,000 underapplication). This underapplication or overapplication is typically disposed of at year-end as a direct addition to or deduction from Cost of Goods Sold, even though it may also pertain to accounts other than Cost of Goods Sold. Conceptually, however, there is justification for prorating it.

☐ THE USE OF VARIABLE AND FIXED APPLICATION RATES

As we have seen, overhead application is the most troublesome aspect of product costing. The presence of fixed costs is the biggest single reason for the costing difficulties. Most companies have made no distinction between variable- and fixed-cost behavior in the design of their accounting systems. For instance, reconsider the development of overhead rates in our illustration. The machining department developed the rate as follows:

$$\text{overhead application rate} = \frac{\text{expected total overhead}}{\text{expected machine-hours}}$$

$$= \frac{\$277,800}{69,450} = \$4 \text{ per machine-hour}$$

Some companies distinguish between variable overhead and fixed overhead for product costing as well as for control purposes. This distinction could have been made in the machining department. Rent, supervision, depreciation, and insurance would have been considered the fixed portion of the total manufacturing overhead, and two rates could have been developed:

$$\text{variable-overhead application rate} = \frac{\text{expected total variable overhead}}{\text{expected machine-hours}}$$

$$= \frac{\$114,000}{69,450}$$

$$= \$1.64 \text{ per machine-hour}$$

$$\text{fixed-overhead application rate} = \frac{\text{expected total fixed overhead}}{\text{expected machine-hours}^1}$$

$$= \frac{\$163,800}{69,450}$$

$$= \$2.36 \text{ per machine-hour}$$

As the next chapter explains, such rates can be used for product costing, and distinctions between variable and fixed overhead incurrence can also be made for control purposes.

☐ ACTUAL VERSUS NORMAL COSTING

The overall system we have just described is sometimes called an actual costing system, because every effort is made to trace the actual costs, as incurred, to the physical units benefited. However, it is only partly an actual system, because the overhead, by definition, cannot be definitely assigned to physical products. Instead, overhead is applied on an average or normalized basis, in order to get representative or normal inventory valuations. Hence we shall label the system a *normal* system. The cost of the manufactured product is composed of *actual* direct material, *actual* direct labor, and *normal* applied overhead.

The two job-order costing approaches described in this chapter may be compared as follows:

	ACTUAL COSTING	NORMAL COSTING
Direct materials	Actual	Actual
Direct labor	Actual	Actual
Manufacturing overhead:		
Variable	Actual	Predetermined rates*
Fixed	Actual	Predetermined rates*

*Actual inputs (such as direct-labor hours or direct-labor costs) multiplied by predetermined overhead rates (computed by dividing total budgeted manufacturing overhead by a budgeted application base such as direct-labor hours).

Reconsider the factory overhead cost in Exhibit 13-4. Actual factory overhead incurred, item 4a, would be the same under actual and normal costing: $290,000 + $102,000 = $392,000. However, applied factory overhead, item 4b, would differ. Under normal costing, it would be as shown in Exhibit 13-4. That is, the total applications, which would occur as the jobs were worked on, would be: $280,000 + $95,000 = $375,000.

In contrast, under actual costing no overhead would be applied as jobs were worked on. Instead, overhead would be applied only after all overhead costs for the year were known. Then, using an "actual" average rate(s) instead of a predetermined rate(s), costs would be applied to all jobs that had been worked on throughout the year. In such a case, entry 4b for application under actual costing would be $392,000 instead of the $375,000 used under normal costing. All costs incurred would be exactly offset by costs applied to the Work-in-Process Inventory.

[1]Alternatively, the denominator could be a measure of practical capacity, that is, a measure of the *maximum* feasible number of machine-hours.

Normal costing has replaced actual costing in many organizations precisely because the latter approach fails to provide costs of products as they are worked on during the year. It is possible to use a normal costing system plus year-end adjustments to produce final results that closely approximate the results under actual costing. To do so in our illustration, the underapplied overhead is prorated among Work in Process, Finished Goods, and Cost of Goods Sold, as shown earlier in this chapter (Method I in Exhibit 13-6). Thus, because of the desire for yearly "actual" costing results, we often see normal costing used for inventory costing throughout the year supplemented by once-a-year prorations.

☐ PRODUCT COSTING IN NONPROFIT ORGANIZATIONS

This chapter has concentrated on how to apply costs to manufactured products. However, the job-costing approach is used in nonmanufacturing situations too. Examples include appliance repair, auto repair, dentistry, auditing, income tax preparation, and medical care.

In nonprofit organizations the "product" is usually not called a "job order." Instead, it may be called a program or a class of service. A "program" is an identifiable segment of activities that frequently produce outputs in the form of services rather than goods. Examples include a safety program, an education program, a family counseling program. Often many departments work simultaneously on many programs, so the "job-order" costing challenge is to "apply" the various department costs to the various programs. Then wiser management decisions may be made regarding the allocation of limited resources among competing programs.

The appraisal of nonprofit programs has special problems. The difficulties of *cost* measurement are similar to those in commercial enterprises. However, the *benefits* are tougher to evaluate, because there is seldom a marketplace. How do you measure the benefits from educating the mentally handicapped, placing children in foster homes, saving lives? Because market prices are rarely available, indirect measurements of value are used. (For further discussion, see Chapter 10.)

summary

Accounting systems should be designed to satisfy control and product-costing purposes simultaneously. Costs are initially charged to department responsibility centers (cost centers); then they are applied to products in order to get inventory costs for balance sheets and income statements and in order to guide pricing and to evaluate product performance.

Product costing is an averaging process. Process costing deals with broad averages and great masses of like units. Job costing deals with narrow averages and a unique unit or a small batch of like units.

Indirect manufacturing costs (factory overhead) are often applied to products using predetermined overhead rates. The rates are computed by dividing total budgeted overhead by a measure of total activity such as expected labor-hours or machine-hours. These rates are usually annual averages. The resulting product costs are normal costs, consisting of actual direct material plus actual direct labor plus applied overhead using predetermined rates.

This chapter was written for readers who may or may not have familiarity with journals and ledgers. If you wish to understand the concepts with the help of these accounting tools, please study the first appendix to this chapter together with its pertinent assignment material.

summary problem for your review

■ PROBLEM

The Menlo Co. began business on January 2, 19X1. It made a variety of products, each batch requiring varying attention and effort. Predetermined overhead rates were computed on January 2, 19X1, as follows:

$$\text{variable overhead} = \frac{\text{budgeted variable overhead}}{\text{total expected activity}} = \frac{\$50,000}{25,000 \text{ hrs}} = \$2$$

$$\text{fixed overhead} = \frac{\text{budgeted fixed overhead}}{\text{total expected activity}} = \frac{\$150,000}{25,000 \text{ hrs}} = \$6$$

A summary of results follow:

Direct materials purchased	$110,000
Direct materials used	99,000
Direct labor incurred	
(21,250 hours @ $12.20)	259,250
Variable factory overhead incurred	42,000
Fixed factory overhead incurred	150,000

There was no ending work in process. A normal costing system is used. The cost of goods sold (before considering underapplied overhead) was $396,188.

REQUIRED

1. Prepare an exhibit like Exhibit 13-4, which provides an overview of how the costs would be accounted for to satisfy control and product-costing purposes.
2. Suppose the following: sales, $600,000; selling and administrative expenses, $100,000. Prepare an income statement where the underapplied overhead is considered as a direct adjustment of cost of goods sold. Ignore income taxes.

EXHIBIT 13-7. Solution to requirement 1—in dollars

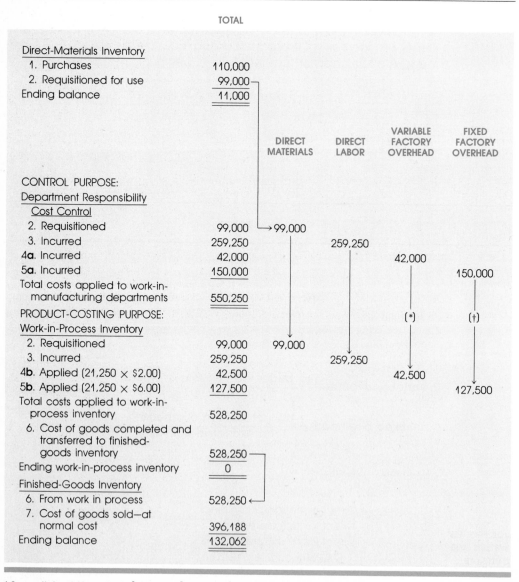

	TOTAL	DIRECT MATERIALS	DIRECT LABOR	VARIABLE FACTORY OVERHEAD	FIXED FACTORY OVERHEAD
Direct-Materials Inventory					
1. Purchases	110,000				
2. Requisitioned for use	99,000				
Ending balance	11,000				
CONTROL PURPOSE:					
Department Responsibility					
Cost Control					
2. Requisitioned	99,000	99,000			
3. Incurred	259,250		259,250		
4a. Incurred	42,000			42,000	
5a. Incurred	150,000				150,000
Total costs applied to work-in-manufacturing departments	550,250				
PRODUCT-COSTING PURPOSE:				(*)	(†)
Work-in-Process Inventory					
2. Requisitioned	99,000	99,000			
3. Incurred	259,250		259,250		
4b. Applied (21,250 × $2.00)	42,500			42,500	
5b. Applied (21,250 × $6.00)	127,500				127,500
Total costs applied to work-in-process inventory	528,250				
6. Cost of goods completed and transferred to finished-goods inventory	528,250				
Ending work-in-process inventory	0				
Finished-Goods Inventory					
6. From work in process	528,250				
7. Cost of goods sold—at normal cost	396,188				
Ending balance	132,062				

*Overapplied variable overhead, $42,500 − $42,000 = $500
†Underapplied fixed overhead, $150,000 − $127,500 = $22,500
Total overhead underapplied, $22,500 − $500 = $22,000

■ SOLUTION

1. See Exhibit 13-7.
2.

MENLO CO. Income Statement For the Year Ended December 31, 19X1	
Sales	$600,000
Cost of goods sold at normal cost	$396,188
Add underapplied overhead	22,000
Cost of goods sold, actual cost	$418,188
Gross profit	$181,812
Selling and administrative expenses	100,000
Net income	$ 81,812

Appendix 13A:
job-costing details: journal entries and ledgers

Exhibit 13-1 provides an overall perspective of the control and product-costing purposes of accounting systems. This appendix uses the examples in the chapter as a basis for presenting the details of a job-order cost accounting system. To understand this appendix, you must possess a familiarity with the fundamentals of double-entry bookkeeping. In short, this appendix provides a grasp of how a cost bookkeeping system actually works. However, the overall conceptual framework described in the chapter is not expanded here.

□ GENERAL SYSTEMS DESIGN

In principle, the general system design is straightforward and rests on a rigid distinction between control and product costing (see Exhibit 13-8). There is wide agreement among accountants, managers, and systems experts that control is best attained in *any* organization by initially charging the departments with the costs subject to their control. There is a wide divergence in theory and practice, however, as to the best way for *applying*[2] overhead costs to products.

Exhibit 13-8 illustrates the foregoing conceptual points and provides the focus for the journal entries in this appendix. However, company systems use a variety of approaches, including many shortcuts in the general ledger. For example, entries 1*a* and 1*b* are often condensed into a single entry:

Work-in-process inventory	10,000	
Direct-materials inventory		10,000

[2]The credit side of the Department Responsibility Cost Control account is often represented by a completely separate offsetting account, which could be termed "Department Responsibility Costs Applied." Such an *applied* account is roughly similar to Allowance for Depreciation and Allowance for Uncollectible Accounts, which are offsets to Plant and Equipment and Accounts Receivable.

EXHIBIT 13-8

PURPOSE	JOURNAL ENTRIES		
	1. Direct-Material Usage, $10,000		
Control	(1a) Department A responsibility cost control	10,000	
	Direct materials inventory		10,000
Product costing	(1b) Work-in-process inventory	10,000	
	Department A responsibility cost control		10,000
	2. Direct-Labor Usage, $8,000		
Control	(2a) Department A responsibility cost control	8,000	
	Accrued payroll or cash		8,000
Product costing	(2b) Work-in-process inventory	8,000	
	Department A responsibility cost control		8,000
	3. Manufacturing Overhead Incurred, $4,000		
Control	(3a) Department A responsibility cost control	4,000	
	Accounts Payable, Allowance for Depreciation,		
	Accrued Payroll, and various other accounts		4,000
Product costing	(3b) Work-in-process inventory	4,000	
	Department A responsibility cost control		4,000

There is no harm in shortcuts, as long as the underlying concepts dominate the thinking about systems design. For example, departmental responsibility for *control* of direct-material usage is usually maintained by means other than general journals and ledgers. If so, the above journal entry illustrates the product-costing purpose alone.

Again one must distinguish between costs for control and for product costing. Whether a process-cost or a job-cost approach is used, costs must be allocated to departments for control purposes. The typical job-order approach uses one account for tracing product costs and another account or accounts for accumulating department costs.

☐ BASIC RECORDS

The basic record for the accumulation of job costs is the **job order** or **job cost sheet.** Exhibit 13-9 shows a job cost sheet and the related source documents. A file of current job cost sheets becomes the subsidiary ledger for the general ledger account, Work-in-Process Inventory.

While job cost sheets are the primary scorekeeping device for *product costing,* department responsibility control sheets serve *control* purposes. For example, Exhibit 13-10 shows how the details of various costs charged to a particular department may be accumulated. The file of these sheets forms a subsidiary ledger for the general ledger account, Department Responsibility Cost Control, or a similar account.

Exhibit 13-11 shows how the general ledger accounts would be affected by the transactions originally analyzed in Exhibit 13-4. A careful study of this exhibit should yield insight into many relationships, particularly those between

EXHIBIT 13-9. Source documents

SOURCE DOCUMENTS

JOB COST SHEET

Job Order No. _____

Description

Reference	Date	Amount	Summary
Direct material: (Requisition No. or Bill of Materials)	xx xx xx	xx xx xx	xx
Direct labor: (Work Ticket No.)	xx xx xx	xx xx xx	xx
Factory overhead applied: (Predetermined rate multiplied by actual machine hours or labor dollars or labor hours)	xx	xx	
Total product cost			xx

Direct Material Requisition

Job No. _____   Date _____

Department _____   Account _Work in process_

Description	Quantity	Unit Cost	Amount
	xx	x	xx

Work Ticket

Job No. _____   Date _____

Department _A_   Account _Work in process_

Operation _Drill_

Units: Start _3:00 P.M._   Rate _____
Worked   _10_
Rejected —   Stop _4:15 P.M._   Amount _____
Completed _10_

Estimated factory overhead for the year $277,800
Estimated machine hours   69,450
Predetermined overhead rate per labor hour* $4

*Explained in the chapter.

EXHIBIT 13-10. Machining department responsibility cost control sheet

MACHINING DEPARTMENT RESPONSIBILITY COST CONTROL SHEET

Month of ____

Date	Source Document	Direct Material	Direct Labor	Indirect Labor	Supplies	Utilities	Repairs	Rent	Supervision	Depreciation	Insurance
	Requisitions	xx			xx						
	Labor work tickets, analyses, or recapitulations		xx	xx					xx		
	Invoices					xx	xx	xx			
	Special memos on accruals, prepayments, etc.						xx			xx	xx

EXHIBIT 13-11. Summary effects of job costing: normal costing system

GENERAL JOURNAL

1.	Direct materials inventory	$1,900,000	
	Accounts payable or cash		$1,900,000
	Purchases		
2a.	Deparment responsibility cost control	1,890,000	
	Direct materials inventory		1,890,000
	Requisitions charged to departments for control purposes		
2b.	Work in process	1,890,000	
	Department responsibility cost control		1,890,000
	Requisitions applied to jobs for product costing purposes		
3a.	Department responsibility cost control	390,000	
	Accrued payroll or cash		390,000
	Work tickets charged to departments for control purposes		
3b.	Work in process	390,000	
	Department responsibility cost control		390,000
	Work tickets applied to jobs for product costing purposes		
4a.	Department responsibility cost control	392,000	
	Cash, accounts payable, and various accounts		392,000
	Overhead charged to departments as incurred for control purposes		
4b.	Work in process	375,000	
	Department responsibility cost control		375,000
	Overhead applied to products, using predetermined application rates		
5.	Finished goods	2,500,000	
	Work in process		2,500,000
	To transfer costs of goods completed		
6a.	Accounts receivable or cash	4,000,000	
	Sales		4,000,000
6b.	Cost of goods sold	2,480,000	
	Finished goods		2,480,000

GENERAL LEDGER (Selected accounts)

Department Responsibility Cost Control

Control Purpose:		Product Costing Purpose:	
2a. Direct material	$1,890,000	2b. Applied	$1,890,000
3a. Direct labor	390,000	3b. Applied	390,000
4a. Factory overhead	392,000	4b. Applied	375,000

Direct Materials

Bal.	$ 110,000	2a.	$1,890,000
1.	1,900,000		

Work in Process

2b.	$1,890,000	5.	$2,500,000
3b.	390,000		
4b.	375,000		

Finished Goods

Bal.	12,000	6b.	2,480,000
5.	2,500,000		

Cost of Goods Sold

6b.	2,480,000	

SUBSIDIARY LEDGER (Selected)

Department Cost Sheets

Assembly

Machining

Direct Material	Direct Labor	In-direct Labor	Supplies	Various

Job Cost Sheets

Direct material

Direct Labor

Applied Overhead

the subsidiary ledgers and the general ledger. A file of department cost sheets supports the charges to Department Responsibility Cost Control, while a file of job cost sheets supports Work in Process.

☐ RELATIONSHIPS AMONG SOURCE DOCUMENTS, SUBSIDIARY LEDGERS, AND GENERAL LEDGER

The source documents, such as material requisitions or work tickets, which were illustrated in Exhibit 13-9, are usually made in multiple copies, each being used for a specific task. For example, a materials requisition could be executed by a foreman in as many as six copies and disposed of as follows:

1. Kept by storekeeper who issues the materials.
2. Used by stores ledger clerk for posting to perpetual inventory cards for materials.
3. Used by job order cost clerk to post the Job Cost Sheet (Exhibit 13-9).
4. Used by cost control clerk to post the Direct Material Used column of Department Responsibility Cost Control Sheet (Exhibit 13-10).
5. Used by general ledger clerk as a basis for a summary monthly entry for all of the month's requisitions (Exhibit 13-11).
6. Retained by the foreman. He can use the requisition as a cross check against the performance reports which show his usage of material.

Of course, machine accounting and electronic computer systems can use a single punched card as a requisition. Sorting, re-sorting, classifications, reclassifications, summaries, and re-summaries can easily provide any desired information. Because these source documents are the foundation for data accumulation and reports, the importance of accurate initial recording cannot be overemphasized.

Copies of these source documents are used for direct postings to subsidiary ledgers. Sometimes the subsidiary ledgers will contain summarized postings of daily batches of source documents, rather than individual direct postings. Accounting data are most condensed in the general ledger and most detailed on the source documents, as the following listing shows:

ITEM	
Work in Process	General ledger (usually monthly totals only)
Job Cost Sheets	Subsidiary ledgers (perhaps daily summaries)
Material Requisitions or Work Tickets	Source documents (minute to minute, hour to hour)

The daily scorekeeping duties are accomplished with source documents and subsidiary ledgers. Copies of the source documents are independently summarized and are usually posted to the general ledger only once a month. See entry 2a, Exhibit 13-11, where, for convenience, a year was used, rather than a month.

In order to obtain a bird's-eye view of a system, we have been concentrating on general ledger relationships. However, keep in mind that the general ledger is a very small part of the accountant's daily work. Furthermore, current control is aided by hourly, daily, or weekly flash reports of material, labor, and machine usage. The general ledger itself is a summary device. Reliance on the general ledger for current control is ill-advised, because the resulting reports come too late and are often too stale for management control use.

☐ DISPOSITION OF FACTORY OVERHEAD

As incurred, factory overhead is allocated to departments and accumulates on the left side of the Department Responsibility Control account. The applied factory overhead accumulates on the right-hand side, and the difference between incurred and applied fluctuates from month to month. As Exhibit 13-6 demonstrates, there are two fundamental ways to eliminate the year-end difference. The journal entries are:

Either	1. Work in process	994	
	Finished goods	205	
	Cost of goods sold	15,801	
	Department responsibility cost control		17,000
	To prorate ending underapplied overhead among the accounts where the costs of the 19X2 jobs worked on are now lodged.		
or	2. Cost of goods sold (or a separate charge against revenue)	17,000	
	Department responsibility cost control		17,000
	To close ending underapplied overhead directly to Cost of Goods Sold.		

As is discussed near the end of the chapter, factory overhead is accounted for differently under actual costing and normal costing. Reconsider entry 4 in Exhibit 13-11 (in thousands of dollars):

		ACTUAL COSTING		NORMAL COSTING	
4a.	Department responsibility cost control	392		392	
	Cash, accounts payable, etc.		392		392
4b.	Work in process	—		375	
	Department responsibility cost control		—		375
At end of year:	Work in process	392		—	
	Department responsibility cost control		392		—
	Cost of goods sold	—		17	
	Department responsibility cost control		—		17

Appendix 13B:
illustration of process costing

The major illustration in this chapter featured job-order costing. The same concepts pertain to process costing, but the application of costs to products is much easier.

Assume that the same company produced transistor radios in large quantities. Suppose it completed 1 million units during the year. Then the unit cost of goods completed would simply be the total cost of $2,500,000 ÷ 1,000,000, or $2.50.

The major difficulty in process costing is applying costs to uncompleted products—goods still in process at the end of the accounting period. For example, suppose 100,000 radios were still in process at year-end; only 900,000 were started and completed. All the parts had been made or requisitioned, but only half of the assembly labor had been completed for each of the 100,000 radios.

What was the output for the year? An obvious answer would be 900,000 completed units plus 100,000 half-completed units. But we should hesitate to express the sum of the output as 1 million units. After all, each of the partially completed units has received only half the assembly labor and overhead inputs applied to the fully completed output. Instead, we express output not as *physical* units, but as *equivalent* units.

Equivalent units is the expression of output in terms of *doses* or *amount* of work applied thereto. In process costing, a physical unit is looked upon as a collection of work applications (material and conversion costs).

Conversion costs are defined as direct labor plus manufacturing overhead. To illustrate the basic approach, we use the data in the assembly department only from Exhibit 13-4:

	physical flow	EQUIVALENT UNITS direct materials	EQUIVALENT UNITS conversion costs
Units started and completed	900,000	900,000	900,000
Work in process, end:	100,000		
Materials added: 100,000 × 1		100,000	
Conversion costs: 100,000 × 1/2			50,000
Units accounted for	1,000,000		
Total work done		1,000,000	950,000
Assembly costs:			
Direct materials added		$890,000	
Conversion costs ($190,000 + $102,000)			$292,000
Divide by equivalent units		1,000,000	950,000
Unit costs added in assembly		$.89	$.3073684

Note that costs are applied on the basis of costs per equivalent unit. The ending work-in-process inventory (assembly department cost component only) would be:[3]

Direct materials, 100,000 × $.89   = $ 89,000
Conversion costs, 50,000 × $.3073684 =   15,368
Assembly department component   = $104,368

Processing industries (engaging in mass production of like units) tend to use standard product costing rather than the actual product costing or normal product costing described in this chapter.[4] Standard product costing is discussed in the next chapter.

Process costing and job-order costing, as described here, represent two extremes of how product costing is accomplished. Each manufacturing company develops its own hybrid to suit its desires. For example, many companies will have so-called operation costing systems. The cost of each operation is computed using process costing; then the final cost of the product is compiled depending on what operations were conducted in its manufacture. Thus a product that has one coat of paint, one polishing, and no hand-finishing operation will bear less cost than a similar product that has three coats, two polishings, and one hand-finishing operation.

assignment material

■ FUNDAMENTAL ASSIGNMENT MATERIAL

13-1. **Terminology.** Define *job order; job-order costing; normal cost system; overapplied factory overhead; process costing;* and *underapplied factory overhead.*

13-2. **Balance sheets and income statements.** Consider the following (in millions of dollars):

---

[3]The idea of equivalent units extends to all types of organizations, even though the terminology differs. For example, clinical laboratories often measure volume in terms of weight units. A *weight unit* is an arbitrary unit by which various lab procedures are ranked in terms of the relative combination of labor, supplies, and related costs devoted to each. For instance, a procedure with a weight of two is deemed to use twice the resources as a procedure with a weight of one. An average cost per weight unit is developed, which is then multiplied by the average number of weight units per laboratory procedure to obtain an average unit cost for each laboratory procedure. Radiology departments use a similar "process costing" system. For another example, the beer industry translates its productions into equivalent barrels, even though its output is in the form of various sizes of kegs, cans, and bottles.

[4]For an expanded discussion of process costing, see Charles T. Horngren, *Cost Accounting: A Managerial Emphasis,* 4th ed. (Englewood Cliffs, N.J.: Prentice-Hall, 1977), Chaps. 18 and 19.

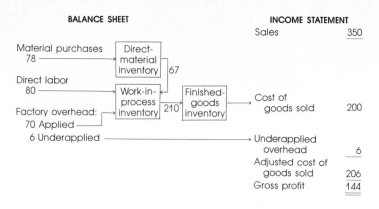

BALANCE SHEET

INCOME STATEMENT

Sales 350

Material purchases
78 → Direct-material inventory 67

Direct labor
80 → Work-in-process inventory 210 → Finished-goods inventory → Cost of goods sold 200

Factory overhead:
70 Applied
6 Underapplied → Underapplied overhead 6

Adjusted cost of goods sold 206

Gross profit 144

REQUIRED

The beginning inventory balances were (in millions): direct material, $20; work in process, $26; and finished goods, $60.

1. Compute the ending balances of the three inventories.
2. Compute the actual factory overhead incurred.

13-3. **Disposition of overhead.** Refer to the preceding problem. Assume that overhead was overapplied by $30 and that the ending inventories were $30, $20, and $80, respectively. Unadjusted cost of goods sold is still $200. Management has decided to prorate the $30 to the pertinent accounts (using their unadjusted ending balances) instead of writing it off solely as an adjustment of current cost of goods sold.

REQUIRED

1. What accounts would be affected by the proration and by what amounts?
2. Your answer to Requirement 1 would affect current gross profit differently than if the $30 were all written off solely as an adjustment of current cost of goods sold. By how much? Would the current gross profit be higher or lower?

■ ADDITIONAL ASSIGNMENT MATERIAL

13-4. "The special decision purpose of accounting is difficult to satisfy on a routine basis." Why?

13-5. "Cost application or absorption is terminology related to the product-costing purpose." Why?

13-6. "I was looking at a trial balance the other day and was mystified by the account Department Responsibility Cost Applied. I just didn't know what it meant or where it fit." Briefly unravel the mystery.

13-7. What are some reasons for *incurred* and *applied* overhead differing?

13-8. Sometimes five copies of a stores requisition are needed. What are their uses?

13-9. "The general ledger is an incidental part of the accountant's daily work." Explain.

13-10. "Costs of inefficiency cannot be regarded as assets." Explain.

13-11. "Under actual overhead application, unit costs soar as volume increases, and vice versa." Do you agree? Explain.

13-12. "Overhead application is overhead allocation." Do you agree? Explain.

13-13. Distinguish between job costing and process costing.

13-14. "The basic distinction between job-order costing and process costing is the breadth of the denominator." Explain.

13-15. What is the subsidiary ledger for work in process in a job-cost system?

13-16. Define *normal costing*.

13-17. What is the best theoretical method of allocating underapplied or over-applied overhead, assuming that the objective is to obtain as accurate a cost allocation as possible?

13-18. **Direct materials.** The GH Company has a beginning inventory of direct materials of $8 million. During the year it acquired $100 million in additional materials. Its ending inventory was $10 million. How much direct materials were used during the year?

13-19. **Normal costing system.** The following data summarize the factory operations of the Leavitt Manufacturing Co. for the year 19X1, its first year in business (in thousands):

1.	Direct materials purchased for cash	$ 840
2.	Direct materials issued and used	790
3.	Labor used directly on production	200
4a.	Indirect labor	90
4b.	Depreciation of plant and equipment	140
4c.	Miscellaneous factory overhead (ordinarily would be detailed)	130
5.	Overhead: 190 percent of direct labor	?
6.	Cost of production completed	1,300
7.	Cost of goods sold	1,100

REQUIRED

Prepare an analysis similar to that in Exhibit 13-4. Show the ending balances in direct-materials inventory, work in process, and finished goods. For purposes of this analysis, combine the items in 4 as "overhead incurred." (For more detailed analysis of this problem, see Problems 13-33 and 13-34. Furthermore, Problem 13-26 is an alternate for this problem.)

13-20. **Accounting for overhead, predetermined rates.** Catherine Electronics Co. uses a predetermined overhead rate in applying overhead to individual job orders on a *machine-hour* basis for Department No. 1 and on a *direct-labor-hour* basis for Department No. 2. At the beginning of 19X4, the company's management made the following budget predictions:

	DEPT. NO. 1	DEPT. NO. 2
Direct-labor hours	100,000	200,000
Machine-hours	300,000	41,000
Direct-labor cost	$2,200,000	$4,000,000
Factory overhead	$2,400,000	$2,000,000

Cost records of recent months show the following accumulations for Job Order No. 341:

	DEPT. NO. 1	DEPT. NO. 2
Direct-labor cost	$15,400	$ 7,000
Material placed in production	$22,000	$40,000
Machine-hours	2,300	60
Direct-labor hours	700	350

REQUIRED

1. What is the predetermined overhead *rate* that should be applied in Department No. 1? In Department No. 2?
2. What is the *total overhead* cost of Job Order No. 341?
3. If Job Order No. 341 consists of 1,000 units of product, what is the *unit cost* of this job?

4. At the *end* of 19X4, actual results for the year's operations were as follows:

	DEPT. NO. 1	DEPT. NO. 2
Actual machine-hours	275,000	39,500
Actual direct-labor hours	105,000	210,000
Actual overhead costs incurred	$2,500,000	$1,900,000

Find the underapplied or overapplied overhead for each department and for the factory as a whole.

13-21. **Underapplied and overapplied overhead.** Manwell Bandage Corporation applies factory overhead at a rate of $3.50 per direct-labor hour. Selected data for 19X3 operations are (in thousands):

	CASE 1	CASE 2
Direct-labor cost	$120	$210
Direct-labor hours	50	55
Indirect-labor cost	$ 25	$ 35
Sales commissions	$ 15	$ 10
Depreciation, manufacturing equipment	$ 10	$ 15
Direct-material cost	$200	$230
Factory fuel costs	$ 12	$ 18
Depreciation, finished-goods warehouse	$ 4	$ 14
Cost of goods sold	$380	$490
All other factory costs	$119	$138

REQUIRED

Compute for both cases:

1. Factory overhead applied.
2. Total factory overhead incurred.
3. Amount of underapplied or overapplied factory overhead.

13-22. **Comparison of overhead accounting for control and for product costing.** The Faston Company has an overhead rate of $3 per direct-labor hour, based on expected variable overhead of $100,000 per year, expected fixed overhead of $200,000 per year, and expected direct-labor hours of 100,000 per year.

Data for the year's operations follow:

	DIRECT-LABOR HOURS USED	OVERHEAD COSTS INCURRED*
First six months	60,000	$168,000
Last six months	36,000	$136,000

*Fixed costs incurred were exactly equal to budgeted amounts throughout the year.

1. What is the underapplied or overapplied overhead for each six-month period? Label your answer as underapplied or overapplied.
2. Explain *briefly* (not over 50 words for each part) the probable reasons for the exact figures attributable to the causes you cite.

13-23. **Disposition of overhead.** Consider the following balances at the end of the year 19X2 (in thousands):

Indirect manufacturing costs incurred	$490
Indirect manufacturing costs applied	544
Work-in-process inventory	100
Finished-goods inventory	200
Cost of goods sold	600

1. Assume that underapplied or overapplied overhead is regarded as a reduction or addition to current income via adding or deducting the amount from the unadjusted cost of goods sold. What is the adjusted cost of goods sold?
2. Assume that the underapplied or overapplied overhead is prorated among the pertinent accounts in proportion to their ending unadjusted balances. What is the adjusted cost of goods sold?
   For a more detailed examination of the data, see Problem 13-32.
3. By how much would gross profit be affected by adopting the approach in Requirement 2 rather than Requirement 1? Would the gross profit be higher or lower?

13-24. Disposition of overhead. A company uses a job-order system. At the end of 19X4 the following balances existed (in millions):

Cost of goods sold	$50
Finished goods	20
Work in process	30
Factory overhead (actual)	50
Factory overhead (applied)	40

1. Demonstrate two different ways to dispose of the underapplied overhead.
2. Gross profit, before considering the effects in Requirement 1, was $40 million. What is the adjusted gross profit under the two methods demonstrated?

13-25. Relationships of manufacturing costs. (CMA.) Selected data concerning the past fiscal year's operations (000 omitted) of the Televans Manufacturing Company are presented below:

	INVENTORIES	
	beginning	ending
Raw materials	$75	$85
Work in process	80	30
Finished goods	90	110
Other data:		
Raw materials used		$326
Total manufacturing costs charged to production during the year (includes raw materials, direct labor, and factory overhead applied at a rate of 60% of direct-labor cost)		686
Cost of goods available for sale		826
Selling and general expenses		25

Select the best answer for each of the following items:
1. The cost of raw materials purchased during the year amounted to
   a. $411.   b. $360.   c. $316.   d. $336.
   e. none of the preceding responses is correct.
2. Direct-labor costs charged to production during the year amounted to
   a. $135.   b. $225.   c. $360.   d. $216.
   e. none of the preceding responses is correct.
3. The cost of goods manufactured during the year was
   a. $636.   b. $766.   c. $736.   d. $716
   e. none of the preceding responses is correct.
4. The cost of goods sold during the year was
   a. $736.   b. $716.   c. $691.   d. $801.
   e. none of the preceding responses is correct.

13-26. Straightforward job costing. Conerly Machine Tool Company is a huge company that makes special machinery and components in response to job orders, mostly from even larger companies on the West Coast. Conerly also makes a limited number of specialized parts that are held in stock for sale to machine shops.

The company has two major departments: Machining and Finishing. Manufacturing overhead is applied using predetermined rates; the allocation base in Machining is machine-hours, and in Finishing it is direct-labor cost. All the data below are in millions.

The beginning inventories for 19X6 were:

Finished goods	$12
Direct materials (132 types)	40
Work in process (in finishing department)	38

The factory overhead budget for 19X6 was:

	MACHINING	FINISHING
Supplies (lubricants, coolants, etc.)	$ 40	$ 5
Utilities	60	15
Repairs and maintenance	35	10
Indirect labor	190	90
Depreciation on equipment	100	20
Factory rent	30	15
Property taxes, insurance, etc.	20	5
Supervision	25	20
Total	$500	$180
Budgeted direct-labor cost	$ 90	$200
Budgeted machine-hours	25	5

The following actually occurred during 19X6:

		MACHINING	FINISHING	TOTAL
1.	Direct materials purchased			$ 400
2.	Direct materials requisitioned	$360	$ 70	430
3.	Direct-labor costs incurred	85	190	275
4a.	Factory overhead incurred	480	221	701
4b.	Factory overhead applied	440	?	?
5.	Cost of goods completed			1,234
6a.	Sales			2,000
6b.	Cost of goods sold			1,226

1. Compute the predetermined overhead rates.
2. Compute the amount of the machine-hours actually worked.
3. Compute the amount of factory overhead applied in the finishing department.
4. Prepare an exhibit similar to Exhibit 13-4, which shows how the costs are accounted for to satisfy control and product-costing purposes. Show the ending inventory balances for direct materials, work in process, and finished goods.
5. Prepare a partial income statement similar to the one illustrated in Exhibit 13-5. Overapplied or underapplied overhead is written off as an adjustment of current cost of goods sold.

This problem is pursued in more detail in Problem 13-35.

13-27. Nonprofit job costing. Job-order costing is usually identified with manufacturing companies. However, service industries and nonprofit organizations also use the method. Suppose that a social service agency has a cost accounting system that tracks cost by department (for example, family counseling, general welfare, and foster children) and by case. In this way, the manager of the agency is better able to determine how her limited resources (mostly professional social workers) should be allocated. Furthermore, her interchanges with her superiors and various politicians are more fruitful when she can cite the costs of various types of cases.

The condensed line-item budget for the general welfare department of the agency for 19X6 showed:

Professional salaries:

Level 12	6 @ $32,000 = $192,000	
Level 10	18 @ $24,000 = 432,000	
Level 8	30 @ $16,000 = 480,000	$1,104,000
Other costs		441,600
Total costs		$1,545,600

For costing various cases, the manager favored using a single overhead application rate based on the ratio of total overhead to direct labor. The latter was defined as those professional salaries assigned to specific cases.

The professional workers filled out a weekly "case time" report, which approximated the hours spent for each case.

The instructions on the report were: "Indicate how much time (in hours) you spent on each case. Unassigned time should be listed separately." About 20 percent of available time was unassigned to specific cases. It was used for professional development (for example, continuing education programs). "Unassigned time" became a part of "overhead," as distinguished from the direct labor.

REQUIRED

1. Compute the "overhead rate" as a percentage of direct labor (that is, the assignable professional salaries).
2. Suppose that last week a welfare case, Client No. 462, required two hours of Level 12 time, four hours of Level 10 time, and nine hours of Level 8 time. How much job cost should be allocated to Client No. 462 for the week? Assume that all professional employees work a 1,650-hour year.

13-28. **Job costing in a consulting firm.** AB Engineering Consultants is a firm of professional civil engineers. It mostly has surveying jobs for the heavy construction industry throughout California and Nevada. The firm obtains its jobs by giving fixed-price quotations, so profitability is highly dependent on the ability to predict the time required for the various subtasks on the job. (This situation is similar to that in the auditing profession, where times are budgeted for such audit steps as reconciling cash and confirming accounts receivable.)

A client may be served by various professional staff, who hold positions in the hierarchy from partners to managers to senior engineers to assistants. In addition, there are secretaries and other employees.

AB Engineering has the following budget for 19X4:

Compensation of professional staff	$2,000,000
Other costs	800,000
Total budgeted costs	$2,800,000

Each professional staff member must submit a weekly time report, which is used for charging hours to a client job-order sheet. The time report has seven columns, one for each day of the week. Its rows are as follows:

Chargeable hours:
Client 234
Client 262
Etc.

Nonchargeable hours:
Attending seminar on new equipment
Unassigned time
Etc.

In turn, these time reports are used for charging hours and costs to the client job-order sheets. The managing partner regards these job sheets as absolutely essential for measuring the profitability of various jobs and for providing an "experience base for improving predictions on future jobs."

REQUIRED

1. This firm applies overhead to jobs at a predetermined percentage of the professional compensation charged directly to the job ("direct labor"). For all categories of professional personnel, chargeable hours average 85 percent of available hours. The nonchargeable hours are regarded as additional overhead. What is the overhead rate as a percentage of the "direct labor," the chargeable professional compensation cost?
2. A senior engineer works 48 weeks per year, 40 hours per week. His compensation is $36,000. He has worked on two jobs during the past week, devoting 10 hours to Job 234 and 30 hours to Job 262. How much cost should be charged to Job 234 because of his work there?

13-29. **Normal versus actual costing.** Drew Company has compiled the following costs:

Actual manufacturing overhead incurred	$951,000
Direct labor	480,000
Direct materials used	786,000

There were no beginning inventories. At the end of the year, one-third of the production is unsold and is held as finished-goods inventory. The costs in finished-goods inventory are in the same proportion as in cost of goods sold.

REQUIRED

1. Assume that normal costing is used. Manufacturing overhead is at a rate of 190 percent of direct labor. Underapplied or overapplied overhead is written off as an expense. Compute the finished-goods inventory.
2. Assume that actual costing is used. Compute the finished-goods inventory.
3. What is the major difficulty with using actual costing? Do you favor proration of underapplied overhead when normal costing is used? Why?

13-30. **Finding unknowns.** The Kroeger Company has the following balances on December 31, 19X7. All amounts are in millions:

Factory overhead applied	$180
Cost of goods sold	400
Factory overhead incurred	200
Direct-materials inventory	40
Finished-goods inventory	140
Work-in-process inventory	80

The cost of goods completed was $380. The cost of direct materials requisitioned for production during 19X7 was $170. The cost of direct materials purchased was $190. Factory overhead was applied to production at a rate of 180 percent of direct-labor cost.

REQUIRED

Compute the beginning inventory balances of direct materials, work in process, and finished goods. These computations can be made without considering any possible adjustments for overapplied or underapplied overhead.

13-31. **Appendix A problem**
1. Prepare journal entries to record the information in the "Summary Problem for Your Review" at the end of the chapter. See Exhibit 13-11 for guidance.

2. Show the postings of the journal entries to T-accounts for Department Responsibility Cost Control, for Work in Process, and for Finished Goods.

13-32. Appendix A problem: overhead. Refer to Problem 13-23. For Requirement 1, show the journal entry. Also show all the year's postings to the T-accounts for all inventories, and show their closing balances. For Requirement 2, show the journal entry only.

13-33. Appendix A problem: journal entries. Refer to the data in Problem 13-19.

REQUIRED

1. Prepare general journal entries for a normal cost system. Number your entries.
2. Present the T-account for Department Responsibility Cost Control. Sketch how this account's subsidiary ledger would appear, assuming that there are four factory departments. You need not show any numbers in the subsidiary ledger.

This problem is probed in more detail in Problem 13-34.

13-34. Appendix A problem: source documents. Refer to Problems 13-19 and 13-33. For each journal entry, indicate (a) the most likely name for the source documents that would authorize the entry, and (b) how the subsidiary ledgers, if any, would be affected.

13-35. Appendix A problem. Refer to Problem 13-26. Use those data to prepare an exhibit similar to Exhibit 13-11, which shows general journal entries and the major T-accounts. Work solely with the total amounts, not the details for Machining and Finishing. Explanations for the journal entries are not required, nor are subsidiary ledgers.

13-36. Process costing. Study the second appendix to this chapter. In the illustration there, suppose that 300,000 radios instead of 100,000 were in the ending work in process. The units started were 1.1 million. Direct materials added were $990,000. Conversion costs were $285,000. Prepare a statement that shows the total work done in equivalent units, the unit costs added in assembly, and the ending work in process (assembly department cost component only).

13-37. Nonprofit process costing. Study the second appendix to this chapter. The California State Franchise Tax Board must process millions of income tax returns yearly. Because of recent negative votes by the citizens, the tax board must work with fewer personnel in the early 1980s than it did in the early 1970s. To find ways to improve productivity, some work-measurement experts have been closely observing the processing of tax returns.

When the taxpayer sends in his or her return, documents such as checks and withholding statements are compared with the data on the return. Other inspections of the return are also conducted. Although the processing time taken depends on the complexity of the return, the expected time allowed is based on an "average" return.

Assume that 1.2 million returns were received on April 15. On April 23, the work-measurement experts found that all processing steps had been fully completed on 40 percent of the returns. However, 60 percent still had to be submitted for final inspection.

REQUIRED

1. The final inspection process represents 25 percent of the complete processing time. Compute the total work done in terms of equivalent units.
2. Various materials and supplies amounting to $144,000 were consumed in processing the returns (punched cards, inspection check-sheets, clips, staples, and so

on). For these calculations, materials and supplies are regarded as direct materials. The conversion costs were $3,060,000. Compute the unit costs of materials and supplies and of conversion.

3. Compute the cost of the tax returns still in process.

13-38. **Process costing.** Study the second appendix to this chapter. A company manufactures and sells small portable fans. Business is booming because, to save on costs of electricity, many households are using fans instead of air conditioners. Various materials are added at various stages in the assembly department. Costs are accounted for on a process-cost basis. The end of the process involves adding an outer shell of the fan, conducting a final inspection, and adding a cardboard carton.

The final inspection requires 5 percent of the total processing time. All materials besides the shell and the carton are added by the time the fans reach an 80 percent stage of completion of conversion.

There were no beginning inventories. One hundred thousand fans were started in production during 19X3. At the end of the year, which was not a busy time, 4,000 fans were in various stages of completion. All of the ending units in work in process were at the 95 percent stage. They awaited final inspection and being placed in cartons.

Total materials consumed in production, except for cartons, were $1.5 million. Cartons used were $172,800. Total conversion costs were $798,400.

REQUIRED

1. Present a schedule of physical flow, equivalent units, and unit costs of direct materials except cartons.
2. Present a summary of the cost of goods completed and the cost of ending work in process.

chapter 14

OVERHEAD APPLICATION: DIRECT AND ABSORPTION COSTING

learning objectives

When you have finished studying this chapter, you should be able to:

1. Identify the basic feature that distinguishes the direct-costing approach from the absorption approach.
2. Construct an income statement, using each of the two product-costing approaches.
3. Prepare a reconciliation of the net incomes reported by these two approaches.
4. Contrast the treatment of fixed-overhead costs for budgeting and control purposes with their treatment for product-costing purposes.
5. Identify the nature of the denominator variance, compute it, and state how it should appear in the income statement.
6. Identify the two methods and their rationale for disposing of the standard cost variances at the end of a year.
7. Identify the differences among the three alternative cost bases of an absorption-costing system: actual, normal, and standard.
8. Analyze and compare all the major variances in a standard cost system. (Appendix 14)

The preceding chapter concentrated on how an accounting system is used to *accumulate* costs by departments and to *apply* costs to the products (or services) that are produced by those departments. This chapter[1] concentrates on two major variations of product costing. We use a standard product-costing system here for illustrative purposes. However, these variations can be used in non-standard product-costing systems too.

Direct versus absorption costing

□ ACCOUNTING FOR FIXED MANUFACTURING OVERHEAD

Two major methods of product costing will be compared in this chapter: **direct costing** (the contribution approach) and **absorption costing** (the functional, full-costing, or traditional approach). These methods differ in only one conceptual respect: Fixed manufacturing overhead is excluded from the cost of products under direct costing but included in the cost of products under absorption costing. In other words, direct costing signifies that fixed factory overhead is not inventoried. In contrast, absorption costing signifies that fixed factory overhead is inventoried.

Direct costing is more accurately called **variable** or **marginal costing,** because in substance it applies only the *variable* production costs to the product. As Exhibit 14-1 shows, fixed manufacturing overhead is regarded as an expired cost to be immediately charged against sales rather than as an unexpired cost to be held back as inventory and charged against sales later as a part of cost of goods sold.

The term "direct" costing is widely used, but "variable" costing is a more accurate description. Why? Because, as Exhibit 14-1 shows, the "direct" costing approach to the inventorying of costs is not confined to only "direct" materials and labor; it also includes an "indirect" cost—the *variable* manufacturing overhead. Such terminological confusion is unfortunate but apparently unavoidable in a field such as management accounting, where new analytical ideas or approaches arise in isolated fashion. Newly coined terms, which may not be accurately descriptive, often become embedded too deeply to be supplanted later.

Take a moment to reflect on Exhibit 14-1. Also, reexamine Exhibit 3-2, which provides an overview of income statement and balance sheet relationships. (Exhibit 3-2 is on p. 63.)

Absorption costing is much more widely used than direct costing, although the growing use of the contribution approach in performance measurement and cost analysis has led to increasing use of direct costing for internal-reporting purposes. Neither the public accounting profession nor the Internal Revenue Service approves of direct costing for external-reporting purposes.

---

[1]Chapter 14 may be studied without having studied Chapter 13. However, Chapter 3 (particularly the first half, which is worth reviewing now) and Chapter 7 should be studied before undertaking Chapter 14. This book was written to permit the utmost flexibility. In particular, many instructors may prefer to follow Chapter 3 with Chapter 13 and then follow Chapter 7 with Chapter 14.

EXHIBIT 14-1. Comparison of flow of costs

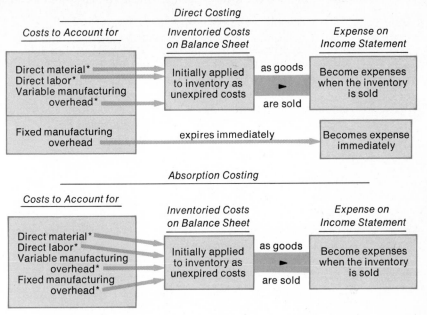

*As goods are manufactured, the costs are "applied" to inventory usually via the use of unit costs.

☐ FACTS FOR ILLUSTRATION

To make these ideas more concrete, consider the following example. The Tolman Company had the following operating characteristics in 19X4 and 19X5:

Basic Production Data at Standard Cost	
Direct material	$1.30
Direct labor	1.50
Variable manufacturing overhead	.20
Standard variable costs per unit	$3.00

Fixed manufacturing overhead was $150,000. Expected production in each year was 150,000 units. Sales price, $5 per unit.

Selling and administrative expense is assumed for simplicity as being all fixed at $65,000 yearly, except for sales commissions at 5 percent of dollar sales.

	19X4	19X5
In units:		
Opening inventory	—	30,000
Production	170,000	140,000
Sales	140,000	160,000
Ending inventory	30,000	10,000

There were no variances from the standard variable manufacturing costs, and fixed manufacturing overhead incurred was exactly $150,000 per year.

REQUIRED

1. Prepare income statements for 19X4 and 19X5 under direct costing.
2. Prepare income statements for 19X4 and 19X5 under absorption costing.
3. Show a reconciliation of the difference in operating income for 19X4, 19X5, and the two years as a whole.

The solution to this problem will be explained, step by step, in subsequent sections. The solution to Requirement 1 is in Exhibit 14-2, to Requirement 2 in Exhibit 14-3, and to Requirement 3 in Exhibit 14-5.

☐ DIRECT-COSTING METHOD

The solution to Requirement 1 is shown in Exhibit 14-2. It has a familiar contribution-approach format, the same format introduced in Chapter 3. The only new characteristic of Exhibit 14-2 is the presence of a detailed calculation of cost of goods sold, which is affected by changes in the beginning and ending inventories. (In contrast, the income statements in Chapters 3 through 7 assumed that there were no changes in the beginning and ending inventories.)

The costs of the product are accounted for by applying all variable manufacturing costs to the goods produced at a rate of $3 per unit; thus inventories are valued at standard variable costs. In contrast, fixed manufacturing costs are not applied to any products but are regarded as expenses as actually incurred.

EXHIBIT 14-2. Direct costing

TOLMAN COMPANY
Comparative Income Statements (In thousands of dollars)
for the Years 19X4 and 19X5
(Data are in text)

		19X4	19X5
Sales, 140,000 and 160,000 units, respectively	(1)	700	800
Opening inventory—at standard variable cost of $3		—	90*
Add variable cost of goods manufactured at standard, 170,000 and 140,000 units, respectively		510	420
Available for sale, 170,000 units in each year		510	510
Deduct ending inventory—at standard variable cost of $3		90*	30†
Variable manufacturing cost of goods sold		420	480
Variable selling expenses—at 5% of dollar sales		35	40
Total variable expenses	(2)	455	520
Contribution margin	(3) = (1) − (2)	245	280
Fixed factory overhead		150	150
Fixed selling and administrative expenses		65	65
Total fixed expenses	(4)	215	215
Operating income	(3) − (4)	30	65

*30,000 units × $3 = $90,000.
†10,000 units × $3 = $30,000.

Again, before reading on, please trace the facts from the illustrative problem to the presentation in Exhibit 14-2, step by step.

☐ ABSORPTION-COSTING METHOD

Exhibit 14-3 contains the following highlights of **standard absorption costing:**

1. The unit product cost is $4, not $3, because variable manufacturing costs ($3) plus fixed manufacturing overhead ($1) are applied to product.
2. The $1 predetermined application rate for fixed overhead was based on a denominator of 150,000 units ($150,000 ÷ 150,000 = $1). A **denominator variance**[2] appears whenever actual production (140,000 units in

EXHIBIT 14-3. Absorption costing

TOLMAN COMPANY
Comparative Income Statements (In thousands of dollars)
for the Years 19X4 and 19X5
(Data are in text)

	19X4	19X5
Sales	700	800
Opening inventory—at standard absorption cost of $4*	—	120
Cost of goods manufactured at standard of $4	680	560
Available for sale	680	680
Deduct ending inventory at standard absorption cost of $4	120	40
Cost of goods sold—at standard	560	640
Gross profit at standard	140	160
Denominator variance†	20 F	10 U
Gross margin or gross profit—at "actual"	160	150
Selling and administrative expenses	100	105
Operating income	60	45

*Variable cost	$3
Fixed cost ($150,000 ÷ 150,000)	1
Standard absorption cost	$4

†*Computation of denominator variance based on denominator volume of 150,000 units:*

19X4	$20,000 F	(170,000 − 150,000) × $1
19X5	10,000 U	(150,000 − 140,000) × $1
Two years together	$10,000 F	(310,000 − 300,000) × $1

U = *Unfavorable;* F = *Favorable.*

---

[2]The term *denominator variance* is relatively new, so it is not widely used in practice. The equivalent terms, *activity variance, capacity variance,* and especially **volume variance,** are widely used. The term *denominator variance* is favored here because it is a more precise description of the fundamental nature of the variance, which arises from the choice of some denominator and is measured by deviations from that denominator. In contrast, volume variance is a much looser term that may be applied to deviations in volume of all kinds for all kinds of costs and revenues.

19X5) deviates from the level of activity selected as the denominator for computing the predetermined product-costing rate. As the footnote in Exhibit 14-3 indicates, the measure of the variance is $1 multiplied by the difference between the actual volume of output and the denominator volume.

3. Denominator variances (and other variances) are usually accounted for as expired costs, that is, as expenses of the current period. They are often accounted for as adjustments that convert the gross profit at standard to gross profit at "actual," as shown in Exhibit 14-3.

The first of these three ideas, overhead application, was explained in the preceding chapter. The denominator variance and the disposition of variances will be discussed in subsequent sections.

Fixed overhead and absorption costs of product

□ VARIABLE AND FIXED UNIT COSTS

A graphical presentation of how an absorption-costing system works for (1) departmental budgeting and control purposes and (2) product-costing purposes may help underscore the assumptions being made. Even though absorption-costing systems rarely split their factory overhead into variable and fixed components, we will do so here to stress the underlying assumptions. For *variable* costs, the graphs are:

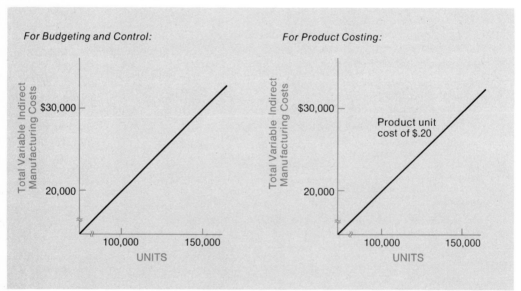

The two graphs are identical, so there is no conflict in the total results if the second graph is used as a basis for predicting how total costs will behave. Variable overhead will increase at a rate of $.20 per unit, as the slope of the graph shows.

Thinking in terms of *total costs* is the most popular way to budget (plan) and control operating activities. In contrast, thinking in terms of *unit costs* is the most popular way to allocate total costs for product-costing purposes.

Under absorption costing, the accounting system for *fixed* manufacturing overhead is shown by the next graphs (which are not to the exact scale of the preceding graphs):

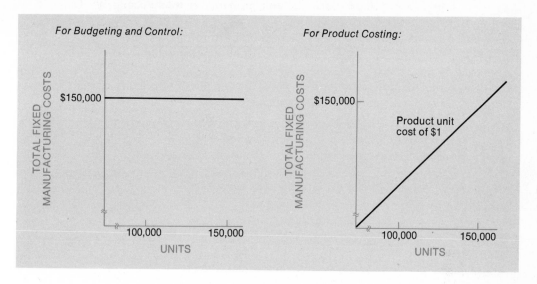

For product-costing purposes, the accountant takes the total costs in the first graph and chooses a method for applying the costs to the product. The accountant typically accomplishes this application via some unitization, using some predicted volume as a denominator:

$$\text{unit product cost} = \frac{\text{predicted total cost}}{\text{denominator volume}} = \frac{\$150{,}000}{150{,}000} = \$1$$

For inventory purposes, as each unit is worked on, a $1 fixed indirect manufacturing cost will be applied to it. Thus the first 100,000 units would bear a total *product cost* of $100,000, the next 100,000 units a total *product cost* of an additional $100,000, as the next graphs demonstrate:

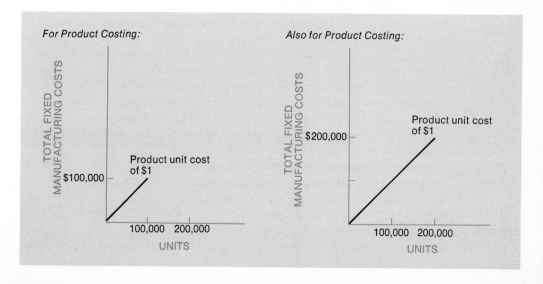

The *total* fixed cost for budgetary planning and control will be unaffected by the specific predicted volume used as a denominator. For instance, when the predicted total fixed cost is $150,000, if the predicted volume were 100,000 instead of 150,000 units, the unit product cost would change:

$$\text{unit product cost} = \frac{\text{predicted total fixed cost}}{\text{denominator volume}} = \$1.50$$

But the first graph for fixed costs, the one that is of primary concern for planning and control, would not change:

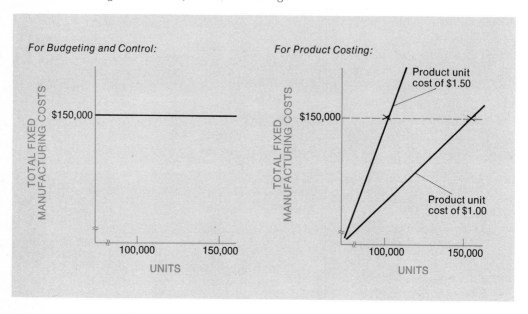

SELECTING THE DENOMINATOR LEVEL

As the immediately preceding graph shows, the unit cost depends on the activity level chosen as the denominator in the computation; the higher the level of activity, the lower the unit cost. The costing difficulty is magnified because management usually desires a single representative standard fixed cost for a product despite month-to-month changes in production volume.

The two graphs dramatize how the two purposes differ. The control-budget purpose regards fixed costs in a straightforward manner, viewing them in accordance with their actual cost behavior pattern. In contrast, as the graphs indicate, the absorption product-costing approach views these fixed costs as though they had a variable cost behavior pattern.

The selection of an appropriate denominator level for the predetermination of fixed-overhead rates is a matter of judgment. Thus the standard product cost would differ, depending on how the rate is set for fixed overhead. Some managers favor using the expected actual activity for the year in question; others favor using some longer-run (three-to-five-year) approximation of "normal" activity; and others favor using maximum or full capacity (often called *practical capacity*) as the denominator.

Although fixed-overhead rates are often important for product costing and long-run pricing, such rates *have limited significance for control purposes*. At the lower levels of supervision, almost no fixed costs are under direct control; even at higher levels of supervision, few fixed costs are controllable in the short run within wide ranges of anticipated activity.

☐ NATURE OF DENOMINATOR VARIANCE

A denominator variance arises whenever the actual outputs achieved deviate from the activity level selected as the denominator for computing the predetermined product-costing rate.

The denominator variance is the conventional measure of the cost of departing from the level of activity originally used to set the fixed-overhead rate.[3] Most companies consider denominator variances to be beyond immediate control, although sometimes the top sales executive has to do some explaining or investigating. Sometimes failure to reach the denominator volume is caused by idleness due to poor production scheduling, unusual machine breakdowns, shortages of skilled workers, strikes, storms, and the like.

There is no denominator variance for variable overhead. The concept of denominator variance arises for fixed overhead because of the conflict between accounting for control (by budgets) and accounting for product costing (by application rates). Note again that the fixed-overhead budget serves the control purpose, whereas the development of a product-costing rate results in the treatment of fixed overhead *as if it were* a variable cost. In other words, the applied line in Exhibit 14-4 is artificial in the sense that, for product-costing purposes, it seemingly transforms a fixed cost into a variable cost. This bit of magic forcefully illustrates the distinction between accounting for control and accounting for product costing.

To summarize, denominator variance arises because the actual production activity level achieved frequently does not coincide with the activity level used as a denominator for selecting a predetermined product-costing rate for fixed factory overhead.

1. When denominator production activity and actual production activity are identical, there is no denominator variance.

2. When actual activity is less than denominator activity, the denominator variance is unfavorable. It is measured in Exhibit 14-4 as follows:

(denominator activity − actual activity) × predetermined fixed-overhead rate = denominator variance
(150,000 hours − 140,000 hours) × \$1 = \$10,000
or
budget minus applied = denominator variance
\$150,000 − \$140,000 = \$10,000

[3]Do not confuse the denominator variance described here with the marketing variance described in Chapter 7. The denominator variance arises because of the peculiarities of historical-cost accounting for fixed overhead in an absorption-cost system. In contrast, the marketing variance in Chapter 7 is an entirely separate measure. It aims at estimating the effects on profit of deviating from an original master budget. It is the budgeted unit contribution margin multiplied by the difference between the master budgeted sales in units and the actual sales in units.

EXHIBIT 14-4. Denominator variance for 19X5
(data are from exhibit 14-3)

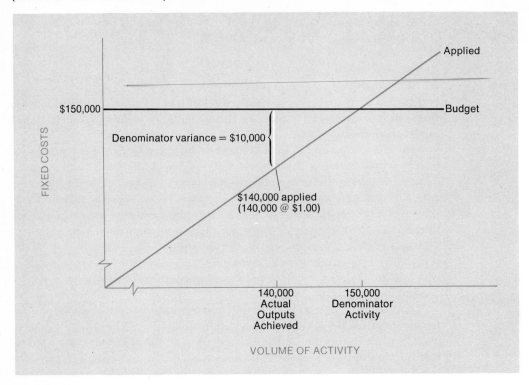

FIXED COSTS

Applied

$150,000 ——— Budget

Denominator variance = $10,000

$140,000 applied
(140,000 @ $1.00)

140,000
Actual
Outputs
Achieved

150,000
Denominator
Activity

VOLUME OF ACTIVITY

3. Where actual activity exceeds denominator activity, as was the case in 19X4, the denominator variance is favorable because it is an index of better-than-expected utilization of facilities.

Note, too, that the dollar amount of the denominator variance depends on what activity level was selected to determine the application rate. In our example, suppose that 200,000 units were selected as the denominator volume level. The predetermined rate would have been $150,000 divided by 200,000, or 75¢. A subsequent volume of 170,000 hours would result in what denominator variance for 19X4? (Compute it before reading on.) The variance would be 30,000 hours multiplied by 75¢, or $22,500, unfavorable, as compared with the $20,000 favorable variance now shown in Exhibit 14-3. This shows how the choice of the volume-level denominator can radically affect the analysis and unit costs for product-costing purposes.

Above all, we should recognize that fixed costs are simply not divisible like variable costs; they come in big chunks and they are related to the provision of big chunks of production or sales capability rather than to the production or sale of a single unit of product.

There are conflicting views on how fixed-overhead variances are best analyzed. Obviously, the "best" way is the one that provides management with the most insight into its company's operations. Consequently, overhead analysis varies from company to company. In many companies denominator variances are most usefully expressed in physical terms only. For instance, a denominator variance could be expressed in machine-hours or kilowatt-hours.

Reconciliation of direct costing and absorption costing

Exhibit 14-5 contains a reconciliation of the net incomes shown in Exhibits 14-2 and 14-3. The difference can be explained in a shortcut way by mutliplying the fixed-overhead product-costing rate by the *change* in the total units in the beginning and ending inventories. Consider 19X5: The change in units was 20,000, so the difference in net income would be 20,000 units multiplied by $1.00 = $20,000.

Exhibit 14-6 gives a more complete explanation of the difference in results. It traces the $30,000 of fixed costs held over from 19X4 under absorption costing, and it shows how the 19X5 income statement must bear these costs as well as the new costs of 19X5 (except for $10,000 lodged in the ending inventory of 19X5).

Effect of other variances

So far, our example has deliberately ignored the possibility of any variance except the denominator variance, which arises solely because of the desire for an application rate for fixed overhead in an absorption-costing situation (and the resultant likelihood that the chosen denominator level will differ from the actual

EXHIBIT 14-5

Reconciliation of Net Income under Direct Costing and Absorption Costing			
	19X4	19X5	TOGETHER
Operating income under:			
Absorption costing (see Exhibit 14-3)	$60,000	$ 45,000	$105,000
Direct costing (see Exhibit 14-2)	30,000	65,000	95,000
Difference to be explained	$30,000	$ −20,000	$ 10,000
The difference can be reconciled by multiplying the fixed-overhead rate by the **change** in the total inventory units:			
Fixed-overhead rate	$1	$1	$1
Change in inventory units:			
Opening inventory	—	30,000	—
Ending inventory	30,000	10,000	10,000
Change	30,000	−20,000	10,000
Difference in operating income explained	$30,000	$ −20,000	$ 10,000

EXHIBIT 14-6

Tracing of Fixed Manufacturing Costs During 19X5
(Data are from Exhibits 14-2 and 14-3)

DIRECT COSTING—
INVENTORIED COSTS

COSTS TO ACCOUNT FOR   **EXPENSE IN 19X5**

No fixed overhead was
unexpired in 19X4

Fixed overhead of $150,000
actually incurred
in 19X5   expires immediately → $150,000

ABSORPTION COSTING—
INVENTORIED COSTS

COSTS TO ACCOUNT FOR   **EXPENSE IN 19X5**

Fixed overhead of $30,000 was
held as unexpired
cost at end of 19X4 → Fixed overhead included
in beginning inventory,
30,000 units × $1 = $ 30,000

Fixed overhead of $150,000:
Applied to product, → Additions to inventory
$140,000   140,000 units × $1 = 140,000

Available for sale   170,000 units $170,000

160,000 units sold   160,000 — expires → Part of cost of
goods sold,
at standard $160,000

Ending inventory
10,000 units $ 10,000

Not applied to
product, $10,000,
expired as a
denominator variance   expires immediately ————→ Denominator variance   10,000

Expired costs $170,000

Note that operating income must be $20,000 lower under absorption costing than under direct costing because $170,000 of fixed costs expire rather than $150,000.

production level achieved). Now we will introduce other variances that were explained in Chapter 7. Let us assume some additional facts for 19X5 (the second of the two years covered by our example):

Direct-material variances	None
Direct-labor variances	$34,000 U
Variable-manufacturing overhead variances	$ 3,000 U
Fixed-overhead budget control variance	$ 7,000 U
Supporting data (used to compute the above variance as shown in the appendix to this chapter):	
Standard direct-labor hours allowed for 140,000 units of output produced	35,000
Standard direct-labor rate per hour	$6.00
Actual direct-labor hours of input	40,000
Actual direct-labor rate per hour	$6.10
Variable manufacturing overhead actually incurred	$31,000
Fixed manufacturing overhead actually incurred	$157,000

Exhibit 14-7 contains the income statement under absorption costing that incorporates these new facts. These new variances hurt income by $44,000 because, like the denominator variance, they are all charged against income in 19X5. When variances are favorable, they increase operating income.

EXHIBIT 14-7

Absorption Costing
Modification of Exhibit 14-3 for 19X5
(Additional facts are in text)

(in thousands)

Sales, 160,000 @ $5		$800
Opening inventory at standard, 30,000 @ $4	$120	
Cost of goods manufactured at standard, 140,000 @ $4	560	
Available for sale, 170,000 @ $4	$680	
Deduct ending inventory at standard, 10,000 @ $4	40	
Cost of goods sold at standard, 160,000 @ $4		640
Gross profit at standard		$160
Net variances for standard variable manufacturing costs ($34,000 + $3,000), unfavorable	$ 37	
Fixed-overhead budget-control variance, unfavorable	7	
Denominator variance (arises only because of fixed overhead), unfavorable	10	
Total variances		54
Gross profit at "actual"		$106
Selling and administrative expenses		105
Operating income		$ 1

Disposition of standard cost variances

The advocates of standard costing, particularly when the standards are viewed as being currently attainable, contend that variances are by and large subject to current control. Therefore variances are not inventoriable and should be considered as adjustments to the income of the period instead of being prorated over inventories and cost of goods sold. In this way, inventory valuations will be more representative of desirable and attainable costs.

The countervailing view favors a proration of the variances[4] over inventories and cost of goods sold. In this way, inventory valuations will be more representative of the **"actual"** costs incurred to obtain the products. In practice, unless the variances are deemed significant in amount, they are usually not prorated because the managers who use standard cost systems favor the views in the preceding paragraph.

Therefore, in practice, variances are typically regarded as adjustments to current income. The form of the disposition is unimportant. Exhibit 14-7 shows the variances as a component of the computation of gross profit at "actual." The variances could also appear as a completely separate section elsewhere in the income statement. This helps to distinguish between product costing (that is, the cost of goods sold, at standard) and loss recognition (unfavorable variances are "lost" or "expired" costs because they represent waste and inefficiency that do not justify them as inventoriable costs. That is, waste is not an asset.)

summary

Standard cost accounting systems are usually designed to satisfy **control** and **product-costing** purposes simultaneously. Many varieties of product costing are in use. For years, manufacturing companies have regularly used a version of absorption costing, which includes fixed factory overhead as a part of the cost of product based on some predetermined application rate (variances are not inventoried). In contrast, direct costing, which is more accurately called **variable costing**, charges fixed factory overhead to the period immediately—that is, fixed overhead is altogether excluded from inventories. Absorption costing continues to be much more widely used than direct costing, although the growing use of the contribution approach in performance measurement has led to increasing use of direct costing for internal purposes.

The denominator variance is linked with absorption costing, not direct costing. It arises from the conflict between the control-budget purpose and the product-costing purpose of cost accounting. The denominator variance is measured by the predetermined fixed-over-

---

[4]For example, the Internal Revenue Service advocates proration. Why? Because most variances tend to be unfavorable. Therefore proration of variances causes higher ending inventory values, higher immediate income, and higher income taxes than lack of proration. For instance, if say, $6,000 of the $54,000 variances in Exhibit 14-7 were prorated to the ending inventory, the income would rise from $1,000 to $7,000.

head rate multiplied by the difference between denominator production volume and actual production volume.

Standard costing uses fully predetermined product costs for direct material, direct labor, and factory overhead. If the standards are currently attainable, the variances are not inventoried. Instead, they are directly charged or credited to current operations.

Readers who study both this and the preceding chapters will readily see that various alternatives of **absorption product costing** are possible:[5]

	ACTUAL COSTING	NORMAL COSTING	STANDARD COSTING
Direct materials	Actual costs	Actual	Standard inputs allowed for actual output achieved × predetermined prices
Direct labor	Actual	Actual	
Variable factory overhead	Actual	Predetermined rates × actual inputs	
Fixed factory overhead	Actual		

summary problems
for your review

■ PROBLEMS

1. Reconsider Exhibits 14-2 and 14-3. Suppose that production in 19X5 was 145,000 units instead of 140,000 units, but sales were 160,000 units. Also assume that the net variances for all variable manufacturing costs were $37,000, unfavorable. Regard these variances as adjustments to standard cost of goods sold. Also assume that actual fixed costs were $157,000. Prepare income statements for 19X5 under direct costing and under absorption costing.

2. Explain why operating income was different under direct costing and absorption costing. Show your calculations.

3. Without regard to Requirement 1, would direct costing or absorption costing give a manager more leeway in influencing his short-run operating income through production-scheduling decisions? Why?

■ SOLUTIONS

1. See Exhibits 14-8 and 14-9. Note that the ending inventory will be 15,000 instead of 10,000 units.

[5]In addition, the same alternatives are available for *direct product costing*. The *only* change in the above tabulation would be to delete fixed factory overhead entirely because it is not a product cost under direct costing assumptions.

EXHIBIT 14-8

TOLMAN COMPANY
Income Statement (Direct Costing)
for the Year 19X5
(In thousands of dollars)

Sales			$800
Opening inventory—at variable standard cost of $3	$ 90		
Add variable cost of goods manufactured	435		
Available for sale	$525		
Deduct ending inventory—at variable standard cost of $3	45		
Variable cost of goods sold, at standard		$480	
Net variances for all variable costs, unfavorable		37	
Variable cost of goods sold, at actual		$517	
Variable selling expenses—at 5% of dollar sales		40	
Total variable costs charged against sales			557
Contribution margin			$243
Fixed factory overhead		$157*	
Fixed selling and administrative expenses		65	
Total fixed expenses			222
Operating income			$ 21†

*This could be shown in two lines, $150,000 budget plus $7,000 variance.
† The difference between this and the $65,000 operating income in Exhibit 14-2 occurs because of the $37,000 unfavorable variable cost variances and the $7,000 unfavorable fixed-cost control-budget variance.

2. Decline in inventory levels is 30,000 − 15,000, or 15,000 units. The fixed-overhead rate per unit in absorption costing is $1. Therefore $15,000 more of fixed overhead was charged against operations under absorption costing than under direct costing. Generally, when inventories decline, absorption costing will show less income than direct costing; when inventories rise, absorption costing will show more income than direct costing.

3. Some version of absorption costing will give a manager more leeway in influencing his operating income via production scheduling. Operating income will fluctuate in harmony with changes in net sales under direct costing, but it is influenced by both production and sales under absorption costing. For example, compare the direct costing in Exhibits 14-2 and 14-8. As the second note to Exhibit 14-8 indicates, the operating income may be affected by assorted variances (but not the denominator variance) under direct costing, but production scheduling *per se* will have no effect on operating income. On the other hand, compare the operating income of Exhibits 14-7 and 14-9. As the third note to Exhibit 14-9 explains, production scheduling as well as sales influence operating income. Production was 145,000 rather than 140,000 units. So $5,000 of fixed overhead became a part of ending inventory (an asset) instead of part of the denominator variance (an expense)—that is, the denominator variance is $5,000 lower and the ending inventory contains $5,000 more fixed overhead in Exhibit 14-9 than in Exhibit 14-7.

EXHIBIT
14-9

TOLMAN COMPANY
Income Statement (Absorption Costing)
for the Year 19X5
(In thousands of dollars)

Sales		$800
Opening inventory at standard cost of $4	$120	
Cost of goods manufactured at standard	580	
Available for sale	$700	
Deduct ending inventory at standard	60	
Cost of goods sold at standard	$640	
Net variances for all variable manufacturing costs, unfavorable	$37	
Fixed factory overhead budget-control variance, unfavorable	7	
Denominator variance, unfavorable	5*	
Total variances	49	
Cost of goods sold at actual		689†
Gross profit at "actual"		$111
Selling and administrative expenses		
Variable	$ 40	
Fixed	65	105
Operating income		$ 6‡

*Denominator variance is $1 × (150,000 denominator volume − 145,000 actual production).

† This format differs slightly from Exhibit 14-7. The difference is deliberate; it illustrates that the formats of income statements are not rigid. (Exhibit 14-7 is on page 417.)

‡ Compare this result with the $1,000 operating income in Exhibit 14-7. The only difference is traceable to the production of 145,000 units instead of 140,000 units, resulting in an unfavorable denominator variance of $5,000 instead of $10,000.

Appendix 14:
comparisons of denominator variances
with other variances

☐ DENOMINATOR VARIANCE IS UNIQUE

The only new variance introduced in this chapter is the denominator variance, which arises because fixed-overhead accounting must serve two masters: the **control-budget** purpose and the product-costing purpose. Let us examine these variances in perspective by using the approach originally demonstrated in Exhibit 7-6. The results of the approach are in Exhibit 14-10, which deserves your careful study, particularly the two notes. Please ponder the exhibit before reading on.

Exhibit 14-11 provides a graphical comparison of the variable and fixed overhead that were analyzed in Exhibit 14-10. Note how the control-budget line and the product-costing line (the applied line) are superimposed in the graph for variable overhead but differ in the graph for fixed overhead.

EXHIBIT 14-10

Analysis of Variances
(Data are from text)

	(A) COST INCURRED: ACTUAL INPUTS × ACTUAL PRICE	(B) FLEXIBLE CONTROL BUDGET BASED ON ACTUAL INPUTS	(C) FLEXIBLE CONTROL BUDGET BASED ON ACTUAL OUTPUTS ACHIEVED	(D) PRODUCT COSTING: APPLIED TO PRODUCT
Direct labor:	40,000 × $6.10 = $244,000	40,000 × $6 = $240,000	(35,000 × $6 or 140,000 × $1.50) = $210,000*	(35,000 × $6 or 140,000 × $1.50) = 210,000*
Variable manufacturing overhead:	(given) $31,000	40,000 × $.80 = $32,000	(35,000 × $.80 or 140,000 × $.20) = $28,000*	28,000*
Fixed manufacturing overhead:	$157,000	Lump sum 150,000	Lump sum $150,000†	140,000 × $1.00 = $140,000

Direct labor:

40,000 × ($6.10 − $6) = Price variance, $4,000 U

5,000 × $6 = Efficiency variance, $30,000 U

No variance

Flexible control-budget variance, $34,000 U

No variance

Variable manufacturing overhead:

Price (spending) variance, $1,000 F

5,000 × $.80 = Efficiency variance, $4,000 U

No variance

Flexible control-budget variance, $3,000 U

No variance

Underapplied overhead, $3,000 U

Fixed manufacturing overhead:

Price (spending), $7,000 U

No variance

Denominator variance, $10,000 U

Flexible control-budget variance, $7,000 U

Denominator variance, $10,000 U

Underapplied overhead, $17,000 U

U = Unfavorable, F = Favorable.

*Note especially that the control budget for variable costs rises and falls in direct proportion to production. Note also that the control-budget purpose and the product-costing purpose harmonize completely; the total costs in the flexible budget will always agree with the standard variable costs applied to product because they are based on standard costs per unit multiplied by units produced.

†In contrast with variable costs, the control-budget total will always be the same regardless of the units produced. However, the control-budget purpose and the product-costing purpose conflict; whenever actual production differs from denominator production, the standard costs applied to product will differ from the control budget. This difference is the denominator variance. In this case, the denominator variance may be computed by multiplying the $1 rate times the difference between the 150,000 denominator volume and the 140,000 units of output achieved.

EXHIBIT 14-11. Comparison of control and product-costing purposes, variable overhead and fixed overhead (not to scale)

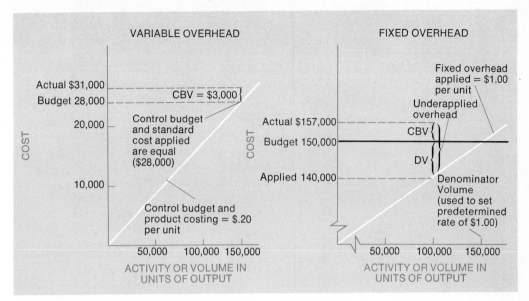

CBV = *Control-budget variance.*
DV = *Denominator variance.*

Underapplied or overapplied overhead is always the difference between the actual overhead incurred and the overhead applied. An analysis may then be made:

underapplied overhead = flexible control-budget variance + denominator variance
for variable overhead = $3,000 + 0 = $3,000
for fixed overhead = $7,000 + $10,000 = $17,000

☐ LOST-CONTRIBUTION MARGINS

Finally, what is the economic significance of unit fixed costs? Unlike variable costs, total fixed costs do not change in the short run as production or sales fluctuate. Management would obtain a better measure of the cost of underutilization of physical facilities by trying to approximate the related lost-contribution margins instead of the related historical fixed costs.[6] Fixed-cost incurrence often involves lump-sum outlays based on a pattern of expected recoupment. But ineffective utilization of existing facilities has no bearing on the amount of fixed costs currently incurred. The economic effects of the inability to reach target volume levels are often directly measured by lost-contribution margins, even if these have to be approximated. The historical-cost approach fails to emphasize the distinction between *fixed-cost incurrence,* on the one hand, and the objective of *maximizing the total contribution margin,* on the other hand. These are separable management problems, and the utilization of existing capacity is more closely related to the latter.

COSTING:
DIRECT AND
ABSORPTION

[6]For an expanded discussion, see C. Horngren, "A Contribution Margin Approach to the Analysis of Capacity Utilization," *Accounting Review,* 42, No. 2, 254–64.

For instance, the denominator variance in our example was computed at $10,000 by multiplying a unit fixed cost of $1 by the 10,000-unit difference between the 150,000 units of denominator activity and 140,000 units produced. This $10,000 figure may be helpful in the sense that management is alerted in some crude way to the probable costs of failure to produce 150,000 units. But the more relevant information is the lost-contribution margins that pertain to the 10,000 units. This information may not be so easy to obtain. The lost-contribution margins may be zero in those cases where there are no opportunities to obtain any contribution margin from alternative uses of available capacity; in other cases, however, the lost-contribution margins may be substantial. For example, if demand is high, the breakdown of key equipment may cost a company many thousands of dollars in lost-contribution margins. Unfortunately, in these cases, existing accounting systems would show denominator variances based on the unitized fixed costs and entirely ignore any lost-contribution margins.

assignment material

■ FUNDAMENTAL ASSIGNMENT MATERIAL

14-1. **Terminology.** Define *absorption costing; actual costing; control-budget variance; denominator variance; direct costing; marginal costing; normal costing; standard absorption costing; standard direct costing; variable costing; volume variance.*

14-2. **Comparison of absorption and direct costing.** Here is some information pertaining to a year's operations:

Fixed selling and administrative expenses	$300,000
Fixed manufacturing overhead	400,000
Direct labor	300,000
Variable manufacturing overhead	100,000
Direct material used	200,000
Variable selling and administrative expenses	250,000

There were no beginning inventories and no ending work in process. Ten thousand units were manufactured, and 8,000 units were sold.

REQUIRED

1. Using absorption costing, compute the ending finished-goods inventory.
2. Using direct costing (also called variable costing), compute the ending finished-goods inventory.
3. Would operating income be higher or lower under direct costing? By how much? The answer is $80,000 lower. Explain why the difference exists.

14-3. **Extension of chapter illustration.** Reconsider Exhibits 14-2 and 14-3. Suppose that in 19X5 production was 156,000 units instead of 140,000 units, and sales were 150,000 units. Also assume that the net variances for all variable manufacturing costs were $23,000, unfavorable. Also assume that actual fixed manufacturing costs were $160,000.

1. Prepare income statements for 19X5 under direct costing and under absorption costing. Use a format similar to Exhibits 14-8 and 14-9.
2. Explain why operating income was different under direct costing and absorption costing. Show your calculations.

14-4. Extension of appendix illustration. Study the analysis of variances in Exhibit 14-10. Suppose that production is 156,000 units. Also assume:

Standard direct-labor hours allowed per unit produced	.25
Standard direct-labor rate per hour	$6.00
Actual direct-labor hours of input	42,000
Actual direct-labor rate per hour	$6.10
Variable manufacturing overhead actually incurred	$32,000
Fixed manufacturing overhead actually incurred	$160,000

REQUIRED   Prepare an analysis of variances similar to that shown in Exhibit 14-10.

ADDITIONAL ASSIGNMENT MATERIAL

14-5. Why do advocates of currently attainable standard costs as a method for product costing claim that it is conceptually superior to actual costing?

14-6. "Direct costing means that only direct material and direct labor are inventoried." Do you agree? Why?

14-7. "The dollar amount of the denominator variance depends on what activity level was chosen to determine the application rate." Explain.

14-8. Why is it artificial to unitize fixed costs?

14-9. "The fixed cost per unit is directly affected by the denominator selected." Do you agree? Explain.

14-10. "Absorption costing regards more categories of costs as product costs." Explain. Be specific.

14-11. "Direct costing is used in several corporate annual reports." Do you agree? Explain.

14-12. How is fixed overhead applied to product?

14-13. Define the *denominator variance* as conventionally measured.

14-14. Simple comparison of direct and absorption costing. B Company began business on January 1, 19X1, with assets of $100,000 cash and equities of $100,000 capital stock. In 19X1 it manufactured some inventory at a cost of $50,000, including $10,000 for factory rent and other fixed factory overhead. In 19X2 it manufactured nothing and sold half of its inventory for $32,000 cash. In 19X3 it manufactured nothing and sold the remaining half for another $32,000 cash. It had no fixed expenses in 19X2 or 19X3.

There are no other transactions of any kind. Ignore income taxes.

REQUIRED   Prepare an ending balance sheet plus an income statement for 19X1, 19X2, and 19X3 under (1) absorption costing and (2) direct costing (variable costing).

14-15. Comparison of direct and absorption costing. The following data pertain to the operations of the Francine Company for 19X4, its first year in business. The company manufactured 16,000 units and sold 9,600:

Contribution margin	$190,000
Beginning inventories	0
Ending inventory, work in process	0
Ending inventory, direct materials	40,000
Fixed factory overhead	640,000
Direct labor	700,000
Variable factory overhead	260,000
Direct materials purchased	840,000
Variable selling and administrative expenses	350,000
Fixed selling and administrative expenses	500,000

REQUIRED

1. Compute the ending finished-goods inventory using (a) absorption costing and (b) direct costing (variable costing).
2. Explain the amount of difference between your answers 1a and 1b.

14-16. Comparison of direct and absorption costing over five years. Two corporations are hotly competitive in the manufacture and sale of farm machinery. Their sales volume, production volume, and fixed indirect manufacturing costs have been practically identical.

Companies A and B	19X1	19X2	19X3	19X4	19X5
Units produced	100,000	100,000	105,000	90,000	90,000
Units sold	90,000	90,000	100,000	100,000	95,000
Fixed indirect manufacturing costs	$100,000	$105,000	$105,000	$105,000	$100,000

Company A uses absorption costing, and Company B uses direct costing. For each of the five years, would Company A's operating income be higher or lower than Company B's? Assume that neither company had inventories at the beginning of 19X1. Assume that there is a first-in, first-out flow of costs.

14-17. Direct and absorption costing. (H. Schaefer.) Data for 19X2:

Sales: 10,000 units at $12 each	
Actual production	12,000 units
Denominator activity	15,000 units
Manufacturing costs **incurred:**	
Variable	$60,000
Fixed	30,000
Nonmanufacturing costs **incurred:**	
Variable	$15,000
Fixed	14,000

REQUIRED

1. Determine net income for 19X2, assuming the firm uses the direct-costing approach to product costing. (Do not prepare a statement.)
2. Assume that (a) there is *no* January 1, 19X2, inventory, (b) *no* variances are allocated to inventory, and (c) the firm uses a "full absorption" approach to product costing. Compute (a) the cost assigned to December 31, 19X2, inventory; and (b) net income for the year ended December 31, 19X2. (Do not prepare a statement.)

14-18. All-fixed costs. (Suggested by Raymond P. Marple.) The Marple Company has built a massive water-desalting factory next to an ocean. The factory is completely automated. It has its own source of power, light, heat, etc. The salt water costs nothing. All producing and other operating costs are fixed; they do not vary with output because the volume is governed by adjusting a few dials on a control panel. The employees have flat annual salaries.

The desalted water is not sold to household consumers. It has a special taste that appeals to local breweries, distilleries, and soft-drink manufacturers. The price, 10¢ per gallon, is expected to remain unchanged for quite some time.

The following are data regarding the first two years of operations:

| | IN GALLONS | | COSTS (ALL FIXED) | |
	sales	production	manufacturing	other
19X1	5,000,000	10,000,000	$450,000	$100,000
19X2	5,000,000	0	450,000	100,000

Orders can be processed in four hours, so management decided, in early 19X2, to gear production strictly to sales.

REQUIRED

1. Prepare three-column income statements for 19X1, for 19X2, and for the two years together using (a) direct costing and (b) absorption costing.
2. What is the break-even point under (a) direct costing and (b) absorption costing?
3. What inventory costs would be carried on the balance sheets on December 31, 19X1 and 19X2, under each method?
4. Comment on your answers in Requirements 1 and 2. Which costing method appears more useful?

14-19. **Semifixed costs.** The McFarland Company differs from the Marple Company (described in Problem 14-18) in only one respect: It has both variable and fixed manufacturing costs. Its variable costs are $.025 per gallon, and its fixed manufacturing costs are $225,000 per year.

REQUIRED

1. Using the same data as in the preceding problem, except for the change in production-cost behavior, prepare three-column income statements for 19X1, for 19X2, and for the two years together using (a) direct costing and (b) absorption costing.
2. Why did McFarland earn a profit for the two-year period while Marple suffered a loss?
3. What inventory costs would be carried on the balance sheets on December 31, 19X1 and 19X2, under each method?

14-20. **Fundamentals of overhead variances.** The Kinnear Company is installing an absorption standard cost system and a flexible overhead budget. Standard costs have recently been developed for its only product and are as follows:

Direct material, 2 pounds @ $15	$30
Direct labor, 6 hours @ $6	36
Variable overhead, 6 hours @ $2	12
Fixed overhead	?
Standard cost per unit of finished product	$?

Denominator activity (expected activity) is expressed as 12,000 standard direct-labor hours per month. Fixed overhead is expected to be $36,000 per month. The predetermined fixed-overhead rate for product costing is not changed from month to month.

REQUIRED

1. Calculate the proper fixed-overhead rate per standard direct-labor hour and per unit.
2. Graph the following for activity from zero to 15,000 hours:
   a. Budgeted variable overhead
   b. Variable overhead applied to product

3. Graph the following for activity from zero to 15,000 hours:
   a. Budgeted fixed overhead
   b. Fixed overhead applied to product
4. Assume that 10,000 standard direct-labor hours are allowed for the output achieved during a given month. Actual variable overhead of $20,400 was incurred; actual fixed overhead amounted to $37,000. Calculate the
   a. Fixed-overhead control-budget variance
   b. Fixed-overhead denominator variance
   c. Variable-overhead control-budget variance
5. Assume that 12,500 standard direct-labor hours are allowed for the output achieved during a given month. Actual overhead incurred amounted to $59,800, $37,800 of which was fixed. Calculate the
   a. Fixed-overhead control-budget variance
   b. Fixed-overhead denominator variance
   c. Variable-overhead control-budget variance

14-21. **Fixed overhead and practical capacity.** The expected activity of the paper-making plant of Scott Paper Company was 36,000 hours per month. Practical capacity was 48,000 hours per month. The standard hours allowed for the actual output achieved in January was 41,000. The budgeted fixed-factory-overhead items were:

Depreciation, equipment	$260,000
Depreciation, factory building	40,000
Supervision	30,000
Indirect labor	180,000
Insurance	10,000
Property taxes	20,000
Total	$540,000

Because of unanticipated scheduling difficulties and the need for more indirect labor, the actual fixed factory overhead was $565,000.

REQUIRED

1. Using practical capacity as the denominator for applying fixed factory overhead, prepare a summary analysis of fixed-overhead variances for January.
2. Using expected activity as the denominator for applying fixed factory overhead, prepare a summary analysis of fixed-overhead variances for January.
3. Explain why some of your variances in Requirements 1 and 2 are the same and why some differ.

14-22. **Review of Chapters 13 and 14.** (CMA, adapted.) Examine the accompanying data regarding Department 203. Answer the multiple choice questions. Show computations.

1. The actual overhead for Department 203 for 19X7 was
   a. $156,000
   b. $123,000
   c. $70,000
   d. $112,000
   e. None of the preceding responses is correct.

2. Department 203 overhead for 19X7 was
   a. $11,000 underapplied
   b. $11,000 overapplied
   c. $44,000 underapplied
   d. $44,000 overapplied
   e. None of the preceding responses is correct.

3. The denominator (volume) variance for Department 203 for 19X7 was
   a. $16,000 unfavorable
   b. $12,000 unfavorable
   c. $0
   d. $15,000 unfavorable
   e. None of the preceding responses is correct.

Department 203—Work in Process—Beginning of Period

JOB NO.	MATERIAL	LABOR	OVERHEAD	TOTAL
1376	$17,500	$22,000	$33,000	$72,500

Department 203 Costs for 19X7

INCURRED BY JOBS	MATERIAL	LABOR	OTHER	TOTAL
1376	$ 1,000	$ 7,000	—	$ 8,000
1377	26,000	53,000	—	79,000
1378	12,000	9,000	—	21,000
1379	4,000	1,000	—	5,000
NOT INCURRED BY JOBS				
Indirect materials and supplies	15,000	—	—	15,000
Indirect labor	—	53,000	—	53,000
Employee benefits	—	—	$23,000	23,000
Depreciation	—	—	12,000	12,000
Supervision	—	20,000	—	20,000
Total	$58,000	$143,000	$35,000	$236,000

Department 203 Overhead Rate for 19X7

Budgeted overhead	
Variable—Indirect materials	$16,000
Indirect labor	56,000
Employee benefits	24,000
Fixed—Supervision	20,000
Depreciation	12,000
Total	$128,000
Budgeted direct-labor dollars	$80,000
Rate per direct-labor dollar ($128,000 ÷ $80,000)	160%

4. The total overhead price (spending) variance for Department 203 for 19X7 was
   a. $5,000 unfavorable
   b. $7,000 unfavorable
   a. $16,000 unfavorable
   d. $12,000 unfavorable
   e. None of the preceding responses is correct.

5. Job number 1376 was the only job completed and sold in 19X7. What amount was included in cost of goods sold for this job?
   a. $72,500
   b. $91,700
   c. $80,500
   d. $19,200
   e. None of the preceding responses is correct.

6. The value of work-in-process inventory at the end of 19X7 was
   a. $105,000
   b. $180,600
   c. $228,000
   d. $205,800
   e. None of the preceding responses is correct.

7. Assume that overhead was underapplied in the amount of $14,000 for Department 203. If underapplied overhead was distributed between cost of goods sold and inventory, how much of the underapplied overhead was charged to the year-end work-in-process inventory? (Distribute in proportion to how overhead was originally applied.)
   a. $9,685
   b. $4,315
   c. $12,600
   d. $1,400
   e. None of the preceding responses is correct.

14-23. **Fill in the blanks.** Read the appendix. Consider the following data regarding factory overhead:

	VARIABLE	FIXED
Budget for actual hours of input	$40,000	$60,000
Applied	37,000	55,000
Budget for standard hours allowed for actual output achieved	?	?
Actual incurred	44,000	59,000

REQUIRED

Using the above data, fill in the blanks below. Use *F* for favorable or *U* for unfavorable for each variance.

	TOTAL OVERHEAD	VARIABLE	FIXED
1. Price (spending) variance	————	————	————
2. Efficiency variance	————	————	————
3. Denominator variance	————	————	————
4. Flexible control-budget variance	————	————	————
5. Underapplied overhead	————	————	—— —

14-24. Straightforward problem on standard cost system. Read the appendix. The Bendex Company uses flexible budgets and a standard cost system. The month's data for a department follow:

Direct-labor costs incurred, 11,000 hours, $125,400
Variable overhead costs incurred, $28,500
Fixed-overhead budget variance, $1,500 favorable
Finished units produced, 2,000
Fixed-overhead costs incurred, $36,000
Variable overhead applied at $2.70 per hour
Standard direct-labor cost, $12 per hour
Denominator production per month, 2,500 units
Standard direct-labor hours per finished unit, 5

REQUIRED

Prepare an analysis of all variances (similar to Exhibit 14-10, page 422).

14-25. Multiple choice. (CMA, adapted.) Read the appendix. Eastern Company manufactures special electrical equipment and parts. Eastern employs a standard cost accounting system with separate standards established for each product.

A special transformer is manufactured in the transformer department. Production volume is measured by direct-labor hours in this department, and a flexible-budget system is used to plan and control department overhead.

Standard costs for the special transformer are determined annually in September for the coming year. The standard cost of a transformer for 19X7 was computed at $67 as shown below:

Direct materials			
Iron	5 sheets	@ $2	$10
Copper	3 spools	@ $3	9
Direct labor	4 hours	@ $7	28
Variable overhead	4 hours	@ $3	12
Fixed overhead	4 hours	@ $2	8
Total			$67

Overhead rates were based upon 4,000 direct-labor hours of monthly activity for 19X7. Variable-overhead costs are expected to vary with the number of direct-labor hours actually used.

During October 19X7, 800 transformers were produced. This was below expectations because a work stoppage occurred during contract negotiations with the labor force. Once the contract was settled, the department scheduled overtime in an attempt to catch up to expected production levels.

The following costs were incurred in October 19X7:

DIRECT MATERIAL	DIRECT MATERIALS PURCHASED	MATERIALS USED
Iron	5,000 sheets @ $2.00 per sheet	3,900 sheets
Copper	2,200 spools @ $3.10 per spool	2,600 spools

Direct labor
Regular time:	2,000 hours @ $7.00	
	1,400 hours @ $7.20	
Overtime:	600 of the 1,400 hours were subject to overtime premium. The total overtime premium of $2,160 is included in variable overhead in accordance with company accounting practices.	

| Variable overhead: | $10,000 |
| Fixed overhead: | $ 8,800 |

REQUIRED

Select the best answer for each of the following eight items. Show computations to support your answer.

1. The most appropriate time to record any variation of actual material prices from standard is
   a. At year end, when all variations will be known
   b. At the time of purchase
   c. At the time of material usage
   d. As needed to evaluate the performance of the purchasing manager
   e. Some time other than those shown above is appropriate

2. The total material efficiency (quantity) variance is
   a. $200 favorable
   b. $400 favorable
   c. $600 favorable
   d. $400 unfavorable
   e. None of the preceding responses is correct.

3. The labor price (rate) variance is
   a. $280 unfavorable
   b. $340 unfavorable
   c. $1,680 unfavorable
   d. $2,440 unfavorable
   e. None of the preceding responses is correct.

4. The variable-overhead price (spending) variance is
   a. $200 favorable
   b. $400 unfavorable
   c. $600 unfavorable
   d. $1,600 unfavorable
   e. None of the preceding responses is correct.

5. The efficiency variance in variable overhead is the standard variable-overhead rate times the difference between standard labor hours of output and
   a. 2,000 hours
   b. 2,600 hours
   c. 2,800 hours
   d. 3,400 hours
   e. None of the preceding responses is correct.

6. The budget variance for fixed overhead is
   a. $2,400 unfavorable
   b. $0
   c. $800 unfavorable
   d. Not calculable from the problem
   e. None of the preceding responses is correct.

7. The fixed-overhead denominator (volume) variance is
   a. $400 unfavorable
   b. $2,200 unfavorable
   c. $2,400 unfavorable
   d. $1,600 unfavorable
   e. None of the preceding responses is correct.

8. An unfavorable fixed-overhead denominator variance is most often caused by
   a. Actual fixed overhead incurred exceeding budgeted fixed overhead
   b. An overapplication of fixed overhead to production
   c. A decrease in the level of the finished inventory of transformers.
   d. Production levels exceeding sales levels
   e. Normal activity exceeding actual production levels

COSTING:
DIRECT AND
ABSORPTION

431

14-26. **Analysis of variances.** (CPA, adapted.) Read the appendix. The Groomer Company manufactures two products, florimene and glyoxide, used in the Singapore plastics industry. The company uses a flexible budget in its standard cost system to develop variances. Selected data follow:

	FLORIMENE	GLYOXIDE
Data on standard costs:		
Raw material per unit	3 pounds at $1.00 per pound	4 pounds at $1.10 per pound
Direct labor per unit	5 hours at $2.00 per hour	6 hours at $2.50 per hour
Variable factory overhead per unit	$3.20 per direct-labor hour	$3.50 per direct-labor hour
Fixed factory overhead per month	$20,700	$26,520
Denominator activity per month	5,750 direct-labor hours	7,800 direct-labor hours
Units produced in September	1,000	1,200
Costs incurred for September:		
Raw material	3,100 pounds at $.90 per pound	4,700 pounds at $1.15 per pound
Direct labor	4,900 hours at $1.95 per hour	7,400 hours at $2.55 per hour
Variable factory overhead	$16,170	$25,234
Fixed factory overhead	$20,930	$26,400

REQUIRED

Select the best answer for each of the following items. Show computations to support your answer.

1. The total variances (that is, the difference between total costs incurred and total standard costs applied to product) to be explained for both products for September are
   a. Florimene, $255, favorable; Glyoxide, $909, unfavorable
   b. Florimene, $7,050 favorable; Glyoxide, $6,080, favorable
   c. Florimene, $4,605, favorable; Glyoxide, $3,431, favorable
   d. Florimene, $2,445, unfavorable; Glyoxide, $2,949, unfavorable
   e. None of the above

2. The labor-efficiency variances for both products for September are
   a. Florimene, $195, favorable; Glyoxide, $510, unfavorable
   b. Florimene, $1,700, favorable; Glyoxide, $1,000, favorable
   c. Florimene, $200, favorable; Glyoxide, $500, unfavorable
   d. Florimene, $195, favorable; Glyoxide, $510 favorable
   e. None of the above

3. The labor-price (rate) variances for both products for September are
   a. Florimene, $245, favorable; Glyoxide, $370, unfavorable
   b. Florimene, $200, favorable; Glyoxide, $500, unfavorable
   c. Florimene, $1,945, favorable; Glyoxide, $630 favorable
   d. Florimene, $245, unfavorable; Glyoxide, $370, favorable
   e. None of the above

4. The "price" variances for variable overhead for both products for September are
   a. Florimene, $490, unfavorable; Glyoxide, $666, favorable
   b. Florimene, $167, unfavorable; Glyoxide, $35, unfavorable
   c. Florimene, $170, unfavorable; Glyoxide, $34, unfavorable
   d. Florimene, $1,900, favorable; Glyoxide, $1,960, favorable
   e. None of the above

14-27. Inventory measures, production scheduling, and evaluating divisional performance. The Dore Company stresses competition between the heads of its various divisions, and it rewards stellar performance with year-end bonuses that vary between 5 and 10 percent of division net operating income (before considering the bonus or income taxes). The divisional managers have great discretion in setting production schedules.

Division Y produces and sells a product for which there is a longstanding demand but which can have marked seasonal and year-to-year fluctuations. On November 30, 19X2, Robert Smith, the Division Y manager, is preparing a production schedule for December. The following data are available for January 1 through November 30:

Beginning inventory, January 1, in units	10,000
Sales price, per unit	$ 500
Total fixed costs incurred for manufacturing	$11,000,000
Total fixed costs: other (not inventoriable)	$11,000,000
Total variable costs for manufacturing	$22,000,000
Total other variable costs (fluctuate with units sold)	$ 5,000,000
Units produced	110,000
Units sold	100,000
Variances	None

Production in October and November was 10,000 units each month. Practical capacity is 12,000 units per month. Maximum available storage space for inventory is 25,000 units. The sales outlook, for December through February, is 6,000 units monthly. In order to retain a core of key employees, monthly production cannot be scheduled at less than 4,000 units without special permission from the president. Inventory is never to be less than 10,000 units.

The denominator used for applying fixed factory overhead is regarded as 120,000 units annually. The company uses a standard absorption-costing system. All variances are disposed of at year-end as an adjustment to standard cost of goods sold.

1. Given the restrictions as stated, and assuming that the manager wants to maximize the company's net income for 19X2:
   a. How many units should be scheduled for production in December?
   b. What net operating income will be reported for 19X2 as a whole, assuming that the implied cost behavior patterns will continue in December as they did throughout the year, to date? Show your computations.
   c. If December production is scheduled at 4,000 units, what would reported net income be?
2. Assume that standard direct costing is used rather than standard absorption costing:
   a. What would net income for 19X2 be, assuming that the December production schedule is the one in Requirement 1, part *a*?
   b. Assuming that December production was 4,000 units?
   c. Reconcile the net incomes in this requirement with those in Requirement 1.
3. From the viewpoint of the long-run interests of the company as a whole, what production schedule should the division manager set? Explain fully. Include in your explanation a comparison of the motivating influence of absorption and direct costing in this situation.
4. Assume standard absorption costing. The manager wants to maximize his after-income-tax performance over the long run. Given the data at the beginning of the problem, assume that income tax rates will be halved in 19X3. Assume also that year-end write-offs of variances are acceptable for income tax purposes.
   How many units should be scheduled for production in December? Why?

14-28. Comparing the performance of two plants. On your first day as assistant to the president of Holland Systems, Inc., your in-box contains the following memo:

> To: Assistant to the President
> From: The President
> Subject: Mickey Mouse Watch Situation
>
> This note is to bring you up-to-date on one of our acquisition problem areas. Market research detected the current nostalgia wave almost a year ago and concluded that HSI should acquire a position in this market. Research data showed that Mickey Mouse Watches could become profitable ($2 contribution margin on a $5 sales price) at a volume of 100,000 units per plant if they became popular again. Consequently, we picked up closed-down facilities on each coast, staffed them, and asked them to keep us posted on operations.
> Friday I got preliminary information from accounting that is unclear. I want you to find out why their costs of goods sold are far apart and how we should have them report in the future to avoid confusion. This is particularly important in the Mickey Mouse case, as market projections look bad and we may have to close one plant. I guess we'll close the West Coast plant unless you can show otherwise.

Preliminary Accounting Report

	EAST	WEST
Sales	$500,000	$500,000
Cost of goods sold	300,000	480,000
Gross margin	$200,000	$ 20,000
Administration costs (fixed)	20,000	20,000
Net income	$180,000	$ 0
Production	200,000 units	100,000 units
Variances (included in Cost of goods sold)	$180,000, favorable	$ 90,000, unfavorable

REQUIRED

Reconstruct the given income statements in as much detail as possible. Then explain in detail why the income statements differ, and clarify the situation confronting the president. Assume that there are no price or efficiency variances.

INFLUENCES OF QUANTITATIVE TECHNIQUES ON MANAGEMENT ACCOUNTING

learning objectives

When you have finished studying this chapter, you should be able to:

1. Distinguish between making decisions under certainty and making decisions under uncertainty.
2. Construct a decision table involving probabilities and compute the expected value of each action.
3. Use standard deviation and expected value to compute the coefficient of variation, and indicate how it can measure the relative degrees of risk among alternatives.
4. Compute the expected value of perfect information.
5. Construct a graph for a linear-programming solution.
6. Develop the equations and inequalities for a linear-programming solution.
7. Determine the economic-order quantity (EOQ) by using the formula, and estimate the EOQ by preparing a schedule of the relevant costs of various selected order sizes.
8. Determine the safety stock and the reorder point in a simple inventory situation.

Because the branches of knowledge overlap, it is always an oversimplification to specify where the field of accounting starts and where it ends. Some accountants take the view that accounting should restrict itself to scorekeeping, the compilation of financial history. Others feel that if accountants do not move quickly to assimilate a working knowledge of computer technology and assorted mathematical techniques, their attention-directing and problem-solving functions will be seized by the expanding field of management science.

We need not be concerned with the controversy over what accounting is and what it is not. Regardless of its label, the subject matter of this chapter has a bearing on management planning and control and is therefore important to accountants and to managers. One of the marks of an educated person is his or her ability to recognize and accept changes that promise better ways of accomplishing objectives. The accountant is still the top quantitative expert in nearly all organizations, and few companies employ full-time mathematics specialists. To retain and improve his or her status, the accountant should be aware of how mathematical models may improve planning and control. The alert managers would naturally expect their accountants to keep abreast of the newer quantitative techniques.

This chapter is a survey. Technical competence in any of the areas mentioned can be achieved only by thorough specialized study. We shall explore decision theory and uncertainty, linear-programming models, and inventory-control models.

The accountant often provides many of the data that are included in these decision models. An understanding of the nature of decision models should have a direct effect on how the accountant designs a formal information system.

Decision theory and uncertainty

☐ FORMAL DECISION MODELS

A **model** is a depiction of the interrelationships among the recognized factors in a real situation. Most models spotlight the key interrelationships and de-emphasize the unimportant factors. Models take many forms. Museums contain model rockets and model ships. Automobile companies distribute miniature model cars. Accountants continually work with accounting systems and financial reports, which are models. Operations researchers principally use mathematical equations as models.

Decision models are often expressed in mathematical form. The careful use of mathematical models supplements hunches and implicit rules of thumb with explicit assumptions and criteria. Mathematical models have been criticized because they may oversimplify and ignore important underlying factors. Still, many examples of successful applications can be cited. For example, inventory-control and linear-programming models are widely used. The test of success is not whether mathematical models lead to perfect decisions, but whether such models lead to better decisions than via alternative techniques. How is this test applied? Sometimes it is difficult, but conceptually the test is to compare the net financial impact (after deducting the cost of accumulating the information used in the decision) of the decision generated by the mathematical model versus the net financial impact of the decision generated by other techniques. In other words, the relative attractiveness of using mathematical decision models is again subject to the cost-benefit test.

Decision theory is a complex, somewhat ill-defined body of knowledge developed by statisticians, mathematicians, economists, and psychologists that tries to prescribe how decisions should be made and to describe systematically which variables affect choices. The basic approach of decision theory has the following characteristics:

1. An organizational objective that can be quantified. This objective can take many forms. Most often, it is expressed as a maximization (or minimization) of some form of profit (or cost). This quantification is often called a *choice criterion* or an *objective function*. This objective function is used to evaluate the courses of action and to provide a basis for choosing the best alternative.

2. A set of the alternative courses of action under explicit consideration. This set of *actions* should be collectively exhaustive and mutually exclusive.

3. A set of all relevant *events* (sometimes called *states*) that can occur. This set should also be collectively exhaustive and mutually exclusive. Therefore only one of the states will actually occur.

4. A set of *probabilities* that describes the likelihood of occurrence for each event.

5. A set of *outcomes* (often called *payoffs*) that measure the consequences of the various possible actions in terms of the objective function. Each outcome is conditionally dependent on a specific course of action and a specific event.

□ PAYOFF TABLES AND DECISION TABLES

An example may clarify the essential ingredients of a formal model. Suppose a decision maker has two mutually exclusive and exhaustive alternative courses of action regarding the quality-control aspects of a project: accept a unit of product or reject the unit of product. The decision maker also predicts that two mutually exclusive and exhaustive events will affect the outcomes: either the product unit conforms to the quality standards, or it does not conform. The combination of actions, events, and outcomes can be presented in a **payoff table:**

ALTERNATIVE ACTIONS	ALTERNATIVE EVENTS AND OUTCOMES	
	conform	nonconform
Accept	$12[1]	$2[2]
Reject	$ 7[3]	$7[4]

Note: The number references in this table relate to the corresponding numbers in the list that follows.

The outcomes in this example are the dollar contributions to profit; they are assumed to take the pattern shown here because

1. Acceptance and conformance should produce the normal contribution to profit.

2. Acceptance and nonconformance eventually results in expensive rework after the product is processed through later stages, so the contribution is lower.

3. Rejection and conformance results in immediate unnecessary rework that reduces the normal contribution.

4. Rejection and nonconformance results in the same immediate necessary rework described in item 3.

The payoff table includes three of the five ingredients of the formal model: actions, events, and outcomes. The other two ingredients are the probabilities and the choice criterion. Assume that the probability of conform is 0.6 and that of nonconform is 0.4. Assume also that the choice criterion is to maximize the expected value of the outcome, the contribution to profit. The payoff table can now be expanded to a **decision table:**

	EVENTS		
PROBABILITY OF EVENT:	conform 0.6 contribution	nonconform 0.4 contribution	EXPECTED VALUE OF CONTRIBUTION
Actions:			
Accept	$12	$2	$8
Reject	$ 7	$7	$7

Given this model, the decision maker would always accept the product, because the expected value of the outcome is larger for Accept than for Reject. Let $\bar{A}$ = the "average" or expected value;[1] then:

if accept, $\bar{A} = \$12(0.6) + \$2(0.4) = \$7.20 + \$.80 = \$8$

if reject, $\bar{A} = \$7(0.6) + \$7(0.4) = \$4.20 + \$2.80 = \$7$

As you can see, an expected value is simply a weighted average using the probability of each event to weight the outcomes for each action. (Incidentally, $\bar{A}$ is pronounced A-*bar*.)

□ DECISIONS UNDER CERTAINTY

Decisions are frequently classified as those made under certainty and those made under uncertainty. Certainty exists when there is absolutely no doubt

---

[1] An expected value is an arithmetic mean, a weighted average using the probabilities as weights. The formula is

$$\bar{A} = \sum_{x=1}^{n} A_x P_x$$

where A_x is the outcome or payoff or cost or cash flow for the xth possible event or state of nature, P_x is the probability of occurrence of that outcome, $\bar{A}$ is the expected value of the outcome, and n is the number of events.

about which event will occur and when there is a single outcome for each possible action. The payoff table would appear as follows (data assumed):

ACTION	OUTCOME
Buy **A**	$1,000
Buy **B**	1,400
Buy **C**	1,900
Buy **D**	800

Note that there is only one column in the payoff table because there is only one possible event. The decision obviously consists of choosing the action that will produce the best outcome. However, decisions under certainty are not *always* obvious. There are often countless alternative actions, each of which may offer certain outcomes. The problem, then, is finding the best one. For example, the problem of allocating 20 different job orders to 20 different machines, any one of which could do the job, can involve literally *billions* of different combinations. Each way of assigning these jobs is another possible action. The payoff table would have only one outcome *column*, because the costs of production using the various machines are assumed as known; however, it would have 2½ quintillion *rows*. This demonstrates that decision making under certainty can be more than just a trivial problem.

When an outcome is certain for a particular (or given) action, the prediction is a single point with no dispersion on either side. There is a 100 percent chance of occurrence if the action is taken; in other words, the probability is 1.0. For example, the expected cash inflow on the action, buying a federal Treasury note, might be, say, $4,000 for next year. This might be graphed as follows:

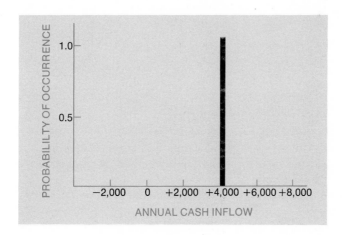

□ DECISIONS UNDER RISK OR UNCERTAINTY

Of course, decision makers must frequently contend with uncertainty rather than certainty; they face a number of possible events, given a particular course of action. The distinction among various degrees of uncertainty centers on the degree of objectivity by which probabilities are assigned. The probabilities may be assigned with a high degree of objectivity.[2] That is, if decision makers know the probability of occurrence of each of a number of events, their assignment of probabilities is "objective," because of mathematical proofs or the compilation of historical evidence. For example, the probability of obtaining a head in the toss of a symmetrical coin is 0.5; that of drawing a particular playing card from a well-shuffled deck, 1/52. In a business, the probability of having a specified percentage of spoiled units may be assigned with great confidence, which is based on production experience with thousands of units.

If decision makers have no basis in past experience or in mathematical proofs for assigning the probabilities of occurrence of the various events, they must resort to the *subjective* assignment of probabilities. For example, the probability of the success or failure of a new product may have to be assessed without the help of any related experience. This assignment is subjective, because no two individuals assessing a situation will necessarily assign the same probabilities. Executives may be virtually certain about the *range* of possible events or possible outcomes, but they may differ about the likelihoods of various possibilities within that range.

The concept of uncertainty can be illustrated by considering two investment proposals on new projects.[3] The manager has carefully considered the risks and has subjectively determined the following discrete probability distribution of expected cash flows for the next year (assume that the useful life of the project is one year):

PROPOSAL A		PROPOSAL B	
probability	cash inflow	probability	cash inflow
0.10	$3,000	0.10	$2,000
0.20	3,500	0.25	3,000
0.40	4,000	0.30	4,000
0.20	4,500	0.25	5,000
0.10	5,000	0.10	6,000

☐ EXPECTED VALUE AND STANDARD DEVIATION

Exhibit 15-1 shows a graphical comparison of the probability distributions. The usual approach to this problem is to compute an **expected value** for each probability distribution.

The expected value of the cash inflow in Proposal A is

$$\bar{A} = 0.1(3,000) + 0.2(3,500) + 0.4(4,000) + 0.2(4,500) + 0.1(5,000)$$
$$= \$4,000$$

---

[2]This is sometimes called decision making under risk, as distinguished from decision making under certainty. The distinction between risk and uncertainty in the current literature and in practice is so blurred that the terms are used interchangeably here.

[3]James C. Van Horne, *Fundamentals of Financial Management*, 4th ed. (Englewood Cliffs, N.J.: Prentice-Hall, 1980, Chap. 15.

EXHIBIT 15-1. Comparison of probability distributions

The expected value for the cash inflow in Proposal B is also $4,000:

$$\bar{A} = 0.1(2,000) + 0.25(3,000) + 0.3(4,000) + 0.25(5,000) + 0.1(6,000)$$
$$= \$4,000$$

Incidentally, the expected value of the cash inflow in the federal Treasury note is also $4,000:

$$\bar{A} = 1.0(4,000) = \$4,000$$

Note that mere comparison of these $4,000 expected values is an oversimplification. These three single figures are not strictly comparable; one represents certainty, whereas the other two represent the expected values over a range of possible outcomes. Decision makers must explicitly or implicitly (by "feel" or hunch) recognize that they are comparing figures that are really representations of probability distributions; otherwise the reporting of the expected value alone may mislead them.[4]

To give the decision maker more information, the accountant could provide the complete probability distribution for each proposal. However, often that course means flooding the manager with too much data for convenient comprehension. Therefore a middle ground is often used. A summary measure of the underlying dispersion is supplied. The conventional measure of the dispersion of a probability distribution for a single variable is the *standard deviation*—the square root of the mean of the squared deviations from the expected value. The standard deviation is denoted by σ, which is *sigma*, the lowercase Greek letter for *s:*

$$\sigma = \sqrt{\sum_{x=1}^{n} (A_x - \bar{A})^2 \, P_x}$$

[4]For example, how would you feel about choosing between the following two investments? First, invest $10 today with a probability of 1.0 of obtaining $11 in two days. Second, invest $10 today with a probability of 0.5 of obtaining $22 in two days and 0.5 of obtaining $0. The expected value is $11 in both cases.

The standard deviation for Proposal A is smaller than that for Proposal B:

$$\text{for a: } \sigma = [0.1(3{,}000 - 4{,}000)^2 + 0.2(3{,}500 - 4{,}000)^2$$
$$+ 0.4(4{,}000 - 4{,}000)^2 + 0.2(4{,}500 - 4{,}000)^2$$
$$+ 0.1(5{,}000 - 4{,}000)^2]^{1/2}$$
$$= [300{,}000]^{1/2} = \$548$$

$$\text{for b: } \sigma = [0.1(2{,}000 - 4{,}000)^2 + 0.25(3{,}000 - 4{,}000)^2$$
$$+ 0.3(4{,}000 - 4{,}000)^2 + 0.25(5{,}000 - 4{,}000)^2$$
$$+ 0.1(6{,}000 - 4{,}000)^2]^{1/2}$$
$$= [1{,}300{,}000]^{1/2} = \$1{,}140$$

$$\text{for the treasury note: } \sigma = \sqrt{1.0(4{,}000 - 4{,}000)^2} = 0$$

A measure of relative dispersion is the *coefficient of variation,* which is the standard deviation divided by expected value. The coefficient for Proposal B is $1{,}140 \div 4{,}000 = 0.29$; for A it is $548 \div 4{,}000 = 0.14$; and for the Treasury note it is $0 \div 4{,}000 = 0$. Therefore, because the coefficient is a relative measure of risk or uncertainty, B is said to have a greater degree of risk than A, which, in turn, has a greater degree of risk than the Treasury note.

□ THE ACCOUNTANT AND UNCERTAINTY

Many accounting practitioners and managers shudder at the notion of using subjective probabilities to quantify things that are supposedly "intangible" or "unmeasurable" or "qualitative" or "unquantifiable." However, their position is weak, simply because decisions *do* have to be made. The attempts by statisticians, mathematicians, and modern accountants to measure the unmeasurable is an old and natural chore that scientists have performed for centuries. The use of subjective probabilities merely formalizes the intuitive judgments and hunches that managers so often use. It forces decision makers to expose and evaluate what they may have done unconsciously for years.

Many statisticians and accountants favor presenting the entire probability distribution directly to the decision maker. Others first divide the information into a threefold classification of optimistic, middle, and pessimistic categories. Still others provide summary measures of dispersion, such as the standard deviation or the coefficient of variation. In any event, we are likely to see the accountant's formal recognition of uncertainty and probability distributions in his or her reporting. In this way, the information will portray underlying phenomena in a more realistic fashion instead of as if there were only a world of certainty.

□ EXAMPLE OF GENERAL APPROACH TO UNCERTAINTY

An example of the general approach to dealing with uncertainty may clarify some of the preceding ideas.

▪ PROBLEM

Once a day, a retailer stocks bunches of fresh-cut flowers, each of which costs 40¢ and sells for $1. The retailer never reduces his price; leftovers are given to a nearby church. He estimates characteristics as follows:

DEMAND	PROBABILITY
0	0.05
1	0.20
2	0.40
3	0.25
4	0.10
5 or more	0.00
	1.00

REQUIRED

The retailer wants to know how many units he should stock in order to maximize profits. Try to solve before consulting the solution that follows.

SOLUTION

The profit, per unit sold, is 60¢; the loss, per unit unsold, is 40¢. All the alternatives may be assessed in the following *decision table.*

EVENTS: DEMAND OF PROBABILITY OF EVENT	0 0.05	1 0.20	2 0.40	3 0.25	4 0.10	EXPECTED VALUE
Actions, Units Purchased:						
0	$ 0	$ 0	$ 0	$ 0	$ 0	$ 0
1	− .40	.60	.60	.60	.60	.55
2	− .80	.20	1.20	1.20	1.20	.90
3	−1.20	− .20	.80	1.80	1.80	.85
4	−1.60	− .60	.40*	1.40	2.40	.55

Example of computation: $(2 \times \$1.00) - (4 \times \$.40) = \$.40$

As shown in an earlier section, the computation of expected value $(\overline{A})$ for each action is affected by the probability weights and the conditional payoff associated with each combination of actions and events:

$$\overline{A} \text{ (Stock 1)} = 0.05(-.40) + 0.20(.60) + 0.40(.60) + 0.25(.60) + 0.10(.60)$$
$$= \$.55$$

$$\overline{A} \text{ (Stock 2)} = 0.05(-.80) + 0.20(.20) + 0.40(1.20) + 0.25(1.20) + 0.10(1.20)$$
$$= \$.90$$

and so on.

To maximize expected payoff, the retailer should stock two units $(\overline{A} = \$.90)$.

☐ OBTAINING ADDITIONAL INFORMATION

Sometimes the executive is hesitant about making a decision. He or she wants more information before making a final choice. Some additional information is nearly always obtainable—at a price. Consider a popular technique for computing the maximum amount that should be paid for such additional information. The general idea is to compute the expected value under ideal circumstances—that is, circumstances that would permit the retailer to predict, with absolute certainty, the number of units to be sold on any given day. A decision table *with perfect information* would appear as follows:

EVENT: DEMAND OF	0	1	2	3	4	EXPECTED
PROBABILITY OF EVENT	0.05	0.20	0.40	0.25	0.10	VALUE
Actions, Units Purchased:						
0	$0					$ 0
1		$.60				.12
2			$1.20			.48
3				$1.80		.45
4					$2.40	.24
Total expected value						$1.29

The total expected value with perfect information is computed as follows:

$$\bar{A} \text{ (perfect information)} = 0.05(0) + 0.20(.60) + 0.40(1.20) + 0.25(1.80) + 0.10(2.40) = \$1.29$$

In this table, it is assumed that the retailer will never err in his forecasts and that demand will fluctuate from zero to four exactly as indicated by the probabilities. The maximum day-in, day-out profit is $1.29. Consequently, the most the retailer should be willing to pay for perfect advance information would be the difference between the expected value with perfect information and the expected value with existing information—$1.29 minus the $.90 expected value computed in the previous example, or 39¢. The latter is usually called the expected value of perfect information, the top price the retailer should pay for additional knowledge.

In the real world, of course, the retailer would not pay 39¢, because no amount of additional information is likely to provide perfect knowledge. But businesses often obtain additional knowledge through sampling, and sampling costs money. The executive needs a method (a) for assessing the probable benefits, in relation to its cost, of additional information from sampling; and (b) for determining the best sample size. In the present example, no sampling technique would be attractive if its cost allocated to each day's operations equaled or exceeded the 39¢ ceiling price.

Linear-programming models

☐ CHARACTERISTICS

Linear programming is a potent mathematical approach to a group of business problems that contain many interacting variables and that basically involve the utilization of limited resources in such a way as to increase profit or decrease cost. There are nearly always limiting factors or scarce resources that are restrictions, restraints, or constraints on available alternatives. Linear programming has been applied to a vast number of business decisions, such as machine scheduling, product mix, raw-material mix, scheduling flight crews, production routing, shipping schedules, transportation routes, blending gasoline, blending sausage ingredients, and designing transformers. In general, linear programming is the best available technique for combining materials, labor, and facilities to best advantage when all the relationships are approximately linear and many combinations are possible.

Note that linear programming is a decision model under conditions of *certainty*, where constraints affect the allocation of resources among competing uses. That is, the model analyzes a total list of actions whose outcomes are known with certainty and chooses the combination of actions that will maximize profit or minimize cost.

☐ THE TECHNIQUES, THE ACCOUNTANT, AND THE MANAGER

All of us are familiar with linear equations (e.g., $X + 3 = 9$). We also know that simultaneous linear equations with two or three unknowns become progressively more difficult to solve with pencil and paper. Linear programming essentially involves (1) constructing a set of simultaneous linear equations, which represent the model of the problem and which include many variables; and (2) solving the equations with the help of the digital computer.

The formulation of the equations—that is, the building of the model—is far more challenging than the mechanics of the solution. The model aims at being a valid and accurate portrayal of the problem. Computer programmers can then take the equations and process the solution.

As a minimum, accountants and executives should be able to recognize the types of problems in their organizations that are most susceptible to analysis by linear programming. They should be able to help in the construction of the model—i.e., in specifying the objectives, the constraints, and the variables. Ideally, they should understand the mathematics and should be able to talk comfortably with the operations researchers who are attempting to express their problem mathematically. However, the position taken here is that the accountant and the manager should concentrate on formulating the model and *analyzing* the solution and not worry too much about the technical intricacies of *obtaining* the solution. The latter may be delegated to the mathematicians; the feasibility and advisability of delegating the former is highly doubtful.

☐ ILLUSTRATION OF PRODUCT MIX

Consider the following illustration: Machine 1 is available for 24 hours, and Machine 2 is available for 20 hours, for the processing of two products. Product X has a contribution margin of $2 per unit; Product Y, $1 per unit. These products must be sold in such combination that the quantity of X must be equal to or less than the quantity of Y. X requires 6 hours of time on Machine 1 and 10 hours of time on Machine 2. Product Y requires 4 hours of time on Machine 1 only. What daily production combination will produce the maximum profit?

The linear-programming approach may be divided into four steps, although variations and shortcuts are available in unique situations:

1. Formulate the objectives. The objective is usually to maximize profit or minimize cost.

2. Determine the basic relationships, particularly the constraints.
3. Determine the feasible alternatives.
4. Compute the optimum solution.

Techniques may differ. In the uncomplicated situation in our example, the graphic approach is easiest to understand. In practice, the *simplex method* is used—a step-by-step process that is extremely efficient. Basically, the simplex method begins with one feasible solution and tests it algebraically, by substitution, to see if it can be improved. These substitutions continue until further improvement is impossible, given the constraints. The optimum solution is therefore achieved.

These four steps may be applied to the example.

Step 1. **Formulate the objectives.** In our case, find the product combination that results in the maximum total contribution margin. Maximize:

$$\text{total contribution margin} = \$2X + \$1Y \qquad (1)$$

This is called the objective function. X represents the number of X product units, and Y represents the number of Y units.

Step 2. **Determine the basic relationships.** The relationships may be depicted by the following inequalities:

For Machine 1:	$6X + 4Y \leq 24$
For Machine 2:	$10X \leq 20$
Sales of X and Y:	$X - Y \leq 0$
Because negative production is impossible:	$X \geq 0 \text{ and } Y \geq 0$

The three solid lines in Exhibit 15-2 will help you to visualize the machine constraints and the product-mix constraint. (To plot a constraint line, assume for Machine 1 that $X = 0$; then $Y = 6$. If $Y = 0$, then $X = 4$. Connect points (0,6) and (4,0) with a straight line.)

Step 3. **Determine the feasible alternatives.** Alternatives are feasible if they are technically possible. We do not want to bother with computations for impossible solutions. The shaded area in Exhibit 15-2 shows the boundaries of the feasible product combinations—that is, combinations of X and Y that satisfy all constraining factors.

Step 4. **Compute the optimum solution.** Steps 2 and 3 focused on physical relationships alone. We now return to the economic relationships expressed as the objective in step 1. We test various feasible product combinations to see which one results in a maximum total contribution margin. It so happens that the best solution must lie on one of the corners of the Area of Feasible Product Combinations in Exhibit 15-2. The corners represent the limits of at least two constraints, so those constraints (resources) are being fully utilized. Intuitively, full utilization suggests optimality. The total contribution margin is calculated for each corner. The steps, which are similar to the simplex method, which uses digital computers, are:

a. Start with one possible combination.
b. Compute the profit.

EXHIBIT 15-2. Linear programming: graphic solution

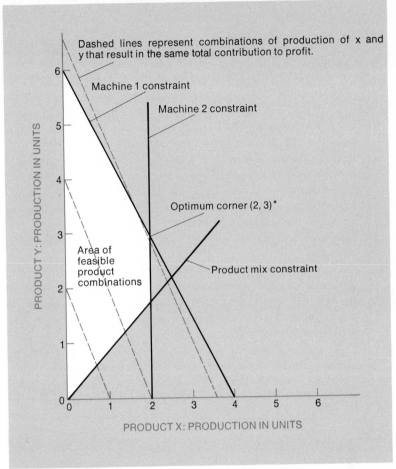

Dashed lines represent combinations of production of x and y that result in the same total contribution to profit.

Machine 1 constraint

Machine 2 constraint

Optimum corner (2, 3)*

Area of feasible product combinations

Product mix constraint

PRODUCT Y: PRODUCTION IN UNITS

PRODUCT X: PRODUCTION IN UNITS

Here, the coordinates of the corners may be obvious. However, if they are not obvious, they can be computed easily by using simultaneous equations for the constraints that intersect at the corners:

Trial 3: (1) $6X + 4Y = 24$
  (2) $10X = 20; X = 2$
  (1) $(6 \times 2) + 4Y = 24$
  (1) $4Y = 24 - 12 = 12; Y = 12 \div 4 = 3$
Thus, coordinates are (2,3).
Trial 4: (2) $10X = 20; X = 2$
  (3) $X - Y = 0$
  (3) $2 - Y = 0; Y = 2$
Thus, coordinates are (2,2).

c. Move to another possible combination to see if it will improve the result in step b. Keep moving from corner to corner until no further improvement is possible. (The simplex method is more efficient because it does not necessitate testing all possible combinations before finding the best solution.)

These steps are summarized below. They show that the optimum combination is two units of X and three units of Y:

TRIAL	CORNER	COMBINATION PRODUCT X	PRODUCT Y	$2X + $1Y = TOTAL CONTRIBUTION MARGIN
1	0,0	0	0	$2(0) + $1(0) = $0
2	0,6	0	6	2(0) + 1(6) = 6
3	2,3	2	3	2(2) + 1(3) = 7
4	2,2	2	2	2(2) + 1(2) = 6

Why must the best solution lie on a corner? Consider all possible combinations that will produce a total contribution margin of $1 ($2X + 1Y = 1). This is a straight line through (0,2) and (1,0). Other total contribution margins are represented by the dashed lines parallel to this one. Their associated total contribution margins increase the further the lines get from the origin. The optimum line is the one furthest from the origin that has a feasible point on it; intuitively, we know that this happens at a corner (2,3). Furthermore, if you put a ruler on the graph and move it parallel with the $1 line, the optimum corner becomes apparent.

As these trials show, the central problem of linear programming is to find the specific combination of variables that satisfies all constraints and achieves the objective sought. Moving from corner to corner (which is really moving from one possible solution to another) implies that the scarce resource, productive capacity, is being transferred between products. Each four-hour period that Machine 1 is productively used to produce one unit of Y may be sacrificed (i.e., given or traded) for one six-hour period required to produce one unit of X. Consider the exchange of twelve hours of time. This means that three units of Y will be traded for two units of X. Will this exchange add to profits? Yes:

Total contribution margin at corner (0, 6)	$6
Additional contribution margin from Product X:	
2 units, @ $2	$4
Lost contribution margin, Product Y:	
3 units, @ $1	3
Net additional contribution margin	1
Total contribution margin at corner (2, 3)	$7

It is not simply a matter of comparing margins per unit of *product* and jumping to the conclusion that the production of Product X, which has the greater margin per unit of product, should be maximized.[5] These substitutions are a matter of trading a given contribution margin per unit of a limiting factor (i.e., a critical resource) for some other contribution margin per unit of a limiting factor.

448

[5]This point is also discussed in Chapter 4 in the section "Contribution to Profit per Unit of Limiting Factor."

Inventory planning and control models

Comprehensive inventory-planning and control systems have been successfully installed in many companies. The major objective of inventory management is to discover and maintain the optimum level of investment in the inventory. Inventories may be too high or too low. If too high, there are unnecessary carrying costs and risks of obsolescence. If too low, production may be disrupted or sales permanently lost. The optimum inventory level is that which minimizes the total costs associated with inventory.

The purchase costs or the manufacturing costs of the inventory (that is, the acquisition costs) would usually be irrelevant to the inventory-control decisions considered here, because we assume that the total annual quantity required would be the same for the various alternatives. Exhibit 15-3 shows the main relevant costs that must be considered, the costs of ordering plus the costs of carrying.

The two significant cost items tend to offset one another. The total relevant costs of carrying, including interest, rise as orders decrease in frequency and grow in size, but the total costs of ordering, delivery, etc., decrease; and vice versa.

□ HOW MUCH TO ORDER?

The two main questions in inventory control are how much to order at a time and when to order. A key factor in inventory policy is computing the optimum

EXHIBIT 15-3

Some Relevant Costs of Inventories

COSTS OF ORDERING

1. Preparing purchase or production orders
2. Receiving (unloading, unpacking, inspecting)
3. Processing all related documents
4. Extra purchasing or transportation costs for frequent orders
5. Extra costs of numerous small production runs, overtime, setups, and training

plus

COSTS OF CARRYING

1. Desired rate of return on investment*
2. Risk of obsolescence and deterioration
3. Storage-space costs
4. Personal property taxes
5. Insurance

Cost that ordinarily does not explicitly appear on formal accounting records.

size of either a normal purchase order for raw materials or a shop order for a production run. This optimum size is called the **economic order quantity,** the size that will result in minimum total annual costs of the item in question. Consider this example:

PROBLEM

A refrigerator manufacturer buys certain steel shelving in sets from outside suppliers at $4 per set. Total annual needs are 5,000 sets at a rate of twenty sets per working day. The following cost data are available:

Desired annual return on inventory investment,		
10% × $4	$.40	
Rent, insurance, taxes, per unit per year	.10	
Carrying costs per unit per year		$ .50
Costs per purchase order:		
Clerical costs, stationery, postage, telephone, etc.		$10.00

What is the economic order quantity?

SOLUTION

Exhibit 15-4 shows a tabulation of total relevant costs under various alternatives. The column with the least cost will indicate the economic order quantity.

Exhibit 15-4 shows minimum costs at two levels, 400 and 500 units. The next step would be to see if costs are lower somewhere between 400 and 500 units—say, at 450 units:

EXHIBIT 15-4

Annualized Relevant Costs of Various Standard Orders (250 working days)

SYMBOLS

E	Order size	50	100	200	400	500	600	800	1,000	5,000
E/2	Average inventory in units*	25	50	100	200	250	300	400	500	2,500
A/E	Number of purchase orders†	100	50	25	12.5	10	8.3	6.3	5	1
S(E/2)	Annual carrying cost @ $.50	$ 13	$ 25	$ 50	$100	$125	$150	$200	$ 250	$1,250
P(A/E)	Annual purchase-order cost @ $10	1,000	500	250	125	100	83	63	50	10
C	Total annual relevant costs	$1,013	$525	$300	$225	$225	$233	$263	$ 300	$1,260

Least cost

E = Order size
A = Annual quantity used in units
S = Annual cost of carrying one unit in stock one year
P = Cost of placing a purchase order
C = Total annual relevant costs

*Assume that stock is zero when each order arrives. (Even if a certain minimum inventory were assumed, it has no bearing on the choice here as long as the minimum is the same for each alternative.) Therefore the average inventory relevant to the problem will be one-half the order quantity. For example, if 600 units are purchased, the inventory on arrival will contain 600. It will gradually diminish until no units are on hand. The average inventory would be 300; the carrying cost, $.50 × 300, or $150.
†Number to meet the total annual need for 5,000 sets.

Average inventory, 225 × $.50   = $113 Carrying costs
Number of orders (5,000/450), 11.1 × $10 =   111 Purchase-order costs
                                                              $224 Total relevant costs

The dollar differences here are extremely small, but the approach is important. The same approach may be shown in graphic form. See Exhibit 15-5. Note that in this case, total cost is at a minimum where total purchase-order cost and total carrying cost are equal.

EXHIBIT 15-5. Graphic solution of economic lot size

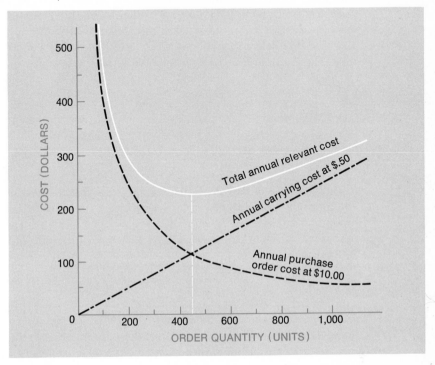

□ ORDER-SIZE FORMULA

The graphic approach has been expressed as a formula (derived via calculus):

$$E = \sqrt{\frac{2AP}{S}}$$

where E = order size; A = annual quantity used in units; P = cost of placing an order; and S = annual cost of carrying one unit in stock for one year.
    Substituting:

$$E = \sqrt{\frac{2(5,000)(\$10)}{\$.50}} = \sqrt{\frac{\$100,000}{\$.50}} = \sqrt{200,000}$$

E = 448, the economic order quantity (often referred to as EOQ)

As we may expect, the order size gets larger as A or P gets larger or as S gets smaller.
    Note in Exhibit 15-5 that the approach to economic lot size centers on

locating a minimum-cost *range* rather than a minimum-cost *point*. *The total-cost curve tends to flatten between 400 and 800 units.* In practice, there is a definite tendency to (a) find the range, and (b) select a lot size at the lower end of the range. In our example, there would be a tendency to select a lot size of 400 or slightly more.

□ WHEN TO ORDER?

Although we have seen how to compute economic order quantity, we have not yet considered another key decision: When to order? This question is easy to answer only if we know the *lead time,* the time interval between placing an order and receiving delivery, know the EOQ, and are *certain* of demand during lead time. The graph in Exhibit 15-6 will clarify the relationships among the following facts:

Economic order quantity	448 sets of steel shelving
Lead time	2 weeks
Average usage	100 sets per week

Exhibit 15-6, Part A, shows that the *reorder point*—the quantity level that automatically triggers a new order—is dependent on expected usage during lead time; that is, if shelving is being used at a rate of 100 sets per week and the lead time is two weeks, a new order will be placed when the inventory level reaches 200 sets.

□ MINIMUM INVENTORY: SAFETY ALLOWANCE

Our previous example assumed that 100 sets would be used per week—a demand pattern that was known with certainty. Businesses are seldom blessed with such accurate forecasting; instead, demand may fluctuate from day to day, from week to week, or from month to month. Thus the company will run out of stock if there are sudden spurts in usage beyond 100 per week, delays in processing orders, or delivery delays. Obviously, then, nearly all companies must provide for some **safety stock**—some minimum or buffer inventory as a cushion against reasonable expected maximum usage. Part B of Exhibit 15-6 is based on the same facts as Part A, except that reasonable expected maximum usage is 140 sets per week. The safety stock might be, say, 80 sets (excess usage of 40 sets per week multiplied by two weeks). The reorder point is commonly computed as safety stock plus the average usage during the lead time.

The foregoing discussion of inventory control revolved around the so-called two-bin or constant-order-quantity system: When inventory levels recede to *X,* then order *Y.* Another widely used model is the constant-order-cycle system. For example, every month, review the inventory level on hand and order enough to bring the quantity on hand and on order up to some predetermined level of units. The reorder date is fixed, and the quantity ordered depends on the usage since the previous order and the outlook during the lead time. Demand forecasts and seasonal patterns should also be considered in specifying the size of orders during the year.

EXHIBIT 15-6. Demand in relation to inventory levels

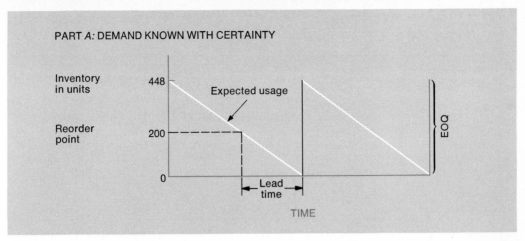

PART A: DEMAND KNOWN WITH CERTAINTY

Inventory in units — 448

Expected usage

Reorder point — 200

EOQ

0

Lead time

TIME

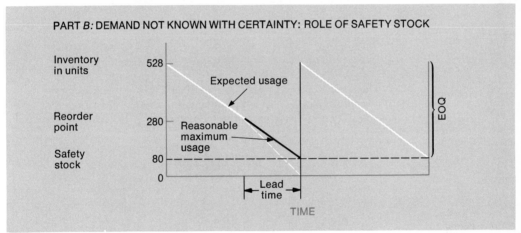

PART B: DEMAND NOT KNOWN WITH CERTAINTY: ROLE OF SAFETY STOCK

Inventory in units — 528

Expected usage

Reorder point — 280

Reasonable maximum usage

Safety stock — 80

EOQ

0

Lead time

TIME

summary

Mathematical decision models are increasingly being used because they replace or supplement hunches with explicit assumptions and criteria. As these decision models become more widely utilized, accounting reports for decision making will tend to give more formal, explicit recognition of uncertainty. For example, the reporting of some measure of probability distributions is more likely.

Accountants often provide inputs to assorted decision models, such as linear-programming models and inventory-control models. Therefore both accountants and managers need to understand the uses and limitations of the models.

summary problem for your review

Review this chapter's examples on statistical probability theory, linear programming, and inventory control by trying to solve them before studying their solutions.

assignment material

FUNDAMENTAL ASSIGNMENT MATERIAL

15-1. Terminology. Define *conditional value; decision table; economic order quantity; expected value; lead time; linear programming; model; payoff table; safety stock.*

15-2. Uncertainty of forecasts. This and other textbooks tend to specify future amounts of revenues and expenses as though they were errorless predictions. For example, a problem might state that "sales are expected to be $X per year." However, the sales personnel may really prepare three predictions:

EVENT	PERCENTAGE CHANCE OF OCCURRENCE	SALES
Optimistic	30%	$1,000,000
Most likely	50	800,000
Pessimistic	20	600,000

REQUIRED | Using an expected-value table, show what predicted sales are for the next year.

15-3. Inventory levels and sales forecasting. Each Sunday, Holman, the proprietor of a sidewalk stand, stocks bunches of fresh flowers, which cost $.80 and sell for $2.00 each. Leftovers are given to a nearby nursing home. Demand characteristics are quite stable, but there is some uncertainty:

DEMAND	PROBABILITY
Less than 60	.00
60	.20
61	.30
62	.40
63	.10
64 or more	.00

REQUIRED | How many units should be stocked to maximize operating income? Show your calculations.

15-4. Perfect information. Suppose Jane Holman, the owner of the sidewalk stand in the preceding problem, could hire a fortune teller who would perfectly forecast the demand each day. Holman would then stock the exact number of bunches of flowers needed. Compute Holman's expected operating income per day. Compute the maximum price she should be willing to pay for perfect information.

15-5. Linear programming. A company manufactures two kinds of precision tools, C (cheap) and E (expensive). The contribution margin of C is \$4 per unit, while E's contribution margin per unit is \$5. The tools are produced in three operations: machining, assembling, and finishing. The following is the average time, in hours, required for each tool:

	MACHINING	ASSEMBLING	FINISHING
C	1	5	3
E	2	4	2
Maximum time available for each operation	700	1,700	850

REQUIRED

Assume that the time available can be allocated to either type of tool. Express the relationships as inequalities. Using graphic analysis, show which product mix will result in the maximum total contribution margin.

■ ADDITIONAL ASSIGNMENT MATERIAL

15-6. "The management accountant must be technically competent in computer technology and modern mathematics." Do you agree? Explain.

15-7. What is a payoff table?

15-8. "I'm not certain what uncertainty is." Explain *uncertainty* briefly.

15-9. Consider the following probability distribution:

DAILY SALES EVENT IN UNITS	PROBABILITY
1,000	0.1
1,500	0.5
2,000	0.2
2,500	0.1
3,000	0.1
	1.0

A student commented: "If a manager has perfect information, he will always sell 3,000 units." Do you agree? Explain.

15-10. Which of the following are linear equations?

$$x + y + 4z + 6a = 8c + 4m$$
$$x^2 = y$$
$$x^2 - y = 4$$
$$4c = 27$$

15-11. What is the minimum competence in linear programming that managers should have?

15-12. "Lead time is the interval between placing an order and the use of inventory." Do you agree? Explain.

15-13. "The major objective of inventory management is to minimize cash outlays for inventories." Do you agree? Explain.

15-14. What are the principal costs of having too much inventory? Too little inventory?

15-15. "The safety stock is the average amount of inventory used during lead time." Do you agree? Explain.

15-16. "If demand and lead time were known with certainty, no safety stock would be needed." Do you agree? Explain.

15-17. Money on the table. The search for oil is a chancy and costly undertaking. For example, in December 1972 the United States government sold a parcel of Louisiana offshore oil leases covering 536,000 acres for $1.6 billion. The previous record was $900 million in the Alaska North Slope in 1969.

The leases are sold on blocks of acreage. Sealed bids are received on various blocks from joint ventures of several oil companies or from a single company. A news item concerning the bidding stated:

> The left-on-the-table aggregate this time came to a stunning $660 million or 40% of the winning total. By far, the most open-handed bidder was the group headed by Shell which grabbed fourteen tracts with bids totaling $230 million or more than twice the $93 million sum of the runner-up bids.

REQUIRED Describe what you think is meant by *money-on-the-table*. Why does it occur? Who collects it?

15-18. Long-distance phone calls. A memorandum from the president of Stanford University contained the following:

> As of October 20, 1972, the placement of person-to-person telephone calls from the University extensions will cease; rather, you are asked to place station-to-station calls instead. . . . We anticipate that this change in policy will save over $30,000 per year in toll charges.
>
> You will be interested to know that for the same cost approximately two station-to-station calls can be made for each person-to-person call. Further, a sampling of Stanford users indicates that there is the probability of 66 ⅔% that a station-to-station call will be successfully completed the first time.

REQUIRED Using the data given, compute the annual Stanford long-distance phone bill for person-to-person calls before the new policy took effect. In all cases, assume that two station-to-station calls will obtain the desired person.

15-19. Probabilities: automatic or semiautomatic equipment. The Clarion Company is going to produce a new product. Two types of production equipment are being considered. The more costly equipment will result in lower labor and related variable costs:

EQUIPMENT	TOTAL ORIGINAL COST	SALVAGE VALUE	VARIABLE COSTS, PER UNIT OF PRODUCT
Semiautomatic	$40,000	—	$4
Automatic	95,000	—	3

Marketing executives believe that this unique product will be salable only over the next year. The unit selling price is $5. Their best estimate of potential sales follows:

TOTAL UNITS	PROBABILITY
30,000	0.2
50,000	0.4
60,000	0.2
70,000	0.2

REQUIRED Prepare an analysis to indicate the best course of action.

15-20. Probabilities and multiple choice. (CMA.) Select the best answer for each of the accompanying items. Show computations where applicable.

The ARC Radio Company is trying to decide whether or not to introduce as a new product a wrist "radiowatch" designed for shortwave reception of exact time as broadcast by the National Bureau of Standards. The "radiowatch" would be priced at $60, which is exactly twice the variable cost per unit to manufacture and sell it. The incremental fixed costs necessitated by introducing this new product would amount to $240,000 per year. Subjective estimates of the probable demand for the product are shown in the following probability distribution:

ANNUAL DEMAND	PROBABILITY
6,000 units	0.2
8,000 units	0.2
10,000 units	0.2
12,000 units	0.2
14,000 units	0.1
16,000 units	0.1

1. The above probability distribution is a
   a. normal distribution
   b. symmetric distribution
   c. continuous distribution
   d. binomial distribution
   e. discrete distribution.
2. The expected value of demand for the new product is
   a. 11,000 units
   b. 10,200 units
   c. 9,000 units
   d. 10,600 units
   e. 9,800 units
3. The probability that the introduction of this new product will not increase company's profit is
   a. 0.00
   b. 0.04
   c. 0.40
   d. 0.50
   e. 0.60

15-21. **Probability assessment and new product.** A new manager, David Fong, has just been hired by the Batten Company. He is considering the market potential for a new toy, Thrillo, which, like many toys, may have great fad appeal.

Fong is experienced in the fad market and is well qualified to assess Thrillo's chances for success. He is certain that sales will not be less than 25,000 units. Plant capacity limits total sales to a maximum of 80,000 units during Thrillo's brief life. Fong thinks that there are two chances in five for a sales volume of 50,000 units. The probability that sales will exceed 50,000 units is four times the probability that they will be less than 50,000.

If sales are less than 50,000, he feels quite certain that they will be 25,000 units. If sales exceed 50,000, unit volumes of 60,000 and 80,000 are equally likely. A 70,000-unit volume is four times as likely as either.

Variable production costs are $3 per unit, selling price is $5, and the special manufacturing equipment (which has no salvage value or alternate use) costs $125,000. Assume, for simplicity, that the above-mentioned are the only possible sales volumes.

REQUIRED

Should Thrillo be produced? Show detailed computations to support your answer.

15-22. **Computation of expected value.** (CMA.) The Unimat Company manufactures a unique thermostat which yields dramatic cost savings from effective climatic control of large buildings. The efficiency of the thermostat is dependent upon the quality of a specialized thermocoupler. These thermocouplers are purchased from Cosmic Company for $15 each.

Since early 19X6, an average of 10 percent of the thermocouplers purchased from Cosmic have not met Unimat's quality requirements. The number of unusable thermocouplers has ranged from 5 to 25 percent of the total number purchased and has resulted in failures to meet production schedules. In addition, Unimat has incurred additional costs to replace the defective units because the rejection rate of the units is within the range agreed upon in the contract.

Unimat is considering a proposal to manufacture the thermocouplers. The company has the facilities and equipment to produce the components. The engineering department has designed a manufacturing system which will produce the thermocouplers with a defective rate of 4 percent of the number of units produced. The schedule presents the engineers' estimates of the probabilities that different levels of variable manufacturing cost per thermocoupler will be incurred under this system. The variable manufacturing cost per unit includes a cost adjustment for the defective units at the 4 percent rate. Additional annual fixed costs incurred by Unimat if it manufactures the thermocoupler will amount to $32,500.

ESTIMATED VARIABLE MANUFACTURING COST PER GOOD THERMOCOUPLER UNIT	PROBABILITY OF OCCURRENCE
$10	10%
12	30
14	40
16	20
	100%

Unimat Company will need 18,000 thermocouplers to meet its annual demand requirements.

REQUIRED

Prepare an expected value analysis to determine whether Unimat Company should manufacture the thermocouplers.

15-23. **Net present values, probabilities, and capital budgeting.** At the recent stockholders' meeting of a large utility company, a stockholder raised the question of the profitability of the satellite communications project undertaken by the company. The project was undertaken two years ago. The president stated that $10 million had been invested in the project in each of the previous years and that an equal amount must be invested in each of the next three years. There would be no income from the project until the total investment was completed. At that time the probability of receiving $4 million cash inflow from operations would be 0.8; the probability of receiving $8 million in the second year after completion would be 0.7; the probability of receiving $15 million in the third year after completion would be 0.6; the probability of receiving $30 million for the following seven years would be 0.5.

This company expects a minimum rate of return of 10 percent on investments.

REQUIRED

As a stockholder, would you have approved of this project when it was first undertaken? Support your answer with figures, using the net-present-value approach.

15-24. **Evaluation of degree of risk: standard deviation and coefficient of variation.** Suppose that you are the manager of a bottling company. You are trying to choose between two types of equipment, F and G. The proposals on the top of the next page have discrete probability distributions of cash flows in each of the next four years.

REQUIRED

1. For each proposal, compute (a) the expected value of the cash inflows in each of the next three years, (b) the standard deviation, and (c) the coefficient of variation.
2. Which proposal has the greater degree of risk? Why?

PROPOSAL F		PROPOSAL G	
probability	net cash inflow	probability	net cash inflow
0.10	$3,000	0.10	$1,000
0.25	4,000	0.25	2,000
0.30	5,000	0.30	3,000
0.25	6,000	0.25	4,000
0.10	7,000	0.10	5,000

15-25. Expected value, standard deviation, and risk. Suppose that the Van Horne Company is planning to invest in a common stock for one year. An investigation of the expected dividends and expected market price has been conducted. The probability distribution of expected returns for the year, as a percentage, is:

PROBABILITY OF OCCURRENCE	POSSIBLE RETURN
0.05	.284
0.10	.224
0.20	.160
0.30	.100
0.20	.040
0.10	−.024
0.05	−.084

REQUIRED

1. Compute the expected value of possible returns, the standard deviation of the probability distribution, and the coefficient of variation.
2. Van Horne could also earn 6 percent for certain on federal bonds. What are the standard deviation and the coefficient of variation of such an investment?
3. Relate the computations in Requirement 1 with those in Requirement 2. That is, what role does the coefficient of variation play in determining the relative attractiveness of various investments?

15-26. Probabilities and costs of rework versus costs of setup. The Schlaifer Company has an automatic machine ready and set to make a production run of 2,000 parts. For simplicity, only four events are assumed possible:

FAULTY PARTS	PROBABILITY
30	0.6
200	0.2
600	0.1
900	0.1

The incremental cost of reworking a faulty part is 20¢. An expert mechanic can check the setting. He can, without fail, bring the faulty parts down to thirty, but this is time-consuming and costs $25 per setting.

Should the setting be checked?

15-27. Cost and value of information. An oil-well driller, Mr. George, is thinking of investing $50,000 in an oil-well lease. He estimates the probability of finding a producing well as 0.4. Such a discovery would result in a net gain of $100,000 ($150,000 revenue − $50,000 cost). There is a 0.6 probability of not getting any oil, resulting in the complete loss of the $50,000.

REQUIRED

1. What is the net expected value of investing?
2. Mr. George desires more information because of the vast uncertainty and the large costs of making a wrong decision. There will be an unrecoverable $50,000 outlay if no oil is found; there will be a $100,000 opportunity cost if he does not invest and the oil is really there. What is the most he should be willing to pay for perfect information regarding the presence or absence of oil? Explain.

15-28. Payoff tables and perfect information. (CMA, adapted.) Vendo, Inc., has been operating the concession stands at a university's football stadium. The university has had successful football teams for many years; as a result the stadium is always full. The university is located in an area that suffers no rain during the football season. From time to time, Vendo has found itself very short of popcorn and at other times it has had many units left. A review of the records of sales of the past nine seasons revealed the following frequency of popcorn sold:

	GAMES
10,000 units	5
20,000 units	10
30,000 units	20
40,000 units	15
	50

Popcorn sells for 50¢ each and costs Vendo 30¢ each. Unsold popcorn is given to a local orphanage without charge.

REQUIRED

1. Assuming that only the four quantities listed were ever sold and that the occurrences were random events, prepare a payoff table (ignore income taxes) to represent the four possible strategies of ordering 10,000, 20,000, 30,000, or 40,000 units.
2. Using the expected value decision rule, determine the best strategy.
3. What is the dollar value of perfect information?

15-29. LP multiple choice. (CMA.) The Marlan Metal Products Company has just established a department for the production of two new products—metal trays and storage devices. This department is ready to begin operations with five metal-forming machines and five metal-cutting machines, which have been rented for $300 each per month from a local machine company. Both products require production time on both machines. Each of the machines is capable of 400 hours of production per month. No additional machines can be obtained.

	MACHINE-HOURS PER UNIT		TOTAL AVAILABLE MACHINE-HOURS PER MONTH
	trays	storage devices	
Metal-cutting machines	1	2	2,000
Metal-forming machines	2	2	2,000

The controller's department has summarized expected costs and revenues as follows:

	trays	storage devices
Selling price per unit	$18	$27
Variable cost per unit	14	20

Demand for the storage devices is unlimited, but Marlan believes that no more than 800 units of the trays can be sold per month.

The following linear-programming formulation and accompanying graph represent the facts described above. Marlan must operate within the specified constraints as it tries to maximize the contribution margin from this new operation. Marlan intends to operate at the optimal level, which it has determined to be the point labeled "OP" on the graph.

maximize Z = $4T + $7S
subject to:

$$T + 2S \le 2,000$$
$$2T + 2S \le 2,000$$
$$T \le 800$$
$$T,S \ge 0$$

where:
T = number of units of trays produced
S = number of units of storage devices produced
Z = contribution margin

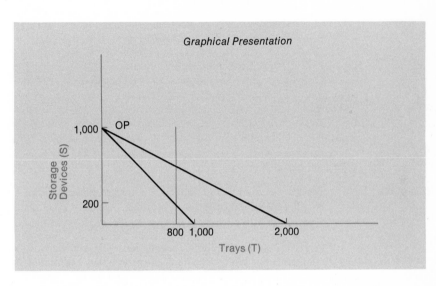

Graphical Presentation

REQUIRED

Select the best answer for each of the following items:

1. If the selling price of storage devices is lowered from $27 to $23, the maximum total contribution margin Marlan could earn would
   a. decrease by $3,800.
   b. decrease by $4,000
   c. increase by $4,000
   d. decrease by $3,200
   e. not be expected to change

2. The maximum amount Marlan should be willing to spend on advertising in order to increase the demand for trays to 1,000 units per month would be
   a. $0
   b. $600
   c. $1,400
   d. $5,400
   e. $7,000

3. If one metal-forming machine is returned to the rental agency and the rent can be avoided on the returned machine, Marlan's total profit would
   a. be unaffected
   b. increase by $300
   c. decrease by $1,100
   d. decrease by $1,400
   e. decrease by $4,300

4. Marlan has just realized that a material needed for the production of both products is in short supply. The company can obtain enough of this material to produce 1,200 trays. Each tray requires 2/3 as much of this material as the storage devices. Which of the following constraints will incorporate completely and correctly this additional information into the formulation of the problem?
   a. T $\le$ 1,200
   b. 2/3 S $\le$ 1,200
   c. T + 2/3 S $\le$ 1,200
   d. 2/3 T + 1 S $\le$ 800
   e. T − 3/2 S = 0

15-30. Production scheduling and linear programming. A factory can produce either Product A or Product B. Machine 1 can produce 15 units of B or 20 units of A per hour. Machine 2 can produce 20 units of B or 12 units of A per hour. Machine 1 has a maximum capacity of 10,000 hours, and Machine 2 a maximum capacity of 8,000 hours.

Product A has a unit contribution margin of 20¢; B, 16¢. There is an unlimited demand for either product; however, both products must be produced together through each machine in a combination such that the quantity of B is at least 20 percent of the quantity of A.

REQUIRED Which combination of products should be produced? Solve by graphic analysis. Express all relationships as inequalities.

15-31. Linear programming and minimum cost. The local agricultural center has advised George Junker to spread at least 4,800 pounds of a special nitrogen fertilizer ingredient and at least 5,000 pounds of a special phosphate fertilizer ingredient in order to increase his crops. Neither ingredient is available in pure form.

A dealer has offered 100-pound bags of VIM @ $1 each. VIM contains the equivalent of 20 pounds of nitrogen and 80 pounds of phosphate. VOOM is available in 100-pound bags @ $3 each; it contains the equivalent of 75 pounds of nitrogen and 25 pounds of phosphate.

REQUIRED Express the relationships as inequalities. How many bags of VIM and VOOM should Junker buy in order to obtain the required fertilizer at minimum cost? Solve graphically.

15-32. Linear-programming formulation. (CMA.) Excelsion Corporation manufactures and sells two kinds of containers—paperboard and plastic. The company produced and sold 100,000 paperboard containers and 75,000 plastic containers during the month of April. A total of 4,000 and 6,000 direct-labor hours were used in producing the paperboard and plastic containers, respectively.

The company has not been able to maintain an inventory of either product, due to the high demand; this situation is expected to continue in the future. Workers can be shifted from the production of paperboard to plastic containers and vice versa, but additional labor is not available in the community. In addition, there will be a shortage of plastic material used in the manufacture of the plastic container in the coming months due to a labor strike at the facilities of a key supplier. Management has estimated there will only be enough raw material to produce 60,000 plastic containers during June.

The income statement for Excelsion Corporation for the month of April is shown on page 463. The costs presented in the statement are representative of prior periods and are expected to continue at the same rates or levels in the future.

REQUIRED 1. The management of Excelsion Corporation plans to use linear programming to determine the optimal mix of paperboard and plastic containers for the month of June to achieve maximum profits. Using data presented in the April income statement, formulate and label the
   a. Objective function
   b. Constraint functions
2. Identify the underlying assumptions of linear programming.
3. What contribution would the management accountant normally make to a team established to develop the linear-programming model and apply it to a decision problem?

15-33. Economic order quantity. (CMA.) Hermit Company manufactures a line of walnut office products. Hermit executives estimate the demand for the double walnut

EXCELSION CORPORATION
Income Statement
For the Month ended April 30, 19X8

	PAPERBOARD CONTAINERS	PLASTIC CONTAINERS
Sales	$220,800	$222,900
Less: Returns and allowances	$ 6,360	$ 7,200
Discounts	2,440	3,450
	$ 8,800	$ 10,650
Net sales	$212,000	$212,250
Cost of sales		
Raw-material cost	$123,000	$120,750
Direct labor	26,000	28,500
Indirect labor (variable with direct-labor hours)	4,000	4,500
Depreciation—machinery	14,000	12,250
Depreciation—building	10,000	10,000
Cost of sales	$177,000	$176,000
Gross profit	$ 35,000	$ 36,250
Selling and general expenses		
General expenses—variable	$ 8,000	$ 7,500
General expenses—fixed	1,000	1,000
Commissions	11,000	15,750
Total operating expenses	$ 20,000	$ 24,250
Income before tax	$ 15,000	$ 12,000
Income taxes (40%)	6,000	4,800
Net income	$ 9,000	$ 7,200

letter tray, one of the company's products, at 6,000 units. The letter tray sells for $80 per unit. The costs relating to the letter tray are estimated to be as follows for 19X7:

1. Standard manufacturing cost per letter tray unit—$50
2. Costs to initiate a production run—$300
3. Annual cost of carrying the letter tray in inventory—20 percent of standard manufacturing cost

In prior years, Hermit Company has scheduled the production for the letter tray in two equal production runs. The company is aware that the economic order quantity (EOQ) model can be employed to determine optimum size for production runs. The EOQ formula as it applies to inventories for determining the optimum order quantity is as follows:

$$\text{EOQ} = \sqrt{\frac{2 \text{ (Annual demand)(Cost per order)}}{\text{(Cost per unit)(Carrying cost)}}}$$

REQUIRED

Calculate the expected annual cost savings Hermit Company could experience if it employed the economic order quantity model to determine the number of production runs that should be initiated during the year for the manufacture of the double walnut letter trays.

15-34. **Inventory control and television tubes.** The Nemmers Company assembles private-brand television sets for a retail chain, under a contract requiring delivery of 100 sets per day for each of 250 business days per year. Each set requires a picture tube, which Nemmers buys outside for $20 each. The tubes are loaded on trucks at the supplier's factory door and are then delivered by a trucking service at a charge of $100 per trip, regardless of the size of the shipment. The cost of storing the tubes (including the desired rate of return on investment) is $2 per tube per year. Because production is stable throughout the year, the average inventory is one-half the size of the truck lot. Tabulate the relevant annual cost of various truck-lot sizes at 5, 10, 15, 25, 50, and 250 trips per year. Show your results graphically. (Note that the $20 unit cost of tubes is common to all alternatives and hence may be ignored.)

15-35. Reorder point. A utility company uses 5,000 tons of coal per year to generate power at one of its plants. The company orders 500 tons at a time. Lead time for the orders is five days, and the safety stock is a three-day supply. Usage is assumed to be constant over a 360-day year. Calculate the reorder point.

15-36. Inventory policy. (CMA.) Breakon, Inc., manufactures and distributes machine tools. The tools are assembled from approximately 2,000 components manufactured by the company. For several years the production schedule called for one production run of each component each month. This schedule has resulted in a high inventory turnover rate of 4.0 times but requires 12 setups for each component every year. In a normal year $3,500 of cost is incurred for each component to produce the number of units sold. The company has been successful in not letting the year-end inventory drop below $100 for each component.

The production manager recommends that the company gradually switch to a schedule of producing the annual needs of each component in one yearly production run. He believes this would reduce costs, because only one setup cost would be incurred each year for every component rather than 12. At the present time the costs for each setup are $36. Estimated annual costs associated with carrying inventory, per $1 of inventory value, are: property tax, 4 percent; insurance, 2 percent; and storage cost, 20 percent. The firm estimates its cost of capital to be 10 percent after taxes and pays income taxes at 40 percent of taxable income.

REQUIRED

1. If Breakon converts to the "once-a-year" production schedule for its components, calculate the total investment released or additional investment required once the changeover is completed.
2. If Breakon converts to the "once-a-year" production schedule, calculate the after-tax savings or added expenses once the changeover is completed.
3. What factors other than those referred to in Requirements 1 and 2 should be considered in reaching a decision to change the production policy?
4. Do your calculations support a change to the proposed policy? Explain your answer.

suggested readings

BIERMAN, HAROLD, and THOMAS R. DYCKMAN, *Managerial Cost Accounting,* 2nd ed. New York: Macmillan, 1976.

DEMSKI, JOEL S., *Information Analysis,* 2nd ed. Reading, Mass.: Addison-Wesley, 1980.

FELTHAM, GERALD A., *Information Evaluation.* Sarasota, Fla.: American Accounting Association, 1972.

HOLLOWAY, CHARLES A., *Decision Making under Uncertainty.* Englewood Cliffs, N.J.: Prentice-Hall, 1979.

HORNGREN, C., *Cost Accounting: A Managerial Emphasis,* 4th ed., Chaps. 14, 24–27. Englewood Cliffs, N.J.: Prentice-Hall, 1977.

LIVINGSTONE, JOHN LESLIE, ed., *Management Planning and Control: Mathematical Models.* New York: McGraw-Hill, 1970.

MILLER, D. W., and M. K. STARR, *Executive Decisions and Operations Research,* 2nd ed. Englewood Cliffs, N.J.: Prentice-Hall, 1969.

STOCKTON, R. STANSBURY, *Introduction to Linear Programming.* Homewood, Ill.: Richard D. Irwin, 1971.

WAGNER, HARVEY M., *Principles of Operations Research with Applications to Managerial Decisions,* 2nd ed. Englewood Cliffs, N.J.: Prentice-Hall, 1975.

part four

basic
financial
accounting
for managers

chapter **16**

BASIC ACCOUNTING: CONCEPTS, TECHNIQUES, AND CONVENTIONS

learning objectives

When you have finished studying this chapter, you should be able to:

1. Identify the meanings and interrelationships of the principal elements of financial statements: assets, liabilities, owners' equity, revenues, expenses, dividends, and others.
2. Analyze typical business transactions to determine their effects on the principal elements of financial statements.
3. Distinguish between the accrual basis of accounting and the cash basis of accounting.
4. Select relevant items from a list of data and assemble them into a balance sheet, an income statement, and a statement of retained income.
5. Distinguish between the reporting of corporate owners' equity and the reporting of owners' equity for partnerships and sole proprietorships.
6. Identify the generally accepted accounting principles and the main conventions that underlie financial reporting for external purposes.

This chapter provides an overview of the accounting process for individuals with little or no background in accounting and for those who want to review some fundamental ideas.[1] We shall become acquainted with some terminology and with what financial statements say and do not say. Knowing what financial statements do *not* communicate is just as important as knowing what they do communicate. We shall mainly be concerned with how to measure the managers' custodial or stewardship responsibilities for the assets entrusted to them. This is basically a scorekeeping task.

This chapter covers the fundamentals without employing some of the bookkeeping techniques (for example, ledger accounts) and language (for example, debit and credit) that are commonplace in accounting. The chapter appendixes probe the ideas of the chapter in greater depth, using a more technical approach.

We consider the essence of profit-making activities and how the accountant portrays them. As we examine what the accountant does, we shall introduce the concepts and conventions that he or she uses. Although the major focus will be on profit-seeking organizations, the main ideas also apply to not-for-profit organizations. Moreover, managers of the latter usually have personal investments in profit-seeking organizations or must interact with businesses in some way.

Entities and accounting transactions

Managers, investors, and other interested groups usually want the answers to two important questions about an organization: How well did the organization perform for a given period of time? and Where does the organization stand at a given point in time? The accountant answers these questions with two major financial statements—an **income statement** and a **balance sheet.** To obtain these statements, he or she continually records the history of an organization. Through the **financial accounting** process, the accountant accumulates, analyzes, quantifies, classifies, summarizes, and reports the seemingly countless events and their effects on the **entity.** An entity is a specific area of accountability. The entity concept is important because accounting usually focuses on the financial impact of events as they affect a particular entity. An example of an entity is a university, which also encompasses many smaller entities such as the School of Law and the School of Engineering.

In terms of their financial impact on economies throughout the world, **corporations** are the principal form of entity. *Corporations* are organizations created by individual state laws. The owners are identified as stockholders (also called shareholders). When approved by the state, the corporation becomes a separate entity, an "artificial person" that conducts its business completely apart from its owners.

The accounting process focuses upon **transactions** as they affect an entity. A *transaction* is any event that affects the financial position of an entity and requires recording. Through the years, many concepts, conventions, and rules

---

[1]The aim of this section of the book (Chapters 16–19) is to provide an introduction and overview of an area that has come to be known as financial accounting. Thus, readers of the companion volume, *Introduction to Financial Accounting,* will find that these chapters provide a review rather than new material. For expanded coverage, see *Introduction to Financial Accounting.*

have been developed regarding what events are to be recorded as *accounting transactions* and how their financial impact is measured. These concepts will be introduced gradually over the remaining chapters.

Financial statements

Financial statements are summarized reports of accounting transactions. They can apply to any point in time and to any span of time.

An efficient way to learn about accounting is to study a specific illustration. Suppose that Retailer No. 1 began business as a corporation on March 1. An opening balance sheet (more accurately called **statement of financial position** or **statement of financial condition**) follows:

RETAILER NO. 1
Balance Sheet (Statement of Financial Position)
As of March 1, 19X1

ASSETS		EQUITIES	
Cash	$100,000	Paid-in capital	$100,000

The balance sheet is a photograph of financial status at an instant of time. It has two counterbalancing sections—assets and equities. **Assets** are economic resources that are expected to benefit future activities. **Equities** are the claims against, or interests in, the assets.

The accountant conceives of the balance sheet as an equation:

$$\text{assets} = \text{equities}$$

The equities side of this fundamental equation is often divided as follows:

$$\text{assets} = \text{liabilities} + \text{owners' equity}$$

The **liabilities** are the economic obligations of the entity. The **owners' equity** is the excess of the assets over the liabilities. For a corporation, the owners' equity is called **stockholders' equity.** In turn, the stockholders' equity is composed of the ownership claim against, or interest in, the total assets arising from any paid-in investment **(paid-in capital),** plus the ownership claim arising as a result of profitable operations **(retained income** or **retained earnings**).

The following is a summary of the *transactions* that occurred in March:

1. Initial investment by owners, $100,000 cash.
2. Acquisition of inventory for $75,000 cash.
3. Acquisition of inventory for $35,000 on open account. A purchase (or a sale) on open account is an agreement whereby the buyer pays cash some time after the date of sale, often in thirty days. Amounts owed on open accounts are usually called **accounts payable.**
4. Merchandise carried in inventory at a cost of $100,000 was sold on open account for $120,000. These open customer accounts are called **accounts receivable.**

5. Collections of accounts receivable, $30,000.

6. Payments of accounts payable, $10,000.

7. On March 1, $3,000 cash was disbursed for store rent for March, April, and May. Rent is $1,000 per month, payable quarterly in advance, beginning March 1.

Note that these are indeed *summarized* transactions. For example, all the sales will not take place at once, nor will purchases of inventory, collections from customers, or disbursements to suppliers. A vast number of repetitive transactions occur in practice, and specialized data-collection techniques are used to measure their effects on the entity.

The above transactions can be analyzed using the balance sheet equation, as shown in Exhibit 16-1.

Transaction 1 has been explained previously. Note, in this illustration, that paid-in capital represents the claim arising from the owners' total initial investment in the corporation.[2]

Transactions 2 and 3, the purchases of inventory, are steps toward the ultimate goal—the earning of a profit. But stockholders' equity is not affected. That is, no profit is realized until a sale is made.

Transaction 4 is the sale of $100,000 of inventory for $120,000. Two things happen simultaneously: A new asset, Accounts Receivable, is acquired (4a) in exchange for the giving up of Inventory (4b).

Transaction 5, the collection, is an example of an event that has no impact on stockholders' equity. It is merely the transformation of one asset (Accounts Receivable) into another (Cash).

Transaction 6, the payment, also has no effect on stockholders' equity—it affects assets and liabilities only. In general, collections from customers and payments to suppliers of the *principal* amounts of debt have no direct impact on stockholders' equity. Of course, as will be seen in a subsequent section, *interest* on debt does affect stockholders' equity as an item of expense.

Transaction 7, the rent disbursement, is made to acquire the right to use store facilities for the next three months. At March 1, the $3,000 measures the future benefit from these services, so the asset *Prepaid Rent* is created (7a). *Assets* are defined as economic resources. They are not confined to items that you can see or touch, such as cash or inventory. Assets also includes legal rights to future services such as the use of facilities.

Transaction 7b recognizes that one-third of the rental services have expired, so the asset is reduced and stockholders' equity is also reduced by $1,000 as rent expense for March. This recognition of rent *expense* means that $1,000 of the asset Prepaid Rent has been "used up" (or has flowed out of the entity) in the conduct of operations during March.

For simplicity, we have assumed no expenses other than *cost of goods sold* and *rent*. The accountant would ordinarily prepare at least two financial statements.

---

[2] Stock certificates usually bear some nominal "par or stated value" that is far below the actual cash invested. For example, the par or stated value of the certificates might be only $10,000; if so, the formal recording of an ownership claim arising from the investment might be split between two subparts, one for $10,000 "capital stock, at par" and another for $90,000 "paid-in capital in excess of par value of capital stock." See the next chapter for additional discussion.

EXHIBIT 16-1 (*Put a clip on this page for easy reference.*)

RETAILER NO. 1
Analysis of Transactions (in dollars)
For March 19X1

| | | assets | | | = | liabilities + | stockholders' equity | |
| | | | | | | | paid-in | retained |
Transactions	cash +	accounts receivable +	inventory +	prepaid rent	=	accounts payable +	capital +	income
1. Initial investment	+100,000				=		+100,000	
2. Acquire inventory for cash	−75,000		+75,000		=			
3. Acquire inventory on credit			+35,000		=	+35,000		
4a. Sales on credit		+120,000			=			+120,000 (revenue)
4b. Cost of inventory sold			−100,000		=			−100,000 (expense)
5. Collect from customers	+30,000	−30,000			=			
6. Pay accounts of suppliers	−10,000				=	−10,000		
7a. Pay rent in advance	−3,000			+3,000	=			
7b. Recognize expiration of rental services				−1,000	=			−1,000 (expense)
Balance, 3/31/X1	+42,000	+90,000	+10,000	+2,000	=	+25,000	+100,000	+19,000
	144,000				=	144,000		

RETAILER NO. 1
Income Statement
For the Month Ended March 31, 19X1

Sales (revenue)		$120,000
Expenses:		
Cost of goods sold	$100,000	
Rent	1,000	
Total expenses		101,000
Net income		$ 19,000

RETAILER NO. 1
Balance Sheet
March 31, 19X1

Cash	$ 42,000	Liabilities: Accounts payable		$ 25,000
Accounts				
receivable	90,000	Stockholders' equity:		
Inventory	10,000	Paid-in capital	$100,000	
Prepaid rent	2,000	Retained income	19,000	119,000
Total assets	$144,000	Total equities		$144,000

Relationship of balance sheet and income statement

The income statement has measured the operating performance of the corporation by matching its accomplishments (revenue from customers, which usually is called *sales*) and its efforts (**cost of goods sold** and other expenses). The balance sheet shows the financial position at an instant of time, but the income statement measures performance for a span of time, whether it be a month, a quarter, or longer. The income statement is the major link between balance sheets:

Examine the changes in stockholders' equity in Exhibit 16-1. The accountant records **revenue** and **expense** so that they represent increases (revenues) and decreases (expenses) in the owners' claims. At the end of a given period, these items are summarized in the form of an income statement.

Each item in a financial statement is frequently called an *account,* so that term will be used occasionally in the rest of this book. In the above example, the outflows of assets are represented by decreases in the Inventory and Prepaid Rent accounts and corresponding decreases in stockholders' equity in the form of Cost of Goods Sold and Rent Expense. Expense accounts are basically negative elements of stockholders' equity. Similarly, the Sales (revenue) account is a positive element of stockholders' equity.

Revenues and expenses

Reflect further on transaction 4. As Exhibit 16-1 shows, this transaction has two phases, a revenue phase (4a) and an expense phase (4b) (dollar signs omitted):

DESCRIPTION OF TRANSACTIONS	ASSETS = EQUITIES	
Balances after Transaction 3 in Exhibit 16-1	135,000 =	135,000
4a. Sales on account (inflow)	Accounts receivable +120,000 = Stockholders' equity,	+120,000
4b. Cost of inventory sold (outflow)	Inventory −100,000 = Stockholders' equity,	−100,000
Balances, after Transaction 4	155,000 =	155,000

Transaction 4a illustrates the realization of *revenue*. *Revenues* are generally gross increases in assets from delivering goods or services. To be **realized** (that is, formally recognized in the accounting records as revenue earned during the current period), revenue must ordinarily meet three tests. First, the goods or services must be fully rendered (for example, delivery to customers). Second, an exchange of resources evidenced by a market transaction must occur (for example, the buyer pays or promises to pay cash and the seller delivers merchandise). Third, the collectibility of the asset (for example, an account receivable) must be reasonably assured.

Transaction 4b illustrates the incurrence of an expense. *Expenses* are generally gross decreases in assets from delivering goods or services. Both revenues and expenses have been characterized as flows of resources (revenues are inflows and expenses are outflows).

Transactions 4a and 4b also illustrate the fundamental meaning of **profits** or **earnings** or **income,** which can simply be defined as the excess of revenues over expenses.

As the Retained Income column in Exhibit 16-1 shows, increases in revenues increase stockholders' equity. In contrast, increases in expenses decrease stockholders' equity. So expenses are negative stockholders' equity accounts.

Transactions 3 and 4 were purchases of merchandise inventory. They were steps toward the ultimate goal—the earning of a profit. But by themselves purchases earn no profit; remember that stockholders' equity was unaffected by the inventory acquisitions in transactions 2 and 3. That is, no profit is realized until a sale is actually made to customers.

Transaction 4 is the $120,000 sale on open account of inventory that had cost $100,000. Two things happen simultaneously: an inflow of assets in the form of accounts receivable (4a) in exchange for an outflow of assets in the form of inventory (4b). Liabilities are completely unaffected, so owners' equity rises by $120,000 − $100,000, or $20,000.

Users of financial statements desire an answer to the question: How well did the organization perform for a given period of time? The income statement helps answer this question. For Retailer No. 1, there has been a change in stockholders' equity attributable solely to operations. This change is measured by the revenue and expenses for the period in question.

The analytical power of the balance sheet equation

As you study Exhibit 16-1, the following points should become clearer about how accountants use the fundamental balance sheet equation as their framework for analyzing and reporting the effects of transactions:

$$\text{assets (A)} = \text{liabilities (L)} + \text{stockholders' equity (SE)} \qquad (1)$$

SE equals original ownership claim plus the increase in ownership claim due to profitable operations. That is, *SE* equals the claim arising from paid-in capital plus the claim arising from retained income. Therefore,

$$A = L + \text{paid-in capital} + \text{retained income} \qquad (2)$$

But, ignoring dividends for the moment, Retained income equals Revenue minus Expenses. Therefore,

$$A = L + \text{paid-in capital} + \text{revenue} - \text{expenses} \qquad (3)$$

Revenue and *expense accounts* are nothing more than subdivisions of stockholders' equity—temporary stockholders' equity accounts, as it were. Their purpose is to summarize the volume of sales and the various expenses, so that management is kept informed of the reasons for the constant increases and decreases in stockholders' equity in the course of ordinary operations. In this way comparisons can be made, standards or goals can be set, and control can be better exercised.

The entire accounting system is based on the simple balance sheet equation. As you know, equations in general possess enormous analytical potential because of the dual algebraic manipulations that they permit. The equation is always kept in balance because of the duality feature.

Exhibit 16-1 illustrates the dual nature of the accountant's analysis. For each transaction, the equation is *always* kept in balance. If the items affected are confined to one side of the equation, you will find the total amount added equal to the total amount subtracted on that side. If the items affected are on both sides, then equal amounts are simultaneously added or subtracted on each side.

The striking feature of the balance sheet equation is its universal applicability. No transaction has ever been conceived, no matter how simple or complex, that cannot be analyzed via the equation. The top technical partners in the world's largest professional accounting firms, when confronted with the most intricate transactions of multinational companies, will inevitably discuss and think about their analyses in terms of the balance sheet equation and its major components: assets, liabilities, and owners' equity (including the explanations of changes in owners' equity that most often take the form of revenues and expenses).

Accrual basis and cash basis

The process of determining income and financial position is anchored to the **accrual basis** of accounting, as distinguished from the **cash basis**. In accrual accounting, the impact of events on assets and equities is recognized in the time periods when services are rendered or utilized instead of when cash is paid or received. That is, revenue is recognized as it is *earned,* and expenses are recognized as they are *incurred*—not when cash changes hands. For example, Transaction 4*a* in Exhibit 16-1 recognizes revenue when sales are made on credit. Similarly, Transactions 4*b* and 7*b* show that expenses are recognized as efforts are expended or services utilized to obtain the revenue (regardless of when cash is disbursed). Therefore income is affected by measurements of noncash resources and obligations. The accrual basis is the principal conceptual framework for matching accomplishments (revenue) with efforts (expenses).

If the cash basis of accounting were used instead of the accrual basis, revenue and expense would depend on the timing of various cash receipts and disbursements. In our Retailer No. 1 example, the March income statement would contain the following:

Revenue (cash collected from customers)		$ 30,000
Expenses:		
Cash disbursed for merchandise ($75,000 in Transaction 2 plus $10,000 in Transaction 6)	$85,000	
Cash disbursement for rent	3,000	
Total expenses		88,000
Net loss		−$58,000

The March 31 balance sheet would have:

Cash	$42,000	Paid-in capital	$ 100,000
		Retained income	−58,000
		Stockholders' equity	$ 42,000

The major deficiencies of the cash basis of accounting are apparent from this example: It ignores the impact on net income and financial position of the liability for accounts payable and the impact of such very real assets as accounts receivable, inventory, and prepaid rent.

Despite the incompleteness of the cash basis of accounting, it is used widely by individuals when they measure their income for personal income tax purposes. For this limited purpose, the cash basis often gives a good approximation of what might also be reported on the accrual basis. Long ago, however, accountants and managers found cash-basis financial statements, such as those above, to be unsatisfactory as a measure of both performance and position. Now more than 95 percent of all business is conducted on a credit basis; cash receipts and disbursements are not the critical transactions as far as the recognition of revenue and expense is concerned. Thus the accrual basis evolved in response to a desire for a more complete, and therefore more accurate, report of the financial impact of various events.

Adjustments to the accounts

To measure income under the accrual basis, the accountant uses **adjustments** at the end of each reporting period. *Adjustments* (also called *adjusting the books, adjusting entries, adjusting the accounts*) may be defined as the key final process that ensures the assignment of financial effects of transactions to the appropriate time periods. Thus adjustments are made at periodic intervals, that is, just before the computation of ending balances when the financial statements are about to be prepared.

Earlier a *transaction* was defined as any economic event that should be recorded by the accountant. Note that this definition is *not* confined to market transactions, which are actual exchanges of goods and services between the entity and another party. For instance, the losses of assets from fire or theft are also transactions even though no market exchange occurs.

Adjustments are a special category of transactions. The principal adjustments may be classified into four types:

I. Expiration of Unexpired Costs
II. Realization (Earning) of Previously Deferred Revenues
III. Accrual of Previously Unrecorded Expenses
IV. Accrual of Previously Unrecorded Revenues

As we shall see, all of these adjustments have an important common characteristic. They reflect **implicit transactions,** in contrast to the **explicit transactions** that trigger nearly all day-to-day routine entries.

To illustrate, entries for credit sales, credit purchases, cash received on account, and cash disbursed on account are supported by explicit evidence. This evidence is usually in the form of **source documents** (for example, sales slips, purchase invoices, employee time records). On the other hand, adjustments for wages, prepaid rent, depreciation, and the like are prepared from special schedules or memorandums that recognize events (like the passage of time) that are temporarily ignored in day-to-day recording procedures.

Adjustments refine the accountant's accuracy and provide a more complete and significant measure of efforts, accomplishments, and financial position. They are an essential part of accrual accounting.

Assets frequently expire because of the passage of time. This first type of adjustment was illustrated in Exhibit 16-1 by the recognition of rent expense in transaction 7b.

Other examples of adjusting for asset expirations include the write-offs to expense of such assets as Office Supplies Inventory, Advertising Supplies Inventory, and Prepaid Fire Insurance. The other three types of adjustments are discussed later in this chapter.

☐ THE MEASUREMENT OF EXPENSES: ASSETS EXPIRE

Transactions 4*b* and 7*b* demonstrate how assets may be viewed as bundles of economic services awaiting future use or expiration. It is helpful to think of assets, other than cash and receivables, as prepaid or stored costs (for example, inventories or plant assets) that are carried forward to future periods rather than immediately charged against revenue:

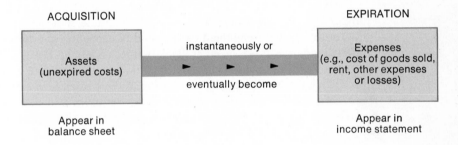

Expenses are used-up assets. Thus assets are **unexpired costs** held back from the expense stream and carried in the balance sheet to await expiration in future periods.

The analysis of the inventory and rent transactions in Exhibit 16-1 maintains this distinction of acquisition and expiration. The unexpired costs of inventory and prepaid rent are assets until they are used up and become expenses.

Sometimes services are acquired and utilized almost instantaneously. Examples are advertising services, interest services (the cost of money, which is a service), miscellaneous supplies, and sales salaries and commissions. Conceptually, these costs should, at least momentarily, be viewed as assets upon acquisition before being written off as expenses. For example, suppose there was an eighth transaction in Exhibit 16-1, whereby newspaper advertising was acquired for $1,000 cash. To abide by the acquisition-expiration sequence, the transaction might be analyzed in two phases:

		ASSETS		= LIABILITIES +	STOCKHOLDERS' EQUITY	
trans-action	cash	+ other assets +	unexpired advertising =		paid-in capital +	retained income
8a.	−1,000		+1,000 =			
8b.			−1,000 =			−1,000 (expense)

Frequently, services are acquired and used up so quickly that accountants do not bother recording an asset such as Unexpired Advertising or Prepaid Rent for them. Instead, a shortcut is taken:

trans-action	cash	+ other assets	= liabilities	+ paid-in capital	+ retained income
8	−1,000		=		−1,000 (expense)

Making the entry in two steps instead of one may seem cumbersome, and it is—from a practical bookkeeping viewpoint. But our purpose is not to learn how to be efficient bookkeepers. We want an orderly way of thinking about what the manager does. The manager acquires goods and services, not expenses *per se.* These goods and services become expenses as they are utilized in obtaining revenue.

Some of the most difficult issues in accounting center on when an unexpired cost expires to become an expense. For example, some accountants believe that research and development costs should be accounted for as unexpired costs (often found on balance sheets as "Deferred Research and Development Costs") and written off (amortized) in some systematic manner over a period of years. But the regulators of financial accounting in the United States have ruled that such costs have vague future benefits that are difficult to measure. Thus, research costs must be written off as expenses immediately; hence, research costs would never be found on balance sheets.

☐ PAUSE FOR REFLECTION

This is an unusually long chapter, so pause. If you have never studied accounting before, or if you studied it long ago, you should not proceed further with your study of this chapter until you have solved the following problem. There are no shortcuts. Pushing a pencil is an absolute necessity for becoming comfortable with accounting concepts. The cost-benefit test will easily be met; your gain in knowledge will exceed your investment of time.

Another suggestion is to do the work on your own. In particular, do not ask for help from any professional accountant if he or she introduces any new terms beyond those already covered. For example, the technical terms of debits, credits, and ledger accounts will only confuse, not clarify, at this stage. Instead, scrutinize Exhibit 16-1. Note how the balance sheet equation is affected by each transaction. Then do the review problem that follows.

summary problem
for your review

PROBLEM ONE

The Retailer No. 1 transactions for March were analyzed early in this chapter. The balance sheet showed the following balances as of March 31, 19X1:

Cash	$ 42,000	
Accounts receivable	90,000	
Inventory	10,000	
Prepaid rent	2,000	
Accounts payable		$ 25,000
Paid-in capital		100,000
Retained income		19,000
	$144,000	$144,000

The following is a summary of the transactions that occurred during the next month, April:

1. Collections of accounts receivable, $88,000.
2. Payments of accounts payable, $24,000.
3. Acquisitions of inventory on open account, $80,000.
4. Merchandise carried in inventory at a cost of $70,000 was sold on open account for $85,000.
5. Adjustment for recognition of rent expense for April.
6. Some customers paid $3,000 in advance for merchandise they ordered but that is not expected in inventory until mid-May. (What asset must rise? Does this transaction increase liabilities or stockholders' equity?)
7. Total wages of $6,000 (which were ignored for simplicity in March) were paid on four Fridays in April. These payments for employee services were recognized by increasing Wages Expense and decreasing Cash.
8. Wages of $2,000 were incurred near the end of April, but the employees had not been paid as of April 30. Accordingly, the accountant increased Wages Expense and increased a liability, Accrued Wages Payable.
9. Cash dividends declared and disbursed to stockholders on April 29 equaled $18,000. (What account besides Cash is affected?)

REQUIRED

1. Using the *accrual basis* of accounting, prepare an analysis of transactions, employing the equation approach demonstrated in Exhibit 16-1. To have plenty of room for new accounts, put your analysis sideways.
2. Prepare a balance sheet as of April 30, 19X1, and an income statement for the month of April. Also prepare a new report, the Statement of Retained Income, which should show the beginning balance, followed by a description of any major changes, and end with the balance as of April 30, 19X1.
3. Using the *cash basis* of accounting, prepare an income statement for April. Compare the net income with that computed in Requirement 2. Which net income figure do you prefer as a measure of the economic performance for April? Why?

Entries 6 through 9 and the statement of retained income have not been explained. However, as a learning step, try to respond to the requirements here anyway. Explanations follow almost immediately.

Part 1. *Analysis of transactions.* The answer is in Exhibit 16-2. The first five transactions are straightforward extensions or repetitions of the March transactions. But the rest of the transactions are new. They are discussed in the sections that follow the solutions to the second and third parts of this problem.

Part 2. *Preparation of financial statements.* See Exhibits 16-3, 16-4, and 16-5. The first two of these exhibits show financial statements already described in this chapter: the balance sheet and the income statement. Exhibit 16-5 presents a new statement, the *Statement of Retained Income,* which is merely a formal reconciliation of the retained income. It consists of the beginning balance, adds net income for the period in question, and deducts cash dividends to arrive at the ending balance. Frequently, this statement is tacked on to the bottom of an income statement. If so, the result is a *combined* statement of income and statement of retained income.

Part 3. *Cash basis income statement.* See Exhibit 16-6. The net income is $61,000 on the cash basis, but only $6,000 on the accrual basis. Accountants prefer the accrual basis because it provides a more complete and precise measurement of economic performance, a better matching of accomplishments with efforts. For example, the timing of disbursements to reduce accounts payable obviously is not as closely related to sales in April as the cost of inventory that was sold.

Accounting for deferred revenue

Entry 6 is an example of **deferred revenue,** sometimes called **unearned revenue,** which is a liability because the retailer is obligated to deliver the goods ordered or to refund the money if the goods are not delivered. Some managers might prefer to call this account *advances from customers,* or *customer deposits,* instead of *deferred sales revenue,* but it is a deferred revenue account no matter what its label. That is, it is revenue collected in advance that has not been earned as yet. Advance collections of rent and magazine subscriptions are other examples.

Sometimes it is easier to see how accountants analyze transactions by visualizing the financial positions of both parties to a contract. For instance, for the rent transaction of March 1 compare the financial impact on Retailer No. 1 with the impact on the landlord who received the rental payment:

	LANDLORD				RETAILER NO. 1		
	A	=	L	+ SE	A	= L	+ SE
	cash		deferred rent revenue	rent revenue	cash	prepaid rent	rent expense
1. Prepayment	+3,000	=	+3,000		−3,000	+3,000 =	
2. March expiration		=	−1,000	+1,000		−1,000 =	−1,000
3. April expiration		=	−1,000	+1,000		−1,000 =	−1,000

You are already familiar with the Retailer No. 1 analysis. The $1,000 monthly entries for Retailer No. 1 are examples of the first type of adjustments, the expiration of unexpired costs.

Study the transactions from the viewpoint of the owner of the rental prop-

EXHIBIT 16-2 *(Place a clip on this page for easy reference.)*

RETAILER NO. 1
Analysis of Transactions (In dollars)
For April 19X1

Transaction	cash	+ accounts receivable	+ inventory	+ prepaid rent	=	accounts payable	+ accrued wages payable	+ deferred sales revenue*	paid-in capital	+ retained income
Bal. 3/31/X1	+42,000	+90,000	+10,000	+2,000	=	+25,000			+100,000	+19,000
1.	+88,000	−88,000			=					
2.	−24,000				=	−24,000				
3.			+80,000		=	+80,000				
4a.		+85,000			=					+85,000 (revenue)
4b.			−70,000		=					−70,000 (expense)
5.				−1,000	=					− 1,000 (expense)
6.	+3,000				=			+3,000*		
7.	−6,000				=					− 6,000 (expense)
8.					=		+2,000			− 2,000 (expense)
9.	−18,000				=					−18,000 (dividend)
Bal. 4/30/X1	+85,000	+87,000	+20,000	+1,000	=	+81,000	+2,000	+3,000	+100,000	+7,000
	193,000									193,000

assets = liabilities + stockholder's equity

Some managers and accountants would call this account "Customer Deposits" or "Advances from Customers."

EXHIBIT 16-3

ASSETS		EQUITIES		
Cash	$ 85,000	Liabilities:		
Accounts receivable	87,000	Acounts payable	$ 81,000	
Inventory	20,000	Accrued wages		
Prepaid rent	1,000	payable	2,000	
		Deferred sales		
		revenue	3,000	$ 86,000
		Stockholders' equity:		
		Paid-in capital	$100,000	
		Retained income	7,000	107,000
Total assets	$193,000	Total equities		$193,000

EXHIBIT 16-4

Sales		$85,000
Cost of goods sold		70,000
Gross profit		$15,000
Operating expenses:		
Rent	$1,000	
Wages	8,000	9,000
Net income		$ 6,000

*A **"single-step" statement** *would not draw the gross profit figure but would merely list all the expenses—including cost of goods sold—and deduct the total from sales.* **Gross profit** *is defined as the excess of sales over the cost of the inventory that was sold. It is sometimes called* **gross margin.**

EXHIBIT 16-5

Retained income, March 31, 19X1	$19,000
Net income for April	6,000
Total	$25,000
Cash dividends	18,000
Retained income, April 30, 19X1	$ 7,000

EXHIBIT 16-6

RETAILER NO. 1
Income Statement (Cash Basis)
For the Month Ended April 30, 19X1

Sales (collections from customers, including advance payments)		$91,000
Expenses:		
Disbursements for merchandise	$24,000	
Wages	6,000	30,000
Net income		$61,000

erty. The first transaction recognizes *deferred revenue,* sometimes called *unearned revenue,* which is a *liability* because the lessor is obligated to deliver the rental services (or to refund the money if the services are not delivered).

The first two types of adjustments are often really mirror images of each other. If one party to a contract has a prepaid expense, the other has a deferred revenue. A similar analysis could be conducted for, say, a three-year fire insurance policy or a three-year magazine subscription. The buyer recognizes a prepaid expense (asset) and uses adjustments to spread the initial cost to expense over the useful life of the services. In turn, the seller, such as a magazine publisher, must initially recognize its liability, Deferred Subscription Revenue. The *deferred* revenue is then systematically recognized as *earned* revenue as magazines are delivered throughout the life of the subscription. The diagrams below show that explicit cash transactions in such situations are initially recognized as balance sheet items and are later transformed into income statement items via periodic adjustments:

You have now seen how two types of adjustments might occur: (1) expiration of unexpired costs and (2) realization (earnings) of previously deferred revenues. Next we consider the third type of adjustment: accrual of previously unrecorded expenses, as illustrated by wages.

Accrual of previously unrecorded expenses (wages)

An entity usually "incurs" an expense and "accrues" a debt or liability during a given period even though no explicit transaction occurs. Examples are wages of employees and interest on borrowed money. The liabilities grow as the clock ticks or as some services are continuously acquired and used, so they are said to **accrue** (accumulate).

It is awkward and unnecessary to make hourly, daily, or even weekly formal recordings in the accounts for many accruals. Consequently, a series of adjustments are made to bring each expense (and corresponding liability) account up to date just before the formal financial statements are prepared.

☐ ACCOUNTING FOR PAYMENT OF WAGES

Consider wages. Most companies pay their employees at predetermined times. Here is a sample calendar for April:

APRIL						
S	M	T	W	T	F	S
	1	2	3	4	5	6
7	8	9	10	11	12	13
14	15	16	17	18	19	20
21	22	23	24	25	26	27
28	29	30				

Suppose Retailer No. 1 pays its employees each Friday for services rendered during that week. For example, wages paid on April 26 would be compensation for the week ended April 26. The cumulative total wages paid on the Fridays during April were $6,000. Although day-to-day and week-to-week procedures may differ from entity to entity, a popular way to account for wages expense is the shortcut procedure described earlier for goods and services that are routinely consumed in the period of their purchase:

assets (A) = liabilities (L) + stockholders' equity (SE)

	cash		wages expense
7. Routine entry for explicit transactions	−6,000	=	−6,000

☐ ACCOUNTING FOR ACCRUAL OF WAGES

The company expanded its work force on April 29. Moreover, in addition to the $6,000 already paid, Retailer No. 1 owes $2,000 for employee services rendered during the last two days of April. The employees will not be paid for these services until May. No matter how simple or complex a set of accounting procedures may be in a particular entity, periodic adjustments ensure that the financial statements adhere to accrual accounting. The tabulation that follows repeats entry 7 for convenience and then adds entry 8.

	A	=	L	+	SE
	cash		accrued wages payable		wages expense
7. Routine entry for explicit transactions	−6,000	=			−6,000
8. Adjustment for implicit transaction, the accrual of previously unrecorded wages		=	+2,000		−2,000
Total effects	−6,000	=	+2,000		−8,000

Entry 8 is the first example in this book of the impact of the analytical shortcut that bypasses the asset account and produces an expense that is offset by an increase in a liability. Conceptually, entries 7 and 8 could each be subdivided into the asset acquisition–asset expiration sequence, but this two-step sequence is not generally used in practice for such expenses that represent the immediate consumption of services.

Other examples of accrued expenses include sales commissions, property taxes, income taxes, and interest on borrowed money. Interest is rent paid for the use of money, just as rent is paid for the use of buildings or automobiles. The interest accumulates (accrues) as time unfolds, regardless of when the actual cash for interest is paid.

Accrual of previously unrecorded revenues

The final type of adjustment, which is not illustrated in the "Summary Problem for Your Review," is the realization of revenues that have been earned but not yet shown in the accounts. It is the mirror image of the accrual of previously unrecorded expenses. Consider a financial institution that lends cash to Retailer No. 1 on a three-month promissory note for $50,000 with interest at 1.5 percent per month payable at maturity. The following tabulation shows the mirror-image effect of the adjustment for interest at the end of the first month (.015 × $50,000 = $750):

FINANCIAL INSTITUTION, AS A LENDER			RETAILER NO. 1 AS A BORROWER		
A	= L +	SE	A =	L	+	SE
accrued interest receivable		interest revenue		accrued interest payable	interest expense
+750	=	+750		=	+750	−750

To recapitulate, you have now seen examples of the four major types of the adjustments needed to implement the accrual basis of accounting:

TYPE	DESCRIPTION	ILLUSTRATION
1	Expiration of unexpired costs	Rent expense (Exhibit 16-2, page 481, entry 5)
2	Realization (earning) of previously deferred revenues	The mirror image of type 1, whereby the landlord recognizes rent revenue and decreases deferred rent revenue (rent collected in advance)
3	Accrual of previously un-recorded expenses	Wage expense (Exhibit 16-2, entry 8)
4	Accrual of previously un-recorded revenues	Interest revenue earned but un-collected by a financial institu-tion

Dividends and retained income

☐ DIVIDENDS ARE NOT EXPENSES

As transaction 9 shows, cash dividends are not expenses like rent and wages. They should not be deducted from revenues because dividends are not directly related to the generation of sales or the conduct of operations. Cash dividends are distributions of assets to stockholders that reduce retained income. The abil-ity to pay dividends is fundamentally caused by profitable operations. Retained income increases as profits accumulate and decreases as dividends occur.

The entire right-hand side of the balance sheet can be thought of as claims against the total assets. The liabilities are the claims of creditors. The stockhold-ers' equity represents the claims of owners arising out of their initial investment (paid-in capital) and subsequent profitable operations (retained income). **Re-tained income** is also called **retained earnings, undistributed earnings,** or **reinvested earnings.** As a company grows, this account can soar enormously if dividends are not paid. Retained income can easily be the largest stockholders' equity account.

☐ RETAINED INCOME IS NOT CASH

Retained income is *not* a pot of cash that is awaiting distribution to stockholders. Consider the following illustration:

Step 1. Assume an opening balance sheet of:

Cash	$100	Paid-in capital	$100

Step 2. Purchase inventory for $50 cash. The balance sheet now reads:

Cash	$50	Paid-in capital	$100
Inventory	50		
	$100		

Steps 1 and 2 demonstrate a fundamental point. Ownership equity is an undivided claim against the total assets (in the aggregate). For example, half the shareholders do not have a specific claim on cash, and the other half do not have a specific claim on inventory. Instead, all the shareholders have an undivided claim against (or, if you prefer, an undivided interest in) all the assets.

Step 3. Now sell the inventory for $80:

Cash	$130	Paid-in capital	$100
		Retained income	30
		Total equities	$130

At this stage, the retained income might be reflected by a $30 increase in cash. But the $30 in retained income connotes only a *general* claim against *total* assets. This may be clarified by the transaction that follows.

Step 4. Purchase equipment and inventory, in the amounts of $40 and $50, respectively. Now:

Cash	$ 40	Paid-in capital	$100
Inventory	50	Retained income	30
Equipment	40		
Total assets	$130	Total equities	$130

Where is the $30 in retained income reflected? Is it reflected in Cash, in Inventory, or in Equipment? The answer is indeterminate. This example helps to explain the nature of the Retained Income account. It is a *claim,* not a pot of gold. Retained income is increased by profitable operations, but the cash inflow from sales is an increment in assets (see step 3). When the cash inflow takes place, management will use the cash, most often to buy more inventory or equipment (step 4). Retained income is a *general* claim against, or undivided interest in, *total* assets, *not* a specific claim against cash or against any other particular asset.

A term that is virtually archaic, **earned surplus,** is sometimes still found in stockholders' equity sections. Fortunately, its use is fading fast. Earned surplus is an interchangeable term for retained income. The trouble with the term is that *surplus* is misleading. It connotes something superfluous or unessential or left over; therefore, consequent misunderstandings of the term might be expected. As the above example shows, earned surplus (retained income) is not an asset, nor does it represent an unnecessary ownership interest.

As stated above, **dividends** are distributions of assets that reduce ownership claims. The cash assets that are distributed typically arose from profitable operations. Thus dividends or withdrawals are often spoken of as "distributions of profits" or "distributions of retained income." Dividends are often erroneously described as being "paid *out of* retained income." In reality, cash dividends are distributions of assets and liquidate a portion of the ownership claim. The distribution is made possible by profitable operations.

The amount of cash dividends declared by the board of directors of a company depends on many factors, the least important of which is the balance in Retained Income. Although profitable operations are generally essential, dividend policy is also influenced by the company's cash position and future needs for cash to pay debts or to purchase additional assets. It is also influenced by whether the company is committed to a stable dividend policy or to a policy that normally ties dividends to fluctuations in net income. Under a stable policy, dividends may be paid consistently even if a company encounters a few years of little or no net income.

Proprietorships and partnerships

The owners' equity section of the balance sheet can be affected by four basic types of transactions, (1) investments, (2) withdrawals, (3) revenues, and (4) expenses:

Assets = Liabilities + Owners' Equity

−Owners' withdrawals + Owners' investments
(e.g., corporate cash
dividends)
−Expenses + Revenues

The basic accounting concepts that underlie the owners' equity are unchanged regardless of whether ownership takes the form of a corporation, sole proprietorship, or partnership. However, in **proprietorships** and **partnerships,** distinctions between contributed capital (that is, the investments by owners) and retained income are rarely made. Compare the possibilities for Retailer No. 1 as of April 30:

Owners' Equity for a Corporation

Stockholders' equity:		
Capital stock (paid-in capital)	$100,000	
Retained income	7,000	
Total stockholders' equity		$107,000

Owners' Equity for a Sole Proprietorship

Alice Walsh, capital	$107,000

Owners' Equity for a Partnership

Susan Zingler, capital	$ 53,500
John Martin, capital	53,500
Total partners' equity	$107,000

In contrast to corporations, sole proprietorships and partnerships are not legally required to account separately for contributed capital (that is, proceeds from issuances of capital stock) and for retained income. Instead, they typically accumulate a single amount for each owner's original investments, subsequent investments, share of net income, and withdrawals. In the case of a sole proprietorship, then, the owner's equity will consist of a lone capital account.

Other terms for owners' equity are **equity capital** and **net worth.** The latter term is fading (the faster, the better). Net worth is a poor term because it implies that the owners' equity is a measure of the "current value" of the business. The total owners' equity is a measure of the ownership claim against the total assets, but it does not necessarily yield an accurate approximation of what some outsider is willing to pay for such an ownership interest. The selling price of a business is the subject of independent bargaining that seldom has a direct relationship to the accounting records of the assets or equities of the entity.

Nonprofit organizations

The examples in this chapter have focused on profit-seeking organizations, but balance sheets and income statements are also used by not-for-profit organizations. For example, hospitals and universities have income statements, although they are called *statements of revenue and expense*. The "bottom line" is frequently called "excess of revenue over expense" rather than "net income."

The basic concepts of assets, liabilities, revenue, and expense are applicable to all organizations, whether they be utilities, symphony orchestras, private, public, American, Asian, and so forth. However, some nonprofit organizations have been slow to adopt several ideas that are widespread in progressive companies. For example, in many governmental organizations the accrual basis of accounting has not supplanted the cash basis. This has hampered the evaluation of the performance of such organizations.

Generally accepted accounting principles

☐ "PRINCIPLES" IS A MISNOMER

The financial statements of publicly held corporations and many other corporations are subject to an independent **audit** that forms the basis for a professional accounting firm's opinion, typically including the following key phrasing:

> In our opinion, the accompanying financial statements present fairly the financial position of the ABC Company at December 31, 19X1, and the results of its operations for the year then ended, in conformity with generally accepted accounting principles applied on a basis consistent with that of the preceding year.

We will explore the meaning of such key phrases as "present fairly" and "generally accepted accounting principles." Reflect on the fact that the accounting firm must conduct an audit before it can render the above opinion. An *audit* is an "examination" that is made in accordance with generally accepted auditing standards (which have been developed primarily by the American Institute of Certified Public Accountants). Such examination includes miscellaneous tests of the accounting records, internal control systems, and other auditing procedures as deemed necessary. The examination culminates with the rendering of the accountant's **independent opinion.** This opinion (sometimes called **certificate**) is the accountant's stamp of approval on *management's* financial statements.

The auditor's opinion, usually appearing at the end of annual reports prepared for stockholders and other external users, is often mistakenly relied on as an infallible guarantee of financial truth. Somehow accounting is thought to be an exact science, perhaps because of the aura of precision that financial statements possess. But accounting is more art than science. The financial reports may appear accurate because of their neatly integrated numbers, but they are the results of a complex measurement process that rests on a huge bundle of assumptions and conventions called **generally accepted accounting principles (GAAP).**

What are these generally accepted accounting principles? This technical term covers much territory. It includes both broad concepts or guidelines and detailed practices. It includes all conventions, rules, and procedures that together make up accepted accounting practice at any given time.

Accounting principles become "generally accepted" by agreement. Such agreement is not influenced solely by formal logical analysis. Experience, custom, usage, and practical necessity contribute to the set of principles. Accordingly, it might be better to call them *conventions,* because principles connotes that they are the product of airtight logic.

☐ FASB, APB, AND SEC

Every technical area seems to have regulatory bodies or professional associations whose names are often abbreviated. Accounting is no exception.

During the 1970s and 1980s, American generally accepted accounting principles have been most heavily influenced by the **Financial Accounting Standards Board (FASB)** and its predecessor body, the **Accounting Principles Board (APB).** The FASB consists of seven qualified individuals who work full time. The board is supported by a large staff and an annual $10 million budget.

The board is an independent creature of the private sector and is financially supported by various professional accounting associations (such as the leading organization of the auditors, the American Institute of Certified Public Accountants, the AICPA).

The FASB was established in 1973 as the replacement for the Accounting Principles Board (APB). The APB consisted of a group of eighteen accountants (mostly partners in large accounting firms) who worked part time. The board issued a series of thirty-one opinions during 1962–73, many of which are still the accounting law of the land. Many of these **APB Opinions** and **FASB Statements** will be referred to in succeeding chapters of this book.

The U.S. Congress has designated the **Securities and Exchange Commission (SEC)** as holding the ultimate responsibility for authorizing the generally accepted accounting principles for companies whose stock is held by the general investing public. However, the SEC has informally delegated much rule-making power to the FASB. This public sector–private sector relationship may be sketched as follows:

Issues pronouncements on various accounting issues. These pronouncements govern the preparation of typical financial statements.

Independent auditing firms **(Certified Public Accountants)** issue opinions concerning the fairness of financial statements prepared for external use (for example, corporate annual reports). These auditors are required to see that the statements do not depart from the FASB Statements and the APB Opinions.

Reconsider the three-tiered structure above. Note that Congress can overrule both the SEC and the FASB, and the SEC can overrule the FASB. Such undermining of the FASB occurs rarely, but pressure is exerted on all three tiers by corporations if they think an impending pronouncement is "wrong." Hence the setting of accounting principles is a complex process involving heavy interactions among the affected parties: public regulators (Congress and SEC), private regulators (FASB), companies, the public accounting profession, representatives of investors, and other interested groups.[3]

In sum, the public body (the SEC) has informally delegated much rulemaking power regarding accounting theory to the private bodies (the APB and FASB). These boards have rendered a series of pronouncements on various accounting issues. Independent auditing firms, which issue opinions concerning the fairness of corporate financial statements prepared for external use, are required to see that corporate statements do not depart from these pronouncements.

Three measurement conventions

Three broad measurement or valuation conventions (principles) establish the basis for implementing accrual accounting: realization (when to recognize revenue), matching (when to recognize expense), and the stable dollar (what unit of measure to use).

[3]For a fuller description, see the following in the *Journal of Accountancy* by Charles T. Horngren: "Accounting Principles: Private or Public Sector?" May 1972; "The Marketing of Accounting Standards," October 1973; and "Will the FASB Be There in the 1980s?" November 1976.

☐ REALIZATION

The first broad measurement or valuation convention, *realization,* was discussed earlier in this chapter in the section "Revenues and Expenses." In general, revenue is realized when the goods or services in question are delivered to customers.

☐ MATCHING AND COST RECOVERY

Generally accepted accounting principles are based on the concepts of accrual accounting described earlier in this chapter. You may often encounter a favorite buzzword in accounting: **matching.** The process of matching is the relating of accomplishments or revenues (as measured by the selling prices of goods and services delivered) and efforts or expenses (as measured by the cost of goods and services used) to a *particular period* for which a measurement of income is desired. In short, matching is a short description of the accrual basis for measuring income.

The heart of recognizing expense is the **"cost recovery"** concept. That is, assets such as inventories, prepayments, and equipment are carried forward as assets because their costs are expected to be recovered in the form of cash inflows (or reduced cash outflows) in future periods. At the end of each period, the accountant (especially the outside auditor at the end of each year) carefully examines the evidence to be assured that these assets—these prepaid costs—should not be written off as an expense of the current period. For instance, in our chapter example, prepaid rent of $2,000 was carried forward as an asset as of March 31 because the accountant is virtually certain that it represents a future benefit. Why? Because without the prepayment, cash outflows of $2,000 would have to be made for April and May. So the presence of the prepayment is a benefit in the sense that future cash outflows will be reduced by $2,000. Furthermore, future revenue (sales) will be high enough to ensure the recovery of the $2,000.

☐ STABLE MONETARY UNIT

The monetary unit (the dollar in the United States, Canada, Australia, New Zealand, and elsewhere) is the principal means for measuring assets and equities. It is the common denominator for quantifying the effects of a wide variety of transactions. Accountants record, classify, summarize, and report in terms of the dollar.

Such measurement assumes that the principal counter—the dollar—is an unchanging yardstick. Yet we all know that a 1980 dollar does not have the same purchasing power as a 1970 or 1960 dollar. Therefore accounting statements that include different dollars must be interpreted and compared with full consciousness of the limitations of the basic measurement unit. (For an expanded discussion, see Chapter 19.)

Accountants have been extensively criticized for not making explicit and formal adjustments to remedy the defects of their measuring unit. In the face of this, some accountants maintain that price-level adjustments would lessen objectivity and would add to the general confusion. They claim that the price-level problem has been exaggerated, and that the adjustments would not significantly affect the vast bulk of corporate statements because most accounts are in current or nearly current dollars.

On the other hand, inflation has been steady and its effects are sometimes surprisingly pervasive. We can expect to see increasing experimentation with reporting that measures the effects of changes in the general economywide price level and in the prices of specific assets. The most troublesome aspect, however, is how to interpret the results after they are measured. Investors and managers are accustomed to the conventional statements. The intelligent interpretation of statements adjusted for changes in the price level will require extensive changes in the habits of users.

The body of generally accepted accounting principles contains more than just the measurement conventions just discussed. Other major concepts include going concern, objectivity, materiality, and cost-benefit. These are discussed in the first appendix of this chapter.

summary

An underlying structure of concepts, techniques, and conventions provides a basis for accounting practice. The three major measurement conventions are: realization, matching and cost recovery, and stable monetary unit. The accrual basis is the heart of accounting, whereby revenues are recognized as earned and expenses as incurred rather than as related cash is received or disbursed.

At the end of each accounting period, adjustments must be made so that financial statements may be presented on a full-fledged accrual basis. The major adjustments are for (1) the expiration of unexpired costs, (2) realization (earning) of previously deferred revenues, (3) accrual of previously unrecorded expenses, and (4) accrual of previously unrecorded revenues.

Income statements usually appear in single-step, condensed form in published annual reports and in multiple-step, detailed form in the reports used within an organization.

Finally, readers who have had no or little exposure to accounting should solve the "Summary Problems for Your Review" before proceeding to the next chapter. To read about basic accounting concepts is not enough. Work some problems too—the more, the better.

summary problem for your review

The first problem appeared earlier in the chapter.

PROBLEM TWO

The following interpretations and remarks are sometimes encountered with regard to financial statements. Do you agree or disagree? Explain fully.

1. "If I purchase 100 shares of the outstanding common stock of General Motors Corporation (or Retailer No. 1), I invest my money directly in that corporation. General Motors must record that transaction."

2. "Sales show the cash coming in from customers and the various expenses show the cash going out for goods and services. The difference is net income."

3. "Why can't that big steel company pay higher wages and dividends too? It can use its hundreds of millions of dollars of retained income to do so."

4. "The total stockholders' equity measures the amount that the shareholders would get today if the corporation were liquidated."

5. "Conservatism is desirable because investors will be misled if the financial report is too rosy."

SOLUTION TO PROBLEM TWO

1. Money is invested directly in a corporation only upon original issuance of the stock by the corporation. For example, 100,000 shares of stock may be issued at $80 per share, bringing in $8 million to the corporation. This is a transaction between the corporation and the stockholders. It affects the corporate financial position:

Cash	$8,000,000	Stockholders' equity	$8,000,000

In turn, 100 shares of that stock may be sold by an original stockholder (A) to another individual (B) for $130 per share. This is a private transaction; no funds come to the corporation. Of course, the corporation records the fact that 100 shares originally owned by A are now owned by B, but the corporate financial position is unchanged. Accounting focuses on the business entity; the private dealings of the owners have no direct effect on the financial position of the entity and hence are unrecorded except for detailed records of the owners' identities.

In sum, B invests his money in the shares of the corporation when he buys them from A. However, individual dealings in shares already issued and held by stockholders have no direct effect on the financial position of the corporation.

2. Cash receipts and disbursements are not the fundamental basis for the accounting recognition of revenues and expenses. Credit, not cash, lubricates the economy. Therefore, if services or goods have been rendered to a customer, a legal claim to cash in the form of a receivable is deemed sufficient justification for recognizing revenue; similarly, if services or goods have been used up, a legal obligation in the form of a payable is justification for recognizing expense.

This approach to the measurement of net income is known as the accrual method. Revenue is recognized as it is earned by (a) goods or services rendered and (b) an exchange in a market transaction. Expenses or losses are recognized when goods or services are used up in the obtaining of revenue (or when such goods or services cannot justifiably be carried forward as an asset because they have no potential future benefit). The expenses and losses are deducted from the revenue, and the result of this matching process is net income, the net increase in stockholders' equity from the conduct of operations.

3. As the chapter indicated, retained income is not cash. It is a stockholders' equity account that represents the accumulated increase in ownership claims due to profitable operations. This claim or interest may be partially liquidated by the payment of cash dividends, but a growing company will reinvest cash in sustaining the added investments in receivables, inventories, plant, equipment, and other assets so necessary for expansion. As a result, the ownership claims become "permanent" in the sense that, as a practical matter, they will never be liquidated as long as the company remains a going concern.

This linking of retained income and cash is only one example of fallacious interpretation. As a general rule, there is no direct relationship between the individual items on the two sides of the balance sheet.

4. Stockholders' equity is a difference, the excess of assets over liabilities. If the assets were carried in the accounting records at their liquidating value today, and the liabilities were carried at the exact amounts needed for their extinguishment, the remark would be true. But such valuations would be coincidental, because assets are customarily carried at historical cost expressed in an unchanging monetary unit. Intervening changes in markets and general price levels in inflationary times may mean that the assets are woefully understated. Investors may make a critical error if they think that balance sheets indicate current values.

5. Conservatism is an entrenched practice among accountants, and it is also favored by many managers and investors. However, it has some ramifications that should be remembered. Conservatism will result in fast write-offs of assets with consequent lower balance sheet values and lower net incomes. But later years may show higher net incomes because of the heavier write-offs in early years.

So being conservative has some long-run countereffects because, for any asset, early fast write-offs will lighten expenses in later years. This countervailing effect is especially noteworthy when a company is having trouble making any net income. In such cases, the tendency is to wipe the slate clean by massive write-offs that result in an enormous net loss for a particular year. Without such assets to burden future years, the prospects brighten for reporting future net profits rather than net losses.

Conservatism has another boomerang effect. The understatement of assets and net income may prompt anxious stockholders to sell their shares when they should hold them. A dreary picture may be every bit as misleading as a rosy one.

Appendix 16A: Additional accounting concepts

This appendix describes the following concepts, which are prominent parts of the body of generally accepted accounting principles: going concern or continuity, objectivity or verifiability, materiality, and cost-benefit.

☐ THE GOING CONCERN OR CONTINUITY CONVENTION

Many accountants would regard **going concern** as a fact of life rather than as a convention or assumption. To view an entity as a going concern is to assume that it will continue indefinitely or at least that it will not be liquidated in the near future. This notion implies that existing *resources,* such as plant assets, *will be used* to fulfill the general purposes of a continuing entity *rather than sold* in tomorrow's real estate or equipment markets. It also implies that existing liabilities will be paid at maturity in an orderly manner.

Suppose some old specialized equipment has a depreciated cost of $10,000, a replacement cost of $12,000, and a realizable value of $7,000 in the used-equipment market. The going concern convention is often cited as the justification for adhering to acquisition cost (or acquisition cost less depreciation, $10,000 in this example) as the primary basis for valuing assets such as inventories, land, buildings, and equipment. Some critics of these accounting practices believe that such valuations are not as informative as their replacement cost ($12,000) or their realizable values upon liquidation ($7,000). Defenders of using $10,000 as an appropriate asset valuation argue that a going concern will generally use the asset as originally intended. Therefore the recorded cost (the acquisition cost less depreciation) is the preferable basis for accountability and evaluation of performance. Hence other values are not germane because replacement or disposal will not occur en masse as of the balance sheet date.

The opposite view to this going concern or **continuity convention** is an immediate-liquidation assumption, whereby all items on a balance sheet are valued at the amounts appropriate if the entity were to be liquidated in piecemeal fashion within a few days or months . This liquidation approach to valuation is usually used only when the entity is in severe, near-bankrupt straits.

☐ OBJECTIVITY OR VERIFIABILITY

Users want assurance that the numbers in the financial statements are not fabricated by management or by accountants in order to mislead or to falsify the financial position and performance. Consequently, accountants seek and prize **objectivity** as one of their principal strengths and regard it as an essential characteristic of measurement. Objectivity results in accuracy that is supported by convincing evidence that can be verified by independent accountants. It is a relative rather than an absolute concept. Some measurements can be extremely objective (such as cash in a cash register) in the sense that the same measurement would be produced by each of a dozen CPAs. But there are gradations of objectivity. A dozen CPAs are less likely to arrive at the same balances for receivables, inventories, plant and equipment, and miscellaneous assets. Yet they strive for measurement rules that will produce results that are subject to independent check. That is why accountants are generally satisfied with existing tests of realization: requiring an exchange to occur before revenue is realized helps ensure **verifiability**.

Many critics of existing accounting practices want to trade objectivity (accuracy) for what they conceive as more relevant or valid information. For example, the accounting literature is peppered with suggestions that accounting should attempt to measure "economic income," even though objectivity may be lessened. This particular suggestion often involves introducing asset valuations at replacement costs when these are higher than historical costs. The accounting profession has generally rejected these suggestions, even when reliable replacement price quotations are available, because no evidence short of a bona fide sale is regarded as sufficient to justify income recognition. However, inflation during the past decade has led to experimentation with the use of replacement costs and other versions of current values for external purposes. (See Chapter 19 for a fuller discussion.)

□ MATERIALITY

Because accounting is a practical art, the practitioner often tempers accounting reports by applying the convention of materiality. Many outlays that theoretically should be recorded as assets are immediately written off as expenses because of their lack of significance. For example, many corporations have a rule that requires the immediate write-off to expense of all outlays under a specified minimum of, say, $100, regardless of the useful life of the asset acquired. In such a case, coat hangers may be acquired that may last indefinitely but may never appear in the balance sheet as assets. The resulting $100 understatement of assets and stockholders' equity would be too trivial to worry about.

When is an item material? There will probably never be a universal clear-cut answer. What is trivial to General Motors may be material to Joe's Tavern. An item is material if its omission or misstatement would tend to mislead the user of the financial statements under consideration. A working rule is that an item is material if its proper accounting would probably affect the decision of a knowledgeable user. In sum, materiality is an important convention. But it is difficult to use anything other than prudent judgment to tell whether an item is material.

□ COST-BENEFIT

Accounting systems vary in complexity from the minimum crude records kept to satisfy governmental authorities to the sophisticated budgeting and feedback schemes that are at the heart of management planning and controlling. As a system is changed, its potential benefits usually must exceed its additional costs. Often the benefits are difficult to measure, but this **cost-benefit criterion** at least implicitly underlies the decisions about the design of accounting systems. The reluctance to adopt suggestions for new ways of measuring financial position and performance is frequently because of inertia, but it is often because the apparent benefits do not exceed the obvious costs of gathering and interpreting the information.

□ ROOM FOR JUDGMENT

Accounting is commonly misunderstood as being a precise discipline that produces exact measurements of a company's financial position and performance. As a result, many individuals regard accountants as little more than mechanical tabulators who grind out financial reports after processing an imposing amount of detail in accordance with stringent predetermined rules. Although accountants take methodical steps with masses of data, their rules of measurement allow much room for judgment. Managers and accountants who exercise this judgment have more influence on financial reporting than is commonly believed. These judgments are guided by the basic concepts, techniques, and conventions called generally accepted accounting principles (GAAP). Examples of the latter include the basic concepts just discussed. Their meaning will become clearer as these concepts are applied in future chapters.

This chapter offered some insight into the overall approach of the accountant to the measuring of economic activity. This appendix focuses on some of the main techniques that the accountant would use to analyze the illustration in the chapter.

☐ THE ACCOUNT

To begin, consider how the accountant would record the Retailer No. 1 transactions that were introduced in the chapter. Recall their effects on the elements of the balance sheet equation:

	A		=	L	+	SE
	cash	inventory	=	accounts payable		paid-in capital
1. Initial investment by owners	+100,000		=			+100,000
2. Acquire inventory for cash	−75,000	+75,000	=			
3. Acquire inventory on credit	+35,000		=	+35,000		

This balance sheet equation approach emphasizes the concepts, but it can obviously become unwieldy if many transactions occur. You can readily see that changes in the balance sheet equation can occur many times daily. In large businesses, such as in a department store, hundreds or thousands of repetitive transactions occur hourly. In practice, **ledger accounts** must be used to keep track of how these multitudes of transactions affect each particular asset, liability, revenue, expense, and so forth. The accounts used here are simplified versions of those used in practice. They are called T-accounts because they take the form of the capital letter *T*. The above transactions would be shown in T-accounts as follows:

assets = equities

or

assets = liabilities + stockholders' equity

Cash			
Increases		Decreases	
(1)	100,000	(2)	75,000
Bal.	25,000		

Accounts Payable			
Decreases		Increases	
		(3)	35,000

Inventory			
Increases		Decreases	
(2)	75,000		
(3)	35,000		
Bal.	110,000		

Paid-in Capital			
Decreases		Increases	
		(1)	100,000

The above entries were made in accordance with the rules of a *double-entry system*, whereby at least two accounts are affected by each transaction. Asset accounts have left-hand balances. They are increased by entries on the left-hand side and decreased by entries on the right-hand side.

Equity accounts (liabilities and stockholders' equity) have right-hand balances. They are increased by entries on the right-hand side and decreased by entries on the left-hand side.

Each T-account summarizes the changes in a particular asset or equity. Each transaction is keyed in some way, such as by the numbering used in this illustration or by date or both. This keying facilitates the rechecking (auditing) process by aiding the tracing of transactions to original sources. A balance of an account is computed by deducting the smaller total amount from the larger and placing the remainder on the side with the larger total amount. These accounts can be kept in various forms, from fancy account paper with pen and ink to magnetic computer tape. Whatever their form, their objective is to keep an up-to-date summary of the changes in specific asset and equity accounts.

A balance sheet can apply to any point in time. The necessary information is tabulated in the accounts. For example, the balance sheet after the first three transactions would contain:

ASSETS		EQUITIES	
Cash	$ 25,000	Liabilities:	
Inventory	110,000	Accounts payable	$ 35,000
		Stockholders' equity:	
		Paid-in capital	100,000
Total assets	$135,000	Total equities	$135,000

☐ GENERAL LEDGER

Exhibit 16-7 is the *general ledger* of Retailer No. 1. The *general ledger* is defined as the group of accounts that supports the accounts shown in the major financial statements.[4] Exhibit 16-7 is merely a recasting of the facts that were analyzed in Exhibit 16-1. Study Exhibit 16-7 by comparing its analysis of each transaction against its corresponding analysis in Exhibit 16-1.

☐ DEBITS AND CREDITS

The balance sheet equation has often been mentioned in this chapter. Recall:

$$A = L + \text{paid-in capital} \tag{1}$$

$$A = L + \text{paid-in capital} + \text{retained income} \tag{2}$$

$$A = L + \text{paid-in capital} + \text{revenue} - \text{expense} \tag{3}$$

---

[4] The general ledger is usually supported by various *subsidiary ledgers,* which provide details for several accounts in the general ledger. For instance, an accounts receivable subsidiary ledger would contain a separate account for each credit customer. The accounts receivable balance that appears in the Sears balance sheet is in a single account in the Sears general ledger. However, that lone balance is buttressed by detailed individual accounts receivable with millions of credit customers. You can readily visualize how some accounts in general ledgers might have subsidiary ledgers supported by subsubsidiary ledgers, and so on. Thus a subsidiary accounts receivable ledger might be subdivided alphabetically into Customers A–D, E–H, and so forth.

EXHIBIT 16-7

General Ledger of RETAILER NO. 1

1. Initial investment
2. Acquire inventory for cash
3. Acquire inventory on credit
4a. Sales on credit
4b. Cost of inventory sold
5. Collect from customers
6. Pay accounts of suppliers
7a. Pay rent in advance
7b. Recognize expiration of rental services

ASSETS (INCREASES ON LEFT, DECREASES ON RIGHT)

Cash

(1)	100,000	(2)	75,000
(5)	30,000	(6)	10,000
		(7a)	3,000
3/31 Bal.	42,000		

Accounts Receivable

(4a)	120,000	(5)	30,000

Inventory

(2)	75,000	(4b)	100,000
(3)	35,000		
3/31 Bal.	10,000		

Prepaid Rent

(7a)	3,000	(7b)	1,000

EQUITIES (DECREASES ON LEFT, INCREASES ON RIGHT)

Accounts Payable

(6)	10,000	(3)	35,000

Paid-in Capital

		(1)	100,000

Retained Income

		3/31 Bal.	19,000 *

EXPENSE AND REVENUE ACCOUNTS

Cost of Goods Sold

(4b)	100,000		

Sales

		(4a)	120,000

Rent Expense

(7b)	1,000		

*The details of the revenue and expense accounts appear in the income statement. Their net effect is then transferred to a single account, Retained Income, in the balance sheet. Note: An ending balance should be drawn for each account, but all balances are not shown here because some can be computed easily by inspection.

The accountant often talks about entries in a technical way:

Transposing, $\qquad$ A + expenses = L + paid-in capital + revenue $\qquad$ (4)

Finally, $\qquad\qquad\qquad$ left = right $\qquad\qquad\qquad$ (5)

$$\text{debit} = \text{credit}$$

Debit means one thing and one thing only—"left" (not "bad," "something coming," etc.). **Credit** means one thing and one thing only—"right" (not "good," "something owed," etc.). The word *charge* is often used instead of *debit,* but no single word is used as a synonym for *credit.*

For example, if you asked an accountant what entry to make for Transaction 4*b,* the answer would be: "I would debit (or charge) Cost of Goods Sold for $100,000; and I would credit Inventory for $100,000." Note that the total dollar amount of the debits (entries on the left side of the account(s) affected) will *always* equal the total dollar amount of the credits (entries on the right side of the account(s) affected) because the whole accounting system is based on an equation. The symmetry and power of this analytical debit-credit technique is indeed impressive.

Assets are traditionally carried as left-hand balances. Why do assets and expenses both carry debit balances? They carry left-hand balances for different reasons. *Expenses* are temporary stockholders' equity accounts. Decreases in stockholders' equity are entered on the left side of the accounts because they offset the normal (i.e., right-hand) stockholders' equity balances. Because expenses decrease stockholders' equity, they are carried as left-hand balances.

To recapitulate:

assets		=	liabilities		+	stockholders' equity	
increase	decrease	=	decrease	increase	+	decrease	increase
+	–		–	+		–	+
debit	credit		debit	credit		debit	credit
left	right		left	right		left	right

Because revenues increase stockholders' equity, they are recorded as credits. Because expenses decrease stockholders' equity, they are recorded as debits.

You have just seen an example of *double-entry* accounting, so named because at least two accounts are *always* affected in each transaction.

☐ THE STRANGE DEBIT-CREDIT LANGUAGE

Beginners in the study of accounting are frequently confused by the words *debit* and *credit.* Perhaps the best way to minimize confusion is to ask what words would be used as substitutes? *Left* would be used instead of debit, and *right* would be used instead of credit.

The words *debit* and *credit* have a Latin origin. They were used centuries ago when double-entry bookkeeping was introduced by Paciolo, an Italian monk. Even though *left* and *right* are more descriptive words, *debit* and *credit* are too deeply entrenched to avoid.

Debit and credit are used as verbs, adjectives, or nouns. That is, "debit $1,000 to cash and credit $1,000 to accounts receivable" are examples of uses as verbs, meaning that $1,000 should be placed on the left-hand side of the cash account and on the right-hand side of the accounts receivable account. Similarly, if "a debit is made to cash" or "cash has a debit balance of $12,000," the *debit* is a noun or adjective that describes the status of a particular account. Thus debit and credit are short words that are packed with meaning.

In our everyday conversation we sometimes use the words *debits* and *credits* in a general sense that may completely diverge from their technical accounting uses. For instance, we may give praise by saying "She deserves plenty of credit for her good deed" or "That misplay is a debit on his ledger." When you study accounting, forget these general uses and misuses of the words. Merely think right (or left).

assignment material

FUNDAMENTAL ASSIGNMENT MATERIAL

16-1. Terminology. More new terms were introduced in this chapter than in any other, so be sure that you understand the following. Define *account; Accounting Principles Board (APB); accounts payable; accounts receivable; accrual basis; accrue; adjusting entries; adjustments; APB Opinions; assets; audit; balance sheet; capital; cash basis; certificate; Certified Public Accountant; common stock; continuity convention; contributed capital; corporation; cost-benefit criterion; cost of goods sold; cost of sales; credit; debit; deferred income; deferred revenue; depreciation; dividends; earned surplus; earnings; entity; equities; expense; expired costs; explicit transactions; FASB Statements; financial accounting; Financial Accounting Standards Board (FASB); generally accepted accounting principles (GAAP); going concern convention; gross margin; gross profit; implicit transactions; income; income statement; independent opinion; ledger; legal value; liabilities; limited liability; matching and cost recovery; materiality; net worth; notes payable; objectivity; open account; operating cycle; owners' equity; paid-in capital; partnership; par value; preferred stock; profits; proprietorship; realization; reinvested earnings; residual interest; retained earnings; retained income; revenue; Securities and Exchange Commission (SEC); single-step income statement; source documents; stated value; statement of financial condition; statement of financial position; stockholders' equity; transaction; unbilled revenue; undistributed earnings; unearned revenue; unexpired costs; verifiability.*

16-2. Balance sheet equation. Find the unknowns (in thousands), showing computations to support your answers. Consider each case independently.

	CASE		
	1	2	3
Assets, beginning of period	$ 80	$ C	$ G
Assets, end of period	90	290	F
Liabilities, beginning of period	C	100	95
Liabilities, end of period	G	G	85
Paid-in capital, beginning of period	10	20	E
Paid-in capital, end of period	F	F	75
Retained income, beginning of period	25	70	90
Retained income, end of period	E	E	100
Revenues	100	D	300
Expenses	85	180	260
Net income	D	30	C
Dividends	-0-	10	D
Additional investment by stockholders	-0-	40	25

16-3. True or false. Use *T* or *F* to indicate whether each of the following statements is true or false.

1. The cash balance is the best evidence of stockholders' equity.

2. From a single balance sheet, you can find stockholders' equity for a period of time but not for a specific day.

3. It is not possible to determine change in the condition of a business from a single balance sheet.

4. Retained Earnings should be accounted for as a current asset item.

5. Cash should be classified as a stockholders' equity item.

6. Machinery used in the business should be recorded as a noncurrent asset item.

16-4. Analysis of transactions, preparation of statements. (An alternate is Problem 16-28.) The Dorian Company was incorporated on March 1, 19X1. Dorian had six holders of common stock. Alice Dorian, who was the president and chief executive officer, held 60 percent of the shares. The company rented space in department stores and specialized in selling costume jewelry. Dorian's first venture was in the Goliath Department Store.

The following events occurred during March.

1. The company was incorporated. Common stockholders invested $80,000 cash.

2. Purchased merchandise inventory for cash, $50,000.

3. Purchased merchandise inventory on open account, $10,000.

4. Merchandise carried in inventory at a cost of $35,000 was sold for cash for $20,000 and on open account for $60,000, a grand total of $80,000. Dorian (not Goliath) carries and collects these accounts receivable.

5. Collection of the above accounts receivable, $12,000.

6. Payments of accounts payable, $6,000. See Transaction 3.

7. Special display equipment and fixtures were acquired on March 1 for $21,000. Their expected useful life was twenty-one months, with no terminal scrap value. Straight-line depreciation was adopted. This equipment was removable. Dorian paid $5,000 as a down payment and signed a promissory note for $16,000.

8. On March 1, Dorian signed a rental agreement with Goliath. The agreement called for a flat $3,000 per month, payable quarterly in advance. Therefore Dorian paid $9,000 cash on March 1.

9. The rental agreement also called for a payment of 10 percent of all sales. This payment is in addition to the flat $3,000 per month. In this way, Goliath would share in any success of the venture and be compensated for general services such as cleaning and utilities. This payment was to be made in cash on the last day of each month as soon as the sales for the month were tabulated.

10. Wages, salaries, and sales commissions were all paid in cash for all earnings by employees. The amount was $32,000.

11. Depreciation expense was recognized. See Transaction 7.

12. The expiration of an appropriate amount of prepaid rental services was recognized. See Transaction 8.

REQUIRED

1. Prepare an analysis of Dorian Company's transactions, employing the equation approach demonstrated in Exhibit 16-1. Show all amounts in thousands.
2. Prepare a balance sheet as of March 31, 19X1, and an income statement for the month of March. Ignore income taxes.
3. Given these sparse facts, analyze Dorian's performance for March and its financial position as of March 31, 19X1.

BASIC
ACCOUNTING

16-5. Comparison of cash versus accrual basis. Refer to the preceding problem. Prepare an income statement on the cash basis for March. Compare it with the income statement on the accrual basis. Which basis provides a better measure of economic performance? Why?

16-6. Give five examples of accounting entities.

16-7. Define *going concern.*

16-8. What is the major criticism of the dollar as the principal accounting measure?

16-9. What does the accountant mean by *objectivity?*

16-10. Criticize: "Assets are things of value owned by the entity."

16-11. Criticize: "Net income is the difference in the ownership capital account balances at two points in time."

16-12. Distinguish between the accrual basis and the cash basis.

16-13. How do adjusting entries differ from routine entries?

16-14. Why is it better to refer to the *costs,* rather than *values,* of assets such as plant or inventories?

16-15. Give at least two synonymous terms for each of the following: *balance sheet; income statement; assets.*

16-16. Give at least three other terms for *retained earnings.*

16-17. Criticize: "As a stockholder, I have a right to more dividends. You have millions stashed away in retained earnings. It's about time that you let the true owners get their hands on that pot of gold."

16-18. Criticize: "Dividends are distributions of profits."

16-19. Explain why advertising should be viewed as an asset upon acquisition.

16-20. What is the role of cost-benefit (economic feasibility) in the development of accounting principles?

16-21. If gross profit is 60 percent, express the relationship of cost of goods sold to gross profit in percentage terms.

16-22. **Income statement.** Here is a statement of an automobile dealer:

MARVEL CARS, INC.
Statement of Profit and Loss
December 31, 19X3

Revenues:		
Sales	$1,000,000	
Increase in market value of land and building	200,000	$1,200,000
Deduct expenses:		
Advertising	$ 100,000	
Sales commissions	50,000	
Utilities	20,000	
Wages	150,000	
Dividends	100,000	
Cost of cars purchased	700,000	1,120,000
Net profit		$ 80,000

REQUIRED | List and describe any shortcomings of this statement.

16-23. Nature of retained income. This is an exercise on the relationships between assets, liabilities, and ownership equities. The numbers are small, but the underlying concepts are large.

1. Assume an opening balance sheet of:

Cash	$1,000	Paid-in capital	$1,000

2. Purchase inventory for $600 cash. Prepare a balance sheet. A heading is unnecessary in this and subsequent requirements.

3. Sell the entire inventory for $850 cash. Prepare a balance sheet. Where is the retained income in terms of relationships within the balance sheet? That is, what is the meaning of the retained income? Explain in your own words.

4. Buy inventory for $400 cash and equipment for $700 cash. Prepare a balance sheet. Where is the retained income in terms of relationships within the balance sheet? That is, what is the meaning of the retained income? Explain in your own words.

5. Buy inventory for $300 on open account. Prepare a balance sheet. Where is the retained income and account payable in terms of the relationships within the balance sheet? That is, what is the meaning of the account payable and the retained income? Explain in your own words.

16-24. Find unknowns. The following data pertain to the Bunce Corporation. Total assets at January 1, 19X1, were $100,000; at December 31, 19X1, $120,000. During 19X1, sales were $200,000, cash dividends were $4,000, and operating expenses (exclusive of cost of goods sold) were $50,000. Total liabilities at December 31, 19X1, were $55,000; at January 1, 19X1, $40,000. There was no additional capital paid in during 19X1.

REQUIRED

(These need not be computed in any particular order.)
1. Net income for 19X1.
2. Cost of goods sold for 19X1.
3. Stockholders' equity, January 1, 19X1.

16-25. Tenant and landlord. The Iglehart Company, a retail hardware store, pays quarterly rent on its store at the beginning of each quarter. The rent per quarter is $9,000. The owner of the building in which the store is located is the Rouse Corporation.

REQUIRED

Using the balance sheet equation format, analyze the effects of the following on the tenant's and the landlord's financial position:
1. Iglehart pays $9,000 rent on July 1.
2. Adjustment for July.
3. Adjustment for August.
4. Adjustment for September.

16-26. Customer and airline. The Levitz Furniture Company decided to hold a managers' meeting in Hawaii in February. To take advantage of special fares, Levitz purchased airline tickets in advance from United Airlines at a total cost of $90,000. These were acquired on December 1 for cash.

REQUIRED

Using the balance sheet equation format, analyze the impact of the December payment and the February travel on the financial position of both Levitz and United.

16-27. **Balance sheet equation; solving for unknowns.** Compute the unknowns (V, W, X, Y, and Z) in each of the individual cases, Columns **A** through **G**.

GIVEN	A	B	C	D	E	F	G
Assets at beginning of period		$10,000				Z	$ 8,200
Assets at end of period		11,000					9,600
Liabilities at beginning of period		6,000				$12,000	4,000
Liabilities at end of period		Y					6,000
Stockholders equity at beginning of period	$5,000	Z				V	X
Stockholders' equity at end of period	X	5,000				10,000	W
Sales			$15,000		X	14,000	20,000
Inventory at beginning of period			6,000	$ 8,000		Y	
Inventory at end of period			7,000	6,000		7,000	
Purchases of inventory			10,000	10,000		6,000	
Gross profit			Y		2,000	6,000	V
Cost of goods sold*			X	X	4,500	X	Z
Other expenses			4,000			4,000	5,000
Net profit	3,000	X	Z			W	Y
Dividends	1,000	-0-				1,500	400
Additional investments by stockholders						5,000	-0-

Note that Cost of goods sold = Beginning inventory + Purchases − Ending inventory.

16-28. **Fundamental transaction analysis and preparation of statements.** (An alternate is Problem 16-4.) Three women who were college classmates have decided to pool a variety of work experiences by opening a women's clothing store. The business has been incorporated as Sartorial Choice, Inc. The following transactions occurred during April.

1. On April 1, 19X1, each woman invested $9,000 in cash in exchange for 1,000 shares of stock each.

2. The corporation quickly acquired $50,000 in inventory, half of which had to be paid for in cash. The other half was acquired on open accounts that were payable after thirty days.

3. A store was rented for $500 monthly. A lease was signed for one year on April 1. The first two months' rents were paid in advance. Other payments were to be made on the second of each month.

4. Advertising during April was purchased on open account for $3,000 from a newspaper owned by one of the stockholders. Additional advertising services of $6,000 were acquired for cash.

5. Sales were $65,000. The average markup above the cost of the merchandise was two-thirds of cost. Eighty percent of the sales were on open account.

6. Wages and salaries incurred in April amounted to $11,000, of which $5,000 was paid.

7. Miscellaneous services paid for in cash were $1,410.

8. On April 1, fixtures and equipment were purchased for $6,000 with a down payment of $1,000 plus a $5,000 note payable in one year.

9. See Transaction 8 and make the April 30 adjustment for interest expense *accrued* at 9.6 percent. (The interest is not *due* until the note matures.)

10. See Transaction 8 and make the April 30 adjustment for depreciation expense on a straight-line basis. The estimated life of the fixtures and equipment is ten years with no expected terminal scrap value.

11. Cash dividends of $300 were declared and disbursed to stockholders on April 29.

REQUIRED

1. Using the accrual basis of accounting, prepare an analysis of transactions, employing the equation approach demonstrated in Exhibit 16-1. Place your analysis sideways; to save space, use abbreviated headings. Work slowly. Use the following headings: Cash, Accounts Receivable, Inventory, Prepaid Rent, Fixtures and Equipment, Accounts Payable, Notes Payable, Accrued Wages Payable, Accrued Interest Payable, Paid-in Capital, and Retained Income.

2. Prepare a balance sheet and a multiple-step income statement. Also prepare a statement of retained income.

3. What advice would you give the owners based on the information compiled in the financial statements?

16-29. Measuring income for tax and other purposes. The following are the summarized transactions of Dr. Cristina Faragher, a dentist, for 19X7, her first year in practice.

1. Acquired equipment and furniture for $50,000. Its expected useful life is five years. Straight-line depreciation will be used.

2. Fees collected, $80,000. These fees included $2,000 paid in advance by some patients on December 31, 19X7.

3. Rent is paid at the rate of $500 monthly, payable on the twenty-fifth of each month for the following month. Total disbursements during 19X7 for rent were $6,500.

4. Fees billed but uncollected, December 31, 19X7, $15,000.

5. Utilities expense paid in cash, $600. Additional utility bills unpaid at December 31, 19X7, $100.

6. Salaries expense of dental assistant and secretary, $16,000 paid in cash. In addition, $1,000 was earned but unpaid on December 31, 19X7.

Dr. Faragher may elect either the cash basis or the accrual basis of measuring income for income tax purposes, provided that she uses it consistently in subsequent years. Under either alternative, the original cost of the equipment and furniture must be written off over its five-year useful life rather than being regarded as a lump-sum expense in the first year.

REQUIRED

1. Prepare a comparative income statement on both the cash and accrual bases, using one column for each basis.

2. Which basis do you prefer as a measure of Dr. Faragher's performance? Why? What is the justification for the government's allowing the use of the cash basis for income tax purposes?

16-30. Accrual basis of accounting. Christiane Jose runs a small consulting-engineering firm that specializes in designing and overseeing the installation of environmental-control systems. However, even though she is the president, she has had no formal training in management. She has been in business one year and has prepared the following income statement for her fiscal year ended June 30, 19X4.

JOSE CONSULTING ENGINEERS, INC.
Income Statement
For the Year Ended June 30, 19X4

Fees collected in cash		$500,000
Expenses paid in cash except for depreciation:		
Rent	$ 12,500	
Utilities	10,000	
Wages	200,000	
President's salary	46,000	
Office supplies	14,000	
Travel	30,000	
Miscellaneous	80,000	
Depreciation	10,000	402,500
Operating income		$ 97,500

Jose realized that the entire $50,000 cost of the equipment acquired on July 1, 19X3, should not be an expense of one year. She predicted a useful life of five years, a terminal value of zero, and deducted $10,000 as depreciation for the first year.

Jose is thinking about future needs for her expanding business. For example, although she now uses rented space in an office building, she is considering buying a small building. She showed her income statement to a local banker, who reacted: "Christiane, this statement may suffice for filing income tax forms, but the bank will not consider any long-term financing until it receives a balance sheet and income statement prepared on the accrual basis of accounting. Moreover, the statements must be subjected to an audit by an independent certified public accountant."

As a CPA, you are asked to audit her records and fulfill the bank's request. The following data are gathered.

1. On July 1, 19X3, Jose invested $25,000 cash, and two friends each invested $2,000 cash in the firm in return for capital stock.

2. Jose acquired $50,000 of equipment on July 1, 19X3. A down payment of $20,000 cash was made. A $30,000 two-year note bearing an annual interest rate of 15 percent was signed. Principal plus interest were both payable at maturity.

3. On June 30, 19X4, clients owed Jose $95,000 on open accounts.

4. Salaries are paid on the fifteenth of every month. As business expanded throughout the fiscal year, additional employees were added. The total payroll paid on June 15, 19X4, including the president's monthly salary of $4,000, was $40,000.

5. Rent was paid in advance on the fifteenth of every month. An initial payment of $1,500 covered July 1, 19X3–August 15, 19X4. Payments of $1,000 monthly were paid beginning August 15, 19X3.

6. Office supplies on hand on June 30, 19X4, were $5,000.

7. On April 1, 19X4, a local oil refinery gave Jose a retainer fee of $60,000 cash in exchange for twelve months of consulting services beginning at that date.

REQUIRED

1. Using the accrual basis of accounting, prepare an income statement for the fisal year. Submit supporting computations properly labeled.
2. Prepare a balance sheet, dated June 30, 19X4. Assume that the cash balance is $116,500.

16-31. **Reconstruct the cash account.** Refer to the preceding problem. Show a summary analysis of the cash receipts and disbursements that proves that the ending cash balance is indeed $116,500. Label your analysis fully.

16-32. **Debits and credits.** Read the appendix on ledger accounts. Determine for the following transactions whether the account *named in parentheses* is to be debited or credited.

1. Sold merchandise (Merchandise Inventory), $1,000.
2. Paid Johnson Associates $3,000 owed them (Accounts Payable).
3. Bought merchandise on account (Merchandise Inventory), $2,000.
4. Received cash from customers on accounts due (Accounts Receivable), $1,000.
5. Bought merchandise on open account (Accounts Payable), $5,000.
6. Borrowed money from a bank (Notes Payable), $10,000.

16-33. True or false. Read the appendix on ledger accounts. Use *T* or *F* to indicate whether each of the following statements is true or false.
1. Debit entries must always be recorded on the left.
2. Decreases in accounts must be shown on the debit side.
3. Both increases in liabilities and decreases in assets should be entered on the right.
4. Money borrowed from the bank should be credited to Cash and debited to Notes Payable.
5. Purchase of inventory on account should be credited to Inventory and debited to Accounts Payable.
6. Decreases in liability accounts should be recorded on the right.
7. Increases in asset accounts must always be entered on the left.
8. Increases in stockholders' equity always should be entered as credits.
9. Equipment purchases for cash should be debited to Equipment and credited to Cash.
10. Asset credits should be on the right and liability credits on the left.
11. Payments on mortgages should be debited to Cash and credited to Mortgages Payable. Mortgages are long-term debts.

16-34. Using T-accounts. Read the appendix on ledger accounts. Refer to Problem 16-4. Make entries for March in T-accounts. Key your entries and check to see that the ending balances agree with the financial statements.

16-35. Using T-accounts. Read the appendix on ledger accounts. Refer to Problem One of the "Summary Problems for Your Review." The transactions are analyzed in Exhibit 16-2. Make entries in T-accounts and check to see that the ending balances agree with the financial statements in Exhibits 16-3, 16-4, 16-5 on page 482.

16-36. T-accounts. Read the appendix on ledger accounts. Refer to Problem 16-28. Use T-accounts to present an analysis of April transactions. Key your entries and check to see that the ending balances agree with the financial statements.

UNDERSTANDING PUBLISHED FINANCIAL REPORTS

16-37. Balance sheet effects. The Wells Fargo Bank showed the following items (among others) on its balance sheet at December 31, 19X1:

Cash	$ 947,000,000
Total deposits	$6,383,000,000

REQUIRED

BASIC
ACCOUNTING

1. Suppose that you made a deposit of $1,000 in the Wells Fargo Bank. How would each of the bank's assets and equities be affected? How would each of your personal assets and equities be affected? Be specific.
2. Suppose that a savings and loan association makes an $800,000 loan to a local hospital for remodeling. What would be the effect on each of the association's assets and equities immediately after the loan is made? Be specific.

3. Suppose that you borrowed $10,000 from the Household Finance Company on a personal loan. How would such a transaction affect each of your personal assets and equities?

16-38. Prepare balance sheet. Crown Zellerbach Company is a large producer of timber, wood products, pulp, and paper. The company's annual report for 1978 included the following balance sheet items as of December 31, 1978 (in thousands of dollars):

Various notes payable	$ 563,213
Cash	(1)
Total shareholders' equity	(2)
Total liabilities	(3)
Accounts receivable	230,370
Capital stock	140,061
Inventories	305,609
Accounts payable	138,211
Properties	1,151,742
Additional shareholders' equity	822,380
Other assets	272,820
Other liabilities	299,844
Total assets	1,963,709

REQUIRED

Prepare a condensed balance sheet, including amounts for
1. Cash. What do you think of its relative size?
2. Total shareholders' equity.
3. Total liabilities.

16-39. McDonald's Financial Statements. McDonald's Corporation is a well-known fast-food restaurant company. The following data are from a recent annual report (in thousands):

Retained earnings, end of year	$ 554,106	Dividends paid on common stock	$ 6,073
Revenues	1,406,148	General, administrative, and selling expenses	149,818
Interest expense	56,042	Depreciation	58,115
Income tax expense	130,100	Rent	29,810
Food and paper	429,519	Retained earnings, beginning of year	423,483
Wages and salaries	242,098	Other operating expenses	173,950

REQUIRED

1. Prepare the following for the year:
   a. Income statement
   b. Statement of retained income
2. Comment briefly on the relative size of the cash dividend.

16-40. The case of the president's wealth. From the *Chicago Tribune*, August 20, 1964:

Accountants acting on President Johnson's orders today reported his family wealth totaled $3,484,098.

The statement of capital, arrived at through conservative procedures of evaluation, contrasted with a recent estimate published by *Life* magazine, which put the total at 14 million dollars.

The family fortune, which is held in trust while the Johnsons are in the White House, was set forth in terms of book values. The figures represent original cost rather than current market values on what the holdings would be worth if sold now.

Announced by the White House press office, but turned over to reporters by a national accounting firm at their Washington branch office, the financial statement apparently was intended to still a flow of quasi-official and unofficial estimates of the Johnson fortune. . . .

ASSETS

Cash	$ 132,547
Bonds	398,540
Interest in Texas Broadcasting Corp.	2,543,838
Ranch properties and other real estate	525,791
Other assets, including insurance policies	82,054
Total assets	$3,682,770

LIABILITIES

Note payable on real estate holding, 5 percent due 1971	$ 150,000
Accounts payable, accrued interest, and income taxes	48,672
Total liabilities	$ 198,672
Capital	$3,484,098

The report apportions the capital among the family, with $378,081 credited to the President; $2,126,298 to his wife Claudia T., who uses the name Lady Bird; $490,141 to their daughter Lynda Bird; and $489,578 to their daughter Luci Baines.

The statement said the family holdings—under the names of the President, his wife, and his two daughters, Lynda Bird and Luci Baines—had increased from $737,730 on January 1, 1954, a year after Johnson became Democratic leader of the Senate, to $3,484,098 on July 31 this year, a gain of $2,746,368. . . .

A covering letter addressed to Johnson said the statement was made "in conformity with generally accepted accounting principles applied on a consistent basis."

By far the largest part of the fortune was listed as the Johnsons' interest in the Texas Broadcasting Corporation, carried on the books as worth $2,543,838.

The accountants stated that this valuation was arrived at on the basis of the cost of the stock when the Johnsons bought control of the debt-ridden radio station between 1943 and 1947, plus accumulated earnings ploughed back as equity, less 25 percent capital gains tax.[5]

Editorial, *Chicago Tribune,* August 22, 1964:

An accounting firm acting on Mr. Johnson's instructions and employing what it termed "generally accepted auditing standards" has released a statement putting the current worth of the Lyndon Johnson family at a little less than 3 1/2 million dollars. . . .

Dean Burch, chairman of the Republican National Committee, has remarked that the method used to list the Johnson assets was comparable to placing the value of Manhattan Island at $24, the price at which it was purchased from the Indians. The Johnson accounting firm conceded that its report was "not intended to indicate the values that might be realized if the investment were sold."

---

[5]You need not be concerned about the details of this method of accounting until you study Chapter 18. In brief, when an investor holds a large enough stake in a corporation, such investment is accounted for at its acquisition cost plus the investor's pro-rata share of the investee's net income (or net loss) minus the investor's share of dividends. For example, suppose the Texas Broadcasting Company earned $100,000 in a given year and that Johnson owned 100 percent of the company. In this situation, the Johnson financial statements would show an increase in Interest in Texas Broadcasting Corp. of $100,000 less the $25,000 income tax that would become payable upon disposition of the investment. (Today's accountants would prefer to increase the Investment account by the full $100,000 and the liabilities by $25,000. See the Carter financial statements.)

In fact, it would be interesting to observe the response of the Johnson family if a syndicate of investors were to offer to take Texas Broadcasting off the family's hands at double the publicly reported worth of the operation. . . .

1. Evaluate the criticisms, making special reference to fundamental accounting concepts or "principles."
2. The financial statements of President and Mrs. Carter are shown in an accompanying exhibit. Do you prefer the approach taken by the Carter statements as compared with the Johnson statements? Explain.

JAMES EARL CARTER, JR. AND ROSALYNN CARTER
Financial Statements
December 31, 1977

Perry, Chambliss, Sheppard and Thompson
Certified Public Accountants
Americus, Georgia

JAMES EARL CARTER, JR. AND ROSALYNN CARTER
STATEMENT OF ASSETS AND LIABILITIES
DECEMBER 31, 1977
(UNAUDITED)

ASSETS

	COST BASIS	ESTIMATED CURRENT VALUE
Cash	$204,979.04	$204,979.04
Cash Value of Life Insurance	45,506.88	45,506.88
U.S. Savings Bonds, Series E	1,425.00	1,550.94
Loan Receivable	50,000.00	50,000.00
Overpayment of 1977 Income Taxes	51,121.27	51,121.27
Personal Assets Trust—Note 3	151,097.87	557,717.11
Residence, Plains, Georgia	45,000.00	54,090.00
Lots in Plains, Georgia	1,100.00	3,155.00
Automobile	4,550.75	2,737.50
Total Assets	$554,780.81	$970,857.74

LIABILITIES

Miscellaneous Accounts Payable, Estimated	$ 1,500.00	$ 1,500.00
Provision for Possible Income Taxes on Unrealized Asset Appreciation—Note 4	0	174,000.00
Total Liabilities	$ 1,500.00	$175,500.00
Excess of Assets Over Liabilities	$553,280.81	$795,357.74

JAMES E. CARTER, JR. AND ROSALYNN CARTER
NOTES TO FINANCIAL STATEMENTS
DECEMBER 31, 1977

NOTE 1: *Estimated market values of real estate are 100% of the fair market values as determined by county tax assessors except as to certain assets held in the personal assets trust, which are stated at book value.*

NOTE 2: *This statement excludes campaign fund assets and liabilities.*

NOTE 3: *The interest in Carter's Warehouse partnership, the capital stock of Carter's Farms, Inc., the remainder interest in certain real estate and securities and a commercial lot in Plains, Georgia, were transferred to a personal assets trust in January, 1977. The primary purpose of the trust is to isolate the President from those of his assets which are most likely to be affected by actions of the federal government. The President was responsible as a general partner for obligations of the partnership before his partnership interest was transferred to the trust. The transfer to the trust did not affect such responsibility.*

NOTE 4: *If the market values of the assets were realized, income taxes would be payable at an uncertain rate. A provision for such income taxes has been made at rates in effect for 1977.*

NOTE 5: *The amounts in the accompanying statements are based principally upon the accrual basis method of accounting.*

chapter 17

UNDERSTANDING CORPORATE ANNUAL REPORTS

learning objectives

When you have finished studying this chapter, you should be able to:

1. Identify the meanings and interrelationships of the main types of items in the classified balance sheet of a corporation.
2. Measure the financial effects of various transactions, especially stock splits, stock dividends, and cash dividends.
3. Distinguish between reserves and funds in the financial statements.
4. Identify the meanings and interrelationships of the principal elements in the income statement of a corporation.
5. Identify the meanings and interrelationships of the elements in the retained income statement.
6. Prepare the statement of changes in financial position.
7. Identify the relationship of depreciation to the statement of changes in financial position and indicate the effects of depreciation on income taxes, cash, and working capital.

Accounting has often been called the language of business. But it is a language with a special vocabulary aimed at conveying the financial story of organizations. To understand corporate annual reports, a reader must learn at least the fundamentals of the language. This chapter presents the basic meanings of the terms and relationships used in the financial statements found in annual reports.

Accounting is commonly misunderstood as being a precise discipline that produces exact measurements of a company's financial position and performance. As a result, many individuals regard accountants as little more than mechanical tabulators who grind out financial reports after processing an imposing amount of detail in accordance with stringent predetermined rules. Although accountants take methodical steps with masses of data, their rules of measurement allow much room for judgment. Managers and accountants who exercise this judgment have more influence on financial reporting than is commonly believed.

This chapter extends the discussion of the financial statements in the preceding chapter. It also introduces the Statement of Changes in Financial Position. Additional coverage (including investments in subsidiaries, consolidated statements, and accounting for inflation) will be found in the final two chapters of this book.

Classified balance sheet

☐ CURRENT ASSETS

Assets are usually grouped in the manner shown in Exhibit 17-1. The *current assets* are cash plus assets that are reasonably expected to be converted to cash or sold or consumed during the normal operating cycle. They are the assets directly involved in the operating cycle, including cash; temporary investments in marketable securities; receivables of nearly all kinds, including installment accounts and notes receivable if they conform to normal industry practice and terms; inventories; and prepaid expenses.

Most organizations exist to serve a desire for some type of goods or services. Whether they are profit seeking or not, they typically follow a similar, somewhat rhythmic, pattern of economic activity. An **operating cycle** (also called a *cash cycle* or *earnings cycle*) is the time span during which cash is used to acquire goods and services, which in turn are sold to customers, who in turn pay for their purchases with cash. Consider the following example. A retail business usually engages in some version of the following operating cycle in order to earn profits (figures assumed):

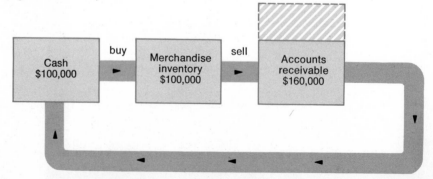

EXHIBIT
17-1

(*Place a clip on this page for easy reference.*)

ASSETS	DECEMBER 31 19X1	DECEMBER 31 19X0
Current assets:		
Cash	$ 2,600	$ 2,200
Temporary investments in marketable securities	600	600
Receivables, net of allowance for doubtful accounts	5,300	5,100
Inventories at cost	14,600	14,400
Prepaid expenses	600	600
Total current assets	$23,700	$22,900
Plant assets:		
Land	$ 300	$ 300
Buildings and equipment, net of accumulated depreciation	7,000	5,800
Total plant assets	$ 7,300	$ 6,100
Total assets	$31,000	$29,000

EQUITIES

Current liabilities:		
Accounts payable	$ 7,100	$ 5,200
Accrued expenses payable	1,600	1,700
Accrued income taxes payable	500	400
Total current liabilities	$ 9,200	$ 7,300
5% Mortgage bonds payable	$16,000	$16,000
Total liabilities	$25,200	$23,300
Stockholders' equity:		
Preferred stock, 6%, $100 par value, $100 liquidating value	$ 1,600	$ 1,600
Common stock, $10 par value	2,000	2,000
Additional paid-in capital	1,000	1,000
Retained income	1,200	1,100
Total stockholders' equity	$ 5,800	$ 5,700
Total equities	$31,000	$29,000

The box for Accounts Receivable (amounts owed to the business by customers) is larger than the other two boxes because the objective is to sell goods at a price higher than acquisition cost. Retailers and nearly all other businesses buy goods and services and perform acts (such as placing them in a convenient location or changing their form) that merit selling prices that hopefully will yield a profit. The total amount of profit earned during a particular period heavily depends on the excess of the selling prices over the costs of the goods and additional expenses and on the speed of the operating cycle.

Several operating cycles may occur during one year. But some businesses need more than one year to complete a single cycle. The distillery, tobacco, and lumber industries are examples. Inventories in such industries are nevertheless regarded as current assets. Similarly, installment accounts and notes receivable are typically classified as current assets even though they will not be fully collected within one year.

Some comments on specific kinds of current assets follow:

Cash consists of bank deposits in checking accounts plus money on hand. Incidentally, visualize how a deposit would be accounted for by a bank. Its cash will increase and its liabilities increase in the form of "Deposits," which are really "Deposits Payable."

Marketable securities is a misnomer, although the expression is encountered frequently. Strictly speaking, marketable securities may be held for either a short-term or a long-term purpose. A better expression would be *temporary or short-term investments* (as distinguished from *long-term investments* in capital stock or bonds of other companies, which are not current assets). They represent an investment of excess cash not needed immediately. The idea is to get earnings on otherwise idle cash. The money is typically invested in securities that are highly liquid (easily convertible into cash) and that have relatively stable prices, such as short-term notes or government bonds. These securities are usually shown at cost or market price, whichever is lower. The market price is disclosed parenthetically if it is above cost.

Accounts receivable is the total amount owed to the company by its customers. Because some accounts will ultimately be uncollectible, the total is reduced by an allowance or provision for doubtful accounts (that is, possible "bad debts" arising from credit extended to customers who do not pay). The difference represents the net amount that will probably be collected.

Inventories consist of merchandise, finished products of manufacturers, goods in the process of being manufactured, and raw materials. These are frequently carried at cost or market (defined as replacement cost), whichever is lower. Cost of manufactured products normally is composed of raw material plus the costs of its conversion (direct labor and manufacturing overhead) into a finished product.

Once the total cost of goods purchased or produced by a company is measured, how should it be allocated between the goods sold (an expense) and the goods still on hand (an asset)? This is easy to do if the products are readily identifiable, like the cars of an automobile dealer or the expensive merchandise of a jewelry store. But it is infeasible to have an elaborate identification system for goods that are purchased and sold in vast numbers and variety. Therefore one of the following assumptions regarding cost flows is typically used: average cost, first-in, first-out, or last-in, first-out.[1]

Prepaid expenses are usually unimportant in relation to other assets. They are short-term prepayments or advance payments to suppliers. Examples are short-term prepaid expenses such as rent, operating supplies, and insurance that will be used up within the current operating cycle. They belong in current

[1]Accounting for manufacturing costs is discussed in Chapters 13 and 14. Incidentally, recent progress in data-processing capabilities at lower and lower costs has made specific identification more and more economical.

assets, because if they were not present more cash would be needed to conduct current operations.[2]

☐ PLANT ASSETS

Plant assets are sometimes called **fixed assets** or *property, plant, and equipment.* Because they are physical items that can be seen and touched, they are often called *tangible assets.*

Land is typically accounted for as a separate item and is carried indefinitely at its original cost.

Plant and equipment are initially recorded at cost: the invoice amount, plus freight and installation, less cash discounts. The major difficulties of measurement center on the choice of a pattern of depreciation—that is, the allocation of the original cost to the particular periods or products that benefit from the utilization of the assets.

Accountants often stress that depreciation is a process of allocation of the original cost of acquisition; it is not a process of valuation in the ordinary sense of the term. The usual balance sheet presentation does *not* show replacement cost, resale value, or the price changes since acquisition. The accounting for the latter is discussed in the final chapter.

The amount of original cost to be allocated over the total useful life of the asset as depreciation is the difference between the total acquisition cost and the estimated **terminal disposal value.** The depreciation allocation to each year may be made on the basis of time or service. The estimate of useful life, which is an important factor in determining the yearly allocation of depreciation, is influenced by estimates of physical wear and tear, technological change, and economic obsolescence.

For example, suppose that equipment with an estimated useful life of four years is acquired for $41,000. Its estimated scrap value is $1,000. Exhibit 17-2 shows how the asset would be displayed in the balance sheet if a straight-line method of depreciation were used. The annual depreciation expense that would appear on the income statement would be:

$$\frac{\text{original cost} - \text{estimated terminal value}}{\text{years of useful life}}$$

or

$$\frac{\$41,000 - \$1,000}{4} = \$10,000 \text{ per year}$$

☐ DEPRECIATION IS NOT CASH

An understanding of how the accountant reports plant assets and depreciation will highlight the limitations of financial statements. Professor William A. Paton, a leading scholar in accounting for more than sixty years, once compared

---

[2]Sometimes prepaid expenses are lumped with **deferred charges** as a single amount, *prepaid expenses and deferred charges,* that appears at the bottom of the current asset classification or at the bottom of all the assets as an "other asset." Deferred charges are like prepaid expenses, but they have longer-term benefits. For example, the costs of relocating a mass of employees to a different geographical area or the costs of rearranging an assembly line may be carried forward as deferred charges and written off as expense over a three- to five-year period.

EXHIBIT 17-2

Straight-Line Depreciation* (figures assumed)				
	BALANCES AT END OF YEAR			
	1	2	3	4
Plant and equipment (at original acquisition cost)	$41,000	$41,000	$41,000	$41,000
Less: Accumulated depreciation (the portion of original cost that has already been charged to operations as expense)	10,000	20,000	30,000	40,000
Net book value (the portion of original cost that will be charged to future operations as expense)	$31,000	$21,000	$11,000	$ 1,000

Other patterns of depreciation are discussed later in this chapter.

accounting for fixed assets with a boy's acquisition of a jelly-filled doughnut (the original cost, $41,000). The boy is so eager to taste the jelly that he licks it and creates a hole in the center of the doughnut (the accumulated depreciation of $10,000 at the end of Year 1). He continues his attack on the doughnut, and the hole enlarges. The hole is the **accumulated depreciation.** The *net book value* or *carrying amount* of the asset diminishes as the hole gradually becomes larger throughout the useful life of the doughnut. At the end of the useful life, the **book value** consists of the original doughnut ($41,000) less its gaping hole ($40,000), leaving a crumbly $1,000.

If you remember that accumulated depreciation is like a hole in a doughnut, you will be less likely to fall into the trap of those who think that accumulated depreciation is a sum of cash being accumulated for the replacement of plant assets.

Some accountants despise the likening of accumulated depreciation to the hole in the doughnut. Regardless of your degree of fondness for the doughnut analogy, remember that accumulated depreciation is not cash. If a company does actually decide to accumulate specific cash for the replacement of assets, such cash would be an asset that should be specifically labeled as a cash fund for replacement and expansion or a fund of marketable securities for replacement and expansion. Holiday Inns, Inc., has such a fund, calling it a *capital construction fund.* Such funds are quite rare, because most companies can earn better returns by investing any available cash in ordinary operations rather than in special funds. Typically, companies will use or acquire cash for the replacement and expansion of plant assets only as specific needs arise.

Leasehold improvements are not illustrated in the Exhibit 17-1 balance sheet, but they are often grouped with plant assets. Such improvements may be made by a lessee (tenant) who invests in painting, decorating, fixtures, and air-conditioning equipment that cannot be removed from the premises when a lease expires. The costs of leasehold improvements are written off in the same manner as depreciation; however, their periodic write-off is called **amortization.**

Natural resources such as mineral deposits are not illustrated here, but they are typically grouped with plant assets. Their original cost is written off in the form of *depletion* as the resources are used. For example, a coal mine may cost $10 million and originally contain an estimated 5 million tons. The depletion rate would be $2 per ton. If 500,000 tons were mined during the first year, depletion would be $1 million for that year; if 300,000 tons were mined the second year, depletion would be $600,000; and so forth.

☐ INTANGIBLE ASSETS

Intangible assets are a fuzzy class of **long-lived assets** that are not physical in nature. They are not illustrated in the Exhibit 17-1 balance sheet, but examples are goodwill, franchises, patents, trademarks, and copyrights.

Goodwill, which is discussed in more detail in the next chapter, is defined as the excess of the cost of an acquired company over the sum of the fair market value of its identifiable individual assets less the liabilities. For example, suppose Company A acquires Company B at a cost to A of $10 million and can assign only $9 million to various identifiable assets such as receivables, plant, and patents less liabilities assumed by the buyer; the remainder, $1 million, is goodwill. Identifiable intangible assets, such as franchises and patents, may be acquired singly, but goodwill cannot be acquired separately from a related business. This excess of the purchase price over the fair market value is called "goodwill" or "purchased goodwill" or, more accurately, "excess of cost over fair value of net identifiable assets of businesses acquired."

The accounting for goodwill illustrates how an *exchange* transaction is a basic concept of accounting. After all, there are many owners who could command a premium price for their companies. But such goodwill is never recorded. Only the acquired goodwill arising from arm's-length bargaining is shown as an asset on the purchaser's records.

For shareholder-reporting purposes, goodwill must be amortized, generally in a straight-line manner, over the periods benefited. The maximum amortization period should not be longer than forty years. The minimum amortization period was not specified by the Accounting Principles Board (APB *Opinion No. 17*), but a lump-sum write-off on acquisition is forbidden.

Research and development costs are those resulting from planned search or critical investigation aimed at obtaining new products or processes or significant improvements in existing products or processes. The Financial Accounting Standards Board (*Statement No. 2*) has required that all such costs be charged to expense when incurred. The FASB recognized that research and development costs may generate many long-term benefits, but the general high degree of uncertainty about the extent and measurement of future benefits led to conservative accounting in the form of immediate write-off.

☐ HISTORICAL THRUST TOWARD CONSERVATISM

Many managers and accountants insist that some intangible assets have unlimited lives. But the Accounting Principles Board ruled that the values of all intangible assets eventually disappear. The attitudes of the regulatory bodies toward accounting for intangible assets became increasingly conservative during the 1970s. For example, before October 31, 1970, the amortization of good-will, trademarks, and franchises with indefinite useful lives was not mandatory. The new requirement for amortization was not imposed retroactively. Consequently, many companies *are* currently amortizing goodwill acquired after October 31, 1970, but *are not* amortizing goodwill acquired before that date.

Before 1975, many companies regarded research and development costs as assets. Research costs were treated as deferred charges to future operations and amortized over the years of expected benefit, usually three to six years. But, as already mentioned, the FASB banned deferral and required write-off of these costs as incurred.

The contrast between the accounting for tangible and intangible long-lived assets raises some provocative and knotty theoretical issues. Accountants are sometimes overly concerned with physical objects or contractual rights, tending to overlook the underlying reality of future economic benefits. This preoccupation with physical evidence often results in the expensing of outlays that should be treated as assets. Thus expenditures for research, advertising, employee training, and the like are generally expensed, although it seems clear that in an economic sense such expenditures represent expected future benefit. The difficulty of measuring future benefits is the reason usually advanced for expensing these items.

In summary, accounting practice for intangible assets is not consistent, as this excerpt from the 1979 Annual Report of Omark Industries exemplifies: "Costs incurred for internally developed patents, trademarks and formulae are charged to current operations. The costs of purchased patents, trademarks and formulae are amortized over their respective legal or economic lives. The excess of purchase price over value ascribed to assets of businesses purchased is amortized over periods presently ranging up to 20 years."

☐ INCOME TAX REPORTING AND SHAREHOLDER REPORTING

Throughout this discussion of long-lived assets, please distinguish between reporting to stockholders and reporting to the income tax authorities. Reports to stockholders must abide by "generally accepted accounting principles." In contrast, reports to income tax authorities must abide by the income tax rules and regulations. These rules are in accordance with GAAP in many respects, but they frequently diverge.

Keep in mind that the income tax laws are patchworks that often are designed to give taxpayers special incentives for making investments. For example, England permits a taxpayer to write off the full cost of new equipment as expense in the year acquired. Although a total write-off may be permitted for income tax purposes, it is not permitted for shareholder-reporting purposes.

American companies are generally not required to follow the same valuations or depreciation schedules for both shareholder-reporting and income tax purposes. Therefore there is nothing immoral or unethical about "keeping two sets of records." For example, consider how the accounting for perpetual franchises, trademarks, and goodwill differs. Their acquisition costs *must* be amortized for shareholder reporting but *must not* be amortized for income tax purposes; the Internal Revenue Service will not allow amortization because of the indefinite duration of their usefulness.

The following table summarizes how accounting for two purposes can conflict:

	maximum* useful lives in years for measuring annual amortization	
	to shareholders	to internal revenue service
Patents	17	Same as first column
Copyrights	40	Same
Sports player contracts	Length of contract	Same
Franchise and licenses	Length of contract or 40 if length is unlimited	Same or no amortization permitted†
Trademarks	40	No amortization permitted†
Goodwill	40	No amortization permitted†
Research and development	Full write-off as incurred	Same

*These maximums are frequently far in excess of the economic lives. Thus patents and copyrights are often written off in two or three years because the related products have short lives.

† The Internal Revenue Service does not permit amortization of intangible assets with indefinite useful lives. Examples are franchises of unlimited duration, such as a football franchise, goodwill, and trademarks.

☐ LIABILITIES

Current liabilities are those that fall due within the coming year or within the normal operating cycle if longer than a year. *Accounts payable* are amounts owed to suppliers who extended credit for purchases on open account. These open account purchases from trade creditors are ordinarily supported by signatures on purchase orders or similar business documents. *Notes payable* are backed by formal promissory notes held by a bank or business creditors.

Accrued expenses payable are recognized for wages, salaries, interest, and similar items. The accountant tries to recognize expenses as they occur in relation to the operations of a given time period regardless of when they are paid for in cash. *Accrued income taxes payable* is a special accrued expense of enough magnitude to warrant a separate classification.

Long-term liabilities are those that fall due beyond one year. Bonds payable are formal certificates of indebtedness that are accompanied by a promise to pay interest at a specified annual rate.

Mortgage bonds are supposed to provide some additional safety for the bondholders in case the company is unable to meet its regular obligations on the bonds. If such an undesirable event occurs, the bondholders will have a prior lien on a specific asset(s). This means that such an asset may be sold and the proceeds used to liquidate the obligations to the bondholders. If no such lien exists, the bondholders have no special claims against the assets beyond the general claim against the *total* assets enjoyed by the general creditors such as trade creditors.

Subordinated debentures (not illustrated in Exhibit 17-1) are like any long-term debt except that *subordinated* means such bondholders are junior to the other general creditors in exercising claims against assets, and *debenture* means a general claim against all unencumbered assets rather than a specific claim against particular assets.

The following example should clarify these ideas. Suppose a company is liquidated. *Liquidation* means converting assets to cash and terminating outside claims. The company had miscellaneous assets, including a building, that were converted into $110,000 cash.

ASSETS		EQUITIES	
Cash	$110,000	Accounts payable	$ 30,000
		First-mortgage bonds payable	90,000
		Subordinated debentures payable	40,000
		Total liabilities	$160,000
		Stockholders' equity (negative)	(50,000)
Total assets	$110,000	Total equities	$110,000

The mortgage bonds would be paid in full, the trade creditors would get paid two-thirds on the dollar ($20,000 for a $30,000 claim), and the other claimants would get nothing. If the debentures were *unsubordinated,* the $20,000 of cash remaining after paying $90,000 to the mortgage holders would be used to settle the $70,000 claims of the unsecured creditors as follows:

To trade creditors	$\frac{3}{7} \times \$20,000 =$	$ 8,571
To debenture holders	$\frac{4}{7} \times \$20,000 =$	11,429
Total cash distributed		$20,000

Deferred income taxes, which arise because the timing of income tax payments is delayed beyond the current operating cycle, are not shown in Exhibit 17-1 but are commonly found in the annual reports of American companies.

☐ STOCKHOLDERS' EQUITY

Stockholders' equity (also called *owners' equity* or *capital* or *net worth*) as an overall class is the total residual interest in the business. It is a balance sheet difference, the excess of total assets over total liabilities. There may be many subclasses. It arises from two main sources: (1) contributed or paid-in capital and (2) retained income.

Paid-in capital typically comes from owners who invest in the business in exchange for stock certificates, which are issued as evidence of shareholder rights. It is often composed of a number of classes of capital stock with a variety of different attributes. *Preferred stock* typically has some priority over other shares regarding dividends or the distribution of assets upon liquidation. A *cumulative* preferred stock means that if a specified annual dividend of, say, $5 per share is not paid, this preferred claim accumulates and must be paid in full before any dividends are paid to any other classes of stock. Preferred shareholders do not ordinarily have voting privileges regarding the management of the corporation.

Stock frequently has a designated **par** or **legal** or **stated** value that is printed on the face of the certificate. For preferred stock (and bonds), par is a basis for designating the amount of dividends or interest. Many preferred stocks have $100 par values; therefore a 9 percent, $100-par preferred stock would carry a $9 annual dividend. Similarly, an 8 percent bond usually means that the investor is entitled to annual interest of $80 because most bonds have par values of $1,000. Par value of common stock has no practical importance. Historically, it was used for establishing the maximum legal liability of the stockholder in case the corporation could not pay its debts. Currently, it is set at a nominal amount (for example, $5) in relation to the market value of the stock upon issuance (for example, $70). It is generally illegal for a corporation to sell an original issue of its common stock below par. Common shareholders typically have *limited liability,* which means that creditors cannot resort to them as individuals if the corporation itself cannot pay its debts.

Common stock has no predetermined rate of dividends and is the last to obtain a share in the assets when the corporation is dissolved. Common shares usually have voting power in the management of the corporation. Common stock is usually the riskiest investment in a corporation, being unattractive in dire times but attractive in prosperous times because, unlike other stocks, there is no limit to the stockholder's potential participation in earnings.

Paid-in capital in excess of par (formerly called *capital surplus* or *paid-in surplus*) is the excess received over the par or stated or legal value of the shares issued. Common shares are often issued at a price substantially greater than par. The balance sheet effects of selling 100,000 shares of $5 par common at $80 per share would be:

Cash	$8,000,000	Common stock	$ 500,000
		Paid-in capital in excess of par	7,500,000
		Stockholders' equity	$8,000,000

Retained income, also called *retained earnings* or *reinvested earnings,* is the increase in stockholders' equity due to profitable operations. It was explained more fully in Chapter 16. Retained income is the dominant item of stockholders' equity for most companies. For instance, as of January 1, 1980, Caterpillar Tractor Co. had a stockholders' equity of $3,065 million, of which $2,888 million was retained income.

Treasury stock is a corporation's issued stock that has subsequently been repurchased by the company. Such repurchase is a liquidation of an ownership claim. It should therefore appear on a balance sheet as a deduction from total stockholders' equity. The stock is not retired; it is only held temporarily "in the treasury" to be distributed later as a part of an employee stock purchase plan or as an executive bonus or for use in an acquisition of another company. Cash dividends are not paid on shares held in the treasury; cash dividends are distributed only to the shares outstanding (in the hands of stockholders), and treasury stock is not outstanding stock. Treasury stock is usually of minor significance in the financial picture of a corporation.

☐ STOCK SPLITS

Many companies occasionally split their stock. A **stock split** or split-up refers to the issuance of additional shares for no payments by stockholders and under conditions indicating that the objective is to increase the number of outstanding shares for the purpose of reducing their unit market price, in order to bring the stock price down into a more popular range. This supposedly encourages wider distribution and a higher total market value for the same ownership interest. Corporate management naturally wants the stock to be as attractive as possible, easing the task of raising additional investment capital when needed. For a given ownership interest, the higher the total market value, the more capital can be raised by issuance of additional shares.

Stock split-ups can be achieved by issuing new shares for old shares or simply by issuing additional shares to conform to the size of the split. Suppose that Company A has the following stockholders' equity section:

	BEFORE 2-FOR-1 SPLIT	CHANGES	AFTER 2-FOR-1 SPLIT
Common stock, 100,000 shares @ $10 par	$ 1,000,000	⎡−100,000 shares @ $10 par⎤ +200,000 shares @ $5 par	$ 1,000,000
Additional paid-in capital	4,000,000		4,000,000
Total paid-in capital	$ 5,000,000		$ 5,000,000
Retained income	6,000,000		6,000,000
Stockholders' equity	$11,000,000		$11,000,000
Overall market value of stock @ assumed $150 per share	$15,000,000	@ assumed $80 per share	$16,000,000

There is no effect on the reported amount of the total stockholders' equity. A person who previously owned 1,000 shares (a 1 percent interest) now owns 2,000 shares (still a 1 percent interest). Professor Willard Graham explained a stock split as being akin to taking a gallon of whiskey and pouring it into five individual bottles. The resulting packaging will attract a price for each fifth that will produce a higher total value than if the gallon were not split (less the amount spilled when pouring into the five bottles—that's the legal, printing, and clerical costs). Therefore Company A splits its stock with the hope that the market value of the total ownership interest will increase from $15 million to $16 million because one share that previously sold for $150 will now be in the form of two shares that might sell for $80 each, or a total of $160.[3]

[3]This hope is not justified by the evidence. See Linda Snyder Hayes, "The Myth of the Stock Split," *Fortune*, February 26, 1979, pp. 101–2. The myth is that a lower price will enhance total demand and total market value. But investors are not easily fooled by new wrappers placed on unchanged merchandise.

Cash dividends are a straightforward means of rewarding the shareholder for investing in the corporation. In contrast, so-called stock dividends are often misunderstood. The term **stock dividends** is a misnomer because such dividends are totally different from cash dividends. A stock dividend is a distribution to stockholders of additional shares of any class of the distributing company's stock; the stockholders make no additional investment in the corporation. The most frequently encountered type of stock dividend is the distribution of additional common stock to existing holders of common stock already outstanding; usually anywhere from 1 to 10 percent of the number of common shares already outstanding are distributed.

In substance, stock dividends are not dividends at all, as the term is usually understood. Each shareholder's proportionate interest in the corporation is unchanged; the unit market price of each share tends to decline in response to the additional shares outstanding without any corresponding infusion of new shareholder investment in the corporation. Reconsider our example of Company A (before the split). Suppose the market value of common shares is $150 at the time of issuance of the stock dividend. A "common-on-common" stock dividend of 2 percent would affect the stockholders' equity section as follows:

	BEFORE 2% STOCK DIVIDEND	CHANGES	AFTER 2% STOCK DIVIDEND
Common stock, 100,000 shares @ $10 par	$ 1,000,000	+(2,000 shares @ $10 par) = +20,000	$ 1,020,000
Paid-in capital in excess of par	4,000,000	+[2,000 shares @ ($150 − $10)] = +280,000	4,280,000
Retained income	6,000,000	−(2,000 @ $150) = −300,000	5,700,000
Stockholders' equity	$11,000,000		$11,000,000
Overall market value of stock @ assumed $150 per share	$15,000,000	@ assumed $147.06 per share*	$15,000,000*
Total shares outstanding	100,000		102,000
Individual shareholder:			
Assumed ownership of shares	1,000		1,020
Percentage ownership interest	1%		Still 1%

*Many simultaneous events affect the level of stock prices, including expectations regarding the general economy, the industry, and the specific company. Thus the market price of the stock may move in either direction when the stock dividend is declared. Theory and complicated case studies indicate that a stock dividend should have zero effect on the total market value of the firm. Accordingly, the net market price per share should be $15,000,000 ÷ 102,000 shares = $147.06.

First, note that the individual shareholder receives no assets from the corporation.[4] Moreover, the shareholder's fractional interest is unchanged; if the shareholder sells the dividend shares, his or her proportionate ownership interest in the company will decrease.

[4]For additional reading, see R. Watts, "The Information Content of Dividends," *Journal of Business,* April 1973, pp. 191–211; and S. Bar-Yosef and L. Brown, "A Reexamination of Stock Splits Using Moving Betas," *Journal of Finance,* September 1977, pp. 1069–80.

Second, the company records the transaction by transferring the market value of the additional shares from retained income to common stock and "paid-in capital in excess of par." This entry is often referred to as being a "capitalization of retained income." It is basically a signal to the shareholder that $300,000 of retained income is no longer available as a claim to future cash dividends.

Stock dividends are prime examples of have-your-cake-and-eat-it-too manipulations that in substance are meaningless but that seemingly leave all interested parties happy. The company pays a "dividend" but gives up no assets. The stockholders may think they are getting a dividend even though to realize it in cash they must sell some of their fractional interest in the company.

The stock dividend device is particularly effective where a low percentage, such as 1 or 2 percent, of additional shares are issued that may have an imperceptible effect on the market price. The recipient, who is not particularly concerned about his or her fractional ownership interest anyway, may hold 1,000 shares at a $150 market price before the dividend and 1,020 shares at the same $150 market price after the dividend. The recipient's reaction is likely to be favorable because the dividend increased his or her wealth by $20 \times \$150 = \$3,000$. Why? Because the peculiarities of the stock market somehow avoided the logical lowering of the market price per share, and not because the corporation gave the recipient anything directly.

☐ STOCK SPLITS AND DIVIDENDS

The U.S. accounting authorities differentiate among sizes of stock dividends. That is, the low-percentage dividends just described are really "stock dividends" and must be accounted for on the basis of the market prices of the shares. However, high-percentage dividends (typically those 20 percent or higher) must be accounted for as stock splits.

A stock split is often achieved via the use of the stock dividend device by issuing an enormous stock "dividend" of 50 or 100 percent or more. The use of such high-percentage stock dividends is merely another way of obtaining a stock split. Such a transaction should not really be called a stock dividend; it would be better to call it a "split-up effected in the form of a stock dividend." This requires a decrease in Retained Income and an increase in Common Stock in the amount of only the *par value* (rather than the market value) of the additional shares. For example, if the two-for-one split described earlier (see the section entitled "Stock Splits") were achieved through an equivalent 100 percent stock dividend, the total amount of stockholders' equity would be unaffected. However, its composition would change:

	BEFORE 100% STOCK DIVIDEND	CHANGES	AFTER 100% STOCK DIVIDEND
Common stock, 100,000 shares @ $10 par	$ 1,000,000	+(100,000 shares @ $10 = $1,000,000)	$ 2,000,000
Paid-in capital in excess of par	4,000,000		4,000,000
Total paid-in capital	$ 5,000,000		$ 6,000,000
Retained income	6,000,000	−$1,000,000 par value of "dividend"	5,000,000
Stockholders' equity	$11,000,000		$11,000,000

Stock splits frequently occur in this form of a stock "dividend" instead of in the classical form described earlier. Why? The major reason is to save clerical costs and the bothering of shareholders. After all, the swapping of old certificates for new certificates is more expensive than the mere printing and mailing of additional certificates.

☐ RESERVES AND FUNDS

Accountants frequently use the term **reserve** in their reports. To a layperson, reserve normally means setting aside a specific amount of cash or securities for a special purpose such as vacations, illness, and birthday gifts. Accountants *never* use the word reserve to describe such an amount; instead they call such assets a **fund**. For example, a *pension fund* is cash or other highly liquid assets segregated for meeting the pension obligations. Similarly, a *sinking fund* is usually cash or securities segregated for meeting obligations on bonded debt. Holiday Inns, Inc., has a *construction fund* for building new hotels.

The word *reserve* is on the wane, but it is used frequently enough to warrant an acquaintance with its three broad meanings in accounting:

1. *Retained income reserve.* A restriction of intent or authority to *declare* dividends, denoted by a specific subdivision of retained income. The term *appropriated* or *restricted* is better terminology than reserve. Examples are reserves for contingencies (which can refer to any possible *future* losses from such miscellany as foreign devaluations of currency, lawsuits, and natural disasters) and reserves for self-insurance (which refer to possible *future* losses from fires or other casualty losses). This reserve is *not* a reduction of total retained income; it is merely an earmarking or subdividing of part of retained income. The 1977 annual report of Delta Air Lines provides an illustration in the stockholders' equity section:

> Retained earnings (of which $284,631,000 is restricted at June 30, 1977 as to the payment of cash dividends under credit agreements) $480,853,000

2. *Asset valuation.* An offset to an asset. Examples: reserves for depreciation, depletion, uncollectible accounts, or reduction of inventory or investments to market value. "Allowance for . . ." is much better terminology.

3. *Liability.* An estimate of a definite liability of indefinite or uncertain amount. Examples: reserves for income taxes, warranties, pensions, and vacation pay. "Estimated liability for . . ." is much better terminology. An example of a liability reserve is provided by the annual report of Pitney-Bowes, Inc. (the major manufacturer of postage meters). It contains the following liability account: Reserve for Future Windup Costs of Discontinued Operations.

Income statement

☐ USE OF SUBTOTALS

Most investors are vitally concerned about the company's ability to produce long-run earnings and dividends. In this regard, income statements are much more important than balance sheets. The income statement is straightforward and, for the most part, is stated in terms of current dollars. Revenue is shown first; this represents the total sales value of products delivered and services rendered to customers. Expenses are then listed and deducted. The statement can take two major forms: single-step and multiple-step. The single-step statement merely lists all expenses without drawing subtotals, whereas the multiple-step statement contains one or more subtotals, as illustrated in Exhibit 17-3.

EXHIBIT
17-3

THE GREEN CO.
Statement of Income
For the Year Ended December 31, 19X1
(In thousands of dollars)

Sales		$55,000
Cost of goods sold		40,000
Gross profit on sales		$15,000
Operating expenses:		
Selling expenses	$8,900	
Administrative expenses	2,000	
Depreciation expense	1,000	11,900
Operating income		$ 3,100
Interest expense		800
Income before income taxes		$ 2,300
Income taxes		1,150
Net income		$ 1,150
Earnings per share of common stock		$5.27*

*Computation of earnings per share:

Net income	$1,150,000
Deduct preferred dividends	96,000
Net income for holders of common stock	$1,054,000
Divide by common shares	200,000
Earnings per share of common stock	$5.27

Subtotals often highlight significant relationships. As explained in the preceding chapter, sometimes cost of goods sold is deducted from sales to show gross profit or gross margin. This indicates the size of the margin above merchandise costs—an important statistic for many managers and analysts.

Depreciation expense, various selling expenses, and various administrative expenses are often grouped as "operating expenses" and deducted from the gross profit to obtain *operating income,* which is also called *operating profit.* (Of course, cost of goods sold can actually be viewed as an operating expense, because it is also deducted from sales revenue to obtain "operating income.")

☐ OPERATING AND FINANCIAL MANAGEMENT

Operating income is a popular subtotal because of the oft-made distinction between operating management and financial management. *Operating management* is mainly concerned with the major day-to-day activities that generate sales revenue (that is, utilizing a given set of resources). In contrast, *financial management* is mainly concerned with where to get cash and how to use cash for the benefit of the entity (that is, obtaining and investing the needed capital). **Examples of questions of financial management include:** How much cash should be held in checking accounts? Should we pay a dividend? Should we borrow or issue common stock? The best managements perform both operating management and financial management superbly. However, many managers are superior operating managers and inferior financial managers, or vice versa.

Because interest expense is usually a result of financial rather than operating decisions, it appears as a separate item after operating income. In this way, comparisons of operating income between years and between companies are facilitated. Some companies make heavy use of debt, which causes high interest expenses, whereas other companies incur little debt and interest expenses.

☐ INCOME, EARNINGS, PROFITS

Although this book does tend to use *income* most often, the terms *income, earnings,* and *profits* are often used as synonyms. The income statement is also called the *statement of earnings,* the *statement of profit and loss,* and the *P & L statement.* For some strange reason, many companies, as illustrated in Exhibits 17-3 and 17-4, will use net *income* on their income statements but will refer to retained income as retained *earnings.*

The term *net income* is the residual after deducting income taxes. The term "net" is seldom used for any subtotals that precede the calculation of net income; instead, the subtotals are called "income." Thus the appropriate term is "operating income" or "income from operations," not "net operating income."

Income taxes are often a prominent expense and are not merely listed with operating expenses. Instead, income taxes are often deducted as a separate item immediately before net income.

Statement of retained earnings

The analysis of the changes in retained earnings is frequently placed in a separate statement, the statement of retained earnings, also called statement of retained income. As Exhibit 17-4 demonstrates, the major reasons for changes in

EXHIBIT 17-4	THE GREEN COMPANY Statement of Retained Earnings For the Year Ended December 31, 19X1 (In thousands of dollars)		
	Retained earnings, December 31, 19X0		$ 900
	Net income (Exhibit 17-3)		1,150
	Total		$2,050
	Deduct dividends:		
	On preferred stock	$ 96	
	On common stock	954	1,050
	Retained earnings, December 31, 19X1		$1,000

retained income are dividends and net income. Note especially that dividends are *not* expenses. They are not deductions in computing net income, as Chapter 16 explained in more detail. (This is a long chapter. Pause and read p. 541 before proceeding.)

Statement of changes in financial position

☐ CONCEPT OF CHANGES STATEMENT

In 1971, in *Opinion No. 19*, the Accounting Principles Board added another financial report to its requirements. A **statement of changes in financial position** must be presented as a basic financial statement in corporate annual reports. Before 1971, the statement was most widely known as a **statement of sources and applications of funds.** For brevity in the ensuing discussion, the statement will frequently be called a **changes statement.** Many accountants call it a *funds statement;* the term is convenient, but not descriptive.

The major purpose of the statement of changes in financial position is to provide a detailed presentation of the results of financial management, as distinguished from operating management. The changes statement summarizes the financing and investing activities of the enterprise. The statement shows directly information that readers of financial reports could otherwise obtain only by makeshift analysis and interpretation of published balance sheets and statements of income and retained income.

Balance sheets are statements of financial position, whereas changes statements are obviously statements of *changes* in financial position. Balance sheets show the status at a day in time. In contrast, changes statements, income statements, and retained income statements cover periods of time; they provide the explanations of why the balance sheet items have changed. This linkage may be depicted as shown in the accompanying diagram.

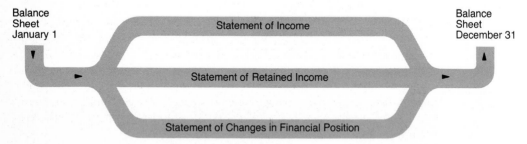

Balance Sheet January 1

Statement of Income

Statement of Retained Income

Statement of Changes in Financial Position

Balance Sheet December 31

The overall idea of the statement of changes in financial position may be most easily summarized by calling it a *where got, where gone statement,* a term used to describe the statement in its early stages of development. It was devised to provide the reader with a glimpse of where the resources came from during the year and where they have gone.

☐ FOCUS ON WORKING CAPITAL

The statement of changes in financial position is still in its infancy as a required major financial report. It is undergoing experimentation as more experience is being gained with it. There has been long-standing disagreement on the concept and format of the changes statement.[5] By far the most popular approach has been to view it as an explanation of why **working capital** has changed for a given period. The probable reason that the changes statement has focused on working capital is the perspective it provides on the entire natural operating cycle rather than just one part thereof (such as cash or cash plus receivables).

Accountants define *working capital* as the excess of current assets over current liabilities. Pure, unrestricted cash is working capital in its finest sense. However, *working capital* is broader than *cash* alone. It is a "net" concept; that is, it is the *difference* between a category of assets and a category of liabilities.

☐ TYPICAL SOURCES AND USES

Most changes statements have displayed the sources and uses of working capital, as follows:

Sources of working capital (or working capital provided):
Operations (excess of revenue over charges against revenue requiring working capital)
Sale of noncurrent assets (plant, equipment, long-term investments in securities)
Issuance of long-term debt
Issuance of capital stock

Uses of working capital (or working capital applied):
Declaration of cash dividends
Purchase of noncurrent assets (plant, equipment, long-term investments in securities)
Reduction of long-term debt
Repurchase of outstanding capital stock

Financial analysts have cited the following useful information as being revealed by a changes statement: the major sources from which working capital has been obtained (that is, profitable operations, borrowing, sale of capital stock); clues as to the financial management habits of the executives (that is, management attitudes toward spending and financing); the proportion of working capital applied to plant, dividends, debt retirement, and so forth; indications of the impact of working capital flows upon future dividend-paying probabilities; and an indication of the company's trend toward general financial strength or weakness.

☐ EXAMPLE OF CHANGES STATEMENT

The preparation of a changes statement can become complex in some instances, but the basic ideas are straightforward. Generally, as the example will show, a changes statement can simply be prepared from a visual inspection of the changes in balance sheet items, the use of a few additional facts, and a familiarity with the typical sources and uses of working capital listed above.

[5]For example, see Loyd C. Heath, "Let's Scrap the Funds Statement," *Journal of Accountancy,* October 1978, p. 94.

Consider the example of the B Company, which had the following condensed income statement for 19X2:

B COMPANY Statement of Income For the Year Ended December 31, 19X2 (in thousands)		
Sales		$200
Deduct expenses:		
Expenses requiring working capital	$140	
Depreciation	17	157
Net income		$ 43

The B Company had the following condensed balance sheets (in thousands of dollars):

	DECEMBER 31				DECEMBER 31		
	19X2	19X1	CHANGE		19X2	19X1	CHANGE
Current assets:				Current			
Cash	$ 5	$ 25	$ (20)	liabilities	$100	$ 10	$ 90
Net receivables	45	25	20	Long-term debt	105	5	100
Inventories	100	60	40	Total liabilities	$205	$ 15	$190
Total current				Stockholders'			
assets	$150	$110	$ 40	equity	425	315	110
Plant assets, net							
of accumulated							
depreciation	480	220	260				
Total assets	$630	$330	$300	Total equities	$630	$330	$300

Additional information: In 19X2 the company issued long-term debt and capital stock for cash of $100,000 and $87,000, respectively. Cash dividends were $20,000. New equipment was acquired for $277,000 cash.

Because the changes statement explains the *causes* for the change in working capital, the first step is to compute the amount of the change (which represents the net *effect*):

	DECEMBER 31		
	19X2	19X1	
Current assets	$150	$110	
Current liabilities	100	10	
Working capital	$ 50	$100	
Net decrease in working capital			$50

(Exhibit 17-5 illustrates how this computation is usually shown in detail in the lower part of the changes statement in the section called changes in components of working capital.

Exhibit 17-5

B COMPANY
Statement of Changes in Financial Position
For the Year Ended December 31, 19X2
(in thousands of dollars)

SOURCES AND USES OF WORKING CAPITAL

Sources:		
Working capital provided by operations (Schedule A)		$ 60
Issuance of long-term debt		100
Issuance of additional capital stock		87
Total sources		$247
Uses:		
Payment of cash dividends	$ 20	
Acquisition of plant and equipment	277	
Total uses		297
Decrease in working capital		$(50)

CHANGES IN COMPONENTS OF WORKING CAPITAL

	DECEMBER 31		INCREASE (DECREASE) IN WORKING CAPITAL
	19X2	19X1	
Current assets:			
Cash	$ 5	$ 25	$(20)
Net receivables	45	25	20
Inventories	100	60	40
Total current assets	$150	$110	$ 40
Current liabilities (detailed)	100	10	(90)
Working capital	$ 50	$100	
Decrease in working capital			$(50)

SCHEDULE A
WORKING CAPITAL PROVIDED BY OPERATIONS

First Alternative Presentation (Using the Addback Method):	
Net income (from income statement)	$ 43
Add: Charges against income not requiring working capital:	
Depreciation	17
Working capital provided by operations	$ 60
Second Alternative Presentation* (Using the Straightforward Method):	
Sales	$200
Deduct: All expenses requiring working capital (detailed)	140
Working capital provided by operations	$ 60

*Although the straightforward method is frequently easier to understand, the addback method is used almost exclusively in annual reports.

When business expansion occurs, as in this case where there is a strong working-capital position at the outset, working capital will probably decline. Why? Because the managers tend to let their short-term payables get as high as seems prudent. Cash balances will also tend to fall to a bare minimum because the cash is usually needed for investment in miscellaneous business assets required for expansion.

The statement in Exhibit 17-5 gives a direct picture of where the working capital came from and where it has gone. In this instance, the excess of uses over sources reduced working capital by $50,000. Without the statement of changes, the reader of the annual report would have to conduct his or her own analysis of the balance sheets, income statement, and statement of retained income to get a grasp of the impact of financial management decisions.

☐ CHANGES IN BALANCE SHEET EQUATION

The balance sheet equation is again useful because it can provide the conceptual framework underlying the statement of changes in financial position. Consider the following:

$$\text{assets} = \text{liabilities} + \text{stockholders' equity}$$

$$\begin{aligned}\text{current assets (CA)} + \\ \text{noncurrent assets (NCA)} = \end{aligned} \begin{aligned}\text{current liabilities (CL)} + \\ \text{noncurrent liabilities (NCL)} + \\ \text{paid-in capital (PC)} + \text{retained} \\ \text{income (RI)}\end{aligned}$$

$$CA - CL = NCL + PC + RI - NCA$$

therefore, working capital (WC),
which is CA − CL $= NCL + PC + RI - NCA$

Change (Δ) in working capital between balance sheet dates:

$$\Delta WC = \Delta NCL + \Delta PC + \Delta RI - \Delta NCA$$

or

change in working capital $=$ change in all nonworking capital accounts

The statement of changes in financial position focuses on the changes in the nonworking capital accounts (that is, the noncurrent accounts) as a way of explaining how and *why* the level of working capital has gone up or down during a given period. Thus the major changes in the accounts on the right-hand side of the above equation appear in the statement of changes in financial position as *causes* of the change in working capital. The left side of the equation measures the *net effect* of the change in working capital.

Applying the equation to our data, we can see, step by step, how the changes statement in Exhibit 17-5 is based on the same theoretical foundation that underlies the other financial statements (in thousands of dollars):

	ΔWC	=	ΔNCL	+	ΔPC	+	ΔRI	−	ΔNCA
Sales	+ 200 =						+200		
Expenses requiring working capital	− 140 =						− 140		
Working capital provided by operations	+ 60 =						+ 60		
Expense not requiring working capital: depreciation	0 =						− 17	−	(−17)
Net income, a subtotal							+ 43		
Issuance of long-term debt	+100 =		+100						
Issuance of capital stock	+ 87 =				+87				
Cash dividends	− 20 =						− 20		
Acquisition of new equipment	−277 =							−	(+277)
Net changes	− 50 =		+100		+87		+ 23	−	(+260)

$$-50$$

When statements become complicated, accountants prefer to use work sheets or T-accounts to help their analysis. In any event, the totals shown in the tabulation indicate that all transactions affecting working capital have been accounted for. The $50,000 *change* in working capital is offset by the *changes* in the nonworking capital accounts. Each noncurrent account can be analyzed in detail if desired.

☐ STEPS IN PREPARATION

Although balance sheet equations, T-accounts, or work sheets are frequently helpful, the statement of changes in financial position can also be prepared in a less-formal way:

1. Prepare a schedule of changes in the components of working capital. (See the second section of Exhibit 17-5).

2. Prepare the sources section, which customarily starts with working capital provided by operations. (See the top part of Exhibit 17-5.)

3. Determine other sources and uses of working capital by gathering additional information (given in this illustration). In an actual case, the keys to this approach are (a) to know the typical sources and uses and (b) to search systematically for them through the annual report.

4. If all the necessary information is not directly available, the changes should be analyzed for all balance sheet items *except* current assets and current liabilities. To illustrate such analysis, consider the B Company balance sheets on page 532:

a. The change in long-term debt is an increase of $105,000 − $5,000 = $100,000. The indication is that additional long-term debt was issued, a source of working capital.

b. The change in stockholders' equity was an increase of $425,000 − $315,000 = $110,000, to be explained. What are the typical explanations for changes in stockholders' equity? Issuances of capital stock, net income (or loss), and dividends. Thus:

$$\text{net increase} = \text{new issuance} + \text{net income} - \text{dividends}$$

$$\$110,000 = \text{new issuance} + \$43,000 - \$20,000$$

$$\text{new issuance} = \$110,000 - \$43,000 + \$20,000$$

$$\text{new issuance} = \$87,000, \text{ a source of working capital}[6]$$

c. Turning to uses, the only other noncurrent account not fully explained is net plant assets. The net change is an increase of $480,000 − $220,000 = $260,000. Changes therein are usually explained by assets acquired, asset disposals (none in this example), and depreciation expense for the period:

$$\text{net increase} = \text{acquisitions} - \text{disposals} - \text{depreciation expense}$$

$$\$260,000 = \text{acquisitions} - 0 - \$17,000$$

$$\text{acquisitions} = \$260,000 + \$17,000$$

$$\text{acquisitions} = \$277,000, \text{ a use or application of working capital}[7]$$

5. The difference between the total sources and uses of working capital is the net change in working capital, which must agree with the amount computed in step 1, a $50,000 decrease in this illustration.

6. APB *Opinion No. 19* requires that major financing and investing activities be included in the changes statement even though working capital is unaffected. For example, the statement would show the acquisition of a building (a use) in exchange for the issuance of capital stock (a source). Other examples are the exchanging of one type of long-term debt for another, the conversion of long-term debt into common stock, and the swapping of plant assets. Our illustration does not include such transactions.

☐ WORKING CAPITAL PROVIDED BY OPERATIONS

The first major item in the sources section is **working capital provided by operations.** There are two ways to compute this item: the **addback method** and the **straightforward method,** shown in Schedule A of Exhibit 17-5. Because it is easier to understand, please initially consider the *straightforward method.* Sales to customers are almost always *the* major source of working capital. Correspondingly, outlays for cost of goods sold and operating expenses are almost always *the* major use of working capital. The excess of sales over all the expenses requiring working capital is, by definition, the working capital provided by operations. The direct way to compute this figure is shown as the second alternative presentation in Schedule A, sales of $200,000 minus expenses of $140,000 equals working capital provided by operations, $60,000.

An alternative, often convenient, way to compute working capital provided by operations is to begin with net income. Then adjust for those items that

---

[6]The $87,000 new issuance was disclosed in the given data. Even if the $87,000 were not specifically revealed, it could be deduced from the other known amounts, as shown above in the equation approach.

[7]Here again, the amount was included in the given data, but if it were not, it could be computed in the manner demonstrated above in the equation approach.

entered the computation of net income but did *not* affect working capital. This can be called the *addback method.* Using the balance sheet equation, compare the two methods:

EFFECTS OF OPERATIONS	$\Delta WC = \Delta NCL + \Delta PC + \Delta RI$	$- \Delta NCA$
Straightforward method:		
Sales	+200,000 =	+200,000
Expenses requiring working capital	−140,000 =	−140,000
Expenses not requiring working capital:		
depreciation	0 =	− 17,000 − (−17,000)
Working capital provided by operations	+60,000 =	+ 43,000 − (−17,000)
Addback method:		
Begin with net income	+ 43,000 =	+ 43,000
Add charges to income not requiring working capital: depreciation*	+ 17,000 =	− (−17,000)
Working capital provided by operations	+ 60,000 =	+ 43,000 − (−17,000)

The depreciation of $17,000 was deducted in computing the net income of $43,000. Its effect on the equation was to decrease RI and decrease NCA, so it had no effect on working capital. Therefore, unless the $17,000 is added back to net income, working capital provided by operations would be understated as being $43,000 instead of $60,000. Note that both methods have the same final effects on net changes in the equation.

As the footnote to Schedule A indicates, the first alternative presentation, here called the *addback method,* is used almost exclusively in annual reports even though it may require a bit more effort to understand. The usual presentation would omit schedule A and appear as follows:

Sources:	
Net income	$ 43,000
Add charges not requiring working capital:	
Depreciation	17,000
Working capital provided by operations	$ 60,000
Other sources:	
Issuance of long-term debt	100,000
Issuance of additional capital stock	87,000
Total sources	$247,000

If the addback method is somewhat more difficult to fathom, why is it used so heavily? There are two main reasons besides the unsatisfying reason: "Because we've always done it that way." First, beginning with net income shows the important link with the income statement. Second, the straightforward method (which begins with sales) can require a detailed listing of expenses that is cumbersome and duplicates much of what is already contained in the income statement. The addback method is really a shortcut computation of the target number, working capital provided by operations.

The most crucial aspect of a changes statement is how **depreciation** and other expenses that do not require working capital relate to the flow of working capital. There is widespread misunderstanding of the role of depreciation in financial reporting, so let us examine this point in detail.

Accountants view depreciation as an allocation of historical cost to expense. Therefore depreciation expense does not entail a current outflow of resources in the form of cash, which is the prime form of working capital. Exhibit 17-6 shows the typical relationship of current operations to the production of working capital. Net income is a residual; by itself, it provides no working capital. Instead of beginning with the Sales total and working down, accountants usually start with Net Income and work up (E + D = $60,000 in Exhibit 17-6) by adding back all charges not requiring working capital, as previously explained.

Unfortunately, the use of this shortcut method may at first glance create an erroneous impression that depreciation is, by itself, a source of working capital. If that were really true, a corporation could merely double or triple its bookkeeping entry for depreciation expense when working capital were badly needed! What would happen? Working capital provided by operations would be unaffected. Suppose that depreciation in Exhibit 17-6 is doubled:

Sales	$200,000
Less: All expenses requiring working capital (detailed)	140,000
Working capital provided by operations	$ 60,000
Less: Depreciation	34,000
Net income	$ 26,000

The doubling affects depreciation *and* net income, but it has no direct influence on working capital provided by operations, which, of course, still amounts to $60,000, the sum of net income and depreciation.

EXHIBIT 17-6

Analysis of Income Statement to Show Effects of Operations on Working Capital

Sales	$200,000	(A)
Less: All expenses requiring working capital (detailed)	140,000	(B)
Working capital provided by operations	$ 60,000	(C)
Less: Depreciation	17,000	(D)
Net income	$ 43,000	(E)

Note: Figures are from the preceding example. In this example, depreciation is the only expense not requiring working capital.

Depreciation, income taxes, and working capital

A major objective of this chapter is to pinpoint the relationships between depreciation expense, income tax expense, cash as a major item of working capital, and accumulated depreciation. Too often, these relationships are confused. For instance, the business press frequently contains misleading quotations such as the following (*Business Week,* November 20, 1979, p. 115): ". . . we're looking for financing $3.75 billion. Of that, about 60% will be recovered in depreciation and amortization." Accountants quarrel with such phrasing because depreciation itself is not a direct source of cash, as we saw earlier in this chapter.

To encourage investment in plant and equipment, federal income tax laws permit faster write-offs for depreciation than straight-line. These faster write-offs, called **accelerated depreciation,** are illustrated in Exhibit 17-7.

Depreciation is a deductible noncash expense for income tax purposes. Hence the higher the depreciation allowed to be deducted in any given year, the lower the taxable income and the cash disbursements for income taxes. In short, if depreciation expense is higher, more cash is conserved and kept for various uses. Therefore, compared with the straight-line method, accelerated depreciation methods result in a higher cash balance *after* income tax. Compare an accelerated method with the straight-line method, using the numbers in Exhibit 17-7:

	STRAIGHT-LINE DEPRECIATION	DOUBLE-DECLINING-BALANCE-DEPRECIATION
(C) Income before depreciation	$60,000	$60,000
Depreciation deduction on income tax return	17,000	34,000
Income before income taxes	$43,000	$26,000
(T) Income taxes @ 40%	17,200	10,400
Net income	$25,800	$15,600
Net after-tax working capital provided by operations:		
C − T = $60,000 − $17,200 =	$42,800	
= $60,000 − $10,400 =		$49,600

Some strange results occur here. The reported net income is *lower* under accelerated depreciation than under straight-line depreciation, but the cash balance is *higher*. Thus, suppose managers were forced to use one depreciation method for all purposes. Managers who are concerned about reported net income to shareholders may prefer straight-line to accelerated depreciation. This dilemma is not faced by managers in the United States, where straight-line depreciation is often used for shareholder purposes while accelerated depreciation is used for income tax purposes. (See page 520 for additional explanation.)

There is only one source of working capital provided by operations: *sales to customers.* As our example shows, the effect of more depreciation on cash or working capital is *indirect:* it reduces income taxes by 40 percent of the extra

EXHIBIT
17-7

Annual Depreciation Expense: Three Methods
Assume equipment costs $85,000, no scrap value,
five-year life.

| | | ACCELERATED DEPRECIATION | |
| | | declining balance at twice the straight-line rate† | sum-of-years' digits‡ |
year	straight-line*		
1	$17,000	$34,000	$28,333
2	17,000	20,400	22,667
3	17,000	12,240	17,000
4	17,000	7,344	11,333
5	17,000	4,406	5,667
Total	$85,000	$78,390	$85,000

*20% of $85,000 each year.
†40% of $85,000; 40% of ($85,000 − $34,000); etc. This method will never fully depreciate the existing balance. Therefore, in the later years of an asset's life, companies typically switch to a straight-line method.
‡Sum of digits is 1 + 2 + 3 + 4 + 5 = 15. Then 5/15 × $85,000: 4/15 × $85,000; etc.

depreciation deduction of $17,000, or $6,800. Therefore accelerated depreciation keeps more cash in the business for a longer span of time because of the postponement of disbursements for income taxes.

Consider the account for accumulated depreciation. No cash is there. It is a negative asset, a hole in the doughnut regardless of whether income tax rates are zero, 20 percent, or 90 percent.

summary

This chapter explained the meaning of the account titles most often found in the major financial statements. Accountants have narrow meanings for many of their terms, including **funds, reserves, working capital, depreciation,** and others. In particular, the term **depreciation** is misunderstood. Unless these terms are clear, the user is likely to misinterpret financial reports.

Statements of changes in financial position, also (less accurately) called **funds statements,** are increasing in importance because they yield direct insights into the financial management policies of a company. They also directly explain why a company with high net income may nevertheless be unable to pay dividends because of the weight of other financial commitments to plant expansion or retirement of debt.

summary problems
for your review

PROBLEM ONE

"The book value of plant assets is the amount that would be spent today for their replacement." Do you agree? Explain.

PROBLEM TWO

On December 31, 19X1, a magazine publishing company receives $300,000 in cash for three-year subscriptions. This is regarded as deferred revenue. Show the balances in that account at December 31, 19X2, 19X3, and 19X4. How much revenue would be earned in each of those three years?

PROBLEM THREE

B Company splits its $10 par common stock 5 for 1. How will its balance sheet be affected? Its earnings per share?

PROBLEM FOUR

C Company distributes a 2 percent stock dividend on its 1 million outstanding $5 par common shares. Its stockholders' equity section before the dividend was:

Common stock, 1,000,000 shares @ $5 par	$ 5,000,000
Paid-in capital in excess of par	20,000,000
Retained income	75,000,000
Total stockholders' equity	$100,000,000

The common was selling on the open market for $150 per share when the dividend was distributed.

How will the stockholders' equity section be affected? If net income were $10.2 million next year, what would earnings per share be before considering the effects of the stock dividend? After considering the effects of the stock dividend?

PROBLEM FIVE

"A reserve for depreciation provides cash for the replacement of fixed assets." Do you agree? Explain.

PROBLEM SIX

"A reserve for taxes is cash set aside in a special bank account so that the cash is readily available when taxes are due." Do you agree? Explain.

PROBLEM SEVEN

"A reserve for contingencies is cash earmarked for use in case of losses on lawsuits or fires." Do you agree? Explain.

PROBLEM EIGHT

1. Using Exhibits 17-1, 17-3, and 17-4, prepare a statement of changes in financial position for the Green Company.

2. In your own words, explain why working capital declined. What other sources of funds are likely to be available?

SOLUTION TO PROBLEM ONE

Net book value of the plant assets is the result of deducting accumulated depreciation from original cost. This process does not attempt to capture all the technological and economic events that may affect replacement value. Consequently, there is little likelihood that net book value will approximate replacement cost.

SOLUTION TO PROBLEM TWO

The balance in Deferred Revenue would decline at the rate of $100,000 yearly; $100,000 would be recognized as earned revenue in each of three years.

SOLUTION TO PROBLEM THREE

Total stockholders' equity would be unaffected, but there would be five times more outstanding shares than previously at $2 par rather than $10 par. Earnings per share would be one-fifth of that previously reported, assuming no change in total net income applicable to the common stock.

SOLUTION TO PROBLEM FOUR

Stockholders' equity:

	BEFORE 2% STOCK DIVIDEND	CHANGES	AFTER 2% STOCK DIVIDEND
Common stock 1,000,000 shares @ $5 par	$ 5,000,000	+ (20,000 @ $5)	$ 5,100,000
Paid-in capital in excess of par	20,000,000	+ [20,000 @ ($150 − $5)]	22,900,000
Retained income	75,000,000	− (20,000 @ $150)	72,000,000
	$100,000,000		$100,000,000

Earnings per share before considering the effects of the stock dividend would be $10,200,000 ÷ 1,000,000, or $10.20. After the dividend: $10,200,000 ÷ 1,020,000, or $10.

Note that the dividend has no effect on net income, the numerator of the earnings-per-share computation. But it does affect the denominator and causes a mild dilution which, in theory, should be reflected by a slight decline in the market price of the stock.

SOLUTION TO PROBLEM FIVE

542

Reserve for depreciation is a synonym for *accumulated depreciation.* It is a negative asset, an offset to or deduction from original cost. It is a "hole in a doughnut" and in no way represents a direct stockpile of cash for replacement.

SOLUTION TO PROBLEM SIX

Reserve for taxes is a liability reserve, not a fund gathered for a particular purpose. It is a misleading label because it means "estimated income taxes payable." This does not preclude the establishment of a special *fund* if one is desired, although this is seldom done in practice.

SOLUTION TO PROBLEM SEVEN

Reserve for contingencies is a retained income reserve, a formal restriction of intent or authority to *declare* dividends, often made voluntarily by a board of directors. Its purpose is to warn stockholders that future dividend possibilities are constrained by future possible events that might bear sad economic consequences.

Often restrictions of authority to *declare* dividends are the result of legal agreements with bondholders or other creditors who do not want resources paid to shareholders in the form of dividends until creditor claims are met.

SOLUTION TO PROBLEM EIGHT

1.

GREEN CO.
Statement of Changes in Financial Position
For the Year Ended December 31, 19X1

Sources:		
Net income	$1,150,000	
Add charges against income not requiring working capital: depreciation	1,000,000	
Working capital provided by operations		$2,150,000
Other sources		—
Total sources		$2,150,000
Applications:		
Purchases of plant and equipment	$ 2,200,000*	
Cash dividends:		
On preferred stock	96,000	
On common stock	954,000	
Total applications		3,250,000
Decrease in working capital (see schedule)		$(1,100,000)

Changes in Components of Working Capital

	19X1	19X0
Current assets:		
Cash	$ 2,600,000	$ 2,200,000
Temporary investments in marketable securities	600,000	600,000
Receivables, net	5,300,000	5,100,000
Inventories	14,600,000	14,400,000
Prepaid expenses	600,000	600,000
Total current assets	$23,700,000	$22,900,000
Current liabilities:		
Notes payable	$ 3,900,000	$ 2,800,000
Accounts payable	3,200,000	2,400,000
Accrued expenses payable	1,600,000	1,700,000
Accrued income taxes payable	500,000	400,000
Total current liabilities	$ 9,200,000	$ 7,300,000
Working capital	$14,500,000	$15,600,000
Decrease in working capital (explained above)		($1,100,000)

*($7,000,000 − $5,800,000) + *depreciation of $1,000,000 = $2,200,000.*

2. The decline in working capital came from the inability to generate enough working capital from operations to cover expenditures for plant and equipment and dividends. In view of the pressure on working capital, one may question the wisdom of paying a $954,000 cash dividend to common shareholders. Other sources of working capital might be sales of long-term investments, if any; sales of plant and equipment; issuance of long-term debt; or sale of capital stock.

assignment material

FUNDAMENTAL ASSIGNMENT MATERIAL

17-1. Terminology. Define *accelerated depreciation; accumulated depreciation; addback method; amortization; book value; changes statement; deferred charges; depreciation; double-declining-balance depreciation; fixed assets; fund; funds provided by operations; goodwill; intangible assets; legal value; long-lived assets; marketable securities; operating cycle; par value; prepaid expenses; reserve; residual value; scrap value; stated value; statement of changes in financial position; statement of sources and applications of funds; stock dividend; stock split; sum-of-the-years'-digits depreciation; tangible assets; terminal value; trademarks; working capital; working-capital cycle; working capital provided by operations.*

17-2. Meaning of book value. Y Company purchased an office building twenty years ago for $1 million, $200,000 of which was attributable to land. The mortgage has been fully paid. The current balance sheet follows:

Cash		$400,000	Stockholders'
Land		200,000	equity	$750,000
Building at cost	$800,000		
Accumulated depreciation	650,000		
Book value		150,000	
Total assets		$750,000	

The company is about to borrow $1.8 million on a first mortgage to modernize and expand the building. This amounts to 60 percent of the combined appraised value of the land and building before the modernization and expansion.

REQUIRED

Prepare a balance sheet after the loan is made and the building is expanded and modernized. Comment on its significance.

17-3. Depreciation, income taxes, and cash flow. Mr. Hawtrey, president of the Vaunt Transportation Company, had read a newspaper story that stated: "The Zenith Steel Company had a cash flow last year of $1,500,000, consisting of $1,000,000 of net income plus $500,000 of depreciation. New plant facilities helped the cash flow, because depreciation was 25 percent higher than in the preceding year." "Cash flow" is frequently used as a synonym for "cash provided by operations," which, in turn, is cash revenue less cash operating expenses and income taxes.

Hawtrey was encouraged by the quotation because the Vaunt Company had just acquired a vast amount of new transportation equipment. These acquisitions had placed a severe financial strain on the company. Hawtrey was heartened because he thought that the added cash flow provided by the depreciation on the new equipment should ease the financial pressures on the company.

The income before income taxes of the Vaunt Company last year (19X2) was $200,000. Depreciation was $200,000; it will also be $200,000 on the old equipment in 19X3.

Revenue in 19X2 was $1.9 million (all in cash), and operating expenses other than depreciation were $1.5 million (all in cash).

In 19X3 the new equipment is expected to help increase revenue by $1 million. However, operating expenses other than depreciation will increase by $800,000.

REQUIRED

1. Suppose that depreciation on the new equipment for financial-reporting purposes is $100,000. What would be the "cash flow" from operations (cash provided by operations) for 19X3? Show computations. Ignore income taxes.
2. Repeat Requirement 1, assuming that the depreciation on the new equipment is $50,000. Ignore income taxes.
3. Assume an income tax rate of 40 percent. (a) Repeat Requirement 1; (b) repeat Requirement 2. Assume that the same amount of depreciation is shown for tax purposes and for financial-reporting purposes.
4. In your own words, state as accurately as possible the effects on "cash flow" of depreciation. Comment on Requirements 1, 2, and 3 above in order to bring out your points. This is a more important requirement than Requirements 1, 2, and 3.

17-4. **Changes statement and analysis of growth.** (An alternate is Problem 17-53.) The Denny Company has the following balance sheets (in millions):

	December 31 19X7	December 31 19X6		December 31 19X7	December 31 19X6
Current assets:			Current liabilities		
Cash	$ 2	$ 10	(detailed)	$105	$ 30
Receivables, net	60	30	Long-term debt	150	—
Inventories	100	50	Stockholders'		
Total current			equity	207	160
assets	$162	$ 90			
Plant assets (net of					
accumulated					
depreciation)	300	100			
Total assets	$462	$190	Total equities	$462	$190

Net income was $54 million. Cash dividends paid were $7 million. Depreciation was $20 million. Fixed assets were purchased for $220 million, $150 million of which was financed via the issuance of long-term debt outright for cash.

Denny Alain, the president and majority stockholder, was a superb operating executive. He was an imaginative, aggressive marketing man and an ingenious, creative production man. But he had little patience with financial matters. After examining the most recent balance sheet and income statement he muttered, "We've enjoyed ten years of steady growth; 19X7 was our most profitable ever. Despite such profitability, we're in the worst cash position in our history. Just look at those current liabilities in relation to our available cash! This whole picture of the more you make, the poorer you get, just does not make sense. These statements must be cockeyed."

REQUIRED

1. Prepare a statement of changes in financial position (sources and applications of working capital).
2. Using the changes statement and other information, write a short memorandum to Mr. Alain, explaining why there is such a squeeze on cash.

17-5. "The schedule of changes in components of working capital is an integral part of the statement of changes in financial position." Do you agree? Explain.

17-6. Demonstrate how the fundamental balance sheet equation can be recast to focus on working capital.

17-7. "Cash flow per share (or working capital provided by operations per share) can be downright misleading." Why?

17-8. What are the major sources of working capital? Applications?

17-9. What type of insights are provided by a changes statement?

17-10. Define *funds statement.*

17-11. What is working capital?

17-12. What are some examples of expenses and losses not affecting working capital?

17-13. What are the two major ways of computing working capital provided by operations?

17-14. "The ordinary purchase of inventory has no effect on working capital." Why?

17-15. "Net losses mean drains on working capital." Do you agree? Explain.

17-16. "Depreciation is usually a big source of working capital." Do you agree? Explain.

17-17. What are some weaknesses of the idea that funds are working capital?

17-18. Give other definitions of *funds.*

17-19. What is the major difference between a statement of changes in working capital and a cash flow statement?

17-20. Criticize the following presentation of part of a changes statement:

Sources:	
Sales	$100,000
Less expenses requiring working capital	70,000
Funds provided by operations	$ 30,000

17-21. The gain on the sale of a fixed asset represents part of the working capital received by the X Company. How should this item be presented on a changes statement? Why?

17-22. What are the effects on working capital flows of the following transaction: The purchase of fixed assets at a cost of $100,000, of inventories at a cost of $200,000, and of receivables at a cost of $50,000, paid for by the assumption of a $70,000 mortgage on the fixed assets and the giving of a ninety-day promissory note for $280,000.

17-23. The net income of the Lear Company was $1.5 million. Included on the income statement are the following:

Uninsured loss of inventory, by flood (classified as a part of operating expenses)	$100,000
Gain on the sale of equipment	200,000
Dividend income	10,000
Interest income, including $5,000 not yet received	20,000
Amortization of patents	50,000
Depreciation	400,000

Compute the working capital provided by operations, assuming that interest and dividend income are a part of operating income.

17-24. "Asset valuation reserves are created by charges to stockholders' equity." Do you agree? Explain.

17-25. Why is the term *marketable securities* a misnomer?

17-26. "Accumulated depreciation is a hole in a doughnut." Explain.

17-27. "Accumulated depreciation is a sum of cash being accumulated for the replacement of fixed assets." Do you agree? Explain.

17-28. "Goodwill may have nothing to do with the personality of the manager or employees." Do you agree? Explain.

17-29. Why should short-term prepaid expenses be classified as current assets?

17-30. Why are intangible assets and deferred charges usually swiftly amortized?

17-31. What is a subordinated debenture?

17-32. "Mortgage bonds are always safer investments than debentures." Do you agree? Explain.

17-33. What is the role of a par value of stock or bonds?

17-34. "Common shareholders have limited liability." Explain.

17-35. "Treasury stock is negative stockholders' equity." Do you agree? Explain.

17-36. How can a stock split be achieved via the use of a stock dividend?

17-37. What are the three major types of reserves?

17-38. Enumerate the items most commonly classified as current assets.

17-39. "Sometimes 100 shares of stock should be classified as current assets and sometimes not." Explain.

17-40. What is the proper measure for an asset newly acquired through an exchange (e.g., an exchange of land for securities)? Explain.

17-41. Criticize: "Depreciation is the loss in value of a fixed asset over a given span of time."

17-42. What factors influence the estimate of useful life in depreciation accounting?

17-43. "Accountants sometimes are too concerned with physical objects or contractual rights." Explain.

17-44. How may the distinction between contributed and accumulated capital be blurred by traditional accounting?

17-45. **Various intangible assets.** Consider the following:

1. On December 28, 19X1, Bach Company purchased a patent for a tape recorder for $340,000. The patent has ten years of its legal life remaining. Technology changes fast, so Bach expects the patent to be worthless in four years. What will be the amortization for 19X2?

2. On December 29, 19X1, a publisher acquires the copyright for a book by Jimmy Carter for $2 million. Most sales of the book are expected during 19X2 and 19X3. What will be the amortization for 19X2?

3. On January 4, 19X1, Company X acquires Company Y for $30 million and can assign only $25 million to identifiable individual assets. What is the minimum amount of amortization of the goodwill for 19X1? Could the entire amount be written off in 19X1? Why?

4. In 19X1, Company C spent $10 million in its research department that resulted in new valuable patents. In December 19X1, Company D paid $10 million to an outside inventor for some valuable new patents. How would the income statements for

19X1 for each company be affected? How would the balance sheets as of December 31, 19X1, be affected?

17-46. Stockholders' equity section. From the following data, prepare for the Ramirez Corporation a detailed stockholders' equity section as it would appear in the balance sheet at December 31, 19X3:

Dividends payable	$ 64,000
Unappropriated retained income	7,000,000
Additional paid-in capital, preferred stock	1,000,000
Common stock, $5 par value per share, authorized 900,000 shares, issued 600,000 shares of which 30,000 are held in the treasury	3,000,000
8% preferred stock, $40 par value, callable at $42, authorized 100,000 shares, issued and outstanding 80,000 shares	3,200,000
Treasury stock, common (at cost)	6,000,000
Fund for replacement of plant	1,250,000
Additional paid-in capital, common stock	9,000,000
Appropriated retained earnings because of loan agreement	5,000,000

17-47. Effects on stockholders' equity. Indicate the effect $(+, -,$ or $0)$ on *total* stockholders' equity of General Motors Corporation of each of the following:

1. Declaration of a cash dividend
2. Payment of item 1
3. Declaration of a stock dividend (common on common)
4. Issuance of a stock dividend (common on common)
5. Failing to declare a regular dividend on cumulative preferred stock
6. Sale of 100 shares of General Motors by David Rockefeller to Tom Jones
7. Operating loss for the period
8. Purchase of ten shares of treasury stock for $1,000 cash
9. Sale of treasury stock, purchased in item 8, for $1,200
10. Sale of treasury stock, purchased in item 8, for $900
11. Creation of a reserve for contingencies
12. Creation of a construction fund
13. Creation of a reserve for current income taxes
14. Creation of a reserve for depreciation

17-48. Balance sheet classification of reserves and funds. Designate whether each of the following is essentially an asset account (A); asset valuation account (AV); liability account (L); or retained earnings account (R).

1. Reserve for sinking fund
2. Reserve for vacation pay
3. Reserve for possible future losses in foreign operations
4. Sinking fund for retirement of bonds
5. Reserve for employees' bonuses
6. Reserve for purchases of other companies
7. Construction fund
8. Reserve for impending economic recession
9. Reserve for replacement of facilities at higher price levels
10. Reserve to reduce investments from cost to market value

17-49. Comparison of popular depreciation methods. Speas Company acquired equipment for $32,000 with an expected useful life of five years and a $2,000 expected residual value. Prepare a tabular comparison of the annual depreciation and book value for each year under straight-line, sum-of-years'-digits, and double-declining-balance depreciation.

17-50. Depreciation and working capital. Dyle Company has the following data for 19X5: all expenses requiring working capital, $610,000; depreciation, $70,000; sales, $980,000. Ignore income taxes.

REQUIRED

1. Compute working capital provided by operations and net income.
2. Assume that depreciation is tripled. Compute working capital provided by operations and net income.

17-51. Changes statement. (The next problem is an alternate.) The D Company has the following balance sheets (in millions of dollars):

	AS OF DECEMBER 31			AS OF DECEMBER 31	
	19X4	19X3		19X4	19X3
Current assets (detailed)	$ 90	$ 80	Current liabilities (detailed)	$ 50	$ 45
Fixed assets (net of depreciation)	60	40	Long-term debt	5	—
Goodwill	5	10	Stockholders' equity	100	85
	$155	$130		$155	$130

Net income was $25 million. Cash dividends paid were $10 million. Depreciation was $7 million. Half the goodwill was amortized. Fixed assets of $27 million were purchased.

REQUIRED

Prepare a statement of changes in financial position (sources and applications of working capital).

17-52. Changes statement. (The preceding problem is an alternate.) G Company had a net income of $80,000 in 19X3. Sales were $990,000; expenses requiring working capital, $790,000; and depreciation, $120,000. G Company had the following balance sheets (in thousands):

	DECEMBER 31			DECEMBER 31	
	19X3	19X2		19X3	19X2
Current assets:			Current liabilities:		
Cash	$ 20	$ 60	Accounts payable	$ 560	$ 300
Net receivables	240	150	Accrued payables	100	10
Inventories	450	350	Subtotal	$ 660	$ 310
Total current assets	$ 710	$ 560	Long-term debt	—	400
Plant assets, net of accu-			Stockholders'		
mulated depreciation	850	670	equity	900	520
Total assets	$1,560	$1,230	Total equities	$1,560	$1,230

In 19X3 the company issued additional capital stock for $400,000 cash. The long-term debt was retired for cash. Cash dividends declared and paid were $100,000. New equipment was acquired for $300,000 cash.

REQUIRED

1. Prepare a statement of changes in financial position, including two alternative presentations of a supporting schedule of working capital provided by opera-tions.
2. Write a short memorandum summarizing the information contained in the statement.
3. Refer to Requirement 1. Support your financial statement by using a form of the balance sheet equation. Step by step, show in equation form how each item in the changes statement affects working capital.

ANNUAL REPORTS

17-53. Changes statement. (An alternate is Problem 17-4.) The Weinberg Co. has assembled the following data (in millions):

	TRIAL BALANCE DEC. 31		
DEBITS	**19X2**	**19X1**	**change**
Cash	$ 10	$ 25	$(15)
Accounts receivable	40	28	12
Inventory	70	50	20
Prepaid general expenses	4	3	1
Plant assets, net	202	150	52
	$326	$256	$ 70
CREDITS			
Accounts payable for merchandise	$ 74	$ 60	$ 14
Accrued property tax payable	3	2	1
Mortgage payable in 19X9	50	—	50
Capital stock	100	100	—
Retained earnings	99	94	5
	$326	$256	$ 70

WEINBERG CO.
Income Statement and Reconciliation of Retained Earnings
For the Year Ended Dec. 31, 19X2
(In millions)

Sales		$250
Less cost of goods sold:		
Inventory, Dec. 31, 19X1	$ 50	
Purchases	160	
Cost of goods available for sale	$210	
Inventory, Dec. 31, 19X2	70	140
Gross profit		$110
Less other expenses:		
General expense	$ 51	
Depreciation	40	
Property taxes	10	101
Net income		$ 9
Dividends		4
Net income of the period retained		$ 5
Retained earnings, Dec. 31, 19X1		94
Retained earnings, Dec. 31, 19X2		$ 99

On December 30, 19X2, Weinberg paid $42 million in cash and signed a $50 million mortgage on a new plant acquired to expand operations. Because net income was $9 million, the highest in the company's history, Ms. Weinberg, the chief executive officer, was distressed by the company's extremely low cash balance.

1. Prepare a statement of changes in financial position that focuses on working capital. You may wish to use Exhibit 17-5 as a guide. However, incorporate the First Alternative Presentation (as illustrated there in Schedule A) into the body of your changes statement. That is, the sources section will begin with net income.
2. What is revealed by the statement of changes in financial position? Does it help you reduce Ms. Weinberg's distress? Why?
3. Briefly explain to Ms. Weinberg why cash has decreased even though working capital has increased and net income was $9 million.

4. Refer to Requirement 1. Support your financial statement by using a form of the balance sheet equation. Step by step, show in equation form how each item in the changes statement affects working capital.

■ UNDERSTANDING PUBLISHED FINANCIAL REPORTS

17-54. Airplane crash. A DC-10 airplane owned by American Airlines crashed in May 1979. It had been purchased for $18 million but was carried on American's books at $10.8 million. The plane's replacement cost, reflected in the insurance payment, was $37 million.

A news story reported: "American Airlines reported yesterday second-quarter earnings jumped 117.1 percent over those a year earlier. The quarter's profits included a $24.3 million after-tax gain from the proceeds of insurance . . ."

REQUIRED

1. Prepare an analysis of the above facts, including the acquisition of a new airplane. Use the format of the balance sheet equation. Because of various complications, the applicable income tax was relatively small.
2. Do you think a casualty should generate a reported gain? Why?

17-55. Stock dividends. The St. Regis Paper Company had 13.7 million shares of $5 par value common stock issued and outstanding in 19X8 when a 2 percent stock dividend was issued. The market value of the stock at the time was $36 per share.

REQUIRED

Indicate what accounts would be affected by the issuance of the dividend and by how much.

17-56. Stock split. The 19X7 annual report of Essex International Corporation included the following in the statement of consolidated retained earnings:

Charge relating to stock split in May 19X7 $4,392,800

The comparative balance sheets showed:

| | DECEMBER 31 | |
	19X7	19X6
Common stock $1 par value	$8,785,600	$4,392,800

REQUIRED

Define *stock split*. What did Essex International do to achieve its stock split? Does it conflict with your definition? Explain fully.

17-57. Valuation of intangible assets of football team. New owners acquired the Los Angeles Rams football team in 19X2 for $7.2 million. They valued the contracts of their forty players at a total of $3.5 million, the franchise at $3.6 million, and other assets at $100,000. For income tax purposes, the Rams amortized the $3.5 million over five years; therefore they took a tax deduction of $700,000 annually.

The Internal Revenue Service challenged the deductions. It maintained that only $300,000 of the $7.2 million purchase price was attributable to the player contracts and that the $3.2 million of the $3.5 million in dispute should be attributed to the league franchise rights. Such franchise rights are regarded by the Internal Revenue Service as a valuable asset with an indefinite future life; therefore no amortization is permitted for tax-reporting purposes.

Suppose the operating income for each of the five years (before any amortization) was $1 million.

1. Consider the reporting to the Internal Revenue Service. Tabulate a comparison of annual operating income (after amortization) according to two approaches: (a) the Rams and (b) the IRS. What is the difference in annual operating income?

2. Reports to shareholders by American companies do not have to adhere to the same basis used for income tax purposes. Consider the reporting to shareholders. The Rams had been using a five-year life for player contracts and a forty-year life for the league franchise rights. Tabulate a comparison of operating income (after amortization) using (a) this initial approach and (b) the approach whereby only $300,000 would have been attributed to player contracts. What is the difference in operating income?

3. Comment on the results in Requirements 1 and 2. Which alternative do you think provides the most informative report of operating results? Why?

chapter 18

INTERCORPORATE INVESTMENTS, INCLUDING CONSOLIDATIONS

learning objectives

When you have finished studying this chapter, you should be able to:

1. Contrast the equity method with the cost method for reporting intercorporate investments.
2. Identify the concept of consolidating financial statements and the purposes, assumptions, and principles that underlie consolidated statements.
3. Describe the main features of consolidated financial statements and construct the statements from a set of data.
4. Explain the nature of goodwill and how it is measured and reported in the consolidated financial statements.

The major aim of this chapter is to unravel the mysteries of intercorporate investments and consolidated statements, which are inevitably present in annual reports. The nature of goodwill is also explained.

Equity method of accounting for intercorporate investments

Investments in the equity securities of one company by another company are accounted for in different ways, depending on the type of the relationship between the "investor" and the "investee." For example, the ordinary stockholder is a passive investor who follows the **cost method,** whereby the initial investment is recorded at cost and dividends are recorded as income when received.

Beginning in 1970 (APB *Opinion No. 18*), U.S. companies were required to use the **equity method** instead of the cost method if the investor exerts a "significant influence" over the operating and financial policies of an investee, even though the investor holds 50 percent or less of the outstanding voting stock. The *equity method* is defined as the cost at date of acquisition adjusted for the investor's share of dividends and earnings or losses of the investee subsequent to the date of investment. The carrying amount of the investment is reduced by dividends received from the investee and by the investor's share of investee's losses. The carrying amount of the investment is increased by the investor's share of investee's earnings. The equity method is generally used for a 20 through 50 percent interest, because such a level of ownership is regarded as a presumption that the owner has the ability to exert significant influence, whereas the cost method is generally used to account for interests of less than 20 percent. The treatment of an interest in excess of 50 percent is explained in the following section on consolidated financial statements.

The equity method is relatively new. Long-term investments in equity securities were carried at acquisition cost for many years by U.S. companies and are still carried at cost by parent companies in many countries.

Compare the cost and equity methods. Suppose Company A acquires 40 percent of the voting stock of Company B for $80 million. In Year 1, B has a net income of $30 million and pays cash dividends of $10 million. A's 40 percent shares would be $12 million and $4 million, respectively.

The balance sheet equation of A would be affected as follows:

	EQUITY METHOD			COST METHOD		
	assets	=	equities	assets	=	equities
	cash + investments	=	liab. + stk. eq.	cash + investments	=	liab. + stk. equity
1. Acquisition	−80 +80	=		−80 +80	=	
2. Net income of B	+12	=	+12	No entry and no effect		
3. Dividends from B	+4 −4	=		+4	=	+4
Effects for year	−76 +88	=	+12	−76 +80	=	+4

The investment account will have a net increase of $8 million for the year. The dividend will increase the cash account by $4 million.

The investment account will be unaffected. The dividend will increase the cash account by $4 million.

Under the equity method, income is recognized by A as it is earned by B rather than when dividends are received. Cash dividends do not affect net income; they increase Cash and decrease the Investment balance. In a sense, the dividend is a partial liquidation of the investor's "claim" against the investee. The receipt of a dividend is similar to the collection of an account receivable. The revenue from a sale of merchandise on account is recognized when the receivable is created; to include the collection also as revenue would be double-counting. Similarly, it would be double-counting to include the $4 million of dividends as income after the $12 million of income is already recognized as it is earned.

The major justification for requiring the use of the equity method is that it is more appropriate than the cost method for recognizing increases or decreases in the economic resources underlying the investments. The most striking difference between the two methods is that the cost method allows management to influence reported net income. Under the cost method, the reported net income of the investor could be directly affected by the dividend policies of the investee, over whom the investor might have significant influence. Under the equity method, the reported net income could not be influenced by the manipulation of dividend policies.

Sears, the world's largest retailer of general merchandise, holds ownership interests in several companies. An example is Sears's 40.2 percent interest in Roper Corporation, a manufacturer of household appliances. Sears must use the equity method in accounting for such investments because an ownership interest in excess of 20 percent is presumed to be evidence of ability to exert significant influence.

Consolidated financial statements

United States companies having substantial ownership of other companies must issue **consolidated financial statements,** which are explained in this section. An American cannot hope to understand a corporate annual report without understanding the assumptions underlying consolidations. Furthermore, the 1970s were marked by a worldwide movement toward requiring consolidated financial statements instead of parent-company-only statements.[1]

A publicly held business is typically composed of two or more separate legal entities that constitute a single overall economic unit. This is almost always a **parent-subsidiary** relationship where one corporation (the parent) owns more than 50 percent of the outstanding voting shares of another corporation (the subsidiary).

Why have subsidiaries? Why not have the corporation take the form of a single legal entity? The reasons include limiting the liabilities in a risky venture, saving income taxes, conforming with government regulations with respect to a part of the business, doing business in a foreign country, and expanding in an orderly way. For example, there are often tax advantages in acquiring the capital stock of a going concern rather than its individual assets.

Consolidated statements combine the financial positions and earnings reports of the parent company with those of various subsidiaries into an overall report as if they were a single entity. The aim is to give the reader better perspective than could be obtained by his or her examining a large number of separate reports of individual companies.

[1]For example, in 1977 Japanese companies were required to use consolidated statements. See "Japan's Accounting Shake-up," *Business Week,* April 25, 1977, pp. 112–14.

When parent and subsidiary financial statements are consolidated, double-counting of assets and equities must be avoided via "intercompany eliminations." Suppose Company P acquired a 100 percent voting interest in S for $213 million cash at the beginning of the year. Their balance sheet accounts are analyzed in the equation form below. Investment in S is presented in the first column because it is a focal point in this chapter, not because it appears first in actual balance sheets. Figures in this and subsequent tables are in millions of dollars and are assumed:

	ASSETS		= LIABILITIES +	STOCKHOLDERS' EQUITY
	investment + in S	cash and other assets	= accounts payable, + etc.	stockholders' equity
P's accounts, Jan. 1:				
Before acquisition		650 =	200 +	450
Acquisition of S	+213	−213 =		
S's accounts, Jan. 1:		400 =	187 +	213
Intercompany eliminations	−213		=	−213
Consolidated, Jan. 1	0 +	837 =	387 +	450

Note that the $213 million is paid to the *former owners* of S as private investors. The $213 million is *not* an addition to the existing assets and stockholders' equity of S.

The consolidated entity shows the details of *all* assets and liabilities of *both* the parent and the subsidiary. The Investment in S account is the evidence of an ownership interest, which is held by P but which is really composed of all of the S assets and the S liabilities. The consolidated statements cannot show both the evidence of interest *plus* the detailed underlying assets and liabilities. So this double-counting is avoided by eliminating the reciprocal evidence of ownership present in two places: (a) the Investment in S on P's books and (b) the Stockholders' Equity on S's books.

Thus we see that each legal entity has its individual set of books, but the consolidated entity is the summation of the individual assets and liabilities after the elimination of any duplications. If the $213 million elimination of the reciprocal accounts did not occur, there would be a double-counting in the consolidated statement.

□ AFTER ACQUISITION

Long-term investments in equity securities, such as this investment in S, are carried in the investor's balance sheet by the equity method, the same method of accounting for an unconsolidated ownership interest of 20 through 50 percent, as previously described. Suppose S has a net income of $50 million for the year. If the parent company were reporting alone, it would have to account for the net income of its subsidiary by increasing its Investment in S account and its Stockholders' Equity account (in the form of Retained Income) by 100 percent of $50 million.

The income statements for the year would contain (numbers in millions assumed):

	P	S	CONSOLIDATED
Sales	$900	$300	$1,200
Expenses	800	250	1,050
Operating income	$100	$ 50	$ 150
Pro-rata share (100%) of subsidiary net income	50	—	
Net income	$150	$ 50	

P's parent-company-only income statement would show its own sales and expenses plus its pro-rata share of S's net income (as the equity method requires). Reflect on the changes in P's accounts, S's accounts, and the consolidated accounts (in millions of dollars):

	ASSETS		= LIABILITIES +	STOCKHOLDERS' EQUITY
	investment + in S	cash and other assets	= accounts payable, + etc.	stockholders' equity
P's accounts:				
Beginning of year	213 +	437	= 200 +	450
Operating income		+100	=	+100 in retained income
Share of S income	+50		=	+50 in retained income
End of year	263 +	537	= 200 +	600
S's accounts:				
Beginning of year		400	= 187 +	213
Net income		+50	=	+50 in retained income
End of year		450	= 187 +	263
Intercompany eliminations	−263		=	−263
Consolidated, end of year	0 +	987	= 387 +	600

Review at this point to see that consolidated statements are the summation of the individual accounts of two or more separate legal entities. They are prepared periodically via work sheets. The consolidated entity does not have a separate continuous set of books like the legal entities. Moreover, a consolidated income statement is merely the summation of the revenue and expenses of the separate legal entities being consolidated after eliminating double-counting. The income statement for P shows a $150 million net income; for S, a $50 million net income; for consolidated, a $150 million net income.

☐ MINORITY INTERESTS

A consolidated balance sheet usually includes an account on the equities side called **Outside Stockholders' Interest in Subsidiaries,** often also termed simply **Minority Interests.** It arises because the consolidated balance sheet is a combination of all the assets and liabilities of a subsidiary. If the parent owns, for example, 90 percent of the subsidiary stock, then outsiders to the consolidated group own the other 10 percent. The account Outside Stockholders' Interest in Subsidiaries is a measure of this minority interest. The diagram that follows shows the area encompassed by the consolidated statements; it includes all the subsidiary assets, item by item. The creation of an account for minority interests, in effect, corrects this overstatement:

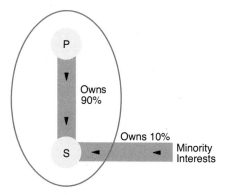

The next table, using the basic figures of the previous example, shows the overall approach to a consolidated balance sheet immediately after the acquisition. P owns 90 percent of the stock of S for a cost of .90 × $213, or $192 million. The minority interest is 10 percent, or $21 million.

	ASSETS		=	LIABILITIES	+	STOCKHOLDERS' EQUITY
	investment + in S	cash and other assets	= accounts payable etc.	+ minority interest	+	stockholders' equity
P's accounts, Jan. 1:						
Before acquisition		650	= 200		+	450
Acquisition of 90% of S	+192	−192	=			
S's accounts, Jan. 1:		400	= 187		+	213
Intercompany eliminations	−192		=	+21		−213
Consolidated, Jan. 1	0	+ 858	= 387	+ 21	+	450

Again, suppose S has a net income of $50 million for the year. The same basic procedures are followed by P and by S regardless of whether S is 100 percent owned or 90 percent owned. However, the presence of a minority interest changes the *consolidated* statements slightly. The income statements would include:

	P	S	CONSOLIDATED
Sales	$900	$300	$1,200
Expenses	800	250	1,050
Operating income	$100	$ 50	$ 150
Pro-rata share (90%) of subsidiary net income	45	—	
Net income	$145	$ 50	
Outside interest (10%) in subsidiaries' net income (minority interest in income)			5
Net income to consolidated entity			$ 145

Consolidated balance sheets at the end of the year would be prepared as follows:

	ASSETS		=	LIABILITIES	+	+ STOCKHOLDERS' EQUITY
	investment in S	+ cash and other assets	=	accounts payable, etc.	+ minority interest	+ stockholders' equity
P's accounts:						
Beginning of year	192	+ 458*	=	200	+	450
Operating income		+100	=			+100
Share of S income	+45		=			+45
End of year	237	+ 558	=	200	+	595
S's accounts:						
Beginning of year		400	=	187	+	213
Net income		+50	=			+50
End of year		+ 450	=	187	+	263
Intercompany eliminations	−237		=		+26†	−263
Consolidated, end of year	0	+ 1,008	=	387	+ 26 +	595

*650 beginning of year − 192 for acquisition = 458.
†21 beginning of year + .10 (50) = 21 + 5 = 26.

Perspective on Consolidated Statements

□ CONSOLIDATED SUBSIDIARIES

Exhibits 18-1 through 18-3 provide an overall look at how financial statements appear in corporate annual reports. The circled items 1 and 2 deserve special mention:

1. The headings indicate that these are *consolidated* financial statements.
2. On balance sheets, the minority interest typically appears just above the stockholders' equity section, as Exhibit 18-1 shows. On income statements, the minority interest in net income is deducted as if it were an expense of the consolidated entity, as Exhibit 18-2 shows. Remember that minority interest is a claim of outside stockholders' interest in a *consolidated subsidiary* company. Note also that minority interests arise only in conjunction with *consolidated* financial statements.

To help understanding, consider the following hypothetical relationships that exist for Goliath Corporation, which for more realism could be viewed as a simplified version of Sears:

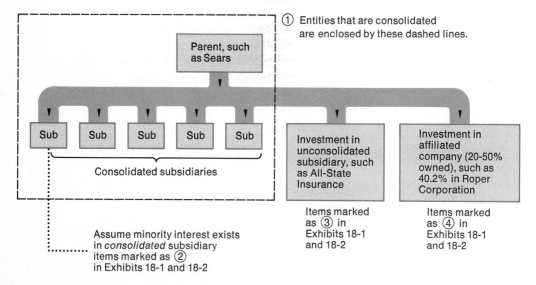

① Entities that are consolidated are enclosed by these dashed lines.

Parent, such as Sears

Sub Sub Sub Sub Sub

Consolidated subsidiaries

Investment in unconsolidated subsidiary, such as All-State Insurance

Investment in affiliated company (20-50% owned), such as 40.2% in Roper Corporation

Assume minority interest exists in *consolidated* subsidiary items marked as ② in Exhibits 18-1 and 18-2

Items marked as ③ in Exhibits 18-1 and 18-2

Items marked as ④ in Exhibits 18-1 and 18-2

□ UNCONSOLIDATED SUBSIDIARIES

We have already seen how the equity method is used on a parent company's books to account for its investment in subsidiaries. Most often, such investment accounts are eliminated when consolidated statements are prepared, as was just illustrated. Sometimes there is justification for not consolidating one or two subsidiaries with businesses totally different from the parent and other subsidiaries. Examples are a merchandiser's subsidiary finance companies and insurance companies. For instance, a consolidated statement of Sears and Allstate Insurance Company would produce a meaningless hodgepodge, so the Allstate interest is shown as an Investment on the Sears consolidated balance sheet, even

EXHIBIT 18-1 *(Place a clip on this page for easy reference.)*

GOLIATH CORPORATION
① Consolidated Balance Sheets
As of December 31
(In millions of dollars)

ASSETS	19X3	19X2	CHANGE
Current assets:			
Cash	$90	$56	
Short-term investments in debt securities at cost (which approximates market value)	—	28	
Accounts receivable (less allowance for doubtful accounts of $2,000,000 and $2,100,000 at their respective dates)	91	95	
Inventories at average cost	120	130	
Total current assets	301	309	(8)
③ Investments in unconsolidated subsidiaries	63	55	8
④ Investments in affiliated companies	10	9	1
Property, plant, and equipment:			
Land at original cost	50	39	11
Plant and equipment 19X3 $192 19X2 $135			
Original cost			
Accumulated depreciation 126 112			
Net plant and equipment	66	23	
Total property, plant, and equipment	116	62	57
Other assets:			
Franchises and trademarks	15	16	
Deferred charges and prepayments	3	4	
Total other assets	18	20	(2)
Total assets	$508	$455	53

EQUITIES	19X3	19X2	CHANGE
Current liabilities:			
Accounts payable	$100	$ 84	
Notes payable	10	—	
Accrued expenses payable	32	22	
Accrued income taxes payable	34	38	
Total current liabilities	176	144	32
Long-term liabilities:			
First mortgage bonds, 5% interest, due Dec. 31, 19X6	25	25	
Subordinated debentures 6% interest, due Dec. 31, 19X9	30	20	10
Total long-term liabilities	55	45	
Deferred Income*	12	9.3	2.7
② Outside stockholders' interest in consolidated subsidiaries (minority interests)	6	5.7	0.3
Total liabilities	249	204	
Stockholders' equity:			
Preferred stock, 100,000 shares $30 par	3	3	
Common stock, 1,000,000 shares, $1 par	1	1	
Paid-in capital in excess of par	55	55	
Retained income	200	192	8
Total stockholders' equity	259	251	
Total equities	$508	$455	53

*Advances from customers on long-term contracts. Other examples are collections for rent and subscriptions, which often are classified as current liabilities.

†Dividend rate is $5 per share; each share is convertible into two shares of common stock. The shares were originally issued for $100. The excess over par is included in "paid-in capital in excess of par." Liquidating value is $100 per share.

EXHIBIT 18-2

GOLIATH CORPORATION
①Consolidated Income Statements
For the Year Ended December 31
(000's omitted)

	19X3	19X2
Net sales and other operating revenue	$499,000	$599,100
Cost of goods sold and operating expenses, exclusive of depreciation	468,750	554,550
Depreciation	14,000	11,000
Total operating expenses	482,750	565,550
Operating income	16,250	33,550
④Equity in earnings of affiliates	1,000	900
③Equity in earnings of unconsolidated subsidiary	8,000	10,000
Total income before interest expense and income taxes	25,250	44,450
Interest expense	2,450	2,450
Income before income taxes	22,800	42,000
Income taxes	12,000	21,900
Income before minority interests	10,800	20,100
②Outside stockholders' interest (minority interests) in consolidated subsidiaries' net income	300	600
Net consolidated income to Goliath Corporation*	10,500	19,500
Preferred dividends	500	500
Net income to Goliath Corporation common stock	$ 10,000	$ 19,000
Earnings per share of common stock:		
on shares outstanding (1,000,000 shares)	$10.00†	$19.00
Assuming full dilution, reflecting conversion of all convertible securities (1,200,000 shares)	$ 8.75‡	$16.25

*This is the total figure in dollars that the accountant traditionally labels net income. It is reported accordingly in the financial press.
† This is the figure most widely quoted by the investment community: $10,000,000 ÷ 1,000,000 = $10.00; $19,000,000 ÷ 1,000,000 = $19.00.
‡ Computed, respectively: $10,500,000 ÷ 1,200,000 = $8.75; $19,500,000 ÷ 1,200,000 = $16.25.

though the Sears interest is 100 percent. A separate set of Allsate statements is included in the Sears annual report.

Investments in domestic unconsolidated subsidiaries are carried via the equity method. The use of the equity method necessitates recognition of the parent's share of unconsolidated subsidiary net income. Exhibit 18-2 is an example of how this income usually appears as a separate item in the consolidated income statement. Note also that the beginning balance of the Investment account in Exhibit 18-1 was $55 million. It has risen by $8 million for the year because of the consolidated enterprise's share in the unconsolidated subsidiary net income.

EXHIBIT
18-3

GOLIATH CORPORATION
Consolidated Statement of Retained Income
For the Year Ended December 31
(000's omitted)

	19X3	19X2
Balance beginning of year	$192,000	$176,000
Add: Net income to Goliath Corporation	10,500	19,500
Total	202,500	195,500
Deduct:		
Cash dividends on preferred stock (also shown in Exhibit 18-2)	500	500
Cash dividends on common stock	2,000	3,000
Total dividends	2,500	3,500
Balance, end of year	$200,000	$192,000

Exhibits 18-1 and 18-2 indicate that the unconsolidated subsidiary did not declare dividends during 19X3. But suppose that the parent received $6 million in dividends. The equity method would have the following effects:

Equity Method:

Original investment	$55	
Share of subsidiary net income	8	→ Same as now appears in the
Balance	$63	income statement in
Dividends received	6	Exhibit 18-2
Balance, December 31, 19X3	$57	

The $6 million dividend would not appear in the income statement because it would represent a double-counting. Instead, it is regarded as a partial liquidation of the $63 million ownership "claim" as measured in the Investment account. Thus net income of the subsidiary increases this claim, and dividends reduce this claim.

Investments in foreign subsidiaries are often carried at cost because of a longstanding reluctance to recognize gains prior to the receipt of a corresponding amount of funds from the foreign subsidiaries. This conservative approach is an outgrowth of many unhappy experiences with wars, expropriations of assets, devaluations of currencies, and currency restrictions.

☐ INVESTMENTS IN AFFILIATES

INTER-CORPORATE INVESTMENTS

As described earlier in the chapter, investments in equity securities that represent 20 to 50 percent ownership are usually accounted for under the equity method. These investments are frequently called Investments in Affiliates. For example, see the items marked as 4 in Exhibits 18-1 and 18-2. Sears accounts for its Investment in Roper Corporation in this manner. Exhibit 18-1 shows how the

Investment account in the balance sheet has risen by the pro-rata share of the current earnings of affiliates, the $1 million shown in the income statement in Exhibit 18-2.

Recapitulation of investments in equity securities

Exhibit 18-4 summarizes all the relationships depicted in the preceding exhibits. Take a few moments to review Exhibits 18-1 and 18-2 in conjunction with Exhibit 18-4. In particular, note that minority interests arise only in conjunction with *consolidated* subsidiaries. Why? Because consolidated balance sheets and income statements aggregate 100 percent of the detailed assets, liabilities, sales, and expenses of the subsidiary companies. Thus, if a minority interest were not recognized, the stockholders' equity and net income of the consolidated enterprise would be overstated.

In contrast, minority interests do not arise in connection with the accounting for investments in *unconsolidated* subsidiaries or investments in affiliated companies. Why? Because no detailed assets, liabilities, revenues, and expenses of the unconsolidated subsidiaries or affiliated companies are included in the consolidated statements. The investor's interests in these companies have been recognized on a pro-rata basis only.

EXHIBIT 18-4

Summary of Consolidations and Equity Method

ITEM IN EXHIBITS 18-1 AND 18-2	PERCENTAGE OF OWNER-SHIP	TYPE OF ACCOUNT-ING	BALANCE SHEET EFFECTS	INCOME STATEMENT EFFECTS
①	100%	Consoli-dation	Individual assets, individual liabilities added together	Individual revenues, individual expenses added together
②	Greater than 50% and less than 100%	Consoli-dation	Same as 1, but recognition given to minority interest in liability section	Same as 1, but recognition given to minority interest near bottom of statement when consolidated net income is computed
③	Greater than 50% up to 100%, but subsidiary in totally different business, so not consolidated	Equity method	Investment carried at cost plus pro-rata share of subsidiary earnings less dividends received	Equity in earnings of **unconsolidated subsidiary** shown on one line as addition to income
④	20% to and including 50%	Equity method	Same as 3	Same as 3, often called equity in earnings of **affiliated** companies

As we have seen, the accounting for investments in voting stock depends on the nature of the investment:

1. Except for those subsidiaries in insurance and finance activities, nearly all investments that represent more than a 50 percent ownership interest are usually consolidated. A subsidiary is a corporation controlled by another corporation. The usual condition for control is ownership of a majority (more than 50 percent) of the outstanding voting stock.

2. a. If the subsidiary is not consolidated, it is carried by the parent under the equity method, which is cost at date of acquisition adjusted for the investor's share of the earnings or losses of the investee subsequent to the date of investment. Dividends received from the investee reduce the carrying amount of the investment.

   b. The equity method is also generally used for a 20 through 50 percent interest because such a level of ownership is regarded as a presumption that the owner has the ability to exert significant influence.

   c. Investments in corporate joint ventures should also be accounted for under the equity method. "Corporate joint ventures" are corporations owned and operated by a small group of businesses (the "joint venturers") as a separate business or project for the mutual benefit of the members of the group. Joint ventures are common in the petroleum and construction industries.

3. Marketable equity securities held as short-term investments are generally carried at the lower of cost or market value.[2] These investments are typically passive in the sense that the investor exerts no significant influence on the investee.

Accounting for goodwill

□ PURCHASED GOODWILL

The major example on intercorporate investments assumed that the acquisition cost of Company S by Company P was equal to the *book values* of Company S. However, the total purchase price paid by P often exceeds the book values of the assets acquired. In fact, the purchase price also often exceeds the sum of the fair market values (current values) of the identifiable individual assets less the liabilities. Such excess of purchase price over fair market value is called **"goodwill"** or "purchased goodwill" or, more accurately, "excess of cost over fair value of net identifiable assets of businesses acquired." Recall that Chapter 17 briefly discusses the nature of goodwill.

To see the impact on the consolidated statements, refer to our initial example on consolidations, where there was an acquisition of a 100 percent interest in S by P for $213 million. Suppose that the price were $40 million higher, or a

[2]FASB *Statement No. 12*, "Accounting for Certain Marketable Securities," requires that a portfolio of securities (rather than each security as an individual investment) should be stated at the lower of cost or market. If the investment is classified as a current asset, any write-downs to market should affect current net income. If the investment is a noncurrent asset, the write-down shall be recorded directly in the stockholders' equity section of the balance sheet as a separate valuation account and not as a component of the determination of net income.

total of $253 million. For simplicity, assume that all other assets and liabilities in P and S were unaffected by paying $253 million. Also assume that the fair values of the individual assets of S are equal to their book values. The balance sheets immediately after the acquisition are:

	investment in S	+	cash and other assets	=	accounts payable, etc.	+	stockholders' equity
	ASSETS			**= LIABILITIES +**			**STOCKHOLDERS' EQUITY**
P's accounts:							
Before acquisition			650	=	200	+	450
Acquisition	+253		−253	=			
S's accounts:			400	=	187	+	213
Intercompany eliminations	−213			=			−213
Consolidated	40*	+	797	=	387	+	450

The $40 million "goodwill" would appear in the consolidated balance sheet as a separate intangible asset account. It is often shown as the final item in a listing of assets. It is usually amortized in a straight-line manner as an expense in the consolidated income statement over a span of no greater than 40 years.

If the book values of the S individual assets are not equal to their fair values, the usual procedures are:

1. S continues as a going concern and keeps its accounts on the same basis as before.
2. P records its investment at its acquisition cost (the agreed purchase price).
3. For consolidated reporting purposes, the excess of the acquisition cost over the book values of S is identified with the individual assets, item by item. (In effect, they are revalued at the current market prices prevailing when P acquired S). Any *remaining excess* that cannot be identified is labeled as purchased goodwill.

Suppose in our example that the fair value of the other assets of S (e.g., machinery and equipment) exceeded their book value by $30 million. The balance sheets immediately after acquisition would be the same as above, with a single exception. The $40 million goodwill would now be only $10 million. The remaining $30 million would appear in the consolidated balance sheet as an integral part of the "other assets." That is, the S equipment would be shown at $30 million higher in the consolidated balance sheet than the carrying amount on the S books. Similarly, the depreciation expense on the consolidated income statement would be higher. For instance, if the equipment had five years of useful life remaining, the straight-line depreciation would be $30 ÷ 5, or $6 million higher per year.

As in the preceding tabulation, the $10 million "goodwill" would appear in the consolidated balance sheet as a separate intangible asset account.

☐ GOODWILL AND ABNORMAL EARNINGS

Goodwill is frequently misunderstood. The layperson often thinks of goodwill as being the friendly attitude of the neighborhood store manager. But goodwill has many aspects that some observers have divided into causes (sources) and effects (fruits). A purchaser may be willing to pay more than the current values of the individual assets received because the acquired company is able to generate abnormally high earnings (the effects or fruits). The causes of this excess earning power may be traceable to personalities, skills, locations, operating methods, and so forth. For example, a purchaser may be willing to pay extra (the fruits) because excess earnings can be forthcoming from

1. Saving in time and costs by purchasing a corporation having a share of the market in a type of business or in a geographical area where the acquiring corporation planned expansion;
2. Excellent general management skills or a unique product line;
3. Potential efficiency by combination, rearrangement, or elimination of duplicate facilities and administration.

Of course, "goodwill" is originally generated internally. For example, a happy combination of advertising, research, management talent, and timing may give a particular company a dominant market position (the cause) for which another company is willing to pay dearly (the fruit). This ability to command a premium price for the total business is goodwill. Nevertheless, such goodwill is never recorded by the selling company. Therefore the *only goodwill* generally recognized as an asset is that identified when one company is purchased by another. The consolidated company then must show in its financial statements the purchased goodwill.

summary

Nearly all corporate annual reports contain consolidated financial statements, as well as "investment" accounts of various sorts. Therefore, acquiring a fundamental understanding of accounting for intercorporate investments is essential for intelligent usage of financial reports.

Exhibits 18-1 and 18-2 summarize how intercorporate investments are accounted for. Note how the equity method is applied. The $8 million increase in the Investments account is attributable to the pro-rata share of the unconsolidated subsidiary net income shown in Exhibit 18-2. (See pages 561 and 562.)

Minority interests are also displayed in Exhibits 18-1 and 18-2. Consider the $300,000 increase (Exhibit 18-1) in Outside Stockholders' Interest in Consolidated Subsidiaries. It is attributable to the increase in minority interests' share of the income of consolidated subsidiaries, as indicated in the income statement in Exhibit 18-2.

summary problem
for your review

PROBLEM

1. Review the section on minority interests. Suppose that P owns 60 percent of the stock of S for a cost of .60 × $213, or $128 million. The total assets of P consist of this $128 million plus $522 million of other assets, a total of $650 million. The S assets and equities are unchanged from the amount given in the example on page 556. Prepare an analysis showing what amounts would appear in a consolidated balance sheet immediately after the acquisition.

2. Suppose S has a net income of $50 million for the year, and P has an operating income of $100 million. Other details are described in the example on page 557. Prepare an analysis showing what amounts would appear in a consolidated income statement and year-end balance sheet.

SOLUTION

1.

	ASSETS		=	LIABILITIES	+	STOCKHOLDERS' EQUITY
	investment in S	+ cash and other assets	=	accounts payable, etc.	+ minority interest	+ stockholders' equity
P's accounts, Jan. 1:						
Before acquisition		650	=	200	+	450
Acquisition of 60% of S	+128	−128	=			
S's accounts, Jan. 1		400	=	187	+	213
Intercompany eliminations	−128		=		+85	−213
Consolidated, Jan. 1	0	+ 922	=	387	+ 85 +	450

2.

	P	S	CONSOLIDATED
Sales	$900	$300	$1,200
Expenses	800	250	1,050
Operating income	$100	$ 50	$ 150
Pro-rata share (60%) of unconsolidated subsidiary net income	30	—	
Net income	$130	$ 50	
Outside interest (40%) in consolidated subsidiary net income (minority interest in income)			20
Net income to consolidated entity			$ 130

	investment in S		cash and other assets		accounts payable, etc.		minority interest		stockholders' equity
						ASSETS = LIABILITIES + STOCKHOLDERS' EQUITY			
P's accounts:									
Beginning of year	128	+	522*	=	200			+	450
Operating income			+100	=					+100
Share of S income	+30			=					+30
End of year	158	+	622	=	200			+	580
S's accounts:									
Beginning of year			400	=	187			+	213
Net income			+50	=					+50
End of year			450	=	187			+.	263
Intercompany eliminations	−158			=			+105†		−263
Consolidated, end of year	0	+	1,072	=	387	+	105	+	580

*650 beginning of year − 128 for acquisition = 522.
†85 beginning of year + .40 (50) = 85 + 20 = 105.

assignment material

FUNDAMENTAL ASSIGNMENT MATERIAL

18-1. Terminology. Define *consolidated statements; cost method for investments; equity method; goodwill; minority interests; subsidiary.*

18-2. Cost or equity method. (An alternate is Problem 18-18.) Company D acquired 30 percent of the voting stock of Company E for $30 million cash. In Year 1, E had a net income of $20 million and paid a cash dividend of $13,333,333.

REQUIRED

Using the equity and the cost methods, show the effects of the three transactions on the accounts of D. Use the balance sheet equation format.

18-3. Consolidated financial statements. (An alternate is Problem 18-19.) Company P acquired a 100 percent voting interest in Company S for $110 million cash at the beginning of the year. Immediately before the business combination, each company had the following condensed balance sheet accounts (in millions):

	P	S
Cash and other assets	$600	$200
Accounts payable, etc.	$250	$ 90
Stockholders' equity	350	110
Total equities	$600	$200

REQUIRED

1. Prepare a tabulation of the consolidated balance sheet accounts immediately after the acquisition. Use the balance sheet equation format.
2. Suppose P and S have the following results for the year:

	P	S
Sales	$700	$400
Expenses	550	360

INTER-CORPORATE INVESTMENTS

Prepare income statements for the year for P, S, and the consolidated entity.

3. Present the effects of the operations for the year on P's accounts and on S's accounts, using the balance sheet equation. Also tabulate the consolidated balance sheet accounts at the end of the year. Assume that liabilities are unchanged.
4. Suppose S paid a cash dividend of $30 million. What accounts in Requirement 3 would be affected and by how much?

18-4. **Minority interests.** This extends the preceding problem. However, this problem is self-contained because all the facts are reproduced below. Company P acquired a 70 percent voting interest in Company S for $77 million cash at the beginning of the year. Immediately before the business combination, each company had the following condensed balance sheet accounts (in millions):

	P	S
Cash and other assets	$600	$200
Accounts payable, etc.	$250	$ 90
Stockholders' equity	350	110
Total equities	$600	$200

1. Prepare a tabulation of the consolidated balance sheet accounts immediately after the acquisition. Use the balance sheet equation format.
2. Suppose P and S have the following results for the year:

	P	S
Sales	$700	$400
Expenses	550	360

Prepare income statements for the year for P, S, and the consolidated entity.
3. Using the balance sheet equation format, present the effects of the operations for the year on P's accounts and S's accounts. Also tabulate consolidated balance sheet accounts at the end of the year. Assume that liabilities are unchanged.
4. Suppose S paid a cash dividend of $30 million. What accounts in Requirement 3 would be affected and by how much?

18-5. **Goodwill and consolidations.** This extends Problem 18-3. However, this problem is self-contained because all the facts are reproduced below. Company P acquired a 100 percent voting interest in Company S for $170 million cash at the beginning of the year. Immediately before the business combination, each company had the following condensed balance sheet accounts (in millions):

	P	S
Cash and other assets	$600	$200
Accounts payable, etc.	$250	$ 90
Stockholders' equity	350	110
Total equities	$600	$200

Assume that the fair values of the individual assets of S were equal to their book values.

1. Prepare a tabulation of the consolidated balance sheet accounts immediately after the acquisition.
2. If goodwill is going to be amortized over forty years, how much was amortized for the first year? If over five years, how much was amortized for the first year?
3. Suppose the book values of the S individual assets are equal to their fair market values except for equipment. The net book value of equipment is $30 million

and its fair market value is $70 million. The equipment has a remaining useful life of four years. Straight-line depreciation is used.

a. Describe how the consolidated balance sheet accounts immediately after the acquisition would differ from those in Requirement 1. Be specific as to accounts and amounts.

b. By how much will consolidated income differ in comparison with the consolidated income that would be reported in Requirement 2? Assume amortization of goodwill over a forty-year period.

18-6. **Prepare consolidated financial statements.** From the following data, prepare a consolidated balance sheet and income statement of the Lumsden Corporation. All data are in millions and pertain to operations for 19X2 or to December 31, 19X2:

Retained income	$198
Accrued income taxes payable	30
Investments in unconsolidated subsidiaries (which are two insurance companies)	60
Cost of goods sold and operating expenses, exclusive of depreciation and amortization	700
Paid-in capital in excess of par	82
Interest expense	25
Subordinated debentures, 11% interest, due December 31, 19X9	100
Outside stockholders' interest in consolidated subsidiaries' net income	15
Goodwill	120
Net sales and other operating revenue	900
Investments in affiliated companies	20
Common stock, 10 million shares, $1 par	10
Depreciation and amortization	20
Accounts payable	200
Equity in earnings of unconsolidated subsidiary	18
Cash	50
First-mortgage bonds, 10% interest, due December 31, 19X8	80
Property, plant, and equipment, net	120
Preferred stock, 2 million shares, $50 par, dividend rate is $5 per share, each share is convertible into five shares of common stock	100
Short-term investments at cost, which approximates current market	40
Income tax expense	70
Accounts receivable, net	100
Outside stockholders' interest in subsidiaries (minority interests)	90
Inventories at average cost	400
Dividends declared and paid on preferred stock	10
Equity in earnings of affiliated companies	2

ADDITIONAL ASSIGNMENT MATERIAL

18-7. "The equity method is usually used for long-term investments." Do you think this is appropriate? Explain.

18-8. "A consolidated balance sheet can contain an asset, Investment in Unconsolidated Subsidiary." Do you agree that this is appropriate? Explain.

18-9. Distinguish between control of a company and significant influence over a company.

18-10. "Goodwill is the excess of purchase price over the book values of the individual assets acquired." Do you agree? Explain.

18-11. What criterion is used to determine whether a parent-subsidiary relationship exists?

18-12. Why have subsidiaries? Why not have the corporation take the form of a single legal entity?

18-13. What is a *minority interest?*

18-14. When is there justification for not considering subsidiaries in accounting reports?

18-15. What is the *equity method?*

18-16. Contrast the cost method and the equity method.

18-17. "A company can carry some investments in unconsolidated subsidiaries at cost." Under what circumstances is this a correct statement?

18-18. Equity method. (An alternate is Problem 18-2). Company A acquired 30 percent of the voting stock of Company B for $90 million cash. In Year 1, B had a net income of $50 million and paid cash dividends of $30 million.

REQUIRED

Prepare a tabulation that compares the equity method and the cost method of accounting for A's investment in B. Show the effects on the balance sheet equation under each method. What is the year-end balance in the Investment in B account under the equity method? Under the cost method?

18-19. Consolidated financial statements. (An alternate is Problem 18-3.) Suppose Company P acquired a 100 percent voting interest in Company S for $200 million cash at the beginning of the year. Their balance sheet accounts immediately after the acquisition were (in millions):

	P	S
Investment in S	$200	$ —
Cash and other assets	600	450
Total assets	$800	$450
Accounts payable, etc.	$300	$250
Stockholders' equity	500	200
Total equities	$800	$450

REQUIRED

1. Using the balance sheet equation format, prepare a tabulation of the consolidated balance sheet accounts immediately after the acquisition.
2. Suppose S had sales of $400 million and expenses of $360 million for the year. P had sales of $950 million and expenses of $825 million. Prepare income statements for P, for S, and for the consolidated company.
3. Using the balance sheet equation, present the effects of the operations for the year on P's accounts and S's accounts. Also tabulate the consolidated balance sheet accounts at the end of the year. Assume that liabilities are unchanged.
4. Suppose S paid a cash dividend of $40 million. What accounts in Requirement 3 would be affected and by how much?

18-20. Consolidated statements. Consider the following for D Company as of December 31, 19X4:

	PARENT	SUBSIDIARY*
Assets	$700,000	$200,000
Liabilities to creditors	$200,000	$ 80,000
Stockholders' equity	500,000	120,000
Total equities	$700,000	$200,000

80 percent owned by parent

The $700,000 of assets of the parent include a $96,000 investment in the subsidiary. The $96,000 includes the parent's pro-rata share of the subsidiary's net income for 19X4. The parent's sales were $990,000 and the operating expenses were $922,000. These figures exclude any pro-rata share of the subsidiary's net income. The subsidiary's sales were $700,000 and operating expenses were $660,000. Prepare a consolidated income statement and a consolidated balance sheet.

18-21. **Consolidated financial statements.** Fresno Company (the parent) owns 100 percent of the common stock of Grand Company (the subsidiary), which was acquired at the beginning of 19X3. Their financial statements follow:

Income Statements
for the Year Ended
December 31, 19X3

	PARENT	SUBSIDIARY
Revenue and "other income"	$40,000,000	$10,000,000
Expenses	38,000,000	9,000,000
Net income	$ 2,000,000	$ 1,000,000

Balance Sheets
December 31, 19X3

	PARENT	SUBSIDIARY
Assets	$10,000,000	$4,000,000
Liabilities to creditors	$ 4,500,000	$1,000,000
Stockholders' equity	5,500,000	3,000,000
Total equities	$10,000,000	$4,000,000

REQUIRED

1. The subsidiary had enjoyed a fantastically profitable year in 19X3. The parent's income statement had been prepared by showing the parent's claim to the subsidiary's income as a part of the parent's "other income." On the other hand, the parent's balance sheet is really not completed. The $10 million of assets of the parent company include a $2 million investment in the subsidiary and do *not* include the parent's claim to subsidiary's 19X3 net income.

   Prepare a consolidated income statement and a consolidated balance sheet. Use the balance sheet equation format for the latter.

2. Suppose that Fresno Company owned 60 percent of the Grand Company. Liabilities to creditors are unchanged. The assets of the parent company include a $1.2 million investment in the subsidiary instead of $2.0 million. However, assume the total assets are $10 million. The balance sheet is really not completed because the investment account does not reflect the claim to the subsidiary's 19X3 net income. Similarly, the parent's revenue and other income is $39.6 million, not $40.0 million.

   Prepare a consolidated income statement and a consolidated balance sheet. Use the balance sheet equation format for the latter.

18-22. **Determination of goodwill.** Refer to the preceding problem, Requirement 1. Suppose that the investment in the subsidiary in Requirement 1 was $2.8 million instead of the $2.0 million as stated. This would mean that the "other assets" would be $7.2 million instead of $8.0 million. Would the consolidated income differ? How? Be as specific as possible. Would the consolidated balance sheet differ? How? Be as specific as possible.

18-23. **Purchased goodwill.** Consider the following balance sheets (in millions of dollars):

	COMPANY X	COMPANY Y
Cash	150	20
Inventories	60	30
Plant assets, net	60	30
Total assets	270	80
Common stock and paid-in capital	70	30
Retained income	200	50
Total equities	270	80

X paid $120 million to Y stockholders for all of their stock. The "fair value" of the plant assets of Y is $70 million. The fair value of cash and inventories is equal to their carrying amounts. X and Y continued to keep separate books as individual entities.

REQUIRED

1. Prepare a tabulation showing the balance sheets of X, of Y, Intercompany Eliminations, and Consolidated immediately after the acquisition.
2. Suppose that only $60 million rather than $70 million of the total purchase price of $120 million could be logically assigned to the plant assets. How would the consolidated accounts be affected?
3. Refer to the facts in Requirement 1. Suppose X had paid $144 million rather than $120 million. State how your tabulation in Requirement 1 would change.

18-24. **Amortization and depreciation.** Refer to the preceding problem, Requirement 3. Suppose a year passes, and X and Y generate individual net incomes of $20 million and $13 million, respectively. The latter is after a deduction by Y of $6 million of straight-line depreciation. Compute the consolidated net income if goodwill is amortized (1) over forty years and (2) over ten years. Ignore income taxes.

18-25. **Allocating total purchase price to assets.** Two entities had the following balance sheet accounts as of December 31, 19X1 (in millions):

	GREY-MONT	PARA-DELT		GREY-MONT	PARA-DELT
Cash and receivables	$ 30	$ 22	Current liabilities	$ 50	$ 20
Inventories	120	3	Common stock	100	10
Plant assets, net	150	95	Retained income	150	90
Total assets	$300	$120	Total equities	$300	$120
Net income for 19X1	$ 19	$ 4			

On January 4, 19X2, these entities combined. Greymont issued $180 million of its shares (at market value) in exchange for all of the shares of Paradelt, a motion picture division of a large company. The inventory of films acquired through the combination had been fully amortized on Paradelt's books.

During 19X2 Greymont entered into many television distribution contracts that called for $21 million in film rentals over a prolonged span of years. These rentals were to be collected over this period of time, but the contracts were used as support for immediate recognition of revenue (and consequent net income).

Greymont earned $20 million on its other operations during 19X2. Paradelt broke even on its other operations during 19X2.

REQUIRED

1. Prepare a consolidated balance sheet for the combined company immediately after the combination on a purchase basis. Assume that on a purchase basis $80 million would be assigned to the inventory of films.

2. Prepare a comparison of net income between 19X1 and 19X2 where 25 percent of the cost of the film inventories would be properly matched against the revenue from the television contracts. What would be the net income for 19X2 if the $80 million were assigned to goodwill rather than to the library of films, and goodwill were amortized over forty years?

18-26. **Changes statement.** (This is more difficult than the other problems on the changes statement.) Using Exhibits 18-1, 18-2, and 18-3, prepare a consolidated statement of changes in financial position using the working capital concept of "funds" for the Goliath Corporation.

■ UNDERSTANDING PUBLISHED FINANCIAL REPORTS

18-27. **Classification on balance sheet.** The following accounts appeared in the annual report of the Jewel Companies, Inc.:

1. Accumulated earnings—reserved for self-insured losses and general contingencies
2. Long-term indebtedness, due within one year
3. Investments: minority interest in foreign affiliates (at cost)
4. Prepaid expenses and supplies
5. Dividends payable
6. Treasury stock at cost

REQUIRED | Indicate in detail in what section of the balance sheet each account should appear.

18-28. **Meaning of account descriptions.** The following account descriptions were found in various annual reports:

Montgomery Ward: Net earnings of subsidiaries not consolidated
Tenneco: Equity in undistributed earnings of 50% owned companies
St. Regis Paper: Equity in net earnings of subsidiaries not consolidated and associated companies

In your own words, explain what this type of account represents.

18-29. **Consolidations in Japan.** *Business Week* (April 25, 1977, p. 112) reported that Japan's finance ministry issued a directive requiring the six hundred largest Japanese companies to produce consolidated financial statements after April 1, 1977. The story said: "Financial observers hope that the move will help end the tradition-honored Japanese practice of 'window dressing' the parent company financial results by shoving losses onto hapless subsidiaries, whose red ink was seldom revealed. . . . When companies needed to show a bigger profit, they would sell their product to subsidiaries at an inflated price. . . . Or the parent company charged a higher rent to a subsidiary company using its building."

REQUIRED | Could a parent company follow the quoted practices and achieve window dressing in its parent-only financial statements if it used the equity method of accounting for its intercorporate investments? The cost method? Explain.

18-30. **Investments in equity securities.** Clark Equipment Company is a multinational corporation with subsidiaries and affiliations throughout the world. Its annual report for 1980 showed total assets of $900.1 million. Investments in companies in which

Clark owned 20 percent or more minority interest was $25.0 million. The remaining investments in companies in which Clark owned less than 20 percent amounted to $4.3 million.

REQUIRED How did Clark report the investments in which it owned more than 50 percent interest? Indicate briefly how the following three classes of investments should be accounted for: (a) greater than 50 percent interest; (b) 20 percent through 50 percent interest; and (c) less than 20 percent interest.

18-31. Equity method of accounting for unconsolidated subsidiaries. Trans World Airlines owns 100 percent of Hilton International Company. The airline and hotel operations are now being reported on a consolidated basis. However, in past years the hotel operations have not been consolidated with the airline operations for financial-reporting purposes. The following data are extracted from the TWA 1972 annual report (in millions):

	12-31-72	12-31-71
From statement of consolidated income:		
Income from airline operations	(5.3)	
Income from hotel operations	8.8	
Net income for the year	$ 3.5	
From consolidated balance sheet:		
Investments: equity in Hilton International	$47.0	$38.2

REQUIRED If Hilton International had paid cash dividends of $4.1 million in 1972, how would the payment have affected TWA net income for the year? How would it have affected the investment balance at December 31, 1972?

18-32. Effect of transactions under the equity method. (J. Patell, adapted.) Koppers Company Inc. is a diversified manufacturer. Its balance sheets showed (in thousands):

	DECEMBER 31	
	1976	1975
Investments, affiliated companies, at equity	$15,153	$13,134

These affiliated companies were owned by Koppers in various proportions from 20 to 50 percent. Dividends received from these companies during 1976 totaled $1,739,000.

The income statement for 1976 showed (in thousands):

Equity in earnings of affiliates	$2,922

REQUIRED 1. Did Koppers purchase more shares in affiliated companies during 1976 or sell off part of its holdings (in aggregate)? Give the dollar amount of the transaction, and label it as a purchase or a sale. *Hint:* Use a balance sheet equation or a T-account to aid your analysis.
2. Income before taxes in 1976 was $107,931,000. What would Kopper's 1976 net income before taxes have been if it had accounted for its Investment in affiliated companies by the cost method?

chapter 19

FINANCIAL REPORTING AND CHANGING PRICES

learning objectives

When you have finished studying this chapter, you should be able to:

1. Explain and illustrate four different ways of measuring income: (a) historical cost/nominal dollars; (b) current cost/nominal dollars; (c) historical cost/constant dollars; and (d) current cost/constant dollars.
2. Explain and illustrate the distinctions between realized and unrealized income under current-cost accounting. (Appendix 19)
3. Explain the difference between monetary and nonmonetary items. (Appendix 19).
4. Compute general purchasing-power gains and losses. (Appendix 19)
5. Describe the major provisions of FASB **Statement No. 33**, "Financial Reporting and Changing Prices." (Appendix 19)

The measurement of income is easily the most controversial subject in accounting. This chapter focuses on how inflation is portrayed by the income statement. An appendix explores the problems of accounting for inflation in more depth, although still at an introductory level. This chapter provides an overview of the imprecision of a reported net income figure and of the uses, assumptions, and limitations of the typical financial statements.

Inflation and income measurement

Throughout the 1970s a pet theme of politicians and others was the "unconscionable" or "obscene" profits reported by American companies. In turn, business executives have maintained that our well-known historical cost basis for measuring income produces misleading results, especially during a time of rising prices. Some managers have complained that the reported profits are so badly overstated that income taxes have been unfairly levied. In many cases, capital, rather than income, has been taxed. This chapter concentrates on these issues. Its purpose is to deepen your understanding of the various concepts of income and capital.

Recent years have been marked by unprecedented levels of inflation in nearly all countries. As a result, influential persons have attacked the traditional financial statements as being "unrealistic," "misleading," "useless," and so on. Suggestions for change have led to regulatory actions that departed from historical-cost measures, which had almost exclusively dominated financial reporting throughout the century. These departures will now be described. In essence, the controversies center on how income and capital should be defined. Different sets of concepts of income and capital will lead to different measurement methods.

☐ INCOME OR CAPITAL

At first glance, the concept of income seems straightforward. Income is increase in wealth. But what is wealth? It is capital. But what is capital? An endless chain of similar questions can be constructed. The heart of the issue is the distinction between invested capital and income. The time-honored interpretation is that invested capital is a *financial* concept (rather than a *physical* concept). The focus is on the potential profitability of the money (the financial resources) invested, no matter what types of inventory, equipment, or other physical resources have been acquired.

The G Company situation described below will be used to compare various concepts of income and capital. Four basic methods of income measurement are presented, two using nominal dollars and two using constant dollars. **Nominal dollars** are dollar measurements that are not restated for fluctuations in the general purchasing power of the monetary unit, whereas **constant dollars** are nominal dollars restated in terms of current purchasing power.

G Company has the comparative balance sheets at December 31 (based on historical costs in nominal dollars) shown on the top of the next page.

The company had acquired all of its four hundred units of inventory at $20 per unit (total of $8,000) on December 31, 19X1, and had held the units until December 31, 19X2. Three hundred units were sold for $35 per unit (total of $10,500 cash) on December 31, 19X2. The replacement cost of the inventory

	19X1	19X2
Cash	$ 0	$10,500
Inventory, 400 and 100 units, respectively	8,000	2,000
Total assets	$8,000	$12,500
Original paid-in capital	$8,000	$ 8,000
Retained income	—	4,500
Stockholders' equity	$8,000	$12,500

at that date was $30 per unit. The general-price-level index was 100 on December 31, 19X1, and 110 on December 31, 19X2. Assume that these are the only transactions. Ignore income taxes.

□ HISTORICAL COST/NOMINAL DOLLARS

Exhibit 19-1 is the basis for the explanations that follow in the next several pages. The first set of financial statements in Exhibit 19-1 shows the time-honored method that uses historical cost/nominal dollars (Method 1). Basically, this method measures invested capital in nominal dollars. It is the most popular approach to income measurement and is commonly called the historical-cost method. Operating income (equals net income in this case) is the excess of realized revenue ($10,500 in 19X2) over the "not restated" historical costs of assets used in obtaining that revenue. As we have already seen, when the conventional accrual basis of accounting is used, an exchange transaction is ordinarily necessary before revenues (and resulting incomes) are deemed to be realized. Thus, no income generally appears until the asset is sold; intervening price fluctuations are ignored.

□ CURRENT COST/NOMINAL DOLLARS

The second set of financial statements in Exhibit 19-1 illustrates a **current-cost** method that has especially strong advocates in Canada, the United Kingdom, and Australia (Method 2). This method uses current cost/nominal dollars. The focus is on income from continuing operations. As shown in the column for the income statements, this model emphasizes that operating income should be "distributable" income. That is, G Company could pay dividends in an amount of only $1,500, leaving enough assets to allow for replacement of the inventory that has just been sold.

Critics of the historical-cost approach claim that the $4,500 measure of income from continuing operations is misleading because it inaccurately reflects (it overstates) the net increment in distributable assets. If a $4,500 dividend were paid, the company would be less able to continue operations at the same level as before. The $3,000 difference between the two operating incomes ($4,500 − $1,500 = $3,000) is frequently referred to as an "inventory profit" or an "inflated profit." Why? Because $9,000 instead of $6,000 is now necessary to replace the 300 units sold (300 × the increase in price from $20 to $30 equals the $3,000 difference).

The focus on "distributable" income raises serious issues regarding definitions of income and invested capital. Is invested capital a financial or a physical

EXHIBIT 19-1 *(Put a clip on this page.)*

Four Major Methods to Measure Income and Capital

| | NOMINAL DOLLARS* | | | | CONSTANT DOLLARS* | | | |
| | (method 1) historical cost | | (method 2) current cost | | (method 3) historical cost | | (method 4) current cost | |
Balance Sheets as of December 31	19X1	19X2	19X1	19X2	19X1	19X2	19X1	19X2
Cash	—	10,500	—	10,500	—	10,500	—	10,500
Inventory, 400 and 100 units, respectively	8,000	2,000ᵇ	8,000	3,000ᶜ	8,800ᵉ	2,200ᵉ	8,800	3,000ᶜ
Total assets	8,000	12,500	8,000	13,500	8,800	12,700	8,800	13,500
Original paid-in capital	8,000	8,000	8,000	8,000	8,000ᶠ	8,800ᶠ	8,800ᶠ	8,800ᶠ
Retained income (confined to income from continuing operations)		4,500		1,500		3,900		1,500
Revaluation equity:								
Realized holding gainsᵃ				3,000				2,400ᵍ
Unrealized holding gainsᵃ				1,000				800ᵍ
Total equities	8,000	12,500	8,000	13,500	8,800	12,700	8,800	13,500

Income Statement for 19X2				
Sales, 300 units @ $35	10,500	10,500	10,500	10,500
Cost of goods sold, 300 units	6,000ᵇ	9,000ᶜ	6,600ᵉ	9,000ᶜ
Income from continuing operations (to retained income)	4,500	1,500	3,900	1,500
Holding gains:ᵃ				
Realized holding gains on 300 units sold		3,000ᵈ		2,400ᵍ
Unrealized holding gains on 100 units unsold		1,000ᵈ		800ᵍ
Total holding gainsᵃ		4,000		3,200

*Nominal dollars are not restated for a general price index, whereas constant dollars are restated.

(a) Many advocates of this current-cost method favor showing these gains in a completely separate statement of holding gains rather than as a part of the income statement. Moreover, many favor including some or all of these gains as a part of income for the year; see Appendix 19 for further discussion.

(b) $100 \times \$20$ (c) $100 \times \$30$ (d) $300 \times (\$30 - \$20)$ (e) $110/100 \times \$8,000$ (f) $110/100 \times \$8,000$
   $300 \times \$20$ $300 \times \$30$ $100 \times (\$30 - \$20)$ $110/100 \times \$2,000$
                                                $110/100 \times \$6,000$

(g) $\$9,000 - $ Restated cost of $\$6,600 = \$2,400$ $\$3,000 - $ Restated cost of $\$2,200 = \$800$
   or   or
   $300 \times (\$30 - 110\% \text{ of } \$20) = \$2,400$ $100 \times (\$30 - 110\% \text{ of } \$20) = \$800$

concept? Adherents of the current cost/nominal dollar method insist that no income can result until enough financial resources are generated to maintain *physical capacity*. All holding gains and losses, realized or unrealized, would be *excluded* from income. **Holding gains** (or *losses*) are generally defined as increases (or decreases) in the replacement costs of the assets held during a given period. (Other interpretations of whether some or all holding gains should be *included* in income are presented in Appendix 19.)

     For simplicity, income taxes are ignored in Exhibit 19-1. The historical cost/nominal dollar method (Method 1) is the only acceptable method for reporting on income tax returns in English-speaking countries. As Appendix 19 discusses in more detail, many managers of heavy industries like steel and aluminum claim that their capital is being taxed under the historical cost/nominal dollar method. These managers maintain that taxes should be levied only on *income from continuing operations,* as computed under the current cost/nominal dollar method (Method 2).

☐ REGULATORY ACTIONS

During the late 1970s, accountants in many countries struggled with the problem of measuring the current cost of assets. For example, in 1976 the U.S. Securities and Exchange Commission issued a revolutionary requirement for supplementary footnote disclosure (as distinguished from a full-fledged balance sheet and income statement) of the replacement cost of inventories; replacement cost of productive capacity of plant and equipment; cost of goods sold based on replacement cost as of time of sale; and depreciation based on average replacement cost for the period.

After extensive public hearings, the Financial Accounting Standards Board issued similar but more extensive disclosure requirements in 1979. Its *Statement No. 33,* "Financial Reporting and Changing Prices," applies to public companies that have either (1) inventories and property, plant, and equipment (before deducting accumulated depreciation) amounting to more than $125 million or (2) total assets amounting to more than $1 billion (after deducting accumulated depreciation). No changes must be made in the primary financial statements. All information required by the statement is to be presented as supplementary schedules in published annual reports. Appendix 19 has a fuller description of the FASB requirements.

☐ HISTORICAL COST/CONSTANT DOLLARS

Method 3 of Exhibit 19-1 shows the results of applying general index numbers to historical costs. Essentially, the income measurements in each year are restated in terms of *constant dollars* (possessing the same general purchasing power of the current year) instead of the *nominal dollars* (possessing different general purchasing power of various years).

The fundamental reasoning underlying the Method 3 approach goes to the heart of measurement theory itself. Additions or subtractions must use a *common measuring unit,* be it dollars, francs, meters, ounces, or any chosen measure.

Consider the objections to Method 1. Deducting 6,000 19X1 dollars from 10,500 19X2 dollars to obtain $4,500 is akin to deducting 60 centimeters from 105 meters and calling the result 45. Grade-school tests are marked wrong when such nonsensical arithmetic is discovered, but accountants have been paid well for years for performing similar arithmetic.

Method 3, historical cost/constant dollars, shows how general indexes may be used to restate the historical cost/nominal dollar amounts of Method 1 and thereby remedy the foregoing objections. An example of such an index is the Gross National Product Implicit Price Deflator. Anyone who has lived long enough to be able to read this book is aware that the purchasing power of the dollar is unstable. Index numbers are used to gauge the relationship between current conditions and some norm or base condition (which is assigned the index number of 100). For our purposes, a general price index compares the average price of a group of goods and services at one date with the average price of a similar group at another date. A price index is an average: It does not measure the behavior of the individual component prices. Some individual prices may move in one direction and some in another. The general consumer price level may soar while the prices of eggs and chickens decline.

Do not confuse *general* indexes, which are used in constant-dollar accounting, with *specific* indexes. The two have entirely different purposes. Sometimes specific price indexes are used as a means of approximating the *current costs* of particular assets or types of assets. That is, companies have found specialized indexes to be good enough to get approximations of current costs. This avoids the hiring of professional appraisers or the employing of other expensive means of valuation. For example, Inland Steel uses the Engineering News Record Construction Cost Index to value most of its property, plant, and equipment for purposes of using the current-cost method.

☐ MAINTAINING INVESTED CAPITAL

The historical cost/constant dollar approach (Method 3) is *not* a fundamental departure from historical costs. Instead, it maintains that all historical costs to be matched against revenue should be restated on some constant-dollar basis so that all revenue and all expenses can be expressed in dollars of the same (usually current) purchasing power. The restated figures *are historical costs* expressed in constant dollars via the use of a general price index.

The current dollar is typically employed because users of financial statements tend to think in such terms instead of in terms of old dollars with significantly different purchasing power. The original units in inventory would be updated on each year's balance sheet along with its effect on stockholders' equity. For example, the December 31, 19X1, balance sheet would be restated for comparative purposes on December 31, 19X2:

	NOT RESTATED COST	MULTIPLIER	RESTATED COST
Inventory	$8,000	110/100	$8,800
Original paid-in capital	8,000	110/100	8,800

To extend the illustration, suppose all the inventory was held for two full years. The general price index rose from 110 to 132 during 19X3. The December 31, 19X2, balance sheet items would be restated for comparative purposes on December 31, 19X3:

	RESTATED COST 12/31/X2	MULTIPLIER	RESTATED COST 12/31/X3
Inventory	$8,800	132/110	$10,560*
Original paid-in capital	8,800	132/110	10,560*

*The same result could be tied to the year of acquisition:
Inventory $8,000 × 132/100 = $10,560
Original paid-in capital   8,000 × 132/100 = 10,560

The restated amount is just that—a restatement of original *cost* in terms of current dollars—not a gain in any sense. Therefore this approach should *not* be labeled as an adoption of "current-cost" accounting. Thus, under this approach, if the specific current cost of the inventory goes up or down, the restated cost is unaffected.

The restated historical-cost approach harmonizes with the concept of maintaining the general purchasing power of the invested capital (a financial concept of capital maintenance) in total rather than maintaining "specific invested capital," item by item. More will be said about this distinction after we examine Method 4.

☐ CURRENT COST/CONSTANT DOLLARS

Method 4 of Exhibit 19-1 shows the results of applying general index numbers to current costs. As the footnotes of the exhibit explain in more detail, the nominal gains reported in column 2 are adjusted so that only gains in constant dollars are reported. For example, suppose you buy 100 units on December 31, 19X1, for $2,000 cash. If the current replacement cost of your inventory at December 31, 19X2, is $3,000 but the general price index has risen from 100 to 110, your nominal gain is $1,000 but your "real" gain in constant dollars in 19X2 is only $800: the $3,000 current cost minus the restated historical cost of $2,000 × 1.10 = $2,200.

Suppose the 100 units are held throughout 19X3. The general price index rises from 110 to 132. The replacement cost rises from $30 to $34, a nominal holding gain for 19X3 of $4 × 100 = $400. However, the current cost/constant dollar approach (Method 4) would report a real holding loss:

Current cost, restated, December 31, 19X2:	
$3,000 × 132/110	$3,600
Current cost, December 31, 19X3, 100 × $34	3,400
Holding loss	$ 200

Many theorists disagree on the relative merits of historical-cost approaches versus miscellaneous versions of current-cost approaches to income measurement. But there is general agreement among the theorists that restatements in constant dollars would be an improvement (ignoring practical barriers), because otherwise income includes illusory gains caused by using an unstable measuring unit.

☐ MISINTERPRETATIONS OF CURRENT-COST ACCOUNTING

Restatements in constant dollars can be applied to both the historical-cost and the current-cost basis of income measurement, as Methods 3 and 4 illustrate. Avoid the misconception that the choices are among the first three methods only. In fact, many advocates of the current-cost/constant dollar method insist that it provides the most useful approximation of net income. In any event, any measurement of income should be based on constant dollars.

When inflation accounting is discussed, accountants and managers frequently confuse and blur the various concepts of income just covered. Highlights of Exhibit 19-1 include:

1. The choice among accounting measures is often expressed as either historical-cost accounting or general-price-level accounting or current-cost (specific-price-level) accounting. But this is an inaccurate statement of choices. A correct statement would be that there are four major concepts. General-price-level (constant dollar) accounting may be combined with either historical-cost accounting (Method 3) or current-cost accounting (Method 4).

2. Method 3, the historical cost/constant dollar method, is *not* concerned with current-cost concepts of income, whatever their strengths and weaknesses.

3. The current-cost Methods 2 and 4 are based on **physical** rather than **financial** concepts of **maintenance** of **invested capital**. The variations in interpretation of realized and unrealized gains are discussed in Appendix 19.

4. Write-ups of nonmonetary assets (inventory in this example) under Method 3 do *not* result in the recognition of gains. They are restatements of *costs* in dollars of equivalent purchasing power. See Appendix 19 for a discussion of the distinction between monetary and nonmonetary assets, as well as other aspects of inflation accounting.

summary

The matching of historical costs with revenue is the generally accepted means of measuring net income. But basing such computations on some version of current costs has been proposed as a better gauge of the distinctions between income (the return **on** capital) and capital maintenance (the return **of** capital).

General price indexes are used to adjust historical costs so that all expenses are measured in current dollars of the same purchasing power. Such adjustments do not represent a departure from historical cost. In contrast, specific price indexes are often used to implement the current-cost approach to measuring income and capital.

summary problem for your review

▪ PROBLEM ONE

In 1930 a parcel of land was purchased for $1,200. An identical parcel was purchased today for $3,600. The general-price-level index has risen from 100 in 1930 to 300 now. Fill in the blanks.

PARCEL	(1) HISTORICAL COST MEASURED IN 1930 PURCHASING POWER	(2) HISTORICAL COST MEASURED IN CURRENT PURCHASING POWER	(3) HISTORICAL COST AS ORIGINALLY MEASURED
1			
2			
Total			

1. Compare the figures in the three columns. Which total presents a nonsense result? Why?

2. Does the write-up of parcel 1 in column 2 result in a gain? Why? Assume that these parcels are the only assets of the business. There are no liabilities. Prepare a complete balance sheet for each of the three columns.

You are also urged to review Exhibit 19-1 together with its accompanying explanation.

SOLUTION TO PROBLEM ONE

1.

PARCEL	(1) HISTORICAL COST MEASURED IN 1930 PURCHASING POWER	(2) HISTORICAL COST MEASURED IN CURRENT PURCHASING POWER	(3) HISTORICAL COST AS ORIGINALLY MEASURED
1	$1,200	$3,600	$1,200
2	1,200	3,600	3,600
Total	$2,400	$7,200	$4,800

The addition in column 3 produces a nonsense result. In contrast, the other sums are the results of applying a standard unit of measure. The computations in columns 1 and 2 are illustrations of a restatement of historical cost in terms of a common dollar, a standard unit of measure. Such computations have frequently been termed as adjustments for changes in the general price level. Whether the restatement is made using the 1930 dollar or the current dollar is a matter of personal preference; columns 1 and 2 yield equivalent results. The preponderance of opinion seems to favor restatement in terms of the current dollar (column 2) because the current dollar has more meaning than the old dollar to the reader of the financial statements.

The mere restatement of identical assets in terms of different but equivalent measuring units cannot be regarded as a gain. Expressing parcel 1 as $1,200 in column 1 and $3,600 in column 2 is like expressing parcel 1 in terms of, say, either 1,200 square yards or $9 \times 1,200 = 10,800$ square feet. Surely, the "write-up" from 1,200 square yards to 10,800 square feet is not a gain; it is merely another way of measuring the same asset. The 1,200 square yards and the 10,800 square feet are equivalent; they are different ways of describing the same asset. That is basically what general-price-level accounting is all about. It says you cannot measure one plot of land in square yards and another in square feet and add them together before converting to some common measure. Unfortunately, column 3 fails to perform such a conversion before adding the two parcels together; hence the total is internally inconsistent.

2. Note especially that write-ups under general-price-level accounting do not result in the recognition of gains. They are *restatements* of costs in dollars of equivalent purchasing power. The balance sheets would be:

	(1)	(2)	(3)
Land	$2,400	$7,200	$4,800
Stockholders' equity	$2,400	$7,200	$4,800

Appendix 19: more on inflation accounting

This appendix expands the discussion of the first section of the chapter. Topics include realized and unrealized holding gains, depreciation, and monetary items. Then a summary review problem shows how the significant concepts interrelate.

Interpretations of current-cost accounting

☐ REALIZED AND UNREALIZED HOLDING GAINS

Current cost is the most popular term for describing the fundamental basis for valuing the inventory as shown in the second set of columns in Exhibit 19-1. However, it is a general term having several variations. Be on guard as to its meaning in a particular situation. As illustrated in Exhibit 19-1, the current-cost method stresses that income cannot emerge without deducting the current (or reproduction) cost of replenishing the item at today's prices. The regulatory authorities in most of the English-speaking countries have proposed that the current-cost approach be based on replacement costs. In most instances, replacement cost means today's cost of obtaining a similar asset that would produce the same expected cash flows as the existing asset. For a particular company, these replacement costs would be obtained via price quotations, specific appraisals, or specific indexes for material or construction.

Although replacement cost is the most highly favored version of current cost, some accountants prefer a net realizable value approach to valuation of assets. **Net realizable value** is the estimated selling price in the ordinary course of business, less reasonably predictable costs of completion and disposal. For some assets (for example, marketable securities), net realizable value and replacement cost should be approximately equal (the difference being the costs of executing a transaction, such as brokerage commissions). However, many assets have inactive markets (for example, highly specialized equipment), so net realizable value and replacement cost may vary significantly.

☐ HOLDING GAINS AND PHYSICAL CAPITAL

The current-cost method stresses a separation between *income from continuing operations,* which is defined as the excess of revenue over the replacement costs of the assets consumed in obtaining that revenue, and *holding gains* (or *losses*), which are increases (or decreases) in the replacement costs of the assets held during the current period. Accountants differ sharply on how to account for holding gains. The "correct" accounting depends on distinctions between capital and income. That is, income cannot occur until invested capital is "recovered" or "maintained." The issue of capital versus income is concretely illustrated in Exhibit 19-1. The advocates of a physical concept of capital maintenance claim that *all* holding gains (both those realized gains related to the units sold and the unrealized gains related to the units unsold) should be excluded from income and become a part of revalued capital, called **revaluation equity.** That is, for a going concern no income can result unless the physical capital devoted to operations during the current period can be replaced.

The data for Method 2 in Exhibit 19-1 are listed in detail so that three major alternative interpretations of holding gains may be compared. Exhibit 19-2 tabulates the comparisons.

The first and second tabulations in Exhibit 19-2 take extreme positions. The first tabulation claims that price increases in assets to be replaced are, in effect, restatements of capital. Therefore no current income is recognized. The second tabulation maintains that *all* value increases, whether or not they have been "realized" in the form of a sale, are income of the period when prices rose. This is sometimes called the "economic income" approach, which makes no distinction among the types of assets affected by the increases in prices.

The third tabulation is favored by accountants who want to *recognize* the price increases affecting unsold assets but want to exclude such increases from income until the assets are sold. Thus the second and third tabulations recognize income much sooner than the first tabulation. Indeed, the realized-unrealized distinction of the third tabulation would report the same income for 19X2 as the historical-cost concept ($4,500 in each case). However, the historical cost/nominal dollar concept does not ordinarily identify holding gains as such, nor does it report unrealized gains on inventories.

Essentially, the third tabulation in Exhibit 19-2 *recognizes* all gains as they occur (in the economic sense), but they are divided between realized gains and unrealized gains. The unrealized gains are held "in suspense" in a special stockholders' equity account, called Revaluation Equity in Exhibit 19-1. This concept is really a halfway house between the tabulations one and two in Exhibit 19-2. Why? Because the reported net income for 19X2 would be $4,500. At the

---

EXHIBIT 19-2

Relationships of Holding Gains to Current Income

As shown in Exhibit 19-1, Method 2, page 580:

Income from continuing operations	$1,500
Realized holding gains	3,000
Unrealized holding gains	1,000
Total to account for	$5,500

Alternative effects, depending on distinctions between income and capital:

	TABULATION OF EFFECTS		
	(1)	(2)	(3)
Total current income and increase in retained Income	$1,500	$5,500	$4,500
Revaluation equity	4,000	—	1,000
Total accounted for (from above)	$5,500	$5,500	$5,500

(1) All holding gains are revaluations of capital.
(2) No holding gains are revaluations of capital. They are current income.
(3) Unrealized holding gains are revaluations of capital. Realized holding gains are current income.

same time the $1,000 value increase in unsold inventory would appear as an unrealized gain of 19X2.

Does the $1,000 unrealized gain appear in the income statement as well as in the balance sheet? No, at least not as a part of realized income. The $1,000 gain is a direct increase in Revaluation Equity; of course, it would appear in a statement of changes in stockholders' equity or of changes in Revaluation Equity. When the inventory is sold, the $1,000 is transferred to current income and thus becomes "realized" in the income statement and is therefore a part of Retained Income.

☐ INCOME TAX EFFECTS OF CURRENT COST

The first tabulation in Exhibit 19-2 is the one most heavily advocated by business managers, particularly if current cost eventually becomes acceptable for income tax purposes. In times of rising prices, this version of current cost shows the least income ($1,500 in our example). In this way, income taxes would be postponed and not levied until the assets were sold for cash *and not replaced.*

Keep in mind that the income tax laws in the English-speaking countries have not been changed to permit departures from the historical-cost concept. However, many accelerated write-offs of historical cost are permitted. Indeed, the United Kingdom permits the 100 percent first-year write-off of many investments in long-lived physical assets.

Although, for simplicity, depreciation is not shown in our initial example, it too would be based on replacement cost for Method 2 in Exhibit 19-1. (See the next section of this appendix for an explanation.) Therefore managers in capital-goods industries would especially favor the current-cost concept for income tax purposes because of the prominence of depreciation expenses. In times of rising prices, replacement cost depreciation would increase depreciation expenses, reduce income subject to tax, and decrease income tax outflows—as long as no holding gains were subject to taxes.[1]

☐ DEPRECIATION AND INFLATION

The four methods applied in Exhibit 19-1 to measuring inventories also apply to depreciable assets. Suppose that on January 1, 19X3, $5,000 of the $10,500 cash was used to buy sales equipment. The equipment was being fully depreciated over a five-year life on a straight-line basis. The replacement cost of the equipment (new) at the end of 19X3 was $8,000. The general price index was 110 at the end of 19X2 and 132 at the end of 19X3. Exhibit 19-3 shows the effects and why manufacturers of heavy goods favor the current-cost approach. That is, the manufacturers would want depreciation expense of $1,600 to be deductible for income tax purposes. At the same time, the realized "holding gain" of $3,000 on goods sold should not be subject to tax because it represents capital maintenance rather than income.

---

[1]If taxes were levied as indicated, the capital-goods industries would have relatively lower incomes subject to tax than other industries. However, keep in mind that a country usually has the same target *total* income taxes to be generated by the corporate sector. If the taxable income of all corporations declined, all income tax *rates* would undoubtedly be raised so as to produce the same *total* tax collections as before. Thus a replacement-cost basis may redistribute the tax burden among companies so that capital-goods industries pay less total tax. But the chances are high that the overall percentage rate would increase, so that the tax savings would not be as large as indicated.

EXHIBIT 19-3

	NOMINAL DOLLARS				CONSTANT DOLLARS			
	(method 1) historical cost		(method 2) current cost		(method 3) historical cost		(method 4) current cost	
Balance Sheet Accounts as of December 31	19X2	19X3	19X2	19X3	19X2	19X3	19X2	19X3
Equipment	5,000	5,000	5,000	8,000	6,000[d]	6,000	6,000	8,000
Accumulated depreciation	—	1,000	—	1,600	—	1,200	—	1,600
Net carrying amount	5,000	4,000	5,000	6,400	6,000	4,800	6,000	6,400

Income Statement Effects for 19X3

Depreciation expense	1,000[a]		1,600[b]		1,200[e]		1,600	
Holding gain, equipment			3,000[c]				2,000[f]	

(a) $1/5 \times 5,000$ (e) $1/5 \times 6,000$
(b) $1/5 \times 8,000$ (f) $8,000 - 6,000$
(c) $8,000 - 5,000$
(d) $132/110 \times 5,000$

General purchasing-power gains and losses

Now we return to historical cost/nominal dollar accounting, the comparison of Methods 1 and 3 in Exhibit 19-1 that was introduced in the body of this chapter.

☐ MONETARY ITEMS

A **monetary item** is a claim receivable or payable in a specified number of dollars; the claim remains fixed regardless of changes in either specific or general price levels. Examples are cash, accounts receivable, accounts payable, and bonds payable. In contrast, nonmonetary items have prices that can vary. Examples are inventory, land, equipment, and liabilities for product warranties.

The distinction between monetary and nonmonetary assets is the key to understanding the impact of constant-dollar accounting on income measurement and stockholders' equity. Reconsider the facts depicted in Exhibit 19-1, except that we extend matters throughout 19X3. Suppose the inventory was not replaced. Instead, the $10,500 cash received on December 31, 19X2, was held through 19X3 in a non-interest-bearing checking account. Furthermore, assume that the 100 units of inventory on December 31, 19X2, were held throughout 19X3 and remained unsold on December 31, 19X3. The general-price-level index rose from 110 to 132 during 19X3. The familiar historical cost/nominal dollar (Method 1) statement appears on the top of the next page.

Before reading on, reflect on the intuitive meaning of holding cash during a time of inflation. The holders of cash or claims to cash get burned by inflation. In contrast, the debtors benefit from inflation because they can pay their credi-

Balance Sheets as of December 31	19X2	19X3
Cash	$10,500	$10,500
Inventory	2,000	2,000
Total assets	$12,500	$12,500
Original paid-in capital	$ 8,000	$ 8,000
Retained income	4,500	4,500
Total stockholders' equity	$12,500	$12,500

Income Statement for 19X3

None (no revenue or expenses)

tors with a fixed amount of dollars that have less current purchasing power than when the debt was originally contracted.

How do we measure the economic effects of holding cash during inflation? Using the basic historical cost/constant dollar method in Exhibit 19-1, let us restate in constant dollars, using 19X3 dollars. Because the general-price-level index rose from 110 to 132, the restatements would be:

Balance Sheets as of December 31	19X2	19X3
Cash: 132/110 × 10,500 19X2 dollars	$12,600	$10,500
Inventory: 132/100 × 2,000 19X1 dollars	2,640	2,640
Total assets	$15,240	$13,140
Original paid-in capital: 132/100 × 8,000 19X1 dollars	$10,560	$10,560
Retained income	4,680*	2,580†
Total stockholders' equity	$15,240	$13,140

*$15,240 − $10,560
†$13,140 − $10,560

Income Statement for 19X3

Purchasing-power loss on monetary item	$ 2,100

The cash balance is not restated in 19X3 because it is already measured in 19X3 dollars. The formal constant-dollar income statement, assuming no operating activities, would consist of the lone item as indicated above: purchasing power loss on monetary item, $2,100. The monetary item in this case is cash; its loss of purchasing power is $12,600 − $10,500 = $2,100. In turn, retained income would be reduced as shown, $4,680 − $2,100 = $2,580.

□ NONMONETARY ITEMS

Before reading on, reflect on the intuitive meaning of holding a nonmonetary asset during a time of inflation. Assets in the form of physical things have prices that can fluctuate and thus, unlike cash, offer more protection against the risks of inflation.

As of the end of 19X2, the $10,500 cash balance represented the equivalent of $12,600 in terms of 19X3 purchasing power, but at the end of 19X3 it is worth only $10,500. In contrast, the $2,000 historical investment in inventory, which does not represent a fixed monetary claim, represented $2,640 in terms of 19X3 *purchasing power;* its purchasing power has not been eroded. The inventory is *restated* to an amount of $2,640. But the $2,640 investment in inventory is unaffected by changes in the general-price-level index during 19X3.

Two difficulties and subtleties of constant-dollar accounting deserve emphasis here. First, all past balance sheets are restated in today's dollars. Second, the balance sheet changes are computed among the *monetary* items to produce purchasing-power gains or losses. No such gains or losses will ever appear for nonmonetary items. For example, suppose the $10,500 cash had been immediately reinvested in 300 more units of inventory. How would the constant-dollar statements be affected? No purchasing-power loss or gain would have occurred in 19X3:

	DECEMBER 31, 19X2	DECEMBER 31, 19X3
Inventory (instead of cash)		
132/110 × $10,500	$12,600	$12,600
Inventory (as before)	2,640	2,640
Total assets	$15,240	$15,240
Original capital	$10,560	$10,560
Retained income	4,680	4,680
Total stockholders' equity	$15,240	$15,240

Many accountants and managers confuse these restatements of *historical-cost* statements with current-cost notions of income. However, these constant-dollar statements (Method 3 in Exhibit 19-1) adhere to historical cost. The aim is to see whether the *general* purchasing power of the original invested capital has been maintained. Hence,whether *specific* inventory prices have gone up, down, or sideways is of no concern.

In sum, constant-dollar accounting will modify historical-cost statements in two major ways. First, historical costs are restated in constant dollars. Second, purchasing-power gains and losses arising from holding monetary assets and monetary liabilities will be recognized and will affect net income.[2]

Finally, constant-dollar accounting may be linked with *either* historical-cost statements or current-cost statements. Thus the $2,100 purchasing-power loss computed above would also appear under the current cost/constant dollar method as well as the historical cost/constant dollar method of Exhibit 19-1.

To get a better perspective on how depreciable assets and monetary items are accounted for, you are urged to solve the following "Summary Problem for Your Review."

[2]Many advocate showing these purchasing-power gains and losses as a separate stockholders' equity account apart from retained income. Thus these gains and losses would not be included in current net income. Note that "unrealized" holding gains on monetary items are linked with constant-dollar accounting. They do not exist under nominal-dollar accounting. "Unrealized" holding gains on nonmonetary items are associated exclusively with "current-cost" accounting and are not an integral part of "historical-cost" accounting.

summary problem for your review

The other summary problem appeared earlier in the chapter.

▨ PROBLEM TWO

You purchased a parcel of land ten years ago for $40,000, when the general-price-level index was 90. You also placed $40,000 cash in a safety deposit box. The general-price-level index now is 180. A local real estate appraiser maintains that you could obtain $220,000 for the land today.

REQUIRED

1. Prepare a four-column tabulation of the general purchasing-power gain (loss) and holding gain (loss) on the land for the ten-year period. Show four methods of measurement: historical cost/nominal dollar, current cost/nominal dollar, historical cost/constant dollar, and current cost/constant dollar.
2. Tabulate which of the four methods recognizes purchasing-power gains and which recognizes holding gains on nonmonetary items.
3. Of the four methods, which do you prefer as the most accurate measure of income? Why?

▨ SOLUTION TO PROBLEM TWO

1. All amounts are in thousands of dollars.

MEASUREMENT METHOD

	(1) historical cost/ nominal dollar	(2) current cost/ nominal dollar	(3) historical cost/ constant dollar	(4) current cost/ constant dollar
Holding loss on monetary item, commonly called loss in general purchasing power	—	—	(40)*	(40)*
Holding gain on nonmonetary item	—	180†	—	140‡
Total	—	180	(40)	100

*Cash held today, expressed in current purchasing power = 40
Cash held ten years ago, expressed
  in current purchasing power:

$$40 = \frac{180}{90} = 80$$

Purchasing-power loss (40)

†Current value of 220 − Historical cost of 40 = 180

‡Current value of 220 − (Restated historical cost of $40 \times \dfrac{180}{90}$, or 80) = 140

2. The relationships among the four methods can be tabulated as follows:

MEASUREMENT METHOD

	(1) historical cost/ nominal dollar	(2) current cost/ nominal dollar	(3) historical cost/ constant dollar	(4) current cost/ constant dollar
Recognizes holding gains (losses) on monetary items commonly called gain (loss) in general purchasing power?	No	No	Yes	Yes
Recognizes holding gains (losses) on nonmonetary items?	No*	Yes	No	Yes

*Recognizes losses, not gains, under lower-of-cost-or-market valuations, which are most often applicable in accounting for inventories and marketable equity securities.

3. Accountants and others have been unable to agree on which method (or model) provides the "most accurate" measure of income. Those who favor Method 1 maintain that no income emerges until an actual sale occurs. Those who favor Method 2 assert that there has been an overall increase in wealth of $180,000 and that the actual sale of land is an incidental factor. Those who favor Method 3 essentially favor the historical-cost approach to measuring income but believe that gains or losses on monetary items are actually realized by mere holding.

Economists tend to favor Method 4 as the most comprehensive way of calibrating an entity's income because it aims at measuring changes in overall command over goods and services, measured in constant purchasing power.

Economists have frequently distinguished between "real" and "nominal" income and capital. The historical-cost method has been severely criticized because it uses a "nominal" measure in the form of unrestated dollars rather than a "real" measure in the form of restated dollars with constant purchasing power. Adherents of the current cost/constant dollar model insist that no income can emerge without the maintenance of real capital, that is, nominal capital restated in terms of constant purchasing power.

Requirements of FASB

As briefly described in the body of this chapter, FASB *Statement No. 33*, "Financial Reporting and Changing Prices," requires large companies to report the effects of inflation *as supplementary information*. Exhibit 19-4 shows a format suggested by the FASB for disclosure of the required information. How does this format compare with the presentations in Exhibit 19-1? The middle column is similar to the Method 3 format used in Exhibit 19-1, historical cost/constant

EXHIBIT 19-4

Statement of Income from Continuing Operations Adjusted for Changing Prices
For the Year Ended December 31, 1980
(Figures assumed, in thousands of average 1980 dollars)

	AS REPORTED IN THE PRIMARY STATEMENTS	ADJUSTED FOR GENERAL INFLATION	ADJUSTED FOR CHANGES IN SPECIFIC PRICES (CURRENT COSTS)
Net sales and other operating revenues	$253,000	$253,000	$253,000
Cost of goods sold	197,000	204,384	205,408
Depreciation and amortization expense	10,000	14,130	19,500
Other operating expense	20,835	20,835	20,835
Interest expense	7,165	7,165	7,165
Provision for income taxes	9,000	9,000	9,000
	244,000	255,514	261,908
Income (loss) from continuing operations	$ 9,000	$(2,514)	$(8,908)
Gain from decline in purchasing power of net amounts owed		$ 7,729	$ 7,729
Increase in specific prices (current cost) of inventories and property, plant, and equipment held during the year*†			$ 24,608
Effect of increase in general price level			18,959
Excess of increase in specific prices over increase in the general price level			$ 5,649

*FASB description of holding gain.
†At December 31, 1980, current cost of inventory was $65,700 and current cost of property, plant, and equipment, net of accumulated depreciation, was $85,100.

dollar. The final column is similar to the Method 4 format, current cost/ constant dollar. Note that there is no column similar to the Method 2 format, current cost/nominal dollar.

The $7,729 in Exhibit 19-4 is similar to the gain in general purchasing power, net monetary items, described earlier in this appendix. Moreover, the $5,649 is similar to the holding gains on inventory and equipment. Also note in both exhibits that these numbers are reported but are not added to income from continuing operations. Why? Because opinion continues unsettled as to which, if any, of such numbers are "really" net income.

Although there are similarities to Exhibit 19-1, there is a major difference: The FASB has not required a complete new model of income, nor has it required revamped balance sheets. Instead, the board has taken a piecemeal approach. To comply with *Statement No. 33*, an enterprise must measure the effects of changing prices on inventory, property, plant and equipment, cost of goods sold, and depreciation, depletion, and amortization expense. No adjustments are required to other revenues, expenses, gains, and losses.

Why did the FASB settle for half a loaf? Why did the board fail to require a complete set of financial statements based on at least one model beyond the primary model of historical cost/nominal dollars? The board believes that its approach is simpler and thus easier to understand than a full-fledged set of supplementary financial statements. Furthermore, in 1979 the board and affected parties had been unable to agree on a single answer regarding whether the supplementary information should focus on general or specific price effects. Many preparers and public accounting firms stressed the need to deal with the effects of general inflation; in contrast, users preferred information dealing with the effects of specific price changes.

The FASB intends to undertake a comprehensive review of *Statement No. 33* no later than 1984. The board will then decide what types of supplementary information should be continued. Meanwhile the information required by the statement will be the biggest experiment to date in published financial reports with respect to changing prices.

assignment material

■ FUNDAMENTAL ASSIGNMENT MATERIAL

This collection of fundamental assignment materials covers the whole chapter, excluding the appendix. Some instructors may assign only one or two major topics in the chapter.

Special note: For coverage of the basic ideas of inflation accounting, Problem 19-2 is especially recommended; for a closer but still fundamental look, Problem 19-28 is especially recommended.

19-1. Terminology. Define *constant dollars; current-cost method; financial capital maintenance; holding gains; monetary items; net monetary position; net realizable value; nominal dollars; physical capital maintenance; revaluation equity.*

19-2. Four versions of income and capital. J Company has the following comparative balance sheets as of December 31 (based on historical costs in nominal dollars):

	19X4	19X5
Cash	$ —	$4,500
Inventory, 50 and 20 units, respectively	5,000	2,000
Total assets	$5,000	$6,500
Paid-in capital	$5,000	$5,000
Retained income	—	1,500
Stockholders' equity	$5,000	$6,500

The general-price-level index was 160 on December 31, 19X4, and 208 on December 31, 19X5. The company had acquired fifty units of inventory on December 31, 19X4, for $100 each and had held them throughout 19X5. Thirty units were sold on December 31, 19X5, for $150 cash each. The replacement cost of the inventory at that date was $120 per unit. Assume that these are the only transactions. Ignore income taxes.

REQUIRED

Use four sets of columns to prepare comparative balance sheets as of December 31, 19X4 and 19X5, and income statements for 19X5 under (1) historical cost/nominal dollars, (2) current cost/nominal dollars, (3) historical cost/constant dollars, and (4) current cost/constant dollars.

■ ADDITIONAL ASSIGNMENT MATERIAL

19-3. What are the two polar approaches to income measurement?

19-4. Explain how net income is measured under the current-cost approach.

19-5. What is *distributable income*?

19-6. Explain what a general price index represents.

19-7. Distinguish between general indexes and specific indexes.

19-8. Enumerate four ways to measure income.

19-9. "Specific indexes are used in nominal-dollar accounting but not in constant-dollar accounting." Do you agree? Explain.

19-10. "The choice among accounting measures of income is often expressed as either historical-cost accounting or general-price-level accounting or current-cost accounting." Do you agree? Explain.

19-11. "A holding gain may simultaneously be a holding loss." Do you agree? Explain.

19-12. "General-price-level accounting is a loose way of achieving replacement-cost income accounting." Do you agree? Explain.

19-13. Distinguish between the physical and the financial concepts of maintenance of invested capital.

19-14. "Holding gains on nonmonetary items are not recognized in historical cost/constant dollar accounting." Do you agree? Explain.

19-15. What is the most common meaning of *current cost*?

19-16. "Net realizable value and replacement cost are generally equal." Do you agree? Explain.

19-17. "All holding gains should be excluded from income." What is the major logic behind this statement?

19-18. What are the three basic positions regarding whether holding gains are income?

19-19. "A holding gain can be recognized but unrealized." Do you agree? Explain.

19-20. Why do managers in heavy industries like steel favor the current-cost concept for income tax purposes?

19-21. "The debtor benefits from inflation." Why?

19-22. "Constant-dollar accounting modifies historical-cost accounting in two major ways." Describe the two ways.

19-23. "Net monetary position is the relationship of current assets to current liabilities." Do you agree? Explain.

19-24. What is the argument for departing from the use of historical cost as a basis of recording depreciation of fixed assets?

19-25. Meaning of general index applications and choice of base year. Mays Company acquired land in mid-1961 for $2 million. In mid-1981 it acquired a substantially identical parcel of land for $4 million. The gross national product implicit price deflator annual averages were:

$$1981—160.0 \qquad 1971—100.0 \qquad 1961—66.7$$

REQUIRED

1. In four columns, show the computations of the total cost of the two parcels of land expressed in (a) costs as traditionally recorded, (b) dollars of 1981 purchasing power, (c) 1971 purchasing power, and (d) 1961 purchasing power.
2. Explain the meaning of the figures that you computed in Requirement 1.

19-26. Four ways to compute income. Suppose that a parcel of land is acquired at the end of 19X3 for $100,000 when the general price index is 100. Its current value at the end of 19X4 is $140,000; the general price index is 115. There are at least four ways to portray these events:

(1) Historical cost—not restated for general-price-level effects
(2) Historical cost—restated for general-price-level effects
(3) Current cost (specific price level)—not restated for general-price-level effects
(4) Current cost (specific price level)—restated for general-price-level effects

REQUIRED

1. Using the above four ways as column headings, tabulate the amounts to be shown at the end of 19X4 for land, original capital, retained earnings, and "gain" on the income statement.
2. Suppose that one more year transpires with absolutely no change in either the general price level or the specific price of the land. Suppose that the land is sold for $140,000 cash. Repeat Requirement 1 for 19X5.
3. Explain the composition of the gain that you show in Requirements 1 and 2. What other major points flow from the tabulations in Requirements 1 and 2?

19-27. Depreciation and price-level adjustments. The Klaman Company purchased a computer for $260,000. It has an expected life of four years and an expected residual value of zero. Straight-line depreciation is used. The general price index is 100 at the date of acquisition; it increases 20 points annually during the next three years. The results follow:

YEAR	PRICE-LEVEL INDEX	UNADJUSTED DEPRECIATION	MULTIPLIER	ADJUSTED DEPRECIATION AS RECORDED
1	100	$ 65,000	100/100	$ 65,000
2	120	65,000	120/100	78,000
3	140	65,000	140/100	91,000
4	160	65,000	160/100	104,000
		$260,000		

1. Convert the figures in the last column so that they are expressed in terms of fourth-year dollars.
2. Suppose in Requirement 1 that revenue easily exceeds expenses for each year and that cash equal to the annual depreciation charge was invested in a non-interest-bearing cash account. If amounts equal to the unadjusted depreciation charge were invested each year, would sufficient cash have accumulated to equal the general purchasing power of $260,000 invested in the asset four years ago? If not, what is the extent of the total financial deficiency measured in terms of fourth-year dollars?
3. Suppose in Requirement 2 that amounts equal to the adjusted depreciation for each year were used. What is the extent of the total financial deficiency?
4. Suppose in Requirement 3 that the amounts were invested each year in assets that increased in value at the same rate as the increase in the general price level. What is the extent of the total financial deficiency?

19-28. **Monetary and nonmonetary items.** Read the appendix. H Company began business on December 31, 19X1, with the following balance sheet. The assets were held throughout 19X2, when the general-price-level index rose from 120 to 144. The familiar historical cost/nominal dollar statements would be:

Balance Sheets as of December 31	19X1	19X2
Cash	$ 80,000	$ 80,000
Land	50,000	50,000
Total assets	$130,000	$130,000
Paid-in capital	$130,000	$130,000

1. Using the historical cost/constant dollar approach, prepare comparative balance sheets and an income statement. Ignore interest and income taxes.
2. Repeat Requirement 1. However, assume that a long-term note payable was issued for $45,000 on December 31, 19X1, and that, therefore, paid-in capital was $130,000 − $45,000 = $85,000.

19-29. **Monetary items.** Read the appendix. Refer to Assignment 19-26. Suppose the same company also had $100,000 of cash, which it had acquired at the end of 19X3. It held the cash in a safety deposit box through the end of 19X4.

1. Fill in the blanks for the cash held in the safety box:

	(1) MEASURED IN 19X3 PURCHASING POWER	(2) MEASURED IN 19X4 PURCHASING POWER	(3) AS CONVENTIONALLY MEASURED
Cash balance, December 31, 19X3			
Cash balance, December 31, 19X4	_____	_____	_____
Purchasing-power loss from holding monetary item.	_____	_____	_____

2. Prepare a similar tabulation for the land balance, except that the final line would refer to a "nonmonetary" rather than a "monetary" item.

19-30. **Monetary versus nonmonetary assets.** Read the appendix. Sloan Company owns land acquired for $100,000 one year ago when the general price index was 100. It also owns $100,000 of government bonds acquired at the same time. The index today is 110. Operating expenses and operating revenue, including interest income, resulted in net income (and an increase of cash) of $4,000 measured in historical-dollar terms. Assume that all income and expense transactions occurred yesterday. The Sloan Company has no other assets and no liabilities. Its cash balance one year ago was zero.

1. Prepare comparative balance sheets for the two instants of time plus an income statement summary based on the historical cost/nominal dollar method. Then prepare such statements using the historical cost/constant dollar method.

2. This is a more important requirement. In your own words, explain the meaning of the historical cost/constant dollar statements. Why should the holding of a monetary asset generate a monetary loss while the holding of land causes neither a loss nor a gain?

19-31. Historical cost/constant dollar questionnaire. (J. Shank.) Read the appendix. Multiple choice:

1. In historical cost/constant dollar financial statements, "monetary" items consist of

a. Only cash

b. Cash, other assets expected to be converted into cash, and current liabilities

c. Assets and liabilities with amounts fixed by contract or otherwise in terms of dollars, regardless of price-level changes

d. Assets and liabilities that are classified as current on the balance sheet

e. None of the above

2. An unacceptable practice in presenting historical cost/constant dollar financial statements is

a. The inclusion of general-price-level gains and losses on monetary items in the general-price-level adjusted income statement

b. The inclusion of extraordinary gains and losses in the general-price-level adjusted income statement

c. The use of charts, ratios, and narrative information

d. The use of specific price indices to restate inventories, plant and equipment

e. None of the above

3. Historical cost/constant dollar financial statements do not incorporate

a. The "lower-of-cost-or-market" rule in the valuation of inventories

b. Replacement cost in the valuation of plant assets

c. The historical-cost basis in reporting income tax expense

d. The actual amounts payable in reporting liabilities on the balance sheet

e. Any of the above

4. During a period of rising price levels, if a firm's combined holdings of cash, short-term marketable securities, and accounts receivable exceed its total liabilities, the historical cost/constant dollar financial statements will exhibit

a. Purchasing-power gains increasing net income

b. Purchasing-power losses decreasing net income

c. Purchasing-power gains with no effect on net income

d. Purchasing-power losses with no effect on net income

e. None of the above

5. With regard to a firm's holdings of plant and equipment, when general price levels are rising, its historical cost/constant dollar financial statements will show

a. Holding gains that increase net income

b. Holding gains credited directly to capital with no effect on net income

c. Holding losses that reduce net income

d. Holding losses charged directly against capital with no effect on net income

e. None of the above.

The following information is applicable to items 6 and 7: Equipment was purchased for $120,000 on January 1, Year 1, when the general price index was 100. It was sold on December 31, Year 3, at a price of $85,000. The equipment originally was expected to last six years with no salvage value and was depreciated on a straight-line basis. The general price index at the end of Year 1 was 125, at the end of Year 2 was 150, and at the end of Year 3 was 175.

6. In comparative historical cost/constant dollar balance sheets prepared at the end of Year 2, the end-of-Year 1 balance sheet would show equipment (net of accumulated depreciation) at

a. $150,000

b. $125,000

c. $100,000

d. $80,000

e. None of the above

7. The historical cost/constant dollar income statement prepared at the end of Year 2 should include depreciation expense of

a. $35,000

b. $30,000

c. $24,000

d. $20,000

e. None of the above

19-32. **Comprehensive review of appendix.** A company has the following comparative balance sheets at December 31 (based on historical costs in nominal dollars):

	19X1	19X2
Cash	$2,000	$3,400
Inventory, 20 units and 10 units, respectively	2,000	1,000
Total assets	$4,000	$4,400
Original capital	$4,000	$4,000
Retained income	—	400
Stockholders' equity	$4,000	$4,400
General-price-level index	160	176

The company had acquired all the inventory at $100 per unit on December 31, 19X1, and had held the inventory throughout 19X2; ten units were sold for $140 cash each on December 31, 19X2. The replacement cost of the inventory at that date was $125.

Note: If you are going to solve the next problem too, ignore the requirements of this problem and proceed directly to the more comprehensive problem that follows.

REQUIRED

Prepare a four-column tabulation of income statements: (1) historical cost/nominal dollars; (2) current cost/nominal dollars; (3) historical cost/constant dollars, and (4) current cost/constant dollars. Also show beginning and ending balance sheet accounts for each of the four columns. For example, the above accounts accompany column 1.

19-33. **Extension of appendix problem.** Suppose that in the preceding problem the sales equipment had been purchased on December 31, 19X1, for $1,000 cash provided by an extra $1,000 of capital. The equipment was being fully depreciated over a ten-year life on a straight-line basis. The replacement cost of the equipment (new) at the end of 19X2 was $1,500.

Prepare a four-column tabulation in the same manner described in the requirement to the preceding problem.

▪ UNDERSTANDING PUBLISHED FINANCIAL REPORTS

Problem 19-34 does not require knowledge of Appendix 19, but Problem 19-35 does.

19-34. **Replacement costs.** (P. Griffin.) Accompanying this problem are excerpts from the 1974 Annual Report of Barber-Ellis Limited of Canada. Note 1 to the financial report includes the following passage:

The current replacement costs of inventories and of property, plant and equipment are shown on the balance sheet and earnings are determined by matching current costs with current revenues. Adjustments of the historical cost of physical assets to their current replacement cost are considered as restatements of shareholders' equity and are shown on the balance sheet under "Revaluation Surplus."

Since 1974 is the first year that the company has prepared current replacement cost financial statements, comparative figures are not available.

REQUIRED

From information in the Balance Sheet, Statement of Earnings and Retained Earnings, and Statement of Revaluation Surplus determine, as of December 31, 1974:

1. Current replacement cost "Inventories."
2. Current replacement cost "Property, Plant and Equipment."
3. Current replacement cost "Accumulated Depreciation."
4. Current replacement cost "Total Assets."
5. Current replacement cost "Retained Earnings."

Also, for the year ended December 31, 1974, determine:

6. Current replacement cost "Cost of Products Sold."
7. Current replacement cost "Net Earnings."

Finally, explain in words the nature of:

8. The difference between the current-replacement-cost "Net Earnings" and the historical-cost "Net Earnings" for the year ended December 31, 1974.

BARBER-ELLIS OF CANADA, LIMITED
Current Replacement Cost Balance Sheet
As at December 31, 1974

	CURRENT REPLACEMENT COST	HISTORICAL COST		CURRENT REPLACEMENT COST	HISTORICAL COST
ASSETS			**LIABILITIES**		
Current:			Current:		
Cash	$ 29,783	$ 29,783	Bank indebtedness	$ 7,573,983	$ 7,573,983
Accounts receivable	12,074,945	12,074,945	Accounts payable and accrued liabilities	4,109,189	4,109,189
Inventories	(1)	10,117,804	Income taxes	1,296,693	1,296,693
Prepaid expenses	249,545	249,545	Dividends—preference shares	700	700
Current assets	$22,721,077	$22,472,077	Current portion of long-term debt	486,650	486,650
			Current liabilities	$13,467,215	$13,467,215
Property, plant and equipment	(2)	11,261,927	Deferred income taxes	278,362	278,362
Accumulated depreciation	(3)	(5,817,772)	Long-term debt (Note 1)	4,133,650	4,133,650
Unamortized excess of purchase price of subsidiaries over fair value of net assets acquired	—	816,067	Total liabilities	$17,879,227	$17,879,227
			SHAREHOLDERS' EQUITY		
			Capital stock	$ 565,705	$ 565,705
			Contributed surplus	45,000	45,000
			Retained earnings	(5)	10,242,367
			Revaluation surplus	4,319,204	—
Total assets	$ (4)	$28,732,299	Total equities	$ (4)	$28,732,299

Current Replacement Cost Statement
of Earnings and Retained Earnings
for the year ended December 31, 1974

	CURRENT REPLACEMENT COST	HISTORICAL COST
Net sales	$69,058,300	$69,058,300
Cost of products sold	$ (6)	$50,389,580
Selling, general and administration	10,705,281	10,705,281
Depreciation and amortization	1,095,567	786,969
Interest—long-term debt	381,884	381,884
Interest—current	590,284	590,284
Cost and expenses	$	$62,853,998
Earnings before income taxes	$	$ 6,204,302
Provision for income taxes	2,927,442	2,927,442
Net Earnings	$ (7)	$ 3,276,860
Retained earnings, beginning of year	7,939,344	7,939,344
Sub-total	$	$11,216,204
Adjustment of prior years' depreciation on current replacement cost of plant and equipment	$ 1,948,116	—
Dividends	973,837	$ 973,837
Retained Earnings, End of Year	$	$10,242,367
Earnings per Share:		
Basic	$ 4.30	$ 7.09
Fully diluted	4.22	6.96

Statement of Revaluation Surplus
for the year ended December 31, 1974

Revaluation of physical assets to reflect current replacement cost as at December 31, 1974

Inventories	$ 249,000
Property, plant and equipment	3,902,271
Excess of purchase price over fair value of assets acquired	(816,067)

Revaluation of cost of products sold during the year ended December 31, 1974

Portion of 1974 earnings determined on historical cost basis which are required to replace inventory sold at the current cost in effect at the date of sale	984,000
Revaluation surplus December 31, 1974	$4,319,204

Report on Supplementary Financial Statements

To the Shareholders,
Barber-Ellis of Canada, Limited

In conjunction with our examination of and report on the financial statements of Barber-Ellis of Canada, Limited for 1974 we have also examined the accompanying supplementary financial statements, which have been prepared on a current replacement cost basis.

Uniform criteria for the preparation and presentation of such supplementary financial information have not yet been established and accordingly, acceptable alternatives are available as to their nature and content. In our opinion, however, the accounting basis described in the notes to the supplementary financial statements has been applied as stated and is appropriate in these circumstances.

Touche Ross & Co.
Chartered Accountants

Toronto, Ontario
February 21, 1975

19-35. **Holding gains and purchasing-power gains.** Study the appendix. Refer to the preceding problem. The following additional information is available:

Items from the Historical Cost Balance Sheet of Barber-Ellis dated December 31, 1973

Cash: $25,200
Long-term debt: $4,133,650

General-Price-Level Index
Dec. 31, 1973: 140
Dec. 31, 1974: 154
Average for the year 1974: 147

REQUIRED

1. Calculate the purchasing-power gain or loss associated with long-term debt (a monetary item). Label it as a gain or loss.
2. Calculate the purchasing-power gain or loss associated with cash and label it as a gain or loss. You may assume that the increase in cash occurred uniformly throughout the year.
3. Assume that Barber-Ellis purchased *all* its inventory on January 1, 1974 (no

other purchases prior to or subsequent to that date). Under that assumption, what are the following numbers? Questions *a* through *c* are based on the current cost/nominal dollar model:

a. Total holding gain on inventory in 1974
b. Realized holding gain on inventory in 1974
c. Unrealized holding gain on inventory in 1974
d. Holding gain on inventory in 1974 *net* of inflation (that is, based on the current cost/constant dollar model)

part five

appendixes

appendix a:
recommended readings

The following readings are suggested as an aid to those readers who want to pursue some topics in more depth than is possible in this book. Of course, many of the chapters have footnotes or suggested readings on a particular topic. Therefore the specific chapters should be consulted for direct references.

There is a hazard in compiling a group of recommended readings. Inevitably, some worthwhile books or periodicals are overlooked. Moreover, such a list cannot include books published subsequent to the compilation here.

Professional journals are typically available in university libraries. *Management Accounting* and the *Financial Executive* tend to stress articles on management accounting. The *Journal of Accountancy* emphasizes financial accounting and is directed at the practicing CPA. The *Harvard Business Review* and *Fortune*, which are aimed at general managers, contain many articles on planning and control.

The *Accounting Review* and the *Journal of Accounting Research* cover all phases of accounting at a more theoretical level than the preceding publications.

The *Opinions* of the Accounting Principles Board are available from the American Institute of CPAs, 1211 Avenue of the Americas, New York, N.Y. 10036. The institute also has a series of research studies on a variety of topics. The pronouncements of the Financial Accounting Standards Board are available from the board's offices, High Ridge Park, Stamford, Conn. 06905.

The Financial Executives Institute, 633 Third Ave., New York, N.Y. 10017, and the National Association of Accountants, 919 Third Avenue, New York, N.Y. 10022, have long lists of accounting research publications.

There are many books on elementary management accounting. Also, many books entitled *Cost Accounting* stress a management approach, including those published since 1977 by Charles Horngren (Prentice-Hall), and Gordon Shillinglaw (Richard D. Irwin).

The following books on planning and control should be helpful:

ANTHONY, R. N., and JOHN DEARDEN, *Management Control Systems,* 4th ed. Homewood, Ill.: Richard D. Irwin, 1980.

BEYER, ROBERT, and DONALD TRAWICKI, *Profitability Accounting for Planning and Control,* 2nd ed. New York: Ronald Press, 1972.

DERMER, J., *Management Planning and Control Systems.* Homewood, Ill.: Richard D. Irwin, 1977.

LORANGE, P., and R. VANCIL, *Strategic Planning Systems.* Englewood Cliffs, N.J.: Prentice-Hall, 1977.

SOLOMONS, DAVID, *Divisional Performance: Measurement and Control.* Homewood, Ill.: Richard D. Irwin, 1968. This book has an extensive bibliography. It is especially strong on transfer pricing.

Vancil, Richard, *Decentralization: Managerial Ambiguity by Design.* New York: Financial Executives Research Foundation, 1979.

Books of readings on management accounting topics published since 1974 include:

Anton, Hector R., Peter A. Firmin, and Hugh D. Grove, eds., *Contemporary Issues in Cost and Managerial Accounting,* 3rd ed. Boston: Houghton Mifflin, 1978.

Benston, George J., *Contemporary Cost Accounting and Control,* 2nd ed. Belmont, Calif.: Dickenson, 1977.

DeCoster, D., K. Ramanthan, and G. Sundem, eds., *Accounting for Managerial Decision Making,* 2nd ed. Los Angeles: Melville, 1978.

Rappaport, Alfred, ed., *Information for Decision Making: Quantitative and Behavioral Dimensions,* 2nd ed. Englewood Cliffs, N.J.: Prentice-Hall, 1974.

Rosen, L. S., ed., *Topics in Managerial Accounting,* 2nd ed. Toronto: McGraw-Hill Ryerson, 1974.

Schiff, Jonathan B., *Readings in Managerial Accounting.* Princeton N.J.: Dow Jones/Arno Press, 1980.

Schiff, Michael, and Arie Y. Lewin, eds., *Behavioral Aspects of Accounting.* Englewood Cliffs, N.J.: Prentice-Hall, 1974.

Thomas, W., ed., *Readings in Cost Accounting, Budgeting and Control,* 5th ed. Cincinnati: South-Western Publishing, 1978.

For a book-length study of management accounting in not-for-profit organizations, see:

Anthony, R. N., and R. Herzlinger, *Management Control in Nonprofit Organizations,* rev. ed. Homewood, Ill.: Richard D. Irwin, 1980.

appendix b:
fundamentals of compound interest and the use of present-value tables

Nature of interest

Interest is the cost of using money. It is the rental charge for cash, just as rental charges are often made for the use of automobiles or boats.

Interest does not always entail an outlay of cash. The concept of interest applies to ownership funds as well as to borrowed funds. The reason why interest must be considered on *all* funds in use, regardless of their source, is that the selection of one alternative necessarily commits funds that could otherwise be invested in some other opportunity. The measure of the interest in such cases is the return forgone by rejecting the alternative use. For instance, a wholly owned home or business asset is not cost-free. The funds so invested could alternatively be invested in government bonds or in some other venture. The measure of this opportunity cost depends on what alternative incomes are available.

Interest cost is often unimportant when short-term projects are under consideration, but it becomes extremely important when long-run plans are being considered. The longer the time span, the higher the interest or rental charge. If you place $10,000 in a savings account at 4 percent interest, compounded annually, you accumulate "interest on interest," which is what "compounding" means. The original $10,000 will grow to $10,400 at the end of Year 1 ($10,000 $\times$ 1.04); to $10,816 at the end of Year 2 ($10,400 $\times$ 1.04); to $11,249 at the end of Year 3 ($10,816 $\times$ 1.04); and to $21,911 at the end of Year 20 ($10,000 $\times$ 1.04^{20}). If the rate of interest were 10 percent compounded annually, the original $10,000 would grow to $13,310 at the end of Year 3 ($10,000 $\times$ 1.10^3); and to $67,276 at the end of Year 20 ($10,000 $\times$ 1.10^{20}).

Table 1: present value of $1

Two basic tables are used in capital budgeting. The first table (Table 1, p. 611), the Present Value of $1, deals with a single lump-sum cash inflow or outflow at a given instant of time, the *end* of the period in question. An example should clarify the reasoning underlying the construction and use of the table.

Illustration: Assume that a prominent corporation is issuing a three-year non-interest-bearing note payable that promises to pay a lump sum of $1,000 exactly three years from now. You desire a rate of return of exactly 6 percent, compounded annually. How much would you be willing to pay now for the three-year note? The situation is sketched as follows:

607

Let us examine the chart, period by period. First, let us assume that you are to purchase the $1,000 note at the end of Year 2 instead of at time zero. How much would you be willing to pay? If you wish to earn 6¢ annually on every $1 invested, you would want to receive $1.06 after one year for every $1 you invest today. Therefore, at the end of Year 2 you would be willing to pay $\dfrac{\$1.00}{\$1.06} \times \$1,000$ for the right to receive $1,000 at the end of Year 3, or $.943 \times \$1,000 = \$943$. Let us enter this in a tabular calculation:

END OF YEAR	INTEREST PER YEAR	CUMULATIVE DISCOUNT, CALLED COMPOUND DISCOUNT	PRESENT VALUE AT THE END OF YEAR
3	$57	$ 57	$1,000
2	53	110	943
1	50	160	890
0	—	—	840

Note that what is really being done in the tabulation is a series of computations that could be formulated as follows:

$$PV_2 = \$1,000 \left[\frac{1.00}{1.06}\right] = \$943$$

$$PV_1 = \$1,000 \left[\frac{1.00}{(1.06)^2}\right] = \$890$$

$$PV_0 = \$1,000 \left[\frac{1.00}{(1.06)^3}\right] = \$840$$

This can be written as a formula for the present value of $1:

$$PV = \frac{S}{(1 + i)^n}$$

where PV = Present value at time zero; S = Future amount; i = Interest rate; and n = Number of periods.

Check the answers in the tabulation by using Table 1 (p. 611). For example, the Period 3 row and the 6 percent column show a factor of .840. Multiply this factor by the future cash flow, $1,000, to obtain its present value, $840. Use Table 1 to obtain the present values of

1. $1,600, @ 20 percent, at the end of 20 years.
2. $8,300, @ 10 percent, at the end of 12 years.
3. $8,000, @ 4 percent, at the end of 4 years.

Answers:

1. $1,600 (.026) = $41.60.
2. $8,300 (.319) = $2,648.
3. $8,000 (.855) = $6,840.

Table 2: present value of an ordinary annuity of $1

An ordinary annuity is a series of equal cash flows that take place at the *end* of successive periods of equal length. Assume that you buy a non-interest-bearing serial note from a corporation that promises to pay $1,000 at the end of each of three years. How much should you be willing to pay if you desire a rate of return of 6 percent, compounded annually?

The tabulation of Exhibit B-1 shows how the formula for PV_A, *the present value of an ordinary annuity*, is developed.

EXHIBIT B-1

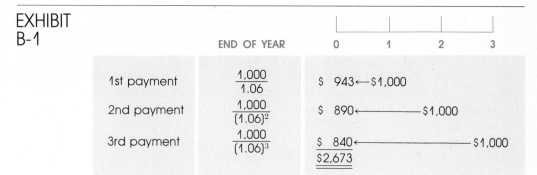

$$PV_A = \text{sum of present values of each item} \qquad (1)$$

For the general case, the present value of an ordinary annuity of $1 may be expressed as follows:

$$PV_A = \frac{1}{1 + i} + \frac{1}{(1 + i)^2} + \frac{1}{(1 + i)^3} \qquad (2)$$

Substituting values from our illustration:

$$PV_A = \frac{1}{1.06} + \frac{1}{(1.06)^2} + \frac{1}{(1.06)^2} \qquad (3)$$

Multiply by $\dfrac{1}{1.06}$:

$$PV_A \left(\frac{1}{1.06} \right) = \frac{1}{(1.06)^2} + \frac{1}{(1.06)^3} + \frac{1}{(1.06)^4} \qquad (4)$$

Subtract Equation 4 from Equation 3:

$$PV_A - PV_A \left(\frac{1}{1.06} \right) = \frac{1}{1.06} - \frac{1}{(1.06)^4} \qquad (5)$$

Factor:

$$PV_A \left(1 - \frac{1}{1.06} \right) = \frac{1}{1.06} \left[1 - \frac{1}{(1.06)^3} \right] \qquad (6)$$

or

$$PV_A \left(\frac{.06}{1.06} \right) = \frac{1}{1.06} \left[1 - \frac{1}{(1.06)^3} \right] \qquad (7)$$

Multiply by $\dfrac{1.06}{.06}$:

$$PV_A = \frac{1}{06}\left[1 - \frac{1}{(1.06)^3}\right] \tag{8}$$

The general formula for the present worth of an annuity of $1 is:

$$PV_A = \frac{1}{i}\left[1 - \frac{1}{(1+i)^n}\right] \tag{9}$$

Solving:
$$PV_A = \frac{1}{.06}(1 - .840) = \frac{.160}{.06} = 2.67 \tag{10}$$

This formula is the basis for Table 2 (p. 612). Check the answer in the table. Minor differences are due to rounding.

Finally, note that Table 2 is convenient, but it is really a compilation of the basic data in Table 1. For example, the present value of each of the three payments could be computed individually, using Table 1:

PV
Factor

$$.943 \times \$1,000 = \$ \ 943$$
$$.890 \times \$1,000 = \ \ \ \ 890$$
$$.840 \times \$1,000 = \ \ \ \ 840$$
$$\$2,673$$

Alternatively, a shortcut computation would use the present-value factor from Table 2, which is merely the sum of the three individual factors = .943 + .890 + .840 = 2.673. Therefore the shortcut computation would be 2.673 × $1,000 = $2,673. If you were marooned on a desert island with one table, Table 1 would be preferable to Table 2.[1]

Use Table 2 to obtain the present values of the following ordinary annuities.

1. $1,600 at 20 percent for 20 years.
2. $8,300 at 10 percent for 12 years.
3. $8,000 at 4 percent for 4 years.

Answers:

1. $1,600 (4.870) = $7,792.
2. $8,300 (6.814) = $56,556.
3. $8,000 (3.630) = $29,040.

[1]For additional tables, see D. Thorndike, *The Thorndike Encyclopedia of Banking and Financial Tables* (Boston: Warren, Gorham & Lamont, 1977).

TABLE 1: (Put a clip on this page for easy reference.)

Present Value of $1

$$PV = \frac{S}{(1+i)^n}$$

PERIODS	3%	4%	5%	6%	7%	8%	10%	12%	14%	16%	18%	20%	22%	24%	26%	28%	30%	40%
1	0.971	0.962	0.952	0.943	0.935	0.926	0.909	0.893	0.877	0.862	0.847	0.833	0.820	0.806	0.794	0.781	0.769	0.714
2	0.943	0.925	0.907	0.890	0.873	0.857	0.826	0.797	0.769	0.743	0.718	0.694	0.672	0.650	0.630	0.610	0.592	0.510
3	0.915	0.889	0.864	0.840	0.816	0.794	0.751	0.712	0.675	0.641	0.609	0.579	0.551	0.524	0.500	0.477	0.455	0.364
4	0.888	0.855	0.823	0.792	0.763	0.735	0.683	0.636	0.592	0.552	0.516	0.482	0.451	0.423	0.397	0.373	0.350	0.260
5	0.863	0.822	0.784	0.747	0.713	0.681	0.621	0.567	0.519	0.476	0.437	0.402	0.370	0.341	0.315	0.291	0.269	0.186
6	0.837	0.790	0.746	0.705	0.666	0.630	0.564	0.507	0.456	0.410	0.370	0.335	0.303	0.275	0.250	0.227	0.207	0.133
7	0.813	0.760	0.711	0.665	0.623	0.583	0.513	0.452	0.400	0.354	0.314	0.279	0.249	0.222	0.198	0.178	0.159	0.095
8	0.789	0.731	0.677	0.627	0.582	0.540	0.467	0.404	0.351	0.305	0.266	0.233	0.204	0.179	0.157	0.139	0.123	0.068
9	0.766	0.703	0.645	0.592	0.544	0.500	0.424	0.361	0.308	0.263	0.225	0.194	0.167	0.144	0.125	0.108	0.094	0.048
10	0.744	0.676	0.614	0.558	0.508	0.463	0.386	0.322	0.270	0.227	0.191	0.162	0.137	0.116	0.099	0.085	0.073	0.035
11	0.722	0.650	0.585	0.527	0.475	0.429	0.350	0.287	0.237	0.195	0.162	0.135	0.112	0.094	0.079	0.066	0.056	0.025
12	0.701	0.625	0.557	0.497	0.444	0.397	0.319	0.257	0.208	0.168	0.137	0.112	0.092	0.076	0.062	0.052	0.043	0.018
13	0.681	0.601	0.530	0.469	0.415	0.368	0.290	0.229	0.182	0.145	0.116	0.093	0.075	0.061	0.050	0.040	0.033	0.013
14	0.661	0.577	0.505	0.442	0.388	0.340	0.263	0.205	0.160	0.125	0.099	0.078	0.062	0.049	0.039	0.032	0.025	0.009
15	0.641	0.555	0.481	0.417	0.362	0.315	0.239	0.183	0.140	0.108	0.084	0.065	0.051	0.040	0.031	0.025	0.020	0.006
16	0.623	0.534	0.458	0.394	0.339	0.292	0.218	0.163	0.123	0.093	0.071	0.054	0.042	0.032	0.025	0.019	0.015	0.005
17	0.605	0.513	0.436	0.371	0.317	0.270	0.198	0.146	0.108	0.080	0.060	0.045	0.034	0.026	0.020	0.015	0.012	0.003
18	0.587	0.494	0.416	0.350	0.293	0.250	0.180	0.130	0.095	0.069	0.051	0.038	0.028	0.021	0.016	0.012	0.009	0.002
19	0.570	0.475	0.396	0.331	0.277	0.232	0.164	0.116	0.083	0.060	0.043	0.031	0.023	0.017	0.012	0.009	0.007	0.002
20	0.554	0.456	0.377	0.312	0.258	0.215	0.149	0.104	0.073	0.051	0.037	0.026	0.019	0.014	0.010	0.007	0.005	0.001
21	0.538	0.439	0.359	0.294	0.242	0.199	0.135	0.093	0.064	0.044	0.031	0.022	0.015	0.011	0.008	0.006	0.004	0.001
22	0.522	0.422	0.342	0.278	0.226	0.184	0.123	0.083	0.056	0.038	0.026	0.018	0.013	0.009	0.006	0.004	0.003	0.001
23	0.507	0.406	0.326	0.262	0.211	0.170	0.112	0.074	0.049	0.033	0.022	0.015	0.010	0.007	0.005	0.003	0.002	
24	0.492	0.390	0.310	0.247	0.197	0.158	0.102	0.066	0.043	0.028	0.019	0.013	0.008	0.006	0.004	0.003	0.002	
25	0.478	0.375	0.295	0.233	0.184	0.146	0.092	0.059	0.038	0.024	0.016	0.010	0.007	0.005	0.003	0.002	0.001	
26	0.464	0.361	0.281	0.220	0.172	0.135	0.084	0.053	0.033	0.021	0.014	0.009	0.006	0.004	0.002	0.002	0.001	
27	0.450	0.347	0.268	0.207	0.161	0.125	0.076	0.047	0.029	0.018	0.011	0.007	0.005	0.003	0.002	0.001	0.001	
28	0.437	0.333	0.255	0.196	0.150	0.116	0.069	0.042	0.026	0.016	0.010	0.006	0.004	0.002	0.002	0.001	0.001	
29	0.424	0.321	0.243	0.185	0.141	0.107	0.063	0.037	0.022	0.014	0.008	0.005	0.003	0.002	0.001	0.001	0.001	
30	0.412	0.308	0.231	0.174	0.131	0.099	0.057	0.033	0.020	0.012	0.007	0.004	0.003	0.002	0.001	0.001		
40	0.307	0.208	0.142	0.097	0.067	0.046	0.022	0.011	0.005	0.003	0.001	0.001						

TABLE 2:

Present Value of Ordinary Annuity of $1

$$PV_A = \frac{1}{i}\left[1 - \frac{1}{(1+i)^n}\right]$$

PERIODS	3%	4%	5%	6%	7%	8%	10%	12%	14%	16%	18%	20%	22%	24%	25%	26%	28%	30%	40%
1	0.971	0.962	0.952	0.943	0.935	0.926	0.909	0.893	0.877	0.862	0.847	0.833	0.820	0.806	0.800	0.794	0.781	0.769	0.714
2	1.913	1.886	1.859	1.833	1.808	1.783	1.736	1.690	1.647	1.605	1.566	1.528	1.492	1.457	1.440	1.424	1.392	1.361	1.224
3	2.829	2.775	2.723	2.673	2.624	2.577	2.487	2.402	2.322	2.246	2.174	2.106	2.042	1.981	1.952	1.923	1.868	1.816	1.589
4	3.717	3.630	3.546	3.465	3.387	3.312	3.170	3.037	2.914	2.798	2.690	2.589	2.494	2.404	2.362	2.320	2.241	2.166	1.849
5	4.580	4.452	4.329	4.212	4.100	3.993	3.791	3.605	3.433	3.274	3.127	2.991	2.864	2.745	2.689	2.635	2.532	2.436	2.035
6	5.417	5.242	5.076	4.917	4.767	4.623	4.355	4.111	3.889	3.685	3.498	3.326	3.167	3.020	2.951	2.885	2.759	2.643	2.168
7	6.230	6.002	5.786	5.582	5.389	5.206	4.868	4.564	4.288	4.039	3.812	3.605	3.416	3.242	3.161	3.083	2.937	2.802	2.263
8	7.020	6.733	6.463	6.210	5.971	5.747	5.335	4.968	4.639	4.344	4.078	3.837	3.619	3.421	3.329	3.241	3.076	2.925	2.331
9	7.786	7.435	7.108	6.802	6.515	6.247	5.759	5.328	4.946	4.607	4.303	4.031	3.786	3.566	3.463	3.366	3.184	3.019	2.379
10	8.530	8.111	7.722	7.360	7.024	6.710	6.145	5.650	5.216	4.833	4.494	4.192	3.923	3.682	3.571	3.465	3.269	3.092	2.414
11	9.253	8.760	8.306	7.887	7.499	7.139	6.495	5.938	5.453	5.029	4.656	4.327	4.035	3.776	3.656	3.544	3.335	3.147	2.438
12	9.954	9.385	8.863	8.384	7.943	7.536	6.814	6.194	5.660	5.197	4.793	4.439	4.127	3.851	3.725	3.606	3.387	3.190	2.456
13	10.635	9.986	9.394	8.853	8.358	7.904	7.103	6.424	5.842	5.342	4.910	4.533	4.203	3.912	3.780	3.656	3.427	3.223	2.468
14	11.296	10.563	9.899	9.295	8.745	8.244	7.367	6.628	6.002	5.468	5.008	4.611	4.265	3.962	3.824	3.695	3.459	3.249	2.477
15	11.938	11.118	10.380	9.712	9.108	8.559	7.606	6.811	6.142	5.575	5.092	4.675	4.315	4.001	3.859	3.726	3.483	3.268	2.484
16	12.561	11.652	10.838	10.106	9.447	8.851	7.824	6.974	6.265	5.669	5.162	4.730	4.357	4.033	3.887	3.751	3.503	3.283	2.489
17	13.166	12.166	11.274	10.477	9.763	9.122	8.022	7.120	6.373	5.749	5.222	4.775	4.391	4.059	3.910	3.771	3.518	3.295	2.492
18	13.754	12.659	11.690	10.828	10.059	9.372	8.201	7.250	6.467	5.818	5.273	4.812	4.419	4.080	3.928	3.786	3.529	3.304	2.494
19	14.324	13.134	12.085	11.158	10.336	9.604	8.365	7.366	6.550	5.877	5.316	4.844	4.442	4.097	3.942	3.799	3.539	3.311	2.496
20	14.877	13.590	12.462	11.470	10.594	9.818	8.514	7.469	6.623	5.929	5.353	4.870	4.460	4.110	3.954	3.808	3.546	3.316	2.497
21	15.415	14.029	12.821	11.764	10.836	10.017	8.649	7.562	6.687	5.973	5.384	4.891	4.476	4.121	3.963	3.816	3.551	3.320	2.498
22	15.937	14.451	13.163	12.042	11.061	10.201	8.772	7.645	6.743	6.001	5.410	4.909	4.488	4.130	3.970	3.822	3.556	3.323	2.498
23	16.444	14.857	13.489	12.303	11.272	10.371	8.883	7.718	6.792	6.044	5.432	4.925	4.499	4.137	3.976	3.827	3.559	3.325	2.499
24	16.936	15.247	13.799	12.550	11.469	10.529	8.985	7.784	6.835	6.073	5.451	4.937	4.507	4.143	3.981	3.831	3.562	3.327	2.499
25	17.413	15.622	14.094	12.783	11.654	10.675	9.077	7.843	6.873	6.097	5.467	4.948	4.514	4.147	3.985	3.834	3.564	3.329	2.499
26	17.877	15.983	14.375	13.003	11.826	10.810	9.161	7.896	6.906	6.118	5.480	4.956	4.520	4.151	3.988	3.837	3.566	3.330	2.500
27	18.327	16.330	14.643	13.211	11.987	10.935	9.237	7.943	6.935	6.136	5.492	4.964	4.524	4.154	3.990	3.839	3.567	3.331	2.500
28	18.764	16.663	14.898	13.406	12.137	11.051	9.307	7.984	6.961	6.152	5.502	4.970	4.528	4.157	3.992	3.840	3.568	3.331	2.500
29	19.188	16.984	15.141	13.591	12.278	11.158	9.370	8.022	6.983	6.166	5.510	4.975	4.531	4.159	3.994	3.841	3.569	3.332	2.500
30	19.600	17.292	15.372	13.765	12.409	11.258	9.427	8.055	7.003	6.177	5.517	4.979	4.534	4.160	3.995	3.842	3.569	3.332	2.500
40	23.115	19.793	17.159	15.046	13.332	11.925	9.779	8.244	7.105	6.234	5.548	4.997	4.544	4.166	3.999	3.846	3.571	3.333	2.500

appendix c: glossary

The italicized words within the definitions or explanations are also described in the glossary.

ABSORPTION COSTING. That type of product costing that assigns fixed manufacturing overhead to the units produced as a product cost. Contrast with *direct costing*.

ACCELERATED DEPRECIATION. Any pattern of *depreciation* that systematically writes off depreciable costs so that progressively smaller amounts are allocated each year.

ACCOUNT. Summary of the changes in a particular asset or equity.

ACCOUNTING METHOD. See *Accounting rate of return*.

ACCOUNTING PRINCIPLES BOARD (APB). The top private-sector regulatory body, which existed from 1959 to 1973, when it was succeeded by the *Financial Accounting Standards Board*.

ACCOUNTING RATE OF RETURN. An expression of the utility of a given project as the ratio of the increase in future average annual net income to the initial increase in required investment. Also called *book value rate* and *unadjusted rate*.

ACCOUNTS PAYABLE. The debts shown on the buyer's balance sheet when the buyer has bought goods or services on open account. Usually a *current liability*.

ACCOUNTS RECEIVABLE. The claims against debtors generally arising from sales of goods or services on open account. Usually a *current asset*.

ACCRUAL BASIS. A matching process whereby *revenue* is recognized as services are rendered and *expenses* are recognized as efforts are expended or services utilized to obtain the revenue, regardless of when cash is received or disbursed.

ACCRUE. Accumulation of a receivable or payable during a given period even though no explicit transaction occurs.

ACCUMULATED DEPRECIATION. The cumulative sum of all *depreciation* recognized since the date of acquisition of the particular assets described.

ACQUISITION COST. The original *historical cost* of an *asset* acquired. Usually includes directly associated costs such as freight and installation.

ACTIVITY ACCOUNTING. See *Responsibility accounting*.

ACTUAL COSTING. The method of allocating costs to products using actual direct materials, direct labor, and overhead.

ADDBACK METHOD. The practice of beginning a statement of changes in financial position with *net income* and then adding or deducting income statement items not affecting *working capital*.

ADJUSTING ENTRIES. The records made of an accounting transaction giving effect to the correction of an error, an accrual, a write-off, a prepayment, a provision for bad debts or depreciation, or the like.

ADJUSTMENTS. The key final process (before the computation of ending account balances) that assures the accountant that the financial effects of transactions are assigned to the appropriate time periods.

ALLOCATION. Assigning one or more items of cost or revenue to one or more segments of an organization according to cause, benefits received, responsibilities, or other logical measure of use.

AMORTIZATION. The systematic reduction of a lump-sum amount.

APB. See *Accounting Principles Board*.

APB Opinions. A series of thirty-one Opinions of the Accounting Principles Board issued during 1962–73, many of which are still the accounting law of the land.

Appropriation. An authorization to spend up to a specified dollar ceiling.

Assets. Economic resources that are expected to benefit future activities.

Asset Turnover. The ratio of sales to total assets available.

Attention Directing. That function of the accountant's information-supplying task which focuses on problems in the operation of the firm or which points out imperfections or inefficiencies in certain areas of the firm's operation.

Audit. An examination that is made in accordance with generally accepted auditing standards. Its aim is to give credibility to financial statements.

Auditor's Report. The written description of an auditor's findings together with the auditor's professional opinion regarding the credibility of management's financial statements.

Avoidable Cost. Those costs that will not continue if an ongoing operation is changed or deleted.

Balance. The difference between the total *debits* and the total *credits* in an *account* at any particular time.

Balance Sheet. A statement of financial status at an instant of time.

Bill of Materials. A specification of the quantities of direct material allowed for manufacturing a given quantity of output.

Book Value. The carrying amount in the accounts, net of any *contra accounts*. For example, the book value of equipment is its *acquisition cost* minus its *accumulated depreciation*.

Book Value Method. See *Accounting Rate of Return*.

Budget. A plan of action expressed in figures.

Budget Appropriation. An authority to spend, usually up to a ceiling amount.

Budget Variance. The difference between an actual and a *budget* amount. Also see *Control-budget variance*.

Capacity Costs. An alternate term for fixed costs, emphasizing the fact that fixed costs are needed in order to provide operating facilities and an organization ready to produce and sell at a planned volume of activity.

Capital. In accounting, this word is too general by itself. In most cases, capital implies owners' equity. Money generated by long-term debt is also often called capital.

Capital Budgeting. Long-term planning for proposed capital outlays and their financing.

Capital Surplus. The excess received over the par or stated or legal value of the shares issued.

Capital Turnover. Revenue divided by invested capital.

Cash Basis. A process of accounting whereby *revenue* and *expense* recognition depend solely on the timing of various cash receipts and disbursements.

Cash Budget. A schedule of expected cash receipts and disbursements.

Cash Flow. A general term that must be interpreted carefully. Most strictly, cash flow means inflows or outflows of cash. Frequently, the term is used loosely to represent funds provided by operations.

Certified Management Accountant. A designation given by the Institute of Management Accounting of the National Association of Accountants to those who pass a set of examinations and meet specified experience and continuing education requirements.

Certified Public Accountant. In the U.S., an accountant earns this designation by a combination of education, qualifying experience, and the passing of a three and one-half day written national examination.

Changes Statement. A *statement of changes in financial position*.

CMA. See *Certified Management Accountant.*

COMMITTED COSTS. Those fixed costs arising from the possession of plant and equipment and a basic organization and thus are affected primarily by long-run decisions as to the desired level of capacity.

COMMON COST. A cost that is common to all the segments in question and is not clearly or practically allocable except by some questionable allocation base.

COMMON STOCK. Stock representing the class of owners having a "residual" ownership of a corporation.

COMPTROLLER. See *Controller.*

CONDITIONAL VALUE. The value that will ensue if a particular event occurs.

CONSERVATISM. Selecting that method of measurement which yields the gloomiest immediate results.

CONSOLIDATED STATEMENTS. Statements that combine legally separate companies as though they were a single fused entity.

CONSTANT DOLLARS. Those monetary units restated so as to represent the same general purchasing power.

CONTINUITY CONVENTION. See *Going concern convention.*

CONTINUOUS BUDGET. A budget that perpetually adds a month in the future as the month just ended is dropped.

CONTRA ACCOUNT. A separate offsetting account. Examples are allowance for uncollectible accounts and accumulated depreciation.

CONTRIBUTED CAPITAL. The total amounts invested by owners at the inception of a business or subsequently. Usually distinguished from capital arising from *retained income.*

CONTRIBUTION APPROACH. A method of preparing income statements that separates variable costs from fixed costs in order to emphasize the importance of cost behavior patterns for purposes of planning and control.

CONTRIBUTION MARGIN. Excess of sales price over variable expenses. Also called marginal income. May be expressed as a total, as a ratio, or on a per-unit basis.

CONTROL-BUDGET VARIANCE. The difference between an actual amount incurred and a budget amount based on a *flexible budget.*

CONTROL FACTOR UNIT. A measure of workload. Examples are lines per hour and pieces mailed per hour.

CONTROLLABLE COST. A cost that may be directly regulated at a given level of managerial authority, either in the short run or in the long run.

CONTROLLER. The chief management accounting executive. Also spelled *comptroller.*

CONTROLLING. Obtaining conformity to plans through action and evaluation.

COPYRIGHT. Exclusive right conveyed by federal statute to reproduce and sell a book, design, pamphlet, drawing, or other creations, and to forbid the publication of excerpts or other imitations.

CORPORATION. Organizations that are "artificial beings" created by individual state laws.

COST. Sacrifice made for goods or services. May take the form of an *outlay cost* or an *opportunity cost.*

COST APPLICATION. Also called *cost absorption.* The allocation to products rather than to departments.

COST APPROXIMATION. See *Cost estimation.*

COST BEHAVIOR PATTERN. See *Cost function.*

COST-BENEFIT CRITERION. As a system is changed, its expected additional benefits usually must exceed its expected additional costs.

COST CENTER. An area of responsibility for costs.

COST ESTIMATION. Attempt to specify some underlying relationship between x and y over a stipulated *relevant range* of x that may be of interest. An approximation of how a cost truly behaves. The approximation is in linear rather than nonlinear form.

COST FUNCTION. A relationship between a cost and one or more variables such as the total cost of repairs in relation to miles driven.

COST METHOD FOR INVESTMENTS. The method whereby the initial investment is recorded at cost and *dividends* are recorded as income.

COST OBJECTIVE. Any activity for which a separate measurement of costs is desired. Examples include departments, products, territories, etc.

COST OF GOODS SOLD. Cost of the merchandise that is acquired and resold.

COST OF SALES. See *Cost of goods sold*.

COST POOL. A group of costs that is allocated to cost objectives in some plausible way.

CREDIT. In accounting, means one thing and one thing only—"right," as distinguished from "left." It typically refers to an entry in an *account* or the *balance* of an account.

CURRENT ASSETS. Cash plus those assets that are reasonably expected to be converted to cash or sold or consumed during the normal operating cycle.

CURRENT COST. Cost stated in terms of current market prices instead of historical cost.

CURRENT-COST METHOD. See *Current cost*.

CURRENT LIABILITIES. Liabilities that fall due within the coming year or within the normal operating cycle if longer than a year.

CURRENTLY ATTAINABLE STANDARDS. Standards expressing a level of economic efficiency that can be reached with skilled, diligent, superior effort.

DEBENTURE. A security with a general claim against all unencumbered assets rather than a specific claim against particular assets.

DEBIT. An entry on the left side of an account.

DECENTRALIZATION. The relative freedom to make decisions. The lower the level in the organization that decisions are made, the greater the decentralization.

DECISION MODEL. A formal method for making a choice that often involves quantitative analysis.

DECISION TABLE. A convenient technique for showing the total expected value of each of a number of contemplated acts in the light of the varying probabilities of the events that may take place and the varying values of each act under each of the events.

DEFERRED CHARGE. An expenditure not recognized as a cost of operations of the period in which incurred but carried forward to be written off in one or more future periods.

DEFERRED INCOME. See *Deferred revenue*.

DEFERRED INCOME TAX (LIABILITY). A *liability* in the *balance sheet* that represents the additional federal income taxes that would have been due if a company had not been allowed to deduct greater amounts for expenses for income-tax-reporting purposes than are recorded for financial-reporting purposes. Also see *Interperiod tax allocation*.

DEFERRED REVENUE. Income received or recorded before it is earned.

DENOMINATOR VARIANCE. Difference between *budgeted* fixed overhead and the fixed overhead *applied* to product.

DEPRECIATION. The allocation of the *acquisition cost* of plant, property, and equipment to the particular periods or products that benefit from the utilization of the *assets*.

DIFFERENTIAL COST. See *Incremental cost*.

DIRECT COSTING. That type of product costing which charges fixed manufacturing overhead immediately against the revenue of the period in which it was incurred, without assigning it to specific units produced. Also called *variable costing* or *marginal costing*.

DIRECT LABOR. All labor that is obviously related to and specifically and conveniently traceable to specific products.

DIRECT MATERIAL. All raw material that is an integral part of the finished good and can be conveniently assigned to specific physical units.

DISCRETIONARY COSTS. Fixed costs arising from periodic, usually yearly, appropriation decisions that directly reflect top-management policies. Also called *programmed costs* or *managed costs*.

DIVIDENDS. Ordinarily distributions of *assets* that liquidate a portion of the ownership claim.

DOUBLE-DECLINING-BALANCE DEPRECIATION (DDB). A form of *accelerated depreciation* that results in first-year *depreciation* being twice the amount of *straight-line depreciation*.

DYSFUNCTIONAL BEHAVIOR. Actions taken in conflict with top-management goals.

EARNED SURPLUS. A virtually archaic term for *retained income*.

EARNINGS. The excess of *revenues* over *expenses*.

EARNINGS PER SHARE. Net income divided by the number of common shares outstanding. However, where preferred stock exists, the preferred dividends must be deducted in order to compute the net income applicable to common stock.

ECONOMIC ORDER QUANTITY. The amount of inventory that should be ordered at one time so that the associated annual costs of the inventory can be minimized.

EFFICIENCY. Optimal relationship between inputs and outputs.

EFFICIENCY VARIANCE. The standard price for a given resource, multiplied by the difference between the actual quantity of inputs used and the total standard quantity of inputs allowed for the number of good outputs achieved.

ENTITY. A specific area of accountability that is the focus of the accounting process. It may be a single corporation, a tax district, a department, a papermaking machine, or a consolidated group of many interrelated corporations.

EQUITIES. The claims against or interests in the assets. The creditors' claims are *liabilities* and the owners' claims are *owners' equity* or, in the case of corporations, *stockholders' equity*.

EQUITY METHOD. A basis for carrying long-term investments at cost plus a pro-rata share of accumulated retained income since acquisition.

EQUIVALENT UNITS. The expression of output in terms of doses or amount of work applied thereto.

EXCESS MATERIAL REQUISITIONS. A form to be filled out by the production staff to secure any materials needed in excess of the standard amount allotted for output.

EXPECTED VALUE. A weighted average of all the conditional values of an act. Each conditional value is weighted by its probability.

EXPENDITURE. Cash or other resources paid, or to be paid, for an *asset* purchased or service acquired.

EXPENSES. Generally a gross decrease in *assets* from delivering goods or services.

EXPIRED COSTS. *Expenditures* from which no further benefit is anticipated; an *expense;* a cost absorbed over the period during which benefits were enjoyed or a *loss* incurred.

EXPLICIT TRANSACTIONS. Events such as cash receipts and disbursements that trigger nearly all day-to-day routine entries.

FACTORY BURDEN. See *Factory overhead*.

FACTORY OVERHEAD. All factory costs other than direct labor and direct material. Also called *factory burden, indirect manufacturing costs, manufacturing overhead,* and *manufacturing expense*.

FASB STATEMENTS. Official rules and regulations regarding external financial reporting issued in a numbered series by the *Financial Accounting Standards Board*.

FINANCIAL ACCOUNTING. Is concerned mainly with how accounting can serve external decision makers, as distinguished from *management accounting*.

FINANCIAL ACCOUNTING STANDARDS BOARD (FASB). The primary regulatory body over accounting principles and practices. It is an independent creature of the private sector.

FINANCIAL CAPITAL MAINTENANCE. The quantity of financial resources (usually historical costs), as distinguished from physical resources or operating capability, to be recovered before *income* emerges.

FIRST-IN, FIRST-OUT. The stock of merchandise or material that is acquired earliest is assumed to be used first; the stock acquired latest is assumed to be still on hand.

FIXED ASSETS. Tangible assets or physical items that can be seen and touched, often called property, plant, and equipment or plant assets.

FIXED COST. A cost that, for a given period of time and range of activity called the *relevant range,* does not change in total but becomes progressively smaller on a *per-unit* basis as volume increases.

FLEXIBLE BUDGET. A budget, often referring to overhead costs only, that is prepared for a range, rather than for a single level, of activity—one that can be automatically geared to changes in the level of volume. Also called *variable budget.* Direct material and direct labor are sometimes included in the flexible budget.

FOREIGN CORRUPT PRACTICES ACT. A federal law that requires adequate *internal controls,* among other requirements.

FRANCHISE. A privilege granted by a government, manufacturer, or distributor to sell a product or service in accordance with specified conditions.

FULL COST. Has two commonly used meanings. First, it is often a synonym for *absorption cost.* Second, it often means absorption cost *plus* an allocation of nonmanufacturing cost.

FULL COSTING. See *Full Cost.*

FUNCTIONAL APPROACH. See *Functional costing.*

FUNCTIONAL COSTING. Classifying costs by allocating them to the various functions performed, such as manufacturing, warehousing, delivery, and billing.

FUND. A specific amount of cash or securities earmarked for a special purpose.

FUNDS PROVIDED BY OPERATIONS. The excess of revenue over all expenses requiring working capital.

FUNDS STATEMENT. A statement of sources and applications of working capital.

GENERALLY ACCEPTED ACCOUNTING PRINCIPLES (GAAP). A technical term including both broad concepts or guidelines and detailed practices. It includes all conventions, rules, and procedures that together make up accepted accounting practice at a given time.

GOAL CONGRUENCE. Sharing of the same goals by top managers and their subordinates.

GOING CONCERN CONVENTION. An *entity* that it is assumed will continue indefinitely or at least will not be liquidated in the near future.

GOODWILL. The total purchase price of assets acquired in a lump-sum purchase that exceeds the total of the amounts that can be justifiably assigned to the individual assets.

GROSS MARGIN. Also called *gross profit.* Excess of sales over the *cost of goods sold,* that is, over the cost of the merchandise inventory that is acquired and resold.

GROSS PROFIT. The difference between sales revenue and the cost of inventories sold.

HISTORICAL COST. See *Sunk cost.*

HOLDING GAINS. Increases (or decreases) in the *replacement cost* (or other appropriate measure of current value) of the *assets* held during the current period.

IDEAL CAPACITY. The absolute maximum number of units that could be produced in a given operating situation, with no allowance for work stoppages or repairs. Also called theoretical capacity.

IDLE TIME. A classification of *indirect labor* that constitutes wages paid for unproductive time due to circumstances beyond the worker's control.

IMPLICIT TRANSACTIONS. Events (like the passage of time) that are temporarily ignored in day-to-day recording procedures and that are recognized via end-of-period *adjustments.*

INCENTIVE. The degree of striving for a goal or objective.

INCOME. The excess of *revenues* over *expenses*.

INCOME STATEMENT. A statement that evaluates the operating performance of the corporation by matching its accomplishments (revenue from customers, which usually is called sales) and efforts (cost of goods sold and other expenses).

INCREMENT. See *Incremental.*

INCREMENTAL. The change in total results (such as revenue, expenses, or income) under a new condition in comparison with some given or known condition.

INCREMENTAL APPROACH. A method of determining which of two alternative courses of action is preferable by calculating the present value of the difference in net cash inflow between one alternative and the other.

INCREMENTAL COST. The difference in total cost between two alternatives. Also called *differential cost.*

INDEPENDENT OPINION. See *Auditor's report.*

INDIRECT LABOR. All factory labor that is not *direct labor.*

INDIRECT MANUFACTURING COSTS. All manufacturing costs other than *direct material* and *direct labor.*

INTANGIBLE ASSETS. Rights or economic benefits that are not physical in nature. Examples are *franchises, patents, trademarks, copyrights,* and *goodwill.*

INTERNAL ACCOUNTING CONTROL. Methods and procedures that are mainly concerned with the authorization of transactions, safeguarding of assets, and accuracy of the financial records.

INTERNAL RATE OF RETURN. The rate of interest at which the present value of expected cash inflows from a particular project equals the present value of expected cash outflow of the same project. Also called *time-adjusted rate.*

INTERPERIOD TAX ALLOCATION. Accounting procedures that account for *timing differences* between *revenues* and *expenses* reported to income tax authorities and to others.

INVESTMENT CENTER. An area of responsibility for *costs, revenues,* and related investment.

INVESTMENT TAX CREDIT. Direct reductions of income taxes arising from the acquisition of depreciable assets.

JOB ORDER. A document that shows the costs allocated to a specific batch of product.

JOB ORDER COSTING. The method of allocating costs to products that receive varying attention and effort.

JOINT PRODUCT COSTS. Costs of two or more manufactured goods, of significant sales values, that are produced by a single process and that are not identifiable as individual products up to a certain stage of production, known as the split-off point.

LAST-IN, FIRST-OUT. A cost-flow assumption that the stock acquired earliest is still on hand; the stock of merchandise or material acquired latest is used first.

LEAD TIME. The time interval between placing an order and receiving delivery.

LEDGER. A group of *accounts.*

LEGAL VALUE. *Par* or *stated value* that is almost always far below the actual cash invested by a stockholder.

LIABILITIES. Probable future sacrifices of economic benefits stemming from present legal, equitable, or constructive obligations of a particular enterprise to transfer *assets* or provide services to other entities in the future as a result of past *transactions* or events affecting the enterprise.

LIFO. See *Last-in, First-out.*

LIFO INCREMENT. See *LIFO layer.*

LIFO LAYER. A separately identifiable additional segment of LIFO inventory.

LIFO POOL. See *LIFO layer.*

LIFO RESERVE. The amount of "cushion" or "understatement" of current inventory values that the LIFO method produces in relation to FIFO.

LIMITED LIABILITY. Corporate creditors ordinarily have claims against the corporate *assets* only. Therefore the stockholders as individuals have no liability beyond their original investment in the corporation.

LIMITING FACTOR. The item that restricts or constrains the production or sale of a product or service.

LINEAR PROGRAMMING. A mathematical approach to a group of business problems that contains many interacting variables and basically involves combining limited resources to maximize *profits* or minimize *costs*.

LINE AUTHORITY. Authority that is exerted downward over subordinates.

LONG-LIVED ASSETS. Resources that are held for an extended time, such as land, buildings, equipment, natural resources, and *patents*.

LOSSES. Losses (or other appropriately descriptive terms) are decreases in *owners' equity* (net assets) from peripheral or incidental *transactions* of an enterprise and from all other transactions and other events and circumstances affecting the enterprise during the period except those that result from *expenses* or distributions by the enterprise to owners.

LOWER OF COST OR MARKET. The superimposition of a market-price test on an inventory cost method.

MANAGED COSTS. See *Discretionary costs*.

MANAGEMENT ACCOUNTING. Concerned mainly with how accounting can serve internal decision makers.

MANAGEMENT AUDIT. A review to determine whether the policies and procedures specified by top management have been implemented.

MANAGEMENT BY EXCEPTION. The practice by the executive of focusing his or her attention mainly on significant deviations from expected results. It might also be called management by variance.

MANUFACTURING EXPENSES. See *Factory overhead*.

MANUFACTURING OVERHEAD. See *Factory overhead*.

MARGINAL COSTING. See *Direct costing*.

MARGINAL INCOME. See *Contribution margin*.

MARKETABLE SECURITIES. Any notes, bonds, or stocks that can be readily sold via public markets. The term is often used as a synonym for *short-term investments*.

MARKETING VARIANCE. The budgeted unit contribution margin multiplied by the difference between the master-budgeted sales in units and the actual sales in units.

MASTER BUDGET. The budget that consolidates the organization's overall plans.

MASTER BUDGETED SALES. The expected sales employed in formulating the master budget for the period.

MATCHING. Establishing a relationship between efforts (expenses) and accomplishments (revenues).

MATCHING AND COST RECOVERY. The procedure of accrual accounting whereby *expenses* are either directly attributed to related *revenues* (matching) of a given period or are otherwise regarded as costs that will not be recovered from revenue in future periods. In short, cost recovery is the justification for carrying unexpired costs as assets rather than writing them off as expenses.

MATERIALITY. The accounting convention that justifies the exclusion of insignificant information from financial reports. Whether an item is material (significant) is a matter of professional judgment.

MINORITY INTEREST. The total shareholder interest (other than the parent's) in a *subsidiary corporation*.

MIXED COST. A cost that has both fixed and variable elements.

MODEL. A depiction of interrelationships of recognized factors in a real situation.

MONETARY ITEMS. A claim receivable or payable in a specified number of dollars; the claim remains fixed regardless of changes in either specific or general price levels.

NAA. See *National Association of Accountants.*

NATIONAL ASSOCIATION OF ACCOUNTANTS. The largest U.S. professional organization of accountants whose major interest is management accounting.

NEGOTIATED MARKET PRICE. A transfer price negotiated by the buying and selling segments when there is no market mechanism to fix a price clearly relevant to the situation.

NET BOOK VALUE. See *Book value.*

NET INCOME. The excess of all *revenues* and gains for a period over all *expenses* and *losses.*

NET MONETARY POSITION. Total monetary assets minus total monetary *liabilities.*

NET PRESENT VALUE METHOD. A method of calculating the expected utility of a given project by discounting all expected future cash flows to the present, using some predetermined minimum desired rate of return.

NET REALIZABLE VALUE. Estimated selling price of a product in the ordinary course of business, less reasonably predictable costs of completion and disposal.

NET WORTH. A synonym for *owners' equity;* no longer widely used.

NOMINAL DOLLARS. Those that are not restated for fluctuations in the general purchasing power of the monetary unit.

NORMAL ACTIVITY. The rate of activity needed to meet average sales demand over a period long enough to encompass seasonal and cyclical fluctuations.

NORMAL COSTING. The method of allocating costs to products using actual *direct materials,* actual *direct labor,* and predetermined overhead rates.

NORMAL COST SYSTEM. See *Normal costing.*

NOTES PAYABLE. Promissory notes that are evidence of a debt and state the terms of payment.

OBJECTIVITY. Accuracy supported by convincing evidence that can be verified by independent accountants.

OBJECT OF COSTING. See *Cost objective.*

OPEN ACCOUNT. Buying or selling on credit usually by just an "authorized signature" of the buyer.

OPERATING CYCLE. The time span during which cash is used to acquire goods and services, which in turn are sold to customers, who in turn pay for their purchases with cash.

OPERATIONS RESEARCH. A diffused collection of mathematical and statistical models applied to decision making.

OPPORTUNITY COST. The maximum alternative earning that might have been obtained if the productive good, service, or capacity had been applied to some alternative use.

ORDER-FILLING COST. A marketing cost incurred in the storing, packing, shipping, billing, credit and collection, and in other similar aspects of selling merchandise.

ORDER-GETTING COST. A marketing cost incurred in the effort to attain a desired sales volume and mix.

ORGANIZATION STRUCTURE. The formal relationships among the individuals and segments within an organization.

OUTLAY COST. A cash disbursement, as distinguished from an *opportunity cost.*

OVERABSORBED OVERHEAD. See *Overapplied factory overhead.*

OVERAPPLIED FACTORY OVERHEAD. The excess of overhead applied to products over actual overhead incurred.

OVERTIME PREMIUM. A classification of *indirect labor costs,* consisting of the wages paid to *all* factory workers in excess of their straight-time wage rates.

OWNERS' EQUITY. The interest of stockholders or other owners in the *assets* of an enterprise and, at any time, the cumulative net result of past *transactions* and other events and circumstances affecting the enterprise.

PAID-IN CAPITAL. The *owners' equity* measured by the total amounts invested at the inception of a business and subsequently.

PAID-IN SURPLUS. See *Capital surplus*.

PARAMETER. A constant, such as *a*, or a coefficient, such as *b*, in a model or system of equations, such as $y = a + bx$.

PARTNERSHIP. A special form of organization that joins two or more individuals together as co-owners.

PAR VALUE. The value printed on the face of the security certificate.

PATENTS. Grants by the federal government to inventors, giving them the exclusive right to produce and sell their inventions for a period of seventeen years.

PAYBACK. The measure of the time needed to recoup, in the form of cash inflow from operations, the initial dollars invested. Also called *payout* and *payoff*.

PAYOFF. See *Payback*.

PAYOFF TABLE. See *Decision table*.

PAYOUT. See *Payback*.

PERFORMANCE REPORT. The comparison of actual results with the budget.

PERIOD COSTS. Those costs being deducted as *expenses* during the current period without having been previously classified as *product costs*.

PHYSICAL CAPITAL MAINTENANCE. The capacity to maintain previous levels of output of goods and services.

PLANNING. Selecting objectives and the means for their attainment.

PRACTICAL CAPACITY. The maximum level at which the plant or department can realistically operate most efficiently, i.e., ideal capacity less allowances for unavoidable operating interruptions. Also called practical attainable capacity.

PREFERRED STOCK. Stock that has some priority over other shares regarding *dividends* or the distribution of *assets* upon liquidation.

PREPAID EXPENSES. Assets that exist because operating supplies and rights to services have been acquired in advance of use.

PRICE VARIANCE. The difference between the actual price and the standard price, multiplied by the total number of items acquired. The term "price variance" is usually linked with *direct material;* the term "rate variance," which is conceptually similar to the price variance, is usually linked with *direct labor.*

PROBLEM SOLVING. That function of the accountant's information-supplying task which expresses in concise, quantified terms the relative advantages and disadvantages to the firm of pursuing a possible future course of action, or the relative advantages of any one of several alternative methods of operation.

PROCESS. A series of actions or operations leading to a definite end.

PROCESS COSTING. The method of allocating costs to the products resulting from the mass production of like units.

PRODUCT COSTS. Costs that are identified with goods produced or purchased for resale.

PROFITABILITY ACCOUNTING. See *Responsibility accounting*.

PROFIT CENTER. A segment of a business that is responsible for both *revenue* and *expense*.

PROFITS. The excess of *revenues* over *expenses*.

PRO-FORMA STATEMENTS. Forecasted financial statements.

PROGRAMMED COSTS. See *Discretionary costs*.

PROPRIETORSHIP. A separate *entity* with a single owner.

P/V CHART. A graph showing volume on the horizontal axis and net income on the vertical axis.

QUALITATIVE FACTOR. A factor that is of consequence but cannot be measured precisely and easily in dollars.

QUANTITY VARIANCE. *Efficiency variance* pertaining to materials or direct labor.

QUOTE SHEET. An analysis of costs used as a basis for determining selling prices.

RATE VARIANCE. The difference between actual wages paid and the standard wage rate, multiplied by the total actual hours of direct labor used. See *Price variance*.

REALIZATION. The recognition of *revenue*. Generally three tests must be met. First, the earning process must be virtually complete in that the goods or services must be fully rendered. Second, an exchange of resources evidenced by a market transaction must occur. Third, the *asset* received must be cash or convertible into cash with reasonable certainty.

REALLOCATION. Allocation of the costs of operating the service departments to the various production departments in proportion to the relative benefits or services received by each production department.

REAPPORTIONMENT. See *Reallocation*.

REGRESSION ANALYSIS. The measurement of the average amount of change in one variable (e.g., shipping cost) that is associated with unit increases in the amounts of one or more other variables.

REINVESTED EARNINGS. See *Retained income*.

RELEVANT DATA FOR DECISION MAKING. Expected future data that will differ among alternatives.

RELEVANT INFORMATION. See *Relevant data for decision making*.

RELEVANT RANGE. The band of activity in which budgeted sales and expense relationships will be valid.

REPLACEMENT COST. Cost to replenish a given amount of an *asset*.

RESERVE. Has one of three meanings: (1) a restriction of dividend-declaring power as denoted by a specific subdivision of *retained income;* (2) an offset to an *asset;* and (3) an estimate of a definite *liability* of indefinite or uncertain amount.

RESIDUAL INCOME. The net income of a profit center or investment center, less the "imputed" interest on the net assets used by the center.

RESIDUAL INTEREST. The *owners' equity* in the entity's *assets* after deducting *liabilities* and any other claims with a higher priority.

RESIDUAL VALUE. The predicted disposal value of a *long-lived asset*.

RESPONSIBILITY ACCOUNTING. A system of accounting that recognizes various responsibility centers throughout the organization and reflects the plans and actions of each of these centers by allocating particular *revenues* and *costs* to those having the pertinent responsibilities. Also called *profitability accounting* and *activity accounting*.

RETAINED EARNINGS. See *Retained income*.

RETAINED INCOME. Additional *owners' equity* generated by *profits*.

RETURN ON STOCKHOLDERS' EQUITY. The rate of return on the invested capital of the shareholders.

REVALUATION EQUITY. That portion of *stockholders' equity* that shows all accumulated *holding gains* not otherwise shown in *retained income*.

REVENUES. Generally, a gross increase in net assets from delivering goods or services. More specifically, revenues are inflows or other enhancements of *assets* of an enterprise or settlements of its *liabilities* (or a combination of both) during a period from delivering or producing goods, rendering services, or other activities that constitute the enterprises's ongoing major or central operations.

SAFETY STOCK. A minimum inventory that provides a cushion against reasonably expected maximum demand and against variations in *lead time*.

SALES MIX. The relative combination of the quantities of a variety of company products that compose total sales.

SCOREKEEPING. That data accumulation function of the accountant's information-supplying task which enables both internal and external parties to evaluate the financial performance of the firm.

SCRAP VALUE. See *Residual value*.

SECURITIES AND EXCHANGE COMMISSION (SEC). The federal agency designated by the U.S. Congress as holding the ultimate responsibility for authorizing the generally accepted accounting principles for companies whose stock is held by the general investing public.

SEGMENT. Any line of activity or part of an organization for which separate determination of costs and sales is wanted.

SEGMENT MARGIN. The contribution margin for each segment less all separable fixed costs, both discretionary and committed. A measure of long-run profitability.

SENSITIVITY ANALYSIS. Measuring how the basic predicted results will be affected by variations in the critical data inputs that will influence those results.

SEPARABLE COST. A cost directly identifiable with a particular segment.

SERVICE DEPARTMENTS. Those departments that exist solely to aid the production departments by rendering specialized assistance with certain phases of the work.

SHORT-RUN PERFORMANCE MARGIN. The contribution margin for each segment, less separable discretionary costs.

SHORT-TERM INVESTMENT. A temporary investment in *marketable securities* of otherwise idle cash.

SINGLE-STEP INCOME STATEMENT. One that groups all *revenue* together (sales plus interest and rent revenues) and then lists and deducts all *expenses* together without drawing any intermediate subtotals.

SOURCE DOCUMENTS. The original records of any *transaction*, internal or external, that occurs in the *entity's* operation.

SPECIFIC IDENTIFICATION. This inventory method concentrates on the physical tracing of the particular items sold.

SPENDING VARIANCE. Basically, a *price variance* applied to variable overhead. However, other factors besides price may influence the amount of the *variance*.

SPLIT-OFF POINT. The juncture of production where the *joint products* become individually identifiable.

STAFF AUTHORITY. The authority to *advise* but not to command; it may be exerted laterally or upward.

STANDARD ABSORPTION COSTING. That type of product costing in which the cost of the finished unit is calculated as the sum of the costs of the standard allowances for factors of production, *including* fixed factory overhead, without reference to the costs actually incurred.

STANDARD COST. A carefully predetermined cost that should be attained, usually expressed per unit.

STANDARD DIRECT COSTING. That type of product costing in which the cost of the finished unit is calculated as the sum of the costs of the standard allowances for the factors of production, *excluding* fixed factory overhead, which is treated as a period cost, and without reference to costs actually incurred.

STATED VALUE. A nominal value of a stock certificate that is usually far below the actual cash invested. See *Par value*.

STATEMENT OF CHANGES IN FINANCIAL POSITION. A formal explanation of the sources and uses of resources, usually sources and uses of *working capital*.

STATEMENT OF FINANCIAL CONDITION. A synonym for *balance sheet*.

STATEMENT OF FINANCIAL POSITION. A substitute term for *balance sheet*.

STATEMENT OF PROFIT AND LOSS. The *income statement*.

STATEMENT OF SOURCES AND APPLICATIONS OF FUNDS. See *Statement of changes in financial position*.

STATIC BUDGET. A *budget* prepared for only one level of activity and, consequently, one that does not adjust automatically to changes in the level of volume.

STEP-DOWN METHOD. Allocation of service department costs to other service departments as well as production departments. Once a department's costs are allocated to other departments, no subsequent service department costs are allocated back to it.

STEP-VARIABLE COSTS. Those variable costs that change abruptly at intervals of activity because their acquisition comes in indivisible chunks.

STOCK DIVIDEND. A distribution to stockholders of additional shares of any class of the distributing company's stock, without any payment to the company by the stockholders.

STOCKHOLDERS' EQUITY. The excess of *assets* over *liabilities* of a corporation.

STOCK SPLIT. The issuance of additional shares for no consideration and under conditions indicating that the objective is to increase the number of outstanding shares for the purpose of reducing their unit market price.

STRAIGHT-LINE DEPRECIATION. A method of allocating the cost of plant assets based on units of time (years).

SUBORDINATED. A creditor claim that is junior to other creditor claims.

SUBORDINATED DEBENTURE. See *Subordinated* and *Debenture*.

SUBSIDIARY. A corporation owned or controlled by a parent company, through the ownership of more than 50 percent of the voting stock.

SUM-OF-THE-YEARS'-DIGITS DEPRECIATION (SYD). A popular form of *accelerated depreciation* where the sum of the digits is the total of the numbers representing the years of life.

SUNK COST. A *cost* that has already been incurred and, therefore, is irrelevant to the decision-making process. Also called *historical cost*.

SYSTEM. A formal means of gathering data to aid and coordinate the process of making decisions.

TANGIBLE ASSETS. See *Fixed assets*.

TAX ALLOCATION. See *Interperiod tax allocation*.

TAX SHIELD. Noncash items (e.g., *depreciation*) charged against income, thus protecting that amount from tax.

TERMINAL VALUE. See *Residual value*.

TIME-ADJUSTED RATE OF RETURN. See *Internal rate of return*.

TIMING DIFFERENCES. Differences between the periods in which *transactions* affect pretax income for reporting to income tax authorities and the periods in which they enter into the determination of pretax income for reporting to shareholders.

TOTAL PROJECT APPROACH. A method of comparing two or more alternative courses of action by computing the total expected inflows and outflows of each alternative and then converting these flows to their present value by applying some predetermined minimum rate of return.

TRADEMARKS. Distinctive identifications of a manufactured product or of a service taking the form of a name, a sign, a slogan, or an emblem.

TRADING ON THE EQUITY. Using borrowed money at a fixed interest rate and/or using funds provided by preferred stockholders with the aim of enhancing the rate of return on common stockholders' equity.

TRADITIONAL COSTING. See *Absorption costing*.

TRANSACTION. Any event that affects the financial position of an *entity* and requires recording.

TRANSFER PRICE. The price charged by one segment of an organization for a product or service that it supplies to another segment of the same organization.

TREASURY STOCK. Outstanding stock that has subsequently been repurchased and not canceled by the company.

UNADJUSTED RATE OF RETURN. See *Accounting rate of return*.

UNAVOIDABLE COST. The opposite of *avoidable cost*.

UNBILLED REVENUE. Fees earned in a given period but for which no bills have been sent to the customer.

UNDERAPPLIED FACTORY OVERHEAD. The excess of actual *factory overhead* over the factory overhead applied to products.

UNDISTRIBUTED EARNINGS. See *Retained income.*

UNEARNED REVENUE. See *Deferred revenue.*

UNEXPIRED COSTS. Any *expenditures* benefiting the future; any asset, including prepaid expenses, normally appearing on a *balance sheet.*

USAGE VARIANCE. *Efficiency variance* pertaining to materials or direct labor.

VARIABLE BUDGET. See *Flexible budget.*

VARIABLE COST. A cost that is uniform *per unit* but fluctuates in total in direct proportion to changes in the related total activity or volume.

VARIABLE COSTING. See *Direct costing.*

VARIABLE COST RATIO. See *Variable expense ratio.*

VARIABLE EXPENSE RATIO. All variable *expenses* divided by *revenues.*

VARIANCE. The deviation of actual results from the expected or budgeted result.

VERIFIABILITY. See *Objectivity.*

VOLUME VARIANCE. See *Denominator variance.*

WEIGHTED-AVERAGE COST. This inventory method assumes that all items available for sale during the period are best represented by their weighted-average cost prices.

WORKING CAPITAL. The excess of *current assets* over *current liabilities.*

WORKING-CAPITAL CYCLE. See *Operating cycle.*

WORKING CAPITAL PROVIDED BY OPERATIONS. *Revenues* less all operating *expenses* requiring *working capital.*

WORK MEASUREMENT. The careful analysis of a task, its size, the methods used in its performance, and its efficiency.

ZERO-BASED BUDGETING. Budgeting from the ground up as though the *budget* were being initiated for the first time.

Note, also see the glossary, pages 613–626

U

Unadjusted rate-of-return model, 324–27
Unavoidable costs, 97–99
Uncertainty:
   decision models and, 129, 439–44
      accountants and, 442
      expected value and standard deviation, 440–42
      general approach to, 442–43
      obtaining additional information, 443–44
   sensitivity analysis in, 317–18
Unconsolidated subsidiaries, 560–63
Underapplied overhead, 381–82
Undistributed earnings (*see* Retained income)
Unearned revenue (*see* Deferred revenue)
Unequal lives, 321
Unexpired costs, 477–78, 486
Uniform accounting, 13
Unit costs, 64–65, 90–94, 122, 128–29, 410–12, 423–24
Usage variance, 181n

V

Variable budgets (*see* Flexible budgets)
Variable costing, 70–71, 91–92 (*see also* Direct costing)
Variable-cost pools, 247–48
Variable-cost ratio, 40
Variable costs:
   absorption costing and, 410–12
   in cost-volume-profit analysis, 28–40, 42–43
   defined, 28–29
   discretionary, 207
   engineered:
      defined, 206–7
      vs. discretionary fixed costs, 209–11

work measurement and, 207–9
   vs. fixed costs, 29–31
   on income statement, 68–71
   proportionately, 215
   transfer pricing and, 279
   (*see also* Contribution approach)
Variable expense ratio, 40
Variable factory overhead, 62
Variable-overhead application rate, 382
Variances, 8
   absorption costing and:
      denominator variance, 409–10, 413–15, 421–24
      effect of, 413–15, 417
   controllability and, 185–87
   marketing, 175, 176
   price and efficiency, 176–78, 180–86
      general approach to analysis of, 182, 183
      graphical approach to analysis of, 183–84
      limitations of, 184–85
      mutual effects, 190–91
      responsibility for, 185–86
Variation, coefficient of, 442
Verifiability, 496
Visual-fit, 217

W

Wage expense, 483–86
Working capital, 530–40
Work-in-process inventory, 64–67
Work measurement, 207–9

Z

Zero-based budgeting, 211–12